Taming the Past

Lawyers and judges often make arguments based on history – on the authority of precedent and original constitutional understandings. They argue both to preserve the inspirational, heroic past and to discard its darker pieces – such as feudalism and slavery, the tyranny of princes and priests, and the subordination of women. In doing so, lawyers tame the unruly, ugly, embarrassing elements of the past, smoothing them into reassuring tales of progress. In a series of essays and lectures written over forty years, Robert W. Gordon describes and analyses how lawyers approach the past and the strategies they use to recruit history for present use while erasing or keeping at bay its threatening or inconvenient aspects. Together, the corpus of work featured in *Taming the Past* offers an analysis of American law and society and its leading historians since 1900.

ROBERT W. GORDON is a Professor of Law at Stanford University and Chancellor Kent Professor of Law and Legal History, Emeritus at Yale University. He was President of the American Society for Legal History in 2000–02, has served on several bar association committees and task forces devoted to reform of the profession, and has previously taught at Buffalo, Wisconsin, Harvard and Oxford.

Studies in Legal History

Editors
Sarah Barringer Gordon, *University of Pennsylvania*
Holly Brewer, *University of Maryland, College Park*
Michael Lobban, *London School of Economics and Political Science*

Titles
Felice Batlan, *Women and Justice for the Poor: A History of Legal Aid, 1863–1945*
Paul Garfinkel, *Criminal Law in Liberal and Fascist Italy*
Stefan Jurasinski, *The Old English Penitentials and Anglo-Saxon Law*
Sophia Z. Lee, *The Workplace Constitution from the New Deal to the New Right*
Michael A. Livingston, *The Fascists and the Jews of Italy: Mussolini's Race Laws, 1938–1943*
Michelle A. McKinley, *Fractional Freedoms: Slavery, Intimacy, and Legal Mobilization in Colonial Lima, 1600–1700*
Karen M. Tani, *States of Dependency: Welfare, Rights, and American Governance, 1935–1972*
Mitra Sharafi, *Law and Identity in Colonial South Asia: Parsi Legal Culture, 1772–1947*

Taming the Past

Essays on Law in History and History in Law

ROBERT W. GORDON
Stanford University

CAMBRIDGE
UNIVERSITY PRESS

CAMBRIDGE
UNIVERSITY PRESS

University Printing House, Cambridge CB2 8BS, United Kingdom

One Liberty Plaza, 20th Floor, New York, NY 10006, USA

477 Williamstown Road, Port Melbourne, VIC 3207, Australia

4843/24, 2nd Floor, Ansari Road, Daryaganj, Delhi – 110002, India

79 Anson Road, #06-04/06, Singapore 079906

Cambridge University Press is part of the University of Cambridge.

It furthers the University's mission by disseminating knowledge in the pursuit of education, learning, and research at the highest international levels of excellence.

www.cambridge.org
Information on this title: www.cambridge.org/9781107193239
DOI: 10.1017/9781108147668

First published 2017

Printed in the United States of America by Sheridan Books, Inc.

A catalogue record for this publication is available from the British Library.

Library of Congress Cataloging-in-Publication Data
Names: Gordon, Robert W. (Robert Watson), 1941– author.
Title: Taming the past : essays on law in history and history in law / Robert W. Gordon, Stanford University
Description: New York : Cambridge University Press, 2017. | Series: Studies in legal history | Includes bibliographical references and index.
Identifiers: LCCN 2017003076 | ISBN 9781107193239 (hardback)
Subjects: LCSH: Law–United States–History. | BISAC: LAW / Legal History.
Classification: LCC KF352 .G67 2017 | DDC 349.73–dc23
LC record available at https://lccn.loc.gov/2017003076

ISBN 978-1-107-19323-9 Hardback
ISBN 978-1-316-64400-3 Paperback

To the memory of

Allison Gordon (1909–1987)

Lincoln Gordon (1913–2010)

Contents

Foreword

John Fabian Witt and Sarah Barringer Gordon

Robert W. Gordon has been an active legal historian for almost fifty years. He is an indisputable leader in a flourishing scholarly field. His laurels are many. But the distinguishing feature of his career is the particular combination of accomplishments that mark his still-growing legacy.

Bob (as he is known to one and all) has long been famous for unsurpassed theoretical incisiveness and analytic acuity. From the very beginning of his career, his interventions into the field of legal history have been propelled by a powerful grasp of legal and social theory. His essays, including several reprinted here, established the theoretical foundations for much of the work in the field of legal history – foundations that remain in place to this day. One need think only of the outpouring of work in the field over the past forty years identifying the law's contingency, establishing its constitutive effects in social life, documenting the recursive feedback loops between law and society, and delighting in the subversive character of legal-historical inquiry. In each of these areas and many more, Bob's essays led the way in identifying the paths followed by scholars of the history of the law in the decades since.

Bob is widely known, as well, as a convivial interlocutor, generous commentator, and critic. As a mentor, he has guided generations of legal historians into the field and its historiography. From his first post at SUNY Buffalo to Wisconsin, Yale, and Stanford, Bob's erudition has earned him pride of place among scholars of American legal history. He has served as the president of the American Society for Legal History, his work has been the subject of symposia and honors, and the many friends and admirers who have benefited from his epistolary talents on their behalf have called down praises upon his head. Bob wears such eminence with modesty and grace.

Together, these two characteristic achievements – the analytic rigor he brings to all his work and the generous building of a field – embody the essence of Bob's contribution to the field. He has managed what for most of us is nearly impossible: to build a field while simultaneously endowing it with a sharp and uncompromising theoretical apparatus.

The only gap in the record is remedied by this volume. It is high time that the work of this fine historian of law is made available to the field. Collected here are eighteen articles, essays, and reviews, including four that have not previously been published, and many that are all too obscure and/or entirely unavailable on our standard databases for scholarship. In other words, a treat is in store for the reader of this volume. Here, gentle reader, the Gordonian oeuvre lies before you, and the authors of this Foreword undertake to provide only the briefest overview, to whet the appetite. The collection tracks Bob's central focus on the history of legal thought, especially the complex relationships among law, legal practice, and the American state from 1870 through the present. Equally important, Bob's critical historiographies draw in wide swaths of scholarship, integrating otherwise disparate strands of historical work into breathtakingly new conversations.

Viewed now for the first time as a whole, the Gordonian oeuvre establishes that Bob's work is imbued with craft, based in wide reading and thinking, and situated on the cutting edge of both law and history. Reflecting the image on the cover of this book, Bob thinks of this collection as an exercise in "taming the dragon," by which he means that he sees the historicism wielded by legal historians as an animal dangerous to those (lawyers, especially) in the present who would naturalize the status quo. In Bob's world, this dragon is poised to comfort the afflicted and afflict the comfortable. As an admonition to those who would deploy the past in ways that paper over complexity, contingency, and contestation, Bob's critical historicism has much caution to offer the legal profession and professoriate, and many avenues for those of us in the field of legal history to explore.

We stress three among the many aspects of Bob's work that deserve attention, and no doubt each reader will add others to the list.

The wordsmith: To the extent that legal history, especially work on the history of the legal profession in America – one of Bob's perennial interests – has otherwise been the province of unduly legalistic prose that only an antiquarian lawyer could love, we invite the reader to a most welcome departure. Bob's work sparkles in part because of his unerring quest for the *mot juste* and his evident delight in the richness and subtlety of language.

Consider the opening of Bob's iconic "Critical Legal Histories," which promised something "bound to look like a seed catalogue or a Pocket Guide to the Common and Exotic Varieties of the Social/Legal Histories of North America." Who can forget the "mandarin materials" of the law as "among the richest artifacts of a society's legal consciousness," or the reminder that the best forms of scholarly work (even where flawed) are "always grandly overflowing" their "conceptual channels"? The functionalist model, Bob describes thus: "When commerce summoned loud, 'Thou Must!,' contract whispered low, 'I can!' " In the face of such epigrammatic genius, one can barely help wanting to join the conversation, loudly or with an enthusiastic whisper, as the case may be. For us, the impulse is as powerful today as it was when we first encountered Bob's energizing work decades ago. Great writing stands the test of time.

The theoretician: Bob's work has led and helped sustain the broad expansion in what we think of as relevant to legal history. As a fellow traveler of cultural and intellectual historians, and as a sympathizer with social history, Bob's work has spanned historical genres. In the legal academy, his work explained and validated historicism more generally. Among historians, Bob's evident command of legal developments across time has expanded historical attention to the ways that legal matters reflect – and in turn affect – society more broadly. Bob's historical brilliance, in other words, helped bring history back into what had long been a predominantly internalist tradition in legal history, while his lawyerly sophistication helped bring law back into the literatures on social and political history and the history of ideas.

Bob does all these things gracefully, usually using a scalpel rather than a machete. Contrary to the common reputation of the *enfants terribles* associated with the Critical Legal Studies movement (a reputation that is largely though not entirely undeserved), Bob has found value in an extraordinarily broad array of competing perspectives. With one breath he embraces the historiography of the cultural turn. With the next he celebrates the virtues of social histories. In one sentence, he cites the value of economic histories by Alfred Chandler, Robert Fogel, or Douglass North. And then he makes a deft turn through the bottom-up history of political movements. This is not to say for a minute that Bob doesn't bring out a sledgehammer from time to time: crude, economically deterministic accounts have brought out Bob's unmediated scorn. But such rebukes emanate from the spirit of openness and curiosity about the multifariousness of the human social and legal experience that the objects of his ire aimed to deny. One might say that Willard Hurst inaugurated the modern era of legal history by opening it up to the history of society. Bob himself has said as much! But he expanded significantly Hurst's methodology and reach, and brought it into conversation with both sides of the law–history divide.

And yet, even as he generously synthesizes entire literatures in elegant turns of phrase, Bob has left his own distinctive theoretical mark, one that is still evolving. More than three decades after the iconic twin articles "Historicism in Legal Scholarship" and "Critical Legal Histories," the intricacies of the law-and-society relationship still preoccupy the field. Many of us are left with case studies in the theoretical structures Bob identified. Did law shape society a little bit more, or did society exercise a little more authority over the law? What were the points of contingency in the development of the law? Only the most fearless among us have dared try to think beyond the basic analytic paradigm set out in Bob's work.

The mensch: In part because of Bob's example as a practicing legal historian, but even more importantly because of his selfless kindness to all, he has helped build a field that is now sophisticated, successful, and grateful to him. Bob has earned the respect of many audiences. He is, for example, trained in law, not history, yet speaks fluently the language of both. Through his efforts on behalf of the field, and through his many students in both history departments and law schools, he has sustained the careers of at least two (and growing) generations of legal historians. He is also a friend and mentor to many who have never been his students, but whose good fortune it has been to profit from Bob's genial and capacious desire to be of assistance to all in the field.

Consider, for example, his reprises of the iconic "Critical Legal Histories" article, both of which are republished here. Presented with ample opportunity to settle scores or dole out dollops of approval or disapproval, Bob embraces (with characteristic goodwill) the disorderly reactions and pell-mell critiques his own work has generated.

Across a career marked by such craft and brilliance and caring, Robert W. Gordon has produced a body of fine scholarship and criticism. To see this extraordinary scholar in action, you have only to turn the page.

Permissions

I am grateful to the following for permission to reprint previously published materials:

Introduction

To the *Law & Society Review*, for "Introduction: The Common Law Tradition in American Legal Historiography," 10 *Law & Society Review*. 9–55 (1975).

To the *Law & History Review*, for "Hurst Recaptured," 18 *Law & History Review*. 167–175 (2000).

To the *Yale Journal of Law and the Humanities*, for "The Elusive Transformation," 6 *Yale J. Law & Hum*. 137 (1994).

To Harvard Law School, for "Method and Politics: Morton Horwitz on Lawyers' Uses of History," in 2 *Transformations in Legal History* (Hamilton & Brophy eds., 2010).

To *Georgetown Law Review*, for "E. P. Thompson's Legacies," 82 *Georgetown L. J.* 2005–2011 (1994).

To *Hofstra Law Review*, for "Holmes's Common Law as Legal and Social Science," *10 Hofstra L. Rev.* 719–746 (1982).

To the *Yale Law Journal*, for "Historicism in Legal Scholarship," 90 *Yale L. J.* 1017–1056 (1981).

To the *Stanford Law Review*, for "Critical Legal Histories," 36 *Stanford L. Rev.* 57–125 (1984).

To the University of Michigan Press, for "Legal History: The Past as Authority and Social Critic," in *The Historic Turn in the Human Sciences* 339–367 (Terrence McDonald ed. 1996); and for "Undoing Historical Injustice," in *Justice and Injustice* (Sarat & Kearns eds. 1996), 35–75.

To the *Miami Law Review*, for "The Constitution of Liberal Order at the Troubled Beginnings of the Modern State," 58 *Miami L. Rev.* 373–400 (2004).

Introduction

When, some years ago, the editors of the *Studies in Legal History* series – then Thomas Green, Hendrik Hartog, and Daniel Ernst – first suggested that the series might collect and republish my various essays on legal historiography, I agreed, but with some diffidence. I had moved on to working on the history and current ethics of the legal profession, and was not much motivated to exhume older work. This project would probably have remained comatose had it not been for the kind, but persistent and ultimately irresistible influence of the current editors, Holly Brewer and Sally Barringer Gordon. They persuaded me that there might still be a readership for essays that had first appeared in widely disparate places, some of them now hard to find; and Sally's willingness to write a foreword to the collection with another old friend and colleague, John Witt, finally clinched the deal.

The essays and lectures collected in this volume draw upon about forty years of thinking and writing about the relation of history to law in general and to American law in particular. Most of them have been reprinted with minor revisions from previously published articles or chapters in edited collections. A few others originated as lectures and appear here in print for the first time.

For the writing of legal history, these have been eventful years. When the first essay reprinted here was written (1975) the entire bibliography of books and articles worth reading on American legal history could fit on a list one or two pages long. American law schools might offer at most one course in legal history, usually a "Development of Legal Institutions" course emphasizing the English background to American law. Now the bibliography is in the thousands, probably beyond anyone's capacity to read through in a lifetime. Virtually every law school attentive to its academic reputation has hired at least one faculty member to teach an American legal history course; some schools have several; the field has attracted some of the best talent among law students and doctoral candidates in History departments; and it is now common for its teachers to have a Ph.D. in History as well as the J.D. Both in law schools and History departments, the kind of social-legal history that James Willard Hurst pioneered and for years practiced almost alone, has proliferated and flourished, while at the same time becoming more comparative and cosmopolitan.[1] Some fields of law, especially Constitutional Law, have taken a notably historical turn, in part because of the vogue for "originalist" interpretation of constitutional texts, but also because the visible influence of social movements and public-interest lawyers on lawmaking in and after the civil rights revolution has motivated research into the origins in those movements of legal strategies and doctrinal arguments that have swayed courts and legislatures.[2] The essays in this book are attempts to describe some of this cascade of legal-history writing as it has been happening and to assess its significance for the ways in which we think about law.

Legal historiography comes, crudely speaking, in two varieties: (1) histories of law written by lawyers (who may also have some historical training) and directed largely to an audience of lawmakers and interpreters such as judges, legislatures, jurists, advocates, and law reformers; and (2) histories of law written by historians (who also may have legal training), and intended largely for academics, contemplative lawyers, and other readers who want to understand where law comes from and how it affects and is affected by social change. Some of the essays in this book are primarily about lawyers' uses of history, others about historians' histories of law, and some about both. Legal historiography was for centuries almost the complete monopoly of lawyers – who else would be interested enough to take the trouble to research it? – who looked to history primarily for professional purposes: to investigate the origins of their own legal practices; to preserve what seemed valuable in tradition and to discard what seemed archaic or irrational; and to deploy history in forensic argument or treatises or judicial opinions to persuade others that the legal conclusions they favored were demanded by tradition or custom or precedent or by the imperatives of historical becoming, the march of progress.

Legal writers were also however among the principal pioneers of modern historians' practice, whose governing ethic is the "historicist" aim of recovering as accurately as possible the law as experienced by people in past times and places and different conceptual universes – not (at least, not obviously and overtly) to deploy as authority in current disputes, but to explore law's meanings and operations in those other contexts.

[1] The recent three-volume *Cambridge History of Law in America* (Michael Grossberg & Christopher Tomlins, eds., 3 vols., 2008) is a heroic multi-author attempt to synthesize this burgeoning literature.

[2] Other social sciences have experienced a turn toward history in the same decades. Political scientists have developed a new specialty, "Political Development," that gives a central role to the history of legal institutions. Even law-and-economics scholars have taken to historical research, as part of a project to determine what kinds of legal institutions and doctrine (like property rights or corporate governance) are "efficient" or most conducive to economic growth.

In our time legal historians often blur the boundaries of these two roles, combining scholarly research into legal history with using the results to argue for particular normative conclusions about what law should be, and do, in the future. But the two roles are still, at least in theory, distinct. Some conventional distinctions are that while lawyers are monists, historians are pluralists: that is, lawyers want to recover a single authoritative meaning from a past act or practice, while historians look for plural, contested, or ambiguous meanings. Lawyers engaged in practical or scholarly advocacy, as when they use history in briefing or arguing or (as judges) deciding cases, want to bring past practices into the present to serve present purposes. Historians regard – or at least are supposed to regard – naked presentism as a sin. "What the historian is interested in is a dead past; a past unlike the present. The *differentia* of the historical past lies in its very disparity from what is contemporary."[3]

Historians, committed to contextualizing past practices, will emphasize all the ways in which their meaning depends upon the material conditions, interpretive conventions, and tacit assumptions in which they were embedded. While lawyers are concerned to find continuities between past and present, historians employing "contextual" or "structuralist" approaches will emphasize discontinuous breaks, epistemic shifts in the ways in which social actors construct their worlds.[4] So for example: "Liberty" in the eighteenth century presupposed a world in which slaves or indentured or household servants and women would perform the menial tasks that freed gentleman for participation in politics or the pursuit of new economic opportunities: a liberty of the few premised on the subordination of the many. At the same time, "liberty" often presupposed more, rather than less, equality than it does in the present, because its realization depended upon a roughly equal distribution of property among the politically enfranchised – a republican equality that prevented the corruption and abuses of power that result when the weak are under domination by the strong. Liberty so conceived was the opposite of servility, the condition of being subject to the will of another. Finally, "liberty" in that time had few connotations, except in the work of utopian or speculative thinkers, of what was later to come, an abstract generalized freedom to do as one wills, limited only by the equal freedom of others. Most forms of liberty were concrete "liberties," particular grants or franchises to communities or trades or classes of persons; or particular customary restraints on governmental power. And "liberty" was regularly distinguished from "license": liberty was both subject to and constituted by legal restraints.[5]

[3] Michael Oakeshott, *Experience and its Modes* 106 (1933).

[4] For many useful examples of these historicizing methods applied to legal history, see William W. Fisher III, "Texts and Contexts: The Application to American Legal History of the Methodologies of Intellectual History," 49 *Stan. L. Rev.* 1065 (1997).

[5] On eighteenth-century "liberty," see generally Quentin Skinner, *Liberty Before Liberalism* (1998); Edmund S. Morgan, *American Slavery, American Freedom: The Ordeal of Colonial Virginia* 295–387 (1975); John Philip Reid, *The Concept of Liberty in the Age of The American Revolution* (1988); Gordon Wood, *The Radicalism of the American Revolution* (1992).

The reader will rightly object that these contrasts between lawyers' and historians' methods are overdrawn. Lawyers don't always violate historicist tenets, constructing fictive pasts in order to locate the past on the same continuous plane as the present. As I'll come back to in a moment, sometimes they invoke history precisely to differentiate the present, to show that some bad practices belong to an earlier age that is properly dead and buried. And no moderately sophisticated historian believes that he or she can really escape the pull of the present: whole books have been written on how contemporary events and prejudices have always shaped historians' choices of topics, background assumptions and biases.[6] Historians have often been as culpable as lawyers at writing apologetic history that minimizes the transgressions of dominant groups and exaggerates the extent to which such evils have been overcome – consider the "Dunning school" of Reconstruction historians who sugarcoated the horrors of slavery, suggested that worse horrors were inflicted by black and carpetbagger rule after the Civil War, and celebrated the Redemption of the South from that misrule. It took the moral awakening prompted by the civil rights movement to dent the entrenched complacency of that consensus narrative and to inspire its revision.

Nonetheless, lawyers' legal history is usually conservative and apologetic. Lawyers mostly look to history for *authority*. They argue that the legal enactments or interpretations they favor grow inexorably out of past enactments, precedents, traditions or historical tendencies. This isn't just true of a conspicuous special subclass of jurists, Constitutional "originalists" who believe that judges today must give the words of the federal Constitution the same meanings that people did at the time of its adoption; it's true of legal argument generally. But lawyers also sometimes use history in much the same way historians use it, as whenever they argue that some long-standing legal practice, precedent or interpretation should no longer be followed because changed circumstances or values have rendered it obsolete.

The "taming" image of my title comes from O. W. Holmes's metaphor, in his famous speech on "The Path of the Law," of history as a means of getting a dragon out of his cave:

> The rational study of law is still to a large extent the study of history. History must be a part of the study, because without it we cannot know the precise scope of rules which it is our business to know. It is a part of the rational study, because it is the first step toward an enlightened skepticism, that is, towards a deliberate reconsideration of the worth of those rules. When you get the dragon out of his cave on to the plain and in the daylight, you can count his teeth and claws, and see just what is his strength. But to get him out is only the first step. The next is either to kill him, or to tame him and make him a useful animal.[7]

[6] See, e.g., Peter Novick, *That Noble Dream: The Objectivity Question and the American Historical Profession* (1988).

[7] Oliver Wendell Holmes, Jr., "The Path of the Law," in *Collected Legal Papers* 167, 187 (1920).

Holmes is saying that you need to understand the genealogy of current legal rules, how they originated and how they developed, in order to know what their purposes were, what functions they served in their original context. Once you know that, however, you have to evaluate whether they are still relevant and useful. Quite often, he suggests, they are mere survivals, maintained by unconscious habit and imitation, or by a more subtle process whereby judges artificially prolong the lifespan of rules that ought to be obsolete by periodically outfitting them with fresh policy rationales. (Holmes assigned most of the task of pruning the legal undergrowth to keep the useful rules, and to throw out or refashion the obsolete or counterproductive rules, to scientific legislation, not to judges. Some of his successors, like Benjamin Cardozo and many in the Legal Realist movement, believed that judges should take a more active role in modernizing the law.)

Holmes thus puts himself in the category of lawyers who use history to challenge the current law for its overdependence on past authority. But in conventional legal argument, even such critical moves are usually made within the safety of a larger set of assumptions about historical change that reassure us that we are part of a broader process of development that preserves continuity with the good parts of the past while purging or shedding the bad parts. Indeed one of the main uses of history in legal argument is to relegate the bad parts of our legal-historical experience, the parts we no longer want or need – like the past of legalized subordination of African-Americans and women (in slavery, Jim Crow and coverture) – to a thoroughly dead past that is over and done with.

Now that I see all these essays collected together, it occurs to me that in one way or another they almost all make some version of the same point: that the historicized past poses a perpetual threat to the legal rationalizations of the present. Brought back to life, the past unsettles and destabilizes the stories we tell about the law to make us feel comfortable with the way things are. Often this is done by explaining how meanings and applications of legal terms have changed; or by exposing the origins of a rule in archaic cultural assumptions or barbaric practices or corrupt or authoritarian influences. Sometimes it is done by revealing the traces of such pasts continuing pervasively into the present.

For an elegant demonstration of this form of critique at work, consider a well-known article by Reva Siegel on current equal-protection law.[8] Siegel describes a form of legal reasoning that aims at "preservation through transformation," a technique that discredits and consigns to the scrapheap of history older justifications for status inequality, but at the same time invents new ones. At the end of the nineteenth century, courts that could no longer justify a husband beating his wife or appropriating all the joint earnings of their marriage to himself as incidents of his rights of lordship over her, argued instead

[8] *See* Reva Siegel, "Why Equal Protection No Longer Protects: The Evolving Forms of Status-Enforcing State Action," 49 *Stan. L. Rev.* 1111 (1997).

that the legal system could not intervene (to protect the wife) in the private domain of love and affection. Similarly, in the same period, courts deprived of the rationale for racial subordination that blacks were whites' natural inferiors, fashioned distinctions between "civil," "political," and "social" rights that left decisions to segregate the races in the "social" sphere (education, marriage, association in public places) to the states. In recent times, now that the "social rights" rationale for apartheid has collapsed, the courts have begun to reason that the evil of race discrimination consists in the state's "discriminatory *purpose*," a criterion that makes it hard for blacks to challenge social and governmental practices that are facially neutral but that in their actual effects help to perpetuate racial inequality, yet (ironically) makes it easy for whites to challenge affirmative-action measures. As courts devise the new rationales, they invent fictional pedigrees for them in history and tradition by arguing, for example, that the evil of slavery and segregation lay not in their being systemic social practices that subordinated the black race, but simply in the practice of classifying people by race, violating the norm of color-blindness. Siegel's essay in critical historicism demolishes these fictive continuities; but at the same time reveals deeper and more disturbing continuities – continuing practices of gender and racial subordination, justified by historically familiar and frequently deployed modes of nominally reformist legal rhetoric, which justify the traces of the bad past by inventing new reasons for leaving them undisturbed. *Plessy* v. *Ferguson* is not dead but lives on, as the doctrine of discriminatory purpose.

Now lawyers have a standard and initially quite plausible response to historically minded critics who oppose contextualized, pluralized, discontinuous interpretations of past texts to the lawyers' presentist interpretations: We lawyers are driven by different purposes than are historians; our job is to bring the past into the present and to turn it to present purposes; this task is no less important and legitimate than the historian's task, and it necessarily employs different criteria and methods. A particularly strong form of this argument has been made by John Reid, who is concerned to protect early-modern lawyers from historians' charges that they "invented" a "fictitious" or "mythic" ancient Saxon Constitution as the repository of English liberties. Reid wants sharply to distinguish the lawyers' enterprises from those of historians, particularly modern historians; the lawyers, he says, were doing a different kind of history, "forensic" history for use in legal argument:

> The forensic historian … searches the past for material applicable to a current issue. The purpose of the advocate, unlike that of the historian, is to use the past for the elucidation of the present, to solve some contemporary problem or, most often, to carry an argument. It is the past put in the service of winning the case at bar.[9]

[9] John Phillip Reid, "The Jurisprudence of Liberty: The Ancient Constitution in the Legal Historiography of the Seventeenth and Eighteenth Centuries," in *The Roots of Liberty: Magna Carta, Ancient Constitution, and the Anglo-American Tradition of the Rule of Law* 147, at 158 (Ellis Sandoz ed., 1993). Expanding this point in John Phillip Reid, *The Ancient Constitution*

Reid is saying: Lawyers' arguments from history are not what historians think of as historical arguments at all; to criticize them as bad history is beside the point. Of course in some sense Reid's response is obviously correct, or the past could never be invoked for practical use in contemporary political or legal debate; and it is almost impossible to imagine political or legal debate without its invocation. *Every* legal text is a historical artifact that must be brought into the present in order to be applied; every argument from tradition, precedent, or the authority of an old text wrenches that text from its prior context and puts it to novel uses, sometimes uses wholly unsuspected by its drafter. Almost every important political or legal controversy brings forth arguments for preserving or recovering – or discarding or revising – something in the past, which in turn relies on a narrative account of what is in that past and how it connects with the present.

But Reid's argument surely proves too much. Once the advocate has brought history into the debate, his forensic adversary has an opening to challenge that history, and will not be able to resist looking at the obvious materials to support that challenge, history written by historians. This is of course exactly what has happened in Supreme Court arguments about "original" meanings: in every case to which historical argument is relevant, we get dueling historians' briefs, and dueling accounts of history from majority and dissenting opinions. And how are we supposed to judge between these competing accounts? To be sure, the majority's account becomes law, and therefore acquires "authority" that competing accounts have not; but that may be a transient victory. Even other members of Roger Taney's own Supreme Court didn't accept their Chief Justice's originalist history, in *Dred Scott*'s case, of the status of blacks as a people without rights at the Founding;[10] and subsequent commentary has been very harsh indeed to that history. As soon as the lawyer or judge expressly adopts the historian's purposes and methods – having blurred genres and created an overlap between fields, having added the authority of "history" to his own *ipse dixits* – he leaves open a port of entry to the subversive tendencies of historicism. Lawyers' history may not be – cannot be, given its expressly presentist purposes – the same as historians' history; but historians' history is not irrelevant to evaluating it.

If asked to define the critical historicism that these essays promote, I would say it is any approach to the past that produces disturbances in the familiar, comfortable strategies that lawyers use to tame the past in order to normalize the present.

and the Origins of Anglo-American Liberty (2005), Reid has two more arguments for lawyers' forensic history. One is a pragmatic argument that, as practiced, in the seventeenth and eighteenth century, arguments from ancient custom were more effective in protecting the liberties of Anglo-American peoples than (for example) arguments from abstract right. The other is that constitutional arguments based on history, even invented history, are likely to be narrower in scope than arguments based on open-ended norms, and therefore more likely to limit judicial discretion. See id., at 115–124.

10 See *Scott* v. *Sanford*, 60 U.S. (19 How.) 393, 564, 572–573 (Curtis, J., dissenting).

Critical history may invert or scramble familiar narratives of continuity, recovery or progress; may advance rival perspectives (such of those as the losers rather than the winners) for surveying legal developments, or may posit alternative trajectories that might have led to a very different present. The ever-present implication of critical history is the contingency of present legal arrangements.

Here's a familiar example of such a use of history: Trial lawyers are fond of describing adversary combat in front of juries as a venerable, centuries-old institution of the common law, as if its antiquity and longevity guaranteed its massive solidity and permanence in our legal system. But the actual history of the jury is a more disturbing story. The jury was a medieval institution to be sure, but the modern procedures of jury trial, dominated by the direct and cross-examination of witnesses by lawyers, with judges in a passive role and the jury silent until the verdict, date only from the nineteenth century.[11] And the major story in the development of jury trial since then has not been of its immovable permanence as the palladium of our liberties, but of its fading – both on the civil and criminal side – to the point of near-disappearance in the present.

Exposure to critical historicism is like living in another country. Anyone who lives in a foreign culture can always find ways of doing so that confirm and reinforce preformed beliefs and identities. In Bangkok, you can stay at the Hilton and eat only at McDonald's. You can look in the foreign culture for all the signs that seem to make it identical to one's own – finding "self-interested rational calculation," or "racism and patriarchy" everywhere. Or you can look instead for the differences that identify its otherness, the "pre-modern," barbaric or alien qualities that your own culture has defined itself in opposition to, or alternatively has claimed to have safely buried in its discarded past. But after longer exposure such strategies of self-confirmation tend to wear thin: seeing that people take utterly for granted things you find exotic, starts to unsettle your idea of what it is to be an ordinary person, and gets you thinking about contingency and constructed identity – all the influences and path-dependencies that must have gone into the making of the culture that made you.

As it happens, a good deal of historiography as practiced by modern historians turns out to be critical to some degree if introduced into legal discourse, because its purposes and working assumptions so often conflict with those of lawyers. From historians' studies of the Constitution, for example, we learn that legal texts are contingent, fragile, and ambiguous embodiments of momentary political compromises in a rapid flux of perceptions that shift with social actors' experiences and fortunes; that no sooner are words launched upon the world in legal form that they help to set in motion consequences that cause them to be reevaluated and reinterpreted.[12] Once we are presented with this

[11] See John Langbein, *The Origins of Adversary Criminal Trial* (2003).

[12] For sterling examples, see the leading historical works on the making of the U.S. Constitution, Gordon Wood, *The Creation of the American Republic, 1776–1787* (1969); and Jack Rakove, *Original Meanings: Politics and Ideas in the Making of the Constitution* (1996).

fluid swirl of multiple, sharply contested and rapidly refigured meanings, the notion that we can pluck one faction's construct from a single instant in time, and authoritatively pronounce it to be for all time thenceforth, "The Original Meaning" looks exceedingly presumptuous and tenuous. Any attempt to fix it into settled doctrine must be provisional, and readily revisable by simply picking a different group's construction of the text from a differing context. The choice of which fragments of the past, which narratives connecting that past to the present, which competing interpretations of those fragments and narratives, we wish to claim as our authoritative antecedents, is a political choice, and one best made candidly, in full awareness of the alternatives.

In addition to trying to make us aware of the contingency of our present legal arrangements, and of the different pathways that might have led us – and might lead us in the future – to different presents, many of the essays in this collection have a further aim. That is the aim of trying to unsettle what (at least what I perceived to be) dominant notions or implicit theories of legal intellectuals regarding the linkages between "law," the specialized professional outputs of legal systems, and "society," the social world that surrounds law, makes demands upon law, and responds to law. The first essay in this collection on the "Common Law Tradition" identified two such notions or theories as implicit in traditional legal histories. One was that law, or anyway the law made by judges and jurists, inhabited its own relatively insulated autonomous sphere, that of a "taught legal tradition" (in Roscoe Pound's phrase), with its own sources of authority and modes of reasoning, which used its distinctive professional modes to analyze and process the problems thrown at it by outside social developments. The other – seemingly exactly the opposite – was that law was almost wholly epiphenomenal, a largely determined set of responses to larger general and inexorable forces of economic, social and political development. Entrenched legal doctrines interpreted, and institutions staffed, by a conservative profession might retard the adaptation of law to social change, but eventual adaptation was inevitable.

As long as legal historians kept their focus on the internal details of the legal system, they did not have to inquire too closely into law's interactions with the wider society. But with the coming of age of social-legal histories in and after the 1970s (in the tracks of such pioneers as Willard Hurst, George Haskins, and Richard Morris in the 1950s), questions about the nature of law–society relations became inescapable. A few legal historians, such as Hurst himself and Lawrence Friedman, engaged in explicit theorizing of such issues[13]; most of the new generation addressed them, as historians generally tend to do, only in passing in their work. By the time I wrote the essay on "Critical Legal Histories"

[13] See, e.g., James Willard Hurst, *Law and Social Process in United States History* (1960); James Willard Hurst, *Law and Markets in United States History: Different Modes of Bargaining Among Interests* (1982); Lawrence M. Friedman, *The Legal System: A Social Science Perspective* (1975).

(republished below) in 1984, it seemed clear that alongside the prevailing conceptions of law-as-autonomous and law-as-epiphenomenal or (belatedly) reactive, there was emerging in legal-historical writing a conception of law–society relations according to which law made society as much as society made law. The "economy" was not something outside law to which law reacted, but was partly constituted by legal doctrines and actions, by particular constellations of property–tort–contract and other private law regimes, by police–power regulations and constitutional restraints on them, by government funding and supports such as tariffs, charters for transport infrastructure, public funding of scientific and public health research, slavery law, and aggressive wars to acquire new territories to wrest from their current owners-in-possession like Mexicans or Indians, and to redistribute them to white settlers and railroads. Law could call a purposeful infliction of economic injury a tort or crime and sanction it with damages, fines or injunctions; or turn it back into a privileged act of competition or labor organizing. Law could make a sexual act between two people into a consummation of a lawful marriage, or condonation of an errant spouse, or into criminal fornication, adultery, or sodomy. Law conferred, or withheld, rights of citizenship. The new legal history is thus as much the legal history of societies as the social history of law. The essays here tried to describe these developments in the field as they were happening.

Finally, some of the essays here were meant as interventions in political debates and controversies in which the participants appeal to legal history. In particular, I join many others in trying to challenge some of the methods and assumptions used by conservatives who have been trying to recover and revive what they believe to be virtuous past legal and constitutional orders in order to repel or undo what they perceive as vicious threats of modernity: the New Deal and Great Society taxing, regulatory and welfare states; the upheavals in morals, family and gender roles resulting from the feminist and gay rights movements and the sexual revolutions; the challenges to white male cultural, social and political dominance stemming from the civil rights movements and loosening of immigration restrictions. Conservative movements invoke history to recover virtuous pasts of laissez-faire markets, strict crime control and morals regulation, and hegemonic Christian culture. One role for critical legal history in these debates has been to suggest that such past orders never existed in the forms claimed for them; and, to the extent they did, brought about much unnecessary suffering that we should not wish to revive.

As it happens, most of the essays in this book on how lawyers use history are not about the big Constitutional debates that make explicit arguments about original meanings or customary rights. I see the major presence of history in law as a set of mostly implicit, taken-for-granted assumptions about the relation of the present to the past, about what is or should be permanent or unchanging, and about how we have changed and the general directions of change. That set of background assumptions does a lot of work in the making and understanding of our law, sometimes with good and useful effects, but often with harmful effects as well. To try to tease out these assumptions – to get the dragon out of his cave – is the main ambition of the present collection. The past cannot always be tamed – it is too wild and unruly for taming. But we need to know what it looks like, and how it looms, for good and ill, over our present.

A Note on the Text: The text of previously published essays is reproduced unchanged except for minor corrections. Chapter 13 has been slightly revised to begin with what were, in the original, its concluding sections. With one exception, the footnotes in each essay have been revised to conform to a uniform style (a hybrid of legal and historical citations styles); the exception is Chapter 12, which has been left in the social-science citation format in which it originally appeared. I have appended at the beginning of each essay a short note indicating where each piece was published and in some cases calling attention to relevant later work.

Acknowledgments: A collection like this of work written over a lifetime is bound to pile up a heap of intellectual debts. My heap looks like a mountain.

I have to begin with my teachers and mentors, whose example and personal encouragement got me started on this path:

At Harvard College: Alexander Gerschenkron, Louis Hartz, Stanley Hoffmann, Mark De Wolfe Howe, Barrington Moore, David Riesman;
At and after Harvard Law School: John Dawson, Willard Hurst, Morton Horwitz, Stanley Katz, John Mansfield, Harry Scheiber, and Lawrence Friedman (who remains a beloved colleague as well as continuing influence).

I have been exceptionally lucky to teach at four universities that are extraordinary in their intellectual liveliness and support for the life of the mind. In each I found colleagues and students whose friendship sustained me and whose scholarship enriched my work:

At SUNY/Buffalo: Dianne Avery, David Hollinger, Al Katz, Fred Konefsky, Janet Lindgren, Elizabeth Mensch, John Henry Schlegel;
At the University of Wisconsin-Madison: Marc Galanter, Joel Handler, Leonard Kaplan, Stewart Macaulay, John Robertson, Mark Tushnet, David Trubek, Louise Trubek, William Whitford;
At Stanford: Barbara Babcock, Joe Bankman, Paul Brest, Jud Campbell, Joshua Cohen, John Donohue, John Hart Ely, David Freeman Engstrom, Nora Engstrom, George Fisher, Barbara Fried, Thomas Grey, Gerald Gunther, Janet Halley, Thomas Heller, Pamela Karlan, Mark Kelman, Amalia Kessler, Larry Kramer, Elizabeth Magill, Michael McConnell, Bernadette Meyler, Robert Rabin, Jack Rakove, Deborah Rhode, James Sheehan, William Simon, Norman Spaulding, Robert Weisberg;

At Yale: Bruce Ackerman, Julia Adams, Akhil Amar, Jack Balkin, Peter Brooks, Richard Brooks, Robert Burt, Guido Calabresi, Amy Chua, Nancy Cott, Mirjan Damaŝka, John Demos, Robert Ellickson, William Eskridge, Owen Fiss, Glenda Gilmore, Jennifer Klein, Paul Kahn, Harold Koh, Anthony Kronman, John Langbein, Daniel Markovits, Burke Marshall, Jerry Mashaw, David Montgomery, Nicholas Parrillo, Claire Priest, George Priest, Robert Post, Judith Resnik, Carol Rose, Jed Rubenfeld, Peter Schuck, Vicki Schultz, Reva Siegel, James Whitman, John Witt.

In the 1980s and 90s my work and spirits were greatly refreshed by companions in the Conference on Critical Legal Studies, a merry and committed band who set out to critique the orthodoxies of the legal academy and had a lot of fun along the way. Among them: Richard Abel, Gary Bellow, James Boyle, Clare Dalton, Jay Feinman, Michael Fischl, Jerry Frug, Mary-Jo Frug, Alan Hyde, James Kainen, Mark Kelman, Karl Klare, David Kennedy, Duncan Kennedy, Frank Michelman, John Nockleby, Frances Olsen, Rand Rosenblatt, William Simon, Joseph William Singer, Katherine Stone, Mark Tushnet, Roberto Mangabeira Unger, and Kenneth Vandevelde.

In the early 1980s by a fortunate chance I was invited by David Flaherty to join the faculty of Summer Seminars in legal history and legal philosophy at the University of Western Ontario. Through those seminars and the friendship of the dean of Canadian legal historians, Richard C.B. Risk, I was able to meet a whole cadre of Canadian scholars who have in only two generations created out of almost nothing a flourishing field of Canadian legal history, including Constance Backhouse, Blaine Baker, Paul Craven, Hamar Foster, Philip Girard, William Kaplan, John McLaren, Jim Phillips, Wesley Pue, Paul Romney, Jonathan Swainger, Mariana Valverde, Rob Vipond.

My greatest debt is to the many scholars whose work these essays celebrate, and who have made of the last four decades a Golden Age of legal history. Besides those already mentioned, these include:

Gregory Alexander, Jerold Auerbach, Stuart Banner, Samantha Barbas, Felice Batlan, Christopher Beauchamp, Holly Brewer, Edward Balleisen, Michael Les Benedict, Barbara Black, Susanna Blumenthal, Guyora Binder, Margot Canaday, Susan Carle, Marianne Constable, Tomiko Brown-Nagin, Lyndsay Campbell, Kenneth Casebeer, Nancy Cott, Robert Cottrol, Barry Cushman, Christine Desan, Stephen Diamond, Charles Donahue, Jr., Markus Dubber, Ariela Dubler, Mary Dudziak, Neil Duxbury, Laura Edwards, Daniel Ernst, Angela Fernandez, William W. Fisher III, Joey Fishkin, William Forbath, Jill Fraley, Alan Freeman, Tony Allan Freyer, Christian Fritz, Paul Frymer, Howard Gillman, Mark Graber, Risa Goluboff, Sally Gordon, Thomas Green, Ariela Gross, Michael Grossberg, Lewis Grossman, Jill Hasday, Ron Harris, Douglas Hay, Hendrik Hartog, Daniel Hulsebosch, Wythe Holt, Herbert Hovenkamp, Arthur Jacobson, Laura Kalman, Michael Klarman, James Kloppenberg, Felicia Kornbluh,

Rande Kostal, Roy Kreitner, Alison LaCroix, Sophia Lee, Renee Lettow Lerner, David Lieberman, Assaf Likhovski, Matthew Lindsay, Sandy Levinson, Michael Lobban, Kenneth Mack, Pauline Maier, Bruce Mann, Maeva Marcus, James May, Serena Mayeri, Sara Mayeux, Charles McCurdy, Michelle McKinley, Rebecca McLennan, Ajay Mehrotra, Dalia Tsuk Mitchell, Jennifer Nedelsky, William Nelson, William Novak, Kent Newmyer, Kunal Parker, Rudolph Peritz, Richard Primus, Edward Purcell, Jedediah Purdy, David Rabban, Gautham Rao, John Phillip Reid, Rebecca Rix, Cristina Rodriguez, Jonathan Rose, Richard Ross, Lucy Salyer, Rebecca Scott, Reuel Schiller, Stephen Siegel, Mitra Sharafi, Karl Shoemaker, Jed Handelsman Shugerman, Brian Simpson, Bruce Smith, Rogers Smith, Avi Soifer, Clyde Spillenger, Amy Stanley, Robert Steinfeld, Robert Stevens, David Sugarman, Karen Tani, Steven Teles, Christopher Tomlins, Mark Tushnet, William Twining, Lea VanderVelde, Laura Weinrib, Carol Weisbrod, Barbara Welke, Lucie White, G. Edward White, Michael Willrich, William Wiecek, Steven Wilf, Victoria Saker Woeste. (I am certain that I have inadvertently left important names off this list!)

I feel particular gratitude toward those who first suggested that the Studies in Legal History series bring out this collection, and who persisted against my prolonged inertia: Daniel Ernst, Hendrik Hartog, Thomas Green, Holly Brewer, and especially Sally Gordon, my shepherd and guide through the publication process; and to Sally (again) and John Witt for their excessively generous Foreword.

For acute criticisms and suggestions for revision I am indebted to Laura Kalman and two anonymous reviewers for Cambridge University Press.

For work on preparing the text I am indebted to my assistants, Sara Abarbanel and Ginny Clegg Smith; and especially to Maithreyi Mulupuru, who performed with great care and skill the conversion of text and footnotes to a uniform format.

Finally my deepest gratitude is to my family, for their sustaining love and support:

Joan, Laura, Emily, Kate, Paul, Gino, Julien, Julia, and Jacob.

PART I

THE COMMON LAW TRADITION IN LEGAL HISTORIOGRAPHY

1

The Common Law Tradition in American Legal Historiography*

> [*This essay first appeared in 10* Law & Society Review *9 (1975), as the first part of an introduction to a Festschrift for the Wisconsin social-legal historian James Willard Hurst. Its aim was to sketch the history of American legal historiography before Hurst came on the scene and to explain how Hurst broke with the tradition of largely "internal" legal history. (In this collection, the essay is split into two parts, with the second part on Hurst's contributions – "James Willard Hurst – Social Legal History's Pioneer" – in the section on "Legal Historians" that follows this one.) Since this was written several notable works have amplified and added much valuable detail to the account given here – most especially of legal history-writing in the nineteenth century: John Burrow,* A Liberal Descent: Victorian Historians and the English Past (1981); *Stephen Siegel, "Historism in Late Nineteenth Century Constitutional Thought," 1990* Wis. L. Rev. *1431; Kunal Parker,* Common Law, History and Democracy in America, 1790–1900: Legal Thought Before Modernism (2011); *and David M. Rabban,* Law's History: American Legal Thought and the Transatlantic Turn to History (2012).]

In 1963, the Italian historiographer Arnaldo Momigliano told an assembly of legal historians that they were gathered to celebrate "a historical event of some importance, the end of history of law as an autonomous branch of historical research." At least in the historiography of ancient law, he said, "the elimination of history of law as independent history now seems to me to be settled."

* This essay owes much to conversations with Paul R. Duggan, Marc Galanter, David Hollinger, Stewart Macaulay, John Henry Schlegel, David Trubek, and Mark Tushnet, and to the members of the Faculty Seminar on Law and Development of the SUNY at Buffalo Law School, who heard and criticized an earlier version. They do not by any means all share the views reported here; and are not responsible for errors and distortions.

> Nor is it important to debate whether it was Max Weber or the French school of sociology or the teaching of Marx and Engels or, finally, the influence of Marc Bloch that precipitated this solution. It is inherent in the general recognition that law, as a systematization of social relations at a given level, cannot be understood without an analysis of the sexual orientations, the moral and religious beliefs, the economic production and the military forces that characterize a given society at a given moment, and are expressed in associations of individuals and in conflicts. It is conceivable today that history of literature, history of art, history of science, and history of religion can each retain some sort of autonomy, inasmuch as each is concerned with a specific activity of man. But what is no longer conceivable is that history of law should be autonomous; for by its very nature it is a formulation of human relations rooted in manifold human activities. And if, in some civilizations, there is a class of jurisconsults with special rules of conduct and of reasoning, this too is a social phenomenon to be interpreted.[1]

In the historiography of American law, the process Momigliano thus described as completed is only just beginning, for American legal historians have usually worked on the assumption that, at least for the purpose of dividing academic labor, it makes sense to identify a sphere of "legal" phenomena in society, and to write about how these have changed over time. It has never, of course, been possible to mark off the precise boundaries of such a field, but as a practical matter it almost inevitably turns out that they are drawn around the institutions, the occupations, the ideas and the procedures that have the appearance at any one time of being *distinctively legal*.[2] One might crudely represent this way of looking at law in society as follows:

input → [Law] → output

[1] A. D. Momigliano, "The Consequences of New Trends in the History of Ancient Law," in Momigliano, *Studies in Historiography* 239, 240–241 (1966).

[2] This would seem to imply that no one could write the legal history of a society that had no notion of "law" as a bundle of specialized activities distinct from, and to some extent autonomous of, other social phenomena – e.g., a society that did not distinguish between legal and religious norms. Legal historians usually solve this problem by treating of the aspects of such societies that appear to serve counterpart social functions to those of the relatively autonomous legal systems. For example, courts perform certain dispute settlement functions in modern Western societies which might, in other societies of the past, have been performed by councils of warriors or village elders. The warriors or elders will therefore be treated in the legal history of the other society. Yet though dispute settlement may be done by warriors or elders in modern Western societies also, that is not "law" and is therefore usually of no interest to legal historians. This somewhat curious manner of defining the field of specialization is partly responsible for the fact that focus abruptly shifts (and narrows) whenever a society exhibits traces of an autonomous legal order. On this point, see text at notes 29–31, 40–44, *infra*. On the emergence of "autonomous" legal orders in modern societies, see *Max Weber on Law and Economy in Society* (Rheinstein ed. 1954), especially chs. 7–9, 11; for a brilliant recent reinterpretation, Roberto Mangabeira Unger, *Law in Modern Society* (1976), especially at 52ff.

Inside the box is "the law," whatever appears autonomous about the legal order – courts, equitable maxims, motions for summary judgment; outside lies "society," the wide realm of the nonlegal, the political, economic, religious, social; the "inputs" are social influences upon the shape of the mass of things inside the law-box, the "outputs" the effects, or impact, of the mass upon society. Within the structure of this crude model there is, of course, a great range of possible theories of law, from a theory asserting that law derives its shape almost wholly from sources within the box (i.e., that it is really autonomous as well as seeming so), to one claiming that the box is really empty, the apparent distinctiveness of its contents illusory, since they are all the product of external social forces. Yet even those who incline to the latter view[3] take the contents of the box, epiphenomenal though they may be, as the main subject-matter of concern to the legal historian. Not that this is the only way of treating law historically, as Momigliano's words make clear;[4] but it probably is the only way for someone who defines himself as a "legal" historian; he has no choice.

Where he does have a choice, and an important one, is between writing internal and external legal history.[5] The internal legal historian stays as much as possible within the box of distinctive-appearing legal things; his sources are legal, and so are the basic matters he wants to describe or explain, such as changes in pleading rules, in the jurisdiction of a court, the texts assigned to beginning law students, or the doctrine of contributory negligence. The external

[3] Lawrence M. Friedman probably inclines as far as anyone. See e.g., his *History of American Law* (1973):

> This book treats American law ... not as a kingdom unto itself, not as a set of rules and concepts, not as the province of lawyers alone, but as a mirror of society. It takes nothing as historical accident, nothing as autonomous, everything as relative and molded by economy and society ... The [legal] system works like a blind, insensate machine. It does the bidding of those whose hands are on the controls ... [T]he strongest ingredient in American law, at any given time, is the present: current emotions, real economic interests, concrete political groups.

Id. at 10, 14. Professor Friedman acknowledges the existence of legal phenomena that are purely "internal" or "formal" – technical aspects of the system that can be altered or adjusted without affecting much (if at all) the outside society. See his "Law Reform in Historical Perspective," 13 *St. Louis U.L.J.* 351 (1969). He also recognizes that people living in some societies may perceive their legal order to be autonomous and to associate autonomy with legitimacy; he would classify such beliefs as part of a society's "legal culture" – "values and attitudes which ... determine the place of the legal system in the culture of the society as a whole." See his "Legal Culture and Social Development," 4 *L. & Soc' y. Rev.* 29, 34 (1969).

[4] Some scholars would go further than Momigliano; see, e.g., Richard L. Abel, "A Comparative Theory of Dispute Institutions in Society," 8 *L. & Soc'y Rev.* 217, 221–224 (1973), for the views of a legal anthropologist who has given up on "law" altogether as a useful organizing concept in social research.

[5] These terms are borrowed from T. S. Kuhn's treatments of (remarkably similar!) problems in the historiography of science. See especially his "Relations between History and History of Science," 100 *Daedalus* 271, 279 (1971), "External history" seems to me a better label than "social" history because it is more inclusive; specifically, it includes intellectual and cultural history.

historian writes about the interaction between the boxful of legal things and the wider society of which they are a part, in particular to explore the social context of law and its social effects, and he is usually looking for conclusions about those effects.

Up until very recently, and with few exceptions, American legal history has been of the internal kind. From time to time the few proponents of external history would direct an exasperated complaint against this situation, without much altering it.[6] As it happens, I tend to sympathize with most of these complaints, but writing another one is not my present purpose, since others have already said trenchantly what needed to be said; and in any case the situation is rapidly improving and there is no need for one. At this point it is more interesting to ask how the tradition of internal historiography got itself established, how it managed to last so long, and what the consequences of its ascendancy were for historical writing about American law. With that kind of perspective it might be possible adequately to assess the achievement of James Willard Hurst, the legal historian who broke decisively with the main tradition over thirty years ago, and who has since become the leading exponent and practitioner of an external historiography.

With the purpose of attempting that assessment in mind, the brief essay that follows tries to sketch the broad outlines of the paths taken by American legal historians since the beginnings of their discipline in the 1880s.[7] As I see it, there was a Classical Period from about 1880 to 1900, followed by a long slump lasting until about 1930; a First Revival of interest and activity in legal-historical studies from the 1930s through the early 1960s; then a Second Revival starting around 1970 and still going strong.[8]

[6] The best of these are, I think, Daniel J. Boorstin, "Tradition and Method in Legal History," 54 *Harv. L. Rev.* 424 (1951); George L. Haskins, "Law and Colonial Society," 9 *Am. Q.* 354 (1957); Stanley N. Katz, "Looking Backward: The Early History of American Law," 33 *U. Chi. L. Rev.* 867 (1966); Lawrence M. Friedman, "Some Problems and Possibilities of American Legal History," in *The State of American History* 3 (Bass ed. 1970); Morton J. Horwitz, "The Conservative Tradition in the Writing of American Legal History," 17 *Am. J. Leg. Hist.* 275 (1973); Herbert Alan Johnson, "American Colonial Legal History: A Historiographical Interpretation," *in Perspectives on Early American History* 250 (Vaughan & Billias eds. 1973), hereinafter Johnson, "Colonial Legal History"; and the many historiographical contributions of Willard Hurst, of which the most comprehensive, as well as the most recent, is "Legal Elements in United States History," in *Law in American History* 3 (Fleming & Bailyn eds. 1971), hereinafter Hurst, "Legal Elements." Much acerbic and astute criticism of the state of the art has appeared over the years in the *Annual Survey of American Law's* "Legal History" sections written by John Phillip Reid (1962–66); Reid and William E. Nelson (1969–70); and Nelson (1967–69; 1973–present). I am very indebted to all the articles cited here. One of the many ironies connected with American legal history is that its shortcomings have called forth so useful a historiographical literature.

[7] See Calvin Woodard, "History, Legal History, and Legal Education," 53 *Va. L. Rev.* 89 (1967) for a similar sketch arriving at somewhat different conclusions.

[8] Some readers may find my idea of what constitutes "American legal history" idiosyncratic – both too inclusive and too exclusive. It includes studies in English legal history in the 1880s and 90s, but then drops these; and excludes constitutional, administrative, and other plausible candidates

Some hedges and qualifications are in order. I do not try here to provide a comprehensive bibliographical survey; there are several excellent ones available.[9] I shall have very little to say about the literature of the Second Revival, contemporary historiography, since I plan to write about that on another occasion. And I can't do here what really ought some day to be done: a full-blooded social history of legal historiography in this country, showing the relationship of attempts to reconstruct the legal past to changes in the situation of lawyers generally, not only in the schools but in practice and in politics; and to intellectual developments outside the law, especially in philosophy and the social sciences.[10] In other words, this story is properly a minor subtheme of a much larger one – which remains untold because its telling has had to wait upon the development of an external legal historiography.[11] In this piece there are hints and whispers about the important relationships, but nothing more.

for the category of American legal history throughout. Let me try to justify this. Hardly anything one could call American legal history was written in the 1880s and 90s, but one has to say something about the legal history that was written (English, mostly), because it exerted such a strong influence on what came later. After that I try to stick to the American side, including in the "legal history" field whatever contemporaries were likely to include, which until recently meant the history of "private law" subjects and not much else except perhaps constitutional history, which I do not feel competent to discuss, but which I gather has suffered from comparable if considerably less severe limitations. See the bibliographical note, and sources there cited, in Harold M. Hyman, *A More Perfect Union* (1973), pp. 557–560. Notions of what legal history is about are, of course, rapidly changing, thanks in large part to the work of Willard Hurst and his school. See text at notes 132–135, *infra*.

9 See, e.g., Reid & Nelson, *Ann. Survey Am. L., supra* note 6; Friedman, *History of American Law, supra* note 3, at 596–621; Friedman *supra* note 6; Johnson, "Colonial Legal History"; David H. Flaherty, "An Introduction to Early American Legal History," in *Essays in the History of Early American Law* (Flaherty ed. 1009); Wythe Holt, "Now and Then: The Uncertain State of Nineteenth Century American Legal History," 7 *Ind. L. Rev.* 615 (1974); and Harry N. Scheiber, "Federalism and the American Economic Order," 10 *L. & Soc'y Rev.* 57 (1975) (in this issue, *infra*).

10 For an example of the exciting possibilities of a historiography relating law and lawyers to a wider culture, see William J. Bouwsma, "Lawyers and Early Modern Culture," 73 *Am. Hist. Rev.* 303 (1973) and the contributions already made to such a history cited in *id.* at 304 n.4.

11 Friedman, *History, supra* note 3, at 567–595 sketches a provocative brief outline of twentieth-century American legal history. The best general secondary treatment of the history of the American bar remains, twenty-five years later, James Willard Hurst, *The Growth of American Law: The Lawmakers* [hereinafter Hurst, *Lawmakers*] 249–375 (1950), a circumstance that probably gives the author little satisfaction. The history of legal education has been well treated recently in Robert Stevens, "Two Cheers for 1870: The American Law School," in *Law in American History* 405, *supra* note 6; Jerold S. Auerbach, "Equity and Amity: Law Teachers and Practitioners, 1900–1922," *id.* at 551; and William Twining, *Karl Llewellyn and the Realist Movement* (1973). Two books are especially successful at relating legal to philosophical thought in the twentieth century: Morton White, *Social Thought in America: The Revolt Against Formalism* (2nd edn. 1957) and David A. Hollinger, *Morris R. Cohen and the Scientific Ideal* (1975). There are several studies of Realism: among them Wilfrid E. Rumble, Jr., *American Legal Realism: Skepticism, Reform, and the Judicial Process* (1968); Calvin Woodard, "The Limits of Legal Realism: An historical perspective," 54 *Va. L. Rev.* 689 (1968); Twining, *supra*, this note; Edward A. Purcell, Jr., *The Crisis of Democratic Theory* (1971); and G. Edward

I

At the beginning of professional legal historiography in the United States which, for convenience, may be taken to be the publication by Henry Adams and his students of their *Essays in Anglo-Saxon Law* in 1876, nobody would have drawn a distinction between legal history and any other kind. For the first generation of professional historians in this country borrowed from Germany not only the name and method of "scientific" historiography, but also the idea of the proper subject-matter of that science: the development of political institutions from their remotest origins to the present. In the hands of the leading professionals in England like Freeman and Stubbs, and in America like Herbert Baxter Adams and John W. Burgess, this turned out to mean that virtually all history was to be legal and constitutional history: they were going to do for Anglo-American political forms what their German models had done for the Roman. Thus, there was nothing eccentric about the young Henry Adams's choice of Anglo-Saxon law as his Harvard seminar project in medieval history, or about the young O. W. Holmes's decision to study first Roman law and then the early forms of common law: the most exciting intellectual problems of the day were problems concerning origins of present political and legal forms, and the hottest debates over whether these origins were Roman or Teutonic.[12]

This preoccupation with origins resulted, of course, from the subscription of nineteenth-century historians to various kinds of evolutionary assumptions about the development of political institutions. These assumptions varied greatly in their particulars and patrimony from historian to historian: some learned an idealist historical jurisprudence from Savigny; others picked up Freeman's idea of history as the gradual unfolding of political liberty; still others borrowed metaphors from anthropology or comparative philology. At the common core of these theories were the assumptions that all societies undergo comparable processes of development from the simple to the complex, the primitive to the civilized; that these processes are continuous and progressive; and that the business of scientists was to discover, through the comparative study of developed and undeveloped peoples, the laws governing the growth

White, "From Sociological Jurisprudence to Realism: Jurisprudence and Social Change in Early Twentieth Century America," 58 *Va. L. Rev.* 999 (1972). This literature on Realism, though interesting and useful, still leaves one with the feeling that something important has been left out. Except for Twining, the authors tend to treat the Realists as (rather inept) legal philosophers, quoting from their more speculative work and from their debates on the nature of law with critics like Roscoe Pound and Morris Cohen. What gets slighted in the process is most of the stuff that the Realists themselves considered their most important work: their studies of subjects like procedure and commercial law. Research now being done by John Henry Schlegel should help to correct this. Jerold S. Auerbach, *Unequal Justice: Lawyers and Social Change in Modern America* (1976) appeared too late to be consulted for this essay.

12 On the significance of Henry Adams' seminar, see Helen M. Cam, *Law Finders and Law-Makers* 176–182 (1962); on the influence of German writers on Holmes, Mark DeWolfe Howe, *Justice Oliver Wendell Holmes: The Proving Years*, 1870–1882, ch. 5 (1963).

of civilizations.[13] The particular business of historians was to trace the development of customs and ideals of already developed civilizations back to their ancient beginnings. For the extremely influential historians H.B. Adams and Burgess, who were especially impressed by German conceptions of history as the science of the state, this program dictated studying the development of political institutions, in their legal and constitutional forms.[14] National and racial ethnocentrism then combined to make Anglo-American civilization the focus of study; and this in turn made of the historiography of North America simply the study of the most recent stages of a long, continuous process beginning in the ancient Teutonic forests.[15]

Institutional-evolutionary studies in legal history flourished in the law schools too in the 1880s and 90s, especially at Harvard; it was under the influence of this school (to varying degrees) that Holmes, Bigelow, Thayer and Ames made their contributions to the study of early English law.[16] The point of dwelling on the assumptions of the historical school is not to depreciate the achievement of these men, who were among the few people Maitland found it worthwhile to correspond with on professional subjects;[17] it is that these assumptions have continued to linger around the law schools to the present day, like radioactive matter with an abnormally long half-life. Professional historians – helped and sometimes led by the legal historians – soon repudiated the simpler tenets of this school, such as the theories of a unilinear evolutionary development and of the Teutonic origins of Anglo-Saxon civilization; and most of them went on to shake off its influence almost entirely. What we have to account for is the survival of nineteenth-century evolutionary theory not only in amateur legal writing – the brief "historical introductions" to textbook or article – but in various indirect ways in monographic legal history as well.[18]

The solution to the puzzle lies, I think, in the reasons that the new law schools were so hospitable to legal-historical studies in the first place: their

[13] J. W. Burrow, *Evolution and Society, A Study in Victorian Social Theory* (1966) emphasizes the variety of nineteenth-century evolutionary theories; Robert A. Nisbet, *Social Change and History* 166–188 (1968), their similarity.

[14] See especially Jurgen Herbst, *The German Historical School in American Scholarship* 112–116 (1965); and John Higham, *History: Professional Scholarship in America* 158–161 (1965). Out of fifteen history courses given at Harvard in 1890–91, "twelve were wholly or partly concerned with constitutional development." Cam, *supra* note 12, at 182.

[15] The titles of some of H. B. Adams's articles will convey the flavor of some of his scholarship: "The Germanic Origin of New England Towns," *Johns Hopkins Studies in History and Political Science* (ser. 1, no. 2, 1882); "Saxon Tithing-Men in America," *id.* (ser. 1, no. 4, 1882); "Norman constables in America," *id.* (ser. 1, no. 8, 1883).

[16] James Barr Ames, *Lectures on Legal History and Miscellaneous Legal Essays* (1913); Melville M. Bigelow, *Placita Anglo-Normannica* (1879) and *History of Procedure in England from the Norman Conquest* (1880); Oliver Wendell Holmes, Jr., *The Common Law* (1881); James Bradley Thayer, *A Preliminary Treatise on Evidence at the Common Law* (1898).

[17] See C. H. S. Fifoot, *Frederick William Maitland: A Life*, at viii, 69–70, 75–76, 80 (1971).

[18] See text at notes 23–27, 32–44, *infra*.

faculties (at least initially) perceived no conflict between historical research and the strictly professional ambitions of the schools. To be sure, the founding generation of law teachers defined a role for themselves in the profession differing from the practitioner's. The legal scholar was not simply to train his students in the law as it was, but to ascertain the principles truly underlying the law through scientific research, to the end of reforming existing law by bringing it into conformity with those principles.[19] History was supposed to be the primary field of research. But ultimately the results of research were to be grist for the judicial mill. Ames, for example, thought of historiography simply as one of the useful lawyer's tasks that the professor, because of his freedom from the press of business, could attend to with the greater efficiency that comes from specialization off unction. What was wanted was:

> a high order of treatises on all the important branches of the law, exhibiting the historical development of the subject and containing sound conclusions based on scientific analysis... Too often the just expectations of men are thwarted by the action of the courts, a result largely due to taking a partial view of the subject, or to a failure to grasp the original development and true significance of the rule which is made the basis of the decision.

As an instance he cites the rule denying enforceability to creditors' agreements to release debtors on part payment of the debt: this "unfortunate rule," says Ames "is the result of misunderstanding a *dictum* of Coke. In truth Coke, in an overlooked case, declared in unmistakable terms the legal validity of the creditor's agreement."[20]

If only historians had earlier brought to light Coke's other case! Ames, plainly, felt none of Maitland's skepticism about the results of mixing legal dogma and legal history. Maitland said: "The lawyer must be orthodox otherwise he is no lawyer; an orthodox history seems to me a contradiction in terms."[21] Like most of his colleagues, Ames did not see the contradiction. He hoped to subordinate the development of dogma to historical science. In fact, things turned out exactly the opposite: legal history was subordinated to legal technique, the immediate needs of the profession to keep current dogma rationalized in line with past authority. The historical school's view of law as the continuous development of institutional forms lent itself beautifully to these needs, since that view made it easy to confuse the history of law with the "common law tradition" – the fictional continuity that each generation

[19] See Auerbach, "Equity and Amity," *supra* note 11 at 553–572.

[20] James Barr Ames, "The Vocation of the Law Professor," in Ames, *supra* note 16 at 366. [The reference is clearly to *Foakes* v. *Beer*, 9 App. Cas. 605 (1884), *citing* Pinnel's Case, 5 Co. Rep. 117a (1602).] Ames also saw a role for the law professor as an "expart counselor in legislation," by which he meant advisor on technical law reform. *id.* at 367–368.

[21] "Why the history of law is not written," *Collected Papers*, I, 480, 493 (1911).

of common lawyers imposes, in its own fashion and for its own ends, on the development of judicial doctrine.[22]

Institutional-evolutionary studies prospered in the law schools because they had something to offer the profession: documentation of the unbroken chain of connection between living lawyers and an ancient tradition. The successors in historiographical fashion to the historical school, however, could offer nothing of the kind. The second generation of American institutional historians, C. M. Andrews and H. L. Osgood in particular, rejected the idea of universal and necessary legal development; and picked up from the research of Maine, Brunner, Maitland, and Vinogradoff (among others) the program of studying the effects upon legal forms of specific and local variations in social environment.[23] Meanwhile the New, or Progressive historians led by Turner and Beard were carrying off much of the historical profession in their challenge to the primacy of the study of the development of political institutions, insisting that legal and constitutional forms were only secondary derivatives of economic and social forces. Beard was of course the most influential proponent of a revised notion of law as the expression, not of the evolving ethical ideals of the Anglo-Saxon race, but of economic interests pursued through factional politics.[24]

The law schools had small use for either of these modes of practicing history, even though Holmes and Pound, both law teachers, had been instrumental in promoting them. Very little American history of any distinction in

[22] Horwitz, *supra* note 6 at 282–283, calls attention to the "incredibly striking" parallels between lawyer's legal history and scientists' history of science, quoting T. S. Kuhn, *The Structure of Scientific Revolutions* 137–138 (2nd edn. 1970):

> Textbooks ... begin by truncating the scientist's sense of his discipline's history and then proceed to supply a substitute for what they have eliminated. Characteristically, textbooks of science contain just a bit of history, either in an introductory chapter or, more often, in scattered references to the great heroes of an earlier age. From such references both students and professionals come to feel like participants in a long-standing historical tradition. Yet the textbook tradition in which scientists come to sense their participation is one that, in fact, never existed ... [S]cience textbooks ... refer only to that part of the work of past scientists that can easily be viewed as contributions to the statement and solution of the text's paradigm problems ... No wonder that textbooks and the historical tradition they imply have to be rewritten after each scientific revolution. And no wonder that, as they are rewritten, science once again comes to seem largely cumulative.

[23] On the new institutional (or "imperial") historians, see Higham, *supra* note 14 at 162–166; Johnson, "Colonial Legal History." Maine is usually thought of as an evolutionist; but Kenneth E. Bock has persuasively argued that he was an opponent of the theory of a unilinear evolutionary development, and not interested in hunting for origins among primitive peoples, but instead was concerned to study law in relation to the entire surrounding culture, including its "relatively recent history." (I.e., Maine was disposed to explain ancient law by ancient history, but not modern law.) "Comparison of Histories: The Contribution of Henry Maine," 16 *Comp. Stud. in Soc' y & Hist.* 232, 247 (1974).

[24] On the Progressives, see Richard Hofstadter, *The Progressive Historians* (1968), especially 181–218; and Higham, *supra* note 14 at 171–182.

the institutional vein of Andrews and Osgood was written in the law schools between 1900 and the revival of legal-historical studies in the 1930s; this is probably because history, like liberal learning generally in that period, fell victim to the case method's exclusive claim on the undergraduate law curriculum. Moreover the institutional approach demanded long and patient study in primary materials, time taken away from, and not yielding any particularly valuable results in aid of, treatise and case-book writing.[25] As for Progressive history, it was simply anathema. When the Progressives took over American constitutional history they pretty well wiped out internal-doctrinal and intellectual-approaches among the historians, leaving these to be cultivated (with great distinction, as it turned out) by political scientists like Corwin and McIlwain.[26] They could obviously not have converted many lawyers to their method in the early part of this century, since in its extreme forms it denied the existence of any autonomous content to law, and hence any meaning to legal historiography as traditionally practiced. The Progressives did not themselves produce (at least, until Willard Hurst began to write) any significant body of work on private law; but their hostility helped effectively to split off legal history from the main action in American scholarship and to isolate it in the law schools.[27]

[25] The case method, in Langdell's original conception a way of getting across the basic principles of legal science, rapidly acquired its present-day justification as a pedagogic vehicle for the teaching of legal method. Thus justified, it became the device for teaching every undergraduate law course, tending to drive out subjects (such as legal philosophy and history) not suited to being so taught. See Stevens, *supra* note 11 at 435–449. In 1960, commenting bitterly on the anti-intellectualism accompanying the spread of the Harvard method in the late nineteenth and early twentieth centuries, Karl Llewellyn recounted that when

> [William A.] Keener was called to Columbia in 1890 to put that law school on a footing worthy of a great University, he brought with him two policies: (1) "The" case-system... (2) All that noise which is not "law" must go out; a "law" curriculum must cast out Ishmael. Columbia ... had therefore to amputate from any official "law"-connection what became the Department of Political Science. Thus the Roman Law Perspective of a Munroe Smith, the scholarship and vision of a [Frank J.] Goodnow, the power and range of our greatest international lawyer, John Bassett Moore [who trained, among others, Julius Goebel, Jr.], flourished not within the law curriculum, nor for it, but across the barbarian border ... In 1915, when, already our foremost jurisprude, [Roscoe Pound] became Dean at Harvard Law School, he deliberately took his own Jurisprudence course *out of the undergraduate curriculum.* He kept it out, lest his bulk of graduates be distracted – or contaminated.

Llewellyn, "The Study of Law as a Liberal Art," in *Jurisprudence* 375, 377–378 (1962). [Italics Llewellyn's; interpolations mine.]

[26] See generally, Herman Belz, "The Realist Critique of Constitutionalism in the Era of Reform," 15 *Am. J. Leg. Hist.* 288 (1971); Paul L. Murphy, "Time to Reclaim: The Current Challenge of American Constitutional History," 69 *Am. Hist. Rev.* 64 (1963).

[27] It is not always appreciated how wide the split was. One can get some sense of it from casual remarks made recently by non-lawyer historians who have become interested in law. For example: (a) Eugene Genovese: "[T]he fashionable relegation of law to the rank of a superstructural and derivative phenomenon obscures the degree of autonomy it creates for itself." *Ron, Jordan, Roll* 25 (1974). (b) Harry N. Scheiber, speaking of recent developments in economic history, refers to "*new* lines of inquiry that stress institutional and doctrinal development in American

Confined to the law faculties, reduced to the status of auxiliary service for strictly professional tasks, and written for the most part by amateurs, legal historiography suffered a rapid narrowing of scope. The old historical school had held out the promise of connecting the history of law and of society. In the study of medieval English law, that promise was being fulfilled. In America it was cut short, and legal history was reduced to internal history.

In part this happened because the historical school's organic theory of culture paradoxically encouraged scholars to disregard the social context of law, just as the "comparative method," by generalizing patterns of development in a single civilization to all others, in fact justified ethnocentricity. James Coolidge Carter, Savigny's chief popularizer in this country, gave the game away when he said that the field of research for judges trying to locate the true or just rule of law for a case by the historical method was "the habits, customs, business and manners of the people, *and those previously declared rules which have sprung out of previous similar inquiries into habits, customs, business, and manners*."[28] This was certainly a convenient method for legal scholars: it meant that in practice they carried no greater research burden than would any legal positivist, for whom legal history was only the history of past state commands, rather than the history of an entire culture.

But of course the main reason lawyer's history became, and remained, internal – confined to the boxful of distinctively legal things – is that it was written from inside the box, was itself a "form of professional activity within the legal system – like adjudication, or advocacy, or counseling."[29] As long as the common law tradition was a source of normative authority, the doing of legal history was conceived to be a professional task; as long as it was a professional task it was bound to be internal. Legal scholars not only took the boxful of legal things as their exclusive subject-matter, but whenever possible adduced as factors explaining the development of legal things only other legal things. The rule seemed to be: stay inside the box; the most common application of the rule was explanation of current case-law doctrine by means of prior case-law doctrine.

This is why, long after the discrediting of evolutionary theories of history, legal history was still so frequently written as if these theories still held sway. For the historian who restricts his sources to the strictly legal, there often is no

law ..." "Government and the Economy: Studies of the 'Commonwealth' Policy in Nineteenth Century America," 3 *J. Interdisc. Hist.* 135, 151 n. 44 (1972) [Italics added]. Historians are discovering law, lawyers society.

28 *The Ideal and the Actual in Law* 10–11 (1890).

29 This is how Richard L. Abel describes a "law book," a "study [that] identifies, defines, organizes the rules [that legal institutions apply] by means of criteria proper to the legal system – it *rationalizes* them in Weber's sense." He contrasts such a "law book" to a "book about law," which is a "mode of *reflection* upon the legal system." "Law Books and Books About Law," 26 *Stan. L. Rev.* 175, 176 (1973) [Italics Abel's]. This is another (and very effective) way of stating Maitland's distinction between legal history and legal dogma, text at note 21, *supra*.

explanation available other than the genetic. Suppose one wanted to explain the use of the "fellow-servant" rule to limit liability of employers for the costs of industrial accidents in the nineteenth century, and one's search were confined to the rule's predecessors in form. One would learn a good deal about the common law of master and servant and the writ of trespass on the case, but nothing about nineteenth-century industry, however useful such knowledge might be.[30]

Limitations of method thus kept driving American lawyers backwards in search of the ancestors of current legal categories in early English forms. When they got there they found a historiography that was often extremely technical, but not internal; the further back one went, the more one found law connected to social structure, economic organization, agricultural method, administrative practice, currents of religious and philosophical speculation. The great researchers of the classical period and their successors had given medieval law a context. But as one approached more recent times, legal history started to thin out to the distinctively "legal" again, and explanations for the shape of legal things to revert to the genetic.

Around 1900 then, at the point serious work in legal history slumped in American law schools, scholarly convention in the field suggested it was all right to try to account for old law by external circumstance, but not new law. This way of looking at things matched nicely with the contemporary jurisprudential theory that the common law, though it had started out derived from Custom, had come, as its administration was brought under a professional judiciary, to be based upon Reason.[31] It is tempting to suggest that the law schools were not interested in developments in historiography that would tend to controvert this theory. At any rate, the configurations that legal-historical

[30] The late Professor Goebel employed his gift for Latinate astringency to characterize this method as treating

> the growth of doctrine as something projected on a horizontal plane of rational manipulation unmindful of its perpendicular support in time or circumstance. In expositions of the doctrine of consideration, the judgments of his majesty's judges in the seventeenth century rub shoulders with those from the American backwoods two hundred years later. To legitimate the control of business, Tudor sumptuary statutes are forcibly wedded to the legislative indiscretions of the seventy-third Congress...
>
> That so fantastic a conception of history should prevail as a convention in the bulk of our legal literature is attributable in some degree to the intellectual tyranny which the judicial opinion exerts. It is a truism that to know the common law its history must be known. Our courts, however, seek enlightenment on the past chiefly in the judgments of their predecessors. These judgments are rarely treated as single but complex assessable facts, for the mass of relevant data of which they are merely parts is usually ignored. In consequence, the antecedent judicial opinion is elevated to a status of preposterous importance as a source...

Julius Goebel, Jr., *Felony and Misdemeanor* xvii–xviii (1937).

[31] Beale was expounding this theory to Harvard law students in 1909, according to notes taken by Robert Lee Hale of his lectures on jurisprudence in that year. These notes are published, with an introduction, in Warren J. Samuels, "Joseph Henry Beale's Lectures on Jurisprudence, 1909," 29 *U. Miami L. Rev.* 260 (1975). See *id.* at 288–293.

scholarship achieved by 1900 were decisive for the future shape of the field – especially in American legal history.

Look for example at the Association of American Law Schools' *Select Essays in Anglo-American Legal History* (1907), which purported to collect in three volumes the cream of current scholarship in the field.[32] This includes some wonderful stuff – e.g., Maitland's famous essay on "English Law and the Renaissance" – but is mostly interesting now for the subjects it includes. Most of the essays (after the traditional start with Teutonic Law) have to do with English law; after some broad surveys, the essays tend to be organized by type of court (Chancery, Admiralty, etc.) and doctrinal field (assumpsit, agency, trover, defamation, etc.). The stress is on the common law, though equity receives seven essays in all, and there are brief treatments of canon law, admiralty, and the law merchant. With very few exceptions, the essays are concerned with tracing the early forms of modern practice categories – "The Historical Development of Code Pleading" – "Early Forms of Partnership" – "The Early History of Negotiable Instruments" – and the exceptions are the essays set in early English history and unabashedly making no pretense at current relevance.

The American entries are of most interest. They cluster around colonial legal history and are primarily devoted to exploring the extent to which colonial law was influenced or determined by English models. Then there are treatments of nineteenth-century attempts at procedural reform in the common law, dealing with proposals to simplify pleading and the organization of courts and with the fate of schemes to codify the common law in whole or in part, from Bentham to David Dudley Field. Lacking (as yet) only the addition of something on the reception of English law after the Revolution, the basic canon of American legal history was fixed – and fixed almost before any work had been done! – upon transplantation to America of the common law and the subsequent challenge and defeat, save for partial accommodation in the form of Code Pleading, of the common law's arch rival, codification. Even to the present, general surveys and collections of materials on American legal history are faithful to the broad outlines of this canon. This is a wonderful example of the survival of form beyond its inspiring context, for these subjects are the vital ones of American experience only within a theory such as the old historical school's – by which American history simply records the later stages of the common law's triumphant struggle for continuous development through Anglo-Saxon civilization.

There were two jarring notes in this collection. One was the famous attempt by Reinsch, a disciple of Turner's at Wisconsin, to demonstrate the domination

[32] And did so in fact. Its nearest rival was a compilation of essays in American legal history put out by members of the Yale Law School faculty, *Two Centuries' Growth of American Law, 1701–1901* (1901), sketching the antecedents of some eighteen fields of contemporary practice, and now interesting mostly as revealing how little access even learned lawyers had to their own past.

of colonial law not by English models but the primitive law of the frontier.[33] Oddly enough this environmental (and later proved erroneous[34]) explanation was absorbed along with the rest of the 1907 collection into the orthodox view of the American past. The assumption of the continuity of Anglo-American legal development was neatly rescued despite the Reinsch theory by Roscoe Pound, who simply moved up the period of "reception" of English law in America to a "formative era" after the Revolution.[35] The other oddity in the collection was the presence of contributions by Simeon Baldwin and the young Samuel Williston on early corporation law.[36] Corporation law too was to find a niche in the permanent canon of appropriate subjects, either as a subspecies of commercial law or on its own. These particular articles, like the others, tended to emphasize the most formal aspects of corporations and the earliest forms at that; there was nothing here like Maitland's speculations on the social functions of different forms of group legal personality.[37] Nonetheless, corporation law had so obviously responded to political and economic pressure in recent history that the inclusion of it in the standard canon was prophetic. Sooner or later, it would be the most promising candidate for external historiographical treatment; and so it eventually proved to be.[38]

Anyone who is skeptical about the extraordinary persistence through our time of this late-nineteenth-century view of the proper scope of legal history should pick up any of the standard history texts published for law students.[39] Or he might look at the historical section of any recent law review article. I am looking at one now, chosen because it is near at hand and because it is one of the best things of its kind, not one of the

[33] Paul Samuel Reinsch, "English Common Law in the Early American Colonies," *Select Essays in Anglo-American Legal History*, I, 367 (1907).

[34] By the work of Goebel, Morris, and Haskins in particular. See Johnson, "Colonial Legal History," and the essays collected in Flaherty, *supra* note 9.

[35] Pound, *The Spirit of the Common Law* 113–118 (1921); *The Formative Era of American Law* 6–12, *et passim* (1938). For an account of Pound's "enormous influence on the study of American law" with these two books, see Michael G. Kammen, "Colonial Court Records and the Study of Early American History: A Bibliographical Review," 70 *Am. Hist. Rev.* 732, 738 (1965); and Katz, *supra* note 6.

[36] Baldwin, "History of the Law of Private Corporations in the Colonies and States," in *Select Essays, supra* note 33, at III, 236; Williston, "The History of the Law of Business Corporations Before 1800," *id.* at III, 195.

[37] Maitland's essays on trusts, corporations, and unincorporated bodies are all collected in *Maitland: Selected Essays* (Hazeltine, Lapsley, & Winfield eds. 1936), as well as in Maitland, *supra* note 21.

[38] There is a fuller literature on the history of the American corporation than on any other subject that plausibly belongs in the field of American legal history. See the bibliography in James Willard Hurst, *The Legitimacy of the Business Corporation in the Law of the United States, 1780–1970* at 165 (1970).

[39] See, e.g., William F. Walsh, *A History of Anglo-American Law* [Bobbs-Merrill] (2nd edn. 1932); Max Radin, *Handbook of Anglo-American Legal History* [West Hornbook Series] (1936); Frederick G. Kempin, Jr., *Historical Introduction to Anglo-American Law in a Nutshell* [West Nutshell Series] (1973). Of course these vary greatly in quality: Radin's is the outstanding one.

worst: an excellent synthesis of anthropological and historical literature about contract law.[40] The article is explicitly evolutionary; it begins with economic transactions in "primitive" societies and ends with twentieth-century American contracts; in between lie ancient Rome, England from medieval to modern times, and nineteenth-century America. The sections on primitive society are rich in detail about the relation of forms of transactions to social life – to kinship systems, religion, land tenure, warfare.[41] Even by the time he reaches medieval England, the author is still interested in externals: we learn for example something about theological views of contract.[42] But from the moment the common law courts get into the picture, the focus of the narrative shifts almost exclusively to institutional and doctrinal forms: case, assumpsit, indebitatus assumpsit, consideration, up to Slade's Case in 1602, whereupon, saving a brief "Epilogue," the article ends![43] It ends presumably because the story of doctrinal developments is now complete; the Epilogue treats summarily of the high point of "freedom of contract" in the nineteenth century and of the tendency in the twentieth to limit this freedom by legislation.[44] Except for passing references to the work of Weber, Hurst, and Lawrence Friedman, there is scarcely a word on the tremendous changes that have taken place in the nature of economic exchange relationships between the seventeenth century and the present, no allusion even to the standard economic histories of Europe and America for that time. It would be absurd to blame this situation on the author, who is a scholar of distinction; he was working with materials that are at hand to tell the story that has commonly been thought the one worth telling. The point is to show how deeply ingrained in the consciousness of the modern lawyer is the late-nineteenth-century's subordination of legal history to the common law tradition.

II

American legal historiography began to revive in the late 1920s. It is not clear why this happened. Perhaps in part it was simply because the students whom Andrews and Osgood had interested in the study of primary source material on British imperial administration were starting to turn out their own work; in part because some of the younger law teachers, especially at Columbia, were trying to break down the hedges that had grown up between other university departments and the law schools. In 1930 the American Historical Association

40 E. Allan Farnsworth, "The Past of Promise: An Historical Introduction to Contract," 69 *Colum. L. Rev.* 576 (1969).

41 *Id.* at 578–588.

42 *Id.* at 591.

43 *Id.* at 592–599.

44 *Id.* at 599–607.

organized a conference of lawyers and historians to draw up a program to publish American legal source materials: this resulted in the American Legal Records series.[45] In the same year, private and foundation gifts established the Foundation for Research in Legal History at Columbia Law School, under the direction of Julius Goebel, Jr., which underwrote research and publication expenses of new secondary work.[46]

For the purposes of this essay, the most interesting aspect of this period of revival, which lasted through the mid-1960s (and is perhaps still going on – these periodizations never work out very neatly), is that its scholarship did not bring about any very substantial redefinition of the field of legal history. (There were exceptions, which will be noted.) On the face of it, this is rather surprising. The period was dominated by work in colonial law done by historians of formidable talent – Goebel, George L. Haskins, Mark DeWolfe Howe, Richard B. Morris, Joseph H. Smith. None of these historians believed that law develops primarily according to the logic of an internal dynamic, independently of surrounding political, social, and economic conditions; indeed each thought that belief one of the failings of the amateur historiography of the early twentieth century, for among other errors it propagated the theory of the process of reception and development of English law taking place in a uniform manner and rate across all of early America. Though some members of this fresh group of colonial historians, notably Morris,[47] were eventually again to emphasize similarities among colonial legal patterns, all of them recognized that any generalizations would have to be based upon archival study of local materials in individual colonies.

Yet though a conviction of the importance of the influence of social surroundings on law was what drove historians of this period to research in local sources in the first place, it did not carry most of them so far as to write external legal history. They stayed chiefly within the orthodox canon of subjects – the reception of English common law in America and its nineteenth-century rivalry with "codification" – and continued to take their materials from the box of distinctively legal things. Their teaching materials, enriched by the results of their research in primary sources, were enormously more sophisticated than similar products of the old institutional-evolutionary school; but they were organized by the same categories as the old school's (reception, codification,

45 The committee consisted of Charles McLean Andrews, Carroll T. Bond (Chief Judge of the Maryland Court of Appeals and editor of the first volume in the series), John Dickinson, the ubiquitous Felix Frankfurter, Evarts B. Greene, and Richard B. Morris. See Evarts B. Greene, "Foreword" to *Proceedings of the Maryland Court of Appeals*, 1695–1729 (American Legal Records, I; Bond ed. 1933). Greene acknowledged "the encouragement, given at an early stage of the development of this project, by Mr. Justice Brandeis ..." *Id.* For a list of publications in the series, see Kammen, *supra* note 35 at 733.

46 See Goebel, *supra* note 30 at ix.

47 See his *Studies in the History of American Law* (1958); and Johnson, "Colonial Legal History" at 258–261.

corporations, etc.), and the detail filling the old categories, though new, was all *legal* detail.[48] Symbolically, the most important collective effort of professional American legal historians at the end of the period was of the same kind as at the beginning-publication of colonial legal records.[49]

One must point out immediately that there were significant exceptions to this pattern; and that historians of this period did make major contributions to an external legal historiography. Daniel Boorstin's study of Blackstone's *Commentaries* and Mark DeWolfe Howe's of Holmes's *Common Law* both succeeded in connecting law books to wider regions of the thought of their time.[50] After a series of monographs written in a more cautious mode, George L. Haskins built a new framework for colonial legal studies by taking as his subject not the specialized concerns of lawyers, but the whole governmental and clerical apparatus of social control in seventeenth-century Massachusetts.[51]

But these, like the work of Hurst and his followers to be discussed later, were exceptions. The main business of the period was to make a start at giving American law historicity, localizing it to specific times and places. Under the spell of evolutionism and professional habit, the earlier school of lawyer-historians had ransacked the past for ancestors of their own day's categories, though these categories might have possessed no significance, or a very different one, for the previous generations back through whom they were traced. The researchers of the 1930s and onward corrected this by showing us colonial law through the eyes of contemporaries – but usually through the eyes of contemporary lawyers, and abnormally bookish lawyers at that. Research that adopted a different perspective was not likely to be considered "legal" history at all, even if it relied primarily on legal sources as evidence – e.g., Richard Morris's great study of colonial labor conditions and regulation[52] or the studies of nineteenth-century "public policy" in the states.[53]

[48] See, e.g., Julius Goebel, Jr., *Cases and Materials on the Development of Legal Institutions* (2nd edn. 1937) [*but see* Ch. 3 of this book, on "Social, economic and intellectual factors conditioning legal development," which mostly accords with tradition in confining discussion of such factors to the earlier English law, but not entirely: cf. *id.* at 620–626 on American corporations]; Mark DeWolfe Howe, *Readings in American Legal History* (1949); and Joseph H. Smith, *Cases and Materials on the Development of Legal Institutions* (1965).

[49] The William Nelson Cromwell Foundation underwrote in whole or in part: *Colonial Justice in Western Massachusetts* (1639–1702): *The Pyncheon Court Record* (Smith ed. 1961); *Legal Papers of John Adams* (Wroth & Zobel eds. 1965); and *The Law Practice of Alexander Hamilton* (Goebel et al., eds. 1964). I am not complaining about this; these volumes are superbly edited, and if there is one place where lavish spreading of technical detail is surely justified, it is in the edition of a primary text.

[50] Boorstin, *The Mysterious Science of the Law* (1941); Howe, *supra* note 12.

[51] Haskins, *Law and Authority in Early Massachusetts* (1960). The influence of this approach may be detected in the range (as well as the title) of a recent collection of essays, *Law and Authority in Colonial America* (Billias ed. 1965).

[52] *Government and Labor in Early America* (1946).

[53] See Scheiber, *supra* note 27.

What can account for the almost unrelenting preoccupation with internals? Daniel Boorstin and Calvin Woodard, who at different times both called for a more catholic vision of the scope of legal history, both attributed its unsatisfactory state in part to the pragmatic temper of legal studies since the 1930s. Boorstin said: "[N]early every American contribution to legal history which ought to be considered a classic was made *before* the movement [to integrate law and the social sciences]"; he blamed the law schools' fads for policy science, social science, and clinical education.[54] Woodard reproached legal scholars "somewhat intoxicated with the delusion of complete freedom from the past" for promoting among students the view that law is merely "engineering," or "the vector of so many mid-20th century social forces rationalized in accordance with the personal preference of so many contemporary judges and legislators."[55]

The trouble with this explanation is that it was precisely those people who took the most pragmatic view of present law that tended to urge the study of the past – urged it, indeed, partly for the sake of ridding the present of the deadwood of irrelevant survivals. Maitland took this view, for example;[56] so did Holmes, the founder of American pragmatic legal thought.[57] In fact, a very large number of lawyers associated with the pragmatic movement[58] took more than a passing interest in legal history. Pound's lectures on the "formative era of American law" influenced several generations of historians;[59] Frankfurter was not only instrumental in obtaining research funding for legal history, but also wrote histories of the Commerce Clause, and (with

[54] "The Humane Study of Law," 57 *Yale L.J.* 960, 963–964 (1948).

[55] Woodard, *supra* note 7 at 110–114.

[56] See, e.g., Maitland writing to Dicey in 1896 (cited in Fifoot, *supra* note 17 at 143):

> The only direct utility of legal history (I say nothing of its thrilling interest) lies in the lesson that each generation has an enormous power of shaping its own law. I don't think that the study of legal history would make men fatalists; I doubt it would make them conservatives. I am sure it would free them from superstitions and teach them that they have free hands.

[57] See, e.g., "Law in Science and Science in Law [1899]," in Holmes, *Collected Legal Papers* 210, 225 (1920):

> From a practical point of view, [the use of history] is mainly negative and skeptical ... [I]ts chief good is to burst inflated explanations. Everyone instinctively recognizes that in these days the justification of a law cannot be found in the fact that our fathers have always followed it. It must be found in some help which the law brings toward reaching a social end which the governing power of the community has made up its mind that it wants ... [H]istory is the means by which we measure the power which the past has had to govern the present in spite of ourselves, so to speak, by imposing traditions which no longer meet their original end.

[58] This phrase seems broad enough to encompass Holmes's pragmatism, Pound's sociological jurisprudence, and the many varieties of legal Realism.

[59] See note 35, *supra*.

others) of federal jurisdiction and labor injunctions;[60] Karl Llewellyn, Jerome Hall, Walton Hamilton, Walter Nelles, and Hessel Yntema, all Realists, all did some of their own work in history[61] and followed closely what was done by others. Pragmatic legal studies were at their height during the revival of professional legal historiography in the 1930's; Goebel was one of the young Turks at the Columbia Law School; Howe was a clerk to Holmes and protégé of Frankfurter's; Haskins was inspired by Pound's theory of interests; and – as will be seen – Hurst's work is written out of an explicitly pragmatic theory of law. The failure of the period of revival to develop an extensive external historiography of law does not stem from pragmatic thinking, but – I am persuaded – from loss of nerve in the face of the implications of that thinking;

[60] Frankfurter, *The Commerce Clause under Marshall, Taney, and Waite* (1937); Frankfurter and James M. Landis, *The Business of the Supreme Court, A Study in the Federal Judicial System* (1928); Frankfurter and Nathan Greene, *The Labor Injunction* (1930).

[61] Llewellyn: "On Warranty of Quality and Society," (Pts. 1 & 2) 36 *Colum. L. Rev.* 699 (1936), 37 *Colum. L. Rev.* 341 (1937); "Across Sales on Horseback," 52 *Harv. L. Rev.* 725 (1939); "The First Struggle to Unhorse Sales," 52 *Harv. L. Rev.* 874 (1939). (This superb quartet on the history of sales law may be Llewellyn's most durable work. Yet he said [of "Warranty of Quality," Pt. 1, *supra* this note at 699 n. *] he was not writing "history, ... [but] an appeal for history. It is a sad commentary on our dogmatics that sales cases over a hundred and fifty years and more than fifty jurisdictions have been treated as if they floated free of time, place and person. Whereas it is time, place, person and circumstance which give them meaning. A few major trends are here presented. But not as history. History calls for detailed knowledge, for detailed background, and for discrimination even more detailed.")

Hall: *Theft, Law and Society* (1935).
Hamilton: "The Ancient Maxim Caveat Emptor," 40 *Yale L. J.* 1133 (1931).
Nelles: "Commonwealth v. Hunt," 32 *Colum. L. Rev.* 1128 (1932); "Towards Legal Understanding," (Pts. 1 & 2), 34 *Colum. L. Rev.* 862, 1041 (1934).
Yntema: *Sourcebook on Roman Law* (1929) (with A. Arthur Schiller).

But *see* Grant Gilmore, Book Review, 21 *The Law School Record* (Chicago) 38 (Summer, 1975):

> When I studied law at Yale in the early 1940s there was no suggestion, in any of the instruction which I received, that there was any point in thinking about law as a historical process. The implicit philosophical or jurisprudential bias which the entire law faculty seemed to share was that law was a sort of mystical absolute waiting to be discovered, described, catalogued, mapped out, so to say, reduced to possession. [Gilmore adds that his instructors included some noted Realists.] It was not until considerably later – if we must have a date, 1960 will do as well as any – that a historical approach to law seemed, almost overnight, to become fashionable, at least among academic theorists.

The absence of a historical approach at Yale in the 1940s does not surprise me; the intellectually curious and innovative phase of legal pragmatism was by then over. I am somewhat perplexed by the reference to a new fashion for history starting about 1960. In 1963, Edward Re surveyed law school curricula to find legal history courses other than "development of Anglo-American legal institutions" (often shortened to DLI) virtually non-existent; and even DLI was rare. (DLI was sometimes real history camouflaged as evolutionism, as in John P. Dawson's splendid Harvard Law School version; more often [to judge from course descriptions cited in Re] simply orthodox evolutionism.) Of course this is not necessarily inconsistent with Gilmore's

not from reckless disregard of the common law tradition, but from an anxious solicitude to preserve it.

The program set forth by pragmatists like Holmes and Pound for development of a science of law called for reconnecting legal to social history, since the contribution of historical study to the program was to liberate the present from law that had arisen out of entirely different social contexts and modes of thought and was not, as a consequence, necessarily suited to modern needs. This was potentially quite a radical view, since it repudiated the whole concept of tradition. Scholars like Langdell (and to a lesser extent Ames) tended to equate historical method and legal science: accurate tracing of the historical development of rules would reveal their immanent principles. Holmes and Pound said that since the end of law was the efficient adjustment of conflicting social interests, *real* legal science consisted in accurate measurement of those interests. The role of history was the important but auxiliary one of clearing away the rubbish of pointless old law.[62]

Outside the law schools these ideas had considerable influence on historians, especially constitutional historians, among whom the impact of economic, social and political factors upon judicial decision-making was a commonplace idea well before the ascendancy of legal Realism.[63] Yet among the lawyers the pragmatic prescription for legal science, assisted by a historiography devoted to destroying instead of beatifying the common law tradition, perhaps not surprisingly failed to make complete converts even of its chief proselytizers. Without knowing for sure what cut short the pragmatic movement as a whole, it is hard to tell what happened to the minor appendage of a program for an external historiography. But here are some ideas.

Training in the common law tradition was what gave a significant elite of the American bar its sense of identity as a mandarinate of masters of an ancient technique; the tradition associated law with both science and high culture,

recollection; "a historical approach to law" does not have to mean legal history courses. But legal history courses provide some evidence of the seriousness of commitment to the approach. See Re, "Legal history courses in American law schools," 13 *Am. Univ. L. Rev.* 45 (1963).

[62] See Pound, *Interpretations of Legal History* 152 and Ch. 7 *passim* (1923); Holmes, "The Path of the Law [1897]," in *supra* note 57 at 167, 191–195. The difference between Holmes's and Ames's views on tradition and function in law is really only one of emphasis: in practice they often arrived at the same conclusion. Ames believed that traditional authority, accurately interpreted by means of scientific historiography, would also produce the socially functional results he thought desirable. Holmes rejected, of course, the idea that the past could supply "correct" legal doctrine, but argued nonetheless for judicial conservatism toward reforming traditional doctrine – "... because I believe the claim of our especial code to respect is simply that it exists, that it is the one to which we have become accustomed ..." "Law in Science," *supra* note 57 at 239.

[63] See Belz, *supra* note 26 and "The Constitution in the Gilded Age: The Beginnings of Constitutional Realism in American Scholarship," 13 *Am. J. Leg. Hist.* 110 (1969); Richard Hofstadter, *The Progressive Historians* 200–202 (1968). Charles Beard acknowledged Holmes, Pound and Goodnow as forerunners in *An Economic Interpretation of the Constitution of the United States* 9 (1913).

and justified the prestige and power of its practitioners.[64] Law was authoritative because autonomous; and its autonomy derived from two sources, its formality (or technicality) and its antiquity. An evolutionary and internal legal historiography contributed, like legal scholarship generally, to reinforcing the tradition.[65] To deprive lawyers of the tradition entirely, as the pragmatists apparently (but, as will be seen, only apparently) proposed to do, was to make orphans of them. It was a threatened professionalism, among other things, that squashed legal pragmatism in the end.

This professionalism more likely arose from within than without the law schools. I doubt that the common law tradition had much mythic significance for the great majority of American lawyers, who probably were content to think of themselves as technicians rather than mandarins.[66] Even among the elite practitioners there can have been few who knew or cared much about the kind of legal history that was being done at the law schools; though if they had known it is entirely possible that they would have favored inculcation of the textbook view of Anglo-American legal "development" which still permeates legal rhetoric.[67] But law teachers too think of themselves as lawyers as much as

[64] Beale: "[L]aw is a traditional manner of thought about right behavior; the lawyers and judges are experts in it." *A Treatise on the Conflict of Laws* xiii (2nd edn. 1935). He developed the idea in his 1909 lectures (Samuels, *supra* note 31 at 292–293):

> [The principal characteristic of the common law] is that it requires a scientific knowledge on the part of a legal caste, thus coming back to a characteristic of the most ancient times, where it was in the knowledge of a priestly caste... How can you tell what is the law of Massachusetts today? You can of course ask the judges, as special experts; but they will not say unless a case is brought before them. The law of Massachusetts is what the body of the Massachusetts bar thinks it is.

I use Beale to stand for orthodoxy because the Realists, especially Frank, did so; and Beale did not seem to mind. How seriously members of the bar took the image of a priesthood is another question, which would require much more research to answer.

[65] The point is forcefully made by Horwitz, *supra* note 6, "The Conservative Tradition in the Writing of American Legal History," that preoccupation with formality and technique in legal history is ideological, in that it serves the interests of the profession to write about law as if it were autonomous from politics and inaccessible to the uninitiated. I think this is right but in some need of qualification and elaboration, which the text following this note tries to supply.

[66] See Maxwell Bloomfield, "Law v. Politics: The Self-Image of the American Bar (1830–1860)," 12 *Am. J. Leg. Hist.* 306 (1968), a study of nineteenth-century lawyers suggesting that most of them disavowed intellectual pretensions and presented themselves as practical businessmen and skilled craftsmen. Jerome Carlin's study of individual practitioners found that "[t]hese lawyers although generally handling matters that require little in the way of technical legal skill, still have fairly frequent contact with the courts and are thereby able to find a link with the most commonly accepted image of a lawyer ... [T]he big firm lawyer, in their view, has not only lost his identity as a real lawyer by virtue of his more infrequent contact with the courts ... but his independence as well." *Lawyers on Their Own* 187 (1962). In short, their identification is with the image of the trial lawyer, not with the more mandarin image of the appellate judge.

[67] See, e.g., William D. Guthrie, *Magna Carta and Other Addresses* (1916) and Elihu Root, *Addresses on Government and Citizenship* (1916), for a view of Anglo-American history as the progressive realization of the principle of individual liberty against the state. Guthrie and Root

professors, and usually more so;[68] it was the professional identities of the legal pragmatists themselves that the tendencies of their movement most threatened. As Leslie Stephen said of Gibbon: "Insects who are eating the heart out of an old tree are not generally gratified, it may be supposed, by the crash and thunder of the fall."[69]

The intellectual currents that eventually converged in Realism, one of which was the proposal for a legal historiography relativized to social and economic surroundings, challenged the professional viewpoint in several ways. (1) Pragmatism promoted research into non-legal materials. The amateur legal historians had stuck to the case reports; their professional successors had added legal manuscript sources of all kinds; but pragmatic legal history would apparently require the historian to step outside the box of distinctively legal things entirely. How far outside one could venture and remain a *legal* scholar? (2) Ames's conception of the legal-scholar-scientist gave him an inside role in the legal system, expert confidant to the judge (and in the extreme case where some statutory adjustment might be required) to the legislature. Pragmatic legal science offered at best a "negative and skeptical" role to the legal historian in present-day practice, whose relation to the judge would be the relatively indirect one of pointing out the irrelevance of the past to the solution of current problems – the role of an outsider, and a critical outsider at that. (3) The proposed field of research not only promised to transform legal scholars into some kind of subspecies of social scientist, but also to displace the judge from the center of the intellectual universe. The judge is of course the key figure in studies of the common law tradition, since he is the carrier of the tradition. The pragmatic view of law – that it arises out of social needs and is to be evaluated by the efficiency with which it serves social functions – merges law into administration; the judge becomes simply one kind of official among many, and often not the most important. (4) Finally, and inevitably, the program of studying law in its social context opened up for discussion the whole explosive issue of the relationship between the inside and the outside of the law-box; of how far legal decisions are determined, or influenced by external pressures and how far by internal criteria; in short, of the reality of the idea of an autonomous legal order in modern society.

were the two leading Wall St. practitioners of their time. But it is dangerous to generalize too far. Some Wall St. men belong, now as then, to the quasi-academic bar, which restates the law in the American Law Institute, serves on law reform commissions and the Cromwell Foundation, takes an active and informed interest in the curricula of the schools, and is familiar with scholars' legal history. It is worth remembering that there are several elites of lawyers – a municipal bond elite, a trial elite, etc. – and that they are not much like one another.

68 I have no authority for this beyond my own observation of teachers and colleagues.

69 *History of English Thought in the Eighteenth Century*, I, 379 (1876). Stephen thought Gibbon's skeptical views had helped to bring about the French Revolution which horrified him.

Social research in law along pragmatic lines was a quagmire for legal method and legal ideology. The program of investigating the social contexts and effects of law, to the end of discovering how efficiently it performed its social functions, made potentially relevant to legal study the entire universe of experience outside the law box. Some of those who ventured into that universe to gain broader perspectives on law never came back – Daniel Boorstin and David Riesman, for example. For others immersion in social research brought about something close to religious conversion: the story is told of Underhill Moore that he was found one day in his office,

> pulling drawers from his filing cabinets and dumping the contents into wastebaskets, cursing meanwhile most frightfully. The student inquired what was going on. "It's my life work," said Moore, "all the notes I have taken in a lifetime of research and it's all wrong." Moore had decided to discard everything he had ever done [he was an authority on Bills and Notes] and start over again, devoting the rest of his life to the experiments needed to work out a scientific theory of legal control in terms of behavioristic psychology.[70]

This episode took place at Columbia Law School in the 1920s, where Moore and others who were to form the core of the Realist movement made the first real attempt to institutionalize the "functional" study of law-in-society in a law school. This famous attempt failed; what is especially instructive about it for our purposes is that it began with the strictly professional purpose of reforming the curriculum to prepare students better for "the actual work in modern law practice";[71] and ended with many of its backers convinced that social research in law could not be performed in a professional setting at all.[72] (Some of them went off to found the short-lived Johns Hopkins Institute.) But most of the Columbia reformers – those who went off to Yale as well as those who stayed on – avoided falling into the quagmire by fashioning lifelines of limiting principles on the scope of their legal research, which kept them connected to traditional professional identities.

One such lifeline was the notion that the purpose of social research in law was to explore the gap between "law on the books and law in action," or the "limits of effective legal action." (Both these famous slogans were, of course, coined by Pound, who pioneered not only the pragmatic movement in law but the later retreat from it.[73]) This program solved two problems at one stroke. It gave the study of extralegal "action" a restricted scope symmetrically coextensive with that of the law-box itself: one looked for the counterpart in "reality" of a law in the "book." It also annexed social research to a respectable

[70] Julius Goebel, Jr. *et al.*, *A History of the School of Law*, Columbia University 251 (1955).

[71] Stevens, *supra* note 11 at 472 n. 28.

[72] For the Columbia experiment, see especially Twining, *supra* note 11, ch. 4 (and the annotations to that chapter at 399–402, which contain some useful warnings against generalizing about the Realists too broadly).

[73] See text at notes 88–96, *infra*.

professional and ideological purpose, i.e., closing the gap, making legal action more effective.[74] After the burst of empirical studies done at Yale in the 1930s, research in this mode largely vanished from the law schools. It never did much influence legal history, though it produced a large body of "impact research" in sociology and political science.[75]

The pragmatic lawyers soon found a lifeline that was stronger and more enduring. This was simply to revive Ames's conception of the law professor as a scholar who helps the judge ensure the sound development of case law, and thus to limit research to such social facts as were potentially relevant to judicial decision-making. To be sure, they expected such research to range farther afield than traditional research, because the judge, to be properly advised, would need to know much more than traditional research could tell him.[76] Julius Goebel, for example, thought the judge ought to have an immensely detailed acquaintance with eighteenth-century criminal procedure.

> Our law is one of the few occupations where history is of direct and specific utility. Traditionally it is by an inquiry into what the law was or has been that the solution of present perplexities is sought. The further back in time this quest is pressed, the more difficult is the finding, and it is then that the aid of the legal historian is sought. Where such a historian, therefore, undertakes to speak of the past, since it is something a future court may need and use, he assumes a responsibility not lightly to be dismissed. This is a moral obligation the implications of which are far-reaching, for not only must the judge put trust in his word, but the parties-litigant whose rights and whose fortunes will be affected by it ...[77]

This was all the more astonishing as it came from someone who certainly could not have been accused of writing practitioner's history, and who was one of the fiercest critics of textbook legal history. Yet he was even more hostile to laymen's trespasses on law; for he felt himself to be first and foremost a lawyer. His work locates colonial law in its full political context of imperial administration and shows how much its forms owed to that context; yet the relation of lawyer's detail is so thorough and minute that it tends to occupy almost the whole foreground – presumably because it is the lawyer's detail that will most interest the twentieth-century judge.[78]

74 For the preoccupation of social-legal research with the gap between law on the books and law in action, see Abel, *supra* note 29 at 185–189 and Marc Galanter, "Notes on the Future of Social Research On Law" (unpublished ms. on file with the *Law & Society Review*).

75 For discussions of these impact studies, see Stephen L. Washy, *The Impact of the United States Supreme Court: Some Perspectives* (1970); Richard Lempert, "Strategies of Research Design in the Legal Impact Study: The Control of Plausible Rival Hypotheses," 1 *L. & Soc' y Rev.* 111 (1966); Martin Shapiro, "The Impact of the Supreme Court," 23 *J. Leg. Ed.* 77 (1971).

76 This position probably came easiest to the teachers of commercial law, a field in which facts of business practice had been supposed to have some relevance to adjudication since Mansfield's time.

77 Goebel & T.R. Naughton, *Law Enforcement in Colonial New York* xxxiii–xxxiv (1944).

78 Goebel's legal history materials are the first to stress extralegal influences on law (*supra* note 48); as director of the Foundation for Research in Legal History he sponsored the publication of

The instance of Goebel may seem unique, and in a way it is – no one had a greater command of the legal sources or delighted more in flourishing them in the faces of the ignorant[79] – but the strategy for saving professional identity was entirely typical. The persisting case-law centeredness of legal scholarship hardly needs documentation, but it is worth noting that all those commonly named as principals in the revolt against formalism – Holmes, Gray, Pound, Frank and Llewellyn – contributed to it;[80] and before long I hope a history of American legal pragmatism will properly stress its conservatism in this respect as much as its iconoclasm in others. Pound's life (1870–1964) spanned the entire period. His biographer has related how his professionalism, his dislike (heightened by the New Deal) of administrative regulation, and his increasingly uncritical admiration of the judiciary steadily narrowed his interests to the point where, in the late 1940s, the prophet of "sociological jurisprudence" stopped reading social science altogether in order to give his full time to Anglo-American case reports.[81] Pound had been one of the first to venture outside the law-box. After a while he did not like what he saw, so he went back in and slammed the door.

This was an extreme version of a common process of withdrawal. It is once again necessary to emphasize that this limitation of scope to gathering fodder for the judge, even the fantastically erudite and open-minded judge of the legal pragmatists' imagination, was, in view of their general intellectual program, almost completely arbitrary. They undertook to look at law from the point of view of the functions it performed in society: this led them to the position that for the purpose of organizing research, it was useful to think of law as a system of social control, or as what officials do about disputes, or lawyers do for a living. By any of these standards litigation in courts (especially litigation to appeal) was only a fragment of diverse complex processes, and through the twentieth century a rapidly shrinking one; few of the graduates of the schools where the legal pragmatists taught were ever likely to have much contact

studies of the history of corporations that were the most ambitious attempts yet to relate modern law to social and economic context [Armand DuBois, *English Business Companies after the Bubble Act* (1933); Shaw Livermore, *Early American Land Companies* (1939) l; and his background essays in *The Law Practice of Alexander Hamilton*, *supra* note 49, especially those on "The Law and the Judicial Scene," *id.* at I, 1 and "The Economy in Hamilton's New York," *id.* at II, 29, reveal a grasp on extra-legal detail as sure as on the law. It is especially striking that someone with so much range should have deliberately unbalanced so much of his work toward the internal.

[79] See, e.g., "*Ex parte Clio*," 54 *Colum. L. Rev.* 450 (1954), reviewing W. W. Crosskey, *Politics and the Constitution* (1953).

[80] Frank did try to direct attention away from appellate and toward trial courts in *Courts on Trial* (1949). Llewellyn, in his general work in legal sociology, notably "What Price Contract – An Essay in Perspective," 40 *Yale L. J.* 704 (1931), showed he was perfectly aware of the limits of the case-lawyers' view – which makes it all the more interesting that he settled down into that view in *The Common Law Tradition: Deciding Appeals* (1960). See text at notes 97–99, *infra*.

[81] David Wigdor, *Roscoe Pound, Philosopher of Law* 207–281 (1974).

with it.[82] Yet the continuing preoccupation of legal research, including legal history, with the work of judges is so taken for granted that its extraordinary perversity is rarely even noticed.

Why this should have happened remains something of a mystery. Undoubtedly the great success of the case method as a teaching device had something to do with it: practically the whole curriculum has been organized around criticizing the work of the appellate bench and this has carried over to research because law professors tend to direct their research toward ultimate incorporation in teaching materials. But by itself this explanation will not serve. Judicial opinions cannot, for instance, be *that* much better teaching tools than administrative opinions, yet courses in Administrative Law tend to be about judicial review of administrative action. That is probably because judges have something administrators do not have: the capacity to represent the learned and cultivated side of law practice,[83] immunity from at least the more obvious kinds of client or constituent pressure, and the ideal of the lawgiver who derives his authority from sources independent of the dominant forces in society. Yet the learning, immunity, and authority that judges were supposed to symbolize all followed from their expertise in the common law tradition, which the legal pragmatists had spent two decades deriding.[84] That

[82] On changes in the role of courts and types of law practice, see Hurst, *Lawmakers* 85–87, 301–305; Robert T. Swaine, *The Cravath Firm and its Predecessors*, II, 461–466 *et passim* (1948).

[83] See the extraordinary elegy of Julius Goebel, Jr., "Learning and Style in the Law – An Historian's Lament," 61 *Colum. L. Rev.* 1393 (1961), in which the author calls up the classical learning of great past judges ("Diversion ... was on a level almost incomprehensible to us. I cannot picture Holt, or Hardwicke, or Mansfield viewing a so-called 'better' program on television, or, if trapped into so doing, esteeming what they had looked upon to be a fit subject of conversation." *Id.* at 1395–1396.); and contrasts it invidiously with the present situation:

> A reasoned opinion that rests upon impeccable authority and that carries conviction by reason of this and of its inner logic, unquestionably is difficult to compose. Fortunate it is that there are so many written. Such are, alas, much out- numbered by those patchworks of cases stated, passages from cyclopedias and snippets from a *Restatement*. This is a style highly esteemed in some trans-Appalachian jurisdictions ... [This has been accompanied by] the descresence of allusive and epigrammatic writing, which so conduces to elegance ...
>
> Surely the law must lose something of majesty if its oracles think of their pronouncements in terms of threading a pipe or of contriving a passable mitre joint. Let us leave such ideas to the legislators. To judges and lawyers the past calls out that we should cherish writing as the exercise of art. This let us not forget.

Id. at 1398–1400.

[84] David Riesman pointed this out in 1951:

> To be sure, most lawyers today recognize that their most important work is done in the office, not in the court- room; the elaborate masked ritual of the courtroom holds attraction only for the neophyte and the layman. Yet it is astonishing how strongly the image of the judge stands as the image of the lawyer-hero. While at the better law schools at least one and often nearly three years are spent in debunking upper-court opinions, in showing their largely derivative quality, their endless fallacies, their interminable self-confusion as to what they are "actually" deciding (as against what they say they are deciding), the better products of the better law

was all right when their basic program was critical, e.g., revealing the personal and class bases of Supreme Court decisions invalidating social legislation, or the confusions and contradictions of Langdellian method. When the Court switched directions in 1937, the growth of executive power in the New Deal seemed to some lawyers to portend administrative tyranny unless checked by the courts; and when the Germans reduced their courts to tools of the Nazi Party, even the most skeptical lawyers felt compelled to reassert the idea of legal autonomy.[85] Under this compulsion, perhaps because no better substitute had been found in the meantime, perhaps no better could be found, the notion of the common law tradition revived.[86]

The revival took several forms, all the way from Catholic natural law theory and Hutchins' and Adler's neo-Aristotelianism to Thurman Arnold's view that the idea of neutral and wisely applied law above men is a myth, but one whose general acceptance (by powerholders as well as others) is necessary to civilized society.[87] Two forms that were especially significant for legal historiography found their archetypes in the work of Pound and Llewellyn.

> schools want nothing more exciting when they get out than a chance to serve as clerk [as I did] to an appellate judge – the "upperer" the better. And as members of the bar they will move heaven and earth to get on the bench themselves (which is the source of much dirt in our political system, since many congressmen have partners who itch to be judges), although they know from practical experience how little power the judge has under the American system and how skilled lawyers are in emasculating that little.

"Towards an anthropological science of law and the legal profession," in Riesman, *Individualism Reconsidered* 440–441 (1954). See also *id.* at 462–463.

85 I am uttering here what is rapidly becoming the standard social-political explanation for the decline of Realism. See Edward A. Purcell, Jr., "American Legal Realism Between the Wars: Legal Realism and the Crisis of Democratic Theory," 75 *Am. Hist. Rev.* 424 (1969); G. Edward White, "The Evolution of reasoned Elaboration: Jurisprudential Criticism and Social Change," 59 *Va. L. Rev.* 279, 281–285 (1973); both of which stress the attacks associating the positivism and skepticism of the Realist movement with fascism, and later with communism.

And yet I wonder. One might have thought that the rise of Nazism and Stalinism would as likely have promoted social research in law as put an end to it, would have encouraged Americans to investigate the sociological bases of the rule of law rather than simply to assert its autonomy from social conditions. This is the sort of work that C. J. Friedrich, Franz Neumann, and Friedrich Hayek all did (from rather different perspectives); was there similar work going on in the law schools? I am not sure, but I think the answer is not much even among the émigré lawyers. *The Journal of Legal & Political Sociology*, started in 1942, began to address these issues (Karl Llewellyn and David Riesman were among the first contributors), but it petered out after a few numbers. The retreat from external social perspectives on law in the late 1930s and 40s is only just beginning to be explained. We need to know a lot more about the politics of law teachers, their attitudes toward the New Deal, toward communism and civil liberties in the 1950s; more also about the contribution of the émigré scholars, about how they altered (and failed to alter) our perspectives on study of the legal system.

86 Or perhaps simply survived; it may never have been abandoned.

87 On the Catholic natural lawyers and Hutchins and Adler, see Purcell, *supra* note 11; on Arnold, see his *Symbols of Government* (1962); Rumble, *supra* note 11 at 217–220.

Pound's contribution was his famous idea of a "taught legal tradition." He began to develop this idea well before the general crisis of pragmatic thought in the 1930s (as has been mentioned already, his was one of the earliest retreats from pragmatism), as a method of attacking the "economic interpretation" of legal history, the domesticated and vulgarized Marxism of the historians who assumed law to be nothing more than an instrument for realizing the self-interest of a dominant class, wielded by judicial members of that class.[88] Proponents of this interpretation were most vulnerable when they were most specific, as when they tried to explain results in individual cases by reference to the class position of the winning party or the judges.[89] Pound was able to run rings around them, showing that contemporary judges with the same backgrounds had reached opposite conclusions on the same issues; and that big economic interests had sometimes won in the courts and sometimes lost.[90] It was a completely sterile debate, since both sides assumed that decisions in the appellate courts accurately represent the extent to which the legal system responds to the claims of economic interests[91] (even if this were valid the case samples were too thin to prove anything either way). The interesting aspect of the debate was that when it provoked Pound into insistence upon a degree of autonomy for law, this is what he came up with:

Tenacity of a taught tradition is much more significant in our legal history than the economic conditions of time and place. These conditions have by no means been uniform, while the course of decision has been characteristically steady and uniform, hewing to common-law lines through five generations of rapid political, economic, and social change, and bringing about a *communis opinio* over the country as a whole on the overwhelming majority of legal questions, despite the most divergent geographical, political, economic, social and even racial conditions ... Economic and political conditions of time and place have led to legislative abrogations and alterations of rules and even at times to attempts to alter the course of the taught tradition. But such changes are fitted

[88] For an early American version, see Brooks Adams, *Centralization and the Law* (1906). The "economic interpretation" was most effective in the robust muckraking and debunking histories of the Supreme Court: notably Gustavus Myers, *History of the Supreme Court of the United States* (1918) and Louis B. Boudin, *Government by Judiciary* (1932). Other reductionist theories of law prevalent in the 1930s, such as Watsonian behavioristic psychology, apparently failed to influence historical writing.

[89] Francis H. Bohlen, "The Rule in Rylands v. Fletcher," 59 *U. Pa. L. Rev.* 298 (1911); Walter Nelles, "Commonwealth v. Hunt," *supra* note 61.

[90] Pound's attacks on the "economic interpretation" may be found in "Political and Economic Interpretations of Legal History," *Proc. Am. Polit. Sci. Ass'n* 95 (1912); *Interpretations of Legal History*, ch. 5 (1923); *The Formative Era of American Law, supra* note 35; "The Economic Interpretation and the Law of Torts," 53 *Harv. L. Rev.* 365 (1940).

[91] For example, Pound concluded from the fact that interpretations of corporate and partnership law restricted businessmen's choice of forms of doing business and of ways of operating across state lines that "capitalists" (whom he conceded were the dominant class at the end of the nineteenth century) had suffered as much from courts' hanging on to traditional forms as had "laborers." See his *Interpretations of Legal History, supra* note 90, at 111–112.

into the traditional system in their interpretation and application, and affect slowly or very little the principles, conceptions and doctrines which are the enduring law. The outstanding phenomenon is the extent to which a taught tradition, in the hands of judges drawn from any class one will, and chosen as one will, so they have been trained in the tradition, has stood out against all manner of economically or politically powerful interests.[92]

Have we seen this before? Of course: it is our old friend, the common law tradition, the continuous, uniform development of law over time by masters of a method. The obviously political part of law, legislation, is "fitted into the traditional system" by interpretation, without much affecting it.[93] Otherwise, the only role for economic and social factors is that of supplying problems for the aloof inhabitants of the law-box to resolve by resort to their learned technique.[94]

The "economic interpretation" refused to concede any autonomy to law: your law-box, its authors said, is really empty. Pound rightly denied this, but when pressed to say what was in it, fell back on the old identification of legal autonomy with formal doctrinal development. This had two bad effects: it prevented the leading advocate of a sociological legal history (and most of the legal historians who followed him) from seeing how much American law *could* quite satisfactorily be explained as the outcome of organized economic interest-group pressure.[95] It also prevented them from inquiring further into what could *not* – into the ways in which the specialized activities inside the law-box might be variables independent of and directing, channeling, diverting or obstructing those pressures. If there was one thing that the realists had made clear, and left as their enduring legacy, it was that the autonomous element in law was not – at least not necessarily, not always – its surface formality; that

[92] Pound, *Formative Era*, *supra* note 35, at 83–84.

[93] Pound explained the vulnerability of legislators to economic pressures by their lack of training in the tradition: "The legislator ... has no settled habits of applying an authoritative technique to authoritatively given materials." "Economic Interpretation," *supra* note 90, at 366. A colleague to whom I showed this passage suggested that since many judges are legislators who have failed of re-election, the critical training experience might be the crucible of failure.

[94] The "taught tradition" idea seems particularly hard to square with Pound's historical account of various theories he supposed had influenced American judicial decision-making in the nineteenth century (law-of-nature theory, analytic and historical theories, etc.) or with his frequent criticisms (especially in his earlier years) of late-nineteenth-century courts on the grounds that they had prevented necessary adaptations to social and economic needs, including adaptations sought to be accomplished by legislation. He worked himself into the position of saying that the taught tradition, apparently proof against "all manner of economically or politically powerful interests," fell victim to the influence of any jurisprudential scribbler who happened to be in the neighborhood; and also that the autonomy of courts consisted in their being perpetually out of tune with modern needs – the very quality for which he had once attacked them.

[95] For fine recent examples of what might be called a "neo-Progressive" approach, see Lawrence M. Friedman, "The Usury Laws of Wisconsin: A Study in Legal and Social History," 1963 *Wisc. L. Rev.* 515; Robert S. Hunt, *Law and Locomotives* (1958).

indeed such formality was most likely to mask the unexamined (or at any rate unacknowledged) presence of outside political or economic influences. But if it wasn't that, what was it? Pound's regression to the "taught tradition" discouraged any attempt to find out.[96]

The other contribution that the pragmatic movement made to the eleventh-hour revival of the idea of tradition in law was given its best and fullest expression in the work of Llewellyn. He saw the "common law tradition" not as a continuously developing body of doctrine but as historically diverse methods ("craft-styles") of judicial decision-making:

> the general and pervasive manner over the country at large, at any given time, of going about the job, the general outlook, the ways of professional know ledge, the kinds of thing the men of the law are sensitive to and strive for, the tone and flavor of the working and of the results. [Craft-style] is well described as a "period-style"; it corresponds to what we have long known as period-style in architecture or the graphic arts or furniture or music or drama.[97]

There were thus several traditions, each specific to a period; the period 1820–1860 having been dominated by a "grand style," 1880–1910 by a "formal style;" the period from 1930 onwards, Llewellyn believed, by a renaissance of the "grand style." (It is hopeless to explain Llewellyn's typology properly in a short space, but for those unfamiliar with it, here are the basics: a grand-style judge is concerned not only to harmonize his decisions, wherever feasible, with past case-law, but to justify them as functional; he tries to work out over time general approaches to handling recurrent types of dispute situations, approaches that will "make sense" to people in the disputants' positions. The formal-style judge, by contrast, cares only about making sure that each decision logically fits into a pre-existing doctrinal scheme: "the rules of law are to decide the cases; policy is for the legislature, not the courts."[98]) This was the most ingenious reconciliation yet of tradition and function in law. It did not turn its back on the idea of law as pragmatic method, social engineering; neither did it reject the work of past judges: it married the two in the tradition of the grand style. Tradition was preserved, but as exemplary rather than authoritative. Whatever its merits as jurisprudence,[99] this way of looking at law had incidental benefits for legal history. It encouraged the study of grand-style judges from the point

[96] I don't wish to imply that the net effect of Pound's influence on legal historiography was baneful. In this field as in so many others, he called attention to the right problems and pointed to suggestive lines of inquiry; and the fact that the Dean of the Harvard Law School uttered phrases like "sociological jurisprudence" gave social research in law respectability it could have acquired in no other way.

[97] Llewellyn, *Common Law Tradition, supra* note 80 at 36.

[98] *Id.* at 39. The most effective statement of the concept of craft-style is in Llewellyn, "On the good, the true, the beautiful in law [1942]," in Llewellyn, *supra* note 25 at 167.

[99] For effective criticisms from differing perspectives, see Charles E. Clark & David Trubek, "The Creative Role of the Judge: Restraint and Freedom in the Common Law Tradition," 71 *Yale L. J.* 255 (1961); Duncan Kennedy, "Legal Formality," 2 *J. Legal Studies* 351 (1973).

of view of what made them exemplary, since the historian working in an age of unabashedly "policy-oriented" jurisprudence will try to bring out, rather than suppress as unfortunate or irrelevant, past judges' view of their society and of what law is needed for it. It is possible to see the two best judicial biographies of recent times, Levy's of Shaw and Reid's of Doe,[100] both grand-style judges, as reflecting the influence of pragmatic legal thought in treating their subjects as architects of bodies of socially serviceable case-law. Llewellyn also taught legal scholars to read judicial opinions more carefully, for rhetoric as well as result, for sources of analogy and authority, for facts used and facts ignored, and above all for the characterization of implications for future cases. (His own excursions into history are probably the best examples of the deployment of the method.)[101] Finally, the concept of period-style (though ahistorical in one of its premises, i.e., that present-day judges were recapturing the reasoning modes of nineteenth-century ancestors fundamentally different in mental outlook)[102] suggested possibilities for historical-sociological theories of legal reasoning styles along the lines of Max Weber's, possibilities that are beginning to be realized in the work of Friedman, Horwitz, Nelson, and Tushnet.[103]

Yet though Llewellyn's concept of tradition, unlike Pound's, pointed toward a more expansive historiography, it maintained the insider's perspective on law, specifically that of insider-as- advisor-to-the-judge. And there are disadvantages to the perspective even of the most social-context-conscious, cosmopolitan insider: everything gets filtered through the lens of professional working concerns and categories. This may have any or all of the following consequences.

(1) The insider's categories to which even extra-legal detail tends to be assimilated may, while rendering it familiar and manageable to lawyers, seriously distort it in other ways. A good illustration from our legal history is the category of "codification," under which has been subsumed a vast diversity of behavior: evangelical antilegalism; backwoods resistance to debt collection; merchant creditors' pressure for more efficient debt collection; anglophobe propaganda; small legal practitioners' complaints

[100] Leonard W. Levy, *The Law of the Commonwealth and Chief Justice Shaw* (1957); John Phillip Reid, *Chief Justice: The Judicial World of Charles Doe* (1967). Howe's biography of Holmes, *supra* note 12, doesn't count as "judicial" biography because it ends before Holmes goes on the bench.

[101] See Llewellyn articles cited *supra* note 61.

[102] Though perhaps not so different in their aspects with which Llewellyn was particularly concerned, as judges in commercial cases.

[103] Lawrence M. Friedman, "On Legalistic Reasoning – A Footnote to Weber," 1966 *Wisc. L. Rev.* 148; Morton J. Horwitz, "The Emergence of an Instrumental Conception of Law," 5 *Perspectives in Am. History* 287 (1971); William E. Nelson, "The Impact of the Antislavery Movement upon Styles of Judicial Reasoning in Nineteenth Century America," 87 *Harv. L. Rev.* 513 (1974); Mark Tushnet, "The American Law of Slavery 1810–1860: A Study in the Persistence of Legal Autonomy," 10 *L. & Soc'y Rev.* 119, *infra*. So far as I know, nobody has taken up Llewellyn's hint that it might be valuable to apply methods of art or architectural history to law.

about pleading complexities; aesthetic distaste for the disorderliness, and democratic distaste for the feudal origins, of the common law; Jefferson's, Bentham's, and Field's plans for codes; the Massachusetts Laws and Liberties of 1648, Field's procedural code, the Federal Rules of Civil Procedure, and the Uniform Commercial Code, not to mention the Law of the Twelve Tables and the BGB. There are few purposes indeed for which it makes any sense at all to lump all this stuff together; yet our historiography to a greater or lesser degree repeatedly did so, combining most of it into a single prolonged "codification movement" that supposedly lasted throughout the nineteenth century and achieved its greatest successes in the twentieth.[104] Scholarship is only recently beginning to break this "movement" up into its component parts.[105]

(2) Appellate case-law comes to stand for the whole "legal system." This would be troublesome if only for the obvious reasons that it limits research to the legal business that happens to flow into the appellate courts; prevents institutional comparisons showing how alike courts are to other parts of the system, and how different, and how power and business are allocated among the various parts. (Prevailing jurisprudential theories of appropriate institutional jurisdiction or competence are likely seriously to misrepresent historical actualities in these matters.) It can also lead to a tendency to overintellectualize, to see the law as a

[104] The codification theme can be tracked from Charles M. Hepburn, "The Historical Development of Code Pleading in America and England," in *Select Essays, supra* note 33 at II, 643; through Charles Warren, *A History of the American Bar*, Ch. 19 (1911), Alison Reppy, "The Field Codification Concept," *in David Dudley Field Centenary Essays* (Reppy ed. 1949); Pound, *Formative Era, supra* note 35; and Howe, *supra* note 48. The theme was picked up by Perry Miller in *The Life of the Mind in America* (1965) (Book 2, "The Legal Mentality"); and has recently been sounded again in Carl B. Swisher, *The Taney Period*, 1836–64 at 339–356 (Oliver Wendell Holmes Devise History of the U.S. Supreme Court, V, 1974). One reason for what must be described as the obsession of our legal historians with this theme is that nineteenth-century American lawyers were obsessed with it also; "codification" was the staple topic of their occasional essays, articles in law periodicals, and orations at bar dinners and memorials. They had as great a capacity to assimilate everything to their own categories as we do. Even the great Haskins may have been somewhat taken in by the appeal of the "codification" category: compare his "Codification of Law in Colonial Massachusetts: A Study in Comparative Law," 30 *Indiana L. J.* 1 (1954) (Massachusetts Law and Liberties of 1648 is the first modern law code in the West) with Ronald G. Walters, "New England Society and the Laws and Liberties of Massachusetts," 106 *Essex Inst. Hist. Colls.* 145 (1970) (the "Laws" is not "basically a code of law but rather something more mundane: a handbook for justices, an instrument for the use of a public and a body of magistrates likely to be of uncertain and conflicting knowledge." *Id.* at 167).

[105] See especially Richard E. Ellis, *The Jeffersonian Crisis* (1971); William E. Nelson, *Americanization of the Common Law*, ch. 5 (1975); Friedman, "Law Reform," *supra* note 3; Maxwell Bloomfield, "William Sampson and the Codifiers: The Roots of American Legal Reform, 1820–1830," 11 *Am. J. Leg. Hist.* 234 (1967); Gerald W. Gawalt, "Sources of Anti-Lawyer Sentiment in Massachusetts, 1740–1840," 14 *Am. J. Leg. Hist.* 283 (1970).

complex body of attempted judicial and academic solutions to a set of philosophic puzzles. Obviously an extremely elaborate jurisprudential literature is an important cultural product, worth studying on its own terms; but as an *exclusive* approach to legal history, this can result in a perception of law as an elevated activity engaged in for its own sake by the lawyers and their clients, and thus fundamentally betray the nature of the subject.

(3) Perhaps most important, history from the lawyer's perspective, if it pays any attention to the world outside the law-box, is bound to focus more closely on inputs than on outputs, and mostly on those inputs that the insiders consciously employ as materials of their craft. This is bound to leave out of consideration major (it is not necessary to argue primary) determinants of the shape and content of the law-box – the reasons for there being any law-box in the first place – i.e., what it is that people in society demand, or expect, of their legal order.

2

Holmes's *Common Law* as Legal and Social Science*

[*This piece was published as part of a Symposium commemorating the 100th anniversary of O. W. Holmes, Jr.*, The Common Law in 10 Hofstra Law Review 719 (1982). *Its attempt to place Holmes's legal theory in its formative intellectual context has been followed by a massive and distinguished literature on Holmes. I think the best of this work is a fine intellectual biography by G. Edward White*, Justice Oliver Wendell Holmes: Law and the Inner Self *(1993); a thorough and probing examination of Holmes's contributions to and views on legal history in David M. Rabban*, Law's History: American Legal Thought and the Transatlantic Turn to History *(2013); Louis Menand's illuminating exploration of Holmes's pragmatist Cambridge circle in* The Metaphysical Club: A Story of Ideas in America *(2001); and especially Thomas Grey's penetrating essay on "Holmes and Legal Pragmatism,"* 42 Stanford Law Review 787 *(1989). Grey's essay has convinced me that I was wrong in the piece that follows to see the conceptualism of Holmes's early essays in analytical jurisprudence as existing in unresolved contradiction with his later historicism. Grey persuasively argues that Holmes's purpose in refining the logical arrangement of legal doctrine into conceptual categories was the modest pragmatic one of making current law more accessible and predictable to lawyers. But his historicism taught him that any such arrangements, including his own, must be transient and provisional, saturated as all law is with the contingent and irrational cultural beliefs and political struggles of its time and place.*]

* This paper is adapted from a talk given in honor of the hundredth anniversary of the publication of *The Common Law* at the annual meeting of the American Society for Legal History, October 1981. Tom Grey commented helpfully on an earlier draft. Conversations, over the years, about Holmes with Morton Horwitz have been invaluable. The background work on this article was done in connection with research on the ideology of the American legal profession, 1870–1920. The project has been supported by the American Council on Learned Societies, the American Bar Foundation, and the Graduate School of the University of Wisconsin-Madison.

"My notion in writing these articles," Holmes told a friend, speaking of the *American Law Review* pieces[1] on which he later based his lectures[2] on *The Common Law*,[3] "is to take up from time to time the cardinal principles and conceptions of the law and make a new and more fundamental analysis of them – For the purpose of constructing a new Jurisprudence or New First Book of the law."[4] Holmes's declaration of intent makes explicit what it is hard for a reader of *The Common Law* to doubt: The work is primarily one of legal theory with excursions into legal history to support the theory. Thus it is as a work of theory and not of history that *The Common Law* must be assessed.

The first reaction that a reader – or even a re-reader – is likely to come away with from this famously Delphic text is one of bafflement at its recklessly miscellaneous quality. One is quite as likely, on turning the pages, to run across an anthropological account of animism in primitive societies[5] as an orthodox history of Year Book doctrine,[6] a polemic from political economy against strict tort liability,[7] or a proposal to revise the classification scheme of analytical jurisprudence.[8] The reader's reactions are confirmed upon turning to Mark Howe's masterly explication of the text,[9] for there he learns that Holmes was, in fact, pursuing in the lectures a variety of theories he had suggested earlier in the *American Law Review*: that sources of the common law are largely Teutonic, not Roman;[10] that Kant and Hegel were wrong to see legal rules as manifestations of the free expression of autonomous, self-determining individual wills;[11] and that Austin was wrong in making rights, rather than duties, the primary concept of his analytic apparatus.[12] Though to be sure these projects have in common that they show all of Holmes's most eminent contemporaries to have been in error – not an accidental similarity, in view of Holmes's very

1 "The Arrangement of the Law: Privity," 7 *Am. L. Rev.* 46 (1872); "Codes, and the Arrangement of the Law," 5 *Am. L. Rev.* 1 (1870) (unsigned article written by Holmes); Holmes, "Common carriers and the common law," 13 *Am. L. Rev.* 609 (1879); Holmes, "Possession," 12 *Am. L. Rev.* 688 (1878); Holmes, "Primitive Notions in Modern Law," 10 *Am. L. Rev.* 422 (1876); Holmes, "Primitive Notions in Modern Law No. II," 11 *Am. L. Rev.* 641 (1877); "The Theory of Torts," 7 *Am. L. Rev.* 652 (1873) (unsigned article written by Holmes).

2 *See* 2 Mark DeWolfe Howe, *Justice Oliver Wendell Holmes* 135–136 (1963).

3 Oliver Wendell Holmes, Jr., *The Common Law* (Howe ed. 1963) [hereinafter cited as *Common Law*].

4 Letter from Oliver Wendell Holmes, Jr. to A. G. Sedgwick (July 12, 1879) (Holmes Manuscripts, Harvard Law School Archives) (copy on file in office of *Hofstra law Review*). I am grateful to Professor Grant Gilmore for permission to quote from the Holmes Papers.

5 *See, e.g., Common Law, supra* note 3, at 12–13. For a discussion of Holmes's historical use of animism in primitive societies, *see* 2 Howe, *supra* note 2, at 161–168.

6 *See, e.g.,* Common Law, *supra* note 3, at 177–179.

7 *See id.* at 72–73.

8 *See, e.g., id.* at 115, 173, 235–236.

9 *See* 2 Howe, *supra* note 2, at 135–252.

10 *See, e.g., id.* at 143–144, 146–148, 152–153, 205–207, 211–214, 228, 252, 277.

11 *See, e.g., id.* at 168–177, 202–204.

12 *See id.* at 76–79, 173.

competitive drive toward originality – there is no other obvious thread uniting them, or explaining their all being tossed together in a book.

In the face of such bewildering diversity, the reader does well to try to follow T. S. Kuhn's advice: "When reading the works of an important thinker, look first for the apparent absurdities in the text, and ask how a sensible person could have written them."[13] This useful precept suggests that the secret of this text may lie in its context of intellectual discourse, the Victorian legal and social science that defined the problems for which Holmes and his contemporaries thought it important to offer solutions. Yet my argument here will be that once one has investigated this context, one will not be able to draw from it any single thread of ideas that unifies and integrates *The Common Law*. One will discover, rather, that it contains multiple and contradictory strands of thought, taken from contemporary positions that often conflict sharply with one another. The explanation of *The Common Law* will turn out to be that it is a book at war with itself.

For some time, scholarly writing on Holmes selected a single intellectual movement – American philosophical pragmatism[14] – as the candidate from the surrounding discourse of his time most likely to explain his thought. Pragmatist philosophy seemed promising first because Holmes belonged, along with the acknowledged founders of pragmatism,[15] to the Metaphysical Club of Cambridge,[16] and second because many of Holmes's themes resonated with the general tenor of pragmatism.[17] For example, the principal theme of the majestic overture to *The Common Law*, that societies are constantly reworking and reinterpreting old legal forms to serve new purposes,[18] has been called "evolutionary pragmatism."[19] This view holds that no legal form has a frozen meaning; rather, legal forms are changing and contingent and depend on the specific practical uses to which successive generations wish to put them.[20] The form may stay the same, but the content changes with changing views of policy – the

[13] Thomas Kuhn, *The Essential Tension* xii (1977).

[14] *See, e.g.*, Philip Wiener, *Evolution and the Founders of Pragmatism* (1949).

[15] The founders of pragmatism referred to include Chauncey Wright, Nicholas St. John Green, William James and Charles Sanders Peirce. *See infra* note 16.

[16] *See* Max Fisch, "Was there a metaphysical club in Cambridge?," in *Studies in the Philosophy of Charles Sanders Peirce* 3 (2d ser., Moore & Robin eds. 1964).

[17] *See, e.g., Common Law, supra* note 3, at 120. "Pragmatism" is obviously too loosely and variously used a term to be capable of any exact definition. In this context, I use it to refer to the general position that scientific truths are not absolute and universal but vary according to – and are only realized in – their "operational" uses in "experience." *Legal* pragmatists' application of the general position is that legal concepts, such as "property," "contractual agreement," and "the cause of the accident," may be given meaning only through examination of the operational uses, or "purposes," to which they are put, so that, for example, whether electricity is "property" will depend upon the functional purposes, in a particular social-historical context, for which the classification is made.

[18] *See id.* at 5.

[19] Wiener, *supra* note 14, at 172.

[20] *See id.* at 176–189; *Common Law, supra* note 3, at 5, 8, 31–32.

policy upon which all law must ultimately be grounded.[21] Holmes's prediction theory of law,[22] where the lawyer is asked to respond to a client's query of "If I go ahead with my scheme, what can they [the courts] do to me?," is also a pragmatist notion.[23] Such themes – as well as the political side he appeared to favor on the bench – have led legal scholars to call Holmes the father of Legal Realism[24] and name him a leader of the "revolt against formalism."[25]

More recently, the author of a student Note in the *Yale Law Journal* has explored the relation to pragmatism of yet a third idea of Holmes,[26] which deserves, more than the famous overture theme of not "logic" but "experience,"[27] to be regarded as the central motif of *The Common Law*. This third idea maintains that throughout the growth of the common law, liability for crimes, torts, and contract-breaking has been based decreasingly on personal, moral culpability and increasingly on an objective or external standard.[28] The standard is sometimes derived from behavior that the community, speaking through the legislature or the jury, considers to be blameworthy in the average person, and that it then proscribes;[29] other times, the standard is derived from policy grounds unrelated, even indirectly, to moral blame.[30] The author, in a well-supported argument, has pointed to the resemblances between this external standard idea and C.S. Peirce's pragmatist epistemology,[31] according to which truth cannot be defined subjectively, as what any one person believes, but only socially, as the prevailing consensus in the community of scientific thinkers.[32]

As seductive as these writers' claims are for using pragmatism as a basis for interpreting Holmes's thought, I think that we have to start somewhere else – specifically with positivism – in order to understand *The Common Law*. In particular, I am referring to the scientific positivism[33] of people like William

[21] *See Common Law*, *supra* note 3, at 5, 8, 31–32.

[22] *See* Oliver Wendell Holmes, Jr., "The Path of the Law," in *Collected Legal Papers* 167 (1920) [hereinafter cited as "The Path of the Law"].

[23] *See* Wiener, *supra* note 14, at 182–184.

[24] William Twining, *Karl Llewellyn and the Realist Movement* 15–20 (1973).

[25] Morton White, *Social Thought in America: The Revolt Against Formalism* 11, 15–18 (rev. edn. 1957).

[26] Note, Oliver Wendell Holmes, Jr., "Peirce & Legal Pragmatism," 84 *Yale L. J.* 1123 (1975).

[27] *Common Law*, *supra* note 3, at 5.

[28] *See, e.g.*, *id.* at 119–121, 233–239, 242.

[29] *See, e.g.*, *id.* at 119–121.

[30] *See infra* text accompanying notes 121–128.

[31] *See* Note, *supra* note 26, at 1129–1134.

[32] *See id.* at 1134–1137.

[33] I am not speaking here of the legal positivism that is sometimes tied to Holmes. For a sampling of commentaries on Holmes's legal positivism, *see* Lon Fuller, *The Law in Quest of Itself* (1940); Mark DeWolfe Howe's response to Fuller in Mark Howe, "The Positivism of Mr. Justice Holmes," 64 *Harv. L. Rev.* 529 (1951); Henry M. Hart's response to Howe in Henry Hart, "Holmes' Positivism – an Addendum," 64 *Harv. L. Rev.* 929 (1951); Howe's response in Mark Howe, "Holmes' Positivism – A Brief Rejoinder," 64 *Harv. L. Rev.* 937 (1951); and the famous

Clifford[34] and Herbert Spencer,[35] two of the most aggressive supporters of the tendency "to treat the world as a hard object gradually being discovered by means of the suppression of human subjectivity,"[36] the same tendency on which the pragmatist members of the Metaphysical Club had declared war.[37] Positivism, in this sense, is the belief that explanation must be scientific, and that to be scientific it must confine its investigation to observable phenomena – facts – and its method to induction, from regularities in the occurrence of past facts, of laws or statements of the probability of the occurrence of future events.[38] The method, in short, should enable the scientist to specify or predict the implications of given empirical conditions.[39]

One can read whole sections of *The Common Law* as Holmes's attempt to turn law into something that permits the exercise of this sort of positivist method. The chapter on possession[40] presents a prime example of a positivist's formulation of a legal right:

> A legal right is nothing but a permission to exercise certain natural powers, and upon certain conditions to obtain protection, restitution, or compensation by the aid of the public force. Just so far as the aid of the public force is given a man, he has a legal right, and this right is the same whether his claim is founded in righteousness or iniquity. Just so far as possession is protected, it is as much a source of legal rights as ownership is when it secures the same protection.
>
> Every right is a consequence attached by the law to one or more facts which the law defines, and wherever the law gives anyone special rights not shared by the body of the people, it does so on the ground that certain special facts, not true of the rest of the world, are true of him. When a group of facts thus singled out by the law exists in the case of a given person, he is said to be entitled to the corresponding rights; meaning, thereby, that the law helps him to constrain his neighbors, or some of them, in a way in which it would not, if all the facts in question were not true of him. Hence, any word which denotes such a group of facts connotes the rights attached to it by way of legal consequences, and any word which denotes the rights attached to a group of facts connotes the group of facts in like manner.

exchange between H. L. A. Hart and Lon Fuller: Henry Hart, "Positivism and the Separation of Law and Morals," 71 *Harv. L. Rev.* 593 (1958); Lon Fuller, "Positivism and Fidelity to Law – A Reply to Professor Hart," 71 *Harv. L. Rev.* 630 (1958).

34 *See* William Clifford, *The Common Sense of the Exact Sciences* (1885).

35 *See* Herbert Spencer, *Illustrations of Universal Progress* (1864).

36 David Hollinger, "William James and the Culture of Inquiry," 20 *Mich. Q. Rev.* 264, 267 (1981).

37 *See* Weiner, *supra* note 14, at 26, 28–30.

38 *See* Thomas Heller, "Is the Charitable Exemption from Property Taxation an Easy Case? General Concerns about Legal Economics and Jurisprudence," in *Essays on the Law and Economics of Local Governments* 183, 184–185 (Rubinfeld ed. 1979).

39 For historical accounts of nineteenth-century positivism, see Leszek Kolakowski, *The Alienation of Reason* (1968) and Maurice Mandelbaum, *History, Man, & Reason* 10–20 (1971). My understanding of the relationship between scientific and legal positivisms has been much improved by Heller, *supra* note 38, at 184–207, 236–251.

40 *Common Law*, *supra* note 3, at 163–194.

> The word "possession" denotes such a group of facts. Hence, when we say of a man that he has possession, we affirm directly that all the facts of a certain group are true of him, and we convey indirectly or by implication that the law will give him the advantage of the situation. Contract, or property, or any other substantive notion of the law, may be analyzed in the same way, and should be treated in the same order... When we say that a man owns a thing, we affirm directly that he has the benefit of the consequences attached to a certain group of facts, and, by implication, that the facts are true of him. The important thing to grasp is, that each of these legal compounds, possession, property, and contract, is to be analyzed into fact and right, antecedent and consequent, in like manner as every other... There are always two things to be asked: first, what are the facts which make up the group in question; and then, what are the consequences attached by the law to that group. The former generally offers the only difficulties.[41]

Holmes also uses positivist method to refute Kant's theory that possession should be legally protected because it is an extension of personality, an exercise of free will.[42] Holmes first tries to dispose of the theory through positivist fiat: "[T]he proximate ground of law must be empirical, even when that ground is the fact that a certain ideal or theory of government is generally entertained. Law, being a practical thing, must found itself on actual forces."[43] He then proposes such a grounding in sociobiology: "[M]an, by an instinct which he shares with the domestic dog, and of which the seal gives a most striking example, will not allow himself to be dispossessed ... [of a thing] without trying to get it back again."[44] Holmes also refutes Kant through an empirical falsification, arguing that although Roman law gave possessory remedies only to owners or almost-owners (seemingly supporting Kant's will – personality theory of possession), the common law has always given possessory remedies to evident non-owners such as bailees. The German jurists, Holmes argues, have thus overgeneralized from a limited field of data; from the perspective of the broader field, it is clear that the Roman practice is an anomalous case.[45]

In Holmes's well-known chapters on tort law, there are at least three positivist moments. In the first, the jury determines liability by asking whether the defendant's behavior could, on the basis of experience, be predicted to cause harm.[46] In the second, the judge is encouraged to look over the field of primary data – jury verdicts in negligence cases – and extract from them a prediction regarding future outcomes.[47] The judge is then to freeze the probable verdict in law as a standard,[48] for "[t]he ideal average prudent man... is a constant, and his conduct under given circumstances is theoretically always the same."[49]

41 *Id.* at 169–170.
42 *See id.* at 163–164.
43 *Id.* at 168 (emphasis added) (footnote omitted).
44 *Id.*
45 *Id.* at 165–167, 184.
46 *Id.* at 87–89, 116–119.
47 *Id.* at 88–90.
48 *Id.* at 88–90, 120.
49 *Id.* at 89.

Juries, however, are an imprecise tool of measurement since their verdicts may vary;[50] thus, in formulating the standard, the judge must take readings from several juries, average them, and then dispense with the jury.[51] Finally, Holmes suggests that the lawyer may predict outcomes for a client based on the data synthesized in law reports.[52]

Holmes's method in the chapter on possession[53] and the chapters on tort law[54] seems to be the substitution of the observable for the unobservable: facts plus legal consequences for rights, animal behavior for free will, and decided case law for philosophers' theories. In each instance, the subjective element is suppressed. There is a clear relation here between Holmes's thought and one of the major theses of *The Common Law* that liability should be fixed by an objective, external standard.[55] Subjectivity in the form of actual intentions is suppressed and replaced by a description of observable, outward facts.

> In other words, the standards of the law are external standards, and, however much it may take moral considerations into account, it does so only for the purpose of drawing a line between such bodily motions and rests as it permits, and such as it does not. What the law really forbids, and the only thing it forbids, is the act on the wrong side of the line, be that act blameworthy or otherwise.[56]

I do not claim, however, that scientific positivism is the final secret of *The Common Law*. It was not a mode in which Holmes, with his strong historicist sense of the contingency of experience, could comfortably operate for very long. Moreover, although scientific positivism does serve to unite several themes, it remains violently discordant with others, notably the famous overture on experience rather than logic.[57] Holmes's positivist method and attitude, however, are well and truly entrenched. Indeed, one must be convinced of this if aware of his repeated assertions, both explicit and implicit, that the proper role of the jurist, the role that Holmes is himself performing, is to develop a method to extract from legal materials the regularity and order that is already present inside them,[58] *not* to impose, by a creative act of interpretation, a new order upon them.

[50] *Id.* at 88–89.

[51] *See id.* at 92–93, 119–121. Of course, this is a paraphrase almost to the point of parody, but it seems to me faithful to Holmes's intentions in these passages.

[52] *See id.* at 91–103.

[53] *Id.* at 163–194.

[54] *Id.* at 63–129.

[55] *See supra* note 28 and accompanying text.

[56] *Common Law*, *supra* note 3, at 88.

[57] *Id.* at 5; *see supra* text accompanying note 18.

[58] *See, e.g.*, *Common Law*, *supra* note 3, at 173:

> What may be [the] relation [of legal duties] to moral rights if there are any, and whether moral rights are not in like manner logically the offspring of moral duties, are questions which do not concern us here. These are for the philosopher, who approaches the law from without as part of a larger series of human manifestations. The business of the jurist is to make known

What did Holmes's positivist method in the form of the external standard contribute to the discourse of its time? Certainly, the external standards idea was a tremendous success[59] in that it became generally known and adopted. It was also a great success, however, even among lawyers who could not swallow Holmes's cynical acid, and whose work the critical implications of Holmes's thought would one day help destroy. *The Common Law* is difficult to analyze because Holmes begins to demolish some of the most important premises of the structures that he was, at the same time, assiduously helping to build. I am speaking here of the structures to which Holmes's positivism in the form of the external standard seemed so useful a contribution: formalism, classical-legal, or liberal thought.[60]

The classical-legal science that achieved dominance in the Harvard and Oxford Law Schools of the 1870s and 80s, and among the members of the United States Supreme Court into the 1920s, was a collective construct of many minds whose basic purpose was the reconceptualization of the legal system so that it might more perfectly vindicate the principles of political liberalism. Liberalism in its broadest sense attempts to maximize the freedom of self-regarding individuals to do as they choose as long as such freedom is consistent with a like freedom in other individuals.[61] To accomplish this objective,

> the content of the law; that is, to work upon it from within, or logically, arranging and distributing it, in order, from its *summum genus* to its *infima species*, so far as practicable.

Id. (italics in original).

[59] *See, e.g.*, Letter from Sir Frederick Pollock to Oliver Wendell Holmes (August 1893), reprinted in 1 *Holmes-Pollock Letters* 46 (Howe ed. 1941): "Nemesis is upon us. The reasonable man and the 'external standard' have filtered down to the common examination candidate, who is beginning to write horrible nonsense about them." *Id.* Undoubtedly the external's longest-lived application is the "objective" theory of contract formation, as influentially adopted by Samuel Williston. *See* 1 Samuel Williston, *A Treatise On The Law Of Contracts* §§ 20, 95 (3rd edn. 1957); 13 *id.* § 1536 (3rd edn. 1970).

[60] Others who are more familiar with the secondary literature on Holmes than I am will correct me if I'm wrong to say that it was Karl Llewellyn who first noticed that there was a classic chassis under Holmes's modern chrome and tailfins, and assigned his work on contracts to the formal style. Karl Llewellyn, *The Common Law Tradition: Deciding Appeals* 187–189 (1960). Grant Gilmore followed, crediting to Holmes, as well as to Samuel Williston and C. C. Langdell, the patrimony of the classical law of contracts. Grant Gilmore, *The Death of Contract* 14–53 (1974). G. Edward White similarly places Holmes in his new history of tort law, G. Edward White, *Tort Law In America* 12–19 (1980), and Morton Horwitz explicitly identifies Holmes with formalism in *The Transformation of American Law, 1870–1960: The Crisis of Legal Orthodoxy* (1992), Ch. 4: "The place of Justice Holmes in American legal thought." C. H. S. Fifoot, in a valuable and strangely neglected little book, noted Holmes's contributions to English classical-legal science. Cecil Fifoot, *Judge and Jurist in the Reign of Victoria* 49–52, 90–91, 124–126 (1959).

[61] What follows is heavily indebted to Duncan Kennedy, "Toward an Historical Understanding of Legal Consciousness: The Case of Classical Legal Thought in America, 1850–1940," 3 *Research in Law & Sociology* 3 (1980). *See also* Patrick Atiyah, *The Rise and Fall of Freedom of Contract* 388–397 (1979); Charles McCurdy, "Justice Field and the Jurisprudence of

liberal thought endows people with (or treats them as naturally having) rights that define what they may freely do, and correlative duties not to interfere with the like rights of others. The state is instituted to protect these rights through enforcement. This institution in turn requires a specification of the state's powers vis-à-vis individuals and the individuals' rights vis-à-vis the state. Late-nineteenth-century classical-legal science was an attempt to formulate a systematic general statement of the actual legal rules in force in order to clarify the boundaries of rights and duties, particularly the boundaries between public power and private rights and between one right-holder and another. It was assumed that where one boundary ended another began.[62] Liberal practice, therefore, was to: (1) explain as many rules as possible as necessary derivations of general, all-inclusive principles, such as protection of property, freedom of contract, or responsibility for wrongful conduct; (2) multiply bright-line tests to aid in determining when a state or individual had crossed the boundary of its sphere of appropriate autonomous action into a sphere in which its invasion could be sanctioned; and (3) clearly classify all human activity as either private or public. The aim was to maximize the spheres of individual freedom as the liberals understood it; ensure the rightful and limit the wrongful reach of state power; standardize endowments of rights in order to achieve a formal equality of individuals; and limit judicial action to the protection of either state or individual will: the will of the parties in a contract action, for example, or the will of the state in an exercise of the police power.[63]

We can hardly wonder that liberal theorists latched on to the positivist sections of *The Common Law*, especially the external standard. Holmes had pushed previously for a "comprehensive arrangement of the law"[64] in order to develop standards that would apply to people generally, irrespective of status relations.[65] In *The Common Law*, however, he developed these standards, creating, for example, a standard of negligence holding a prudent man liable for harms he could be expected to avoid with foreknowledge.[66] In addition, in his treatment of contracts, Holmes developed external standards to help courts find the making and meanings of contracts by reference to the objective, or outward, signs of the parties' intentions.[67] A classical lawyer reading these

Government-Business Relations: Some Parameters of Laissez-Faire Constitutionalism, 1863–1897," 61 *J. Am. Hist.* 970 (1975); Robert W. Gordon, "Legal Thought and Legal Practice in the Age of American Enterprise," in Gerald Geison (ed.), *Professions and Professional Ideologies in America* 70 (1983).

[62] Judges Thomas M. Cooley, John Forest Dillon, Samuel Miller and Stephen Field are among the leading pioneers of this enterprise, particularly on the public law side; on the private law side, one thinks first of C. C. Langdell, J. B. Ames, Samuel Williston, and, to a considerable extent, Holmes, and the English jurists William Markby, T. E. Holland, and Frederick Pollock.

[63] *See* Kolakowski, *supra* note 39.

[64] "The Theory of Torts," *supra* note 1, at 660.

[65] *See id.*

[66] *Common Law*, *supra* note 3, at 63–129.

[67] *See id.* at 242.

sections might well have been excused for supposing them a brilliant technical apparatus for putting into effect liberal legal ideas. After all, Holmes's standards for imposing liability were general inclusive standards applicable to everyone. The standards were expressed in a positivist form, suggesting that the enforcing court need only apply regularities observed in similar factual situations to determine the appropriate legal consequence of the facts in the present case. The aim of Holmes's scheme, like that of classical law generally, appears to be to maximize the sphere of autonomous freedom by giving individuals advised by lawyers reliable predictions of where the courts will limit their actions and the actions of others, and equalize the formal legal treatment of persons. Holmes at various points seems to say this is his aim.[68]

Yet, if this was his aim, there can be no doubt that it conflicted with others, for Holmes was at best only ambivalently a liberal. In fact, his work cruelly laid stress on some of the cardinal weaknesses of, and contradictions within, liberal thought. Such elements of his work represent a sharp break with the classical phase of liberalism.

In the overture to *The Common Law*, for example, Holmes marked his determination to bring the historical and social contingency of legal doctrine into the forefront of legal theory.[69] Attacks on the classical economists, utilitarians, and analytical jurists of the previous generation for their aprioristic, abstract, and ahistorical theories of the "individual" and the "sovereign" were not uncommon in the progressive scholarship of Holmes's time.[70] Holmes's emphasis in the overture on experience over logic[71] signals his allegiance to the historicist enemies of classical legalism.

In other words, *The Common Law* opens with a trumpet blast aimed at the demolition of the classical-legal system that his positivism, in the form of the external standard, was designed to fortify.[72] Even this, however, is not the full

[68] *See, e.g., id.* at 46, 77, 88. Holmes observes:

> The true explanation of the reference of liability to a moral standard... is not that it is for the purpose of improving men's hearts, but that it is to give a man a fair chance to avoid doing the harm before he is held responsible for it. It is intended to reconcile the policy of letting accidents lie where they fall, and the reasonable freedom of others with the protection of the individual from injury.

Id. at 115.

[69] *See id.* at 5. The opening lines of *The Common Law* repeat, with some variations, a critical (unsigned) review Holmes wrote in 1880 of Christopher Langdell, *A Selection of Cases on the Law of Contracts* (2nd edn. 1879), which unkindly called the Harvard Law School Dean "the greatest living legal theologian." Book Notices, 14, 233 (1880). For an account of this episode, *see* 2 Howe, *supra* note 2, at 155–157.

[70] Sir Henry Maine was the pioneer in Anglo-American studies of this new program of a return to the historically based jurisprudence of Hume, Smith, and Montesquieu relying on "scientific" historiography on the German model and comparative anthropology, in place of the "conjectural" histories of the Enlightenment. *See* J. Burrow, *Evolution and Society* 65–100 (1966).

[71] *See supra* notes 18–27 and accompanying text.

[72] *See supra* notes 33–60 and accompanying text.

extent of the confusion, because the fact is that after proclaiming his historicist program,[73] Holmes simply fails to follow it through.

The theme of the overture, the reader will recall,[74] is that throughout the history of the common law, old legal forms continually acquire new content; as the social function of a form changes, so too does its legislative rationale. Once this theme has been sounded, the reader naturally expects its frequent repetition; yet one of the puzzles of *The Common Law* is that it fails to undertake any sustained development of what is announced as its major theme. Although Holmes does at times give concrete illustration to his theme, showing how an ancient form has persisted through modern reinterpretations of its policy basis,[75] most of his historical explanations and examples are informed by quite different theories of legal-historical development: theories of underlying psychological unity, survivals, and origins.

Historicists objected to analytical jurisprudence because it pictured isolated individuals connected to one another and the state solely through rights, duties, powers, and contracts, but paid no attention to the culturally created, historically contingent social sources of law and morals. They accused the analytics of postulating an abstract and universal human nature (or – even more absurdly – a nature created and variable at will by each freely choosing subject), instead of one formed by the peculiar historical circumstances and cultural environments of different societies. Holmes seems at first to be operating in this historicist mode in the famous chapter explaining early forms of liability as the product of animism,[76] the imputing of a human-like intent to things or animals that cause harm.[77] Yet Holmes quickly develops these examples in an unexpected direction: a unified theory of legal liability in all societies, primitive and modern, sociobiologically rooted in the instinct for revenge.[78] True, he is able to cite for his theory impeccable social-scientific authority, the anthropologist Tylor and the psychologist Bain;[79] and might as easily have cited Spencer, who believed no explanation of a social form was complete until traced back to pre-historical physical causation.[80] But an authentically historicist approach would try to understand why it might be *meaningful* to a particular people to treat trees and oxen ceremonially as human beings. Holmes's approach here does the opposite: His uses of history and anthropology lead him back through sociobiology to as reductionist a psychology as any of the classical ones.[81]

[73] *See supra* notes 64–71 and accompanying text.

[74] *See supra* notes 18–25 and accompanying text.

[75] *See, e.g., Common Law, supra* note 3, at 28–31.

[76] *See, e.g., Common Law, supra* note 3, at 12–13, 30–31.

[77] *See, e.g., id.* at 10–12, 31.

[78] *E.g., id.* at 6, 31.

[79] *Id.* at 13 n. 25. The works cited are Edward Tylor, *Primitive Culture* (1871) and Alexander Bain, *Mental Science* (1868).

[80] *See, e.g.,* Herbert Spencer, *The Study of Sociology* (1914).

[81] *See, e.g., Common Law, supra* note 3, at 77–78.

Holmes's general method of treating "survivals" is also not fully consistent with the announced theme of the overture. Holmes labeled old forms as mere survivals and made no attempt to give them a modern rationale.[82] His approach to survivals differed both from that of contemporary anthropologists[83] who used them to test the hypothesis of the uniform evolution of societies,[84] and from twentieth-century legal functionalists who seek to discover through an analysis of the new functions they perform, why the old forms have survived.[85] The twentieth-century approach is consistent with Holmes's announced major theme and, as we have seen,[86] Holmes was a forerunner of this approach in his general theory. He failed, however, to follow through on this theory in his actual practice.[87]

In *Commonwealth* v. *Cleary*,[88] for example, Holmes's court[89] had to decide whether it was error to admit, against a rape defendant, the victim's complaint, which had been delayed until the morning after the alleged rape. Judge Holmes first pointed out that the "rule that in trials for rape the government may or must prove that the woman concerned made complaint soon after the commission of the offense is a perverted survival of the ancient requirement that she should make hue and cry as a preliminary to bringing her appeal."[90] Holmes explained how Lord Hale had rejustified the rule as generating useful corroboration of the woman's trial testimony. Hale's "statement of the law

[82] *See, e.g.*, id. at 161, 180.

[83] *See. e.g.*, John McClennan, *Studies in Ancient History* 4 (1st ser. 1886); Tylor, *supra* note 79, at 21.

[84] Victorian anthropologists were interested in "survivals," apparently functionless vestiges of ancient practices, because, as evidence of an earlier stage of developed civilization, they could be compared with similar forms from existing "primitive" societies to test the hypothesis of the uniform evolution of societies. *See* sources cited *supra* note 83.

[85] *See* Bronislaw Malinowski, *A Scientific Theory of Culture* 30–31. (1944); Lawrence Friedman & Jack Ladinsky, "Social Change and the Law of Industrial Accidents," 61 *Colum. L. Rev.* 50, 65, 72, 76 (1967).

[86] *See supra* notes 14–25 and accompanying text.

[87] *See* Mark Tushnet, "The Logic of Experience: Oliver Wendell Holmes on the Supreme Judicial Court," 63 *Va. L. Rev.* 975, 1031–1035 (1977). Had Holmes followed his own advice, he would surely have had little trouble finding a new ground of policy for employers' liability. Holmes had played a significant role in construing the Employers' Liability Act of 1887. 1887 Mass. Acts ch. 270, §1 (current version at *Mass. Gen. Laws Ann.* Ch. 153, § 1 (West 1958)). The policy behind the Act was to remove certain bars from an employee's right to sue his employer and thus extend the employer's liability. *Ryalls* v. *Mechanics' Mills*, 150 Mass. 190, 191, 22 N.E. 766, 766 (1889). Holmes, however, construed the Act narrowly so as to allow employers to raise common law defenses such as assumption of the risk. *See Mellor* v. *Merchants' Mfg. Co.*, 150 Mass. 362, 23 N.E. 100 (1890). For a discussion of Holmes's treatment of industrial accidents under the Employers' Liability Act of 1887, *See* Tushnet, *supra*, at 1029–1035.

[88] 172 Mass. 175, 51 N.E. 746 (1898).

[89] Mark Tushnet has shown that Holmes's elevation to the Massachusetts bench made him even more shy about looking for modern policy rationales for old forms. Tushnet, *supra* note 87, at 1017–1023.

[90] 172 Mass. at 176, 51 N.E. at 746.

has survived as an arbitrary rule in the particular case, notwithstanding the later-developed principles of evidence."[91] Having taken the trouble to give *two* obsolete rationales for the rule, Holmes declined to argue either for discarding the old rule or for formulating a modern rationale.[92] He later labeled the rule "a pure survival, having nothing or very little to back it except that the practice is established."[93]

If Holmes had followed through on his promise to show new policies animating old forms, he would have had to consider modern social history. Instead, Holmes indicates that a rule can best be explained by its "origins," meaning the oldest traces the historian can find of something resembling the rule's present form. This is apparent on the first page of *The Common Law*:

> In Massachusetts to-day, while, on the one hand, there are a great many rules which are quite sufficiently accounted for by their manifest good sense, on the other, there are some which can only be understood by reference to the infancy of procedure among the German tribes, or to the social condition of Rome under the Decemvirs.[94]

The lawyer's hunt for such origins in this sense, if it is not to be the pure antiquarianism that Holmes explicitly disclaims,[95] must be tied to some theory that makes the origin relevant to the understanding of modern law. One such theory is that the exposure of a weird antique origin disqualifies a rule from contemporary use. Holmes sometimes did use history for this critical purpose, though it was not fully consistent with his general thesis.[96] A second theory is that the tracing of a rule from its origins to the present shows the logic, or teleology, of its evolutionary development,[97] the trend-line one can use to argue how it should be developed in the future. Holmes himself used this argument

[91] *Id.* The rule had become an exception to the general evidentiary exclusion of prior consistent statements.

[92] *See id.*

[93] Oliver Wendell Holmes, Jr., "Law in Science and Science in Law," in *Collected Legal Papers* 210, 227 (1920) (footnote omitted) [hereinafter cited as "Law in Science and Science in Law"]. Holmes contemptuously dismissed the rationale usually postulated that "the outrage is so great that there is a natural presumption that a virtuous woman would disclose it at the first suitable opportunity." *Id.* at 226. Rather, Holmes thought it most unlikely that "a sensitive woman would disclose such a horror." *Id.*

[94] *Common Law*, *supra* note 3, at 5. It is clear Holmes does not mean that some rules may be understood only by reference to their current social functions, for he would not have invoked ancient history. Nor could he have meant that rules may be understood only by an explanation as to why such ancient forms have for so long persisted, for such a meaning would require a showing of how the form had adapted to changing social circumstances. He seems in fact to mean that a rule can best be understood by reference to what lawyers call its "origins," meaning the oldest traces the historian can find of something resembling its present form.

[95] "I shall use the history of our law so far as it is necessary to explain a conception or to interpret a rule, but no further." *Id.* at 6.

[96] *See supra* notes 87–93 and accompanying text.

[97] This kind of historical argument was exceedingly common in Holmes's day. *See*, *e.g.*, Peter Stein, *Legal Evolution* (1980).

in his description of the rise of the external standard of liability.[98] But it is hard to see how this inner-logic-of-development theory can be compatible with the major theme that what really determines the content of a rule is shifting and contingent social purposes.

Origin-tracing may also be important to a writer who, in order to justify or condemn some rule in force, asserts that good rules are traceable to one source[99] and bad rules to another.[100] Although Holmes repeatedly argued for Teutonic over Roman sources for the common law,[101] so quaint a political theory of blessed and tainted sources of law seems far removed from Holmes's repeated declarations that law must be judged by how well it meets current needs.[102] One seems reluctantly compelled to conclude that in his origins-hunting Holmes is simply carrying out the genteel antiquarian lawyer's task of tracing the formal antecedents of modern rules, and showing, as indeed it must be said he did show, that he could do it with far greater erudition than any Anglo-American writer had yet brought to that task.

It is not, then, in the historical sections of *The Common Law* that the intellectual payoff from Holmes's pragmatic-historicist perspective is to be sought. It is rather, by a curious irony, in the driest and most abstract sections; those devoted chiefly to categories of analytical jurisprudence, among which his theory of the sovereign and his theory of rights and duties best exemplify Holmes's departure from the classical-legal tradition.

The social theory of the sovereign, which first surfaces in his *American Law Review* articles,[103] is a brilliant flare that unfortunately fizzles out early. According to Holmes, "by whom a duty is imposed must be of less importance than the definiteness of its expression and the certainty of its being enforced."[104] For example, "[I]f I am invited to a dinner party in London I must appear in evening dress under the penalty of not being asked to similar entertainments if I disobey."[105] In law, however, a judge may disregard a precedent, empty the contents of a statute by construction, or fail to enforce the statute at all.[106]

In considering the source from which law is derived, Holmes said: "Any motive for [judicial] action ... which can be relied upon as likely in the generality of cases to prevail, is worthy of consideration as one of the sources of law."[107] Thus, motives for judicial decision-making may derive from custom,

[98] *See Common Law*, *supra* note 3, at 63–103.

[99] For example, the Teutonic forests, Anglo-Saxon dooms and customs, and anti-monarchical movements.

[100] For example, Roman tyrants, Norman jurists, and Tudor-Stuart prerogative courts.

[101] *See supra* note 10.

[102] *See, e.g.*, *Common Law*, *supra* note 3, at 26, 32.

[103] *See e.g.*, "Codes, and the Arrangementof the Law," *supra* note 1, at 4.

[104] *Id.* at 4.

[105] *Id.*

[106] Book Notices, 6 *Am. L. Rev* 723, 724 (1872) (unsigned but written by Holmes).

[107] *Id.*

mercantile usage, or public policy.[108] Elsewhere, Holmes refers to the source of law, or sovereignty, as "the *de facto* supreme power in the community,"[109] meaning the class or group that is able to have its way against all others. Like his notion of legal rights, Holmes's theory of the sovereign presents itself as a matter of much interest to sociologists or historians, for, given Holmes's theory of sovereignty, an historian can determine who a society's sovereign may be by discovering which commands and rules are habitually obeyed by all of society. Sir Henry Maine later made a similar observation regarding sovereignty;[110] Maine, however, had earlier conducted research through his anthropological work on Indian village communities.[111] Holmes never carried out any kind of research program,[112] yet he repeatedly invoked the "actual feelings and demands of the community"[113] to explain the primary source of law. In his practice, however, Holmes's communities, whose de facto supreme powers are supposedly sovereign and whose felt necessities determine the legislative content of legal forms,[114] are almost wholly featureless and depopulated – they have no classes or guilds or corporations, no cities or villages, no families after the patriarchal family of antiquity, a limited economy, no bureaucracies, armies, or assemblies, barely even a state. Here we witness an expressly social theory of law without a society anywhere in sight.[115]

108 *Id.; see* "The Theory of Torts," *supra* note 1, at 656.

109 "Summary of Events: The Gas-Stokers' Strike," 7 *Am. L. Rev* 582, 583 (1873) (unsigned but written by Holmes).

110 *See* Henry Maine, *Lectures on the Early History of Institutions* 342–400 (7th edn. 1914).

111 Henry Maine, *Village-Communities In The East And West* (1880).

112 Holmes *may* have justified this decision to himself on the "practical ground" that *lawyers* (as compared with judges) are only interested in cases and courts. *See* "Codes, and the Arrangement of the Law," *supra* note 1, at 4–5. If so, this would have been a strangely narrow and formal view of practicality. In Holmes's time, as in ours, lawyers were concerned about more than the courts' judgments. It was common, for example, for a corporation's chief counsel to double as its public relations office, *see, e.g.*, Ralph & Muriel Hidy, *Pioneering in Big Business, 1882–1911*, at 217–218 (1955); Gerald White, *Formative Years in the Far West: A History of Standard Oil Co. of California and Predecessors Through 1919*, at 433–459 (1962), since adverse publicity meant reform movements and reform movements meant legislative and administrative nuisances for the counsel's office. They knew where they had to look for predictions of the public force, and it was often not in the law reports.

113 *Common Law*, *supra* note 3, at 36. Tom Grey has pointed out to me that Holmes's idea of "the community" varied both over time and with the context. In the early *American Law Review* articles, the community out of which the common law arises is an organic whole, though legislation is the product of a community split into warring factions and classes. By the time of *The Common Law*, Holmes had assimilated the common law to the model of social struggle. Yet at the same time, as Grey says, Holmes's speeches on the soldier's faith, and his decision to leave all his money to the United States, suggest that in some ways he held on to an idea of community as something more enduring, compelling, and spiritual than numerous interest-groups battling for domination. Letter from Thomas C. Grey to Robert W. Gordon (February 17, 1982).

114 *See supra* notes 107–110 and accompanying text.

115 In his gentle criticism of Holmes, James Willard Hurst makes a similar point. *See* James Willard Hurst, *Justice Holmes On Legal History* 33–34 (1964).

One can understand, however, why Holmes did not follow through on his theory of the sovereign in either his scholarly or his judicial practice. Considering the realities behind the power relations underlying legal enactments is hardly an approved technique of legal reasoning and justification. Imagine what would have happened if Holmes had applied his theoretical method to the "prompt reporting as corroboration" rule in the rape case.[116] He might have argued that the modern function of the prompt reporting requirement is simply to make claims of rape hard to prove, as many people believe that vindictive women persecute men with false accusations of rape.[117] Whether this is or is not true, consider that prospective defendants in such cases are frequently upper class men, the "*de facto* power in the community" and that their "self-preference" is to reduce the risk of being falsely (or even truthfully) accused. They may do so by perpetuating a "survival," the prompt reporting requirement, because it is easier and cheaper than legislation and because it conceals their purpose. Now obviously I am not arguing that this is necessarily the true explanation of the survival of the prompt reporting rule. It is, nonetheless, completely consistent with Holmes's basic legal theories, namely the theory of the sovereign and the overture theme, and may help clarify why he so often declined opportunities to put his theories into practice.[118]

In any event, Holmes's historicizing of the sovereign, brief though it was, represented an important break with the classical-legal tradition. An even more important break with the classical-legal tradition is also apparent in one of his analytical rather than historical modes. The classicists, recall,[119] hoped to fix definite boundaries to the spheres of free action of individuals vis-à-vis one another and the state, each sphere ending where the other's began. Thus, for a person to have rights of free action, everyone else had to have duties not to interfere with those rights.[120] If this program worked out perfectly, every nonconsensual invasion of a sphere of right would be sanctioned as a

[116] *Commonwealth* v. *Cleary*, 172 Mass. 175, 51 N.E. 746 (1898).

[117] *See* 1 John Wigmore, *A Treatise on the Anglo-American System of Evidence* § 200, at 683 (3rd edn. 1940).

[118] *See, e.g.*, *Vegelahn* v. *Guntner*, 167 Mass. 92, 104–109, 44 N.E. 1077, 1079–1082 (1896) (Holmes, J., dissenting). Holmes expressed his displeasure when the court's opinion was later referred to as pro-labor. Letter from Oliver Wendell Holmes to Sir Frederick Pollock (February [September] 23, 1902), *reprinted in* 1 *Holmes-Pollock Letters*, *supra* note 59, at 106; *see* Tushnet, *supra* note 87, at 1035–1040. Holmes was occasionally willing to produce explanations consistent with his thesis once the "dominant power in the community" had spoken through legislation. *See Commonwealth* v. *Perry*, 155 Mass. 117, 124–125, 28 N.E. 1126, 1127–1128 (1891) (Holmes, J., dissenting). In a series of decisions, however, Holmes restricted the scope of legislation that limited employers' common law defenses to liability, without interpreting the statute as reflecting the growing power of the labor class. Tushnet, *supra* note 87, at 1029–1035; *see* discussion *supra* note 87.

[119] *See supra* notes 61–63 and accompanying text.

[120] Connoisseurs of this field will recognize that I am oversimplifying here, but I will rapidly become unintelligible if I don't.

violation of duty. Holmes seemed to take particular pleasure in attacking this system, by pointing to important categories of immunities and liabilities that did not fit within this scheme: duties without correlative rights;[121] legal sanctions viewed as a "tax on conduct" (meaning the law does not forbid you from doing the thing, but merely says that if you do it you must pay the tariff).[122] Yet another, and perhaps the most important category, is the area of damnum absque injuria: "There are certain things which the law allows a man to do, notwithstanding the fact that he foresees that harm to another will follow from them."[123]

The classical lawyers had recognized the existence of the sphere of damnum absque injuria but viewed it as an anomaly. Holmes brought it to the forefront by pointing to areas of social life where people or groups were free to harm others if they were willing to pay the harms tax,[124] and still other areas where they could harm with impunity.[125] Economic competition was the example

[121] As Holmes observes:

> Legal duties then come before legal rights. To put it more broadly, and avoid the word duty, which is open to objection, the direct working of the law is to limit freedom of action or choice on the part of a greater or less number of persons in certain specified ways; while the power of removing or enforcing this limitation which is generally confined to certain other private persons, or, in other words, a right corresponding to the burden, is not a necessary or universal correlative.

Common Law, *supra* note 3, at 173.

[122] *See* Book Notices, *supra* note 106, at 724–725. Much to the distress of his contemporaries, who were somewhat shocked by the amoralism of the external standard carried to this length, Holmes was eventually to explain all civil liability as a tax on conduct, for example, finding a contract obligation to be nothing more than a promisor's option to perform or pay damages. *Common Law*, *supra* note 3, at 235–236; *see* "The Path of the Law," *supra* note 22, at 174–175.

[123] *Common Law*, *supra* note 3, at 115. I could not have appreciated the importance of this contribution of Holmes without the aid of a brilliant recent survey, Joseph Singer, "The Legal Rights Debate in Analytical Jurisprudence from Bentham to Hohfeld," 1982 *Wisc. L. Rev.* 975 (1982). *See* also Duncan Kennedy & Frank Michelman, "Are Property and Contract Efficient?," 8 *Hofstra L. Rev.* 711, 751–758 (1980) (discussing Hohfeldian analysis and its lessons).

A. V. Dicey, in his otherwise perceptive review of *The Common Law*, overlooked this point. He did see that with the external standard Holmes had set up a system of strict liability for harms, regardless of fault, and that this was as much an important departure from the classical scheme as a more scientific means of implementing the standard. Dicey reconciled the apparent amoralism of the external standard with his own notions of morality by pointing out that people often got hurt by actions that were not, judging by the defendant's state of mind, wicked or careless, and that a civilized community would nonetheless try to prevent these acts. Book Review, *The Spectator*, June 3, 1882 (Literary Supplement), at 745, col. 2, 746, col. 1. (I owe this attribution to Dicey to Saul Touster.) I find this to be a rather ironic reading in view of *The Common Law's* famous attempt to defend the status quo of fault-based liability in the fancy new language of external standards. *See Common Law*, *supra* note 3, at 76–78. The point Dicey missed was that the community might also encourage people to harm each other knowingly, without imposing liability. *See infra* note 126 and accompanying text.

[124] *See supra* note 122.

[125] *See supra* note 123 and accompanying text.

par excellence of activity that was privileged even though it destroyed livelihoods,[126] and Holmes was beginning to argue that labor organization should, in principle, be no different.[127] What Holmes had done was extract a perception commonplace in one rational system of interpreting the world and transfer it to another: the formal apparatus of analytical jurisprudence.

To some extent, he adopted the classical economists' view that the appropriate legal framework of rights and duties was a necessary and sufficient condition for a civil society of market relations that would maximize general welfare, at the necessary cost of driving some individuals to the wall.[128] There are hints that he also shared with the classical economists the view that the anarchy of market relations had to be, and could be, softened and regulated by morals,[129] meaning non-legal social sanctions, and that the appropriate moral framework was that of the Victorian middle class, whose morals, inculcated through religion, education, and the family, were slowly becoming the universal morals of society through a process of historical evolution.[130] Holmes sometimes used Hume's and Smith's term "sympathy"[131] in reference to the softening of market relations to describe modern society's distinctive capacity for altruistic behavior, which comes from the ability to analogize others' sufferings to one's own.[132] In addition, Holmes often spoke of men's ingrained sociobiological urges, such as the desire to dominate, wreak retribution on criminals, and enjoy exclusive possession, as being at least somewhat tempered by an educated sympathy.[133] He believed that individuals, to some extent, took the risk of whatever dangers inhered in social situations in which they found themselves[134] and, to the extent they did not, were simply victims of natural

[126] Holmes developed his insight that communities might encourage people to harm each other knowingly and without imposing liability in his seminal essay, "Privilege, Malice, and Intent," in *Collected Legal Papers* 117 (1920). Since the essay appeared after the labor disturbances and vast merger movements of the 1880s and 90s, its point could be more readily appreciated. This essay is the central focus of Horwitz's chapter on Holmes. *See* Horwitz, *supra* note 60.

[127] *See, e.g., Vegelahn* v. *Guntner*, 167 Mass. 92, 105, 44 N.E. 1077, 1080–1081 (1896) (Holmes, J., dissenting).

[128] *See Common Law, supra* note 3, at 37, 86.

[129] *See* Warren Samuels, *The Classical Theory of Economic Policy* 21–76 (1966).

[130] *See* Samuel Beer, *British Politics in the Collectivist Age* 34–37 (1965); Guido Ruggiero, *History of European Liberalism* 425 (1927).

[131] David Hume, *A Treatise of Human Nature* 318–320 (2nd edn. Selby-Bigge ed. 1978); Adam Smith, *The Theory of Moral Sentiments* 3–13 (reprinted edn. 1966) (reprint of new 1853 edn.).

[132] Holmes had read the anthropologist Charles Staniland Wake, who, in the characteristic Victorian sociobiological mode, rooted "sympathy" in the maternal instinct and argued, on the basis of abundant anthropological and historical evidence, for its progressive growth in advanced civilizations. *See* 1 Charles Wake, *The Evolution of Morality* 411–434 (1878).

[133] *See Summary of Events: The Gas-Stokers' Strike, supra* note 109, at 583–584.

[134] *See Lamson* v. *American Ax & Tool Co.*, 177 Mass. 144, 58 N.E. 585 (1900); *Chisholm* v. *New England Tel. & Tel. Co.*, 176 Mass. 125, 57 N.E. 383 (1900); *Campbell* v. *Dearborn*, 175 Mass. 183, 55 N.E. 1042 (1900); *Quinn* v. *New York*, N.H. & H.R.R., 175 Mass. 150, 55 N.E. 891 (1900). I owe these references to Tushnet, *supra* note 87, at 994 n.103.

misfortunes. There is a striking passage where Holmes compares the injury of a victim of non-legally liable, as compared with non-morally liable, conduct, to being struck by lightning instead of the agency of another human being.[135] In these respects, Holmes did not differ from his liberal contemporaries, and yet, to mention a notorious fact, Holmes's chief method of naturalizing the social order was not liberal at all, but Darwinian, as shown in his remarkable comments on "The Gas-Stokers' Strike" in 1873:

> The struggle for life, undoubtedly, is constantly putting the interests of men at variance with those of the lower animals. And the struggle does not stop in the ascending scale with the monkeys, but is equally the law of human existence. Outside of legislation this is undeniable. It is mitigated by sympathy, prudence, and all the social and moral qualities. But in the last resort a man rightly prefers his own interest to that of his neighbors. And this is as true in legislation as in any other form of corporate action. All that can be expected from modern improvements is that legislation should easily and quickly, yet not too quickly, modify itself in accordance with the will of the *de facto* supreme power in the community, and that the spread of an educated sympathy should reduce the sacrifice of minorities to a minimum. But whatever body may possess the supreme power for the moment is certain to have interests inconsistent with others which have competed unsuccessfully. The more powerful interests must be more or less reflected in legislation; which, like every other device of man or beast, must tend in the long run to aid the survival of the fittest. The objection to class legislation is not that it favors a class, but either that it fails to benefit the legislators, or that it is dangerous to them because a competing class has gained in power, or that it transcends the limits of self-preference which are imposed by sympathy. Interference with contracts by usury laws and the like is open to the first objection, that it only makes the burden of borrowers heavier. The law brought to bear upon the gas-stokers is perhaps open to the second, that it requires to be backed by a more unquestioned power than is now possessed by the favored class; and some English statutes are also very probably open to the third. But it is no sufficient condemnation of legislation that it favors one class at the expense of another; for much or all legislation does that; and none the less when the *bona fide* object is the greatest good of the greatest number. Why should the greatest number be preferred? Why not the greatest good of the most intelligent and most highly developed? The greatest good of a minority of our generation may be the greatest good of the greatest number in the long run. But if the welfare of all future ages is to be considered, legislation may as well be abandoned for the present. If the welfare of the living majority is paramount, it can only be on the ground that the majority have the power in their hands. The fact is that legislation in this country, as well as elsewhere, is empirical. It is necessarily made a means by which a body, having the power, put burdens which are disagreeable to them on the shoulders of somebody else. Communism would no more get rid of the difficulty than any other system, unless it limited or put a stop to the propagation of the species. And it may be doubted whether that solution would not be as disagreeable as any other.[136]

[135] *Common Law*, *supra* note 3, at 78.

[136] "Summary of events: The gas-stokers' strike," *supra* note 109, at 583–584.

It has been noted that the only real Social Darwinist on the Court that decided *Lochner* v. *New York*,[137] was, in fact, Holmes.[138] If the Constitution does not embody Herbert Spencer's *Social Statics*,[139] Holmes's thoughts in *Lochner* surely do.[140] The difference between Holmes's and Spencer's philosophies is that Holmes did not think that the Darwinian struggle comes to an end with the triumph of the middle class or that legislation is exempt from becoming its object. Rather, Holmes believed that the working class is entitled to its triumph if it can get it, and should be able to use legislation as its instrument.[141] Although working class legislation may well be futile and self-defeating, it is not for that reason unlawful.

Thus, Holmes took a strong stand against the premises of freedom and formal equality that underlay the classical-liberal vision of law[142] – those very premises that his external standard was welcomed as technically executing in modern scientific form. He even put forth the fascinating suggestion that the formal equality assumed by law, and promoted by his external standards, is nothing more than a pragmatic working assumption – like the rules of a game – made for the limited purpose of facilitating certain kinds of public interactions.[143] Outside these interactions, the assumption of a formal equality is abandoned for the realistic recognition that the world is actually ruled by force.[144]

Holmes elsewhere made clear his belief that formal rules of general application exist more for the promotion of administrative convenience than for the protection of individual autonomy[145] although his external standard often reflects both the liberalism of much of his jurisprudence and the Darwinism of his historical-social vision. Indeed, the standard almost seems to be an attempt to mediate between them. The external standard, as the average of human conduct established by juries, represents a social consensus, although it sacrifices individuals whose personal qualities fall below it to the collective good. The objective theory of contract formation, for example, results in courts enforcing that which does not always reflect the actual will of the parties involved. It will, however, allow individuals to predict legal consequences more accurately and thus will enable them to plan their conduct in such a way so as to be able, in the future, to carry out their intent effectively. Thus, to the extent

137 198 U.S. 45 (1905).

138 *See* Joseph Wall, "Social Darwinism and Constitutional Law with Special Reference to *Lochner* v. *New York*," 33 *Annals Sci.* 465, 475–476 (1976).

139 Herbert Spencer, *Social Statics* (1851).

140 This aphorism was supplied by Abe Chayes in conversation.

141 *See, e.g., Lochner* v. *New York*, 198 U.S. at 75–76 (Holmes, J., dissenting).

142 *See Common Law, supra* note 3, at 165–167.

143 "You cannot argue with your neighbor, except on the admission for the moment that he is as wise as you, although you may by no means believe it." *Id.* at 38.

144 *Id.*

145 *See, e.g., id.* at 86–87.

that public policy, representing some utilitarian general welfare function or the desires of the currently dominant class, sets the standard of liability, individual freedom and equality will be sacrificed completely, but all for the sake of some higher good.

> [W]hen men live in society, a certain average of conduct, a sacrifice of individual peculiarities going beyond a certain point, is necessary to the general welfare. If, for instance, a man is born hasty and awkward, is always having accidents and hurting himself or his neighbors, no doubt his congenital defects will be allowed for in the courts of Heaven, but his slips are no less troublesome to his neighbors than if they sprang from guilty neglect. His neighbors accordingly require him, at his proper peril, to come up to their standard, and the courts which they establish decline to take his personal equation into account.[146]

The conflict apparent here between law as an agent of freedom and law as an agent of collective good or natural necessity as determined by forces external to individual human choice[147] is reproduced at another level of Holmes's thought, which deals with the lawmaker, specifically, the judge. The issue here could be phrased thus: Is the judge only an agent of outside wills or forces that effectively determine all judicial decisions, or is the judge a freely choosing person, an autonomous actor in social life? The classical lawyers had, of course, an answer to this conflict inherent in judicial decision-making: The judge could participate in society but only to the extent permitted by the formal theory of the separation of powers. The judicial function thus permitted was confined to responding to forces outside: the will of the parties to contracts, for example, or the will of the state as understood and applied by the legal science designed to make them and the boundaries between them clear and unmistakable.[148]

Holmes, as I have mentioned,[149] was a pioneer in breaking up this system at the same time that he was engaged in furthering its development. *The Common Law* is a monument to this contradiction. Positivist legal science in one version poses as capable of making predictions from the case law; yet Holmes locates sovereignty in social domination, which is expressed both inside and outside the legal system, saying it is historically contingent and always changing.[150] In another version, the predictive value of legal science is based on clear general principles, such as that of liability for harms the average prudent man could have avoided with foreknowledge. Yet even as he enunciates the principle, Holmes exposes the quality that allows it to apply to all cases: The ease with which results may be changed by moving the time frame for defendant's

[146] *Id.*

[147] For example, the immanent rationality of the market, sociobiological instincts, and evolutionary processes.

[148] *See* Kennedy, *supra* note 61, at 6–8.

[149] *See supra* notes 88–102 and accompanying text.

[150] *See Common Law*, *supra* note 3, at 31–33.

avoidance-choice backwards or forwards.[151] Such a move requires continued legislative policy choices, not only in the decision of anomalous or difficult cases but in the decision of the ordinary and simple ones. We have to wonder what Holmes's intent is here. Is his theory of torts meant to be an operational concept for handling cases or predicting results, or is it a heuristic device for demonstrating the impossibility of solving cases without constant political choice? It seems to mean all of these things simultaneously.

One sees a similar effect in his chapters on contracts,[152] where, as with torts, Holmes tries both to develop generalizations that will apply to empirical instances and to purge the field of subjective moral constructs, such as the actual will of contracting parties. For example, Holmes held the concept of "promise" to extend beyond those instances where the promisor undertakes to act himself, to cases where the promisor agrees to take the risk of the non-occurrence of events over which he has no control.[153] Holmes's objective theory of contract liability[154] will prevent a buyer from rescinding a contract for the sale of "the barrels... and their contents," even where the seller says the barrels are full of mackerel and they are actually full of salt.[155] The objective theory will permit a buyer's rescission on the ground of fraud, however, where the seller makes innocent false statements of material facts if, under the external standard of knowledge imposed by the community, he should have known they were false, or if they were in fact false.[156] In determining the materiality of a false statement, however, Holmes discards the external standard as useless, for in their contractual relations parties may make anything essential, however trivial the community may find it.[157] Holmes concludes that "after all, the most important element of decision is not any technical, or even any general principle of contracts, but a consideration of the nature of the particular transaction as a practical matter."[158]

In his first articles in the *American Law Review*,[159] Holmes's ambition was to refine the existing categories of analytical jurisprudence with a view toward making them more general and inclusive of legal doctrines. It was in this spirit that he contributed to the emerging classical law of tort his important and majestically general conceptualization of the field of negligence as consisting of the duties of care that everyone owes to everyone else;[160] even then, however, he warned of

[151] A systematic application of this technique to criminal law may be found in Mark Kelman, "Interpretive Construction in the Substantive Criminal Law," 33 *Stan. L. Rev.* 591 (1981).

[152] *Common Law*, *supra* note 3, at 195–264.

[153] *Id.* at 234–235.

[154] *See supra* note 67 and accompanying text.

[155] *Common Law*, *supra* note 3, at 253.

[156] *See id.* at 109, 253–254.

[157] *Id.* at 258.

[158] *Id.* at 263 (emphasis added). "[When] does a difference in qualities rise to a difference in kind? It is a question for Mr. Darwin to answer." "The Theory of Torts" *supra* note 1, at 654.

[159] *E.g.*, "Codes and the Arrangement of the Law," *supra* note 1.

[160] "The Theory of Torts," *supra* note 1, at 660–663.

the next phase of his development: "Law," he said, "is not a science, but is essentially empirical."[161] Thus emerged Holmes's scientific-positivist mode, in which he began his quest for generalizations from empirically observed regularities in legal decision-making. Yet ultimately this ascent to new heights of generalization simply gave him a splendid vantage point from which to observe that none of them worked, and that he was looking down into a fragmented chaos of particularistic transactions and miscellaneous policies, varying with historically changing realignments of purposes and power relations.

Holmes sometimes used that old chestnut, the idea of the natural, evolutionary adaptiveness of the common law, whereby the judge would unconsciously refashion the law to suit the felt necessities of the time, to mediate the contradictions here exposed. He made clear, however, that unconscious evolution belonged to the pre-scientific state of law; the new grounds of legal policy should be conscious and articulate:

> Since the ancient forms of action have disappeared, a broader treatment of the subject ought to be possible. Ignorance is the best of law reformers. People are glad to discuss a question on general principles, when they have forgotten the special knowledge necessary for technical reasoning. But the present willingness to generalize is founded on more than merely negative grounds. The philosophical habit of the day, the frequency of legislation, and the ease with which the law may be changed to meet the opinions and wishes of the public, all make it natural and unavoidable that judges as well as others should openly discuss the legislative principles upon which their decisions must always rest in the end, and should base their judgments upon broad considerations of policy to which the traditions of the bench would hardly have tolerated a reference fifty years ago.[162]

How are judges to do this without making their own choices? Holmes offers theories throughout *The Common Law* that appear at least to minimize the occasions for exercise of what he calls the "sovereign prerogative of choice."[163] One theory is that the external standard device will make most cases easy cases for judicial decision; hard cases, where conflicting standards contradict one another, or where the community mood is shifting away from the standard, Holmes suggests, can be thrown to the jury.[164] Another solution for the judge faced with a hard case is apparent in what may be called the "consensus plateaux" theory. Where there are historical periods of struggle for dominance among conflicting interests asserting conflicting views, legal science is impossible because judges must preserve their role as disinterested observers. Some group eventually wins the struggle, however, and its ideas become entrenched. At this point judges can ascertain the opinions of the community and synthesize from them external standards of liability.[165] At other times Holmes appears

161 "Codes, and the Arrangement of the Law," *supra* note 1, at 4.

162 *Common Law*, *supra* note 3, at 64.

163 "Law in Science and Science in Law," *supra* note 93, at 239.

164 For the mediating functions of the notion of hard cases, see generally Heller, *supra* note 38.

165 Oliver Wendell Holmes, Jr., "Law and the Court," in *Collected Legal Papers* 291, 294–295 (1920).

to rely on the Victorian march of science, whose evolution he hoped might one day produce the ideal scientific policy-maker.[166] One can only speculate as to who this ideal policy-maker might be. A guardian? A law-and-economics wizard? "[T]he man of statistics and the master of economics"[167] that he promised in a later essay?[168]

After making the coherence of his view of lawmaking as science explicitly depend on a social-functional theory of law, a theory of historical direction, and a theory of legislation based either on utilitarian notions of general welfare or Darwinian ones of class struggle, Holmes offers us none of them and gives only the vaguest of aphoristic clues about how to think about them. Holmes's stance at times is simply conservative: To avoid taking sides, the judge should rest on the authority of settled cases simply because they are settled. Arbitrary or functionless survivals though they may be, they protect reliance interests.[169]

The main way in which Holmes seems to have resolved the tension between his continually increased recognition of the political role of judges and his desire to maintain their status as disinterested scientists, was to emphasize more and more the determined nature of all social life: "The necessities seem to me the real king, and the dreaded monopolist depends for his power on embodying a true prophecy of the economic must. But people can say damn Rockefeller when they would not dare to damn the order of the universe or its Author."[170]

I have criticized Holmes's inconsistencies in *The Common Law* and his failure to offer a means by which we may reconcile them. Perhaps I have been somewhat ungracious since his book is the occasion for this piece, in making him, in a sense, my host and me his parasite. I am reminded of the occasion when Holmes as a young man showed Emerson a quite critical essay Holmes had written about Plato, and Emerson said, "[W]hen you strike at a king, you must kill him."[171] I have no wish to try to "kill" *The Common Law*, which remains incredibly rich in insights.[172] It is simply because Holmes saw so much deeper than others that I expect more of him and find his persistent reluctance to develop those insights harder to forgive. What I can admire in Holmes the theorist – of course this says nothing about Holmes the judge – is his deft dissection of classical conceptualism, his Nietzschean insight into the power relations underlying systems of rights and morals, his recognition of the historical

[166] *See, e.g.*, "Law in Science and Science in Law," *supra* note 93, at 238–239.

[167] "The Path of the Law," *supra* note 22, at 187.

[168] *Id.*

[169] *See* "Law in Science and Science in Law," *supra* note 93, at 239.

[170] Letter from Oliver Wendell Holmes, Jr. to Franklin Ford (April 26, 1907) (Holmes Manuscripts, Harvard Law School Archives) (first emphasis added) (copy on file in office of *Hofstra Law Review*).

[171] *Quoted* in 1 Howe, *supra* note 2, at 54 (1957) (emphasis in original) (footnote omitted).

[172] But I must say that outside the famous coloratura passages Holmes's insights require much patience to be noticed.

and social contingency of legal rules, and most of all his aspirations for theory grounded in cosmopolitan historical learning and intended to treat the law as a cultural expression of the felt necessities, power struggles, and ideals of actual human beings in social life. Yet, though we may admire and here celebrate Holmes's aspirations, credit for their achievement in his time belongs, I think, more appropriately to others.[173]

[173] To Marx and Weber, for example, or to Maine and Jhering, Mommsen, Gierke, or Maitland.

PART II

LEGAL HISTORIANS

3

Social-Legal History's Pioneer: The Work of James Willard Hurst

[*This was the second part of the Introduction to the* Law & Society Review's *1975 Festschrift for Hurst. Much has since been written on Hurst's contributions to legal history, some of the best of it in a Symposium on Hurst's work in 18* Law & History Review *1 (2000).*]

The readers of Willard Hurst's first major work, *The Growth of American Law* (1950),[1] could tell from the first few pages that although the book purported only to synthesize existing secondary materials, the synthesis represented something new in American legal history. This was a history of law-making agencies – not only courts, but constitutional conventions, chief executives, administrative agencies, and the bar – inquiring into the social functions these agencies had served since the founding of the Republic. Though described with an insider's understanding and grasp of detail, its perspective on the operations of the legal system was that of an outsider: it was a critical Inspector General's report on how legal institutions had served the society that supported them. Hurst had formulated and announced his program of defection from the main line of legal historiography as early as 1942.[2] *The Growth of American Law* was the cornerstone for the imposing body of external legal history that he, and the Wisconsin school of legal studies he founded,[3] have been writing since, and are still adding to.

1 *The Growth of American Law: The Lawmakers* (1950).

2 "Legal History: A Research Program," 1942 *Wisc. L. Rev.* 319.

3 The works of this school on Wisconsin legal history include: Lawrence M. Friedman, *Contract Law in America* (1965); Robert S. Hunt, *Law and Locomotives: The Impact of the Railroad on Wisconsin Law of the Nineteenth Century* (1958); Spencer Kimball, *Insurance and Public Policy* (1960); George J. Kuehnl, *The Wisconsin Business Corporation* (1959); James A. Lake, *Law and Mineral Wealth: The Legal Profile of the Wisconsin Mining Industry* (1962); Francis W. Laurent, *The Business of a Trial Court, 100 Years of Cases* (1959); Samuel Mermin, *Jurisprudence and Statecraft: The Wisconsin Development Authority and its Implications* (1963); Earl F. Murphy, *Water Purity* (1961).

The preceding essay[4] advanced the argument that the actualization of pragmatic legal theory in historical writing was stunted and sometimes choked off entirely by the reluctance of legal scholars to shake off their old roles of interpreters of the common law tradition. But in Hurst's work pragmatic legal theory reached full flowering, probably unexcelled anywhere else in American legal scholarship. Others have appraised, some of them brilliantly,[5] his work in general: my concern here is only to try to show how his ways of thinking about law dissolved the constraints most legal historians had felt upon taking an external approach.

For this purpose, it is useful to consider Hurst's work as an effort to apply the general insights of pragmatic theory, especially as formulated by John Dewey,[6] to the study of the specific historical phenomenon of American law in the nineteenth and twentieth centuries. "Law" is here a general label for several species of applied social intelligence, which may be understood only by reference to the conditions out of which they are generated and by the consequences to which they give rise. The basic function of law, as of any other form of social intelligence, is to increase men's ability to achieve rational control over social change in order to liberate their natural capacity for growth. Men and women achieve rational control through experimental method, which expands their empirical appreciation of the consequences of their conduct; expanded awareness of consequences enlarges their ideas of what is desirable as well as of the most efficient means of attaining it; and this leads to growth in the range and quality of life experience, especially emotional experience, for "reason probably finds justification ultimately as an instrument by which men achieve more subtle, more varied and more shared emotion."[7]

The special focus of Hurst's attention is governmental activity, the work of agencies and of those who interpret and apply it; Hurst calls this "law." (It is not a definition of law, since Hurst does not try to define law; it is a term of convenience without any precise boundaries.) His reason for concentrating on official action is that the state possesses special characteristics that impart to the exercise of directive intelligence through its agencies an exceptional social significance. Of all associations in society, it is the public organized in the state, acting through the legal order, that stands the best chance of increasing rational control over social change. This is not to say that American law has lived up

4 "The Common Law Tradition in American Legal Historiography," *supra* Ch.1.

5 The outstanding ones in my view are: Harry N. Scheiber, "At the Borderland of Law and Economic History: The Contributions of Willard Hurst," 75 *Am. Hist. Rev.* 744 (1969), and Mark Tushnet, "Lumber and the Legal Process," 1972 *Wisc. L. Rev.* 114.

6 There are other significant influences detectable in Hurst's work, notably Max Weber's; but as a factor shaping Hurst's external perspective, American pragmatic thought seems to me to have been more significant.

7 James Willard Hurst, "The Law in United States History," 105 *Proc. Am. Phil. Soc.* 518, 519 (1960). For Dewey on the same themes, see, e.g., *Experience and Nature*, ch. 10 (2nd edn. 1929).

to its potential in this respect. Far from it: one of Hurst's main themes is that social change has usually been permitted to take place by "drift," "default," or "inertia," by which is meant experience transmuted into social action without the intervention of reflective intelligence. The consciousness from which people draw their desires and preferred means of satisfying them tends to be imprisoned in habitual modes and forms,[8] but old forms are continually coming up against and mixing with one another, in different combinations, thus continually producing a new social environment.[9] Acted upon by new conditions, the old forms will of course yield new consequences. The failure of people to subject new conditions to experimental evaluations means that they are constantly being surprised and baffled by experience, instead of being able to achieve some mastery over it in the interests of human growth.

For Hurst, as for American Progressives generally, the most conspicuous example of "drift" is the persistence through the late nineteenth and early twentieth centuries of the habitual consciousness of private-market-and-business-oriented individualism.[10] In the early nineteenth century, this had been a mode of thinking more functional for growth: it had released human talents and energies for the purpose of settling a continent and fulfilling the basic economic conditions for community existence. But at the same time it had defined business as the main arena for the exercise of talent, so that instrumental intelligence was rarely directed toward the elaboration of any but the most short-term economic consequences of social action. Private economic interests had thus in time come to overwhelm social life, with the results that:

> (1) people's consciousness of the desirable and how to reach it came to take account only of immediate economic costs and benefits (a method of thought Hurst calls "bastard pragmatism") and not of longer-run consequences for more various modes of growth; and (2) people had lost the talent for politics, that is, for organizing to promote, through the legal agencies of the state, ideas of the general good of their communities less parochial than purely economic interest.[11]

Hurst thus follows the main tradition of Progressive thought in relating the exercise of social intelligence to conditions of social organization: its effectiveness depends upon the wide dispersal of power among diverse solidary

[8] For Hurst on drift, see *Law and Social Process in United States History* (1960), especially at 66–75; cf. Dewey on habit, *Human Nature and Conduct*, Pt. 1 (1922).

[9] This phrase tries very clumsily to give a brief impression of Hurst's intricate theoretical account of how imprisonment in habit produces social drift. For this account in its most developed form in Hurst's work, see his *Justice Holmes on Legal History* 11–13 *et passim* (1964).

[10] For typical descriptions of this consciousness, see Hurst, *id.* at 39–50; *Law and Social Process*, *supra* note 8 at 54–55.

[11] Hurst's most powerful expression of these ideas remains that in the final chapter of his *Lawmakers*, *supra* note 1, at 439–446 *et passim*; see also *Law and the Conditions of Freedom in the Nineteenth Century United States* (1967). Here the allegiance to Dewey is especially strong: see *The Public and its Problems* (1927).

communities of shared values. Thus rational policy-making, dispersal of power, and community solidarity are all conditions of one another's existence; and all three are conditions of social growth.[12] The importance of law in society (though Hurst keeps insisting that like other forms of rational planning law can never have more than a marginal directive impact on social change) is that it has special equipment to help nudge these conditions into being. In particular, as the monopolist of legitimate force, the state has authority to hold private power accountable to the general welfare and in extreme cases to adjust its distribution in society, either by breaking up power centers or by balancing them with countervailing powers. But perhaps the most important feature of state action is that it is normatively rational, is supposed to operate through forms and procedures designed to encourage deliberate, informed, and accountable decision-making. More than any other association the government is subject to expectations that its decisions will not be habitual reflexes, but will be mediated through careful reflection upon long-run consequences; and it has extraordinary resources (e.g., the ability to call upon a wide range of expert opinion representing diverse interests in legislative investigation, administrative rule-making, etc.) to generate the appropriate laboratory conditions for the operations of experimental intelligence. In other words, the norms of American constitutionalism ought to provide an especially favorable environment for pragmatic method.[13]

The legal historian's task, as Hurst sees it, is to measure the actual past performance of government against this potential. It takes a historian to do this, because only a perspective on several generations can reveal the habitual modes that have conditioned decision-making as well as the long-run consequences of the actual decisions. The present generation of lawyers needs to know, and needs history to inform it, which circumstances promote, and which prevent, intelligent direction of society in favor of growth. Hurst's rebellion against the dominant tradition in legal scholarship was not made in the name of disinterested reconstruction of the past; he is an intensely committed moralist, for whom the past is full of dreadful warnings.

But for the purpose of this essay, I want to look at these issues exactly backwards from the way Hurst does. He is always concerned to see how history

[12] James Willard Hurst, "Legal Elements in United States History," in *Law in American History* (Fleming & Bailyn eds. 1971), at 88–89; see Dewey, *id.*, especially at chs. 5–6. There is an excellent discussion of this aspect of Progressive thought in David E. Price, "Community and Control: Critical Democratic Theory in the Progressive Period," 68 *Am. Polit. Sci. Rev.* 1663, 1672 (1974).

[13] For a representative passage on the constitutional ideal, see Hurst, "Legal Elements," supra note 12, at 3–7. Hurst never goes quite so far as to equate constitutionalism and his own normative pragmatic method (though he is not entirely innocent of sometimes confusing them in his discourse), since the constitutional ideal has held officials and private holders accountable to serve *individual* life, but not (at least not consistently) to serve social or community life. See *Law and Social Process, supra* note 8 at 3.

can contribute to the living lawyer's exercise of pragmatic method in the public interest; but it is also worthwhile to ask how his vision of pragmatic method contributes to his work as a historian. I think the answer is that, while the general theoretical apparatus outlined above creates some troublesome problems of its own in Hurst's work, it is effective in freeing that work from the limitations of the insider's perspective.

For one thing, Hurst does not feel out of place or pulled apart by being an historian in a law school; he sees no opposition between social research in law and lawyer's business. His view is in keeping not only with Dewey's insistence on the unity of thought and action but with the "Wisconsin idea" – that social science research in the university should lead to social reform through legislation. Historical research and legislative drafting are just specialized aspects of the operations of instrumental intelligence. His paradigm example of law's working the way it should work is the development of workmen's compensation in Wisconsin in the early twentieth century: John Commons's university research seminars helped Charles McCarthy's legislative research department develop the legislation; and advisory committees of employers, unions, insurance companies, and the public helped administer it.[14] In fact, if one had to sum up in a phrase Hurst's deviation from the mainstream of legal historiography, it would be that his allegiances are to the Wisconsin Progressive tradition of lawmaking instead of the common law tradition.[15]

This has important consequences for his work. His first book made clear that he had no interest in linking law practice to the authority and complexity of common law tradition, since he thought that a stubborn clinging to traditional images of the profession was in part responsible for the bar's failure since 1870 to realize its possibilities for exercising social leadership: there were too many lawyers who were just technicians with no sense of the larger social effects of their jobs.[16] (The bar's contributions to "law reform" with Restatements,

[14] James Willard Hurst, *Law and Social Process, supra* note 8 at 37–41.

[15] But it would be misleading to conclude that Hurst simply carried on a going tradition at the Wisconsin Law School, since the Law School was only really brought into the Wisconsin tradition after World War II. In the heyday of the Wisconsin idea before World War I, the faculty consisted mostly of part-time practitioners; after World War I, "the faculty's major service contribution related not to legislation, but to law in the courts," i.e., work on the Restatements of the American Law Institute. John E. Conway, "The Law School: Service to the State and Nation," 1968 *Wisc. L. Rev.* 345, 346. The "law-and-society" approach that now distinguishes the Wisconsin Law School was pioneered after World War II by men recruited to the faculty by Dean Lloyd K. Garrison just before it: notably Jacob H. Beuscher and James Willard Hurst. See W. Scott Van Alstyne, Jr., "The University of Wisconsin Law School 1868–1968: An Outline History," *id.* at 321, 330–331; and Fran Thomas, *Law in Action: Legal Frontiers for Natural Resources Planning – The Work of Professor Jacob H. Beuscher* (Land Economics Monographs No. 4, 1972).

Hurst therefore had to cut all his own trails. But of course it is not likely that his enterprise could have prospered anywhere else as well as in Madison.

[16] See Hurst, *Lawmakers* at 370.

uniform laws, and the like don't count; the Wisconsin Progressive wants social reform through law, not technical law reform.[17])

Nor does he need to preserve the centrality of courts in legal study for their symbolic capacity to legitimate the legal order as a whole through their claims to autonomy derived from the distinctiveness of their doctrines and procedures: since far from thinking law achieves its capacity for control over social change from its distinctive forms, he believes one of the common causes of "drift" is mindless adherence to such forms.[18] Like Llewellyn, he replaces tradition-as-doctrine with pragmatic method as the source of what little directive influence law is ever likely to achieve – you don't achieve control by denying you're part of society but by recognizing how much you are a part of it – but does not go on to equate pragmatic method with case-law craftsmanship; because although courts continue to have an important public role as protectors of liberties against arbitrary state action, their pre-Civil War careers as major planners and coordinators of state policy have long since ended.[19]

The great strength that his historical work derives from his pragmatist's vision is the outsider's perspective: everything is to be examined for what it tells us about law's capacity to overcome the heavy odds in favor of social drift. Hurst's masterwork, the huge study of the legal history of the Wisconsin lumber industry,[20] responds to a single accusing question: how did it come about that the legal system so failed in its job of providing rational processes to increase awareness of long-run consequences that it permitted Wisconsin lumbermen to cut 30 million acres of forest to exhaustion?[21] Answering this leads him into (a) an account of the basic social and cultural conditions (scarcity of working capital, abundance of land, an aggressive manipulativeness toward nature, etc.) that engendered the consciousness of nineteenth-century Wisconsin policy-makers; (b) a description of the consciousness itself ("bastard pragmatism," measurement of benefits by short-term money yields); and (c) an analysis of the results of the applications of this consciousness to legal policy toward the lumber industry (fragmentation of decision-making into one-at-a-time resolution of strictly local problems; great ingenuity in promoting – finding non-monetary subsidies for, allocating power and resources in favor of, inventing financing devices to benefit – those interests believed most capable of

[17] For an illuminating discussion of the distinction, see Lawrence Friedman, "Law Reform in Historical Perspective," 13 *St. Louis L. J.* 351 (1969).

[18] See, e.g., *Law and Economic Growth: The Legal History of the Lumber Industry in Wisconsin, 1836–1915* (1964) [hereinafter, Hurst, *Law & Lumber*] at 99, 298.

[19] See Hurst, *supra* note 82; and *Law & Lumber* 249–250 (on built-in institutional limitations of common law litigation as decision-making method).

[20] *Law & Lumber*.

[21] I do not mean that this book is accusing in tone; on the contrary it is a model of scholarly neutrality, full of warnings against applying the criteria of the present age to the nineteenth century. (The earlier *Lawmakers* is much more overtly didactic.) But it is a grim and passionate book all the same, the more impressively so for its outward reserve.

getting timber cut, transported, and marketed; also complete failure to bring to awareness, and hence to deal with, problems like depletion of the forest or the conditions of lumber labor).

By his choice to organize his work around the concept of "law," Hurst has committed himself to a version of the box model[22] of the legal order in society, but it is a wonderfully different box from those of the standard legal histories. It is much larger, of course, since it includes all official activity: its contents are the habitual modes and forms of official thought – dialect variations, as it were, of the dominant consciousness of the surrounding culture – such as a legislative disposition to protect working men through labor liens but not through state accident insurance. The dialects are significant data for Hurst if and only if they are likely to be consequential for a society's growth; this means that although his work is rich in detail, it is all detail accumulated toward generalization about its social function. As a result –

(1) It tends to be what we might call democratic detail. Legal historians have favored aristocratic detail, worked into intricate tapestries by jurisconsults out of the appellate case law; Hurst's concern is with the system's routine business. This is partly because the effectiveness of law as an instrument of growth has to be assessed by its impact on the ordinary people in society[23] but also because habitual consciousness is formed out of the cumulation of tiny decisions. The study of big decisions fundamentally misleads, since it is only by tracking long sequences that it is possible to sketch the dynamics of drift.

(2) A remarkably small proportion of Hurst's detail consists of the technical stuff of doctrine and procedure beloved of internal legal historians. At least in nineteenth-century Wisconsin law related to lumber, on which Hurst has read *everything*, and reported everything he thinks significant, the particular forms of lawyer's law simply do not seem to have possessed much social significance.[24] The legal variables that *do* matter by his criteria tend to be broader institutional or conceptual traits of the system – e.g., adversary process in litigation as a means of organizing facts and bringing them to the awareness of decision-makers; or the survival into new contexts of thought-patterns formed in old ones, such

[22] For the "box model," see "The Common Law Tradition in American Legal Historiography," *supra*.

[23] Cf. Hurst's very Brandeisian early statement of this position:

> Emphasizing the economic setting, [a legal history course] would deal [in part] with the security and values of individual personality in a world increasingly marked by centralized, large-scale power arrangements. The emphasis would be on the small man – laborer, white-collar worker, farmer, small business man.

Hurst, *supra* note 2, at 331.

[24] See, for one of the rare instances in which Hurst cites a pleading form as significant, *Law & Lumber* 354–355 (where he also points out that it wasn't very significant).

as the fee simple as the desirable mode of conveying timberland, or the English practice of treating standing timber as an ordinary commodity of trade.[25] And Hurst always makes it clear that peculiar dialect-forms of the legal order survive and flourish in part *because* of outside social conditions, not (as Pound's "taught tradition" theory holds) despite them; thus, for example, the 700 lumber-industry contract cases Hurst studies have autonomous characteristics (are "contract-law cases first, and lumber industry cases second" and doctrinally stable over the industry's lifetime) because the abstraction of contract doctrine met the industry's immediate needs for security of market dealings; and the lumbermen's modes of thought did not encourage them to seek anything beyond those needs.[26]

(3) Hurst's organization around the concept of social function encourages comparison among official institutions, and between official and unofficial institutions.

It must be added that Hurst's theory also has some disadvantages for his history.[27] Two of a general nature might be mentioned here:

(1) The theory associates normatively adequate exercise of pragmatic method, or instrumental intelligence, with growth, and failure adequately to exercise it with inertia and drift. This makes it hard to deal with historical situations in which, in retrospect, it appears that heightened awareness of consequences would have been dysfunctional for growth (as Hurst conceives it) and a relative lack of awareness functional. This is most likely to happen when people's interests are in fundamental opposition, but at least one side doesn't know that: and Hurst himself suggests this situation has been a common one:

> [O]n the whole contemporary community values supported, acquiesced in, or were indifferent or unseeing toward most of what private interest sought and obtained from law concerning exploitation of the Wisconsin forest. Undoubtedly there would have been more conflict, and more skulduggery, had contemporary attitudes and energies existed to bring more of these matters to explicit issue... [But in this history] the limitations of men's perception, imagination, and will were more significant than their purposes.[28]

[25] See citations to *Law & Lumber*, *supra* notes 122, 123.

[26] *Law & Lumber* 289–290.

[27] For other criticisms (in the course of generally appreciative treatments) of Hurst's work as theory and history, see the articles by Scheiber and Tushnet, *supra* note 5; Julius Stone, Book Review, 78 *Harv. L. Rev.* 1687 (1965); and Richard B. Abrams, Book Review, 24 *Stan. L. Rev.* 765 (1972).

[28] Tushnet, *supra* note 5 at 125–126 points out in this connection (citing Albert Hirschman on unbalanced growth) that economic development may sometimes depend upon concealment of externalities.

To the extent that a condition of growth is the accommodation of conflicting interests, it may be more functional for the legal system to obscure consequences rather than to reveal them,[131] to legitimate social change by pretending that it all accords with comfortable old forms. I am perhaps suggesting here that Hurst's normative view of the decision-making process may somewhat blunt a sense of historical irony.

(2) Hurst's history relies upon a model of the interaction of law and society drawn chiefly from the peculiar context of nineteenth-century American state promotion and regulation of economic enterprise, which may be difficult to apply outside that context. In a way, Hurst has got hold of the easiest case: (a) the social actors to whom legal regulation is addressed may be counted on to look to extract short-term economic advantage from every decision; (b) they have relatively clear access to legal decision-makers (legislature and courts); (c) the decision-makers pretty much share their views of what is generally desirable for the society; they are really part of the same subculture of entrepreneurs; (d) the rest of society shares or passively accepts the same norms as they do; (e) regulation is almost all promotional and facilitative, rather than adversary; so that there are few significant problems of enforcement.

One could go on, but the point is that these particular conditions all combine to minimize the terrible problems of method faced by those who would practice an external historiography. They make it possible to infer social conditions and consequences *to a large extent from the legal materials themselves:*[29] which in other contexts, involving groups whose norms are alien to those of the decision-makers, or whose access is limited, or who seek symbolic legitimacy for themselves and condemnation of others rather than economic gain from the legal system, or seek nothing from it because they can get what they need outside it, or who resist compliance with its decisions, one cannot safely do.

But even for the study of contexts differing from those out of which he developed his theory, Hurst's milking of legal detail for every ounce of social significance has contributed not only a theoretical account of the social function of law, but some extremely refined techniques for what might be called the intellectual history of government action: how the state, through legal process,

[29] Tushnet, *id.* at 122, says that purely legal materials cannot adequately test even Hurst's theory, and that his "law centeredness seems totally ingenuous." This is unfair. Hurst is acutely aware of the problems of law-centered research, and repeatedly qualifies the inferences he thinks permissible to draw from it. See, e.g., "Legal elements" at 21–22; *Law & Lumber* at 225–227 (where Hurst also makes it clear he did not use business records because none existed). But *some* inferences about the effects of law on extra-legal behavior can be drawn from the legal sources: e.g., the output of the legal system may be supposed to be important, or at least to be thought important, to people who resort frequently to it (seek amending acts in the legislature, litigate in the courts); and less important to those who could use it but do not (like the big lumber companies that tended to refrain from litigation). *Law & Lumber* 200, 226, 321 *et passim.*

expresses social values; the devices by which it ratifies and legitimates certain values and ranks them in relation to others. These techniques – which enable the reader to discover basic notions about prevailing views of favored economic interests, the nature of property rights, or the appropriate role of government from such clues as how a statute allocates burdens of proof – are useful in their own right, whether or not the context also permits inferences as to the actual effects of law on social behavior.

Hurst's main contribution has been to expose the hitherto invisible ways in which the apparently most commonplace incidents of a legal order illuminate social values. By so doing he managed, almost single-handed, to lower from inside the drawbridge over the moat isolating American legal from general historiography.

Others had been bridging the moat from the outside – with studies of nineteenth-century public policy and corporations, of public lands, and of administrative history[30] – but it required an insider with unassailable lawyer's as well as historian's credentials to throw open the gates. For a time, Hurst's work was about the only view law students obtained on the social context of the history of their law.[31] But since what I have called the Second Revival of American legal history started a few years ago, his perspective is becoming the dominant one.[32] One of the events signifying the revival was the devotion of an issue of *Perspectives in American History* to legal history. That was a joint effort by lawyers and historians; and of course the leading article was written by Willard Hurst.[33]

[30] See Scheiber, "Federalism and the American Economic Order," *infra* at 57.

[31] See Re, *supra* note 61.

[32] See, e.g., the large number of respondents stressing the necessity of an external approach to legal history (and taking such an approach in their courses and publications) in Joseph H. Smith, *Report on the Teaching of Legal History in American Law Schools* (AALS Legal History Section; Nov. 1973).

[33] This is his "Legal Elements," *supra* note 6.

4

Hurst Recaptured

[*This was my brief contribution to the Symposium on Willard Hurst in 18* Law & History Review *167 (2000). The Symposium generally is the best source of recent reassessments of Hurst's work and influence*].

Anyone who lived and worked within range of Willard Hurst's benign, if also rather insistent, influence is necessarily somewhat disabled from detached assessment of his legacy. We owe him too much. Not just for the continuous rapid fire of comment, criticism, recommendation, and encouragement that rattled off the famous ancient typewriter; but also for his intellectual and moral example. He set himself long-range projects and finished them; he surveyed large themes and explored them to the bottom. He used his authority to try to get us both to read more broadly and get down into the details. We responded because we were touched that he thought our work might matter, and because he did not spare himself. Even when rebelling against that authority (as I for one often did), we wanted his attention and judgment even when we could not hope for his approval, and he gave them generously.

So I have long been curious to see what a younger generation of legal scholars, unattached in its affections and unburdened with personal obligations, would make of Hurst's work. There was reason to think their reception of it might be fairly critical. Last Fall, I read *Law and the Conditions of Freedom* with a group of legal history graduate students. They had a hard time at first getting past their incredulity at what Hurst did not talk about in the book to focus on what he did. As William Novak points out, much of the best American legal history since the 1980s has been devoted to issues missing or minimized in Hurst's vast body of work. He said little about the history of groups partly excluded from or subordinated within the legal system, such as blacks, women, laborers, immigrants, paupers, and Native American peoples. The legal instruments of subordination – slavery, segregation, convict labor, coverture, Indian removal, crop liens, labor injunctions – are mentioned only in passing in his books; the active movements of the excluded to reform or abolish these instruments, such as the civil rights, women's, and labor movements, are mentioned hardly at all. Hurst did not think human beings generally or Americans specifically cared only about business and making money; but his work did primarily concern itself with economic activity and policy. It revealed little interest in the legal regulation of crime, morals, welfare, religion, war and national security, political dissent or the family.

Hurst wrote intellectual-cultural as well as social history; and that field too looks very different now. Hurst's central subject, as Novak and Carl Landauer note in their essays in this Symposium, was that of how "we" (as he called Americans generally, across time and space) brought a practical consciousness, a body of working principles, to the task of generating legal responses to the mundane challenges of making a life for ourselves on the North American continent. He treated that consciousness (a "middle-class outlook") as an inheritance from the Reformation and the constitutional and commercial revolutions of the seventeenth and eighteenth centuries, pretty well fixed in its essentials when it arrived in the New World, persisting mostly unchanged through the nineteenth century, and transforming itself only when the accumulating social consequences of its unreflective application ("drift and inertia") jolted "us" into more deliberative and longer-range modes of legal planning. To any reader of the last generation's historical work, this picture of a largely static and uniform consciousness is bound to be unsatisfactory. Just as recent general and legal history have stressed social conflict, so too they have focused on dissent from the mainstream consensus on values expressed in law and, even more pointedly, on variety, change, and contradiction within the consensus itself: on civic-republicanism, the Scottish Enlightenment, liberal and evangelical Protestantism, classical political economy, race science, European legal thought, and pragmatism, to name just a few, as sources of legal ideology; on the rise, elaboration, and collapse of the "classical" legal thought of the late nineteenth century; on the radically different applications that generally accepted slogans of liberal legalism ("so use your own as not to injure another's," "free labor," "freedom of contract," "equal protection") could have in practice.[1]

[1] Landauer's excellent essay for this symposium [Carl Landauer, "Social Science on a Lawyer's Bookshelf: Willard Hurst's Law and the Conditions of Freedom in the Nineteenth Century United States," 18 *Law & Hist. Rev.* 59 (2000)] on the social-science sources of the 1950s on which Hurst drew for his general ideas greatly helps to clarify why Hurst was inclined to portray the practical consciousness structuring the workings of the legal system as so general and uniform. Landauer tells us that he had adapted from contemporary cultural anthropologists and post-Freudians their theory of a "fully articulated cultural structure ... in which the parts work perfectly together" as the governing value system of a society (80). As Landauer says, pieces of the "puzzle that did not quite fit" – for instance, Jacksonian anti-corporate sentiment, abolitionist, and temperance societies, "controversies over Masonic lodges, Catholic convents and schools and Mormon communities" – Hurst set aside as marginal.

As Hurst's account of consensus has come to seem over-general to latter-day readers, so too his account of social motives seems unduly flat and affectless. He was concerned, and reasonably so, to emphasize the everyday rather than the exceptional in legal history, the practical, local, mundane motives that brought people to sign a contract or file a lawsuit or enact a statute. He wanted to emphasize structural over Great Man explanations for legal change and unintended over intended consequences of social action; to understand crises as the result of accumulated drift rather than Manichaean struggle. It was in this spirit that Hurst, not altogether unjustly, criticized the radical historians of the 1960s and 1970s for over-dramatizing and over-moralizing as well as over-emphasizing social conflict.[2] But in the process he tended to so flatten American mentalities into short-term calculation ("bastard pragmatism" as he called it) as to make invisible the vast "irrationalities" at their core: the strength of racial and ethnic pride and hatred; the power of masculine images of honor and mastery; the allure of violence; the "paranoid style" of politics expressed in fears of sexual license and miscegenation, urban masses, socialists, aliens, bankers, Catholics and Jews; imperial dreams of conquest and missionary zeal for conversion of the world to American ideals; the pervasive utopian longings for promised lands of milk and honey and millennial visions of ecstasy and catastrophe. It is hard to imagine that a nation of such Babbitts as Hurst tended to portray "us" could have been moved to acquire and settle a continent; build a transcontinental railroad system, consolidate steel companies and national unions; fight a bloody civil war and stave off racial reconstruction for a hundred years; create a political party system regularly organized around positions on racial and moral-cultural issues such as temperance, welfare, and abortion; sustain slavery in a liberal polity; sustain a civil rights movement through decades of adversity; sustain a fervently religious culture in a secularizing industrial world; conduct several notably hysterical purges of foreigners and radicals; and send soldiers to die in foreign fields in five major wars.

Since, as I say, the legal history of the last thirty years has mainly emphasized the topics Hurst left out and given particularity to those he treated very

[2] If I may use this occasion to continue an argument to which, alas, my friend can no longer respond: Hurst's critique of radical legal historians always seemed to me a bit indiscriminate. Hurst believed that those who focused on domination overstated the importance of villains, with conscious motives to oppress or subordinate others, to the routine operations of the legal system. Yet the aim of many of the "critical" legal historians he disparaged was not to moralize legal history by turning it into a struggle between virtuous victims and their evil oppressors but rather to produce a structural account, similar to Hurst's own, of legal ideology. They also aimed to use that account to explain how legal ideology had, relatively independently of the specific intentions and interests of the social actors involved in making and maintaining it, facilitated forms of domination. Nor was their point to condemn liberal-legal ideology as irredeemably oppressive; it was rather to argue that, since the ideology was crammed with contradictions and suppressed alternatives, it always presented progressive possibilities as well as conservative ones, some of which had actually been realized in historical and current social arrangements.

generally, one might have expected a cooler response to his work than the principal contributors to this symposium provide. To their great credit, they pass up the occasion for what would be relatively cheap shots and concentrate instead on historicizing Hurst, locating him in the context of the legal-political preoccupations and intellectual influences of his formative years, 1930 to 1960. The results are really illuminating. They considerably clarify what Hurst owed to his major mentors and influences and how he departed from them. They elucidate what he conceived to be the purposes of his life work. Yet ironically, in the process of historicizing Hurst and placing him back in his own formative context, the contributors also highlight the ways in which his project and ideas for realizing it are still living and important. Because of limitations on length, I will confine my comment to the essays of Daniel Ernst[3] and William Novak.[4]

Ernst's article is a fascinating and valuable work of intellectual biography. It does a good job of portraying the young Hurst as already in possession of formidable maturity, integrity, and independence of mind. The essay's centerpiece is the story of Hurst's collaboration with his two powerful mentors, as Professor Frankfurter's research assistant and Justice Brandeis's law clerk. Ernst shows how much of Frankfurter's outlook the young Hurst absorbed – the interest in statutes and administrative law, the belief in a large administrative discretion and in the well-trained lawyer as the coordinator and applier of public-policy initiatives, the repudiation of a narrow originalism in favor of a broad survey of historical trends and tendencies in constitutional interpretation. But Hurst also went well beyond his teacher in some ways, especially in his interest in the substance of administrative decisions as well as in judicial review of them, and in his decisive repudiation of a judge- and court-centered approach to history.

Ernst is even more interesting in describing Hurst's subtle deviations from Brandeis. Both wanted constitutional courts to find a *via media* between *Lochner* and *Schechter*, that is, between inflexible judicial condemnation of the experiments of the regulatory state on the one hand, and a blank check to administrative delegation run amok on the other hand. But even though, interestingly enough, Hurst was if anything more skeptical than Brandeis of the motives of regulators and interests behind much regulation, he was more willing than Brandeis to argue that legislators and administrators had behaved reasonably and to defer to their decisions.

In his essay, Novak argues that Hurst's lifelong enterprise is best understood as an effort to develop an ambitious historical sociology in the tradition of the grand synthesizers such as Marx and Weber. I think Novak has got through to the essence of Hurst in this piece. A lot of people have thought that what was

[3] Daniel Ernst, "Willard Hurst and the Administrative State: From Williams to Wisconsin," 18 *Law & Hist. Rev.* 1 (2000).

[4] William Novak, "Law, Capitalism and the Liberal State: The Historical Sociology of Willard Hurst," 18 *Law & Hist. Rev.* 97 (2000).

distinctive about Hurst's work was its focus on the low-level working detail of the legal system. That is true, but the detail was always marshaled into the service of a grand social-theoretical scheme. Novak gives a very useful account of this scheme, especially through his division of Hurst's project into its "function," "value," and "power" components. He also has an insightful discussion of Hurst's notions of the weight of habit and inarticulate assumptions: as he says, Hurst does not celebrate consensus, but views it as the product of unexamined, tacit habits of mind. And his noting of Hurst's association of time (the weight of unconscious tradition on law) with Holmes, and of context (law's interaction with the nonlegal surround) with Brandeis, is really brilliant.

Novak's account reminds us of both the virtues and the dangers of historical-sociological method. The virtues are of course the spaciousness of perspective and the production of generalizations for use in other contexts. The dangers are that very broad cross-time generalizations tend to flatten out specificity and historicity and that a very high level of abstraction risks vagueness and banality. Novak's fine summary of Hurst's ideas makes at least this reader think that he did not entirely escape the dangers. The generalizations, like the Parsonian theory they so closely resemble, seem to be chiefly taxonomic; they are heuristics for organizing historical material rather than theories about causal sequences or associations. And as Novak notes, many of Hurst's master concepts – such as "individualism" or the "middle-class outlook" – seem to have no history themselves, to come into the world as uncaused causes, and not to change much thereafter. Moreover, a true historical-sociological method probably has to be comparative; and Hurst, by limiting himself to the U.S. and, more specifically, to Wisconsin, always left unclear how much of his story was an exceptionally American or Wisconsin one. My own view is that the evidence for Hurst's (indisputable) greatness as a historian is to be found in his most detailed and specific works, such as the magisterial lumber book,[5] and in the mid-level generalizations (land was cheap and abundant, labor and working capital scarce; application of fee-simple concepts regarding land use to licenses to cut timber was woefully inappropriate, and so forth) he pulled out of this detail, rather than in his ventures into grand theory.

Ernst and Novak differ at some points. Novak sees Hurst's main project as that of developing a historical sociology of law. Ernst sees it as developing a historical-sociological jurisprudence – that is, as a project for training *lawyers* to do the important jobs they need to do: coordinating administrative functions, allocating resources, and holding power accountable. These do not necessarily conflict – the historical sociology could be both an end-in-itself and a handmaiden to training lawyers, and I think it was. But I also think Ernst is right to believe that training reflective lawyer-statesmen through uncovering

[5] James Willard Hurst, *Law and Economic Growth: The Legal History of the Lumber Industry in Wisconsin, 1836–1915* (1964).

the historical "record" – a record largely one of short-sighted legal-regulatory failures and mistakes punctuated by the occasional successful piece of rational planning – was Hurst's primary aim. This aim is nicely revealed in Hurst's repeated references to American history as "the record," as if it were evidence in a pending legal proceeding, for that was exactly how he saw it. After expanding the relevant record beyond prior appellate cases and their facts to all prior legal acts and the social influences on them, and the pending proceedings to the overall task of designing workable legal-regulatory arrangements for the present age, Hurst wrote his books as background briefs for present-day lawmakers.

Ernst and Novak also seem to differ on Hurst's views about the importance of law in constructing markets and the relations of market actors. Novak quotes all the (many) passages in which Hurst seems to insist on the marginality of law to the economy. Ernst however treats Hurst as having very early on adopted the legal-realist view of the "public constitution of private rights" – that the decision to confer discretionary authority on private actors in markets was a legal choice as much as the decision to give that authority to some official. Perhaps this is not a real difference. Ernst is talking about Hurst's ideas about law, especially the constitutional law of the Fourteenth Amendment, in which context Hurst's concern would be to refute the action/omission distinction as a touchstone for distinguishing "state" from "private" action. Novak is talking about Hurst's views of historical causation – what has been the role of official legal agencies and the law they make in constructing market relations? Even so, it is hard to square the legal-realist Hurst with the postwar Hurst – especially because even the post-war Hurst attributed major force to basic legal concepts in the design of market ground rules. For instance, he assigned primary responsibility for the legal-planning defaults that devastated the Wisconsin forests to uncritical applications of fee-simple ownership and freedom-of-contract ideas.

I would like to end by supplementing the principal papers' ideas about what is most vital and useful to be taken from Hurst's work for the education of present-day lawyers and legal scholars with my own brief list of suggestions:

1. **Attention to the economic, understood as culturally shaped.** Hurst may have slighted other motives and fields of conduct. But there is no doubt that the overwhelming bulk of American effort in lawmaking (statutory, administrative, judicial output and the work of lawyers' offices) relates to economic transactions and relations. Though there are some fine legal histories of economic regulation since Hurst's, legal historians have lately tended relatively to neglect business and the economy. By default the field has been largely turned over to legal economists, whose rational-choice models tend to leave out entirely what Hurst (an admirer of Karl Polanyi, as Landauer reminds us) insisted on keeping centrally in view: the embeddedness of economic decision making in a framework of cultural and social assumptions. Economic rationality for Hurst is

always a strictly bounded rationality: the fixation on immediate costs and gains; the highlighting of some risks and prospects; the discounting or ignoring of others.

2. **The critique of laissez-faire.** Hurst was grimly distressed, but not particularly surprised, by the return in the 1980s and 1990s to some of the highest circles of legal policy-making and policy thinking of the libertarian anti-statism that, he believed, had obscured perceptions of reality and frustrated constructive legal responses to it in the nineteenth century. Hurst critiqued laissez-faire both as fact and as guiding constitutional norm, though he recognized its power as ideology. As fact he knew the American night-watchman state was a myth, since he had written a 946-page book chronicling the massive detailed regulation by a single state of a single industry, through its property, tort, contract, and water law and general police power, during the supposed high period of laissez-faire. As a norm he knew that libertarianism was a seriously incomplete account of the aims of American constitutionalism, whose purposes had never been limited to restraining governments, but included holding both public and private power accountable to serve human values and the general ends of "the commonwealth." As ideology he knew laissez-faire was destructive in its effects: indeed one of the most powerful things he ever wrote was his scornful, passionate polemic in the lumber book against the opinion of Wisconsin's Justice Roujet Marshall that invalidated, as an unconstitutional exercise of state power, Wisconsin's attempt to establish a forest reserve by buying up timberlands – a minimal stab at administrative planning to save some of the forest acreage from devastation.[6]

From his study of the timber catastrophe and similar debacles, Hurst was disinclined to romanticize markets or praise their virtues as "spontaneous orders" (in F. A. Hayek's phrase). Though he had a healthy respect for markets as engines of innovation and prosperity, virtually his entire oeuvre is about how by the end of the nineteenth century the unreflective cult of free enterprise had brought about major crises in the form of unforeseen externalities such as resource exhaustion and a dangerous concentration of political and economic power. But neither did he romanticize the administrative state. He was a Progressive New Dealer, but a hard-headed and skeptical one. A reader can readily find in his work all the important elements of modern public-choice theory, especially the policy failures likely to result from the legislative influence of concentrated private special interests at the expense of diffuse and unorganized interests. Like his mentors Brandeis and Reinhold Niebuhr he stressed the limitations of deliberate action to understand and control social change. But he also recognized some policy successes. He thought that pragmatic experimentation in administrative regulation, informed by the knowledge of those

[6] *State ex rel. Owen* v. *Donald*, 160 Wis. 21, 151 N.W. 331 (1915), analyzed in Hurst, *Law and Economic Growth, supra* note 5, 571–591.

successes as well as past failures – the knowledge acquired from legal history – was the only stay against the randomly chaotic destructiveness of unrestrained capitalism and the only hope for orienting public as well as private action toward "commonwealth" values.

3. **The "whole record" and the "working level."** As Ernst shows, Hurst began his scholarly career with a repudiation of "originalism," the idea that legal history was most useful to present-day legal argument and decision making if it were the history of (a) high doctrine and legal theory (b) at constitutional founding moments. He insisted, and helped to instill as the core Wisconsin-Madison ethic, that the relevant historical record for current understanding was the whole sweep of modern history; that the most reliable guides to legal policy in action were the "mine run" of ordinary statutes and cases and administrative actions. From the start he took a broad view of who lawmakers were: not just courts and legislatures, but the executive and administrative agencies, the people assembled in constitutional conventions, and practicing lawyers and the organized bar. From the vantage point of the present he might perhaps have added social movements.[7]
4. **Law as a public profession.** As Aviam Soifer has said, Hurst's study of lawyers as lawmakers is probably his "most radical scholarly departure" and "remains one of the very best analyses of the bar's role in American society."[8] It is also probably the place in which his method of putting dispassionate narration of history to the service of reforming the present is most successful. As no one had done before him, and few since, Hurst brought out the manifold functions that lawyers had performed in American society: adapters of old doctrines and instruments to new purposes, architects of novel corporate-contractual and regulatory structures, administrators of social relations as mediators between private interests and governments, providers of political and civic leadership, and finally "symbol makers" or ideological spokesmen. Having offered

[7] Then again he might not. Alfred Konefsky is surely right to identify Hurst as a democrat in important respects, especially in his view of law as a field of democratic experimentation and of its major purposes as the channeling and holding accountable both public and private power to the service of enhancing the quality of lives for everyone. But he was not a populist: though he considered popular movements to be invaluable signals of social malfunction, he distrusted what he considered to be their limited vision and unreflective enthusiasms; and, like his contemporary Richard Hofstadter, he deplored their suspicion of trained intellect. For informed long-range policy, he looked as a good Progressive to expert (though preferably self-effacing, responsive, and accountable) administrators. Lawrence Goodwyn's work on the agrarian populists, however, converted Hurst from Hofstadterian distrust to respect for their sophistication on issues of money and credit.

[8] Aviam Soifer, "In Retrospect: Willard Hurst, Consensus History, and *The Growth of American Law*," 20 *Reviews in American History* 135, 136 (1992), commenting on "Part V: The Bar," in James Willard Hurst, *The Growth of American Law: The Lawmakers* (1950), 249–375.

> many examples of the constructive social roles lawyers could play at their best, Hurst then characteristically pointed out the ways in which most lawyers had failed to seize the opportunities offered them. He judged the lawyers of his own time, in contrast to founding generation lawyers like Alexander Hamilton and John Marshall, to be cautious, timid, and narrow, to be either "technicians" unconcerned with the larger goals of law and policy, or "partisans," unthinking extensions of clients' short-term values and interests. The role of advisor to business interests who must take account of the policy purposes expressed in new forms of legislation and regulation, and the extension of cost-effective services to unserved clienteles, however, might still redeem the profession from its narrowness. His analysis of the profession seems as fresh and pointed now as it was forty-nine years ago; and his vision of the public functions of the private bar as useful and inspiring.

Willard, thou should'st be with us at this hour!

5

Morton Horwitz and his Critics: A Conflict of Narratives

[*This was written for a Symposium on the work of Morton Horwitz at the University of Tulsa Law School and originally published in 37* Tulsa Law Review *915 (2002).*]

This Symposium contemplates a master scholar and his work, but happily not in an obituary way. The scholar is not only very much still with us, but briskly plugging away at his massive Holmes Devise History of the Warren Court, in debonair defiance of the curse of doom that has struck down so many predecessors in their quest to finish Holmes Devise Histories of the Supreme Court. Since this is the kind of occasion that puts one in a reminiscent frame of mind, I want to recall for you the place and time in which I first saw Morton Horwitz, a seminar room at Harvard Law School in the fall of 1969, where he was teaching his first course in American Legal History as a Warren Fellow, and I was a second-year law student. The time was a slumbering winter of American Legal History. A brilliant, but brief Indian summer of the field had ended. Mark DeWolfe Howe had died in 1967. Willard Hurst, who continued to be astonishingly productive for the next twenty years, had already published his best work.[1] Few could guess at the new growth gestating in the frozen ground – the new legal histories of William Nelson, Harry Scheiber, Lawrence Friedman, Morton Horwitz, and Ted White among others – and the luxuriant spring and summer of the field to come. In Morton Horwitz's classroom, the instructor paced the room like a restless leopard, if one can imagine a chain-smoking leopard. The young Winston Churchill once remarked earnestly to a young woman, "We are all worms. But I do believe that I am a glow-worm."[2]

[1] James Willard Hurst, *The Growth of American Law: The Law Makers* (1950); James Willard Hurst, *Law and the Conditions of Freedom in the Nineteenth Century United States* (1967); James Willard Hurst, *Law and Economic Growth: the Legal History of the Lumber Industry in Wisconsin, 1836–1915* (1964) [hereinafter *Law and Economic Growth*].

[2] Roy Jenkins, *Churchill: a Biography* 137 (2001) (quoting Violet Bonham Carter).

This is how we felt about the young, febrile, Morty Horwitz. He glowed. He was then assembling the pieces of the story that eventually became *The Transformation of American Law, 1780–1860* ("*Transformation I*").[3] Some of us in that class had already read through what was then the slender bibliography – not more than twenty or thirty books and articles in all – of works worth reading in American Legal History; and had an inkling of the originality and daring of the argument Horwitz was developing before us. Stanley Katz was in the class that fall (already an established historian, he was spending the year at Harvard as a liberal arts fellow). One day we walked out of the class together – it was the class in which Horwitz explained how negligence had evolved out of neglect of quasi-contractual duty and been transmuted to mean actions in excess of statutory jurisdiction and thence to something like "fault" – and looked at each other; and Stan said what was on both our minds: "something extraordinary happened in that class today."

When *Transformation I* appeared in 1977, it made a big splash-perhaps not quite as big as Charles Beard's *Economic Interpretation of the Constitution* – but certainly big for a book about legal history, and a pretty complicated and densely written book at that. Historians loved it and gave it the Bancroft Prize in 1978. Some legal historians liked it too – Willard Hurst and (at least initially) Harry Scheiber gave it favorable though cautiously qualified reviews.[4] But many of the reviews from lawyers were negative. There were criticisms both of the broad substantive arguments and of various matters of detail. Some of these were well taken, others less so. I will not undertake in this short essay a comprehensive survey of the reviews. That task has already been admirably performed, first by Wythe Holt twenty years ago, and with wit, spirit and fresh insight by Laura Kalman in this Symposium.[5] But I would like to try to identify and comment on some general themes of the critiques.

In my view, the most justified of the general critiques was that Horwitz had written an intellectual history of legal ideas and doctrines, and then had extrapolated from that history conclusions about social effects. The thesis was, of course that judges of the early republic, working in concert with commercial interests, had worked a revolution in property, tort, and commercial law, which had redistributed wealth away from groups identified as "farmers, workers and consumers" and into the hands of "entrepreneurs." Once this was accomplished, the judges had hardened the new legal status quo into one of absolute rights, in order to protect the property thus expropriated and transferred against further populist redistribution. The most justified critique, I think, was

[3] Morton J. Horwitz, *The Transformation of American Law, 1780–1860* (1977).

[4] James Willard Hurst, "Book Review," 21 *Am. J. Leg. History* 175 (1977); Harry N. Scheiber, "Back to 'The Legal Mind'? Doctrinal Analysis and the History of Law," 5 *Rev. in Am. History* 458 (1977).

[5] Wythe Holt, "Morton Horwitz and the Transformation of American Legal History," 23 *Wm. & Mary L. Rev.* 663 (1982); Laura Kalman, "Transformations," 37 *Tulsa L. Rev.* 849 (2002).

the simple one that Horwitz's evidence, being all of change internal to the legal system and drawn exclusively from appellate cases and treatises, could not support strong conclusions about social alliances and social effects. The law on the books is not the law in action. If he had looked for such evidence, I believe, it would have confirmed his argument about alliances and effects in some respects, and made it problematic in others.

The thesis about alliances would surely not be hard to support. Proving that the top bracket of American lawyers from 1800 onward – the lawyers who tended to become judges – were allied with, or at least held views in common with, "commercial interests," would be like trying to prove the proposition that "bankers were strongly allied with depositors." The bar elite in the nineteenth century was in part defined, as it is today, by the wealth, social standing, and economic importance of its principal clients. Lawyers invested in their clients' business ventures, drew on them to finance their political campaigns, and intermarried with their families.[6] Such connections do not, of course, mean that lawyers who became judges were nothing more than mouthpieces and deputies of their former clients, or that in their roles as interpreters of statutes and developers of common and constitutional law they were incapable of taking a somewhat independent line on what the law required. But they were usually drawn from the same strata of society and shared the same general ways of thinking about what the public interest required.

In their ways of thinking, however, the "commercial interests" themselves were more divided than Horwitz's treatment allows, and divided especially by views on the proper role law should play in economic development and the primacy of economic growth over competing values. In one of the most valuable, though unaccountably and undeservedly neglected, of the many works inspired by the Horwitz thesis, a pioneering study by Tony Freyer of antebellum law and lawyers in New Jersey, Maryland, Delaware, and Pennsylvania discovered sharp conflicts between corporate "capitalists" and local "producers" over how economic development should proceed and who should bear its costs. The "producers" and their lawyers continued to maintain and defend interests in equitable distribution of the proceeds of economic growth and a moralized view of political economy as an instrument of values such as republican citizenship and community cohesion. In legal contests, because of their commonality of interest with local juries, the producers were often able to triumph over the capitalists.[7]

[6] For illustrative studies, *see e.g.*, Maurice Baxter, *One and Inseparable: Daniel Webster and the Union* (1984); Alfred S. Konefsky, "Law and Culture in Antebellum Boston," 40 *Stan. L. Rev.* 1119 (1988); R. Kent Newmyer, *Supreme Court Justice Joseph Story: Statesman of the Old Republic* (1985).

[7] *See generally* Tony A. Freyer, *Producers versus Capitalists: Constitutional Conflict in Antebellum America* (1994).

The thesis about the social effects of changes in legal rules is obviously a lot more complicated. For example, Horwitz argued that tort law in this period shifted from a strict liability (or presumption of compensation for harm) to a negligence standard, with the result that industrial defendants were effectively immunized from liability.[8] In one of the extensive empirical critiques, Gary Schwartz challenged this conclusion, maintaining that fault liability had always been the norm and pointing out that plaintiffs won many of the tort cases, though he conceded that workers generally lost.[9] Subsequent work, not available to Horwitz or his critics in the 1970s, has clarified that both these positions are pretty much beside the point, because the effective prevailing standard in tort – especially personal injury – cases until late in the nineteenth century was neither strict liability nor negligence, but effectively no liability. For a variety of reasons (employer paternalism, strong disincentives to sue employers, low levels of rights – consciousness, conservative judges, lawyers' fees, witness disqualification rules, etc.) almost nobody ever sued.[10] When the injured eventually did begin to litigate, it turns out, the damages and settlements they recovered were so low as to be almost derisory.[11]

Other work has further complicated Horwitz's thesis of a "subsidy" to capitalists affected by immunity or low damage awards for nuisances and takings by eminent domain. Nuisance doctrine remained schizophrenic throughout the nineteenth century, sometimes awarding compensation or injunctions to neighboring landowners for damage from nearby mining and manufacturing operations and sometimes denying them.[12] Freyer found that local landowners who invoked statutory proceedings for assessing compensation for takings by corporate enterprises were often able to recover more than market value because

[8] Horwitz, *supra* note 3, at 97–108.

[9] *See* Gary Schwartz, "Tort Law and the Economy in Nineteenth Century America: A Reinterpretation," 90 *Yale L. J.* 1717 (1981).

[10] *See generally* Robert B. Rabin, "The Historical Development of the Fault Principle: A Reinterpretation," 15 *Ga. L. Rev.* 925 (1981); Lawrence M. Friedman, "Civil Wrongs: Personal Injury Law in the Late 19th Century," 1987 *Am. Bar Found. Res. J.* 351 (1987); John Fabian Witt, "Toward a New History of American Accident Law: Classical Tort Law and the Cooperative First-party Insurance Movement," 114 *Harv. L. Rev.* 690 (2001).

[11] Friedman, *supra* note 10, at 365–367.

[12] *See e.g.*, Robert Bone, "Normative Theory and Legal Doctrine in American Nuisance Law: 1850 to 1920," 59 *S. Cal. L. Rev.* 1101 (1986). Bone discusses a classic set of cases that deal with the protracted litigation between Sanderson, a landowner, and the Pennsylvania Coal Co. In the first case, the Pennsylvania Supreme Court allowed the landowner to enjoin a coal company from emitting coal dust that polluted the plaintiff's stream, on the ground that the plaintiff had an absolute right to undisturbed enjoyment of his property. *Pa. Coal Co.* v. *Sanderson*, 86 Pa. 401 (1878). Eight years later, the same court, in a fourth decision with the same parties before it on the same facts, refused to give any remedy on the ground that the coal company had an absolute right to make "natural" use of its property, which in its case was mining coal, notwithstanding any "incidental" damage to its neighbors. *Sanderson* v. *Pa. Coal Co.*, 113 Pa. 126, 6 A. 453 (1886).

of the sympathy of the local assessors.[13] Appeals to the courts (some of whose judges were indeed investors in developers' ventures, but who were politically connected to local "producer" as well as "capitalist" interests) sometimes lowered such assessments, but usually upheld them.[14]

Some reviews challenged Horwitz's doctrinal rather than his (implicit) social history. The most prominent of these was Brian Simpson's critique of Horwitz's thesis on the transformation of contract law.[15] Horwitz – I am simplifying an intricate technical quarrel – argued that contract law shifted from an eighteenth-century pattern in which juries enforced contracts according to community-based moral expectations of fair and equitable exchange, to a mid-nineteenth-century pattern of awarding expectation damages for breach of the strict terms of express executory promises. He described in short a shift from enforcement of bargains on fair terms to enforcement of the "will of the parties" as expressed in the formal terms of their agreements. Simpson said that Horwitz was wrong to see the will or consent theory as a nineteenth-century innovation; it was already embedded in common law contract doctrine by the mid-eighteenth century. What Horwitz was seeing, Simpson suggested, was something quite different, not a change in the law, but the "progressive dethronement of the jury," "accompanied by the generation or reception of law in order not so much to replace or transform older doctrine as to provide law where before there was little or none."[16]

In the same year as Simpson's article, however, the Horwitz thesis received a significant hormone boost from Patrick Atiyah's massive *Rise and Fall of Freedom of Contract*, which told a story similar to Horwitz's about the evolution of modern English contract law. Through the eighteenth and early nineteenth centuries, Atiyah said, the law of contractual obligations was largely a law enforcing equitable returns (what we would now call reliance or restitution interests) for already executed contract performances. Only in the nineteenth century did the executory contract, and legal enforcement of parties' mutually agreed-upon promises, become the "paradigm of contract theory."[17] In 1992, James Oldham judiciously reviewed the entire controversy in his edition of the manuscripts of Lord Mansfield, the great eighteenth-century English commercial law judge. Oldham granted to Simpson and his allies their point about contract doctrine: the consent theory and the action on the executory promise had certainly been recognized in legal doctrine by Mansfield's time. But, Oldham said, the "great majority" of the decided cases of the time largely support the Horwitz-Atiyah story, since the contracts actually sued on were

[13] Freyer, *supra* note 7, at 152.

[14] *Id.* at 160–165.

[15] A. W. B. Simpson, "The Horwitz Thesis and the History of Contracts," 46 *U. Chi. L. Rev.* 533 (1979).

[16] *Id.* at 600.

[17] P. S. Atiyah, *The Rise and Fall of Freedom of Contract* 419 (1979).

mostly executed contracts and "contract and quasi-contract were congenial parts of an overall philosophy of moral transactional behavior that required the honoring of legitimately created expectations and the return of benefits unjustly acquired."[18]

More interesting, however, were the reviews that did not just criticize the book, or try to pick apart its arguments and evidence, but that obviously hated it. The book genuinely affronted them – much as Beard's *Economic Interpretation of the Constitution* had affronted his readers – and for similar reasons. Horwitz had committed a sort of sacrilege. As John Reid put it, speaking of Horwitz as one of a new clan of left-wing historians, "The iconoclasts have invaded the temple of legal history. They have smashed the fetishes, blotted out the frescoes, and desecrated the tombs. If we do not force them to the evidence, they will even desacralize Clio."[19] This was not quite as good as one of the headlines greeting Charles Beard's book, "SCAVENGERS, HYENA-LIKE, DESECRATE THE DEAD PATRIOTS WE REVERE,"[20] but it was in the same spirit. As Beard had pulled down the Founders from their lofty perch of disinterested farsighted statesmen, and recast them as men with property in speculation to gain or lose in the new political arrangements of the republic, so too had Horwitz charged that judges of the early republic, the "Golden Age" or "Formative Period of American Law" with participation in a grubby conspiracy to line, if not their own pockets, those of commercial or entrepreneurial elites. Horwitz's narrative, in short, ran sharply and rudely into some of the dominant narratives, and the collision hurt.

What were the prevailing narratives? Horwitz in an earlier iconoclastic essay[21] had identified some of them as the "conservative tradition" in American legal historiography: a practice of extolling the great judges of the past as guardians of the common law tradition – a "taught tradition," as Roscoe Pound had called it, celebrated as autonomous from political pressures and economic forces, a tradition of purely legal reasoning about purely legal principles, and yet despite (or rather because of) that the great source of limits on popular impulses to level and redistribute property. John Reid's review spoke for that tradition in its suggestion (which Reid however oddly attributed to Willard Hurst) that nineteenth-century courts, so far from conspiring with any set of economic interests, "acted as neutral referees, intervening only when one party appealed a question from the marketplace, otherwise permitting contending groups to fight for economic survival without close supervision as long

[18] James Oldham, *The Mansfield Manuscripts and the Growth of the Law in the Eighteenth Century vol. 1*, 228, 231 (1992).

[19] John Reid, "A Plot Too Doctrinaire," 55 *Tex. L. Rev.* 1307, 1321 (1977).

[20] Peter Novick, *That Noble Dream: The "Objectivity Question" and the American Historical Profession* 96 (1988) (quoting a Headline in the Marion, Ohio *Star*).

[21] Morton J. Horwitz, "The Conservative Tradition in the Writing of American Legal History," 17 *Am. J. Leg. History* 275 (1973).

as they did so by certain, general rules."[22] Strangely enough, though, it was not until many years later that the authentic ghost of Roscoe Pound materialized in Peter Karsten's *Heart versus Head* to reproach Horwitz for having failed to understand that judges decide out of doctrinally stable principle, not ideology or material interest or even just the desire to pursue specific policies such as economic growth.[23] The main burden of the most severe critiques, including Reid's, was not so much that the judges had been instrumental, but that their work's aims and results were to "subsidize" entrepreneurs and "redistribute" in favor of the rich.

Indeed, had the rest of *Transformation I*'s story remained in the key of Horwitz's opening chapter, I suspect the storm would have been avoided. The book begins with the story of how American judges shift from a view of law as found to law as made, law as a self-conscious engine of social policy. The next chapters identify the main policy as economic development. Judges posed as defenders of vested property rights, when in fact they were Schumpeterian entrepreneurs, destroyers of established property rights, and agents of their reassignment to dynamic developers. Horwitz's story breaks here with the older "conservative traditions" – that judges are guided by principle and that they side with established property. But it is perfectly continuous and consistent with the "commonwealth histories" of Oscar and Mary Handlin, Carter Goodrich, Louis Hartz, and the social-legal histories of Willard Hurst and Harry Scheiber,[24] uncovering a long history of government and legal system promotion of economic development in the early republic and pointing out that it favored dynamic property, not vested property, entrepreneurial rather than *rentier* interests. Horwitz's *Transformation I* fit nicely into this line of work by documenting more thoroughly the contribution of the courts, and legal doctrines in decisions and treatises, to this promotional enterprise.

[22] Reid, *supra* note 19, at 1321. In a similar spirit, see Randall Bridwell, "Theme v. Reality in American Legal History: A Comment on Horwitz, the Transformation of American Law, 1780–1860, and the Common Law in America," 53 *Ind. L. Rev.* 449, 496 (1978) (the common law is a "largely self-ordering system supportive of autonomous individual behavior and experiment, adjusting itself with the aid of limited judicial intervention that does not effectively elevate the narrow interests of 'caste or class' ").

[23] Peter Karsten, *Heart versus Head: Judge-Made Law in Nineteenth Century America* (1997). Karsten did not, however, argue that common law judges functioned in a wholly autonomous and socially insulated legal sphere. Occasionally, they were motivated to soften the cold reason of the law by considerations of fairness and equity (the "Heart" of his title) grounded in Christian morality. But they never seem to have been motivated by political views or allegiances.

[24] Oscar Handlin & Mary Flug Handlin, *Commonwealth; A Study of the Role of Government in the American Economy: Massachusetts, 1774–1861* (rev. edn.1969); Carter Goodrich, *Government Promotion of American Canals and Railroads, 1800–1890* (1960); Louis Hartz, *Economic Policy and Democratic Thought: Pennsylvania 1776–1860* (1948); Hurst's works, *supra* note 1; Harry N. Scheiber, *Ohio Canal Era: A Case Study of Government and the Economy, 1820–1861* (1987).

The difference between Horwitz's narrative and theirs was in part that he was much darker and depressive about the outcomes, because he took a fundamentally dimmer view of capitalist development.[25] (Beard's crime, similarly, was not that he had suggested that the Founders sought to protect property rights against the mob, but that he suggested there was something wrong with that.) These were the vibes the most hostile reviewers picked up and reacted against. I have often heard critics call Horwitz's work "Marxist," though I have never been able to see much of anything Marxist about it, no suggestion whatsoever for example that "in the last instance" struggles between classes produced by dominant relations of production determine social relations or ideological superstructures such as legal doctrines. It seems a more idealist than Marxist story: the lawyers and judges had a choice to make, and they chose to ally themselves with business interests rather than the republican ideals of the Revolution.

Horwitz is drawing on different background narratives of the history of industrial capitalism. One, pretty clearly, is E. P. Thompson's narrative of how the working-class world of English craft artisans was crushed; and how "the moral economy of the English crowd," a communitarian ideology of fair prices and wages and equitable distribution of scarce basic commodities in times of dearth, enforced by the legal system through local magistrates, was displaced by a heartless laissez-faire regime of market prices and wages.[26] Another is Karl Polanyi's brilliant and terrifying narrative of industrial capitalism in *The Great Transformation*, as a total pulverizing of traditional social ties and social life and the conversion of all social relations into relations of calculated exchange of commodities in impersonal markets. The spirits of Thompson and Polanyi loom most visibly over Horwitz's chapter on contract law, with its story of communal conceptions of fair exchange being supplanted by the "will theory" and the legal enforcement of contracts on whatever terms one party could demand or compel from another.[27] But they are present throughout the entire book. When Hurst wrote of law's displacing "vested rights," he was thinking of *rentier* landlords and fox-hunting squires. Horwitz implicitly presents a more Thompsonian story, of customary expectations of fair prices, and of traditional

[25] Not, by the way, that his predecessors were wholly complacent. Hartz had described with biting clarity how mid-century corporations had appropriated the Jacksonians' originally anti-corporate individualist ideology and turned it in their favor against state regulation. Hartz, *supra* note 24, at 113–122. Hurst, a Progressive New Dealer – far from calling nineteenth-century law either efficient or just – said it exuded a "bastard pragmatism" focused on short-term gain and oblivious to larger social ends. Hurst, *Law and Economic Growth*, *supra* note 1, at 34–37 and passim. Scheiber described how courts had aided the expropriation of property on behalf of transport companies. Harry N. Scheiber, "Property Law, Expropriation, and Resource Allocation by Government: The United States, 1789–1910," 33 *J. Econ. History* 232 (1973).

[26] E. P. Thompson, "The Moral Economy of the English Crowd in the Eighteenth Century," in E. P. Thompson, *Customs in Common* 185 (1993).

[27] Horwitz, *supra* note 3, at 160–188.

collective use-rights; of juries settling disputes among neighbors according to communal norms, rather than remote judges enforcing rules favoring commercial strangers and outsiders and unconcerned with equity and morality. And surely, in Horwitz's identification of the winners and losers from capitalist development, there is more than a hint of Charles Beard's economic populism. Horwitz was reaching back into the histories of the Progressive period and the 1930s, and the new left-wing social histories of the 1960s, for narratives to fuel his rebellion against the scholarship of the 1950s, the pages of yesteryear when consensus-minded Cold Warriors kept law and order on the fields of historical scholarship.

Still other background presences to his book are cheering his rebellion from 1950s legal scholarship: the Legal Realists of the 1920s and 30s and contemporary work of the Critical Legal Studies movement, of which he was one of the founders and most eminent members. The signs of these influences are in his distrust – indeed disgust – with legal formalism, meaning here, the pose of judges and treatise-writers that they are speaking for a general, apolitical, neutral body of legal principles. Such principles always conceal, for Horwitz, a right-wing political agenda and ideological bias. He was even led to a severe criticism of the admired E. P. Thompson. In the concluding chapter of *Whigs and Hunters* – a generally Beardian book about how the English upper-class had twisted and manipulated the law to divest traditional rights to take deer, graze cattle, and glean corm from harvests, to protect the landowner's absolute and enclosed property, and to punish customs as crimes – Thompson ended with an unexpected paean of praise for the "rule of law" as an "unqualified human good" – for all its abuses, a great western institution that limits the rulers as well as the ruled.[28] The formalist view of the rule of law, Horwitz chided, always conceals inequalities of wealth and power under a facade of formal equality, and delegitimates attempts to remedy such inequalities.[29]

For their part, some of Horwitz's critics were speaking out of competing narratives of their own, some old, some new. Reid very straightforwardly adopted the traditional narrative of American legal-economic development as progress away from feudalism and mercantilism and toward economic liberalism. For Reid, the law's shift from enforcing just prices to express promises was a lifting of restraints on commerce and freedom. Similarly Chief Justice Shaw's decision in *Farwell*,[30] immunizing employers from vicarious liability for harms caused by fellow-servants, on the ground that workers had impliedly contracted to assume the risk – which Horwitz had called a redistributive rule-change subsidizing railroads at the expenses of workers – was, for Reid, simply the fulfillment of the Revolution's principle of freedom of contract: "the

[28] E. P. Thompson, *Whigs and Hunters: The Origin of the Black Act* 258–269 (1975).

[29] Morton Horwitz, "The Rule of Law: An Unqualified Human Good?," 86 *Yale L. J.* 561, 566 (1977).

[30] *Farwell* v. *Boston & Worcester RR.*, 45 Mass. 49 (1842) (opinion of Shaw, CJ.).

individual, free to enter or reject a perilous employment, was made responsible for his own decisions."[31]

Another of Horwitz's hostile critics, Stephen Williams, then a professor at Colorado law school, now a distinguished federal judge, attacked him from the perspective of Chicago law-and-economics, in a review called *Doubtful Economics Makes Doubtful History*. Williams made some valuable points: he was really puzzled about why Horwitz would want to privilege stable property rights in first occupiers, such as riparian users or farmers, against later-competing users. I agree that this preference, in a man generally speaking of the left, for absolute property rights (and pre-commercial societies) is a little hard to understand: it makes sense, I think, only in a Polanyi/Thomson narrative in which such stable use rights are aspects of stable communities. It also makes sense to an ironic narrative – one in which judges and lawyers totally committed to preserving absolute property rights end up totally subverting them. Williams also asked some good analytic questions: when can a set of legal rule changes with distributional impacts be labeled "subsidies?" What's the baseline? And he also filled a gap Horwitz had left by summarizing some data from economic history about changes in income and wealth distribution in the antebellum United States, though the data was too aggregate to either confirm or refute Horwitz's basic thesis, and of course shed no light either way on how, if at all, legal rule-changes affected basic distributive shares.[32] But Williams's more basic point was to express doubt that law had become more instrumental (or "utilitarian") in the early nineteenth century. He drew on a competing narrative, this one of Chicago law-and-economics (which was I believe itself a completely unconscious repeating of a nineteenth-century narrative of the progressive evolution of the common law) to the effect that the "common law" was generally both utilitarian and efficient, indeed had been efficient for many

[31] Reid, *supra* note 19, at 1317. Reid reasonably asks the historian to interpret the fellow-servant rule in the light of contemporary, rather than modern, views of freedom of contract. Even doing that, however, it is difficult to reconcile the fellow-servant cases with doctrines being developed at the same time to deal with contracts between railroads and shippers and passengers, which explicitly refuse to allow the railroads to contract out of liability even expressly, on the grounds that the other parties have no real opportunity to withhold consent from such contracts. Even in mid-nineteenth-century America, the problems of the one-sided contract of adhesion were perceptible, if only selectively so, to the legal system.

[32] Stephen Williams, "Transforming American Law: Doubtful Economics Makes Doubtful History," 25 *U.C.L.A. L. Rev.* 1187, 1210–1211 (1978). Williams reported the evidence from economic history as showing no significant changes in wealth distribution in the antebellum United States. A more recent review of the data indicates however that "[a]ll the fragments of unsatisfactory evidence taken together may justify a conclusion that wealth inequality increased somewhat during the nineteenth century, at least in the antebellum period." Clayne Pope, "Inequality in the Nineteenth Century," in *The Cambridge Economic History of the United States vol.* 2, 109, 135 (Engerman & Gallman eds. 2000); Jenny Wahl, "Twice-Told Tales: An Economist's Re-Telling of the Transformation of American Law, 1780–1860," 37 *Tulsa L. Rev.* 881 (2002).

centuries, as in its long struggle against restraints on alienation.[33] This argument surely proved a bit too much. For if the law is efficient when it loosens feudal restraints, how can it be efficient when it creates them? And if the law is efficient when it does away with just-price doctrines and enforces contracts according to their strict terms, what was it before it thus reformed itself? If the Mill Acts are efficient because, by converting property to liability rules, they prevent holdout landowners from thwarting progress by injunction, why did the rule have to change?

In hindsight perhaps the most surprising fact about the reviews of *Transformation I* is that Horwitz's severest critics came mostly from the right, not the left. The book appeared after all in 1977, in the full flowering of post-1960s social history "from the bottom up." One would have expected some critics to fault Horwitz's book for focusing on the quarrels of white men who could afford to fight cases to appeal, and leaving out all the law of social relations of novel concern – the law of slavery, indentured servants, the employment relation and labor organizing, the law of sex roles, marriage and the family, the criminal law as an agent of social repression and discipline. The closest to such a critique was Wythe Holt's, but in the course of an exceptionally warm and generous overall review.[34] The answer must be that in the 1970s and 80s the space for any kind of legal left was very small, Horwitz was one of its few occupants, and for once left-wing scholars passed up the usually irresistible opportunity to savage one of their own.

The reception accorded to Horwitz's second volume, *The Transformation of American Law 1870–1960: The Crisis of Legal Orthodoxy* ("*Transformation II*"),[35] was altogether different in kind. I found only one really hostile review, by the conservative lawyer Bruce Fein in *The Washington Times*, which dismissed Horwitz's intellectual history as a story of scholastic disputes, and provided a delicious illustration of the continuing power of "classical" ideology by dismissing all Progressive statutory innovations on the common law – such as minimum wage laws – as rent-seeking by special interests trying to get themselves a better deal than they could get through the market.[36] Most of the major reviews,[37] while politely challenging, were exceedingly respectful, as if trying to temper the howling winds that had surrounded *Transformation I*. Their

[33] Williams, *supra* note 32, at 1200–1205.

[34] Holt, *supra* note 5, at 719–722.

[35] Morton J. Horwitz, *The Transformation of American Law 1870–1960: The Crisis of Legal Orthodoxy* (1992).

[36] Bruce Fein, Straining to Bring Forth a Legal Gnat, *Wash. Times* G3 (August 13, 1992).

[37] *See e.g.*, Daniel R. Ernst, "The Critical Tradition in the Writing of American Legal History," 102 *Yale L. J.* 1019 (1993); Robert W. Gordon, "The Elusive Transformation," 6 *Yale J.L. & Humanities* 137 (1994) [republished as the next chapter in this collection]; James Kloppenberg, "The Theory and Practice of American Legal History," 106 *Harv. L. Rev.* 1332 (1993); John Henry Schlegel, "A Tasty Tidbit," 41 *Buffalo L. Rev.* 1047 (1993); G. Edward White, "Transforming History in the Postmodern Era," 91 *Mich. L. Rev.* 1315 (1993).

emphasis was also different. The reviews of *Transformation I* centered, I have argued, on a conflict of narratives. Those of *Transformation II* were much more about methodology, and especially the vexed connections, on which Horwitz now had a very different take, between intellectual and social history.

Transformation I was mostly about doctrine, and argued that doctrine caused social change. *Transformation II* was mostly about the more abstract legal "thought" of treatises and articles, and argued a more complex view of its relation to social change. In *Transformation II* legal thought sometimes rationalized and legitimated social changes that had already taken place. But sometimes it influenced future social change by operating as an ideological filter of reality as its categories and assumptions shaped the ideological lens through which lawyers looked, one that conditioned their views of what was possible and desirable, public and private, coercive pressure and free contract, faulty or innocent conduct, cause and accident.

Like *Transformation I*, *Transformation II* drew upon background narratives. One remained the standard Progressive story of how Progressive (including Legal-Realist) jurists had challenged the socially conservative formalism of "Classical Legal Thought" (though Horwitz complicated the picture by showing that classical-individualism had actually been hostile to corporate concentration). Another narrative, worked out with his colleague Duncan Kennedy,[38] explained the main contribution of Realism as the smashing of the public–private distinction in classical law, the insight most shrewdly developed by Robert Hale that no legal regime is neutral, and no market is "free," that all legal regimes including "laissez-faire," enable some interests to command and coerce and injure others by means of state power.[39]

But there were two meta-narratives as well, which shaped Horwitz's project much as he argued legal thought had shaped twentieth century legal doctrines and policies. One was borrowed from Thomas Kuhn's *Structure of Scientific Revolutions*, and its theory of paradigm shifts generated by the accumulating strain of disconfirming and anomalous events: at some point, the strain is too much, the old theories lose their plausibility and fall apart, and new ones that appear to promise a more powerful and coherent account of perceived realities supplant them. The other came from Peter Novick's remarkable history of American history-writing in the twentieth century, *That Noble Dream*, in which, one might say, Novick brought the methods of legal-realism to bear on the historical profession's claims to objectivity in historical scholarship. Between them, Kuhn and Novick helped supply Horwitz with both a story-line

[38] Kennedy's pathbreaking and widely influential thesis of his legal history course materials is briefly summarized in Duncan Kennedy, "Toward a Historical Understanding of Legal Conciseness: The Case of Classical Legal Thought in America, 1850–1940," 3 *Research L. and Sociology* 3 (1980).

[39] The best treatment of Hale's ideas is Barbara Fried, *The Assault on Laissez-Faire: Robert Hale and the First Law and Economics Movement* (1998).

for his new book as well as a set of heroes and villains. The story-line was that of the fall of Classical Legal Thought (or formalism), its critique and partial supplanting with Progressive legal thought. This was a Kuhnian narrative. But it was followed by another – the resurgence of legal formalism in the postwar legal system and legal academy. In science, dead paradigms stay dead. In law, they never really get killed off, but hang around and Dracula-like, rise from their coffins to stalk the earth. Horwitz's villains, in the new narrative, were still those of *Transformation I* – the forces of legal formalism, resurgent in the postwar world as Herbert Wechsler's "neutral principles," the "legal process school of jurisprudence," and several generations of purportedly value-free social science, from legal-realist empiricism to law-and-economics. The heroes were the jurists that Novick called "cognitive relativists," fully aware of the value-laden, theory-dependent, necessarily political character of all tools for understanding and regulating the social world, shorn of the illusion that law is or ever can be objectively interpreted or apolitically neutral among contending interests and policies.

Hovering above these two meta-narratives was another methodological commitment, Horwitz's general dislike of overly complex stories and explanations. This commitment too has its roots in the revolt against the 1950s, when historical scholarship worshipped complexity – irony, multiplicity, particularism – as the antidote to the simplifications of "ideology." The cult of complexity in the 1950s, of the tragic sense of limits on human possibilities, as Peter Novick put it, "with its inevitable strong suggestion that any but the most piecemeal and modest tinkering with the social mechanism was ill-fated"[40] – had led into conservative resignation, either complacent or depressed, to the status quo. By way of recoil, Horwitz took from this account a strong preference for clear, vigorous and stripped-down narratives and explanations. This commitment led him to his sharpest point of disagreement with colleagues in Critical Legal Studies, who were disposed to argue that the association of any given set of legal doctrines or principles methods with legal-political outcomes was never anything but contingent, because types of legal argument could be "flipped" so as to be turned to any imaginable purpose. No, Horwitz said: at any given time, legal-argument-types – such as doctrines of causation or absolute-property or strict-liability or the real-entity theory of the corporation – tend to favor privilege, have an inbuilt "tilt" toward particular outcomes and not others.[41] The master-tilt for the second half of *Transformation II* – which if I am not mistaken is completely contrary to or at least very different from the master-tilt of *Transformation I* and the first half of *Transformation II* (in which formalists appear as "Old Conservative" individualists hostile to

[40] Novick, *supra* note 20, at 324.

[41] See e.g., Horwitz, *supra* note 35, at 106 (discussing ideological uses of legal theories of the corporation).

corporate enterprise) – is that formalism, whether of Classical Legal Thought, empirical social science, neutral principles, or law-and-economics, is inherently conservative, and relativism socially progressive. Horwitz's recent short book on the Warren Court carries this theme forward by characterizing the Court as intentionally committed to policy-making for an instrumental purpose, the strengthening of democracy – rather than as, let us say, the elaboration of natural rights.[42]

I have gone into all this because I believe it was precisely this combination of narrative, meta-narrative, and methodological commitments that gave rise to most of the – as I say, comparatively very gentle – quarrels between Horwitz and the reviewers of *Transformation II*. They – and I was one of them – found the paradigms too monolithic, the paradigm-shifts too sharp, and the identification of theoretical with political positions (the major "tilts") too neat. What is one to make of Holmes, for example, a radical skeptic about legal objectivity, but in most respects a rock-ribbed political and economic conservative? Or Morris Cohen, a liberal in politics, but strenuous anti-relativist in methodology? Or Thurman Arnold, an almost pure nominalist in legal theory, a scientific positivist in economic theory, and an ultra-orthodox promoter of competitive capitalism as antitrust chief? More generally, have not most of the great progressive social-legal movements in the American tradition – for universal suffrage, the abolition of slavery and racial segregation, the emancipation of women, labor's rights to organize and strike – drawn upon wholly abstract and formal conceptions of natural equal rights to liberty and justice?

But on one point even the most negative reviewers of Horwitz's two books agreed. This was substantial, original, path-breaking work. Even when apparently mistaken in matters of fact or problematic in matters of interpretation, this was work that probed deeply and provoked, and by so doing aroused legal and historical scholars to wakefulness and effort as well as protest and praise. They might challenge or disagree with it, angrily or respectfully, but they felt they had to engage with it, and by so doing stimulated a large part of the great new flourishing of legal history that began in the late 1970s and is still going strong. Morton Horwitz did a lion's share of the initial hard work, mixed the brew, and stirred the pot. We all owe him a tremendous debt.

[42] Morton J. Horwitz, *The Warren Court and the Pursuit of Justice* 114–115 (1998).

6

The Elusive Transformation*

[*This essay first appeared in 6* Yale Journal of Law and the Humanities 137 (1994) *as a review* of *Morton J. Horwitz*, The Transformation of American Law, 1870–1960: The Crisis of Legal Orthodoxy (*1992*).]

Morton Horwitz's new book is the sequel to his 1977 Bancroft Prize-winning *The Transformation of American Law, 1780–1860*. But as his Preface observes, "it is a very different book."[1] *Transformation I* tells a story in the populist spirit of Charles Beard. It shows how antebellum judges and elite lawyers fashioned an "instrumental" view of law that recruited traditional common law doctrines of property, contract, tort, and commercial law to the service of promoting commercial development. By such means, the legal elites helped business interests to accumulate wealth, property, and power at the expense of workers, farmers, and consumers. *Transformation I* ends with the legal establishment beginning to construct a novel orthodoxy, "legal formalism," to protect the wealth thus accumulated from new threats to redistribute it.

This brings us to the central narrative of *Transformation II*: the crisis and downfall of the late-nineteenth-century way of looking at law, which Horwitz still at times describes as "formalism" but now prefers to call "Classical Legal Thought" ("CLT"), and its critique and displacement by a rival paradigm – "Progressive Legal Thought" ("PLT"). Although others have, of course, written parallel histories of the constitutional law of this period, those are but bits and pieces of the story Horwitz tells – of the "Classical" worldview, of Legal Realism, and of post-World War II legal thought.[2] *Transformation II* is the first full-scale account of this great shift in legal thought.

* I would like to thank Barbara Fried and Tom Grey for helpful comments on an earlier draft.

[1] Morton J. Horwitz, *The Transformation Of American Law, 1870–1960: The Crisis Of Legal Orthodoxy* vi (1992) (hereinafter *Transformation II*).

[2] Among the most interesting of these are Laura Kalman, *Legal Realism At Yale, 1927–1960* (1986); G. Edward White, *Tort Law in America: An Intellectual History* (1980); William W.

Transformation II is a mightily impressive achievement, as one has come to expect from Morton Horwitz. Horwitz displays a magisterial command of an incredibly complicated set of developments. He has synthesized a great deal of scholarship, including much original work of his own, into a story that is organized by a clear point of view. He has strung on this story-line a set of detailed and often brilliant illustrations from different fields of law. Though the whole enterprise has a rather patchwork quality, revealing its origins in separately written essays, some of these essays are quite stunning. The section on Legal Realism (Chs. 5 & 6) is one of the best syntheses on the subject available. The chapters on Justice Holmes (Ch. 4) and on corporate personality (Ch. 3) are especially original in their research and strikingly so in their conclusions.

At the same time this book is a gnarled, cross-grained object, full of twists and knots. Its illustrations and subplots are continually at odds with its dominant themes. To borrow Isaiah Berlin's famous description of Tolstoy, Morton Horwitz is really a "fox" – a historian of many subtle and diverse insights and *aperçus* – who wants to be a "hedgehog," the kind of thinker who tries to organize all experience by means of a single, grand, all-encompassing Idea. Horwitz's Idea is that at the end of the nineteenth century the consciousness of the legal profession was structured by a single governing paradigm. The "transformation" of this consciousness into PLT was a massive paradigm shift in the pattern of one of Thomas Kuhn's scientific revolutions: after a period of accumulating piecemeal critiques and disconfirming experiences, CLT finally fell apart when a rival theory emerged that was powerful enough to replace it. The problem is that Horwitz is too conscientious a historian for his Idea to work. The intricate details of his story keep messing up its architectonic simplicity. In the end, Horwitz's orderly structuralist garden (to switch metaphors) is overrun by its sprawling post-structuralist undergrowth: a luxuriant, unruly proliferation of divergent interpretations.

Fisher III, "The Development of Modern American Legal Theory and the Judicial Interpretation of the Bill of Rights," in *A Culture Of Rights* (Lacey & Haakonssen eds. 1991); Thomas Grey, "Langdell's Orthodoxy," 45 *U. Pitt. L. Rev.* 1 (1983); Duncan Kennedy, "Toward an Historical Understanding of Legal Consciousness: The Case of Classical Legal Thought in America, 1850–1940," 3 *Res. L. & Soc.* 1 (1980); James May, "Antitrust in the Formative Era: Political and Economic Theory in Constitutional and Antitrust Analysis," 50 *Ohio St. L. J.* 257 (1989); Gary Peller, "The Metaphysics of American Law," 73 *Cal. L. Rev.* 1151 (1985); John Henry Schlegel, "American Legal Realism and Empirical Social Science: From the Yale Experience," 28 *Buff. L. Rev.* 459 (1979); Stephen A. Siegel, "Lochner Era Jurisprudence and the American Constitutional Tradition," 70 *N.C. L. Rev.* 1 (1991); Joseph Singer, "Legal Realism Now," 76 *Cal. L. Rev.* 465 (1988); G. Edward White, "From Sociological Jurisprudence to Realism: Jurisprudence and Social Change in Early Twentieth-Century America," 58 *Va. L. Rev.* 999 (1972).

I. THE IDEA OF TRANSFORMATION II

The differences in approach between *Transformation I* and *Transformation II* are subtle but significant. The earlier book takes its main material from appellate doctrine and practical commentaries – Dane, Story, Kent, Greenleaf, and the like. The sequel's domain is legal "thought," a notch above doctrine in generality and abstraction but a notch below legal philosophy or jurisprudence. This is the thought of the high mandarins of the legal system – the efforts of scholars, commentators, and judges to synthesize, systematize, and criticize the law in theoretical and doctrinal writing in treatises and law reviews. *Transformation II* presents the legal system largely from the view of professors or occasional lecturers at the Harvard Law School – except in the chapters on Legal Realism, where the viewpoint shifts to Columbia and Yale. Unlike most historians of high-level legal conceptualization, however, Horwitz does not view this domain as an autonomous island, whose inhabitants go about their business unconcerned with anything else that happens in the world. He aims rather to connect the history of legal concepts with the history both of social change and political reform in the wider society and to parallel movements in philosophy and social science.

Nevertheless, the relation between law and society in *Transformation II* is considerably more diffuse and indirect than it is in *Transformation I*. In *Transformation I*, the legal elite has a political-economic project – the redistribution of property into the hands of entrepreneurs and the protection of it once it gets there – which it executes in a relatively straightforward manner, changing the rules of the legal game in order to immunize industrial developers from liability for takings and torts. In *Transformation II*, Horwitz assigns CLT the much more general ideological function of "legitimating" the legal framework of an entire system of market relations, which the Classical lawyers attempt to serve by promoting the appearance that law is distinct from politics.[3]

The central drama of *Transformation II* is the struggle of "Progressive" legal writers to discredit and replace this dominant "Classical" orthodoxy. As

[3] A nice example is *Transformation II*'s treatment of *Ryan* v. *N.Y. Central Railroad*, 35 N.Y. 210 (1866). The railroad had negligently caused a fire. The New York Court of Appeals held the railroad liable only to the owner of a nearby house, and not to more distant owners whose houses were also destroyed. The Classical jurists, Horwitz says, disdained this decision. Though they too wanted to limit business liability, they wanted even more to promote the view that causation was an objective and apolitical concept. Horwitz comments:

> The explanation gives us some insight into the relative autonomy of legal ideas. The conception of objective causation was too central to the legitimation of the entire system of private law for it to be abandoned even in the interest of erecting another barrier to entrepreneurial liability. Many judges, to be sure, manipulated the proximate-remote distinction in other cases to limit entrepreneurial liability, but few did so as brazenly as in Ryan, threatening to bring the entire intellectual system into disrepute.

Transformation II, *supra* note 1, at 57 (emphasis added).

Horwitz tells it, the Classics aimed at giving systematic and formal expression to a legal worldview that had gradually evolved over the nineteenth century to validate a particular political-economic order, that of decentralized laissez-faire entrepreneurial individualism. The desire to reform that order – to remold the legal system into an active regulatory force capable of taming concentrated corporate power and redistributing wealth – moved the Progressives to their critique. The Classical view of private law was vital, contested ground in this struggle. To the Classics, the common law rules of property, contract, tort, corporations, and unfair competition, together with the common law concepts of objective causation and harm, added up to a natural framework of ground rules, supposedly completely neutral among competing interests, for regulating interactions among individuals and between individuals and the state. In the Classical view, this natural framework was the optimal legal regime for a free and prosperous society. The courts and treatise-writers had even woven the common law ground rules into their theories of constitutional limitations on state power, so that legislatures (by these theories) might not enact regulations tampering with the natural private law order without extraordinary justification.

In Horwitz's account, two main forces worked to break up the Classical paradigm. The first was change in the organization of the economy: the rise to dominance of some sectors by a few giant corporations, the bitter struggles of this newly organized capital with its labor force, and the resultant, evermore conspicuous inequalities in the distribution of wealth and income. All this sharply challenged the Classical claim that because the rules simply encoded the uncoerced choices of contracting individuals, markets structured by common law rules would lead to optimally free, fair, and efficient results. The other force was more internal to legal thought. So successful were the Classics in clarifying their system that in the process they laid bare the weaknesses and contradictions of its underpinnings. For example, they generalized the rights of property that should be protected against private invasion or legislative redistribution to every form of economic expectancy, such as the right to run a business and the right to a reasonable return on invested capital. Once "property" began to mean every form of value, the idea that it all must be legally protected against diminishment disintegrated into incoherence. The distinction between legally protected and unprotected property was revealed for what it was, the result of "political" or "policy" judgments.

The Classical system thus lay exposed to the critiques of Progressives armed with the anti-formalist insights of pragmatist philosophy and institutionalist economics. PLT, in process of formation from the 1880s onwards, reached its peak in the Legal Realist thought of the 1920s and 30s.[4] Progressive/

[4] Horwitz views Legal Realism both as "simply a continuation of the reformist agenda of early twentieth-century Progressivism," *Transformation II*, *supra* note 1, at 169, and as a "distinct intellectual outlook" characterized by a far greater "skepticism about reason and morality" than pre-World War I Progressivism, *id.* at 170.

Realist critics sought to show that the private law system was not "natural," but socially and politically constructed; not neutral, but biased in favor of the economically powerful. They challenged CLT's conceptualism and its claims to be able to derive all the detailed rules of law from a few basic principles such as "property," "will," or "fault." Citing Holmes's famous aphorism that "general propositions do not decide concrete cases,"[5] the Progressives denied that concepts such as "free will" and "property" could determine any unique set of legal outcomes, much less the particular rules of Classical doctrine. Labor strikes and boycotts obviously injured business "property," but so did ordinary competition; thus, knowing that an "owner" had "property" in his business could tell you nothing about whether strikes or boycotts should be treated as enjoinable nuisances or as privileged tactics of competition. The decision had to turn on a debatable, political policy judgment. Similarly, Classical law supposedly enforced the "will of the parties" to freely made contracts but at the same time it objectified contracting parties as "reasonable" people using standardized signs of agreement. How the legal system constructed those objectified intentions and the "ordinary meanings" of their expression, the Progressives pointed out, was a creative, discretionary task, requiring – once again – judgments of policy. The Classics sought to limit business tort liability by restricting it to harms that defendants "objectively" caused; Progressives argued that objective causation was a mirage, since the decision to attribute an event to any one of its potentially infinite causes was inevitably a decision made for a particular purpose, and in law that purpose had to be some goal of policy.

The most powerful Progressive critique – and here Horwitz follows other recent critical scholars paying homage to Robert L. Hale, the Columbia Realist and legal economist of the 1920s and 30s[6] – was of the Classics' public–private distinction. The Classics strictly separated the legal universe into spheres of private (market) and public (state) action. In the Classical world, private action was presumptively voluntary. Private law enforced contracts and corrected (through compensatory damages) harms to private property

[5] *Lochner* v. *New York*, 198 U.S. 45, 76 (1905) (Holmes, J., dissenting).

[6] A previously neglected figure in the history of legal and economic thought, Hale first resurfaced in the 1970s in a study by Warren Samuels, "The Economy as a System of Power and its Legal Bases: The Legal Economics of Robert Lee Hale," 21 *U. Miami L. Rev.* 261 (1973). He was recognized as a trailblazer of the modern Critical Legal Studies movement in Duncan Kennedy and Frank Michelman, "Are Property and Contract Efficient?," 8 *Hofstra L. Rev.* 711 (1980); Singer, *supra* note 2; Mark Kelman, *A Guide To Critical Legal Studies* 103–104 (1987). His insights have since been absorbed into leading works of mainstream legal scholarship. See, e.g., Cass Sunstein, *The Partial Constitution* (1993). For detailed accounts of Hale's work and thought see Neil Duxbury, "Robert Hale and the Economy of Legal Force," 53 *Mod. L. Rev.* 421 (1990) arid especially Barbara Fried, *Robert Hale and Progressive Law and Economics* (1998) which resurrects not only Hale's thought but that of the whole tradition of neo-marginalist and institutionalist legal-economic thought of his period, and is now the definitive treatment.

caused by voluntarily produced (intentional or negligent) wrongs. Public (regulatory) law, on the other hand, was coercive. It was primarily through this division of spheres that the Classics naturalized market relations and made public (legislative and administrative) regulation of those relations seem suspect and artificial – an extraordinary "intervention" into the private sphere. The Progressives insisted that all law, private as well as public, was regulatory and coercive. Contract law enforced some contracts and not others; tort and property law protected against some invasive harms and not others. When the law did enforce, it put state force behind selected types of private actors and decisions. The law privileged some bargaining tactics and coercive threats and prohibited others. Indeed the "rights" of property and contract were best understood as delegations of state power to individuals and corporations, as the Realist John Dawson put it, to "coerce one another" in the marketplace.[7] Wealth and market power were thus always a function of: 1) the legal system's distribution of rights to exclude others or to impose conditions on others' access to one's property, and 2) rights and prohibitions affecting the ability to coordinate and organize.

By such insights, Progressives dissolved the naturalness of the rules constituting the private market. The common law rules were no different from any other kind of regulation, in that they delegated powers to invoke public force according to usually inarticulate, underrationalized, and highly contestable notions of public policy. Some Progressives thought common law judges could do a better job if they understood and analyzed the policy bases of their work. Others assumed Classically trained judges were hopelessly conservative and incompetent to decide important policy issues; only administrators equipped with more realistic and more specialized knowledge of social contexts could do the job.

After a generation of nibbling away at the Classical system, the Progressives brought it crashing down in the New Deal. Yet Horwitz's story ends with an ironic twist. By the time the Progressive/Realist paradigm finally triumphed in legal thought, it had lost most of its critical edge and reformist potential and had instead become technocratic, tamed, and co-opted for relatively conservative political uses. As post-Progressive legal thinkers grew disenchanted with expert bureaucratic rationality, they retreated into the "legalism" and "proceduralism" they had once ridiculed. Some, like Louis Jaffe, expressed renewed support for judicial review of administrative action. Others, like the Harvard "Legal Process" scholars Henry Hart and Albert Sacks, restated all substantive issues of social value and policy as issues of compliance with procedural requirements: in a liberal-pluralist society, the only criterion for evaluating legal decisions was whether they were the "duly arrived at result[s] of duly

[7] John P. Dawson, "Economic Duress-An Essay in Perspective," 45 *Mich. L. Rev.* 253 (1947), quoted in *Transformation II*, *supra* note 1, at 197.

established procedures."[8] The aging Judge Learned Hand retained the earlier Progressive view that Classical law was laden with conservative political judgments, but now found the remedy not in reorienting the legal system toward more liberal ends, but in judicial deference to the "political" branches – even as those branches, in the McCarthy period, were trampling the rights of dissenters.[9] Horwitz's purpose in describing this declension is unmistakable. The underlying aim of his book, sometimes wistfully, sometimes passionately argued, is to recover PLT before it lost its edge, at its moment of highest critical brilliance in the epic contest with Classical formalism, and to dust it off and sharpen it up for battle with the resurgent conservative formalisms of the present day.

II. THE ELUSIVENESS OF THE PARADIGM SHIFT

To keep up the appearance of a harmonious whole, Horwitz continually, at times even rather casually, readjusts his master Idea – redefining the essence of the Classical and Progressive world-views, their relation to social contexts and their political implications, and repositioning the decisive moment of transformation. The running argument between governing Idea and rebellious examples raises many fundamental questions. The following are just a sample.

A. What Is "Legal Thought" and What Is Its Relation to the Rest of Social Life?

Horwitz's category of legal thought, as I said before, seems mostly to be secondary writing by academics or judges, a step in abstraction removed from the body of appellate decisions that constitute the high level ideology of the practicing profession, and many steps from the field or working-level practices of lawyers, judges, and administrative agencies. One of the many interesting questions Horwitz raises – and then responds to in interestingly, if bewilderingly, diverse ways – is that of the relation between legal thought and other social practices, such as the routine work of the rest of the legal system. Other legal historians, such as Lawrence Friedman, doubt that mandarin legal thought has much social significance. For Friedman, the flourishing of legal theory in the Classical period is a sort of child's dress-up game. Lawyers pretended to be scientists because the new prestige of natural science gave them a borrowed glory; otherwise, the mandarin theories were pretty much irrelevant to the working level of the legal system.[10]

[8] Henry M. Hart, Jr. & Albert Sacks, *The Legal Process: Basic Problems In. The Making And Application Of Law* (tent. ed. 1958), quoted in *Transformation II, supra* note 1, at 255.

[9] *Transformation II, supra* note 1, at 258–265.

[10] See Lawrence M. Friedman, *A History of American Law* 618 (2nd edn. 1985).

Obviously, Horwitz thinks otherwise. He is clearly convinced that high-level legal thought is socially significant as a form of ideological ordering. He is rarely very explicit about how legal ideology works, but the main idea seems to be something like this: the function of legal thought is to synthesize a rationalizing order out of the vast miscellany of lower-level practices (doctrine). This ordering is intended to "legitimate" the legal system by showing how its contingent practices may be brought into harmony with what are claimed to be general social norms – though in reality those norms are only the particular political visions of the legal elite and the social groups they represent. ("Ideology," for Horwitz, thus has both its usual meanings: a commonly held coherent set of views of the world that processes experience, and a partial, self-interested set of views that masquerades as a universal vision.) Once assembled, the legal-thought system becomes a self-fulfilling prophecy, exerting a pervasive structuring influence throughout the legal system and society in general, affecting the routine ways in which legal (and other social) actors conceptualize problems, categorize realities, relate causal narratives, argue cases, and justify conclusions. Yet legal thought works as ideology only so long as there is a plausible fit between thought and doctrine, between thought and social reality. When social reality or doctrine (which responds faster than thought to social change) falls out of tune with the thought-system, thought begins to lose its legitimating power.

Horwitz's chapter on corporate theory[11] is probably the most straightforward illustration both of his theory of law as ideology in action and of some of the difficulties his own applications pose for the theory. The chapter opens with CLT already under severe strain – even before it has had a chance to be developed into an influential rationalizing ideology. From its inception, CLT lagged behind economic and doctrinal changes in intra-corporate relations. Seeking to locate the business corporation firmly in the private sphere, to sever it from its origins as a state-created enterprise formed to serve public purposes, the Classics reconceived it in terms of a partnership, nothing more than a contract among individual shareholders.[12] But this contractualism, Horwitz tells us, was "becoming a nostalgic fantasy at the very moment" it was advanced.[13] It could not compass the revolution in corporate structure that was centralizing managerial control in an oligarchy of managers practically unaccountable to the scattered multitude of passive investors who, increasingly, held its stock. In

[11] *Transformation II*, *supra* note l, at ch. 3.

[12] This, Horwitz makes clear, was the view taken in the famous Santa Clara case in which the U.S. Supreme Court said that corporations had the rights of "persons" protected by the Fourteenth Amendment. *Santa Clara* v. *Southern Pac. R.R.*, 118 U.S. 394 (1886). The reasoning was not that the Southern Pacific Railroad itself was a person, either "artificial" or "natural," but rather that it was composed of natural individuals, real persons. *Transformation II*, *supra* note 1, at 69–70.

[13] *Transformation II*, *supra* note 1, at 92.

fact, Horwitz suggests in one of his most surprising insights, the contractualist theory was the creation of "old conservative" individualist lawyers who were hostile to big business and wanted it kept under shareholder control.[14] For a friendlier legal reception and successful legitimation of the new corporation and its control by managers, a new theory was needed (and, evidently, a more sympathetic legal elite to supply it). The theory was in time supplied by jurists who, borrowing from the German jurist Otto von Gierke's neo-medieval conception of associations as "group-persons", reconceived the corporation as a "natural entity," an organic being with its own identity and purposes, as real as any of the natural persons who composed it.

In this new phase, Horwitz suggests, legal thought actually did achieve the power required for it to play a major causal role: its "main effect [rather a strong word, for an intellectual historian] was to legitimate large-scale enterprise and to destroy any special basis for regulation of the corporation that derived from its creation by the state."[15] The natural-entity theory also justified the weakened role of shareholders in governance and the trend away from requiring unanimous shareholder approval for mergers.[16] Indeed, Horwitz wants to insist – against his playful anarchic colleagues in the Critical Legal Studies movement who like to assert that any legal conception can be twisted into the service of almost any purpose or interest – that in context there is usually a "tilt" inherent in a theory toward some specific set of consequences, a natural fit between form and function. In this instance, none of the rival theories, such as contractualism, could have accomplished the necessary legitimating tasks so well. Thus in specific historical settings, "legal theory does powerfully influence the direction of legal understanding."[17]

Yet, is even the case of "natural-entity" theory a good one for Horwitz's view of the influence of legal thought? There are some reasons to doubt it. William Bratton's work on the relation between corporate theory and practice finds, as does Horwitz, that when basic forms of corporate structure change, new theories arise to rationalize them. But, Bratton argues, despite many shifts in high-order theory, there has been an amazing continuity in thinking about the corporation in American history at a level of legal thought closer to the problems of practice, that is, ordinary corporate law doctrine. At that level, Bratton shows, lawyers have regularly, cheerfully, and eclectically mixed up contract, fiduciary, group-entity, and fictive-collective notions of the firm, as necessary, to confront practical problems.[18] Moreover, if there was a "tilt" to natural-entity theory it may quite possibly have been one away from apologists

[14] *Id.* at 103.
[15] *Id.* at 104.
[16] *Id.* at 106.
[17] *Id.* at 107.
[18] William Bratton, "The New Economic Theory of the Firm: Critical Perspectives from History," 41 *Stan. L. Rev.* 1471 (1989).

for unrestrained corporate power. Mark Hager has looked at the Gierkean "natural entity" from another angle, and has found among its most enthusiastic boosters in the early twentieth century a group of social-democratic Progressives. These "left Gierkeans" drew from the theory new rationales for imposing criminal and tort liability on corporate wrongdoers, and for allowing trade unions the same range of natural freedom to act that business corporations had. They realized the theory had some "pro-capital" implications too, but saw these as slight compared to its tilt toward their social-democratic program.[19]

Indeed, in recent years legal apologists for unregulated business have turned not to natural-entity or managerialist notions, but back to the very contractualism – the view of the corporation as nothing more than a "nexus of contracts" between shareholders, managers, creditors, and employees – that Horwitz claims would not have served their purposes in the 1880s.[20]

Modern critics agree with Horwitz and the Progressives that contract theory is terribly deficient as a description of the realities of corporate organization and even of corporate doctrine.[21] But the usefulness of contractualism as ideology may lie precisely in that deficiency: the theory belongs to the long history of classical-liberal ideological enterprises that tries to suppress the non-individualist components of our routine social practices – the collective, authoritarian, communitarian, and fiduciary elements that form the actual glue of economic life. Is legal ideology most useful when it explains and accommodates problematic aspects of social life or when it denies them? Like Ronald Reagan's imagined American past of intact, small-town families whose self-reliant breadwinners made their way on their individual merits, ideology may be most powerful when it appeals to mythic-nostalgic or utopian fantasies that lift people out of ordinary experience. "The power of [Reagan's] appeal," as Garry Wills has suggested, "is the great joint confession that we cannot live with our real past, that we not only prefer but need a substitute."[22] Horwitz himself suggests something very like this mechanism of legitimation-through-denial in his section on agency law,[23] where he pictures legal thought as Hegel's Owl of Minerva, rationalizing an individualistic social vision that was on the point of vanishing as both economic change and new case law made it obsolete. Late-nineteenth-century doctrine adjusted to the realities of delegated power in

[19] Mark M. Hager, "Bodies Politic: The Progressive History of Organizational "Real Entity" Theory," 50 *U. Pitt. L. Rev.* 575 (1989).

[20] *See, e.g.*, Frank H. Easterbrook & Daniel Fischel, *The Economic Structure of Corporate Law* (1991).

[21] *See* William Bratton, "The 'Nexus of Contracts' Corporation: A Critical Appraisal," 74 *Cornell L. Rev.* 407 (1989); Victor Brudney, "Corporate Governance, Agency Costs, and the Rhetoric of Contract," 85 *Colum. L. Rev.* 1403 (1985).

[22] Garry Wills, *Reagan's America* 458 (2nd edn. 1988).

[23] *Transformation II, supra* note 1, at 39–51.

large corporate organizations by charging a company with its agents' contracts even if the agent had only apparent, not actual, authority. The Classical treatises of the time could not reconcile this practice with their grand principle that contractual obligation could only be created by consent. Horwitz comments:

> Perhaps this is a clue to one of the primary functions of the classical legal treatise, which sought not simply to report on the state of the law but to advance a highly abstract and integrated version that was grounded in a picture of a decentralized, individualistic economic and political order.[24]

So Horwitz's own examples, in contrast to his generalizations, suggest a much more complex set of relations between theory and practice than that theory structures practice with a tilt. Don't get me wrong: I am not at all arguing here that practical action is not influenced by theory, including quite formal and abstract theory. The evidence seems overwhelming, for instance, that legal doctrine in fields like antitrust, restraint of trade, labor, and public utilities law has throughout our history been saturated in vulgarized versions of dominant theories of political economy.[25] Legal actors' pictures of cause and effect, of the judge's appropriate role, of what counts as a persuasive description of social reality or the likely consequences of a decision, have to come from somewhere; and the source is often something surprisingly abstract. Many of the grand categories fashioned by the Classical theorists – such as their division of civil liability into tort, contract, and quasi-contract, and of torts into intentional, negligent, and strict liability – continue to pervade legal thought even into the present. Many of the Progressive and Legal Realist devices for analyzing legal problems, such as multi-factor balancing tests, have also dropped into lawyers' common speech. But, of course, not every theory percolates downward from the heights. I very much doubt that the most profound Legal Realist critiques of the given-ness of property and the market, or of the public–private distinction, ever spread very far into the world of practice; though one may detect residues of their influence in particular settings.[26]

[24] *Id.* at 45, This, of course, was a common critique of the Realists: treatises like Williston's were not only out of touch with practical social life, but out of touch with the case law itself.

[25] See, e.g., Herbert Hovenkamp, *Enterprise And American Law, 1836–1937* (1991); May, *supra* note 2; Rudolph Peritz, "A Counter-History of Antitrust Law," 1990 *Duke L. J.* 263. Economic historians are now inclined to explain the major social catastrophe of the Great Depression as having resulted primarily from policy-makers' adherence to an archaic economic doctrine, the gold standard. See Peter Temin, *Lessons from the Great Depression* (1989).

[26] *See Shelley* v. *Kraemer*, 334 U.S. 1 (1948), which invalidated racially restrictive covenants in real-estate contracts on the ground that although private contracts, they had to be enforced by courts and thus could be seen as a form of "state action" under the Fourteenth Amendment. Shelley appears to adopt Robert Hale's view that contract rights are a form of delegated state power. This is not entirely coincidental, since Hale helped brief the case. The case, however, has been much criticized for what the Realists would have thought its outstanding virtue: its blurring of the public–private distinction.

Horwitz's own views on the relation of "legal thought" to context remain mysterious partly because the book delivers only very selectively on its promise to show the "close connection… between social struggle and jurisprudential controversy."[27] Clearly it is the legal story that mainly interests Horwitz, and that story's social and intellectual surroundings are given only brief capsule summaries or, more often, just footnote references. Indeed, the footnotes are crammed with citations to an enormous literature on social and intellectual context, as if the bare cites could somehow raise up that context for the reader and represent all its richness.

One pages through the book wishing fervently to know more about this briefly conjured-up surround – to know more, just to take one example among many, of the elements of classical political economy underlying CLT, and of both the neoclassical (marginalist) and institutionalist challenges to that system. The book scarcely mentions the political movements to which Progressive law and social science were allied – especially Progressive social-legal reform at the state level and in the labor movement. Horwitz wants us to appreciate "the intimate relations between Realists and New Dealers,"[28] but surprisingly says nothing about what specific Realists (such as Jerome Frank, Thurman Arnold, William O. Douglas, or Walton Hamilton) actually did in the New Deal. The chapter on corporate theory has solid accounts of late-nineteenth-century changes in corporate organization; the Holmes chapter recounts contemporary conflicts over tort liability and the labor injunction. But this entire economic context is from the late nineteenth century; after 1900, economic change simply vanishes as an element of context, save for five glancing references to the importance of the Great Depression in delegitimating the Classical scheme.[29] Another large-scale social change agent, the administrative state, enters the narrative for the first time in the New Deal, long after the giant corporation has left it. Where, one has to ask, is the bureaucratic rehearsal for the New Deal in state and municipal agencies, in the Interstate Commerce Commission and War Industries and War Labor Boards, in Commerce Secretary Hoover's "associationism"? Even after the administrative state belatedly appears, Horwitz's main focus is on the dispute over reforming administrative procedure, on the Walter-Logan and Administrative Procedure Acts; there is hardly an actual bureaucracy or program in the story. The New Deal itself puts in only a cameo appearance as an accompaniment to a discussion of the public–private distinction in the Schechter[30] and Carter Coal[31] cases.

Now plainly these are peripheral matters to Horwitz's main concern in this book – he is not writing a study of reciprocal influences of legal thought on

[27] *Transformation II*, *supra* note 1, at 6.

[28] *Id.* at 7.

[29] *Id.* at 187, 190, 207, 220, 240.

[30] *Schechter Poultry Co.* v. *United States*, 295 U.S. 495 (1935).

[31] *Carter* v. *Carter Coal Co.*, 298 U.S. 238 (1936).

social reform movements or of legal on social thought; the reform movements and social thought are background to his main story, and there is nothing wrong with that. Still, his own thesis depends on the argument that they are essential background, with decisive influence upon the pictures of reality and conceptive modes of legal thinkers, and that legal thought in turn is a formative influence on the conduct of social struggles. Of course, a writer cannot do everything at once, and the task Horwitz has set himself is formidable enough for one book. It will be left to the armies of scholars who come after to mine Horwitz's footnotes for the chunks of context missing from his own account.[32]

B. What Are the Defining Characteristics of CLT and PLT?

As with Horwitz's theory of thought–context relations, so too with his account of the substance of his two great protagonists, CLT and PLT: Horwitz the polemical theorist wants the story to be simpler than Horwitz the historian is willing to allow. Thus, contradictions suppressed in one passage to enable the theorist to have his reductive way tend to surface inconveniently a few pages later. Here are some of the key features of CLT and PLT as described in *Transformation II*, along with disconfirming examples, often drawn from the same text, that suggest those descriptions are problematic or incomplete.

1. CLT's "Fear of Redistribution"

In his opening summary of CLT, Horwitz says the "fundamental issue of American political thought was how this most politically democratic country in the world could avoid the threat of coerced economic equality."[33] The obsession of nineteenth-century law, in Horwitz's view, was the fear of Robin Hood democracy, of legal taking from the rich and propertied to give to the not-so-rich. Just as it did in *Transformation I*, the specter of democratic leveling haunts *Transformation II* as the secret motive underlying much juristic thought.

I do not doubt that this was an obsession of many nineteenth-century lawyers, but it is a subset of a larger and more general theme, what Corwin called "the basic doctrine of American Constitutional law,"[34] that the state should not simply take property away from A and give it to B. As Horwitz recognizes in his excellent sections on taxation and on nuisance as the basis of the police power,[35] it is more accurate to say that the nineteenth-century legal elite feared

[32] A splendid example of what one might call "legal-thought-in-action" scholarship is Daniel R. Ernst, "Common Laborers? Industrial Pluralists, Legal Realists, and the Law of Industrial Disputes," 1915–1943, 11 *Law & Hist. Rev.* 59 (1993). Ernst shows how theoretical differences among Progressive lawyers eventually led them to pursue divergent reform strategies.

[33] *Transformation II, supra* note 1, at 9.

[34] Edward Corwin, "The Basic Doctrine of American Constitutional Law," 12 *Mich. L. Rev.* 247 (1914).

[35] *Transformation II, supra* note 1, at 20–31.

democracy as a corrupt cover for "rent-seeking" or special-interest legislation, and feared that private interests – including rich corporate private interests – would seek wealth for themselves through the legislative process at the expense of the general welfare. This more general view of the "basic doctrine" casts the judges not so much as defenders of existing property – for the doctrine was developed in part by Jacksonians hostile to legally established "privileges" and "monopolies" – than as enforcers of legislative generality and neutrality.[36]

The innovation the Classical period's constitutional lawyers grafted onto the "basic doctrine" was to generalize it into a constitutional limitation on "class legislation," on takings from A-group to give to B-group. Horwitz sometimes seems to subscribe to this broader view of what Classical legal principle was about. As we have seen, his chapter on corporate personality is striking for its argument that the Classical "individualist" theory of the firm expressed in the *Santa Clara Railroad Tax Case*, though handy for giving businesses a Fourteenth Amendment shield against regulation, was actually developed by judges hostile to corporate concentration.[37] At many other points, however, Horwitz accepts the Legal-Realist/Progressive critique of CLT as mainly concerned with defending the rich against leveling. Did CLT shift from being a general anti-redistributive regime to a defense-of-the-rich principle? Was it so all along? Or, is Horwitz's point just that its naturalization of common law property endowments and market outcomes legitimated existing distributions, which were becoming *de facto* more unequal in the late nineteenth century?

2. *The "State" of CLT: Neutral State or Minimal State?*

Throughout the book,[38] Horwitz speaks sporadically of the aim of CLT as that of promoting "laissez-faire" or the "night-watchman" state, or minimum interference with the market. This is not quite the same as the aim of promoting "neutrality" among special interests. Of course, the neutrality doctrine could be used and often was used in the service of antiregulatory aims, and Horwitz provides many examples of this. But the doctrine is not inherently antiregulatory; it just insists that state action has to be for general benefit – eminent domain exercised for "public" purposes, taxes "equal, general, and uniform," the police power deployed to serve the public welfare, etc. The official legal ideology, as many scholars[39] (including Horwitz himself,

[36] For elaboration of this point, see Michael Les Benedict, "Laissez-Faire and Liberty: A Re-Evaluation of the Meaning and Origins of Laissez-Faire Constitutionalism," 3 *Law & Hist. Rev.* 293 (1985); see also Howard Gillman, *The Constitution Besieged: The Rise and Demise of Lochner Era Police Powers Jurisprudence* (1993); Alan Jones, "Thomas M. Cooley and Laissez-Faire Constitutionalism," 53 *J. Am. Hist.* 751 (1967); Charles McCurdy, "Justice Field and the Jurisprudence of Government-Business Relations," 61 *J. Am. Hist.* 970 (1975); May, *supra* note 2; Siegel, *supra* note 2.

[37] *Transformation II, supra* note 1, at 75–76.

[38] *See, e.g., id.* at 19.

[39] *See* sources cited *supra* note 36.

at irregular intervals in the book, such as in his treatment of the taxing and police powers[40]) have read it, was that the state of CLT was not the minimal state, that it was instead a state "absolute within its sphere,"[41] with plenary and "inalienable" powers.[42] The generality-neutrality principle was indeed deployed to limit the total size of the public sphere. Yet in the early nineteenth century, as Horwitz might have emphasized much more than he does, both the common law and Whig-mercantilist policy gave broad scope to the "police power" and to "public rights" of property, on the often-voiced premise that all private property was held subject to reasonable limitation for the public good.[43] And the late nineteenth century, the heyday of CLT, was anything but a period of laissez-faire in legislation, either in practice or in legal ideology: the period's outpouring of regulatory statutes and commissions to enforce them were reviewed and almost all approved by orthodox Classical courts.[44] Indeed the great Classical treatises on constitutional limitations and the police power have a quite expansive conception of public goods and of the legitimate scope of state action.[45]

It is positively distressing to see Horwitz helping to perpetuate the surprisingly durable myth that laissez-faire once dominated American economic and legal policy, since he has done as much as any historian to dispel the myth. (*Transformation I*, after all, is all about how the legal system had aggressively intervened to restructure property rights in order to promote the elite's developmental agenda.) To be sure, one can find plenty of instances where American lawyers have mouthed the *rhetoric* of laissez-faire and the night-watchman state, and where that rhetoric has helped to defeat some piece of regulatory legislation or support an argument that the legislation should be held unconstitutional. But at whatever level one cares to inspect it, the marrow of our

[40] *Transformation II*, *supra* note 1, at 20–31.

[41] Kennedy, *supra* note 2.

[42] On the doctrine of the "inalienability" of state powers, see especially McCurdy, *supra* note 36, and Stephen Siegel, "Understanding the Nineteenth Century Contract Clause," 60 *S. Calif. L. Rev.* 1 (1986).

[43] See William J. Novak, "Public Economy and the Well-Ordered Market: Law and Economic Regulation in 19th Century America," 18 *Law & Soc. Inquiry* 1 (1993); Carol M. Rose, "The Comedy of the Commons: Custom, Commerce and Inherently Public Property," 53 *U. Chi. L. Rev.* 711 (1986); Harry N. Scheiber, "Public Rights and the Rule of Law in American Legal History," 15 *Cal. L. Rev.* 415 (1984); Scheiber, "The Road to Munn: Eminent Domain and the Concept of Public Purpose in the State Courts," 5 *Persp. Am. Hist.* 329 (1971).

[44] Charles Warren made this point many years ago. "The Progressiveness of the United States Supreme Court," 13 *Colum. L. Rev.* 294 (1913). For a more detailed restatement, see Janet Lindgren, "Beyond Cases: Reconsidering Judicial Review," 1983 *Wis. L. Rev.* 583. See also Morton Keller, *Affairs Of State: Public Life In Late Nineteenth Century America* (1977); May, *supra* note 2; Melvin Urofsky, "State Courts and Protective Legislation during the Progressive Era," 72 *J. Am. Hist.* 63 (1985).

[45] See Thomas M. Cooley, *Constitutional Limitations* (1868); Christopher G. Tiedeman, *A Treatise on the Limitations of Police Power in the United States* (1886).

legal order has never been libertarian – not in legal theory, not in doctrine, and certainly not in the details of regulatory practice.

3. *Was CLT's View of Property "Natural"?*

Throughout the entire book Horwitz speaks of the pre-Realist belief that property and other rights recognized in the common law ground rules were "natural" rights. True enough, nineteenth-century lawyers did often speak of them as "natural," and the Progressive critics seized on this language. But there are several different plausible meanings of "natural" in this context.

a. One set of ideas is that the market and legal rules constituting it are "natural" in the sense of "pre-political" (as Horwitz often puts it), as opposed to artificial, constructed, and conventional. These rules are nothing less than the rights one would find in a state of nature, which law only recognizes, not constructs. Few sophisticated nineteenth-century lawyers would have endorsed this view, unless in the grip of careless rhetoric. The view that the modern property rights expressed in law are positive, not "natural," is explicit in Hume and Blackstone.[46] Kent's *Commentaries* makes clear that although the instincts to acquire, possess, and defend individual property are "natural," the forms of rights that modern law recognizes (such as those of absentee title-holders against cultivator-squatters) are those conventional rights fashioned for the "convenience" of advanced commercial societies.[47] Horwitz sometimes writes as if it was the Realists who discovered that property was a social creation; but this insight is ancient.[48] He also attributes variously to CLT and to the Realists the notion that "property" could be generalized to extend to all legally protected expectations. It is probably true that the idea did not gain general currency until late in the nineteenth century, but it is already fully explicit in Bentham's work, as is the insight that property gives the holder a sovereign discretion to injure others.[49]
b. I think nineteenth-century lawyers held a much more historicist view that the basic common law ground rules were "natural" in the sense that society was a naturally developing organism which gradually evolved customs that were "naturally" adapted to every stage of its development (there are many references to this idea in the work of James Coolidge Carter, whom Horwitz quotes at length in his Holmes chapter[50]). The

[46] David Hume, *A Treatise of Human Nature* 489 (Selby-Bigge & Nidditch eds., 1978) (1739–40); William Blackstone, 2 *Commentaries on the Law of England* 1–20 (1766).

[47] James Kent, 2 *Commentaries on American Law* 263 (1827).

[48] See Richard Tuck, *Natural Rights Theories* (1979).

[49] See Jeremy Bentham, *Principles of the Civil Code*, in 1 *Works of Jeremy Bentham* 297, 308 (Bowring ed., 1837).

[50] *Transformation II, supra* note 1, at 188–221.

common law encoded these customs.[51] It was this view of evolving social custom as natural that the Progressives turned against the Classics when they claimed that in modern organized society, the natural economic unit was no longer the individual but the large-scale organization, i.e., the corporation or labor union.

c. The hoary view of the common law as gradually adaptive tradition came to merge with a novel view of nature, i.e., the scientific "laws" of modern political economy. The common law rules were natural in this extended sense when they conformed to the "laws of the market"; legislation was "artificial" and hence likely to be futile or pernicious when it contravened these natural laws. Here, the Classical claim was that, while the rules are conventional, they are the optimal rules for a free-market economy, in the sense that following them will assure a return to the talents and efforts of labor in exact proportion to its value.
d. "Natural" can also refer to natural law – higher-law principles above and controlling those of mere positive law. Progressives often accused the Classics of invoking higher law of this sort in judicial review of social legislation. Horwitz considers this charge a Progressive fabrication: the Classics felt constrained by positive law commands, though they thought it appropriate to use natural law principles to fill gaps and resolve conflicts and ambiguities in the positive law.[52] On this point, I think Horwitz has it exactly right.

4. *CLT Is Formalist, But What Exactly Is "Formalism"?*

Formalism is used throughout the book as the main feature of CLT, but it is used in a lot of different ways, and sometimes the differences are very confusing. As I went through the book I found seven (or maybe nine, depending how one counts) different uses. Some of these could be seen as complementary or overlapping uses, diverse facets of a complex portmanteau concept. Others seem – at first glance at least – contradictory. This is a (non-exhaustive) catalogue of the uses of the term in Horwitz's account: Formalism is sometimes (i) what one might call Weberian (or High German) formal rationality, that is, law emptied of all overt non-legal content, a field consisting of strictly juristic categories autonomous from politics, morals, and economics – in short, a self-contained realm of abstract "artificial reason,"[53] wholly indifferent to the probable social consequences of legal decisions.[54] Sometimes it is exactly the opposite, (ii) a legal order committed to enacting a very particular

[51] The most comprehensive account of the leading role in CLT of historical-customary ideas is Stephen Siegel, "Historicism in Late Nineteenth-Century Constitutional Thought," 1990 *Wis. L. Rev.* 1431.

[52] *Transformation II*, *supra* note 1, at 156.

[53] *See, e.g.*, *id.* at 142

[54] *See, e.g.*, *id.* at 17.

substantive view, that of classical liberal views of freedom and political economy; or (iii) a legal order that draws its substance from the bottom up, from gradually evolving social customs.[55] Sometimes its chief defining mark is (iv) conceptualism, the belief that all the specific rules of the legal system may be subsumed under a few headings of very abstract and general concepts such as "free will" or "fault," and then deduced from those concepts (Horwitz calls this "vertical" reasoning); it is also, however, (v) a strong confidence in the power and determinacy of analogical ("horizontal") reasoning from similar cases.[56]

In other places the main formalist idea becomes "categorical thinking," which is really two ideas. On the one hand, the main formalist idea is (vi) a kind of essentialism, the view that legal categories describe natural kinds of things, and that all social phenomena may (with some hard borderline cases) be reliably assigned for legal purposes to one and only one of each kind. On the other hand, it is (vii) formalism in the sense of what Weber called "formal realizability" (and Roscoe Pound derisively labeled "mechanical jurisprudence"), the preference for easy-to-operate "bright-line" rules and objective tests that facilitate certain and predictable (if inevitably somewhat arbitrary) decision-making, in contrast to open-ended particularistic multivariate standards and balancing tests.[57] Elsewhere, formalism represents CLT's commitment to generality in rule-formulation, which may also be subdivided into two somewhat distinct commitments:[58] (1) to generality in the service of neutrality among classes and special interests, that is, to the framing of rules that cut across customary social groupings, treating all parties as abstract A's and B's, and (2) to generality in the service of predictability of results.[59]

Horwitz is hardly alone in the loose pluralism of his account of formalism and, more generally, CLT: late-nineteenth-century American legal thought has proved maddeningly elusive to historians' attempts to chase it down, especially since we are used to seeing it through the eyes of Progressive critics inclined to hostile caricature. Horwitz's multiple and somewhat blurry usages of terms like "natural" and "formalism" may well be more faithful to his sources than clearer and conceptually sharper uses would be. Classical lawyers rarely stopped to ask what exactly they meant by saying rights were "natural," and the Progressive critics of "formalism" likewise were not too troubled by inconsistencies in their critique (formalism was both unduly

[55] *See, e.g., id.* at 121.

[56] *See, e.g., id.* at 155, 202–203.

[57] *See id.* at 17–18, 199–200.

[58] If these additional uses of formalism are added to the previous seven, Horwitz has, in all, nine different uses of formalism. I am not sure, however, whether it is fair to count "generality" as a separate use of formalism, since it may be an inherent attribute of other uses like autonomous-law, conceptualism, and categorical thinking.

[59] *See, e.g., Transformation II, supra* note 1, at 230.

vague and abstract and "mechanical," both removed from politics and the tool of an obsolete political economy, both dependent on abstract and ahistorical principles and tied to a conservative historicism, etc.). But the reader is often left unsure whether what seems like a conflation or confusion of terms is one found in the Classical sources or imposed on them by later critics or the historian himself. It would help us to understand these movements better if we could pick apart their components and then figure out how they were mushed together. Holmes, for example, as Thomas Grey has pointed out, believed strongly in the grouping of doctrines under small numbers of highly abstract categories, as well as rule-formalism or formal realizability. He emphatically did not think that the categories expressed natural essences or that they could determine results in particular cases. Holmes was thus a formalist in some of Horwitz's senses but an anti-formalist in others.[60] Horwitz's view of CLT in fact quite closely tracks the Progressive and Legal Realist accounts of "formalism" – which Horwitz announces from the start, he is trying to challenge.[61] He does challenge the Progressive caricature of CLT as the tool of big business: it was the Progressives who embraced big business, some along with a program to tame it, others happy to let it fulfill its unregulated evolutionary destiny. But Horwitz's description of formalism is basically the Progressive description, and it is, I think, exaggerated in similar ways. American jurists, including even the much-maligned and not very representative Harvard jurists C.C. Langdell and Joseph Beale, never went in for formalism on the High German model of *Pandektenwissenschaft* of the Windscheid variety: the common law is too case-bound for that mode and too dependent upon the individual judge and the concrete precedents. Though not as given to policy analysis and argument as post-Realist thought, even classical opinions and scholarship were suffused with the rhetoric of arguments from convenience and policy.[62] At the same time, I think Horwitz overstates the impact of the Progressive/Realist revolution in legal thought on the prevalence of formalist reasoning as he defines it. True, the impact of Realism on legal scholarship has been deep and pervasive; it outlasted the Legal Process school's retreat to proceduralism in the 1950s, and will probably outlast the many neo-formalist revivals now under way. But judicial reasoning is still primarily doctrinal, categorical, and analogical: judges ask, "Is this a mortgage or a conveyance, a breach of contract or a tort, a gift or

[60] On "formalism" and its multiple meanings, Grey's essays on Langdell and Holmes are especially helpful. Grey, *supra* note 2; Thomas Grey, "Holmes and Legal Pragmatism," 41 *Stan. L. Rev.* 787 (1989). The entire subject could use considerably more analysis. For a valuable, skeptical treatment of the standard uses of "formalism," see Stephen Diamond, "Citizenship, Civilization and Coercion: Justice Holmes on the Tax Power," in *The Legacy Of Oliver Wendell Holmes, Jr.* 115 (Gordon ed.1992).

[61] *Transformation II*, *supra* note 1, at 7.

[62] Some of these are cited in the book. *Id.* at 58. The long quotation from Francis Wharton is a lengthy policy argument against expanded entrepreneurial liability.

a trust?" as if they were matching up the legal category to some natural fact about the world. This is unavoidable, especially in routine practice where "functional" or "purposive" or "consequentialist" policy reasoning of the kind favored by Realists is rare.

I certainly do not mean there is no new law under the sun. Legal reasoning has changed, as one can tell immediately by picking up a law reporter or law review from 1900, or for that matter by reading English law reports or scholarship, which never went through a Realist phase and still largely resemble those from our formalist era. But I do not think any historian has yet found a description that really captures the subtleties of those changes.

5. Political Implications of PLT: Was the Administrative State a Progressive Instrument for Controlling Corporate Power and Redistributing Wealth, or Was It a Captured and Co-opted Instrument of Corporate Power?

This question is, of course, one of the central controversies among modern political scientists, whether they be public choice, "republican," or neo-Marxist theorists, and among historians of the administrative state.[63] Horwitz is as understandably ambivalent about it as most progressive-liberals are. If I read correctly between his lines, he himself reads the history of PLT as a tragic failure of a view of law and regulation that had a chance to further a social-democratic vision, but was tamed and made conservative before that vision was realized. Horwitz also believes that the Realists articulated a potentially profound radical critique of liberal-capitalist legalism, but later retreated in fear of its implications. Sometimes he seems more optimistic, and his account reads as if the Progressive-redistributive vision had really triumphed after all in the New Deal, and only afterwards gone into retreat. Sometimes, however, he adopts the darker, instrumentalist view that the Progressive–New Deal initiatives (and the legal theory that supported them) served large corporate interests from their inception. For example, Horwitz informs us that the Progressive natural-entity conception of the corporation was designed to legitimate the giant firm and to insulate it from regulation.

Progressivism was, of course, all these different things simultaneously, but one wishes Horwitz could have been more explicit about his book's relation to these debates. For instance, he seems to adopt a very Progressive view of the New Deal's administrative agencies, that they really did contain business power. In this mood he is inclined to label critics of the agencies and proponents of heightened judicial scrutiny conservative legalists, reactionary throwbacks

[63] For a small sample of the disputants, see Peter B. Evans *et al.*, *Bringing the State Back In* (1985); Barry D. Karl, *The Uneasy State: The United States from 1915 to 1945* (1983); Gabriel Kolko, *The Triumph of Conservatism* (1963); Theodore Lowi, *The End of Liberalism* (1969); Grant Mcconnell, *Private Power and American Democracy* (1966); George Stigler, *The Citizen and the State: Essays on Regulation* (1975); Cass Sunstein, *After the Rights Revolution* (1990); Thomas K. Mccraw, "Regulation in America: A Review Article," 49 *Bus. Hist. Rev.* 162 (1975).

to CLT.[64] But almost immediately he himself accepts the view that the agencies had become "captured" by the industries they regulated, and that at some point the good guys and bad guys had changed places and judicial review had come to favor liberal causes.[65] The one possibility he doesn't explore is, alas, the most likely one of all: many if not all of the administrative agencies, like the Progressive commissions that preceded them, were (and in some cases were designed to be) "captured" from the start, and as soon as they were created they settled into the familiar triangular alliances between narrow organized-industry interests, their friends in Congress, and the agency staffs. (There were always exceptions – agencies like the early Labor Board and early SEC that, for contingent reasons, were able to assert a relatively autonomous regulatory role.[66]) The industry-orientation of the New Deal agencies was widely noticed at the time[67] and in some ways the wonder is that it took so long for administrative law writers, most of whom had themselves served in those agencies, to notice it too. (The registering of this phenomenon in the group-mind of the Harvard Law School, in the form of Louis Jaffe's articles and the 1960 Landis Report, seems like rather belated notice.[68]) Among political scientists these cozy deals were validated by standard pluralist theory as early as the 1940s and fifties. The understanding here was that administrative officers, like legislators, were just delegates of organized interest-group constituencies, and the resultant compromises were all likely to balance out to something approximating the public interest.[69]

Horwitz's arguments about the political contributions of PLT ultimately remain elusive because – apart from very general references to the legal

[64] See *Transformation II*, *supra* note 1, at 225–240. His main example that signals the retreat to legalism is the adoption of the Administrative Procedure Act, 5 U.S.C. § 551 *et seq*. In the Walter-Logan Act of 1940, conservative lawyers had attempted to hamstring the administrative agencies by forcing them to act through highly formal judicialized procedures. President Roosevelt, on the advice of New Deal administrators attached to the idea that administrative experts should be able to act informally and flexibly, free of internal procedural constraints and judicial review, vetoed Walter-Logan. The two sides compromised in the APA. Horwitz views the compromise as a victory for the conservative-legalist, Walter-Logan forces. *Id.* at 232. This seems exaggerated. The APA only required an agency to use formal procedures in adjudication if Congress specified these in the agency's organic statute. APA rulemaking was presumptively informal, requiring only notice and opportunity for comment.

[65] *Id.* at 240–246.

[66] Actually the problem with the Labor Board was that parts of it, such as the Appeals Division, were exactly like every other administrative agency, biased toward a single constituency. But since the constituency was labor rather than a business group, the bias led to a ferocious Congressional reaction, purge of the Division, and Taft-Hartley. See James A. Gross, *The Reshaping of the National Labor Relations Board* (1981).

[67] *See, e.g.*, Pendleton Herring, *Public Administration and the Public Interest* (1936).

[68] *See Transformation II*, *supra* note 1, at 238–241.

[69] *See* James A. Morone, *The Democratic Wish: Popular Participation and the Limits of American Government* 136 (1990).

system's potential to "redistribute property," "regulate" corporations, promote "social justice," and protect the civil liberties of dissenters – he does not spell out in any detail the Progressive legal thinkers' substantive views, the social agenda that (he believes) their backsliding and compromises in the post-New Deal period left unrealized. Did his Progressives ever mean more by "redistribution" (for example) than a mildly progressive income tax, compulsory unemployment and social insurance schemes, a more generous and efficient accident and workers' compensation system, a broadening of defenses to contract enforcement, recognition of labor unions' rights to organize and bargain collectively, and some enhanced regulatory supervision of corporate structures, public utility rates, and financial markets? If so, what was it? If not, what was left unrealized?[70]

6. *Political Implications of PLT: Progressive and Realist Social Science*

On another aspect of PLT, Horwitz is more openly ambivalent. Some of it, like Robert Hale's and Jerome Frank's work, he thinks was genuinely reformist. Other Realist work, however, he describes as having slipped into sterile technocratic positivism, into the program of trying to derive social-engineering solutions from "value-free" empiricism and of closing the gap between legal conceptions and social practices by readjusting the law to conform to customary practices – a program that was unable to locate values anywhere but in the status quo.[71] In these passages, I think Horwitz occasionally confuses intellectual with political radicalism. The theoretical aspect of Realism he most admires is what (using Peter Novick's term[72]) he calls its "cognitive relativism," its "interpretive or hermeneutic" understanding of the "socially constructed character of frames of reference, categories of thought, and legitimating concepts."[73] The specific Realist project he most admires, as I do, was the work demolishing the Classical categories, breaking the link between rights and remedies, disintegrating the concept of property, trashing the public–private distinction and the presumptions that state action was normally "coercive" and market relations normally "free," and above all, recognizing that the capitalist economy has a socially contingent constitution that is neither natural nor necessary, but alterable by deliberate collective action ("policy choices"). That set of Realist insights was politically reformist in context because it dug away the foundations of a mode of legal thought that had become – though in its

[70] I do not mean to suggest these were trivial ambitions; they were important reforms that required much struggle over a long period to get past the strenuous resistance, intellectual as well as political, of conservative elites. But *Transformation II* often implies that PLT at its height had a more radical agenda, without saying what it might have been.

[71] *Transformation II, supra* note 1, at 208–212.

[72] Peter Novick, *That Noble Dream: The "Objectivity" Question and the American Historical Profession* 288–291 (1988).

[73] *Transformation II, supra* note 1, at 182.

egalitarian antimonopolist origins it had hardly started out that way – the bulwark of an apologetic ideology. But one can recognize that capitalist societies have a constructed and contingent legal constitution without actually wanting to change that constitution very much, or believing that it is politically feasible to change it more than a tiny bit – and few Realists went in for any very radical politics. Thurman Arnold (who curiously appears only once in Horwitz's gallery of Realists) produced some of the wittiest and most devastating critiques ever written of the rhetoric of laissez-faire capitalism.[74] But as chief trustbuster to the New Deal he pursued a cautious, efficiency-based policy, aggressive in the volume of cases brought, but in theory not much different from previous anti-trust enforcement regimes.[75]

On the other hand, some of the Realists' "positivist" social science – to which I think Horwitz is anachronistically unsympathetic – was really illuminating and surprising in its findings, and reformist in its conclusions. It was anything but passively accepting of the status quo.[76] A series of court studies pioneered by Charles Clark made starkly clear to anyone who was willing to listen that trial courts were not tribunals that declared rights and obligations, but factories for routine processing of uncontested debt-collection claims on the civil side and plea-bargains on the criminal. This was all news at the time to the bar elites – indeed news so unwelcome that they refused to believe it.[77] Felix Frankfurter and Nathan Greene's study of labor injunctions revealed the astonishingly prevalent use and sweeping scope of this tactic of labor-capital warfare.[78] Friedrich Kessler's work on adhesion contracts and vertical franchising arrangements was the empirical prop to his theory that the modern capitalist economy was characterized by quasi-"feudal" hierarchies that required legal controls on the overlords and a redistribution of rights in favor of the vassals.[79] And of course Berle and Means's famous work on changes in corporate structure was primarily an empirical study of shareholder diffusion and managerial concentration.[80]

These are just a few among many such studies of the period. Far from normativizing the grubby status quo that it uncovers, this work is often concerned to make the critical point that the law "in action" is not applied uniformly, but in ways that favor the wealthy and powerful. Other Realist empirical work assisted the critical project of undermining CLT, as some of Horwitz's own

[74] Thurman Arnold, *The Folklore of Capitalism* (1938).

[75] See Alan Brinkley, "The New Deal and the Idea of the State," in *The Rise and Fall of the New Deal Order* 85, 89–92 (Fraser & Gerstle eds. 1989).

[76] More sympathetic treatments are in the leading histories of Realist science. *See* Kalman, *supra* note 2; Schlegel, *supra* note 2.

[77] For the court studies and their reception, see Schlegel, *supra* note 2, at 495–519.

[78] Felix Frankfurter & Nathan Greene, *The Labor Injunction* (1930).

[79] Friedrich Kessler, "Contracts of Adhesion: Some Thoughts about Freedom of Contract," 43 *Colum. L. Rev.* 629 (1943).

[80] Adolf A. Berle, Jr. & Gardiner Means, *The Modern Corporation and Private Property* (1933).

examples show: the descriptive sociology of Hale and Jaffe, whose examples of law-in-action – the exercise of law-making authority by private groups – helped make problematic the Classical public–private distinction.[81] In other words, despite its deplorably primitive theoretical bases, its naive functionalism and behaviorism, a good deal of Realist social science is, in context, both interesting and subversive. In this respect it is more a precursor of the modern critical law-and-society movement (which I am sad to see Horwitz leave out of his taxonomy of modern legal thought) than of law and economics. Realist social science in general is a useful reminder of how much science in the Progressive era was assumed not to be value-free in any strict sense, but – because of its ability to continually revise and unsettle complacently accepted and established truths – an instrument in the cause of democratic reform.[82]

There is an interesting parallel and contrast between Horwitz's treatments of CLT and PLT. Both are movements that claimed to be republican movements in the general public interest; both have been criticized as masks for corporate privilege – the first using common and constitutional law as its instrument, the second using legislation and administration. Horwitz by and large accepts the Progressive critique of the Classics, except on the matter of the contractarian theory of the firm. On the other hand, he takes the republican claims of Progressive/Realists at face value (except for their scientism) until the post-New Deal period. These judgments may be on balance fair, if one looks at the political uses actually made of the two legal theories. But the book could emphasize more than it does the bright side of CLT (utopian, republican, and general public interest serving) and the dark side of Progressive/Realism.

III. CONCLUSION

The dialectic between Horwitz's grand Idea and the honesty of his historical detail results in a book of Protean elusiveness: just as you think you have the thesis pinned down, it twists away from you and turns into something else. But this very elusiveness turns out to be remarkably suggestive. Horwitz's subversive subthemes, by rendering his story much more complex than he wants it to be, succeed in making it almost as complex as it probably ought to be.[83]

81 Robert L. Hale, "Law-Making by Unofficial Minorities," 20 *Colum. L. Rev.* 451 (1920); Louis Jaffe, Law-Making by Private Groups, 51 *Harv. L. Rev.* 201 (1937).

82 *See* James Kloppenberg, *Uncertain Victory: Social Democracy and Progressivism in European and American Thought, 1870–1920*, at 319–320, 383–384, 406–407 (1986).

83 Horwitz's aversion to overt complexity – and his preference for the bold assertion and sweeping thesis – are, I suspect, the products of rebellion against his own formative intellectual context: the (very similar) 1950s schools of Legal Process in jurisprudence, "consensus" American historiography, and "end-of-ideology" political theory. These schools all promoted irony, complexity, ambiguity, and tragic resignation to the limits on human capacities to remake societies through deliberate collective action as the necessary antidotes to the sweeping "ideological" commitments that had led to "totalitarianism." This social vision – and the deep political complacency it often induced – is especially well described in Novick, *supra* note 72, at 281–360.

I predict for this book the not unenviable fate of being received like its legendary predecessor, *Transformation I*. It will inspire many to praise and provoke others to furious attempts to refute everything it says. It will supply the questions that must be debated and prod another generation of scholars into evaluating its arguments. From now on anyone who wants to understand this period will have to start with Horwitz and come to grips with his thesis. It will be, as the last book was, seminal: both of new corn and dragon's teeth.

7

Method and Politics: Morton Horwitz on Lawyers' Uses of History

[*This was a contribution to a Symposium on the occasion of Morton Horwitz's retirement as the Charles Warren Professor of American Legal History at Harvard Law School. The Symposium was published in a two-volume edition of its proceedings edited by Daniel Hamilton and Al Brophy as* Transformations in Legal History (*Harvard University Press, 2010*).]

As the many contributions to this Festschrift testify, one of the many achievements of Morton Horwitz's extraordinary career as a legal historian is his deep and pervasive influence on others. As one of his first students, I have absorbed that influence in many ways, among them through Horwitz's essays on legal historiography, or more precisely on lawyers' and legal scholars' uses and abuses of history. These are less well known and cited than his famous *Transformation* books, but they are a substantial and very interesting part of his work. In them we perceive the outlines of a theory, or at least a loose assemblage of views, of connections between historiographical method and politics, of the ways in which lawyers' approaches to the past tend to support political stances – usually conservative but sometimes also reformist. And through his reflections on error, on the ways in which lawyers misuse history, we catch a glimpse of Horwitz's view of the positive uses of history.

By my count there are four major essays in the series.

1. "THE CONSERVATIVE TRADITION IN THE WRITING OF AMERICAN LEGAL HISTORY"

The first is a 1973 review essay: "The Conservative Tradition in the Writing of American Legal History."[1] This is a straightforwardly polemical piece, and

[1] Morton J. Horwitz, "The Conservative Tradition in the Writing of American Legal History," *American Journal of Legal History* 17 (1973): 275–294. The books under review are James McClellan, *Joseph Story and the American Constitution* (Norman: University of Oklahoma

partly for that reason a lot of fun to read. It is also instructive, as it announces many of what will become the major themes of Horwitz's later work. The basic message is simple: history in the hands of lawyers tends to be politically conservative, in several respects:

- It emphasizes continuity in the making of law – either the gradual emergence of modern law by a Burkean process of slow organic change or the consistent adherence through changing social conditions to a core of principle, or both.
- It pretends that law, correctly applied and understood, is autonomous from politics and political ideologies and influences: either an apolitical distillation of tradition or an apolitical science of reason, or both simultaneously. Though uncontaminated by immediate political influences, conservative lawyers' law has an implicit normative content, the characteristically American incongruous and unstable blend of natural law fundamentalism and classical economic liberalism: "Thomistic natural law ... reworked into a glorification of financial and industrial capitalism."[2]
- It is contemptuous of democratic and popular influences on lawmaking and glorifies elite professional judgment and technical skill, especially the learned professional judgment of a "taught tradition." Specifically, it elevates university-trained lawyers in restricted professional guilds over the Jacksonian open profession, legal "science" over commonsense judgment, and judicial – common-law and constitutional – lawmaking over legislating. It suggests that judges properly educated in the common-law tradition and constitutional principle will decide cases correctly, uninfluenced by popular politics and prejudices, and will thus serve as a salutary check on such politics and prejudices.

Horwitz's major critique of the conservative historical tradition is of its politics: it is antidemocratic, and by obscuring the realities of political conflict, class conflict, and distributional conflict in general with a myth of apolitical legal tradition and reason, it tends to rationalize the advantages of the wealthy and powerful. It also confuses mastery of technical legal learning – such as pleading rules and the outlandishly complex English system of estates in land – with superior wisdom and statecraft.

He also believes that the "conservative tradition" produces bad history. It misunderstands the nature of legal change in much the same ways as Thomas Kuhn said that orthodox scientific history misunderstands scientific change – by treating legal change is if it were the product of internal reasoning – the result of professionals applying the same principles and methods consistently

Press, 1971), and Gerald T. Dunne, *Justice Joseph Story and the Rise of the Supreme Court* (New York: Simon & Schuster, 1971).

[2] Ibid., 292.

over time and revising them in the light of new factual discoveries and (in the case of lawyers) changing circumstances. Both scientists' and lawyers' history "emphasize continuity in history in order to make present methods and forms of inquiry appear universal. Both use history to demonstrate that existing categories of thought are historically necessary and not contingent. Both, in short, use history to justify and glorify the present."[3]

Finally, Horwitz argues that conservative historians such as James McClellan (the author of the biography of Story under review) cannot resolve the inherent tension between their contradictory accounts of legal conservatism. Is it founded on unchanging fundamental principles of natural law and/or organic Burkean tradition, or does it promote the legal foundations for a dynamic capitalism? (Horwitz does not put the question quite this way, but I think it is fairly implied from his essay.) The classical jurists of the late nineteenth century (and some strenuous legal libertarians of the present day) liked to argue that there was no contradiction, because basic natural law principles of liberty and property are also the foundations of free markets. But Horwitz thinks the principles are indeed contradictory and embodied in Story's own thought:

> the tension between older principles of simple republican virtue and newer principles of economic expansionism; the strain between an earlier conception of law as the embodiment of morality and an emerging positivist and instrumental view of law based on expediency and ruthless efficiency; a conflict between a traditional view of property as an important element in preserving human autonomy and republican virtue and a later stage of worship of property which accepted it as an instrument of power and domination; a tension between protection of property as necessary for economic growth and a willingness to allow older forms of property to be destroyed with impunity in the interest of economic growth.[4]

Readers of Horwitz's *Transformation of American Law, 1780–1860* (1977) will recognize all the main themes of the book in the quoted paragraph. In *Transformation I*, of course, Horwitz argued that early nineteenth-century lawyers and judges abandoned their commitment to republican virtue to serve masters of commercial and corporate wealth, their commitment to fair and equal exchange to enforce whatever hard bargains superior market power could extract, and their commitment to absolute property rights to promote entrepreneurs' creative destruction of property. Their instrumental, policy-driven views of law recruited law to an economic purpose. But – the story continued – in the late nineteenth century, leading jurists began again to cultivate a view of law as autonomous from politics and policy. This new legal formalism, however, also served an economic purpose, that of insulating the gains that had been realized with the help of legal instrumentalism in an earlier era from populist and labor pressures to redistribute it.

[3] Ibid., 283.

[4] Ibid., 292

In *Transformation I*, in short, Horwitz identified two distinct ways in which dominant legal theories helped leading lawyers rationalize advantages of the wealthy and powerful.

2. PROGRESSIVE LEGAL HISTORIOGRAPHY

In 1984 Horwitz published a lecture, "Progressive Legal Historiography,"[5] that signaled an important revision of his views. This lecture is a disparaging treatment of the Progressive tradition in constitutional historiography, which originated among critics of the Supreme Court around the 1920s and to a large extent continues to dominate constitutional law textbooks and opinions to the present day. Horwitz's critique of Progressive history is somewhat surprising to those who recall his treatment of legal formalism in *Transformation I.* He takes the Progressives to task here for picturing classical legal thought as a mask and apologia for concentrated corporate power, and their own Progressive jurisprudence as an escape from laissez-faire. Horwitz follows revisionist historians (such as Charles McCurdy and Alan Jones) in seeing in the classical lawyers the heirs of the Jacksonian and Free-Soil ideals of equal rights, "free labor," and the competition of smallholders in free markets: they are hostile to corporate concentration and political-economic oligarchy, especially the control of governments by railroads and the "trusts." Their Progressive critics, by contrast, favored corporate consolidation and promoted symbiotic corporate-government alliances. Legal formalism in this view favored the formal equality of individuals and saw concentrated corporate power as the enemy of such equality. The jurisprudence supporting Progressive-corporatist policies was no longer categorical reasoning, but "balancing." Instead of law autonomous from particular interest groups, the Progressives would use law to balance group interests. So in this piece, classical formalist law – which in *Transformation I* had served the function of allowing the beneficiaries of instrumentalist policies of economic growth to preserve their accumulations from redistribution – was intended as a check on corporate power. Horwitz concludes: "In attempting to reconsider Progressive constitutional historiography we need also to consider its attack on legal orthodoxy. By subverting the late-nineteenth-century orthodox claim to legal autonomy – to the independence of law from social conflict – the Progressives may have neutralized one of the most important sources of a critical perspective on American society. There seem to be too few around today."[6]

This lecture presaged Horwitz's full-scale revisionist treatment of classical formalist views of corporate law in *The Transformation of American Law,*

[5] Morton J. Horwitz, "Progressive Legal Historiography," *Oregon Law Review* 63 (1984): 679–687.
[6] Ibid., 687.

1870–1960: The Crisis of Legal Orthodoxy (1992). There he distinguishes between "Old Conservatives" – judges like Cooley, Field, and Miller, who saw the emerging corporate behemoths as threats to individualistic competition – and New Conservatives, who treated corporations as if they were unthreatening individuals themselves, entities, or group persons.

3. THE CONSTITUTION OF CHANGE: LEGAL FUNDAMENTALITY WITHOUT FUNDAMENTALISM

Horwitz's thinking on constitutional lawyers' uses of history continued to evolve. It was given full reconsideration in his great *Harvard Law Review* foreword of 1993 on "The Constitution of Change: Legal Fundamentality without Fundamentalism."[7]

His main argument here is that constitutional "fundamentalism" – the notion that constitutional law is timeless and unchanging, expressed in such theories as those of static textualism or originalism – expresses a pre-modern vision that has somehow survived despite the "destabilizing force of modernism."[8] Constitutional theory that accepted the "modernist insight that meanings are fluid and historically changing"[9] would have to be some form of "living Constitutionalism," acknowledging that legal meanings shift with changes in social context and understandings. The doctrinal product of the justices' historical fundamentalism tends to be a sterile, formal legal science – the proliferation of purportedly neutral abstract categories, bright-line tests, and highly technical distinctions.

The heart of this foreword is a brilliant analysis of the joint opinion in *Planned Parenthood* v. *Casey*,[10] where the justices in the Court's majority who decided not to overrule *Roe* v. *Wade* explain why, in contrast, it *was* proper for the Court to overrule *Plessy* v. *Ferguson* and *Lochner* v. *New York*. It may seem odd that Horwitz would choose, as his principal text to illustrate the Supreme Court's commitment to static views of constitutional meaning, an opinion that justifies overruling prior cases. He explains that the joint opinion's justifications are carefully and narrowly fashioned so as to pose the minimum possible challenge to theories of static meaning.

The joint opinion achieves this by asserting that both cases were simply mistakes – that is, decided on mistaken views of facts. The *Plessy* Court assumed – because the justices simply didn't understand? – that blacks were in fact not stigmatized by compelled segregation in public places, whereas by 1954, as the *Brown* v. *Board of Education* Court recognized, it was clear that

[7] Morton J. Horwitz, "Foreword: The Constitution of Change: Legal Fundamentality without Fundamentalism," *Harvard Law Review* 107 (1993): 30–117.

[8] Ibid., 32.

[9] Ibid., 116.

[10] *Planned Parenthood of Southeast Pa.* v. *Casey*, 505 U.S. 833 (1992).

they were. The *Lochner* Court mistakenly believed that free markets invariably worked; by the time of the Depression, it was clear they did not. The factual assumptions behind the cases having been invalidated, the cases embodying them were properly overruled.[11]

[11] The passage is worth quoting at length:

> In the meantime, the Depression had come and, with it, the lesson that seemed unmistakable to most people by 1937, that the interpretation of contractual freedom protected in *Adkins* rested on fundamentally false factual assumptions about the capacity of a relatively unregulated market to satisfy minimal levels of human welfare. See *West Coast Hotel Co., supra*, at 399. As Justice Jackson wrote of the constitutional crisis of 1937 shortly before he came on the bench: "The older world of *laissez faire* was recognized everywhere outside the Court to be dead." *The Struggle for Judicial Supremacy* 85 (1941). The facts upon which the earlier case had premised a constitutional resolution of social controversy had proven to be untrue, and history's demonstration of their untruth not only justified but required the new choice of constitutional principle that *West Coast Hotel* announced. Of course, it was true that the Court lost something by its misperception, or its lack of prescience, and the Court-packing crisis only magnified the loss; but the clear demonstration that the facts of economic life were different from those previously assumed warranted the repudiation of the old law.
>
> The second comparison that twentieth-century history invites is with the cases employing the separate-but-equal rule for applying the Fourteenth Amendment's equal protection guarantee. They began with *Plessy* v. *Ferguson*, 163 U.S. 537, 41 L. Ed. 256, 16 S. Ct. 1138 (1896), holding that legislatively mandated racial segregation in public transportation works no denial of equal protection, rejecting the argument that racial separation enforced by the legal machinery of American society treats the black race as inferior. The *Plessy* Court considered "the underlying fallacy of the plaintiff's argument to consist in the assumption that the enforced separation of the two races stamps the colored race with a badge of inferiority. If this be so, it is not by reason of anything found in the act, but solely because the colored race chooses to put that construction upon it." *Id.*, at 551. Whether, as a matter of historical fact, the Justices in the *Plessy* majority believed this or not, see *id.*, at 557, 562 (Harlan, J., dissenting), this understanding of the implication of segregation was the stated justification for the Court's opinion. But this understanding of the facts and the rule it was stated to justify were repudiated in *Brown* v. *Board of Education*, 347 U.S. 483, 98 L. Ed. 873, 74 S. Ct. 686 (1954) *(Brown I)*. As one commentator observed, the question before the Court in *Brown* was "whether discrimination inheres in that segregation which is imposed by law in the twentieth century in certain specific states in the American Union. And that question has meaning and can find an answer only on the ground of history and of common knowledge about the facts of life in the times and places aforesaid." Black, The Lawfulness of the Segregation Decisions, 69 Yale L. J. 421, 427 (1960).
>
> The Court in *Brown* addressed these facts of life by observing that whatever may have been the understanding in *Plessy's* time of the power of segregation to stigmatize those who were segregated with a "badge of inferiority," it was clear by 1954 that legally sanctioned segregation had just such an effect, to the point that racially separate public educational facilities were deemed inherently unequal. 347 U.S. at 494–495. Society's understanding of the facts upon which a constitutional ruling was sought in 1954 was thus fundamentally different from the basis claimed for the decision in 1896. While we think *Plessy* was wrong the day it was decided, see *Plessy, supra*, at 552–564 (Harlan, J., dissenting), we must also recognize that the *Plessy* Court's explanation for its decision was so clearly at odds with the facts apparent to the Court in 1954 that the decision to reexamine *Plessy* was on this ground alone not only justified but required.
>
> *West Coast Hotel* and *Brown* each rested on facts, or an understanding of facts, changed from those which furnished the claimed justifications for the earlier constitutional resolutions.

Now as Horwitz says, this is a very bizarre way of understanding constitutional change, as correction of factual error – especially as with respect to both cases the justices cheat considerably by sliding from mistaken facts to changed "social understandings of facts." Horwitz explains these moves, convincingly, as moves to avoid any contact with dynamic constitutionalism, the notion that the U.S. Constitution must change as not only circumstances but social understandings change, in order to uphold a decontextualized, depoliticized, dehistoricized Constitution. The view of *Plessy* as mistaken the day it was decided, in particular, is motivated by the need to isolate that case from the whole course of Reconstruction precedent, to avoid having to condemn the entire jurisprudence as infected by a now officially repudiated assumption about racial inferiority and a desire to narrow the scope of the Reconstruction amendments' promise of equality. "If Plessy was 'wrong the day it was decided,' it was not because the Supreme Court had failed to inform itself about the 'facts' that underlay racial segregation or because the Court was unaware of the social meaning of Jim Crow laws, but rather because almost from the moment the Civil War ended, the Court's decisions constituted betrayal of the 'one pervading purpose' ... of the Civil War Amendments."[12]

Horwitz is, if anything, rather restrained in his critique. The notion that the prior decisions rested on factual mistakes is ludicrous. Both reflected assumptions utterly pervasive among governing classes of the time. *Plessy* reflected a consensus that legal blacks were equal to whites only in their "civil" rights, which were carefully defined to exclude merely "social" rights of association in public accommodations and schools. Such social rights were beyond the scope of the Fourteenth Amendment to enforce. One might, I suppose, argue that these views in turn rested on the undeniably mistaken "factual" assumptions that blacks are inherently inferior to whites or pose a dangerous sexual threat to them. But when such assumptions are widely shared in the majority opinions of entire generations, it is hard to label them simply errors, errors though they may be. Similarly, the *Lochner* decision hardly rested on the "mistake" that unregulated markets invariably maximized human welfare, a mistake only exposed by the Great Depression. The *Lochner* Court majority had managed to live through severe depressions in 1873 and 1893 without realizing the mistake. They would not in any case have used the term *welfare*,

> Each case was comprehensible as the Court's response to facts that the country could understand, or had come to understand already, but which the Court of an earlier day, as its own declarations disclosed, had not been able to perceive. As the decisions were thus comprehensible they were also defensible, not merely as the victories of one doctrinal school over another by dint of numbers (victories though they were), but as applications of constitutional principle to facts as they had not been seen by the Court before. In constitutional adjudication as elsewhere in life, changed circumstances may impose new obligations, and the thoughtful part of the Nation could accept each decision to overrule a prior case as a response to the Court's constitutional duty. (*Casey* at 861–864)

[12] Horwitz, "Foreword," 88.

which connotes economic efficiency; what they believed was that the contracts made by free men in free markets maximized their liberty, and – in a system that returned rewards to free laborers equivalent to the talent, skill, work, thrift, and foresight that they brought to it – were the test of their moral characters. Minimum-wage or maximum-hours regulation fetters free choice with paternalistic controls, distorts the system of rewards to virtue, and corrupts character. That set of beliefs could not have been falsified by the Great Depression, and it is of course still held among libertarians and some evangelicals.

Horwitz's foreword expands the frame around these examples to provide a bravura history of the uses of history in constitutional thought and adjudication. Briefly and crudely, it goes like this. The seventeenth-century lawyers like Edward Coke were static originalists, appealing to an ancient unchanging constitution. Matthew Hale and others discovered a dynamic evolving common law, but the early American founders preferred to rest constitutions on an unchanging fundamental law, like Jefferson's imagined law of the Anglo-Saxons before the Norman Yoke. This static originalism remained the dominant mode of constitutional interpretation through the nineteenth century and came to serve as a support for elite lawyers' bolstering of judicial review as a weapon against democratic leveling. The notion of a dynamic living constitution was a construct of the Progressives, who used it to try to emancipate the Constitution from natural law fundamentalism. The high points were Brandeis's briefs and opinions and the Supreme Court's decision in *Home Building & Loan Association* v. *Blaisdell*.[13] Cardozo's draft opinion in this case asserted the world had changed so as to outdate many of the framers' assumptions, and that if they had the benefit of later experience, they would see the Constitution had to change too; and Chief Justice Hughes's opinion for the Court argued that the Constitution must change to preserve its essential spirit.

Soon afterward, however, the post–New Deal Supreme Court reverted to originalism, the fiction that the New Deal had just continued the nationalizing program of the Marshall Court, and turned to a new source of legitimacy, democracy – which in the nineteenth century had carried negative connotations for elite lawyers.

The current conservative turn back toward static originalism, Horwitz argues, is a move to protect the idea of unchanging fundamental law as a basis of legitimacy from modernism – the assumption of the contingency and context dependence of all ideas. Loosely supported by its associations with scriptural literalism, originalism supplies a spurious objectivity to legal reasoning. As Horwitz truly says, this originalism does not proceed from a conservative Burkean respect for the past or regard for prudential experience, much less for traditional ideals: "There is hardly a trace of wisdom concerning the meaning

[13] 290 U.S. 398 (1934).

of the American past or the possibilities of its future to be found in the opinions of the current Court."[14] The past is ransacked as a source of abstract rules – rules preferably without reasons or purposes – to direct the present.

The irony is that while ritually condemning *Lochner*, the Court has now returned to Lochnerian formalism, if that is viewed not as laissez-faire ideology disguised as natural law, but as neutral abstraction: for example, to an ideal of content neutrality in First Amendment cases, and color-blindness in race cases. As with *Lochner*, the effect is to mask inequalities of power: *Lochner* assumed equality of bargaining power; color-blindness assumes equality of racial advantage, so that state attempts to promote life chances of subordinate groups are just as bad as those to promote dominant groups; the new First Amendment assumes equality of access to money, as if unrestricted political speech took place on a level playing field.

Interestingly, Horwitz adds that a formalist jurisprudence of neutral categories rapidly becomes a complex technical jurisprudence, as formal subcategories of exceptions proliferate to deal with exceptional cases; and legal argument, wholly divorced from substance or purpose, becomes all about to which categories lawyers should assign a set of facts.

This is all remarkably stimulating stuff. I would question some elements of the argument, especially perhaps the history of lawyers' theories of history. Coke's ancient constitutionalism had plenty of dynamic rivals in his own time, well before Hale.[15] In any case, Coke's ancient constitutionalism, as Coke himself was well aware, was a spurious originalism adopted for tactical forensic purposes – as originalism almost invariably is, after all – in the service of a dynamic and modernizing agenda. Coke simply invented and projected back in time the historical traditions he was inclined to follow, just as Justice Scalia does (most recently in the *Heller* opinion on gun control, in which Scalia located the historical precedents most useful to his exposition of a traditional right to guns for self-defense in the home not in the Founding era, but in the nineteenth century[16]). The founders similarly used the language of restoration but in the service of a modernizing cause, the shedding of feudal excrescences and the progress of republican liberty. They completed the conversion of the common law from a crabbed science of pleading and property to a reservoir

[14] Horwitz, "Foreword," 98.

[15] See generally Richard J. Ross, "The Memorial Culture of Early Modern English Lawyers: Memory as Keyword, Shelter and Identity, 1560–1640," *Yale Journal of Law & Humanities* 10 (1998): 229–236, at 255 (after describing many conflicting accounts of immemorial law): "The common lawyers, then, did not embrace the ancient constitution and the myth of their immemorial law as a shared historical account or political strategy so much as participate in a disputation about them, having taught the terms of the conversation to the political nation. The common lawyers were specialists in weaving immemorial lineages out of the threads of legal records and in tearing them apart. Their skill in the process rather than their commitment to a conclusion set them apart as constitutional remembrancers."

[16] 128 S. Ct. 2783, at 2805–2813 (2008).

of public law maxims. I would take particular issue with Horwitz's claim that democracy as a legitimating element of constitutionalism was a post–New Deal invention. In the United States, despite the grumblings of high Federalists about the swinish multitudes and the need for judges to control populist excesses, judicial authority in the early republic was firmly founded on democratic theory.[17] Judges were considered agents of "the people themselves," as Larry Kramer's work emphasizes; at the state level, of course, most of them were elected and, as Jed Shugerman has shown, drew the legitimacy and authority they asserted in exercising the power of judicial review from their election.[18] I would also argue that classical or formalist jurisprudence rested as much on dynamic evolutionary views of law such as those of Cooley, Pomeroy, Dillon, and Carter as on unchanging natural law, and probably more so: freedom of contract was what we had been evolving toward, not what we had to recover from the all-too-mercantilist Founding era.[19]

I also tend to think that Horwitz in this essay draws too tight a set of connections between legal theories and political tendencies. (I'm reviving here an old dispute within critical legal studies: one side asserts that any legal argument can be turned on its head [flipped] to justify the exactly opposite position; the other – Horwitz's side – argues that in any given period, a legal theory tends to favor, or tilt toward, a particular set of political positions.) One can use natural law and even static originalist arguments ad hoc for liberal purposes, and dynamic arguments for conservative ones (the new First Amendment doctrine might be a case of the latter).

In the final essay considered here, Horwitz clarifies that the links between legal theory or method and politics are themselves highly contextual, so that it commonly happens that a method that is liberating or even radical may, a generation later, have become apologia.

4. WHY IS ANGLO-AMERICAN JURISPRUDENCE UNHISTORICAL?

Our last exhibit is "Why Is Anglo-American Jurisprudence Unhistorical?" a remarkably interesting and, I believe, almost unknown article first delivered as the H. L. A. Hart Lecture at Oxford in 1995.[20] Although Horwitz asks the question about English analytical jurisprudence specifically, he also asks it about English common and constitutional law generally. He notes the irony that England, the nation of empiricism and the common law, has an analytic

[17] See generally Larry Kramer, *The People Themselves: Popular Constitutionalism and Judicial Review* (New York: Oxford University Press, 2004).

[18] See Jed Shugerman, "The People's Courts" (unpublished manuscript).

[19] See generally Stephen Siegel, "Historicism in Late Nineteenth-Century Constitutional Thought," *Wisconsin Law Review* 1990: 1431–1548 (1990).

[20] Morton J. Horwitz, "Why Is Anglo-American Jurisprudence Unhistorical?" *Oxford Journal of Legal Studies* 17 (1997): 551–586.

method that is resolutely anti-historical, that screens out history and context to produce an autonomous neutral apolitical mode of legal discourse. By this time it will surprise no one to learn that Horwitz thinks this separation from history serves an ideological function: legal theory avoids historicism, as it avoids hermeneutics, to avoid recognition of the destabilizing insight of "cognitive relativism" that the meanings of words and ideas shift with changing contexts, that meanings are always multiple, not single, and that the quest for stable legal meanings is a chimera. Note that this time Horwitz describes the threat of historicism as meaning proliferation rather than explicitly political. But politics, it is clear, is not far from his mind.

Horwitz then takes his audience on a tour through the modern history of the embrace and rejection of history by legal theorists. Bentham sought to free law from history because in his time legal history meant Blackstone's conservative history of law as evolving custom, used to mystify and justify the status quo. (Horwitz leaves out of his story the progressive legal-historical narratives of the Scottish Enlightenment thinkers, Smith, Hume, and Kames.) In Bentham's time abstraction was the friend of middle-class reformers like himself, anxious to use Parliament to expand the suffrage. After the passage of the Reform Bill of 1832, reformers found a progressive historical narrative of a living and evolving constitution to support their cause of transforming parliamentary sovereignty into popular sovereignty. Now it was the turn of conservatives, led by John Austin, to blunt the reformist edge of utilitarianism – to depoliticize law in the wake of universal suffrage. Rapidly, however, the story undergoes another twist: Henry Maine emerges as a penetrating critic of the ahistorical nature of Austin's analytic jurisprudence. By his time, however, attention to history is meant once more to slow and contain democratic tendencies.

The key figure, in Horwitz's account, responsible for dehistoricizing the study of modern law in England is A. V. Dicey. Dicey wants to distinguish between the legal and political – again, Horwitz suggests, for a political motive – to make the "legal" constitution controlled by lawyers and judges, consisting of a procedural code or bill of rights, a constraint on popular rule, just as it was in the United States. Dicey announces that popular sovereignty controls parliamentary sovereignty, but "like the constitutional thought of the American Federalists, Dicey invokes popular sovereignty in order to restrain it."[21] Dicey explicitly calls for marginalization of history from the study of law. Some of his reasons, Horwitz concedes, are good ones: much constitutional historiography is, for the modern lawyer's purposes, antiquarian and irrelevant. But Dicey uses this excuse to banish all history to the margins. Why? Dicey says that by attending to accounts of how current legal arrangements came to be, people may misunderstand what they actually now are. Horwitz believes that Dicey was trying to suppress controversy about how things are by suppressing

[21] Ibid., 571.

historical accounts that might suggest multiple interpretations. Dicey wanted to expel history from the law curriculum by sending it over to historians and professors of international law. Constitutional law is only law for lawyers with respect to judicially enforceable norms – distinct, therefore, from political constitutional conventions, matters of "high statesmanship" that most of the time cannot and will not be litigated. He admits that lawyers do have somewhat to attend to these conventions (of the unwritten living constitution) because they constrain the courts as well, sometimes even more than statutes do. Yet (he seems to say) to attend too much and too closely to shifting convention would open law to instability. Horwitz says Dicey here mapped out the road to H. L. A. Hart's rule of recognition and the resulting end point of a resolutely ahistorical analytic jurisprudence.[22]

In candor, I don't know quite what to make of Horwitz's concluding section on Hart in this essay. His explanation of Hart's aversion to history, and that of the school of analytic jurisprudence that he revived, takes account of so many factors that it becomes hard to sort out which are the important ones and what their relation is to the larger background narrative of English jurists' uses of history. He gives much significance here to biography:[23] Hart's desire to escape his Jewish origins and his social democratic politics. It was in part Hart's dislike of religion that led him to wish to separate law from custom and law from morality. It was in part his left-wing politics that led him to wish to separate law from history, understood as recognition of unwritten evolving constitutional conventions. During the constitutional crisis of 1931, the young social democrat Hart would, Horwitz thinks, have been revolted by the use of "unwritten constitution" to deprive Labor of the full fruits of its electoral victory. These explanations seem rather ad hoc, especially since some of them could equally well explain opposite conclusions. By the 1940s, one might think, a left-wing social democrat might be quite attracted to a triumphalist story of the unwritten constitution and general progress of society toward the democratic welfare state. Whig history, by then, would seem to lead not toward Blackstonian complacency but toward Clement Atlee, Ernest Bevan, and Lord Beveridge. The reader is left thinking that the undeniably distinct inclinations of British jurists toward analytic and positivist jurisprudence require more general explanations. I would be tempted to locate these in the affinity of such modes of jurisprudence to the formal court-bound modes of teaching ordinary legal subjects, which in turn have resulted from the subordination of British law schools to the profession

[22] Dicey's influence actually seems to me a better explanation for the ahistoricism of English *constitutional law* than of English analytical jurisprudence.

[23] Since Horwitz wrote, these factors have been brilliantly and movingly illuminated in Nicola Lacey, *A Life of H. L. A. Hart: The Nightmare and the Noble Dream* (New York: Oxford University Press, 2004).

and the bench.[24] Law teaching and study have been closely tied to internal professional culture.[25]

CONCLUDING NOTE

One comes away from these essays impressed with their grand sweep and moral passion. This is ambitious, provocative work, bold splashes on a big canvas, with many brilliant points of detail. The world of legal thought depicted here is rather dark. Somehow it seems that no matter how lawyers and judges and jurists use history, whether they embrace the historicity of law or deny it, they usually do so in the service of the powerful. If they admit historical narratives, it is usually to validate the status quo as immemorial tradition or founders' originalism or as the product of gradual perfection of the Constitution or the laws. If they exclude or marginalize history by abstracting away from it or insist that law develops by internal processes autonomous from social context, they usually do so to promote a formalism that masks and rationalizes substantive unfairness and inequality. If they take an instrumental view of law as simply a tool of policy, they use it (as in Horwitz's account of early nineteenth-century judges) to promote a predatory capitalist program of development or (as in his account of the twentieth-century Progressives) to legitimate corporate concentrations of wealth and power.

When E. P. Thompson, in his famous conclusion to *Whigs and Hunters*,[26] suggested that ruling classes, in order to legitimate their rule, build relatively autonomous legal systems that constrain even the rulers themselves, and that these constraints, known as the rule of law, constitute an historical achievement that is "an unqualified human good," Horwitz accepted the description of the ideological process but rejected the praise of the outcome.

> Unless we are prepared to succumb to Hobbesian pessimism "in this dangerous century," I do not see how a Man of the Left can describe the rule of law as "an unqualified human good"! It undoubtedly restrains power, but it also prevents power's benevolent exercise. It creates formal equality – a not inconsiderable virtue – but it promotes substantive inequality by creating a consciousness that radically separates law from politics, means from ends, processes from outcomes. By promoting procedural justice it enables the shrewd, the calculating, and the wealthy to manipulate its forms to their own advantage. And it ratifies and legitimates an adversarial, competitive, and atomistic conception of human relations.[27]

[24] See generally David Sugarman, "The Legal Boundaries of Liberty: Dicey, Liberalism and Legal Science," *Modern Law Review* 46 (1983): 102–111.

[25] One would also expect legal philosophers to be attracted to modes of philosophy dominant elsewhere in university culture: in England, especially at Oxford, analytic philosophy; in America in the 1920s and 1930s, pragmatism.

[26] E. P. Thompson, *Whigs and Hunters: The Origin of the Black Act* (London: Allen Lane, 1975).

[27] Morton J. Horwitz, "The Rule of Law: An Unqualified Human Good?" *Yale Law Journal* 86 (1977): 561–571, at 566.

At first glance it seems that Horwitz is calling Thompson a credulous Pollyanna, all too willing to accept claims of autonomy on their own terms, while Horwitz himself takes a darker and more cynical view of law and its purported autonomy. But look how the paragraph begins – with a *rejection* of "Hobbesian pessimism" and the view that law is nothing but the tool of power. Surely here and elsewhere he is suggesting some hopeful routes out of the dismal history of law's deployment in the service of the powerful. Sometimes he seems to say that the way out is through interpretive multiplicity, that the insights of modernism make it possible to proliferate interpretations of law beyond those that legal establishments try to freeze as canonical, and that rebellious social actors and movements and their lawyers can seize upon and exploit those alternative interpretations.

But he also hints at a much larger normative project: that of how to reconcile the idea of fundamental law, in the sense of basic normative guiding principles of substantive justice, with the modernist insight that meanings are fluid and historically changing. Is there some eventual prospect of uniting in the same person the two Mort Horwitzes – Mort the skeptic, who sees all law as suffused with the ephemeral zeitgeist and the pressures of politics and the Rule of Law as the slogan of the powerful to justify their power and disguise it as neutral principle, and Mort the earnest questing legal idealist, still searching for the beacon of natural fundamental law in the caves of this lamentably fallen world? That is definitely something to look forward to.

8

E. P. Thompson's Legacies

[*This short essay appeared in a Symposium organized by the Georgetown Law Review to memorialize E. P. Thompson after his death in August, 1993. 82* Georgetown Law Review *2005 (1994). Thompson did not see himself as a "legal" historian, but was one of the first to recognize that both official law and popular law and custom pervasively structured social relationships, and he exerted a powerful influence on American as well as British social-legal historiography.*]

Edward Thompson was by common agreement the greatest English-speaking social historian of his age, the presiding genius of an entire generation of historians of the 1960s and after who determined to write history "from the bottom up," through the eyes of people who had been crushed under the wheels of history, especially the wheels of economic "progress." It was Thompson more than anyone else who rescued the lower orders from "the enormous condescension of posterity,"[1] from their reputation as a dumb, illiterate, and violence-prone mob – Burke's "swinish multitude," or less pejoratively but almost as anonymously, Marx and Engels' faceless, mutely suffering "proletariat" – and who showed the New Social Historians how to perform patient, exhaustive archival excavations; whose work gradually revealed a whole underground world of articulate, thoughtful laboring men and women, architects of their own consciousness, active agents who well understood and fiercely resisted the catastrophic changes that were carelessly sweeping them onto history's scrapheap. It was Thompson whose slashing and passionate, while surprisingly precise and delicate, narrative style could make any reader feel – and resolved many to act on the feeling – that writing social history to recruit the understanding of past struggles to present-day social understanding and political action was one of the most important things one could do with one's life.

[1] Edward P. Thompson, *The Making of the English Working Class* 12 (1963).

Thompson's masterpiece, *The Making of the English Working Class*, first appeared in 1963. Reading it through again is like resuming a very old friendship, which intervening time and experience have only improved. The prose is as fresh as ever; the English artisans, laborers, and peasants of 1790–1830 are made as real and immediate as any present-day social movements. All over again one experiences, through Thompson's power of sympathetic recreation, his admiration for their irreverent wit and courage, and his scorn and indignation for the landowners, employers, and magistrates who harassed them endlessly and ultimately wore them out.

Yet at this later re-reading still other qualities, which I was not really equipped to appreciate the first time around, emerge from Thompson's work. One such quality is Thompson's sheer amazing craftsmanship as historian, shown in the hundreds of thousands of scraps of notes from local archives and obscure sources that he gathered and wove into narratives both coherent and grippingly dramatic; in his refusal to be confined by discipline or specialty and his ability to draw freely upon economic, legal, intellectual, political, and social perspectives; in his complete mastery of high and popular cultures reflected in the scraps of poetry, belles-lettres, ballads, and political songs scattered like jewels over every page; and in the intense but restrained (and, for so engaged a writer, remarkably judicious) critical scrutiny that he repeatedly brought to bear on technical and historiographical quarrels. Thompson wore his learning lightly; he almost never (save when exposing an opponent as an ignorant twit) showed off how hard he had been working, what deep quarries of research and theoretical synthesis lay just out of sight, behind his monumental art.

On this re-reading, yet another facet of Thompson's work – one of special interest to this readership of lawyers and legal scholars – also becomes more visible: his extremely sophisticated understanding of the many social roles of law. Like other social critics schooled in Marxist traditions of history and theory, Thompson was well aware of the instrumental functions of law as a bag of weapons and tricks for the rich and powerful to use against the poor. In the period of his special interest, such instrumental uses of law could hardly have been ignored, since they were everywhere: the criminalization of customs, whereby exercises of ancient right such as grazing or deer-taking in common fields and forests were curbed by enclosure; the death penalty; the Combination Acts passed to break up working-men's associations; and the great wave of repressive statutes and prosecutions of "Jacobin" societies and organizations for sedition and riot in England during its early nineteenth-century Red Scare.[2] Thompson's period of interest provided numberless examples of the cynical manipulation and deployment of law by a ruling elite to maintain its

[2] *See generally id.* at Chs. 4, 5. 14, 15; Edward P. Thompson, *Whigs and Hunters: The Origin of the Black Act* (1975).

privileges and to shatter the leadership, morale, and cohesion of working-class organizations.

Thompson, however, never succumbed to a crudely instrumentalist view of law, or to the dismissal of law altogether as expressing merely "bourgeois rights." As always, he drew insight from the radical traditions he admired, and in those traditions law appears in many forms besides class trickery and repression. Law appears, most importantly, as customary right. The claims of easement, or of use-rights such as gleaning, grazing, and taking of fish and deer, made by cottagers, villagers, and tenants upon farmer and gentry landowners were, of course, legal claims – claims to rights of property, not in defiance of property.[3] The claims made by defendants at trials for sedition and riot, for free speech and assembly, free press, fair procedure, and trial by jury were legal claims as well, claims to the rights of "free-born Englishmen" that every radical asserted as his heritage. The eighteenth-century crowd resorted to riot, more often than not, as a carefully regulated remedy aimed at restoring a status-quo-ante after some violation of legal right that regular legal institutions would not or could not redress. Undoubtedly Thompson's famous, spirited defense in *Whigs and Hunters*[4] of the "Rule of Law" as an "unqualified human good" and permanently valuable legacy of Western culture, despite all the long history of law's abuse by rulers and the wealthy for their own ends, draws upon this rich tradition of legalism in English radical dissent.

Seeing law in every corner of social life, Thompson never made the mistake of supposing law was only epiphenomenal, a mere rationalizing ideology or "superstructure" erected on the "real," "material" bases of social life such as technology, relations of production, market structures, or power relations. Law was a crucial element in the constitution of markets and relations of power and of production:

> I found that law did not keep politely to a "level" but was at every bloody level; it was imbricated within the mode of production and productive relations themselves (as property-rights, definitions of agrarian practice) and it was simultaneously present in the philosophy of Locke; it intruded brusquely within alien categories, reappearing bewigged and gowned in the guise of ideology; it danced a cotillion with religion, moralising over the theater of Tyburn; it was an arena of politics and politics was one of its arms; it was an academic discipline, subjected to the rigour of its own autonomous logic; it contributed to the definition of self-identity both of rulers and of ruled; above all, it afforded an arena for class struggle, within which alternative notions of law were fought out.[5]

[3] *See* Edward P. Thompson, "Custom, Law and Common Right," in *Customs in Common* 97 (1991).

[4] *Whigs and Hunters*, *supra* note 2 at 258–269.

[5] Edward P. Thompson, *The Poverty of Theory and Other Essays* 96 (1978).

Still another aspect of Thompson's work that I better understand now is also one of Thompson's most valuable qualities for present-day use – a quality that might be called humanistic concreteness, or particularism. Thompson never wrote a page of history that was not exceptionally dense in detail, in the proper names of persons and places, customs and trades, numbers and events, and quotations from participants. Sometimes he mocked his own habit: "[D]oes it matter a damn who gave Parson Power his instructions; which forms brought 'Vulcan' Gates to the gallows; or how an obscure Richmond publican managed to evade a death sentence…?"[6] The answer, as he well knew, is that it does matter, for (as usual) a complex variety of reasons. One reason was simply fidelity to his project and materials: he was writing about and taking the side of people who were defending against erosion their intensely particular trades, intensely local customs. Not just their livings, but also their dignity and identity, their sense of the right and moral, were all bundled up in these particularities. To understand their situation the historian has to recreate their world in the details that mattered to them – especially because as progress swept them away they mattered not at all to anyone else. One cannot represent men and women as agents unless one can make the reader understand them as real, and reality resides in the details. Thompson learned this lesson from the great Radical polemicists of the period he made his own, especially William Cobbett.[7] Thompson's radicalism, like that of the other great lettered English radicals such as Cobbett, William Morris, R.H. Tawney, or George Orwell, was entirely and doggedly English. Without being chauvinistic or intellectually provincial, Thompson sought to elaborate the distinctness, the local and decentralized nature, the "peculiarities" of English dissent both as factors explaining England's special history and as sources of values worth preserving.

In this celebration of the particular there is concealed, it seems to me, an important and quite general message. Virtually everything Thompson wrote consists as part of a running argument against a kind of reductionist abstraction-mongering, which Thompson truly loathed and believed to be dangerously anti-human wherever it was adopted and applied.[8] In the early-industrial period of his main historical interest, this noxious form of intellectual practice was mainly represented by classical political economy and utilitarian theory and policy; in his own time, by the modern version of the

[6] *Whigs and Hunters*, *supra* note 2 at 260.

[7] For Thompson's tribute to Cobbett, see *The Making of the English Working Class*, supra note 1, at 746–752. Though Thompson's style resembles Cobbett's in its attachment to particularity and proper names, it is actually quite different from Cobbett's, much more ironic, cosmopolitan, and allusive, and in fact more like that of the essayist William Hazlitt, whom Thompson admired as well.

[8] See, e.g., *The Making of The English Working Class*, *supra* note 1, at 267–268, 776–779 (nineteenth-century utilitarians and political economists); *The Poverty of Theory and Other Essays*, *supra* note 5, at 140, 153, 168 (Stalinism and scientism); "The Moral Economy Reviewed," in *Customs in Common*, *supra* note 3, at 259, 303–305 (modern economists).

same things – neo-liberal political economy – but also by functionalist sociology and structuralist Marxism.

The Making of the English Working Class is, among other things, a sustained polemic against impersonal models of "industrialization," "modernization," or "capitalist development," especially the complacent ones like those of F. A. Hayek, T. S. Ashton, R. M. Hartwell, and their school.[9] These writers argued that although the natural workings of markets in the Industrial Revolution may have temporarily displaced a few marginal occupations like cottagers and technologically obsolete craftsmen, "free markets" had also produced a generally higher standard of living for everyone. Thompson set out to refute this smug cost–benefit analysis. The main technique he used was the method of detail – disaggregation of gross statistical claims, of large and lazy economic generalities. He asked, who exactly were the people displaced, how many of them actually were there, and – above all – how did they experience their displacement? He insisted on describing human welfare in non-reductive terms – not just as money incomes, but as independence, dignity, autonomy, and pride in craft. He peered closely at the "natural workings of market forces" and exposed the pervasive coercion behind them – the manipulation of law to reassign property from ancient rights to entrepreneurial uses; the recruitment of tort, trespass, and criminal law to defeat customary practices; the massive repression of political dissent and labor combinations. And indeed Thompson's case is overwhelming that, seen through the eyes of the men and women who lived through them, the Industrial Revolution and the political counter-revolution that accompanied it were nothing short of catastrophic. Thompson was often accused of being a "romantic," of sentimentalizing obsolete and preindustrial forms of community. It is certainly true that he saw value in the lives his subjects had assembled around their customs and trades, and irrecoverable losses – losses not easily valued in a cost–benefit accounting and usually not attempted to be valued at all – in the disappearance of those customs and trades. Though formally a socialist, he was at bottom a Romantic radical in sensibility; he despised both Stalinism and bureaucratic capitalism for their crushing of human personality, especially the eccentric, cantankerous, combative, and lyrical fighting spirit of the sort of radicalism he himself personified.

But to think of Thompson exclusively in this way – for example, as someone who preferred to depict reality with the personal stories of underdogs rather than with abstract models of impersonal processes – is to marginalize him unduly and greatly to underrate his importance as a social thinker. Thompson was a better social analyst, most of the time, than his reductionist opponents because he was a more accurate observer and more hard-headed theorist. He did not disdain economic theory and statistical indices; he used them in his own work, but broke them down, critiqued them, and refined them. He did

[9] See *Capitalism and the Historians* (Hayek ed., 1954).

not suppose that the emphasis he gave to agency in his histories denied the existence or importance of processes or structures. Indeed, one of his persistent criticisms of the New Leftists of 1968 was of their utopian voluntarism, their notion that the world can always spontaneously be remade if you only will it hard enough. But he thought that both economists and structuralist Marxists persistently misdescribed those processes because they were too lazy, or blinded by ideology, to look at them in detail.

Economists, for example, repeatedly asserted that successful forms of capitalist development require markets constituted by fixed and stable legally defined rights of property, and illustrated this proposition with historical examples of societies in which, they contended, such rights had emerged (such as early-modern England). Thompson, sometimes patiently and sometimes not, would respond that there was never anything very fixed about the rights pointed to; that they were a version of rights favored by some courts and social groupings but not others; that they existed in conflict with well-established claims of competing rights; that in any case they were constantly being fought over and renegotiated with every shift in the balance of economic and social power; and that we could not begin to understand property rights until we also understood the webs of local custom, religion, magic, and politics in which they were embedded. Moreover, the webs of customary practice were not just reactionary drags on free markets; but were often highly functional in their own way. For instance, the moral economy of the English crowd in Thompson's classic essay of that title,[10] using law, custom, and calibrated rioting to regulate the price and supply of staple commodities, represented a functional system for preventing famine in times of dearth.[11]

It is heartening to see, in recent economic theorizing and historiography among other places, some tendencies even in the reductionist disciplines to begin to recognize the importance of custom, culture, moral norms, path-dependent institutional forms, religious and family ties, and other solidarities in the formation and enforcement of legal claims and the constitution of markets – in short, to see social science working its long, slow, painful way back to the insights E. P. Thompson had already achieved in 1963. Social-legal historians, who like everyone else familiar with Thompson's work, could hardly avoid being inspired by it, have profitably lived off those insights for some time.[12] But

[10] "The Moral Economy of the English Crowd in the Eighteenth Century," in *Customs In Common*, *supra* note 3, at 185–258.

[11] In a fascinating reply to critics of his thesis on *The Moral Economy of the English Crowd*, Thompson enriched the thesis by comparisons to similar moral economies at work elsewhere in the world, especially in India. See "The Moral Economy Reviewed," *supra* note 8, at 259–351.

[12] Among the legal historians who have seemingly been strongly influenced by Thompson, one thinks of William Forbath, Douglas Hay, Hendrik Hartog, Morton Horwitz, Alfred Konefsky, Elizabeth Mensch, William Novak, Carol Rose, Richard Ross, David Sugarman, and Christopher Tomlins.

now more than ever the terrible simplifiers are roaming the globe, prescribing "shock therapies" for economic stagnation in post-Communist societies and the Third World in the form of "fixed and stable property rights," "privatization," and "free markets." Evidently, they lack the faintest knowledge of the political, legal, and cultural contingencies in which such institutions developed even in the Western capitalist economies – not to mention the human wreckage such development often entailed – and certainly without the slightest reflection on the indigenous political and cultural contexts of their new experiments. More than ever, therefore, social thinkers and social activists, perhaps especially legal thinkers and activists, will have need of Thompson's patient attention to detail, his polemical talent for attacking ideological abstractions and his analytic talent for picking them apart, his engaged sympathy with the men and women whom structural changes leave flattened in their path, and his sharp, disciplined moral indignation. These are his legacies: to strive to imitate his methods, in the service of his ideals of social decency and the most exacting standards of craft, is the best tribute we could pay him.

9

The Constitution of Liberal Order at the Troubled Beginnings of the Modern State*

[*This essay began as a contribution to a Symposium at the University of Miami Law School, March 21–22, 2003, organized to honor Professor Owen Fiss of Yale Law School. The piece uses Fiss's history of the U.S. Supreme Court under Chief Justice Melville Weston Fuller (1888–1910) as a vehicle to explore the legal order of the era and to question whether that order deserves the privileged status it enjoys in modern conservative legal thought. The essay as it appears here is slightly revised from the version originally published in 58* U. Miami L. Rev. *373 (2003)*.]

Many modern conservative politicians, public intellectuals, and lawyers now look back to (what is now generally called) the "classical era" of American law and society – roughly 1880–1930 – with admiring eyes, as a model for the regime of legal-economic and legal-social order they hope to revive. The two main wings of the New Right, economic-libertarians and cultural-conservatives, for obvious reasons look to different facets of classical order. Free-market libertarians admire the "*Lochner* era" for its judicial enforcement of restraints on government regulation of economic bargaining and on progressive redistribution of income. Their program is to dismantle the regulatory-welfare programs and bureaucracies of the Progressive, New Deal and Great Society governments, and to confine the state's role to the protection of property, the enforcement of contracts (with only very narrow defenses) and the supply of a short list of public goods, notably defense. Other New Right intellectuals admire the authoritarian social control of that period, by both state and civil society, of immorality and deviant behavior. They want to undo the cultural and sexual revolutions of the 1960s; the liberalization of divorce; the Warren Court decisions protecting obscenity as free speech and abortion as privacy; the misguidedly soft-hearted

* Thanks to Jules Coleman, Stephen Diamond, Owen Fiss, Alvin Klevorick, Jonathan Simon, and Peter Schuck for helpful comments.

and weak-minded indulgence of the poor with welfare entitlements, minorities with antidiscrimination and affirmative-action laws, and criminals and persons in custody with overscrupulous procedural protections.

The programs of the two wings in some respect overlap: both are hostile to welfare (economic conservatives because it distorts incentives to work and redistributes wealth, social conservatives because it corrupts morals and leads to idleness and promiscuity) and to the "liberal elites" they believe have dominated universities, the media and most governments (economic conservatives because liberals oppose unregulated capitalism, social conservatives because liberals pollute the culture with libertine and secular-humanist values). But these two wings are really very different parties, representing constituencies from very different social and regional backgrounds; and their major programs seem mostly incompatible with one another. Economic conservatives and libertarians resist the intrusion of the heavy hand of authoritarian law into individual free choice in morals and religion as well as in markets. Social conservatives decry a crisis of immorality, but the hero of market society is after all the creative destroyer of tradition, the amoral rational-maximizing entrepreneur. The Ten Commandments say we are not to covet our neighbors' goods, but coveting, or competitive consumption, is what drives the market system. Next only to war, there is nothing more destructive to family ties and traditional communities, customs and values, than global capitalism. Hollywood and TV don't produce all those images of sex, violence, and shallow consumerism that cultural conservatives hate so much because they are liberals out to poison American values, but because those images are what sells.

Notwithstanding these apparently irreconcilable differences, the two wings of the New Right are often able to ally effectively in political coalitions. What enables them to do so is of course largely that they jointly seek political power, don't usually care all that much about the other wing's main issues, and are in battle with common enemies on the left. But their solidarity is also given ideological comfort by shared traditionalist nostalgia for a past order that seems to synthesize the conflicting elements, freedom of contract ideology and social authoritarianism, in their unstable alliance of convenience. Prime Minister Margaret Thatcher nicely evoked this harmonious past when she described the aim of her radically new form of "conservatism" as the restoration of "Victorian values."[1]

1 The English cultural historian Stefan Collini has tartly remarked, "[T]he whole ideological construction of 'Victorian values' was formed in reaction to some equally hypostasized notion of the 'permissive society' of the 1960s and 1970s…[A] crucial element in this emotional dynamic of this reaction was the sense that people – other people, of course – might be getting things they didn't 'deserve', whether it was money or sex. Since it seems pretty clear that in Britain allusions to 'Victorian values' have actually been refracted through memories of lower-middle class childhoods between the wars, what they essentially express is a mean-minded petty-bourgeois *ressentiment* that anyone – anyone else, of course – might get something for nothing." "Victorian Values: From the Clapham Sect to the Clapham Omnibus," in *English Pasts: Essays in History and Culture* (1999) 103, at 107.

For indeed in the classical era judges and lawyers perceived no contradiction in their support for mostly unregulated free bargaining in the economic sphere and for authoritarian paternalism in the social sphere. State-coerced order was not opposed to economic liberty, but a precondition of it (much as, before the Civil War, the enslavement of black persons was a precondition of the liberty of whites). One of the best places to go for an informed and illuminating constitutional history of that period is the volume contributed by Owen Fiss to the *Holmes Devise History of the Supreme Court: Troubled Beginnings of the Modern State, 1888–1910*.[2] This book is not as well known as it should be. It is one of the most important of a series of recent reassessments of the high "classical" period of American public law.[3] The Fuller Court decided among other cases *Lochner*, *Plessy*, *In re Debs*, *Danbury Hatters*, *Adair*, *E.C. Knight*, and the *Insular* and *Chinese Exclusion Cases*, a notable list of "negative examples," as Fiss calls them. His job as he saw it was to historicize those cases, to reconstruct as faithfully as scholarly care makes possible and as sympathetically as the generous spirit and aroused conscience of an Owen Fiss could allow, the mentality of the judges who decided and the lawyers who argued them, and the age that found their reasoning plausible. The result is a Baryshnikov of a book – lithe, muscular and elegant, with moments of acrobatic virtuosity. Only an exceptionally good historian could have maneuvered his mind so closely alongside the categories and assumptions of the opinions; and only an exceptionally good lawyer could have traced their reasoning with such analytic precision.

There are many riches in this book; but my main interest on this occasion is in its largest generalizations, its account of the social vision or conceptual scheme that underlies the cases – its account of a particular version of "liberty" as the fundamental commitment of the Fuller Court. This was, Fiss tells us, a commitment not to anarchy or license, to allowing people to do anything they like, but rather to "ordered liberty" in the "social contract" tradition.

[2] 1993: Volume 8 in the *Holmes Devise History of the Supreme Court of the United States* [hereafter TB].

[3] See, e.g., Charles W. McCurdy, "Justice Field and the Jurisprudence of Government-Business Relations: Some Parameters of Laissez-Faire Constitutionalism," 1863–1897, 61 *J. Am. Hist.* 970 (1975), Michael Les Benedict, "Laissez-Faire and Liberty: A Reevaluation of the Meaning and Origins of Laissez-Faire Constitutionalism," 3 *Law & Hist. Rev.* 293 (1985), Duncan Kennedy, "Towards an Historical Understanding of Legal Consciousness: The Case of Classical Legal Thought in America, 1850–1940," 3 *Res. in Law & Social Theory* 3 (1980); Stephen A. Siegel, "Lochner Era Jurisprudence and the American Constitutional Tradition, 70 *N.C. L. Rev.* 1 (1991), Howard Gillman, *The Constitution Besieged: The Rise and Demise of Lochner Era Police Powers Jurisprudence* (1993), Morton J. Horwitz, *The Transformation of American Law, 1780–1860* (1977), Herbert Hovenkamp, "The Political Economy of Substantive Due Process," 40 *Stan. L. Rev.* 379 (1988); Melvin I. Urofsky, "State Courts and Protective Legislation During the Progressive Era: A Reevaluation," 72 *J. Am. Hist* 63 (1985), Edward A. Purcell Jr., *Litigation and Inequality* (1992); Willliam M. Wiecek, *The Lost World of Classical Legal Thought: Law and Ideology in America, 1886–1937* (1998).

This tradition distinguishes the "social" from the "political," that is, the private from the public. The "social" realm includes "all those activities of individuals that are connected to their happiness or well-being." The "political" sphere is the state.

> The implication is that even without a state, people can achieve a measure of happiness through the pursuit of self-interest and the formation of exchange relationships. As a result the market, growing from the social realm, is treated as the basic ordering mechanism of society and the state as a derivative or supplemental institution. The state is an artificial creation, not part of the social order nor responsible for it. The state is an instrument, created to serve certain discrete ends that exist prior to and independent of it. Its duty is to facilitate exchange in the social realm by protecting property rights, among others, and to bring to an end those activities – for example, outbursts of violence or fraud – that prevent individuals from engaging in exchange or otherwise fully realizing their own ends.[4]

The danger was that the "apparatus of the state might be seized by groups who wished to use it for the purpose of altering or transforming the social order, for example by interfering with exchange relationships or by taking the wealth of some and giving it to others."[5] Against this danger stood the idea of the Constitution as embodying the basic terms of the social contract limiting state authority, enforced by judges. *Lochner* v. *N.Y.*[6], *Adair* v. *U.S.*[7] and, in a somewhat indirect fashion, *Pollock* v. *Farmer's Loan & Trust*[8] (the *Income Tax Case*) are the paradigmatic illustrations. *Lochner* is a decision about "constitutive authority," which Fiss distinguishes from "organic authority," authority in the "social" sphere, such as a parent holds over a child. "[C]onstitutive authority does not arise naturally nor is it intrinsic to some ongoing relationship. Like that of a club or voluntary association, it is artificially created to serve discrete ends." As such it is bound both by general external restraints such as principles of morality, but also by internal restraints, arising from "the very reason for which that authority is created...Such limits require that every exercise of [constitutive authority] be justified in terms of the ends for which that power was created."[9] The exercise of state police power, for instance, was viewed as legitimately serving four discrete ends – health, safety, welfare and morals – and was constitutionally required to economize on, or as we would now say, "narrowly tailor," its means to those ends.

Sometimes Fiss frames the "liberty" protected by enforcing constitutional limits on constitutive authority simply as "the space or area left to the individual after the reasons for the creation of state power were exhausted. Liberty of

4 TB at 47.
5 TB at 48.
6 198 U.S. 45 (1905).
7 208 U.S. 161 (1908).
8 157 U.S. 429 (1895).
9 TB at 158–159.

contract was what remained to the individual after the state reached the outer bounds of its authority."[10] But then he realizes that this account of liberty as residual space is not quite adequate, to the extent it implies that the legal system is indifferent to what people do in that space, that the courts shrug their shoulders and say "Whatever turns you on." On the contrary, the courts meant to valorize, indeed to preserve as a semi-sacred sphere of action, exercises of liberty with a particular content, "the freedom of the parties [in the social sphere] to bargain – a freedom that was seen as the central dynamic of the market and of the social contract tradition"[11] – that is, entrepreneurial liberty, the rights to contract, choose one's calling, manage and invest one's property, and trade one's property and labor on such terms as one could negotiate.

> Contractarianism was devoted to liberty as the end of all social arrangements and identified the state both as a necessary tool to secure the enjoyment of liberty and the principal threat to it. Individuals, it was assumed, would justly order their economic and social relationships through exchange; the state would be needed to enforce those bargains and create the proper conditions of exchange. Legislative majorities might sometimes seek to assign the state more ambitious undertakings, but under the terms of the social contract, fixed once and for all, that option was not available.[12]

I note in passing that this new formulation of the contractarian position gives a rather larger role than Fiss's first version to the state as a "necessary tool" in the operations of the social sphere – the "artificial" has suddenly been inserted into the very constitution of the "natural" – and I will come back to this point. But for now, let me affirm that Fiss thoroughly makes the case for the Fuller Court's commitment to the primacy of liberty. It is all the more striking, therefore, that his book should largely be a record of what, from a modern libertarian's perspective, looks like a cornucopia of illiberal and often starkly repressive actions, most of them blessed, and some even initiated, by the same judicial guardians of liberty. And these actions of the Supreme Court that Fiss records are only fragments of a far-flung archipelago of illiberal state policies around the turn of the century, nearly all of them approved, cheered on, or at least let pass in silence, by orthodox classical liberal courts.

In re Debs,[13] to start with, is of course one of thousands of cases in which courts wielded injunctions to restrain the liberty, as labor saw it, of trade unions to act collectively through strikes, pickets and boycotts to improve their bargaining position to negotiate wages and working conditions. The Court also generally allowed, and indeed cheered on, legislation violating the core premises of entrepreneurial liberty and equal treatment, where the class "protected" by statutory exclusion from the professions and other

[10] TB at 159; see also TB at 357.
[11] TB at 164.
[12] TB at 164.
[13] 158 U.S. 564 (1895).

occupations and limits on hours of work was women rather than men.[14] In the *Insular Cases,*[15] the Court ratified (albeit over vigorous dissents) the exclusion of inhabitants of territories from Constitutional protections of their liberties[16]; in the *Chinese Exclusion* cases, it did the same for Chinese immigrants, allowing the government the unconstrained discretion to expel them at will.[17] In *Plessy* v. *Ferguson,*[18] the Court validated Jim Crow's statutes mandating the expulsion of blacks from spaces in public accommodations reserved for whites, thus enforcing the racial caste hierarchies of the South.[19] In *Mugler* v. *Kansas* (decided just before Fiss's period begins), the Court upheld the authority of states to seize the property of distillers and destroy their businesses, without compensation.[20] In *Turner* v. *Williams,*[21] the Court allowed the government to deport an alien for holding the views of a philosophical anarchist[22]; and in *Patterson* v. *Colorado*[23] allowed state judges to punish for criminal contempt a publisher who had criticized their court[24]: in both cases, the Court casually brushed aside the First Amendment claims of the defendants. In the last case discussed in Fiss's book, *Hodges* v. *U.S.*,[25] the Court is seen declaring the federal government powerless to protect black workers seeking to exercise their fundamental liberty to contract for their labor, against violent white gangs.[26]

Fiss sees some of these cases as consistent with the Court's commitment to contractarian liberty, others more like a betrayal. Of the *Insular Cases* he says "Here all sense of [contractual] limits is gone and the relation of state to subject seems more organic than contractual."[27] But he is careful to demonstrate how in the Court's mind all these decisions *could* have been rationalized to fit into the overall scheme of contractual liberty.

The nationwide Pullman strike of railroad workers led by Eugene Debs represented to the judges a direct coercive interference with the property of employers, their liberty to hire and fire, and with the liberty of non-union workers to contract for their work. But even more basically, it threatened the basic conditions of public peace and order upon which all social relations

[14] TB 176–179.
[15] *Downes* v. *Bidwell,* 182 U.S. 244 (1901); *Hawaii* v. *Mankichi,* 190 U.S. 197 (1903); *Dorr* v. *United States,* 195 U.S. 138 (1904); *Balzac* v. *Porto Rico,* 258 U.S. 298 (1922).
[16] TB 225–226.
[17] TB 298–311.
[18] 163 U.S. 537 (1896).
[19] TB 352–356.
[20] 123 U.S. 623 (1887).
[21] 194 U.S. 279 (1904).
[22] TB 331–339.
[23] 205 U.S. 454 (1907).
[24] TB 340–348.
[25] 203 U.S. 1 (1906)
[26] TB 379–385.
[27] TB at 295.

including market relations were built – so much so that the federal courts felt an imperative of general order-preservation in the public welfare to bypass (potentially nullifying) jury trials and to issue injunctions. Similarly *Turner*, which validated exclusion of anarchists, was broadly justified as an exercise of governmental power to suppress speech with a "bad tendency," the risk however remote of some damage to public order.

The cases dealing with state regulation of women, aliens, and territorials, on the other hand, involved disenfranchised groups, not "members of the constitutional community" and not therefore entitled to liberty and equal treatment as full *sui juris* citizens. Disenfranchisement was not only "a reason for being more tolerant of exercises of state power purportedly on behalf of this group, allowing the state to pursue ends otherwise denied it,"[28] but also a justification for exclusionary or oppressive treatment. Women and children in particular were wards of the state and thus the proper subject of protective or paternal legislation. Groups in the *Insular* and *Chinese Exclusion*[29] cases were not citizens at all, and thus fair game for discriminatory state action.

Plessy v. *Ferguson*, on the other hand, compelled the segregation of a group that had been admitted to full citizenship, African-Americans. But the case was nonetheless an easy one for the Fuller Court judges and most of their contemporaries, who readily found a police-power justification for separating the races in preserving peace and good order, as well as tracking customary usages. Only Justice John Marshall Harlan dissented, on the *Lochner*-like grounds that compelled segregation was redistributive class legislation in favor of whites. Kansas's uncompensated taking of Mugler's brewery's property was justified as a health, safety *and* morals measure, a prophylactic against the "idleness, pauperism and crime" traceable to the evil of alcohol. *Hodges*, on the other hand, though it concerned white gangs violating the core liberties of blacks, fit into the system of court-enforced contractual limits on federal power, once the Court had decided (in the *Civil Rights Cases*) that blacks had no right to federal protection against private action, and for protection of their rights must "take their chances with other citizens in the states where they should make their homes."[30]

To save space I won't multiply Fiss's examples, but as you see their cumulative effect is to leave us with a much more complicated picture than the social-contract system of liberty-protected-by-judicially-enforced-limits-on-constituted-authority that begins his book. Instead of a rather small and limited state, making occasional darting forays into the natural social realm, under

[28] TB at 177.

[29] *Chae Chan Ping* v. *United States*, 130 U.S. 581 (1889) (The Chinese Exclusion Case); *Chew Heong* v. *United States*, 112 U.S. 536 (1884); *United States* v. *Jung Ah Lung*, 124 U.S. 621 (1888); *Fong Yue Ting* v. *United States*, *Wong Quan* v. *United States*, *Fong Yue Ting* v. *United States*, 149 U.S. 698 (1893).

[30] *Hodges* v. *U.S.* 203 U.S. 1, 18–20 (1906).

the watchful eyes of courts of keen to keep the state within its limits, we have a rather pervasive and powerful array of state functions and corresponding actions. The state is not simply stirring a few extra artificial ingredients into an already functioning organic social sphere, but helping to constitute the social sphere – by enforcing property and contract rights, providing the basic conditions of public order underwriting the safety and continued existence of society, and repelling threats to both the appropriate operation of the social sphere and to the foundational order beneath it. Alongside the "social realm" of freely contracting individuals, moreover, the law recognizes a special realm of persons of less than full legal capacity, subject to a much more intrusive range of paternalist and protective state action. And with respect to total outsiders all bets are off, none of the regular limits applies, since they are strangers in the land.

This revised scheme gives us I think a fuller and more accurate picture of late-nineteenth-century conceptions of the role of the courts in enforcing the social contract. But I'd like to suggest it still seriously understates the role that law had come to be assigned in maintaining what Fiss calls the realm of the "social." In my view the "relation of state to subject" had come, to use Fiss's own terms, to be thoroughly "organic"; and – notwithstanding the increasingly activist and notorious enforcement by constitutional courts of some limits on state powers and functions – the use of the state and law to maintain, and defend against threats to, organic social order to be increasingly frequent, intrusive, and not generally subject to much if any constitutional limitation.

Fiss attributes to his judges a paramount concern with promoting and protecting the proper operation of the social realm of property, exchange and free labor, in which all (*sui juris*) individual persons have equal claims with all others to rights, i.e., to legal/political arrangements and institutions protecting their capacity for self-realization through free exercise of their faculties consistent with like rights in others. This seems right to me as at least a partial description of the core concerns of classical liberalism. One of its central institutions is indeed a moralized political economy, the Jacksonian-Ricardian competitive economy of small producers that, if allowed to function correctly, will return to each individual a reward equal to his inputs of effort, talent, and abstinence.

Fiss also attributes to the judges a belief that in the USA the existence and smooth operation of such a social realm was assumed as a more or less "natural" fact, what Friedrich Hayek would later come to call a "spontaneous order."[31] And of course it's true that many nineteenth-century Americans talked as if this social realm were indeed the set of arrangements that uncorrupted human beings, possessed of natural reason, enlightened self-interest and moral sense, would choose for themselves. The main role for law and the state in this vision is to clear away historically created obstructions: to release natural man

[31] Friedrich Hayek, *Law, Legislation and Liberty* 35–54 (1973).

from encrustations of custom, superstition and artificial restraint – restrictions on mobility of land, labor and capital, mercantilist wage and price controls; ecclesiastical hierarchy, aristocracy and monopoly; agrarian and sumptuary laws, and redistribution by confiscation and taxation. Once established, the system is a machine that without undue interference runs of itself – according to the natural laws of moralized political economy – producing the individual characters that will sustain and reproduce it.

Alternatively (and I think more frequently) the social realm was described, in the conservative historicism of nineteenth-century jurists, not as a natural fact but as a complex historical achievement – in the shaping of institutions, but perhaps even more of appropriate characters. The individual character demanded for the appropriate functioning of the sphere of natural liberty is a complex social product; the outcome of a long, slow process of historical evolution toward a civilized society peopled with civilized individuals – of inherited traits, inherited institutions, and a thick web of supporting social arrangements and institutions. The progress of society, civilization, morals, natural religion, learning, and useful arts was gradually producing the ideal individual characters to be bearers of liberal rights: nonconformist Protestant middle-class personalities, pursuers of enlightened self-interest tempered by regard for equal rights of others and possessing strong internalized moral dispositions to self-control, thrift, discipline, and avoidance of license and vice. In the Victorian Anglo-American world (at least outside the "feudal" South) this progress toward liberal society and the liberal characters that sustained it was taken to be a largely established fact – in contrast to Europe, where much struggle, reform, and even middle-class revolution might still be needed as midwives to the birth of liberal society, and personality remained deformed under the yokes of feudalism and religious superstition (a.k.a. Roman Catholicism).

The implications of this position for the governance of evolutionarily stunted peoples were naturally various. Optimists thought that with a change of environment by means of immigration or enlightened colonial government, backward races could assimilate in a generation; racists thought them inherently incapable of ever assimilating; most in between thought they could get there eventually, though it might take hundreds of years. Classical liberal theory was an idealized view of what the Anglo-American middle class thought it had already achieved for itself, and thought could be achieved for virtuous working and lower class people, and even some lesser breeds, with appropriate socialization from above and through their own efforts from below.

Herbert Spencer, whom Fiss identifies as a primary theorist of liberal society,[32] blended the naturalistic and historical accounts into a socio-biological

[32] This identification incidentally seems to me mistaken: American classical judges and lawyers were not generally followers of Spencer or of Social Darwinism; they admired contractual liberty for political-economic and moral reasons, not evolutionary-biological ones. For a nice elaboration of this point, see Herbert Hovenkamp's review of TB, in "The Cultural Crises of the Fuller Court," 104 *Yale L. J.* 2309 (1995).

model, according to which the increasing division of labor and specialization of social functions had gradually over centuries stimulated a responsive evolution of inherited adaptive reflexes and instincts in the human mind. The happy outcome was that coercion would no longer be needed to produce the conditions of self-sustaining market society.[33] J. S. Mill agreed: "Despotism is a legitimate mode of government in dealing with barbarians, provided the end be their improvement...[but in civilized nations] mankind have attained the capacity of being guided to their own improvement by conviction or persuasion..."[34] One conclusion one might draw from these accounts of the equilibrium of liberal society is, certainly, that once it is reached the only job for "artificial" institutions like the state is routine servicing and maintenance of the natural organism of society, and occasional repulsion of threats to its safety or smooth functioning.

The stewards of the legal system in Victorian America often pronounced these libertarian sentiments. But by and large they didn't act as if they believed in them. Their view was rather that sustaining conditions of the social realm and especially of the individual moral characters needed for its operation, couldn't count on taking people as they found them, since the natural state of persons was fallen, weak, and sinful. The sustaining conditions of social life thus depended on very particular types of socializing and "disciplining" institutions and agencies – families, sexual codes, schools, workplaces, correctional institutions, and, of course, properly functioning markets. The glue of society was in bonds of community and authority, what the sociologist Emile Durkheim called the non-contractual foundations of contract.[35] The social sphere of liberty rested on a foundation of both socially produced restraints and coercively maintained order; the order of competition on spheres of social life protected from competition and arms-length bargaining; the order of equal rights on relations of hierarchical subordination. Indeed some of these orders, like the natural authority of the employer and subordination of the employee in the workplace, were actually built into the heart of liberal order itself, not just into its foundations. And all these foundational orders turned out to require much more significant legal reinforcement, legal delegations of discretionary power and legal coercion to make them work, than classical-liberal theory generally liked to recognize except in moments of crisis.

A nice set of illustrations comes from Sarah Barringer Gordon's excellent and revealing recent book about the legal response to Mormon polygamy.[36] From 1860 to 1890 the federal government was mobilized to deploy an extraordinary arsenal of legal resources against Mormon families, Mormon

[33] See generally Herbert Spencer, *Social Statics* (1851), *Principles of Sociology* (1876–95).

[34] Mill, *On Liberty* at 9 (Blackwell 1946 edition).

[35] Emile Durkheim, *The Division of Labor in Society* 206–219 (2nd edn., George Simpson ed. & trans., 1933).

[36] Sarah Barringer Gordon, *The Mormon Question: Polygamy and Constitutional Conflict in Nineteenth Century America* (2002).

churches, Mormon economic institutions and Mormon political arrangements. In just a few years the government disenfranchised polygamists and even those who merely advocated polygamy, repealed women's suffrage in the Utah territory, disqualified polygamists from jury duty, criminalized plural marriage and brought 2,500 prosecutions – a legal campaign to reform sexual behavior "unique in American history… far exceeding that of seventeenth-century Massachusetts"[37] – against polygamists, including 200 against pregnant women for "fornication"; and dissolved the corporation of the Mormon church and escheated its property to the state, limiting its holdings of real property to $50,000.[38] These were of course massive interventions into religious, family and economic life – not to mention massive exercises of federal power with respect to arrangements typically assigned to "local" regulation. And naturally one asks: How could people who supposed they were devoted to freedom of contract, the "voluntary principle" in religion, and the preference for localism in matters of domestic relations, do all this without the slightest hesitation? The campaign against polygamy is one of the many episodes that makes one sharply aware of the primacy to classical liberalism of its moral foundations: monogamy, the channeling of sex into marriage, the differentiation of women in their separate sphere as tamers of male passion and civilizers of male impulses, all essential prerequisites to the functioning of a society and market economy that would render everyone his moral due. "Liberty" was an important protected interest when it served that ultimate goal; but dangerous and vicious when it flowed outside its proper channels.

As Fiss's narrative of the period dramatically indicates, by the 1880s and 90s hardly anybody believed any longer in the most optimistic evolutionary fairytales of progress toward an almost completely self-sustaining economy of virtue, requiring only minimal booster shots of legal force to keep it humming along. Doubtless people in every age perceive their social order as undergoing breakdown. At the end of the last century, it really *was* breaking down. Corporate and labor combinations, subsidies, and special tax breaks that distorted the competitive market, allowing monopolists and unions to reap rents far in excess of their rightful shares; taxation schemes and pauper relief that might give more than their due to either the idle rich or the idle poor; debtor relief and debt repudiation; were all bad for exactly the same reasons polygamy was bad; they interfered with the operations of the moral economy; they corroded the conditions of character-formation.

Why were legal-social reformers – not just the tradition-minded or rural reformers, but modernizing Progressives as well – so obsessed with suppressing obscene literature, gambling, alcohol, prostitution and other forms of vice? Nicola Beisel has plausibly explained these obsessions as the product of middle-class parents' worries that their sons will fall off the wagon of respectability

[37] *Id.* at 156.
[38] *Id. Passim.*

into debauchery and thus jeopardize their futures as self-controlled characters and with them the future of the moral economy itself.[39] Mass unemployment and injuries from industrial accidents threatened the stability of the family as the moral basis of civilization by undermining the independence, founded on his wage-earning capacity, of the male head of household.[40] The tremendous influx of outsiders threatened to swamp liberal society with characters who were not socialized, and perhaps never could be, into habits of industry and self-government: immigrants who were still under the sway of feudal habits – Catholics and socialists, habitually idle paupers; or who were altogether excessively, inhumanly hard workers like the Chinese and Japanese; and, of course, the recently freed slaves.

The most interesting of these threats for my purposes are those that seemed to derive from the market system itself, to be by-products of its routine operations. The most conspicuous among these was the tendency of free contracting and entrepreneurial liberty to beget giant business combinations that put out of business the "small dealers and worthy men," as Justice Peckham called them,[41] who were the sturdy mainstays of the moral economy, and so to call for injections of legal force to restore its healthy functioning. Fiss has a brilliant chapter on antitrust, describing the Fuller Court's judges' contortions to fit the enforcement of the Sherman Act, designed to "save the market from itself,"[42] into their scheme of limits on constituted authority to meddle with the natural workings of the market.

Antitrust was one of several fields in which classical judges repeatedly disagreed about whether an agreement to combine was a normal transaction within the sacred sphere of core liberty/property actions or a threat to that sphere, one that had to be contained to protect the foundational conditions of its natural functioning. All the judges had differing views of what the "natural" conditions were. Justice Peckham, Fiss tells us, "referred to competition as though it were itself a 'rule' or a 'law'. He often spoke of the 'general law of competition' as though the Sherman Act were nothing more or less than the transubstantiation of a law that governed anyway – natural law."[43] Justice Holmes by contrast viewed the growth of business combinations as part of a different natural process altogether, the evolution of social organizations into collective forms, combination as the irresistible organic law of social life. In his remarkable dissent in the Northern Securities case Holmes warned that adoption of the Peckham view, "an interpretation of the [Sherman Act] which

[39] Nicola Beisel, *Imperiled Innocents: Anthony Comstock and Family Reproduction in Victorian America* 49–75 (1997).

[40] See generally John Witt, *The Accidental Republic: Crippled Workingmen, Destitute Widows, and the Remaking of American Law* (2004).

[41] Peckham J., in *U.S.* v. *Trans-Missouri Freight Ass'n*, 166 U.S. 290 at 323 (1897).

[42] TB at 109.

[43] TB at 123.

in my opinion would make eternal the *bellum omnium contra omnes* and disintegrate society so far as it could into individual atoms… would be an attempt to reconstruct society"[44] and would be not only foolish but actually unconstitutional. So even for Holmes – whose relish in upholding legislation usually only increased with his opinion of its absurdity – there were limits: Congress could not be presumed to have attempted to repeal the law of evolution. But the problem remained that by its literal terms the Act seemed to prohibit all contracts in restraint of trade; threatening, as Justice White put it "all liberty of contract and all substantial right to trade, and thus causing that act to be at war with itself by annihilating the fundamental right of freedom to trade which, on the very face of the act, it was enacted to preserve…"[45]

White's eventual compromise in *Standard Oil* and *American Tobacco*'s "rule of reason,"[46] as is well known, drew on Judge William Howard Taft's famous opinion in circuit in the *Addyston Pipe* case,[47] which had said that the Sherman Act simply enacted "common law" principles on restraint of trade. This formula helped to solve the problem of reconciling "artificial" and "coercive" regulation of activity in the "natural" and "social" sphere by naturalizing the form of regulation itself. It suppressed the public-coercive element in regulation by concealing it in the folds of the "common law," viewed as a gradually-unfolding outgrowth of organic custom, which, even though judges enforced it and kept revising it, was somehow not "the state," not an alien excrescence working on the social body from outside, but part of spontaneous order itself. The judges in short solved the problem by defining the social sphere as including built-in natural-law-derived restraints on predation.

Labor combinations posed similar conceptual difficulties for theorists of freedom. It was easy for the judges to see strikes, pickets, and boycotts as interferences with owners' natural-liberty rights to run their businesses (properties) as they saw fit and to hire and fire whom they chose and with other workers' rights to contract individually for their labor. It was even easier for them to perceive potential coercion or violence, from the barest evidences of actual conduct, such as the mere presence of labor pickets, as severe threats to public order that could be suppressed by the police power or the inherent equitable power of courts. But what if the means state legislatures chose to try to solve the public order problem were conciliation rather than repression, as by enacting anti-yellow-dog statutes or other pro-labor legislation? Classical courts for the most part rejected this solution as "class legislation" beyond the bounds of the police power, and capitulation to blackmail (though they had no difficulty accepting the very similar rationale for compelled racial segregation as a safeguard against unlawful violence). Here too, as Fiss points out, there

[44] *Northern Securities Co.* v. *U.S.*, 193 U.S. 197, at 211 (Holmes, J. dissenting) (1904).

[45] *U.S.* v. *American Tobacco Co.*, 221 U.S. 106 at 180 (1911).

[46] *Standard Oil* v. *U.S.*, 221 U.S. 1 (1911), *U.S.* v. *American Tobacco Co.*, 221 U.S. 106 (1911).

[47] *U.S.* v. *Addyston Pipe & Steel Co.*, 85 F. 271 (6th Cir., 1898).

were dissents such as Justice McKenna's in the *Adair* case, which would have justified labor legislation as contributing to industrial peace.[48]

But in general, confronted with threats to the public-order and moral-order foundations of the social sphere – even if the threats arose from the self-undermining effects of routine exercises of contractual liberty itself – legal authorities were disposed to respond with repression to repel the threat and restore order, even if doing so might in the process severely curtail contractual liberty. In order to protect the voluntary selling of self into wage labor as the paradigmatic act of freedom, the legal system criminalized workers' refusal to do so with increasingly repressive and repressively enforced, vagrancy laws – lest idleness and pauperism corrupt the characters of the unemployed.[49] Courts upheld these laws despite their almost total absence of process: police could arrest on bare suspicion, without witnesses to actual begging; suspects were presumed guilty and rapidly dispatched to compulsory workhouse labor. The courts also saw dangers to the organic hierarchies of family order in the expansion of married women's contractual capacities and opportunities. As wives entered the wage workforce and Earnings Acts enabled them to control the proceeds of their labor and thus to achieve some "pecuniary independence" within the household, the courts, as Reva Siegel has shown, refused to allow their new freedom to contract to affect their duties to perform domestic services: these remained personal and unwaivable obligations; and the wife's earnings from third parties still came under her husband's control unless she expressly labored on her "sole and separate account."[50] When young women sold their sexual services to get higher wages and more spending money than they could earn as seamstresses or shop-girls, the legal system (which in earlier decades had generally resigned itself to prostitution as an inevitable evil that had the beneficial side-effects of deflecting male sexual urges away from respectable and onto fallen women) began to resort to more draconian regulation to eradicate this form of exchange.[51]

As with free contract, so with free speech: Mark Graber has convincingly argued that to "conservative libertarians" of the late nineteenth century, free speech was conceptually on a par with contractual liberty as a core liberty to be protected against the state – that is, it was an integral piece of the social sphere. But as Graber concedes, and Fiss demonstrates in his book, if a speaker's

[48] TB at 171, citing *Adair* v. *U.S.*, 208 U.S. 161 (1908), at 185–186 (McKenna, J. dissenting).

[49] See Amy Stanley, *From Bondage to Contract* 103–133 (1998) (describing arrests of thousands of "tramps" in northern cities per year, in sweeps of 20 to 500 per day); William Cohen, *At Freedom's Edge: Black Mobility and the Southern White Quest for Racial Control, 1861–1915* (1991) (use of vagrancy laws to prevent migration of black labor, to assist in compulsory contract enforcement, assert control over defiant or rebellious blacks, and to supply pool through convict labor system for involuntary labor force).

[50] Reva Siegel, "Home as Work: The First Women's Rights Claims Concerning Wives' Household Labor, 1850–1880," 103 *Yale L. J.* 1073, 1170–1189 (1994).

[51] See Ruth Rosen, *The Lost Sisterhood: Prostitution in America, 1900–1918* (1982) 1–37.

words seemed to have any tendency at all, however remote or improbable, to threaten public order, the speech could be suppressed.[52] A nice, dramatic illustration comes just after Fiss's period in *Fox* v. *Washington* (1915), in which the Supreme Court upheld the criminal conviction of an author for writing an article called "The Nude and the Prudes," which praised nudism, protested the arrest of nudists, and called for a boycott of the "prudes" who had instigated the arrests. The Court construed this article as a punishable incitement to breach of the indecent-exposure statutes.[53]

In the South especially, as Peter Bardaglio and Laura Edwards have shown, after slavery disappeared, law and the state took over the paternalistic role of the antebellum patriarchal household as the primary regulator of society's organic relations. The legal system regulated not just "the family," but the whole social-sexual code – the protection of female virtue, most notoriously through savagely punitive legal and extra-legal enforcement of rape and sexual assault laws against black men, but also through refusal to protect women (of any race) who were perceived to flaunt their sexuality against white men; tightening up of anti-incest laws; and a strenuous policy of compelling former slaves who had not been allowed to marry into marriage. Needless to say the enforcement, legal or extra-legal, of the sexual code as of vagrancy laws was most likely to be targeted at blacks who were actually proving their moral worth in the economic order, by acquiring property and moving up the ladder.[54] Preservation of racial status order, rationalized as preservation of sexual and public order, easily trumped contractual liberalism in this setting.

Faced with mounting evidence that the operations of the free-contract-economy themselves might be producing disturbances to its foundational order, legal authorities in this period generally resorted to denial and scapegoating – usually by attributing the disturbance to defects in character introduced by corrupt, impure, or foreign influences. Fiss quotes at length a remarkable speech by Justice Brewer, who admits that free markets produce great inequalities – as is only natural and just, since men differ greatly in their capacities for "self-denial and saving" and "business tact and sagacity." Inequality in turn produces envy and the desire to redistribute wealth. But what inflames envious desire into lawless violence is foreign influence: "the black flag of anarchism, flaunting destruction to property, and, therefore [the] relapse of society to barbarism" and "the red flag of socialism..."[55] In interesting recent work Matthew

[52] Mark A. Graber, *Transforming Free Speech: The Ambiguous Legacy of Civil Libertarianism* 17–49 (1991).

[53] *Fox* v. *Washington*, 236 U.S. 273 (1915).

[54] See generally Peter Bardaglio, *Reconstructing the Household: Families, Sex and the Law in the Nineteenth Century South* (1995); Laura Edwards, *Gendered Strife and Confusion: The Political Culture of Reconstruction* (1997).

[55] David Brewer, The Nation's Safeguard, *Proc. N.Y. State Bar Ass'n.* 37–47 (1893), quoted in TB 54–56.

Lindsay has traced the origins of the Contract Labor Act of 1885, aimed at prohibiting employers from importing cheap foreign labor that would undercut domestic wage rates. The backers were alarmed at the depression of wages below levels that would suffice to enable men to support a family and be independent republican citizens. But rather than admit that market outcomes might not support the moral economy of virtue, they blamed ruinous wage competition on (first) the socially acquired, then (later) the inherent racial, defects of Southern European "pauper laborers" – whose peculiar degeneracy was not refusal to work, but willingness to work for peanuts, as men not accustomed to Anglo-Saxon liberty and thus too degraded to insist on the wages that would maintain them in it.[56]

Classical liberals in short tended to diagnose the basic problem as defective human inputs into the moral economy, rather than the operations of the economy itself. If the human material were the problem the cure must lie in some combination of measures to reshape or repair deficient characters, or if they should prove obdurately refractory, to exclude or expel them. This brings us into the vast territories first mapped by historians of Victorian and Progressive moral and social-legal reform[57] and since occupied and colonized by Foucault and his successors' studies of "disciplines" and "govermentality"[58] – that is, of the elaborate and extensive array of social and state "technologies" deployed to form and "normalize" the individual subjects and citizens who were to be the bearers of liberal rights and obligations. In earlier periods reform entrepreneurs had mostly been content to rely on the spontaneous order of voluntary associations (churches, Bible Societies, temperance societies, and the like) – with the important exceptions of the pioneering big disciplinary institutions of compulsory public schools, prisons, asylums, and workhouses, which were already

[56] Matthew Lindsay, "Preserving the Exceptional Republic: Political Economy, Race, and the Federalization of American Immigration Law," 17 *Yale. J. Law & Human.* 185 (2005). See also Paul T. Ringenbach, *Tramps and Reformers, 1873–1916: The Discovery of Unemployment in New York* (1973), at 24: In a survey of New York charities personnel in 1885, 16 percent attributed the "tramp" problem to unemployment; 70 percent said it resulted from personal deficiencies, "laziness, war drink, dime novels, tobacco, discontent, shiftlessness, vice, love of roving, heredity, socialistic ideas, the Chinese, [or] the devil." (Thanks to Olivia Choe for this reference.)

[57] For a small sample of some of the best work from a large field, see, e.g., David J. Pivar, *Purity Crusade: Sexual Morality and Social Control, 1868–1900* (1973), Paul S. Boyer, *Urban Masses and Moral Order in America, 1820–1920* (1978), Mary E. Odem, *Delinquent Daughters: Protecting and Policing Adolescent Female Sexuality in the United States, 1885–1920* (1995), Richard F. Hamm, *Shaping the 18th Amendment: Temperance Reform, Legal Culture, and the Polity, 1880–1920* (1995), Alan Hunt, *Governing Morals: A Social History of Morals Regulation* (1999), Mariana Valverde, *The Age of Light, Soap and Water: Social Purity and Philanthropy in Canada, 1885–1925* (1991).

[58] See, e.g., Michel Foucault, 3 *The History of Sexuality: The Care of the Self* (1986) and *Power/Knowledge: Selected Interviews and Other Writings, 1972–1977* (Colin Gordon ed., 1980), Jonathan Simon, *Poor Discipline: Parole and the Social Control of the Underclass, 1890–1990* (1993), Nikolas Rose, *Powers of Freedom: Reframing Political Thought* (1999).

up and running by the 1830s and 40s.[59] Moral reformers had also begun by the mid-nineteenth century to turn to the state to regulate the most worrisome and conspicuous forms of vice, such as lotteries, gambling and alcohol.

In Fiss's period, they turned to law and the state for new sources of funding, personnel, legitimacy, and coercive enforcement authority. Sometimes these took the form of new or more punitive criminal laws, sometimes of administrative regimes with rehabilitative mandates, sometimes of new state agencies, perhaps most imaginatively of delegations of state authority to enter, search, investigate, seize, incarcerate and fine to professional groups or citizens groups such as Comstock's Society for the Suppression of Vice, the Child Protection Societies, Commissions on the Social Evil, and the Anti-Saloon Leagues.

I could not even begin to try to summarize all these legal initiatives here; but let me briefly group them into types and give a few examples of each. (1) *Measures to shore up and enhance the capacity of traditional socializing institutions* mostly took the form of protecting the sexual division of labor and gender roles and the monopoly of procreation-within-marriage as the legitimate outlet for sexual urges: such as new legislation outlawing common-law marriage, abortion, selling or distributing information about contraception; banning and seizure of obscene materials; new crackdowns on prostitution; the restriction of professional and other job opportunities to women to prevent them from competing with men for the role of household provider and to safeguard their capacities as wives and mothers; etc. (2) *Codes and institutions to correct the characters of deviants*, especially children: new reformatories for juvenile delinquents and sexually wayward girls, removal of children from working-class homes with bad values, houses of rescue for fallen women; intensive supervision of relief recipients, etc. (3) *Outright repression or exclusion of groups presenting special social dangers*: mass deployment of injunctions (around 2,200 issued between 1880 and 1920[60]) to suppress labor actions; concerted and largely successful campaigns to "purify the electorate" by disenfranchising whole categories of voters – including (in the South) virtually all African-Americans, and (in the North) immigrants, the propertyless, low-income persons unable to pay a poll tax, those unable to read English, mobile populations disabled by residency tests, "paupers" (which included anyone who had received poor or work relief, and workers out on strike), and those unable to meet picky detailed registration requirements[61]; new controls on the unemployed and "sturdy beggars" through stiffer vagrancy laws and (in the

[59] On these institutions see David Rothman, *Discovery of the Asylum; Social Order and Disorder in the New Republic* (1971).

[60] This estimate is that of William Forbath, *Law and the Shaping of the American Labor Movement* (1991) at 193. The bonanza decade for injunctions was the 1920s: 2130, by Forbath's estimate. Id.

[61] Alexander Keyssar, *The Right to Vote* 77–171 (2000). The extension of voting rights to women was a rare countertendency.

South) of black farmers unwilling to work for their former masters through criminalizing contract-breaking[62]; cascades of new laws criminalizing speech, organizations and association of politically threatening groups like "anarchists" or "syndicalists"[63]; and of course exclusion of a whole host of undesirables, from low-wage contract labor, to radicals, anarchists, and the Chinese.[64]

I hasten to emphasize what the best work on these reform movements makes clear: that they emerged from a wide variety of interests and ideological positions; and were by no means all directed to subordinating and controlling the poor and marginal, or to preserving traditional privileges and hierarchies. Though some of these initiatives had precisely those aims, or after more promising beginnings came to be captured by factions with those aims, other movements aspired earnestly and even radically to improve the conditions of the downtrodden and to curtail the powers and reform the characters of the wealthy and mighty. The point is just that the array of legal tools and strategies the reform movements – often spearheaded and staffed by lawyers, by the way – were willing to deploy to address rampant social diseases showed very little disposition to prevent law and the state from invading contractarian boundaries on interference with the self-sustaining and self-reproducing social sphere of natural liberty.

Indeed the judges guarding the boundaries reviewed and approved the vast majority of these initiatives. Sometimes the reason given was that the measure fell within the scope of the police power, which usually turned out, unless it infringed directly on the negotiation of the wage bargain, to be pretty broad. The courts approved what might appear to be blatantly anti-competitive rent-seeking arrangements such as occupational licensing, the exclusion of women from professions and occupations, and the stringent regulation of dairy-product substitutes. They were especially indulgent if the legislative rationale were protection of morals, disposed in such cases to accept the flimsiest and most speculative claims of the risks of social harm posed by the regulated conduct. Sometimes the reason the courts gave was, as in *Debs* (the Pullman Strike case[65]), or *Reynolds* (the Mormon Polygamy case[66]) that the measure was needed to protect the very foundations of social order itself, such as the family or civil peace or political stability, which were prior and superior even to maintenance of the moral economy of the social sphere. And very frequently of course the ground was simply the common device that the legal system uses

[62] Cohen, *supra* note 49.

[63] For an inventory of laws suppressing speech and dissent, see generally Robert J. Goldstein, *Political Repression in Modern America: From 1870 to the Present* (1978).

[64] For the exclusionary measures, see the classic work of John Higham, *Strangers in the Land: Patterns of American Nativism, 1860–1925* (1966); and the recent synthesis of Rogers Smith, *Civic Ideals: Conflicting Visions of Citizenship in U.S. History* (1997) at 347–469.

[65] In re Debs, *supra* note 9.

[66] *Reynolds* v. *U.S.*, 98 U.S. 145 (1879).

to avoid confronting uncomfortable illiberal hierarchies or exercises of discretionary authority – that the claimed anti-liberal practice, like the state's failure to protect the contracting rights of Southern blacks or the rights of women to be free of domestic violence, or its arbitrary exclusion of aliens or dissenters, was simply in somebody's else's jurisdiction.

Does this mean I think Fiss has just invented this libertarian vision of judicially enforced limits on constituted authority – in the same fashion as legal Progressives trumped up the charge (of which Fiss is inclined to acquit them) that the classical judges were mere lackeys of big business? Of course not – the cases are there, and so is a towering heap of briefs and speeches and articles and editorials presenting and justifying this vision. The classical judges' belief in the quasi-natural social sphere or moral economy was entirely sincere – even if it may seem to modern libertarian eyes radically at odds with the entire panoply of state action of the period, which now seems more notable for its impressive array of novel controlling, disciplining, coercing, punishing, and excluding state strategies than it does for restraining heavy-handed state interventions into the social sphere. The tendency of libertarian legal and political-economic theory to ignore or repress awareness of the state and of state-supported coercive preconditions to the functioning of free contracts and free markets has been a favorite theme of critics from Marx, Proudhon, and Hobhouse to legal Progressives like Robert Hale.[67] But this isn't just a story about self-deception or myopia or bad faith: as Fiss points out, social-contract ideology really was in actual practice a powerful tool for structuring much of the judges' decision-making – even if they were prone to deviating from or betraying it in the crunch. And, as he also points out, contractual-liberty ideology had some significant relative-autonomy-feedback effects (my hideous phrasing, not his), moments when classical-liberal judges or lawyers used libertarian arguments against illiberal state initiatives that powerful interests wanted. Fiss's book has many such examples: the vigorous dissenters in the *Insular* Cases; Justice Harlan's dissent in *Plessy*; the *Northern Securities* majority, maybe the majorities who defended the interstate liquor trade against state prohibitionists; the arguments of the consummate classical-liberal James Coolidge Carter[68] – who wrote whole books naturalizing private common-law-structured society as the slow organic growth of custom, a delicate ecology to which ill-conceived popular legislation could cause inestimable damage, but who also argued for the government in favor of the Income Tax and against it in the Chinese Exclusion cases.[69]

[67] See e.g., Karl Marx, "On the Jewish Question [1843]," in Robert C. Tucker (ed.), *The Marx-Engels Reader* 26 (2nd edn. 1978); Pierre-Joseph Proudhon, *General Idea of the Revolution in the Nineteenth Century* [1851], trans. J. B. Robertson (1923) at 294; Robert L. Hale, "Bargaining, Duress and Economic Liberty," 43 *Colum. L. Rev.* 603 (1943).

[68] TB 235, 255–256; 365–366; 133–134; 306–308.

[69] On Carter's relatively progressive liberalism, see Lewis A. Grossman, "James Coolidge Carter and Mugwump Jurisprudence," 20 *Law & History Rev.* 577 (2002).

But even the most aggressive libertarians of the time took for granted the legitimacy of a wide range of legal coercions. Christopher Tiedeman's famous *Treatise on the Limitations of Police Power in the United States* (1886),[70] appearing on the eve of Fiss's period, much cited by lawyers and judges during it, and later much reviled by Progressive critics for its "laissez-faire" views, is a rich storehouse of examples both of the potentially expansive ripple-effects of legal-libertarian ideology and of its limits. Tiedeman rails against many forms of regulation that classical-liberal courts had generally validated – economic regulation of interest charges (usury laws),[71] price and terms of service of public accommodations,[72] and oleomargarine,[73] prohibition of mere consumption of drugs and alcohol,[74] and the private enjoyment of vices such as gambling and fornication (though he thought it all right to regulate the business of vice, gambling-houses and brothels and the liquor trade, even if outright prohibition would probably be futile[75]); laws criminalizing the status of being an "habitual offender"[76]; and many others. He thinks laws preventing women from entering the professions[77] and marriages between people of different races are the results of sheer prejudice, the latter "an uncontrollable prejudice against the black man, and a desire to maintain the inequality of his present social condition."[78] He thinks the process (though not the substance) of vagrancy laws – arrest on suspicion, summary process and reversal of the burden of proof – of dubious validity.[79] For his time this is a courageous and appealing libertarian tract – but one that also, by its long lists of conventionally accepted police-power offenses, shows how ill the "laissez-faire" label fits the law of this period. His chapter on free speech and a free press is only four and a half pages long, and largely defines the rights as freedom from prior restraints;[80] "anarchists and nihilists" may be arrested and their publications seized for publishing "inflammatory

[70] Hereafter cited as Tiedeman.

[71] Tiedeman 238–241.

[72] Tiedeman 233–238.

[73] Tiedeman 295–297.

[74] Tiedeman 148–153; 301–309.

[75] Tiedeman 289–311.

[76] Tiedeman 124–131.

[77] Tiedeman 201–203.

[78] Tiedeman at 536.

[79] Tiedeman 116–122. In justifying the substance of laws punishing vagrancy, the status of being without "visible means of support," Tiedeman had to wage an uphill battle against his honest libertarian conviction that there could be no social harm in idleness or refusing to work per se. "A man has a legal right to live a life of absolute idleness, if he chooses, provided he does not, in so living, violate some clear and well-defined duty to the State." Id. at 118. The "gist of the offense," he reasoned, was "threatening to become a public burden." Id. The best evidence one could hope to find of the general acceptance of vagrancy laws is that a strongly committed libertarian like Tiedeman was willing to find social harm, justifying preventive action, in such a speculative unrealized "threat."

[80] Tiedeman 189–193.

appeals to the passion of discontents,"[81] and blasphemers against the Christian religion may be punished for injuring the public by diminishing respect for religion that sustains the moral basis of the state.[82] And given the severity of the "racial" threat from the abnormally hardworking and morally depraved Chinese, legislatures might reasonably think their exclusion was essential to protect the country from being overrun by the "almond-eyed Asiatic."[83] My favorite passage in the whole treatise, which reveals his characteristic method of balancing liberty and social-order preservation, is his carefully nuanced discussion of legal regulation of cross-dressing, "the prohibition of the appearance in public of men in women's garb, and *vice versa*":

> The use of such dress could serve no useful purpose, and tends to public immorality and the perpetration of frauds. Its prohibition is, therefore, probably constitutional. But it does not follow that a law, which prohibited the use by men of a specific article of women's dress, or to women the use of a particular piece of men's clothing, would be constitutional. The prohibition must be confined to those cases, in which immorality or the practice of deception is facilitated, viz., where one sex appears altogether in the attire of the other sex.[84]

For the classical liberals, then, the order of liberty in the social sphere was deeply, even if not always openly or explicitly, parasitic on foundations of organic order, the basic conditions of social peace and political stability and of the institutions and ethical dispositions counted on to produce the individual characters needed to make the order of liberty function. These conditions in turn were deeply reliant on structuring and coercive law – although theorists like Spencer liked to believe that the need for state coercion was vanishing as liberal behavior became habit and instinct, and legal historicists liked to believe that the essential legal component, private common-law, was itself an evolving organic order rather than an artificial excrescence like state legislation and administration. When this foundational order came under siege – even and perhaps especially when the source of dangerous pollutions was the sphere of liberty itself (new opportunities for women and blacks as potentially equal rights-bearers in the economy, new inequalities and mass unemployment resulting from the industrial system, new national labor organizations and their mass actions to match industries national in scope, new weird religions and political heresies emerging from the pluralist marketplaces of free speech and the voluntary system, and new race threats from the mobility of free labor) – massive new doses of restructuring and coercive law were pumped into the system to repel the threats and restore and refashion the conditions of order. The conditions, made visible, were often strikingly illiberal, thus setting up occasions for battles between the apostles of liberal order and defenders of its illiberal

[81] Tiedeman at 193.
[82] Tiedeman 167.
[83] Tiedeman at 145.
[84] Tiedeman at 156.

foundations. In retrospect, many of the worst things the courts of this age did was to ratify so repeatedly and uncritically the most illiberal of those acts.

Ironically however – as Fiss's consistently penetrating and lucid history, the history that any modern reader seeking to understand the law of this period should start with, makes clear – the Fuller Court made itself more conspicuous, controversial, and politically vulnerable in its preferred self-conception as a defender of the order of liberty than as a legitimator of the authoritarian extravagances of its time. In order to prevent the government from breaching the social contract by overreaching regulation and redistribution, the Court itself assumed the role of Super-Regulator, making itself the supreme arbiter not only of the constitutionality of federal and state legislation and the boundaries of federalism; but also the ultimate supervisor, by virtue of having constitutionalized the right to "fair rates of return on investment" as "property," of the rate-making decisions of every state railroad and public utility commission;[85] the chief government agency, through application of the "rule of reason," for determining the scope and purpose of the antitrust laws;[86] the supreme interpreter, through its exposition of general federal common law in the diversity jurisdiction, of much state tort law;[87] and the ultimate governance authority, through exercise of its equity powers, over interstate labor disputes[88] and bankrupt interstate railroads.[89] At many of these roles, maybe especially that of supervising rate regulation, the justices were conspicuously incompetent; but even the most expert unelected body can't indefinitely withstand the howling whirlwinds it is bound to raise by making itself the supreme magistrate on so many matters of huge public controversy. So Chief Justice Warren's Court found; and so, in time, will its conservative successors.

In part they achieved this happy complacency through compartmentalization. In a perceptive and illuminating essay on classical morals regulation, Herbert Hovenkamp has pointed out that nineteenth-century American legal theory followed social theory in conceptualizing economy and morality as parallel but separate spheres, each to be understood by distinct sciences and subject to distinct modes of regulation.[90] The prolific and popular text writer Francis Wayland, for example, wrote treatises on both economic and moral science.[91] As a moralist Wayland treated men as fallen and sinful, in need of strong community and legal sanctions to restrain their selfish impulses. As an

[85] TB 185–221.

[86] TB 148–154.

[87] See generally Purcell, *supra* note 3.

[88] See generally Forbath, *supra* note 60.

[89] See David Skeel, *Debt's Dominion: A History of Bankruptcy Law in America* 48–70 (2001).

[90] Herbert Hovenkamp, "Law and Morals in Classical Legal Thought," 82 *Iowa L. Rev.* 1427 (1997).

[91] Francis Wayland, *The Elements of Political Economy* (1854); *The Elements of Moral Science* (1856).

economist Wayland took men as he found them, with whatever tastes and preferences they might happen to have, and theorized that markets would work best if such individuals were allowed to freely pursue their self-interest, this side of force and fraud.[92]

The judges of the classical period engaged in similar forms of compartmentalization through the use of categorical reasoning. If they analyzed a case as involving the proper scope of the police power to regulate economic liberty, they insisted that legislatures show a strong health-safety-morals rationale for regulation, by means narrowly tailored to achieve the legitimate end. If the rationale on offer were protection of morals, however, that switched the judges onto another track of reasoning, where they were inclined to credit the thinnest and most speculative arguments of social danger. If the category of the regulated changed – if they were dependents, such as women or children, or constitutional outsiders, such as immigrants – the mode of reasoning about them changed as well.

Hovenkamp's compartmentalization thesis gets us part of the way toward understanding how the classics theorized their bifurcated approach to state regulation of private conduct.[93] Even more important was that the classics assumed that the economic and moral-social spheres generally existed in relations of harmonious interdependence. Men with properly socialized and governed moral characters would, in their economic dealings, want the right things and behave the right ways. The market would in turn reinforce and reproduce moral character, because economic success would reward good (thrifty, hard-working, self-denying, far-seeing, honest, talented) actors, and failure punish bad (idle, shiftless, spendthrift, dishonest) ones.

The great problem for classical law, as for political economy and moral science, was that by the late nineteenth century both the strategy of compartmentalization and the assumption of harmonious interaction of the two spheres were rapidly unraveling. Bad moral characters were infesting market relations; and economic behavior in turn was badly messing up the formation of moral character. The economy was producing mass unemployment and injury, destroying the moral authority of male heads of household, attracting hordes of immigrants with alien values, commercializing vice, producing the twin European pathologies of an unruly urban proletariat and a decadent and idle luxury-loving upper class, generating huge and powerful combinations of capital and counter-combinations of organized labor, and undermining both the foundations in public order and consensual morality and the approximate

[92] Hovenkamp, *supra* note 90, at 135–141.

[93] Again, as I have to keep emphasizing, it was never all that bifurcated. The classical legal system was not even close to a laissez-faire night-watchman state, even though many of its ideological spokesmen liked to claim it was: it approved a very large range of legal regulations of economic conduct, both traditional regulations and the many novel types that were proliferating in late-nineteenth-century state legislatures.

equalities in wealth (among white males) that Americans had always understood to be the prerequisite to an independent republican citizenry.

The responses of the state and law to restore order and morals likewise transgressed the boundaries between spheres. To regulate order and morals *was* to regulate the economy and individual bargaining, big-time. The state destroyed liquor businesses and seized the property of booksellers. When the courts would not allow the state to palliate the losers in the economic struggle with redistributive, compensatory or social-insurance policies or laws enabling labor to improve its bargaining advantage or share some managerial authority with capital, the state's only option to contain the political consequences was more repression. It sent troops to break up combinations of workers. It arrested the unemployed en masse for "choosing" to be out of work. It criminalized labor agitation and advocacy of radical alternatives. The courts, which were supposed to keep the regulatory state within its constitutional limits, remade themselves into powerful regulatory agencies playing a large, and very controversial, role in administering the economy – administering the industrial accident compensation system, repeatedly intervening in labor-capital conflicts, supervising the national network of railroads in receivership, reviewing public-utility rate regulation, and, of course, striking down some legislation with much popular support.

In short, there is no harmonious synthesis of economic laissez-faire and moral authority to be found in the America of 1900 and its legal order. Economic liberty was dissolving the bonds of authority and proving harmful to order and morals, and the efforts to restore order and morals proving harmful to liberty. The chief practical lesson that modern conservatives can learn from their classical counterparts is a cynical one: the ability to keep at bay the awareness that the economic and social spheres may be undermining rather than reinforcing one another by finding scapegoats. The classics, as we've seen, did often try to blame their problems on impurities in the social sphere alone: corrupt and alien foreign elements (Catholics, Chinese, Southern European low-wage labor, communist radicals, etc.) or on blacks and the idle poor. If those were the sources of social problems, they could be addressed by exclusion, repression, and above all resocialization. The current revival of Victorian moral economy, by neo-conservatives such as Charles Murray, Gertrude Himmelfarb, Lawrence Mead, and William Bennett,[94] also aims to use legal-economic-institutional arrangements to promote good and suppress bad values in the poor (though Murray is more prone than the other three to speak of the poor as victims of bad incentives, or bad genes, than of corrupted character): thus welfare (rewarding idleness) and affirmative action (class legislation rewarding

[94] See, e.g., Charles Murray, *Losing Ground: American Social Policy, 1950–1980* (1984); Gertrude Himmelfarb, *The Demoralization of Society: From Victorian Virtues to Modern Values* (1995); William J. Bennett, *The Broken Hearth: Reversing the Moral Collapse of the American Family* (2001); Lawrence Mead, *Beyond Entitlement: The Social Obligations of Citizenship* (1986).

special-interest rent-seeking rather than talent and industry) are especially bad social policies.

But the Victorian social and moral critiques were generally more comprehensive than their modern counterparts: they saw bad values and disorder everywhere, not just among marginals and the lower orders. Their critiques were as much directed upward as downward – to monopoly, concentrated wealth, business predation, subsidies and tax breaks for corporations, and to the conspicuous consumption and love of luxury of the rich. Modern conservative moralists write as if the habits they deplore of self-indulgent consumerism and sexual self-expression were peculiarly the vices of the poor and of a libertine subset of the upper classes, "liberal elites," rather than of the great mass of ordinary people in modern society.[95]

Classical-legal constitutionalism was a far more sophisticated, coherent, plausible and even-handed jurisprudence than the Progressives – who pictured it as a mixture of simple-minded economic theory, nostalgia for a pre-corporate individualistic past, and apologia for corporate business interests of the present – ever gave it credit for. But as a social experiment, the classical legal system was a huge practical failure, on its own terms as well as in historical retrospect. It promised to deliver the optimal mix of liberty, morality, and order. Instead it was either helpless before, or itself helped to produce, higher levels of coercive repression, immorality, and disorder. The decisions of its highest court mostly deserve their reputation as a gallery of illiberal horrors. The vogue in our own age for the revival of the classical system can only arise from an astonishing misapprehension of its actual consequences. And the program to return to the legal-social status quo ante of the 1890s – a society riven by violent class conflict; mass unemployment, industrial injury and poverty-stricken old age, unspeakable levels of urban and rural squalor, corporate domination of politics and systemic racial oppression – is a truly nightmarish prospect to anyone who knows anything at all about it.

[95] An exception is Robert Bork, whose most recent work declares that the whole society is corrupt, immoral and decadent, full of "an increasing number of alienated, restless individuals, individuals without strong ties to others, except in the pursuit of ever more degraded distractions and sensations." *Slouching Towards Gomorrah* (1996) at 63. Bork argues that this condition is the logical culmination that "liberalism" – meaning the doctrines of liberty and equality in the Enlightenment, Declaration of Independence, and Mill's *On Liberty* – "has been moving towards for better than two centuries." *Id.* [For further discussion of Bork's views, see the essay on "Originalism and Nostalgic Traditionalism," *infra*, Ch. 14.]

PART III

HISTORY AND HISTORICISM IN LEGAL HISTORY AND ARGUMENT

10

Historicism in Legal Scholarship*

[*This essay, published in 90* Yale Law Journal *1017 (1981) was written for a Symposium on Legal Scholarship held at Yale Law School in 1981. It was my first attempt to explain the nature of the threat that I believe historicism poses to legal theory and legal reasoning; and to describe the leading ways we have of coping with the threat. Prominent among those ways is what is called here "adaptation theory," which in "Critical Legal Histories," the essay that follows, becomes "evolutionary functionalism."*]

In this chapter, I want to discuss some of the familiar ways in which legal scholarship deals with the fact that law exists in and must to some extent always be understood by reference to particular contexts of space and time. I shall be making and trying to support an argument that historicism,[1] the recognition of the historical and cultural contingency of law, is a perpetual threat to the aims of our legal scholarship as conventionally practiced; that to defend against the threat (or to protect themselves from becoming aware of it) legal scholars have regularly and recurrently resorted to certain strategies of response and evasion; and finally, that these strategies have so influenced the practice of legal scholarship as severely to limit its intellectual options and imaginative range.

* My thanks to David Hollinger for his comments on an early draft of this paper; to Barbara Black and Morton Horwitz for their comments at the symposium; to J. G. A. Pocock (whom I have never met), Charles Gray, and Elizabeth Mensch for teaching me most of what I know about the uses of history in legal thought; and to colleagues at the Buffalo and Wisconsin Law Schools for showing in their work how the "historicist" perspective can transform one's understanding of law.

1 As used here, the elastic term "historicism" refers simply to the perspective that the meanings of words and actions are to some degree dependent on the particular social and historical conditions in which they occur, and to interpretations and criticisms that are suggested by that perspective. It is not intended to describe the view that meanings may be derived *exclusively* by reference to the unique conditions of a specific time and place.

In concluding, I will attempt to suggest some ways in which legal scholarship might break free of these limiting modes of response.

Some cautions and disclaimers before going on. In order to discuss within limited space how our legal scholars have dealt with the problem of historicism, and to cover a time period that is long enough to justify the claim that certain strategies regularly recur, I will have to summarize large bodies of thought rather rapidly and breathlessly, doubtless shearing them in the process of many of their strengths and subtleties. Moreover, as I hope will become clear, to say that work is vulnerable to criticism from the perspective of historicism is not at all to say that it is bad work. Even work whose every specific conclusion has been discredited can stand as a valuable contribution to the conversation of mankind. My project is not to criticize specific pieces of work, but the process by which an intellectual dialogue has risked impoverishment by repeatedly failing to listen or respond to certain conversational moves.

I use "legal scholarship" to mean what might be called the mainstream elite scholarship of this country, the work of the acknowledged intellectual leaders of the profession. In the last century, before the rise of a separate profession of law teachers, this scholarship would have been that of the leading treatise-writers – Kent, Story, Greenleaf, Sedgwick, Parsons, and so forth; afterwards, the scholarship would be that of the writers of books and articles regularly cited or appearing in the leading law reviews. This restriction to "mainstream" scholarship is meant to exclude most of the work on law that emphasizes its historicity, like professional legal history, legal sociology, and legal anthropology; for the most part, this work is neither published nor cited in the leading reviews. But this restriction does not exclude a great deal of work done in other interdisciplinary modes; in particular, it includes the economic analysis of law and legal philosophy in the Anglo-American tradition of Hart, Dworkin, and Rawls.[2]

I. THE THREAT OF HISTORICISM

Mainstream legal scholarship thus defined seems to have three aims.[3] The chief aim is that of rationalizing the real, of showing that the law-making and law-applying activities that go on in our society make sense and may be rationally related to some coherent conceptual ordering scheme. This task, which might be the theoretical attempt to develop or refine the ordering schemes themselves, or simply an effort to fit some specialized pattern of activity into already

[2] *See* Mark Tushnet, "Legal Scholarship: Its Causes and Cure," 90 *Yale L. J.* 1205 (1981).

[3] In the belief that the following account will not be controversial, I have not tried to document it. The skeptical reader is invited to test it out for herself by looking through back numbers of any ten of what she would consider the leading law reviews. See "Summary of Discussion of Historicism in Legal Scholarship," 90 *Yale L.J.* 1060, 1060 (1981) (confirmation of characterization by scholar at symposium) [hereinafter cited as Summary of Discussion].

well-developed schemes, could be approached in almost any spirit, from true agnosticism about whether the real is rational to an assumption that it must be. For most scholars, I would guess, the approach is predetermined by the method: if one is doing legal scholarship at all, one is proceeding as if the real were rational. The second aim goes beyond rationalization to justification, because the basic ordering scheme is not interesting to most legal scholars – even to those who go to some pains to characterize their method as positive and not normative[4] – unless the scheme may be derived from or at least shown to be consistent with some plausible conception of the good. Most writers doing "applied" rather than "basic" scholarship will seek only to refine the already developed justifications of existing ordering schemes, rather than starting from scratch every time. The third aim is a pragmatic one. Legal scholars usually want to persuade their readers that rationalization and justification are practical exercises that will help advocates or policy-makers decide how to act or refrain from acting in social life and how to justify their actions publicly.

An intellectual exercise that satisfies all three of these criteria is necessarily somewhat apologetic, in either a conservative or reformist manner. The conservative reveals the hidden logical fit between what already happens in society and the underlying normative explanatory structure, then seeks to identify deviations or anomalies for the sake of casting them out. The reformer usually points to a whole body of ideas or practices that is out of line with the basic structure, but that can, with appropriate revisions, be made to fit. This exercise is apologetic because the assumption that existing practices are rational and good, or may readily be made so by procedures and options currently available to policy-makers, tends to exclude consideration of other possibilities, such as that the practices are irrational or bad beyond the chance of correction save by fundamental change – in ways of thinking as well as in institutional design. In other words (to overstate somewhat): if the situation cannot be "fixed," it is not a "problem" for the field at all.

The legal activity that is the subject of this scholarship takes place in a society that exists in space and time. This society supplies materials to the rationalizing enterprise in several forms. The first might be called "legal texts." These are the basic data of the field, the work-product of legal agencies and of lawyers doing or anticipating business before them, including cases, statutes, regulations, briefs, pleadings, indentures, deeds, settlement offers, negotiation arguments, advice to clients, and so forth. A second is the "social context," data from the social field in which the legal text is embedded. This could be the "facts" of a dispute, the "social problem" inspiring statutory action, the "difficulties of enforcement" of a tax levy or injunction, or the referent for the word "chicken" in a contract. The third set of materials will be called the "normative

[4] See Frank Michelman, "Norms and Normativity in the Economic Theory of Law," 6 *Minn. L. Rev.* 1015, 1038–1039 (1978).

context," which is the apparatus of normative conceptions to which the legal scholar tries to relate the legal texts. Sometimes these conceptions can be derived from inspection of the texts alone. Sometimes they are imported from outside, from perceptions of customary morality, historical tradition, political economy, ordinary language, moral philosophy, and so forth. I trust that no one will suppose that normative and social contexts are meant to represent categories easily defined to be mutually exclusive.

Any use at all of these social materials, even pure doctrinal scholarship that restricts its scope to legal texts, will expose the user to historicist criticism. The critic will claim that the scholar has, in one way or another, seriously distorted reality by failing to take adequate account of the social and historical contingency of the materials.[5] First, and least interestingly, the critic may try to swamp the rationalizing enterprise by emphasizing the bewildering and dense variety of the data it tries to manipulate. The scholar will come to see his legal texts as heaps of miscellaneous rubbish, and his attempts to sort them out as empty reductionist formalism. Some of the Legal Realists did have this experience,[6] but it is not a common one among legal scholars. A much more common experience is having to fend off the problems that arise because legal texts are "longitudinal" data, assembled by the scholar from earlier times. Principles synthesized from such texts are always open to the challenge that appeal to the old text is inappropriate because the social context has changed; the old text was drawn to respond to conditions that no longer exist. Of course, critical historicism at this level is itself part of the standard apparatus of legal scholarship. It poses no serious threat to the enterprise as a whole if kept on a tight leash, that is, if restricted to relatively trivial differentiation between past and present ("there were no cars traveling at 60 m.p.h. in 1850"), which implies that, saving such details, past and present are continuous. But historicism is dangerous whenever these restraints are loosened, as one can see from the recent powerful assaults by John Ely and Paul Brest on constitutional interpretation bound to textual language or the intentions of the drafters. Ely and Brest break with convention in positing drastic discontinuities, not only in social conditions and technologies, but in basic assumptions about reality[7] – about racial inferiority, the horror of death, or the necessary ineffectuality of judicial power.

The critic might go even further and make the case for discontinuity by reconstituting the political language in which an old text was first written. The old text will be rendered almost wholly archaic if it can be shown to embody a set of conceptions – about human nature, property, virtue, freedom,

[5] Of course, legal scholarship is not unique in its vulnerability to this kind of criticism. See Thomas Kuhn, *The Structure of Scientific Revolutions* 15 (2nd edn. 1970).

[6] *See* Grant Gilmore, *The Ages Of American Law* 80–81 (1977) (discussing Wesley Sturges's "intellectual nihilism").

[7] *See* John Ely, *Democracy and Distrust* 11–41, 45 (1980); Brest, "The Misconceived Quest for the Original Understanding," 60 *B.U.L. Rev.* 204, 220–221 (1980).

representation, necessity, causation, and so forth – that was a unique configuration for its time and in some ways strikingly unlike what we believe to be our own.[8] One naturally thinks in this connection of the remarkable recent work that has made the thought of this country's founders enormously more intelligible by locating its terminology and major preoccupations in a Whig "republican" ideology with a foundation in Renaissance political thought.[9] The lawyer who turns to the best available perspectives on the thinking behind the American Constitution may find herself in the position of the French humanist lawyers who hoped to uncover the universal basis for their own jurisprudence by freeing the Roman Corpus Juris from medieval corruptions, and then did such thorough scholarly work as to persuade many of them of Rome's irrelevance.[10]

Thus far, in this catalogue of perils, I have mentioned chaos and irrelevance. Perhaps more disturbing is the possibility that the critic, searching like the legal scholar for pattern and regularity in legal materials, will uncover a pattern, but not one that the scholar would wish to find. The critic might, for example, attempt to explain legal texts as determined, in an important sense, by some contextual variable such as the politics of a dominant class or temporarily dominant political coalition, the class affiliations of litigant parties or decision-makers, the psychological makeup of officials, or the logic of some long- term historical trend, such as economic growth or the development of internal contradictions in capitalism.[11] Such explanations will frequently be advanced because both ideologues of right and left and scholars in other disciplines have a professional stake in generating them. They are always a potential threat to the assumption that rationalizing legal texts will be a practical means of realizing the social good through law, because they seem to cast law, lawyers, and jurists in the humiliating status of mere epiphenomena, or at best, of people whose job it is to justify change brought about by forces over which they have

[8] *See generally* John Pocock, "Languages and their Implications: The Transformation of the Study of Political Thought," in *Politics, Language, and Time* 5 (1971) (text must be understood in context of mindset embodied in language of the time it was written): Quentin Skinner, "Meaning and Understanding in the History of Ideas," 8 *Hist & Theory* 5 (1969) (historian of ideas should uncover intended meaning of text by examining linguistic context).

[9] *See, e.g.*, John Pocock, *The Machiavellian Moment* 506–545 (1975); Caroline Robbins, *The Eighteenth Century Commonwealthman* 356–377, 85 (1959): Gordon Wood, *The Creation of the American Republic, 1776–1787*, at 48–75 (1969); John Dunn, "The Politics of Locke in England and America in the Eighteenth Century" in *John Locke: Problems And Perspectives* 45, 70–78 (Yolton ed. 1969).

[10] *See* Julian Franklin, *Jean Bodin and the Sixteenth-Century Revolution in the Methodology of Law And History* 36–58 (1963).

[11] *See, e.g.*, Charles Beard, *An Economic Interpretation of the Constitution of the United States* 152–88 (1915) (provisions of Constitution determined by distinct economic interest groups and classes); Lawrence Friedman, *A History of American Law* 10 (1973) (American legal development not autonomous but molded by economy and society).

little control. Curiously enough, however, legal scholarship has enthusiastically embraced certain kinds of social determinism.[12]

More subtle threats than these determinisms arise out of explorations of context that challenge the models of instrumental rationality underlying both the liberal theory of law and the enterprise of legal scholarship. These models assume that legal rules, if they are living up to their potential, are both universalistic and efficacious.[13] Nobody is bothered if the historicist questions this picture by pointing to specific laws that are selectively or ineffectively enforced: these examples simply illustrate the "gap" between law on the books and in action, the deviant practices that it is the function of legal scholars to extirpate.[14] What is troubling to legal scholars is the sociology that demonstrates systematic discontinuities between legal texts and their contexts. There are many different ways of creating this sense of discontinuity. One is an anthropological approach, "legal pluralism," which demotes the legal order to the status of one subculture among many, competing (and often losing) against many other sources of normative order and coercive sanctions, especially the customary orders of private associations.[15] Viewed this way, legal forms may not appear primary and universal, but seem only to express the ideology of a particular official or professional group – lawyers, judges, members of Congress, police officers, school administrators – the content of which is determined by the group's strategy of self-aggrandizement, which may include mystification, the pose of guarding traditional norms, the seizure of initiative from some other agency, or election to political office. Alternatively, the embodiment of a norm in law may be a tribute to its very ineffectiveness, the legal system being assigned the role of expressing as pious hopes norms that no one expects ever to be actualized.[16] Conversely, norms that derive from sources other than the state may be quite effectively enforced: in a society like ours, with strong

[12] *See* discussion of adaptation theory, *infra*.

[13] See David Trubek & Marc Galanter, "Scholars in Self-Estrangement: Some Reflections on the Crisis in Law and Development Studies in the United States," 1974 *Wis. L. Rev.* 1062, 1070–1074 (discussing paradigm of "liberal legalism").

[14] On the "gap" and its functions in legal scholarship, see Richard Abel, "Law Books and Books About Law," 26 *Stan. L. Rev.* 175, 184–189 (1973), and Malcolm Feeley, "The Concept of Laws in Social Science: A Critique and Notes on an Expanded View," 10 *Law & Soc'y Rev.* 497, 498–500 (1976).

[15] *See, e.g.*, Marc Galanter, "Justice in Many Rooms" 3–4 (1979) (unpublished Disputes Processing Research Program Working Paper, #1979-4, University of Wisconsin Law School); Stewart Macaulay, "Non-Contractual Relations in Business: A Preliminary Study," 28 *Am. Soc. Rev.* 55, 62 (1963) (in many business transactions, law of contract and legal sanctions play only a small role); Leon Mayhew, "Stability and Change in Legal Systems," in *Stability and Social Change* 187, 188, 210 (Barber & Inkeles eds. 1971) (legal system cannot exercise control over many autonomous social institutions and organizations).

[16] *See, e.g.*, Murray Edelman, *The Symbolic Uses of Politics* 37–38, 47–49 (1964): Joseph Gusfield, *Symbolic Crusade* 166–171 (1963).

traditions of extralegal[17] and antilegal[18] ideologies, one cannot even assert with confidence that the state has held a monopoly on legitimate violence. What legal scholarship considers the normal case – the law effective according to its announced terms and evident purposes – is relegated to a subclass of events satisfying peculiar and rather unusual social conditions.[19]

Other critics use evidence internal to the legal system to support the thesis of discontinuity, showing, for example, that requirements of procedure clutter every expression of substantive law with elaborate conditions on the means of its application. Rules apparently intended to create liabilities of B to A may submit A to painful assaults on privacy and dignity, may put A to difficult and expensive proof, may be conducted in a language difficult to understand and alien to A's concerns, and may be enforced by an agency congenitally sympathetic to B; such a rule will frequently end up making B stronger than ever. Again, mainstream scholarship expects this result to happen sometimes, and even concedes that it happens in whole areas of law,[20] but docs not admit that it will happen in the typical case.

Many more examples might be given. The point is that these types of social investigation and historicist criticism are profoundly unsettling to the standard rationalizing modes because they suggest that the contributions of texts to contexts are as likely to be harmful or futile as beneficent or practical, for reasons that ordinary legal analysis seems to keep beyond its field of vision. Perhaps more disturbingly, they suggest that the legal text often may not be understood at all in terms of its instrumental relation to a social context, but only as a symbolic statement: a legitimating ideology, a utopian aspiration, or a cultural ritual designed to define boundaries between social cleanliness and defilement. In response, legal scholarship has developed theories of how law relates to society and to history that minimize these threats to its enterprise.

This is not to say that most or even many legal scholars actually feel threatened by criticism from the historicist perspective; far from it.[21] For one thing,

[17] *See, e.g.*, John Reid, *In a Rebellious Spirit* 86–87 (1979); Pauline Maier, "Popular Uprising and Civil Authority in Eighteenth-Century America," 27 *William & Mary Q*. 3, 21–33 (1970). Although both Maier and Reid argue that mob action during the American Revolutionary period could be, and was, rationalized as lawful, that action was nonetheless at odds with officially constituted authority.

[18] *See* Alan Heimert, *Religion and the American Mind* 179–182 passim (1966) (discussing colonial sources of evangelical antilegalism).

[19] *See* William Felstiner, "Influences of Social Organization on Dispute Processing," 9 *Law & Socy Rev*. 65, 80–83 (1974); Marc Galanter, "Why the 'Haves' Come Out Ahead: Speculations on the Limits of Legal Change," 9 *Law & Soc'y Rev*. 95, 149–150 (1974); John Griffiths, "Is Law Important?" 54 *N.Y.U. L. Rev*. 339, 369–374 (1979); William Simon, "The Ideology of Advocacy: Procedural Justice and Professional Ethics," 1978 *Wis. L. Rev*. 29, 119–130.

[20] To some extent administrative regulation and lower level criminal justice administration have been assigned a special status even in mainstream scholarship as examples of persistent discontinuity between overt textual intentions and actual social operation.

[21] Barbara Black and others raised this point at the symposium.

the "applied" work of many middle-level scholars is far enough away from organizing theoretical assumptions that they would not be likely to see assaults on those assumptions as even relevant, much less damaging. To generate the psychological experience of a threat, the critic would first have to encourage such scholars to articulate the theoretical structures they take for granted. For another, the virtue of the "responsive modes" I am about to discuss is precisely that they provide a means to keep any sense of being threatened at bay. This quality is well illustrated by the fact that, although my argument as it has developed has tended to cast legal rationalism in a conservative role, and empiricism and historicism in a subversive and critical one, our experience has been largely the opposite. In the past, legal history has on the whole served to bolster and reassure existing enterprises of legal scholarship[22] and has required powerful assistance from criticism of very different forms – for example, Bentham's analytic demonstration of Blackstone's internal incoherence[23] or Tom Paine's radical fundamentalist attacks based on natural rights[24] – to break up these cozy, historically based systems. Nonetheless, historicist criticism, as I will argue, has also played a part in forcing major shifts in legal scholarship. Indeed, historicist criticism is always ultimately destabilizing to the enterprise. Hence the need for strong defenses.

II. THE FAILURE OF THE RESPONSIVE MODES

I will classify the responsive modes in four categories. The first mode is *denial* that particular contexts of time and place are relevant to the enterprise of legal rationalization. The second is *Cartesianism*, the construction of drastically simplified models of social reality for use in legal analysis. The third is *embrace* of context, or assimilation, in such a way that social and historical contextualization seem to serve rather than to subvert legal rationality. The fourth is *resignation* in the face of social contingency and historical change.

Denial. The purest form of denial is to assert that legal reasoning's exclusive concern should be to work out the relationship of legal texts to a system of suprahistorical norms transcending time and space. In this view, reason is, by definition, deduction from universals, not induction from the temporary and contingent. This style of natural-law thinking need not detain us. In the sixteenth and seventeenth centuries, empirically and historically minded lawyers, among others, helped to ensure its relegation to the margins of elite legal thought by shifting the center of study to positive law – the specific legal practices of actual societies – and by developing a self-consciously inductive

[22] *See* Morton Horwitz, "The Conservative Tradition in the Writing of American Legal History," 17 *Am. J. Legal Hist.* 275, 276, 281 (1973).

[23] See Jeremy Bentham, "A Comment on the Commentaries," in *A Comment on the Commentaries* and *A Fragment on Government* 1 (Burns & Hart eds. 1977).

[24] Thomas Paine, *Rights of Man* (2nd edn. 1791) (1st edn. 1791).

method for deriving legal principles from experience.[25] Of course, natural-law thinking has since remained vital, but I doubt that anyone would claim that its pure form is any longer in the mainstream. To the extent it persists, it is almost always mixed with other modes.

The modern forms of denial are likely to stake out only limited claims for the territory of suprahistorical norms. One example might be the "originalist" view of the interpretation of the Federal Constitution, which claims that at least some texts must be treated as if they had a frozen, noncontingent meaning. For reasons already suggested, this is an exceedingly difficult position to put into practical operation.[26] Another example might be the view that many, though not all, legal rules are technical, facilitative rules used to solve problems of a kind that might arise in any society (such as rules governing the formalities of contract formation) and can therefore be expressed in an abstract form to which any society at any point in its mutation could plug in. Yet denial even in this form cannot successfully defend the rationalizing enterprise. One of the standard, and most effective, historicist attacks made by the Realists on their "formalist" predecessors involved the formalists' claims to have come up with such rules. The supposedly purely technical schemes of offer-and-acceptance rules, for instance, were shown to be indefinitely manipulable in theory to reach the results of "contract formed" or "no contract formed" in any particular case, and to have been regularly manipulated in practice to reach one result or the other in situations that could be distinguished only by close attention to social or economic context.[27]

Cartesianism. The much more common modern strategy for keeping distressing historicity at bay is what I call "Cartesianism": formal modeling, the intellectual strategy of constructing highly simplified models of social reality for the sake of analytic rigor and elegance, in the manner of economic theory. The models are relatively closed games. You cannot play unless you agree in advance to a fairly explicitly specified set of rules about permissible moves. If you change the rules – for example, by admitting a new empirical assumption: the island people produce three goods, not just two, and one person is given a gun – you should change only a few at a time and only with advance notice. Cartesianism is a strategy midway between the denial and the embrace of social contingency: it admits social variables, but only as members of a highly exclusive club, and thus makes itself vulnerable to historicist attack only to the extent it desires.

[25] *See* William Greenleaf, *Order, Empiricism and Politics* 142–205, 262–282 (1964); Pocock, *Machiavellian Moment*, at 3–30.

[26] *See* discussion of originalism, *supra*.

[27] *See, e.g.*, Felix Cohen, "Transcendental Nonsense and the Functional Approach," 55 *Colum. L. Rev.* 809, 839–42 (1935); Karl Llewellyn, "On Our Case-Law of Contract: Offer and Acceptance (pts. 1& 2)," 48 *Yale L. J.* 1, 779 (1938–1939).

The legal formalism of the late nineteenth century was a Cartesian mode in this sense, because many of its practitioners viewed the few core principles on which it was based as socially derived – indeed, as given by history. But history was a subcontractor whose job was finished once it had laid the foundation of principles. The rest of the structure was to be built strictly with such legal texts as could be rationalized according to deductions from those principles,[28] with allowances here and there for quirks of public policy. The Realists had a lot of fun with these structures, pointing out the social contingency of decisions and the policy choices made with the placing of every brick and board.[29] Nonetheless, they too practiced, and bequeathed to us, a quasi-Cartesian method of "policy analysis" that employs a simple model. That model assumes that the rules of appellate doctrine are instantly incorporated in the incentive structures of individuals situated like the litigants, and takes the "facts" as stated in the opinion, for the purpose of analyzing the effect of rules, to represent the litigants' situation. For example: "Adoption of the rule plaintiff wants would ... deter sellers from fraud, cause them to charge higher prices, leave the market in disgust," and so forth. Historicist critics have treated policy analysis harshly, though with no apparent effect upon its incidence. The critics assert that because of high litigation costs, cross-cutting regimes of social custom or domination, total lack of correspondence between the way the judge told the story and the way the litigants experienced it, or the impracticability of general enforcement, announcement of the rule is often likely to have no effect at all, or to have a completely unexpected one.[30]

Yet the vulnerability of Cartesian modes to the battery of historicist criticisms naturally depends on the claims made for the theory. Sir Henry Maine's famous objection to Austin's notion that law is the command of a sovereign – that in many of the world's societies, past and present, one could not find anyone looking like a sovereign issuing anything looking like a command, because their members' habits of obedience are overwhelmingly to orders of custom[31] – was beside the point. Austin was not trying to describe any actual legal system, just proposing a model to sharpen thinking about the idea of law generally. But the moment that positivist theorists like Austin claim the ability to resolve actual social controversies through a reasoning process that is strictly internal to an autonomous legal order, relying exclusively, for example, on the "core meanings" of authoritative legal texts (rules), the historicist is entitled to point out that all language is social, and all meaning contextual.[32] Similarly, modern

[28] See Christopher Langdell, *A Summary of the Law of Contract iv* (2nd edn. 1880) ("a concise statement and exposition of the doctrines" developed in his pioneering casebook).

[29] *See* discussion of Realism, *supra.*

[30] *See, e.g.*, Stewart Macaulay, "Elegant Models, Empirical Pictures, and the Complexities of Contract," 11 *Law & Soc'y Rev*. 507, 508–510 (1977).

[31] Henry Maine, *Lectures on the Early History of Institutions* 357–365 (1888).

[32] *See*, e.g., Lon Fuller, "Positivism and Fidelity to Law – A Reply to Professor Hart," 71 *Harv. L. Rev*. 630, 661–669 (1958).

policy analysts might argue to their critics that the normative enterprise of rationalizing doctrine is one that traditionally proceeds as if the model were empirically valid, so that demonstrations that it is not are irrelevant.[33] Further, if one wishes to converse with judges in their rhetorical reasoning modes, one will adopt their simplifying assumptions, however fanciful they may seem. Yet few legal scholars are willing to see their enterprise as simply one of working within traditional rhetorics. To the extent that, as problem-solvers, they must claim that their models represent social reality well enough to be used as a basis for decision-making, they are fair game for their critics.[34]

Adaptation Theory. Even at the flood tide of formalism in American legal scholarship, at the Harvard Law School of the 1870s and 1880s, the scholars were committed as much to the project of synthesizing legal principles from historical materials as to analytic schematization of those principles. Like Austin himself, who had studied in Germany and was convinced he was pursuing a genuine historical method,[35] they were certain that the historical and analytic methods complemented rather than conflicted with one another. In short, they had found a way of accepting a relationship between legal texts and society, but one seemingly free of historicist perils. This brings us to the third and most important of the responsive modes, the notion that there is an immanent rationality in social life, which it is the business of legal rationalization to incorporate.

One way of embracing history, now rarely used explicitly, is as a curator of timeless traditional wisdom or immemorial custom – the norms of the ancient Gothic Constitution or those of 1787 – which is frequently violated in times of tyranny, but always there to be re-affirmed once people come to their senses.[36] Some versions of this static view of the function of tradition have always been important in our legal thought,[37] but only in combination with much more

[33] Perhaps this answer is rarely given because it is so easily followed by the question: "But if you are not seriously interested in instrumental effects, why do you use a rhetoric of instrumental rationality?" This challenge requires a more complicated (and equally rare) answer, perhaps: "At present instrumental rhetoric is the most legitimate and persuasive."

[34] *Cf.* Mario Rizzo, "The Mirage of Efficiency," 8 *Hofstra L. Rev.* 641, 641–643 (1980) (models of legal economics exclude too many variables to be useful).

[35] *See* 2 John Austin, *Lectures on Jurisprudence* 101–102 (4th rev. Campbell edn. 1813) (1st edn. 1861) (new material in Campbell edition taken from John Stuart Mill's notes); Andreas Schwarz, "John Austin and the German Jurisprudence of His Time," 1 *Politica* 178 (1934).

[36] *See* John Pocock, *The Ancient Constitution and the Feudal Law* 30–55 (1967) (characterizing early seventeenth-century conception of common law as immemorial custom); Rush Welter, *The Mind of America, 1820–1860*, at 26–44 (1975) (post-Revolutionary Americans believed that they had transcended the "macrohistory" of the European old world, and were to live in a "microhistory" in which the problem would be striving to live up to norms already given by the national mission); cf. Sacvan Bercovitch, *The American Jeremiad* 93–131 (1978) (discussing "America's Mission").

[37] *See* Thomas Jefferson, "Whether Christianity is Part of the Common Law?" in 1 *The Writings of Thomas Jefferson, 1760–1775*, at 360 (Ford ed. 1892).

important dynamic views of history. Their exponents have kept up a steady barrage of criticism against the static views without ever managing to expel them entirely. The critical technique is simply to show that the custom or ideal claimed to be immemorial has a specific origin in the circumstances and thinking of a particular period, and survived after it only as a result of inertia.[38] The point of departure for this kind of criticism is the adaptation theory of legal change, which, from its first full articulation (perhaps never since surpassed) by Matthew Hale,[39] has become central to our conventional ways of thought.

Adaptation theorists sometimes say that the function of law is to learn to recognize, or imitate, regimes of spontaneous order already present in social life. Thus, legal rationalization is nothing more than a means to promote accurate encoding of these orders of custom, or "living law." Sometimes they express the role of law more actively, saying that it is a kind of problem-solving technology that responds, or adapts, to "needs" emerging from society. Then the tasks of legal rationalization are to help identify those needs and to improve the adaptive technology. In this century, these views have probably more often been expressed in legal scholarship as a set of vague background assumptions, seemingly too obvious to need any elaboration, than as a full-fledged theory. Blackstone and Adam Smith, both pioneering adaptation theorists, did not shirk the task of trying to spell out in some detail their notions of the adaptive relationship between legal forms and social change,[40] but despite the inspiration that the work of Maine, Vinogradoff, and Weber[41] might have provided, their successors have been uninterested, with only rare exceptions,[42] in trying

[38] *See, e.g.*, Bentham, *supra* note 23, at 234–37; Pocock, *supra* note 36, at 91–123 (discussing work of Sir Henry Spelman).

[39] *See* Mathew Hale, "Considerations Touching the Amendment or Alteration of Lawes," in 1 *A Collection of Tracts Relative to the Law of England* 249 (Hargrave ed. 1787). Describing the dangers of "over much hastiness in changing of old lawes, and introducing of new," he writes:

> It is most certain, that time and long experience is much more ingenious, subtile and judicious, than all the wisest and acutest wits in the world co-existing can be ... So that in truth antient lawes, especially, that have a common concern, are not the issues of the prudence of this or that council or senate, but they are the production of the various experiences and applications of the wisest thing in the inferior world; to wit, time, which as it discovers day after day new inconveniences, so it doth successively apply new remedies; and indeed it is a kind of aggregation of the discoveries, results and applications of ages and events...

Id. at 253–254.

[40] See 2 William Blackstone, *Commentaries* 1–15 (discussing development of legal institution of property); Adam Smith, *Lectures on Jurisprudence* 13–76, 200–292 (Meek, Raphael, & Stein eds. 1978) (relating different modes of acquiring property to hunting, pastoral, agricultural, and commercial stages of social development, and relating different forms of government to same stages).

[41] *See* Henry Maine, *Ancient Law* (1861); Peter Vinogradoff, *Outlines of Historical Jurisprudence* (2 vols.) (1920–1922); Max Weber, *Economy and Society* (2 vols.) (Roth & Wittich eds. 1968).

[42] *See* notes 134–139 *infra* (citing recent work of legal scholars in tradition of Weber).

to develop any systematic social theory of legal change. Thus, when scholars say, as in recent mainstream scholarship they frequently do,[43] that law has changed, or should change, to meet social needs, they do not usually feel that they have to specify what a "social need" is, or how the particular needs they refer to originated and have changed over time.[44]

No matter how loosely they may define their basic concepts, all adaptation theorists must find some way to distinguish adaptive from maladaptive law. The easiest solution to this problem is Hale and Burke's notion of prescriptive experience, which, in an extreme Panglossian form to which neither Hale nor Burke ever subscribed, holds that whatever law exists is on that account presumptively adaptive.[45] Though possibly the most coherent of all the adaptation theories, this one has very little charm for legal scholars, who would have nothing to do if it were valid, and who usually want very much to reject some aspects of the present order. Legal scholars frequently ask, when moving toward evaluation, whether legal interventions in social processes follow the natural grain of such processes or artificially cut across it – naturalness, naturally, being adaptive, and artificiality, maladaptive. This move may be made through a procedural theory of institutional competence, a substantive theory of social processes, or some combination of the two.

The procedural theorist asserts at his crudest that some kinds of law-making are *per se* adaptive, others just as automatically maladaptive. In our scholarly tradition, the assignment of these roles has repeatedly switched back and forth between judges and legislatures, though it occasionally gravitates elsewhere, especially to juries and administrative agencies. Adjudication, for instance, has sometimes been thought to be relatively naturally adaptive because case law, being fact-bound, can simply track social custom in the rich particularity of its form in specific controversies, whereas legislation is necessarily general in form and hence abstract.[46] Alternatively, adjudication is natural because judges possess, through their technical training in case law, vicarious experience of the order of custom, whereas legislators must rely upon the necessarily parochial and limited materials of personal experience or the claims pressed upon

[43] Adaptation theory is so pervasive in the scholarship of the past two centuries that it would be a challenge to find work in which it was not present. For representative modern examples of adaptationism, see Benjamin Cardozo, *The Growth of the Law* (1924), Robert Keeton, "Creative Continuity in the Law of Torts," 15 *Harv. L. Rev.* 463, 484 (1962), and the discussion *infra* of the legal thought of Whigs and Progressives.

[44] Utilitarian legal theory and the current law-and-economics movement have, of course, formulated more or less rigorous theories of the relationship of legal texts to individual wants. But these theories are not, and usually do not pretend to be, social theories, because the social conditions in which preferences arise are treated as exogenous.

[45] *See* John Pocock "Burke and the Ancient Constitution: A Problem in the History of Ideas," *Politics, Language and Time* 202, 215–228 (1971).

[46] *See* James Carter, "The Ideal and the Actual in the Law," 18 *A.B.A. Rep.* 217, 231–236 (1890).

them by lobbyists.[47] Most recently, the argument has surfaced that common law adjudication, for reasons as yet only suspected but having perhaps to do with the survival power of precedents preferred by litigants,[48] seems to produce economically efficient results, whereas legislation is easily captured by special interests to defeat the immanent rationality of the market.[49] On the other hand, the simple case for legislative naturalness, if one is willing to equate "social needs" with "the prevailing political consensus of desires," is that legislation is the outcome of majoritarian processes; if one is not so willing, the case is that legislative committees have more time and expertise than judges to inquire deeply into the social order. A more complex case is that legislation better represents the governing coalitions of "minorities rule." The late Alexander Bickel, for example, ascribed Burkean naturalness to the push and pull of the struggles and compromises of corporate interest groups engaged in pluralist political bargaining. With this lush, jungly background of striving and decaying organic lives he contrasted the artificial activity of adjudication. Adjudication, he argued, is artificial precisely because of the duty of principled reasoning, which, like any abstractly rational design, if extended beyond its appropriate sphere may have unexpected tragic or ironic consequences to the delicate jungle ecology.[50]

Few people are content, however, to rest adaptation theory entirely on the naturally adaptive processes of any single institution. Hale, our prototype theorist, immediately follows his argument that laws should not be rashly amended (because they are presumptively adapted to spontaneous order) with a list of reasons why they should be prudently amended:[51] like Burke, he was a reformer. Spontaneous order has a way of becoming very disorderly. Old texts may be carried into new contexts from insufficient litigation or from force of professional habit, so that the emergence of new rules to meet new needs is stunted. Although presumed to be fundamentally sound, any legal system may develop complexities and anomalies that defeat its own ends, but it may be restored to adaptive capacity through moderate reform, that is, through the deployment of some self-consciously rational equilibrating mechanism. With the theory so qualified, all that is needed is a procedural theory of appropriate equilibrating mechanisms. Hale's own is a common one: see first what may be done through the judiciary and have only last resort to the legislature.[52]

[47] See Roscoe Pound, "The Economic Interpretation and the Law of Torts," 53 *Harv. L. Rev.* 365, 366 (1940).

[48] George Priest, "The Common Law Process and the Selection of Efficient Rules," 6 *J. Legal Stud.* 65, 68 (1977). But *see* George Priest, "Selective Characteristics of Litigation," 9 *J. Legal Stud.* 399, 410 (1980) (addition of new variable to model employed in earlier article causes significant revision in conclusions).

[49] Richard Posner, *Economic Analysis of Law* 404–405 (2nd edn. 1977).

[50] Alexander Bickel, *The Supreme Court and the Idea of Progress* 173–178 (1970).

[51] Hale, *supra* note 39, at 264–271.

[52] *Id.* at 272.

Similarly, if one is a partisan of legislative naturalness, one may advise primary reliance on statutory law-making, subject to correction for gross defect by judicial constitutional review. Most legal writers, of course, have favored multi-tiered systems, in which juries, trial judges, appellate judges, the common-law process, codification by experts, legislation, administration, and judicial review are each given roles both of natural adaptation and of corrective equilibration for different purposes.

To a procedural adaptation theorist, the only valid object of rationalist reform is repair of the natural processes: anything more would be maladaptive intervention. Yet it is a rare scholar who is able to play the game indefinitely – identifying natural mechanisms subject to occasional interruptions for repair by rational ones – without at some point mentioning substantive criteria of adaptability.[53] Once one has gone so far as to distinguish natural from artificial processes and good from bad reforms, one probably has at least some covert substantive notions of what in social life law should adapt to, and what it should promote, restrain, and avoid. One way to identify natural processes and good reforms is simply to make a list of social needs, as banal as you like – for example, political stability, personal security, or maintaining the market.[54] Another way is to infer a list of needs from existing law: to hypothesize that every legal text responds to some need, and then simply to guess what that need might be.[55] However one identifies the needs, the next step is to evaluate how effectively current law serves the need; if it does not, it should be reformed. But this method will get you nowhere without some way to tell current from obsolete needs, since by hypothesis every text responds to some need; what is called for is a theory of social change, or historical direction, that truly adaptive law must follow, and by following which it may be identified. Indeed, the social functionalism of our legal tradition is almost invariably tied to a theory of social-legal development, generally (with some lapses and variations) a theory of progressive development like "modernization," "Whig history," or "legal evolution," which simultaneously licenses most existing law as adaptive and permits historicist criticism of some of it as maladaptively "lagging" behind the course of history.[56]

This discussion must seem a painfully labored journey to arrive at a familiar destination. I have proceeded this way to emphasize that some notion of

[53] *Cf.* Paul Brest, "The Fundamental Rights Controversy: The Essential Contradictions of Normative Constitutional Scholarship," 90 *Yale L. J.* 1063, 1104 (1981) (legal theory cannot avoid making substantive choices); Laurence Tribe, "The Puzzling Persistence of Process-Based Constitutional Theories," 89 *Yale L. J.* 1063, 1064 (1980) (process approach indeterminate if not informed by theory of substantive rights and values).

[54] Surely the longest such list on record is Dean Pound's delineation of individual and societal interests in 3 Roscoe Pound, *Jurisprudence* 25–324 (1959).

[55] This "technique" is nothing more than our accustomed method of classroom "policy analysis."

[56] *See* Part III *infra* (discussing theories of Whigs and Progressives).

historical direction seems to be required by any adaptation theory of law that goes beyond the purely prescriptive. For all their ingenuity in meeting historicist criticism through partial assimilation, however, adaptation theorists actually remain highly vulnerable to it, because the theory's coherence depends on its ability to tell functional from dysfunctional law. This ability can be questioned in several ways.

One attack is the conservative's *reductio* that the rule claimed to be obsolete may actually be fulfilling a valuable, if latent, social function – for example, Blackstone argued that the bizarre quiddities and fictions of the writ system had freed the English land law from feudal restraints[57] – so that the rule is tampered with at the reformer's peril. The latent function might be precisely that of preserving the authority and legitimacy of the legal system by presenting it to the masses as an historical *fait accompli*. Once they have the idea of reform, there is no telling what they may do. The usual response is that a little reform will keep them quiet, but that none at all will enrage them.[58]

A non-conservative variant of this attack has been developed by Lawrence Friedman, who argues that all current law, even what looks like anomalous "survivals," exists for a reason and may be explained by reference to some current social reality. If a rule has not changed for a long time, one should ask why not, and one may often find the answer in a deadlock actively brought about by some clash of interest groups.[59] This perspective absorbs law completely into a determining context by collapsing social "needs" into "interests": law adapts all right, but only to whatever interests happen to get control of it. This view also undermines the normative force of adaptation theory. After all, what could be so wonderful about a law perfectly adapted to the needs of a slave civilization?[60]

A second attack comes from exactly the opposite direction. Many legal texts cannot be explained, and therefore justified, on the ground that they are functional adaptations: they are chronically maladapted to the manifest functions

[57] *See* 5 Blackstone, *supra* note 40, at 195–197.

[58] *See* Douglas Hay, "Property, Authority, and the Criminal Law," in Douglas Hay, Peter Linebaugh, John Rule, Edward Thompson, & Cal Winslow, *Albion's Fatal Tree* 17, 24–26 (1975).

[59] See Friedman, *supra* note 11, at 10, 14; Lawrence Friedman & Jack Ladinsky, "Social Change and the Law of Industrial Accidents," 67 *Colum. L. Rev.* 50, 65, 72, 76 (1967).

[60] Austin made this point very effectively against Blackstone's exaltation of custom:

> During the Middle Ages, the body of the people, throughout Europe, were in the serf or slavish condition. And this slavish condition of the body of the people originated in custom: Although the imperfect rights which custom gave to their masters, together with the imperfect obligations which custom imposed on themselves, were afterwards enforced by Law of which that custom was the basis... Let us turn our eyes in what direction we may, we shall find that there is no connection between customary law, and the well-being of the many.

2 Austin, *supra* note 35, at 559–560.

claimed for them.[61] Nor may they be explained away as "gaps," "lags," or "anomalies": they have almost never worked the way they are supposed to.[62] Such texts can be rationalized only as performing latent functions, which destroys the adaptive/maladaptive boundary.

Adaptation theory's dualism between a "society" that has "needs" and a "legal system" that responds to them can also be attacked. Even if one takes adaptationism in its most romantic form, law unconsciously encodes the customary Zeitgeist in a legal text, placing it on the new grid of a professionally interpreted map of texts, and thereby alters its meaning forever. Moreover, by encoding custom, law transmits it to people in other places and times, and thus acts positively to reproduce the custom (in its altered legal form), and not just passively to reflect it. The "society" that keeps throwing up new needs, therefore, is always partly constituted by its laws, which are helping to make the social needs to which the law-makers pretend only to adapt. Pointing out this kind of circularity was a favorite exercise of the Progressive critics of legal formalism. For example, the Supreme Court said that public utility rate-making was confiscatory unless the rate allowed the utility a reasonable return on the fair value of its property,[63] but of course "fair value" was itself a function of the rate the Court was willing to say was reasonable.[64]

Circularity turned out to be as big a problem for the Progressive jurists, who wanted their law to adapt to the "social facts" of its context instead of to the arid logical consistency worshipped (as they thought) by their predecessors. Yet the "facts" as stated in a case or in a legislative history that describes the social situation to which the legal text is to respond are also in part artifacts of the legal system. If the story were differently told, it would suggest different solutions.[65] The critic can further generalize the point, showing how legal texts participate in the construction of the social world, populating it with creatures of law's own devising, abstract self-determining individuals and artificial corporate persons, ascribing "interests" to them and deciding when their sufferings are recognizable "harms."[66]

[61] *See* Alan Watson, *Society and Legal Change* 7–8, 130–137 (1977). In this very interesting book, Watson accepts the basic tenet of adaptation theory that societies have needs to which their laws should respond, but says that legal systems chronically lag behind such needs, copiously illustrating this claim with examples from Roman and English law.

[62] *See* discussion *supra* of discontinuity between texts and contexts.

[63] *See* Smyth *v.* Ames, 169 U.S. 466, 526, 546–547, *decree modified*, 171 U.S. 361 (1898).

[64] *See* John Dickinson, *Administrative Justice and the Supremacy of Law in the United States* 221–226 (1927).

[65] *See, e.g.*, Richard Danzig, "How Questions Begot Answers in Felix Frankfurter's First Flag Salute Opinion," 1977 *Sup. Ct. Rev.* 257, 258 (1978) (Justice Frankfurter reached opposite conclusions in similar cases by "differential focusing"). An excellent recent treatment of "fact-skepticism" is found in Kenneth Casebeer, "The Judging Glass," 33 *Miami L. Rev.* 59, 98–118 (1978).

[66] *See, e.g.*, Alexander Nékám, *The Personality Conception of the Legal Entity* 116–124 (1938); John Noonan, *Persons and Masks of the Law* 14–25 (1976); Joseph Vining, *Legal Identity*

This last line of criticism suggests a fourth. The social needs usually postulated, besides being partly a construct of the legal system rather than somehow objectively present in society apart from law, are frequently in contradiction with one another.[67] For example, American lawyers of the nineteenth century liked to assert that a main function of law was to protect security in possession and certainty in exchange at the same time that it fostered capital accumulation; they found in practice, however, that they had constantly to choose among these purposes, so that the actual social need served was that of mediating these conflicts by dressing up doctrinal formulae in traditional language to obscure the fact that some people's security and certainty were being promoted at the expense of others'.[68] Interestingly, like other latent functions, this important one is given scant attention in the ordinary scholarly literature.

Finally, the critic can attack the assumptions about the course of history underlying adaptation theory. She can, for example, show that the directional histories are simply wrong. The assumptions of the evolutionary histories of nineteenth-century jurists, especially the assumptions of necessary stage developments in all – at least all "progressive" – societies from communalism toward individualism, and status to contract, were, as Peter Stein has recently reminded us,[69] broken up by historicist critics who found that even English legal development had skipped stages or gone through them in reverse order![70]

I have given a lot of attention to adaptation theory because under one name or another – expediency, convenience, utility, growth, development, modernization, historical or sociological jurisprudence, the functional approach, social engineering, policy analysis, efficiency, or responsive law – it has been a component of virtually all the major movements of Anglo-American juristic writing, and has been a common element cutting across otherwise violent controversies between schools. That is, the idea that law is good if it dynamically adapts to social change is the same idea whether the writer gives primary emphasis to naturally adaptive procedures or to consciously adaptive equilibrating mechanisms; it is also, I believe, vulnerable to the same criticisms. Even theories that at first sight look like pure denial, claiming that legal rationality is not historically contingent, often turn out to be historicist adaptationism in disguise. The idea that the purpose of law is to realize in society certain universally valid norms

20–33 (1978); Mark Kelman, "Consumption Theory, Production Theory, and Ideology in the Coase Theorem," 52 *S. Cal. L. Rev.* 669, 695–696 (1979).

67 This argument is generalized in Duncan Kennedy, "The Structure of Blackstone's Commentaries, 28 *Buffalo L. Rev.* 209, 354–372 (1979).

68 *See, e.g.*, Morton Horwitz, *The Transformation of American Law, 1780–1860*, at 31–62 (1977); Harry Scheiber, "Property Law, Expropriation, and Resource Allocation by Government, 1789–1910," 33 *J. Econ. Hist.* 232, 240–243 (1973).

69 Peter Stein, *Legal Evolution* 107–121 (1980). This book might have been entitled *A brief and lucid history of adaptation theory in nineteenth century England.*

70 *See* 1 Frederick Pollock & Frederick William Maitland, *The History of English Law* 627–634, 654–657, 670–688 (1895) (discussing the "individualism" of early English village communities).

is often tied to a notion of historical development by which the good norms – individual liberty against the state, political equality, freedom of contract, or mixed government, for example – are known to be good because they have been gradually and progressively realizing themselves in history, or because they have been evolving into their present highly developed forms from inferior ones.[71] The idea that law should adapt to follow or promote its dynamically unfolding normative context does not seem to me essentially different from the ideal of adaptation to social context.

Resignation. The last of the responsive modes, resignation, is not really a theory but a set of attitudes. Legal rationality, say the resigned, is only an existential affirmation of order in the midst of nothingness. It satisfies human cravings for meaning and it nourishes myths bolstering the (impliedly necessary and desirable) cohesion of society or the authority of the state. In weaker versions, the resigned admit that legal institutions, like all human works, are naturally imperfect, are always, because of historical contingency, out-of-date, and are inevitably, because of social complexity, problematic in their effects; but that's life. In yet another version, the concession is that all our rationalizing activity is tentative and provisional, all our ideas of the good possibly parochial, but the best that we happen to know. No very definite or systematic patterns are likely to emerge from our inquiries, so we must be content to work out the seemingly pragmatic best solutions case by case.

This attitude is extraordinarily difficult to isolate for discussion because, like denial, it is hardly ever found in pure form, although it is pervasively sprinkled through legal writing[72] and is more of a mood, or tone of voice, than anything one can really grasp. Its strangeness is that while seeming in every way to concede the historicist critics' case, its actual deployment is to justify the orthodox practice of mainstream rationalizing rather than to incorporate the critics' perspective. The effect is like a move in judo: the resigned scholar uses the critics' strength to flip them on their backs and meanwhile keeps doing what he did before. But why, if he recognizes the limitations of his methods? If he sees that current norms and practices are historically contingent, why does he continue writing as if they were natural and necessary? If he is perfectly aware, as he claims he is, that law rarely really works the way it is supposed to, why does he continue to contribute to a style of rationalizing scholarship that accepts at face value an idealized instrumental view of the role of law in society? More generally, if our conventional styles of rationalization are compelled neither by suprahistorical norms nor by the logic of history – nor even by a Cartesian model around which the discipline is organized – why don't we do something else?

[71] *See*, e.g., James Barr Ames, "Law and Morals," 22 *Harv. L. Rev.* 97, 118 (1908) (law has developed through six centuries toward closer "harmony with moral principles").

[72] Resignation occasionally surfaces as the dominant mood in the work of some writers – for example, Holmes, Thurman Arnold, and, more recently, Calvin Woodard and Grant Gilmore.

III. THE PERSISTENCE OF OLD MODES: WHIGS AND PROGRESSIVES

We don't, though. The old modes persist. One way to read the history of our legal thought is as a succession of mixings of the main responsive modes into – "paradigms" is too pretentious, "systems" too suggestive of system – amalgams that command the allegiance of most of the orthodox until they come under attack and are demolished by historicist criticism, among other kinds. But such criticism is strictly limited in its impact by the regrouping, like white cells, of the same old responsive modes into another amalgam uncannily like the one recently demolished.

Let me try briefly to illustrate how this process has worked through a summary account of how the amalgam put together by American antebellum legal writers came under historicist fire around the beginning of our own century, and was then replaced by another and similar amalgam that has dominated our scholarship until very recently.

The principal contributors to what Morton Horwitz has called the "treatise tradition,"[73] the early nineteenth-century's closest analogue to modern legal scholarship, were an elite of primarily Federalist and Whig lawyers[74] anxious to vindicate an ambitious conception of their political role in the new American republic. This role was linked to the enlarged importance of the judiciary in the Federalist scheme, by which the people had delegated governmental authority not simply to representative assemblies but to a complexly interacting system of separated powers, the functioning of each of which was critical to the scheme as a whole. As a result, the state and federal judiciaries, through their authority to say what the law was, were able to claim and to acquire the authority to interpret the fundamental law of the constitutions.[75] Moreover, partly by default of available alternatives, partly by astute political suppression of alternatives occasionally proposed, the profession was able to secure to the federal and state judiciaries, assisted by a learned elite of leaders of their respective bars, the principal responsibility for expounding and developing an American law of private rights.[76] To justify their maintaining this position, these judges and lawyers appealed to their command of a body of legal learning and techniques for working with it ("legal science") that, they said, could guarantee liberty and property far more reliably than its competitors, the temporary whimsies of factional legislative coalitions or the untutored

[73] *See* Horwitz, *supra* note 68, at 257–258 (contributors to this tradition included Chancellor Kent, Joseph Story, and Joseph Angell).

[74] Joseph Story is included in this category, see note 73 *supra*, although of course he started his career as a Jeffersonian.

[75] *See* Wood, *supra* note 9, at 453–463.

[76] Radical reformers in Pennsylvania, for example, "denounced the legal profession, the common law, and the idea of an independent judiciary." Richard E. Ellis, *The Jeffersonian Crisis* 161–164 (1971). Nevertheless, the bar was able to preserve the judiciary's role. *See* Gerard Gawalt, *The Promise Of Power* 81–118 (1979).

non-lawyer's intuitions about natural rights. A potential embarrassment to this claim lay in the fact that English law was the chief component of traditional legal learning. The Revolution had transformed this law into an alien system and one vulnerable to the savage historicist criticism that it was honeycombed by the feudal and superstitious corruptions of centuries, of which, despite progress, "much of the domineering spirit"[77] still remained. Feeling obliged to disentangle their science from its disreputable past while preserving its traditional authority, the Whig-Federalist lawyers deployed against their historicist and natural-rights critics a dazzling array of responsive modes.

One, a *denial* on which they could expect general agreement, was the response that the common law contained certain suprahistorical principles of fundamental law – either the immemorial norms of the ancient Gothic constitution as finally revindicated through historical struggle or simply principles expressive of the law of nature[78] – which Americans had asserted as their birthright in the Revolution and whose best guarantee was adoption of a system known to contain them. This position was undercut somewhat by the elevation of the best known of these principles into written constitutions and bills of rights.

The modes that turned out to be most useful were the several varieties of adaptationism. One was *prescriptive adaptationism*, the argument that the common law was a vast Hale-like repository of collective experience about what ordinary people and wise judges have thought to be useful customs and norms in concrete circumstances.[79] A second was *procedural adaptationism* – judge-made case law had the flexibility to change with changing circumstances. This mode was accompanied by a dash of *resignation*. Because human actions were infinite in their variety and constantly in flux, and legal texts were constantly changing their meaning in new contexts, it was futile and vain to hope to achieve certainty in the law by capturing a rule in a legislative phrase or code. Yet this argument for the constant necessity of reinterpreting texts did not remain a pessimistic one about the indeterminacy of legal language; it quickly became an affirmative argument in favor of entrusting the job of reinterpretation to those specially trained in the science of finding the one "true sense," in the new context, of the old text.[80] Third, the Whig-Federalist lawyers had resort to *equilibrating mechanisms*. Lawyers conceded over and over again to their critics that the common law was full of feudal excrescences, silly fictions,

[77] John Adams, A dissertation on the Canon and the Feudal Law, in I *Papers of John Adams* 103, 127 (Taylor, Kline, & Lint eds. 1977).

[78] *See* Wood, *supra* note 9, at 9–10 (discussing the blending of the ideas that common-law rights were justified because they had "existed from time immemorial" and because they embodied natural law).

[79] *See* James Wilson "Lectures on Law," in I *Works Of James Wilson* 204–207 (1804), for a typical rhapsody in this key.

[80] *See* Francis Lieber, *Legal And Political Hermeneutics* 86 (enlarged ed. Boston 1819).

and parochially English customs and inventions. But Americans, implicitly at the beginning of the colonial settlements and explicitly by the terms of the "reception" statutes, had adopted the common law only insofar as it met their needs and conditions,[81] giving a valuable discretion to their judges to dispense with or vary English precedent. Furthermore, the response continued, England herself had shown what could be accomplished by way of judicial reform, through the example of Lord Mansfield's selective importation of international commercial law and more recent judges' use of European civilian writers to "expand with the exigencies of society," and to suit the "business of a nation increasing in wealth and commerce, and connecting itself with the interests of all the world."[82] *Evolutionary adaptation* was a fourth mode. Despite all its historical archaisms and positive abuses maladaptively implanted during corrupt regimes, the long-term trend of the common law had been a progressive development – for example, away from feudal restraints on alienation, toward a liberal commercial policy[83] – in directions entirely compatible with American republicanism.

By these means and others, legal science was related to something more fundamental than mere politics: to principles of fundamental right as realized teleologically through historical experience and, even more important, to needs spontaneously emerging from social life and to the long-term logic of historical development.

The jurists who put together the "formalist" or "classical" legal schemes of the late nineteenth century did not materially differ in ambitions or assumptions from their antebellum predecessors, though of course their methods were very much more systematic. They believed that the common law had gradually been ridding itself of the archaisms and anomalies preventing its systematization, and was now at the point where, with appropriate rationalizing attention from scholars and law reformers, more and more of its parts might be subsumed under principles of ever greater generality.[84] In other words, pushed along by scientific lawyers, the common law had been *evolving toward* ever-increasing generality and internal consistency, creating as it did so an ever larger scope

[81] *See Van Ness* v. *Pacard*, 27 U.S. (2 Pet.) 137, 144–145 (1829) (Story, J.) (court should not assume, absent authoritative state ruling; that state law includes common-law doctrine that fixtures become part of freehold, because doctrine might have proven not applicable to wilderness conditions); Horwitz, *supra* note 68, at 24–27.

[82] Joseph Story, "Growth of the Commercial Law," in *Miscellaneous Writings Of Joseph Story* 262, 279 (Story ed. 1852).

[83] *See, e.g.*, 3 James Kent, *Commentaries on American Law* 401–413 (1828) (tracing evolution from feudal to allodial estates in land); 4 *id.* at 433–437 (1830) (tracing development of free alienability of land).

[84] *See, e.g.*, John Dillon, *The Laws and Jurisprudence of England and America* 16–89 (1894); Ames, *supra* note 71, at 103, 113; *cf.* Oliver Wendell Holmes, Jr., "Codes, and the Arrangement of The Law," 5 *Am. L. Rev.* l, 12 (1870) (proposing a system for classification and codification of common law that would inform law's future development).

for individual autonomy. Thus, in most cases *historical study* of the origins and development of a legal rule, which should reveal the relation of that rule to an enduring principle (or else that, having no such relation, the rule was only an anachronistic survival), should be a method complementary to *analytic* derivation of the rule from a principle; they should arrive at the same result.[85] Where the results did not coincide, the historical version should be sacrificed, usually on the grounds that it resulted from a textual misreading by some judges in the chain, which had interfered with its proper evolutionary course, and that clarity and certainty in the analytic system required its excision. In this way, the apparently Cartesian abstraction of classical legal science could be seen as responsive both to the current social need for precise definitions of the scope and limits of autonomous conduct and to the long-run course of history.

Hence the classical scheme made itself vulnerable to historicist attack. The main features of the attack are familiar enough not to require more than a quick summary:[86] (1) The model of evolution from "status to contract" underlying classical-legal individualism was oversimplified and distorted. (2) Even if it were correct, evolution had not stopped; if England were taken as the model, modern societies had left individualism behind and entered a new stage of "collectivism."[87] (3) Moreover, said Holmes, giving evolutionism a new Darwinian twist, there is no reason why the struggle to survive should not take the form of a struggle to capture the state and make it legislate in one's favor. Judicial intervention while the struggle continues is an arbitrary taking of sides because truly adaptive law can come about only when the winners are clear.[88] (4) The norms that classical jurists assert as absolute principles immanent in the law are in fact only specific and rather parochial ideologies of certain elites. ("The Fourteenth Amendment does not enact Mr. Herbert Spencer's Social Statics."[89]) (5) The formalist scheme is dysfunctional because it tries to freeze these ideologies in the law, while social development requires the recognition of new needs.[90] (6) The scheme is totally

85 Ames's work typifies the combined historic-analytic method as practiced by a master. *See, e.g.*, James Barr Ames, "Two Theories of Consideration," in *Lectures on Legal History* 323 (1913); James Barr Ames, "The Doctrine of Price v. Neal," in *Lectures On Legal History* 270, 284 (1913).

86 *See* the historicist critiques discussed *supra*.

87 See Albert Venn Dicey, *Lectures on the Relation Between Law & Public Opinion in England During the Nineteenth Century* 299–501 (1905).

88 *See Vegelahn* v. *Guntner*, 167 Mass. 92, 105–106, 44 N.E. 1077, 1080 (1896) (Holmes, J., dissenting); Oliver Wendell Holmes, Jr., "Law and the Court," in *Collected Legal Papers* 291, 294–295 (1920).

89 *Lochner* v. *New York*, 198 U.S. 45, 75–76 (1905) (Holmes, J., dissenting).

90 *See* Roscoe Pound, "Liberty of Contract," 18 *Yale L. J.* 454, 454 (1909) (in holding that liberty of contract is infringed by any legislation that disrupts the equal rights of employers and employees, the courts persisted in applying "an academic theory of equality in the face of practical conditions of inequality")

*non*functional because its abstract formulations can be manipulated to serve any interest whatever.[91]

Implicit, of course, in all these criticisms was an emerging theory of genuinely adaptive law. Indeed, when this critical generation of "Progressives" came to build their own amalgam, most of its emphasis was on adaptation. In Progressive theory, speaking very generally, social needs assert themselves through "interests."[92] Interests are the desires of individuals, but also the programs or aims of concrete social groups in particular relations (bankrupts and creditors, consumers and manufacturers, union members and employers, small stockholders and management) as well as the generally shared purposes of the society as a whole. Interests conflict. The object of law, then, is to ascertain what interests exist, to decide which ones deserve recognition, and to achieve an efficient adjustment of them, approximating their ideal harmonization in the "public interest." Unlike the formalists, who sought to restrict all law-making agencies within carefully bounded spheres, the Progressives had no fixed institutional notion of adaptation, preferring to allocate the workload according to perceived competence to adapt because of expertise, enforcement capability, and so forth. While presuming as an initial matter that when the legislature speaks it is adequately harmonizing interests, they also designed an active adaptive role for courts, both as trackers of custom and as social engineers.

Of special interest to our topic are the ways in which the Progressive scholars, sometimes through exceptionally distinguished historical work, located their own enterprise in time. Pound and Llewellyn, for example, saw twentieth-century judicial method as a continuation of the "Grand Style" of the antebellum "Formative Era," when the courts had brilliantly adapted the old common law to novel social and economic needs.[93] Hurst, Hartz, and the Handlins (only the first strictly speaking a legal scholar) discovered a history of extensive state promotion and regulation of the economy through legislative and administrative as well as judicial action,[94] so that the New Deal, in perspective, could be seen as the culmination of an American tradition of pragmatic response to social needs, without excessive fussing about ideological laissez-faire. All of this work relied upon an implicit or explicit Weberian view of the relationship of law to the social order. The legal system had provided valuable and possibly indispensable institutional support to the development of American capitalism,

[91] *See, e.g.*, Jeremiah Smith, "Legal Cause in Actions of Tort (pt. I)." 25 *Harv. L. Rev.* 103, 106–128 (1911) (manipulating traditional tests of causality in tort).

[92] "Interest" theory in Progressive thought was given its most thorough and abstract treatment by Roscoe Pound. See 3 Pound, note 54, at 15–24.

[93] *See* Karl Llewellyn, *The Common Law Tradition* 86–117 (1960); Roscoe Pound, *The Formative Era of American Law* 93–94 (1938).

[94] *See* Oscar Handlin & Mary Handlin, *Commonwealth* 254–263 (1947); Louis Hartz, *Economic Policy and Democratic Thought* 289–320 (1948); James Willard Hurst, *Law and the Conditions of Freedom* 33–70 (1956).

chiefly through the adoption of legal forms that promoted capital formation, the security of exchange, and demolition of barriers to the interstate mobility of capital and property, and through the development of liability rules that favored dynamic entrepreneurs over static *rentier* interests.

But if antebellum law had been adaptive, the Progressive generation agreed, the law of their late-nineteenth- and twentieth-century predecessors was woefully maladaptive. Harsh liability rules such as the fellow-servant rule, or policies favoring unrestricted accumulation, might have been necessary in the period of industrial takeoff, but these ways of thinking had hardened into dogma, inhibiting reform through legislative or administrative equilibration that could have dealt creatively with the social consequences of organized capitalism. There was a lag; the legal system was mired in immobility or, less kindly, captured by private interests. *Lochner* v. *New York*[95] symbolized the historical low point: it is the counterpart, in the Progressive view, of the old Whigs' Stuart despotism or the corruption of the Walpole ministry. For judicial passivists, the evil was that judges had the nerve to make social policy with broad implications; for activists, that the policy made was maladaptive, out of tune with the course of social development.

The process of historicizing continues, however, so that the Progressive view has suffered some recent shocks, which are exemplified by work on the narrow subject of the Progressive interpretation of history: Lawrence Friedman has restated the entire history of the nineteenth century as one of interests-determined law. Before the Civil War, a broad spectrum of interests united in wanting a law that facilitated business, and got it. In the later period, these interests had to contend with others at cross-purposes. The law was neither more nor less adaptive later than earlier; it simply reflected different constellations of interests.[96] In the other major modern synthesis, Morton Horwitz accepts the Progressive view of the active role of the state and law in antebellum society, but argues that the social functions served were expropriation on behalf of entrepreneurs and protection of their profits from redistribution.[97] In a sense, Horwitz remains within the Progressive tradition in that he presents

[95] 198 U.S. 45 (1905).

[96]

> A legal system *must* respond to the needs of its time and its society. When one speaks of a legal system as out of tune with its society, one is usually referring to quite a different phenomenon: a conflict between parts of society or specific interest groups in which the legal system, or some specialized institution, responds to or reflects some interests but not others. To state, for example, that judges of the late nineteenth century who issued labor injunctions and voided welfare legislation were out of step with their society or unresponsive to social needs is simply to take the victor's view of history. These judges were out of step with a growing, powerful social movement; but their decisions were enunciated in cases brought or defended by real litigants with real economic and social interests.

Lawrence Friedman, 'Heart Against Head: Perry Miller and the Legal Mind' (Book Review), 77 *Yale L. J.* 1244, 1255 (1968). *See generally* Friedman, *supra* note 11.

[97] Horwitz, *supra* note 68, at 99–102.

the republican idea of a government serving all its citizens as betrayed (by lawyers among others) to commercial interests; he departs from it in locating the betrayal at the beginning, rather than the end, of the nineteenth century. With one version or another of the thesis that legal regulatory processes were captured by or designed to favor the regulated,[98] revisionists of both right and left have challenged the Progressives' optimistic conclusion that they reclaimed the law from exclusive service to special interests for the ideally adaptive maximizing of everyone's interest. At the same time, the Progressives' picture of late-nineteenth-century law is being slowly painted over. Posner has sought to vindicate the period's devotion to negligence as the basis of tort liability;[99] and McCurdy, Kennedy, and Atiyah, among others, by taking legal "formalism" seriously on its own terms as a rationalizing enterprise, have made possible an understanding of it as a formidably plausible ideological construct for its time, rather than simply as a vast collective misguidedness or corruption.[100]

Under these and similar shocks, the Progressive amalgam's long domination over the organization of scholarly thinking about law is breaking up, and nothing comparable is in prospect to replace it. Legal scholars can still be found who write in all the traditional responsive modes, but no new amalgam seems to be crystallizing. Perhaps this is because law teachers have been recruited from a much broader political spectrum than ever before, even in the 1930s; perhaps it is also because scholars with totally incompatible intellectual stances have sharpened their weapons against one another.

IV. SOME CONCLUSIONS

In this delightfully heterodox climate there is reason to hope that our mainstream legal scholarship will at last move beyond its standard modes of responding to historicist assertions of the social contingency of law and legal rationalization. Doubtless, there are no solutions to the problems, but the modes as they have been practiced have inhibited the development of more interesting responses, calling forth in their turn new criticisms, and so onward in a dialogue lifted clear of the old gravitational field. Of course, there is also the risk, a serious one if the historical experience is any guide, that the pull of

[98] *See* Thomas McCraw, "Regulation in America: A Review Article," 49 *Bus. Hist. Rev.* 159, 164–179 (1975) (surveying shifting views of regulation among economists, lawyers, historians, and political scientists).

[99] Richard Posner, "A Theory of Negligence," 1 *J. Legal Stud.* 29, 29 (1972) (proposing a theory, based on a sample of American court decisions from the period 1875–1905, of the social function of the fault system of accident liability).

[100] *See, e.g.*, Patrick Atiyah, *The Rise and Fall of Freedom of Contract* 388–397 (1979); Duncan Kennedy, "Form and Substance in Private Law Adjudication," 89 *Harv. L. Rev.* 1685, 1728–17231, 1746–17448 (1976); Charles McCurdy, "Justice Field and the Jurisprudence of Government-Business Relations: Some Parameters of Laissez-Faire Constitutionalism," 1863–1897, 61 *J. Am. Hist.* 970, 1004–1005 (1975).

the old field will be too strong, so that attempts to break clear will be ignored or defeated by misunderstanding. The idea behind this article is that this risk may be avoided if one can identify some of the points of impasse at which the dialogue has traditionally become stuck. Let me conclude by pointing to some examples of how the dialogue is impoverished by sticking at those points, and of how much it could gain by becoming unstuck.

Denial again. Unvarnished denials of the historicity of legal reasoning, for instance, are uninteresting contributions to the dialogue precisely because they deny there is a problem. Take for example a very recent addition to the literature of denial by Richard Epstein,[101] exemplary for the brilliance and baldness with which it puts the case for the universality of basic legal principles. His article's strength is its useful attack on shallow versions of the adaptationist idea that law should change with changing circumstances, such as the notion that we have gone from fault to strict liability in tort in order to adapt to technological change. To this assertion, Epstein says truly, in relevant respects circumstances have not changed in the past century.[102] He admits some kinds of social change might affect the validity of principles expressed in a legal text: changing customs might change the meaning of agreement, changing background regimes of public law might change the need for or impact of a rule of private law, and changing values might change the analysis of the relative costs and benefits of different activities.[103] All other types of change are ruled trivial. "Whereas Romans inflicted harms with poisons, we do it with automobiles,"[104] but their *principles* of liability are the same as ours.

Though unusually breathtaking in the confidence with which it asserts the existence of history-independent legal principles, the article is typical of the standard denial mode in ignoring the problems of the historicity of consciousness itself. Epstein claims that we could profitably discuss tort liability with a Roman lawyer. What could we talk about? Superficially, perhaps quite a lot. We seem to have a common problem, the infliction and compensation of harms, and (along with Holmes's dog[105]) a common perception that intentional are worse than carelessly or accidentally inflicted harms. Even at this level of very great generality, however, our ability to exchange ideas depends on much more than our sharing and attempting to realize some universal moral propositions, such as comparable ideas of property, injuries to it, and compensation

[101] Richard Epstein, "The Static Conception of the Common Law," 9 *J. Legal Stud.* 253 (1980).

[102] He does not, however, have an explanation of his own for why rationales for liability have changed as they have. Indeed, one of the problems with denial theory generally is that its adherents must assert that entire societies, for whole epochs, just get things wrong and adopt false ideas, but they have no way of making intelligible why that should happen.

[103] *Id.* at 266–269.

[104] *Id.* at 259–260.

[105] See Oliver Wendell Holmes, Jr., *The Common Law* 5 (1881) ("[E]ven a dog distinguishes between being stumbled over and being kicked.").

systems, all declared in a rational general form, and enforced by a separate legal system. Of course, in the case of tort, we happen to have still more in common, an impressively large and detailed stock of categories of classification and conventional modes of discourse, because since the twelfth century, with increasing intensity in the nineteenth, legal scholars have made a determined effort to resurrect the Roman categories and appropriate them to modern use. To the extent we think the same way, it is surely in part because we have tried so hard to do so. The taking of a similarity grounded in deliberate cultural appropriation for the common recognition of a universal norm is circularity with a vengeance.

Of course, this borrowing does not mean that the set of norms is not universally valid. As Charles Fried would undoubtedly say, maybe we appropriated the Roman norms because they were the right ones.[106] The trouble here lies in supposing that, because in some formulations their texts can be lifted word for word from their context and still make sense in ours, our norms are theirs. Consider one of Epstein's examples of the proposition that "justifications [of legal rules] are essentially independent of social changes": "In the law of contracts, a promisee who uses force or fraud cannot demand performance of the promise exacted from his promisor."[107] If the other system has a "law" of "contracts" recognizing and enforcing abstract promises subject to abstractly defined defenses, we can be confident of many basic similarities between its universe of concepts and ours. Even this confidence, however, may be premature. On being asked, "why do your laws enforce this promise?" lawyers in the other system might say, "because it was sworn under a banyan tree by the promisee's wife's brother." Ours might say, "in order to support the functioning of the market," an answer quite as mysterious to a world that is familiar with exchange transactions but has no concept of an "economy" as is the

[106] In the same symposium issue in which Epstein's article appears, Fried produces a novel (at least to me) form of denial theory that seeks to account for changes in legal texts by some means other than reference to their contexts. If I read him correctly, he says that law changes when people are persuaded to change it by morally correct arguments, so that the best way to explain why an argument was accepted is to ask whether it was true. If one accepts Fried's premise that there is some suprahistorical means of assessing the moral correctness of, say, arguments on points of medieval land law, and his qualification that this is not a theory of moral progress because bad arguments may persist for a long time (and may even be dominant now), the theory is unassailable from the historicist perspective. If all that he is saying is that lawmakers usually believe in what they are doing, and may be convinced to do something different by an argument that is persuasive in the terms of their moral universe, his claim seems unexceptionable. But the way to vindicate that thesis would be the historical attempt at reconstruction of the lawmakers' moral universe, a necessary first step, it would seem, even for someone who thinks as Fried apparently does that their universe's terms may be translated point for point into some universal moral scheme of reference. *See* Charles Fried, "The Laws of Change: The Cunning of Reason in Moral and Legal History," 9 *J. Legal Stud.* 835, 836–839 (1980).

[107] Epstein, *supra* note 101, at 256.

banyan-oath to ours.[108] So too with force and fraud: any exchange of promises may be regarded as one of mutual threats to withhold performance unless the other side comes across.[109]

Surely what one wants to know about another system is how it draws the line between the voluntary and the coerced exchange, because only by knowing that can one get a sense of the operational meanings it gives to the notions of freedom and coercion. Knowing that it expresses the general norms is about as useful as learning that a nation calls itself a "people's democratic republic."[110] Leon Litwack has recently shown us how, in the Reconstruction South, the idea of "contract" with its happy connotations of free and mutual bargaining was put to work to subject newly emancipated slaves to regimes of domination even worse than their former conditions of servitude.[111] Likewise, "property," with all its associations of the legal watch set about home and hearth, may be used to protect an owner's security or help him express his personality; it may also enable him to exclude others from what they need except on the condition that they submit to his power.[112] By now we are surely accustomed to the idea that "freedom of contract" and "duress" are concepts with such extraordinary historical and cultural pliability that their meanings can be plausibly expounded only at a level of great particularity.[113] If we take just the words, we are likely to become involved in absurd mistranslations – to say "free contract," for example, where, if we knew the context, we might be more likely to say "peonage."

At this stage one listens for the accusation of "Relativist!," but it is really beside the point. One does not have to be a relativist to doubt that our legal

108 See Moses Finley, *The Ancient Economy* 17–23 (1978) (modern economic concepts and models not applicable to study of ancient economy); Karl Polanyi, "Aristotle Discovers the Economy," in *Primitive, Archaic and Modern Economies* 78, 84–85 (1968) (pre-modern communities have no integrated concept of an "economy"). For a contrary view, see Posner's characteristically sweeping argument, based on extensive reading in anthropological literatures, in Richard Posner, "A Theory of Primitive Society, with Special Reference to Primitive Law," 25 *J. L. & Econ.* 1, 2, 4–5 (1980) (explaining customs and institutions of primitive society as economically rational adaptations to high information costs and criticizing "excessively narrow view of what is economic").

109 *See* Robert Hale, "Bargaining, Duress, and Economic Liberty," 48 *Colum. L. Rev.* 603, 604 (1943).

110 Of course, even an interpreter with a fairly full catalogue of instances of applications of the norms may be seriously misled. A scheme of legal norms that narrowly restricts the scope of duties owed to others is one thing in a society that also has strongly sanctioned norms of charitable duties – in such a society, legal restrictions are only limitations on jurisdiction, not definitive statements about right behavior – and quite another thing in a society where religious norms have atrophied.

111 Leon Litwack, *Been in the Storm So Long* 408–420 (1979).

112 The most systematic treatment of this idea is found in Karl Renner, *The Institutions of Private Law* 104–158 (1949).

113 *See* John Dawson, "Economic Duress – An Essay in Perspective," 45 *Mich. L. Rev.* 253, 288–289 (1947).

principles are universal simply because other places and times have used conceptual language sounding rather like our own. One is merely asserting that on closer investigation the resemblance will come to appear superficial, and that anyone who seriously claims that there are normative universals must try to reconstruct the language in which the old text is embedded in sufficient detail to support a theory that something in the old text is comparable to something in the new.[114] The alternatives are almost certainly parochialism (taking the norms we happen to be used to as the universals), banality (positing as universals a list of uselessly general and abstract values), or mistranslation.

Some people would deny that even this more careful reconstruction of other idea systems will make comparisons possible – either on the ground that the other legal ideas have meaning only in the terms of their own contexts, so are not transferable to others, or on the ground that reconstruction of the other system is futile because we can only approach the task with our own apparatus of concepts,[115] and there is no theory-independent conceptual language into which both our own and the other system may be translated for comparative purposes.[116] As Maitland put it:

> If we speak, we must speak with words; if we think, we must think with thoughts. We are moderns and our words and thoughts can not but be modern. Perhaps… it is too late for us to be early English. Every thought will be too sharp, every word will imply too many contrasts.[117]

Others would maintain to the contrary that uncovering the structures deeply underlying all conceptual schemes is possible. I am not taking a position on this controversy because my point is the much more limited one that nobody is going to get very far in meeting the threat of historical contingency by the more elementary denials that it is a problem. And one is cutting oneself off from the prospect of realizing a greatly enriched understanding of one's own system of norms by examining it in comparison with what appear to be very different ones, the first step in that process of comparison being the attempt, doomed though it may be, at reconstructing other systems.

The process of reconstruction may end up convincing us that the other systems – the conceptual world of our Constitution-makers, for example – is indeed discontinuous and unrecapturable. Even this discovery would not

[114] *Cf.* Oliver Wendell Holmes, Jr., "The Path of the Law," in *Collected Legal Papers* 167, 197–98 (1920):

> I assume that, if it is well to study the Roman Law, it is well to study it as a working system. That means mastering a set of technicalities more difficult and less well understood than our own, and studying another course of history by which even more than our own the Roman law must be explained.

[115] *See* Peter Winch, *The Idea of a Social Science and its Relation to Philosophy* 86–91 (1958).

[116] *See* Richard Rorty, *Philosophy and the Mirror of Nature* 315–394 (1979).

[117] Frederic William Maitland, *Township And Borough* 22 (1898).

have made the effort useless; we would at least have learned, as Brest and Ely have tried to teach us,[118] the folly of a literalistic interpretation. And one could learn as well through the contrast. One of the aims of the recent work of Morton Horwitz, William Nelson, and John Reid[119] has been to identify the characteristics of "modern" law (which they severally describe as instrumentalism, adjusting the claims of atomized individuals and interest groups, and law-as-command) by reference to what they see as the "pre-modern" law of the eighteenth century.[120] But reconstruction might do more for us than that: it might demonstrate an actual continuity between the old system and our own. This continuity might be evolutionary, as was assumed by all the nineteenth-century theories of legal progress, but might also be something much more interesting, a relationship of structural analogy such as anthropologists have found, for instance, between pre-scientific and scientific thought.[121] To give an example or two: Douglas Hay's deservedly celebrated essay on *Property, Authority, and the Criminal Law*,[122] which showed the repressive advantages gained when eighteenth-century criminal law combined a paper regime of rarely enforced but terrifying sanctions with an enforcement regime of merciful discretion, abundantly produces insights into modern law, not only modern criminal justice administration but any discretionary administration of a formal system: substitute "street-level bureaucrats" or "political machine" for Hay's "country gentry."

Just lately there has been emerging a remarkable literature on the theme of representation: how our law constitutes artificial entities (abstract individuals, classes of litigants, corporations, states) to represent real persons, then finds real persons to represent the entities thus constituted; also how the law refuses to recognize some persons and collectivities as capable of representing or being represented for some purposes. This theme has been explored in such diverse legal contexts as those of standing,[123] group litigation,[124] cities,[125] and state action.[126] This literature is unusually and in some cases extremely well-informed historically, with rewarding consequences. It is able to show that the forms of representation that we happen to use do not exhaust the stock of

[118] *See supra* note 7.

[119] *See* Horwitz, *supra* note 68, at 16–30; William Nelson, *Americanization Of The Common Law* 173–174 (1975); Reid, *supra* note 17, at 128.

[120] Hendrik Hartog pointed out this similarity to me.

[121] *See, e.g.*, Barry Barnes, "The Comparison of Belief-systems: Anomaly Versus Falsehood," in *Modes Of Thought* 182, 186–188 (Horton & Finnegan eds. 1973).

[122] Hay, *supra* note 58.

[123] *See* Vining, *supra* note 66, at 13–33.

[124] *See* Stephen Yeazell, "From Group Litigation to Class Action, Part II: Interest, Class and Representation," 27 *U.C.L.A. L. Rev.* 1067, 1107–1120 (1980).

[125] *See* Gerald Frug, "The City as a Legal Concept," 93 *Harv. L. Rev.* 1057, 1081–1082 (1980).

[126] *See* Al Katz, "Studies in Boundary Theory: Three Essays in Adjudication and Politics," 28 *Buffalo L. Rev.* 383, 386–408 (1979).

forms that have been historically available, but that we have been unable to perceive or make use of other forms because of basic conceptual limitations in modern liberal political thought. It thus expands the range of possible forms of social organization and at the same time explains why the possibilities have gone unrealized. If there is any hope of attaining the vision of the universal for which the denial theorists long, it seems likely to be realized through studies such as these of historically contingent particulars.

Embrace: Legal Theories of Social and Historical Contingency. After considering denial, moving on to embrace comes as a relief because the scholars who choose this strategy at least recognize the problem of historicity and do not think it can be waved away with assertions that nothing important to legal reasoning ever changes. The basic embrace strategy – some version of adaptation theory – has been a valuable heuristic, because it has directed attention to context and forced legal scholars to elaborate ideas about relationships between texts and their contexts. Anyone could have predicted that at first such ideas would reinforce the usual inclinations of legal scholarship toward conservatism or moderate law reform. The claim would be that if there were differences between ideology and practice (the gap), they could be closed by appropriate equilibrating mechanisms, or that if law had been evolving, its evolution was nearly complete, or proceeding at a very gradual rate, or moving (in the characteristically American conservative teleology) toward the unfolding of a pre-existing ideal.[127] What is frustrating and alarming is that the intellectual development of legal scholarship has so often stalled at this initial level of response, and repelled, retarded, or pushed off to the margins most attempts to go beyond it. I do not think it needs much demonstration that legal history and the sociology of law have become marginal sub-specialties in American law curricula, though there was a time in the founding years at Harvard when every course was partly a legal history course. Likewise, for a moment in the 1920s, much of the Columbia faculty dreamed that every course might be partly one in sociology.

I have tried elsewhere to tell the story of how the law schools ejected legal history when it betrayed them by abandoning evolutionism.[128] John Schlegel, in a fascinating article,[129] has been telling a similarly dispiriting story about Yale's experiments with empiricism. One of Schlegel's stories will serve as a parable. It had long been an article of faith among moderate law reformers in the profession and the schools that the people, as Pound put it, were dissatisfied

[127] *See* Bercovitch, *supra* note 36 (discussing teleology of American mission); Welter, *supra* note 36 (same).

[128] Robert W. Gordon, "J. Willard Hurst and the Common Law Tradition in American Legal Historiography," 10 *Law & Soc'y Rev.* 9, 17–19 (1975).

[129] John Schlegel, "American Legal Realism and Empirical Social Science: From the Yale Experience," 28 *Buffalo L. Rev.* 459 (1979).

with the administration of justice,[130] and that the cause must be the delay and expense of court proceedings, which were in turn caused by unreformed law and procedure. At the high point of the rage for empirical research in the early 1930s, the Wickersham Commission in effect asked Dean Clark of Yale and his research team to verify those propositions. But the Clark team's study of the lower criminal courts found anything but undue delay owing to excessive technicality; the system, they said, "seems almost too efficient; because it presents the spectacle of a long line of orderly offenders, few of whom it is necessary to commit to jail either before or after trial, pleading guilty with systematic regularity... raising no technical objections..."[131] This discovery no longer surprises us, but it did Clark's contemporaries in academic law, who concluded in effect that it must be wrong. Disenchantment with empiricism soon followed; in a few years, it had all but vanished.[132]

Adaptation theory, however, survived. Legal scholars continued to assert that law was an adaptive technology: that legal forms had adapted or could be adapted to serve given social functions, purposes, or interests, and that some forms and institutions were especially adaptive (or "competent") for some functions, and grossly maladaptive (or "incompetent") for others, the most common, but by no means only, assertions being those about what courts were intrinsically good or bad at doing. These arguments – as it is the professional function of one of our best if definitely marginal journals, the *Law & Society Review*, periodically to lament[133] – have in general been carried on in a wilderness almost completely devoid of knowledge or apparent interest in knowledge about what, for example, courts and legislatures in this society actually do.

In particular, one might have hoped that by now our legal scholars would have developed adaptation theory from a set of ad hoc insights into a full-scale

[130] Roscoe Pound, "The Causes of Popular Dissatisfaction with the Administration of Justice," *A.B.A. Rep.* 395, 416–417 (1906).

[131] Schlegel, *supra* note 129, at 504 (quoting Douglas, Arnold, &: Clark, Progress Report on the Study of Business of the Federal Courts 3 (n.d.) (draft) (in Clark Papers, Beinecke Library, Yale University).

[132] Grant Gilmore, "And Now for Something Completely Different" (Book Review), *Law Alumni J.*, Summer 1975, at 38, 39 (Univ. of Chicago) (by early 1940s, "entire law faculty" at Yale viewed law as "a sort of mystical absolute"). The substantive unacceptability of the conclusions of historical and sociological scholarship, is, as the Schlegel article makes clear, only one of the reasons for their disappearance from the legal mainstream. Others are their alien methodologies, the lack of interest taken by most mainstream historians and sociologists in legal subjects, and perhaps above all, their tendency to make any problem on which they are brought to bear seem more complex and ambiguous, and its solution more indeterminate, than it was before they were consulted. As Douglas Hay said to me at the symposium, the maturing of history as a discipline in the late nineteenth century made it increasingly unusable for any immediately practical legal purpose: any field that historians had well trampled was a tremendous battleground of specialized professional controversy.

[133] *See, e.g.*, Ralph Cavanagh & Austin Sarat, "Thinking About Courts: Toward and Beyond a Jurisprudence of Judicial Competence," 14 *Law & Soc'y Rev.* 371 (1980).

historical sociology of law, in the tradition of Weber, that would try to relate in a more or less systematic way changes in legal forms to those in economy and society.[134] But in fact, outside the books of Willard Hurst and his Wisconsin school, I can think of only a handful of such studies in our scholarship, notably Dawson's on contract law in inflationary economies.[135] There are signs of a revival: the entrepreneurial histories of Alfred Chandler have inspired a resurgence of interest among legal scholars in the contribution of legal technologies to corporate concentration in the late nineteenth century;[136] Robert Clark has been developing an unusually detailed neo-Weberian evolutionary model to explain changes in corporate law in a capitalist economy;[137] in extraordinary comparative work, Mirjan Damaska has explored the connection between rules and processes of criminal procedure, and variations in the structures of political authority;[138] and Ian Macneil, Oliver Williamson, and Richard Danzig have developed functional theories of the relation of contract law to patterns of economic organization.[139]

Had more of this work been done earlier, and been absorbed into the bloodstream of the discipline, critical response to it, stressing some of the theoretical limitations of adaptationism – the problems of discontinuity between formal expression and applications, of false dualism between "law" and society, of the indeterminate and contradictory character of regimes of legal form, which makes it difficult to show that any particular one is instrumental to any given economic order – might have stimulated other kinds of historically minded scholarship.

One example might be scholarship that set aside entirely the premise that the primary importance of legal texts lies in their functionally serving some set of manifest social needs, and took discontinuity as its starting point. This approach could lead to an historical perspective on "legal pluralism," state-promoted norms competing with others or for that matter, cooperating with

[134] For recent work explicitly in this tradition, see Roberto Mangabeira Unger, *Law In Modern Society* (1976), and David Trubek, "Toward a Social Theory of Law: An Essay on the Study of Law and Development," 82 *Yale L. J.* 1, 40–50 (1972).

[135] *See* John Dawson, "Effects of Inflation on Private Contracts: Germany, 1914–1924," 33 *Mich. L. Rev.* 171 (1984); John Dawson & Frank Cooper, "Effects of Inflation on Private Contracts: United States, 1861–1879 (pts. l &: 2)," 33 *Mich. L. Rev.* 706, 852 (1985).

[136] *See Managerial Hierarchies* (Chandler & Daems eds. 1980); *Recht und Entwicklung der Grossunternehmen im* 19 *und fruhen* 20. *Jahrhundert* (Horn & Kocka eds. 1979).

[137] *See* Robert Clark, "The Four Stages of Capitalism: Reflections on Investment Management Treatises," 94 *Harv. L. Rev.* 561 (1981); Robert Clark, "The Interdisciplinary Study of Legal Evolution," 90 *Yale L. J.* 1218 (1981).

[138] *See* Mirjan Damaska, "Presentation of Evidence and Factfinding Precision," 123 *U. PA. L. Rev.* 1083 (1975); Mirjan Damaska, "Structures of Authority and Comparative Criminal Procedure, 84 *Yale L. J.* 480 (1975).

[139] *See* Ian Macneil, *The New Social Contract* (1980); Richard Danzig, "Hadley v. Baxendale: A Study in the Industrialization of the Law," 4 *J. Legal Stud.* 249 (1975); Oliver Williamson, "Transaction-Cost Economics: The Governance of Contractual Relations," 22 *J. L. & Econ.* 233 (1979).

others in a division of hegemonic labor; alternatively, it could lead to a focus on the "latent" function of even apparently maladaptive law. Douglas Hay's essay on the criminal law[140] is a stunning example of what can be said about the legitimating functions of unenforced rules. Arthur Leff, in a characteristically bravura performance, has sketched a map of a completely new and potentially valuable territory of symbolic meanings of legal texts that legal scholars who are tired of the old responses can explore.[141]

Adaptation theory in all its forms, as I have pointed out, assumes that the social functions to which law is instrumental – interests, purposes, needs – are exogenous to the legal system. That is, states need security against foreign enemies, economies need growth, business people need security of transactions, everyone needs free expression and protection of property, and so forth. This false dualism makes it hard to see how the legal order also helps to construct the social world whose functions it serves: the "persons" and their "interests" and the "harms" to those interests, not to mention "states" and "markets." We are now suddenly getting a flood of articles that address the legal construction of social categories; this includes the literature on the theme of representation[142] and a novel genre of legal history that treats legal doctrine as ideology, a way of structuring social experience that seems to be a functional response to social needs but is in fact a way of making the existing order seem natural and necessary.[143]

From Cartesianism to Rhetoric. I referred earlier to a quasi-Cartesian mode of response that legal scholars implicitly adopt whenever they say to the historicist critic: "All this social and historical contingency you talk about is no doubt highly interesting, but it is really irrelevant to our task as lawyers, which is to work within a certain well-established framework of normative analysis that takes some basic premises about law-in-society-and-history as stipulated and not open to question." This response is plausible enough, as far as it goes. Many of the criticisms that historians make of lawyers' history are indeed irrelevant to the lawyer's task. At least the immediate interest of historians is always in "historicizing" the past as much as possible, tamping it down firmly into departed times and places.[144] For lawyers, this method is useful only half

[140] *See* Hay, *supra* note 58.

[141] *See* Arthur Leff, "Law and," 87 *Yale L. J.* 989 (1978). Leff has often written in the mode of resignation, but instead of using it as a device for keeping historicism at bay, he has fully incorporated historicist perspectives in his work and helped to advance the dialogue as much as anyone now writing.

[142] *See supra* notes 23–26.

[143] *See, e.g.*, Mark Tushnet, *The American Law of Slavery, 1810–1860: Considerations of Humanity and Interest* (1981). Kennedy, *supra* note 67; Karl Klare, "Judicial Deradicalization of the Wagner Act and the Origins of Modern Legal Consciousness, 1937–1941," 62 *Minn. L. Rev.* 265 (1978).

[144] *See* Michael Oakeshott, "The Activity of being an Historian," in *Rationalism in Politics* 137, 164–167 (1962).

the time, when they want to get rid of some practice justified by tradition. At other times they want not to deaden the past but to make new, mythic, traditions out of it to use in current argument. It is pointless to say that such myths are "inaccurate" from the standpoint of conventional historiography, for they are so by definition. But that does not mean that all historicist criticism of legal rhetorics is irrelevant, because the critic could take the rhetorics on their own terms, instead of the conventional historian's terms, and say, "This is bad mythmaking."

What would such criticism look like? It is hard to say, because the dialogue hypothesized has yet to take place. Perhaps it would take the form of objections that the lawyers' mythic uses of the past are flawed because myopic or incomplete, ignoring aspects of legal traditions that are alternative sources of organizing or inspiring myths. From this perspective, for instance, it might be possible to develop the arguments, sometimes hinted at by historicist critics,[145] that current legal rhetoric, by confining itself to dessicated, liberal individualist or interest-group theories of politics, has cut itself off from the civic humanism of the republican ideology of the founding generation, an ideology that has been periodically resurgent in our politics[146] and that our scholarship should try to reincorporate into our standard normative reasoning modes.

Envoi. There seems, in view of these suddenly blooming wildflowers, reason to hope that our mainstream legal scholarship may at last have been shaken out of its old habits. Yet one cannot be too confident of this. Its basic paradigms, especially adaptation theories, have proved quite amazingly resilient to shock after shock. Because they assume a benign continuity between law and social change, rather than taking it as problematic, such theories have inhibited the development of richly empirical and historical descriptions of how people in society, lawyers and others, actually experience their legal order. While seeking to make the law more effective in the name of a pragmatic empiricism, these theories have restricted thinking about law to minor changes in its present forms, thereby preventing us both from learning what law as experienced in social life is really like and from imagining that law might be other than the way it is. Adaptation theory has been the most subtly apologetic of the responsive modes, because it views "society" and "history" as a largely determined background of forces that nobody can do much about, but sees "law" as the largely free creation of lawyers and jurists, who can adapt to predetermined social change more or less efficiently, depending on how cleverly they design institutions or doctrines. The theory is thus doubly misleading because it denies our

[145] For versions of such arguments, see Brest, *supra* note 53, at 1105–1109, Frug, *supra* note 125, at 1087–1090, and Frank Michelman, "Politics and Values or What's Really Wrong with Rationality Review?" 13 *Creighton L. Rev.* 487, 506–510 (1979).

[146] *See* Dorothy Ross, "The Liberal Tradition Revisited and the Republican Tradition Addressed," in *New Directions in American Intellectual History* 116 (Higham & Conkin eds. 1979).

responsibility for the ways in which legal ideas contribute to the constitution and reproduction of the society "out there" and denies the social contingency of our thinking about law, which drastically (and in my view unnecessarily) restricts its range.

There is no use pretending that some extraordinary new revelation is at hand, but the work that I have described (and much other work as well) seems to help point the way out of this curious impasse, to move legal scholarship beyond its long practiced modes of response. Yet virtually all this work, in one way or another, transgresses the principal ambitions of our scholarship: some of it claims that much of current law, instead of making sense, is contradictory and incoherent; some of it that current law in operation is ineffectual or harmful; and from practically none of it could anyone extract an immediately useful policy proposal. For some people, this last fact alone settles the matter: why are we wasting their time? But even they might pause to consider that if work, otherwise interesting, does not generate what the paradigm considers acceptable conclusions, perhaps the fault lies with the paradigm. What is being proposed here, and in the work I have described, is a kind of reverse Faustian bargain: our sacrifice of immediate influence in the councils of the great for a potentially enormous increase in understanding of our condition.

11

Critical Legal Histories*

[This essay was published in 36 Stanford Law Review *57 (1984), as part of the Review's special Symposium issue on Critical Legal Studies (CLS), a movement of left-leaning intellectuals who were just then coming to prominence in the legal academy. The Symposium included the work of many members of the movement as well as of some of their critics.*

Since much of what CLS stood for has been forgotten (or badly distorted in the remembering), a brief summary of some of its aims and methods may be useful. It was never a unified thing; its views were as diverse as its members; but there was common agreement around the idea that the way law was taught in American law schools, rationalized in legal scholarship, and deployed in legal arguments and decision-making, all tended to contribute to the complacent idea that the legal system in force was just about as efficient, just, and rational a system as it could be ("false legitimation" we called this); and that it could not be reformed except in minor ways without risking economic and political catastrophe ("false necessity"). The motto of the legal system might have been Margaret Thatcher's "There is

* I am grateful to Paul Brest, Tom Heller, Fred Konefsky, Elizabeth Mensch, Deborah Rhode, Mark Tushnet, and especially to Steve Diamond, Lawrence Friedman, Tom Grey, Mark Kelman, Jack Schlegel, Bill Simon, and Dave Trubek for reading earlier drafts and suggesting revisions. Willard Hurst gave the manuscript his usual incredibly close attention, wrote a dozen pages of detailed comments, approved what he could with characteristic generosity, and vigorously challenged what he could not; this article continues a long-standing conversation with him. I owe a special debt to David Sugarman, who has generously shared his ideas with me for years and whose invaluable and (unlike this piece) copiously footnoted manuscript, David Sugarman, "Towards a New History of Law and Material Society in England, 1750–1911," in *Law, Economy and Society: Essays in the History of English Law, 1750–1914* (Rubin and Sugarman eds. forthcoming), which arrived as I started to think about this article, has impressed its influence on every page. [This list of intellectual debts and influences inexplicably left out Duncan Kennedy, not only the progenitor of the distinctive school of doctrinal history described in this piece, but a powerful stimulant to the revisionist thoughts here on law–society relations.]

no alternative." CLS writers launched a volley of critiques of this tragic-complacent set of assumptions, designed to show that there were indeed alternatives, many of which were already embedded in the legal system itself, often as exceptions to prevailing dominant rules and doctrines. Many of the CLS critiques revived and extended the work of Legal Realists of the 1920s and 30s. The critiques began by trying to expose and challenge the implicit political economy of the first year law curriculum, then expanded to critique the emerging theories of the new law-and-economics movement, and eventually law as it was being applied in areas of policy, such as housing, welfare, labor law, corporate law, legal ethics, consumer protection, and many others. CLS went into eclipse in the 1990s, as the limited space for leftist views in the legal academy was increasingly taken up by critical race, feminist, and gay-and-lesbian studies. But many of its insights have been absorbed into mainstream legal scholarship.

This piece (which turns out to have been the most frequently cited of my essays on legal historiography) was partly written to describe a distinctive mode of legal history being written by scholars affiliated with CLS. But it also had a broader aim, that of trying to tease out and make explicit a set of background assumptions (here called "evolutionary functionalism") about the course of Western history, and of the relation of law to that history and to society generally, that American legal scholars tended to take for granted; and to question those assumptions. In 2012 the journal Law & Social Inquiry *invited several legal historians (Hendrik Hartog, Susanna Blumenthal, Laura Edwards, and Christopher Tomlins) to revisit the essay: their comments, and my response, are in 37* Law & Social Inquiry *147–215 (2012). Tomlins has also written an extremely provocative analysis of the program of "critical historicism" described in this and other essays in this volume, recognizing its strengths as critique but deploring its erosion of causal explanation; and proposing ways to retheorize law–society relations: Tomlins, "After Critical Legal History: Scope, Scale, Structure, 8* Ann. Rev. Law & Soc. Sci *(2012): SSRN:* http://ssrn.com/abstract=2034423.]

Critical legal writers pay a lot of attention to history. In fact, they have probably devoted more pages to historical description – particularly the intellectual history of legal doctrine – than to anything else, even law and economics. Such a preoccupation within a radical movement is at first glance surprising. After all, lawyers have, by notorious custom, used history conservatively, appealing to continuity and tradition.[1] And in the less common situations in which lawyers have used history to criticize the status quo, they have usually resorted to social and economic history, to show that the original social context of a legal rule reveals it was adopted for wicked or obsolete reasons, rather than to

[1] Morton Horwitz, Book Review, 17 *Am. J. Legal Hist.* 275, 275–276 (1973).

the history of legal doctrine.[2] What could conceivably be radical – or, as some unkindly ask, even interesting – about rewriting the history of doctrine?

I will attempt, in this article, to give a brief account of the impulses that have prompted the Critical scholars to their chosen ways of writing history (or rather histories, since the movement has actually spawned several different historiographical practices). I'll start by trying to describe a vision of law-in-history that has tended, as I'll argue, to dominate liberal legal scholarship. I will then outline some of the Critical insights that have developed – many of them within liberal scholarship itself – to corrode separate components of that dominant vision. Next, I'll show how Critical writers have tried to build these insights into a more thorough critique and how this critique has affected the ways in which they go about their work. Finally, I will discuss some common attacks on Critical histories, add a few doubting remarks of my own, and proffer some suggestions and exhortations for future directions.[3]

I have little hope, in the pages that follow, of making a new contribution to the long-standing debates over theory and method in socio-legal history.[4] I'm really only concerned with summarizing, in what I would like to think is a clarifying way, some of the main positions in these debates, aware that the outcome of such an effort is bound to look like a seed catalogue or a Pocket Guide to the Common and Exotic Varieties of the Social/Legal Histories of North America. The audience I would most like to reach is that of liberal lawyers who are interested enough in Critical legal writing to be curious about it and who might find it more persuasive as well as more accessible if equipped with such a little guidebook.[5]

[2] Doctrinal history has not always been conservative. Radical legal argument used to draw upon its own notions of the ancient constitution, which was to be reclaimed by revolution from a corrupt present. *See, e.g.*, Christopher Hill, "The Norman Yoke," in *Puritanism and Revolution: Sources in Interpretation of the English Revolution of the 17th Century* 58 (1958).

[3] The knowledgeable reader will have noticed that this outline follows a format (orthodoxy synthesized – partial critiques – total critique and transcendence – critique of the critique) that has become almost as stylized in CLS work as the sonata form was in classical composition. Perhaps it's time for a new format.

[4] Still less does this piece try to join the interesting controversies among Marxist historians and theorists. Although these controversies have counterparts in the literature of American legal scholarship, they are almost never referred to in that literature. Further, any attempt to describe the controversies would require introduction to a lot of specialized concepts and jargon. For a useful recent survey of these controversies, see Gregor McLennan, *Marxism and the Methodologies of History* (1981).

[5] Mine is hardly the first such guidebook. For exceptionally useful treatments of social/theoretical issues in legal historiography, see Alan Hunt, *The Sociological Movement in Law* (1978); Lawrence M. Friedman, "Some Problems and Possibilities of American Legal History," in *The State of American History* 3 (Bass ed. 1970); Wythe Holt, "Morton Horwitz and the Transformation of American Legal History," 23 *Wm. & Mary L. Rev.* 663 (1982); Harry N. Scheiber, "At the Borderland of Law and Economic History: The Contributions of Willard Hurst," 75 *Am. Hist. Rev.* 744 (1970); David Sugarman, "Theory and Practice in Law and History: A Prologue to the Study of the Relationship Between Law and Economy From a Socio-Historical Perspective,"

As the bulk of this piece is committed to describing criticisms of a tradition of historiography called "legal functionalism," I should also say that this is the tradition that has done most to nurture and inspire my own work and there isn't one of its insights, including those I have come to think mistaken, that I haven't found useful. Moreover, as is so often true of really good history, the best writing in this tradition is always grandly overflowing its conceptual channels; one could do worse than to keep trying to imitate the practices of the great functionalist figures even after one has stopped accepting their theories.

I. THE DOMINANT VISION: EVOLUTIONARY FUNCTIONALISM

A. Common Threads

Over the last 150 years or so, enlightened American legal opinion[6] has adhered with remarkable fidelity to what, in broad conception, looks like a single set of notions about historical change and the relation of law to such change. Stated baldly, these notions are that the natural and proper evolution of a society (or at least of a "progressive" society, to use Maine's qualification[7]) is toward the type of liberal capitalism seen in the advanced Western nations (especially the United States), and that the natural and proper function of a legal system is to facilitate such an evolution. (The words "natural" and "proper" stress the normative nature of the theory; deviations from the norm are both atypical and bad.) Let me try to break this very general account down into some more manageable pieces, the handful of propositions that compose its core. Readers will, I hope, understand that what I'm constructing is an "ideal type": a list of the propositions that one could expect most legal writers within the dominant tradition to accept most of the time, even if one could also expect that any individual writer would want to qualify or even violently object to one or two of them.[8]

in *Law, State and Society* (Fryer, Hunt, McBarnet, & Moorhouse eds. 1981); Mark Tushnet, "A Marxist Analyses of American Law," 1 *Marxist Perspectives* 96 (1978); Richard Abel, Book Review, 80 *Mich. L. Rev.* 785 (1980); Stephen Diamond, Book Review, 77 *Mich L. Rev.* 784 (1979); Jay Feinman, Book Review, 78 *Mich. L. Rev.* 722 (1980); Horwitz, *supra* note 1.

6 I'm speaking here not of the work of professional legal historians but of the background assumptions about law-in-history that are present in mainstream legal scholarship generally.

7 *See* Henry Maine, *Ancient Law: Its Connection with the Early History of Society, and Its Relation to Modern Ideas* 21–22 (1861).

8 The danger in trying to set down such a list, of course, is that readers – especially the readers who believe that their own world view is the one about to be made into a target – will say, "Well, who accepts that? I don't know any legal writer who subscribes to *that* view, at least not in such a simple-minded form. Who exactly is Gordon talking about here?" One way to deflect this reaction in advance would be to offer a long list of passages from mainstream legal scholarship that exemplify these core propositions. This might indeed be done, but it would take a lot of space to do it, in part because these propositions are rarely found in the baldly explicit form in which they are stated

1. "Law" and "society" are separate social categories, each describable independently from the other but related to each other through various mechanisms of causal linkage.

Writers in the dominant tradition make an important, though usually silent, move even before they start saying anything substantive about law-in-history: They divide the world into two spheres, one social and one legal. "Society" is the primary realm of social experience. It is "real life": What's immediately and truly important to people, like desire and its fulfillment or frustration, goes on there. This realm is the realm of production, commerce, the market, the family. "Law" or "the legal system," on the other hand, is a distinctly secondary body of phenomena. It is a specialized realm of state and professional activity that is called into being by the primary social world in order to serve that world's needs. Law is auxiliary – an excrescence on social life, even if sometimes a useful excrescence.

Though law and society are separate, they are related. And the big theoretical problem for writers who see the world this way is to work out the secret of that relationship. Thus, they ask questions such as, "Is law a dependent or independent variable?" "Is everything about law – norms, rules, processes, and institutions – determined by society, or does law have "autonomous" internal structures or logic?" "If it has internal structures, do they enable it to have an independent causal effect – to act as a positive feedback loop – on social life?" Writers in the liberal tradition (like those in the Marxist tradition) have resolved these questions in wildly different ways and reached wildly different conclusions,[9] but they all assume that these are the vital questions.

here. They appear in conventional legal discourse more as diffuse background *assumptions*, seemingly too unproblematic to need spelling out. I have decided against trying to document my list in this fashion, less (I hope) out of laziness than out of the expectation that the readers and writers of mainstream legal scholarship will simply *recognize* the propositions as belonging to the ordinary, taken-for-granted, common sense of that scholarship. To supplement this method of recognition, I actually did try in another article to give concrete examples of writers who accepted this set of views. *See* Robert W. Gordon, "Historicism in Legal Scholarship" 90 *Yale L. J.* 1017, 1028–1045 (1981) (the dominant vision was there called "adaptation theory" and more sketchily described than it is here). And in this article I try to provide many more examples at appropriate points.

As for readers who do recognize their own views in my list of the core propositions of the dominant vision but think my account unacceptably reduces, caricatures, or distorts those views, I propose the following procedure: (1) Consider whether the view you want to defend is more accurately categorized as part of the "dominant vision" or as one of the numerous "critiques" of that vision that appear later in this article (it may be that you are really a critic, rather than an adherent, of evolutionary functionalism as I've described it); (2) if after doing that you still find yourself a defender of evolutionary functionalism, but of a far more refined and subtle variety than my caricature, ask yourself whether your variant is or is not vulnerable to the many critiques (it may be that the critiques are as good against the sophisticated as against the crude versions); and finally (3) if you have isolated a strain of the dominant vision that you believe to be immune to the critiques (or, naturally, if you think the critiques are all garbage anyway), write a letter or publish an article in response to this one.

[9] See notes 18–26 *infra* and accompanying text.

2. *Societies have needs.*

This proposition is the functionalist heart of the dominant vision.[10] Social needs may be universal – needs such as survival, stability, maintenance of social order, conflict management, organization of production, security against foreign enemies, allocation of scarce resources, or preservation of continuity in the midst of change or they may be specific to a given stage of social or economic development. One key need is the need to develop along the appropriate social evolutionary path.

Needs operate both as pressures and as constraints. They are the motors driving the society to find means for their fulfillment, and they set the limits on the possibilities of social experimentation – limits beyond which lie dysfunction, futility, failure, and chaos.[11]

3. *There is an objective, determined, progressive social evolutionary path.*

The general idea here is that the causal responsibility for change lies with impersonal forces of historical "becoming." More specifically, the histories of certain advanced Western societies, most notably the United States, describe an evolutionary development that is both natural (in the sense that some version of it will happen in every society unless "artificial" constraints force a deviation) and, on the whole, progressive.

Different generations have described this evolutionary process somewhat differently, but the contemporary United States almost always ends up sitting at the developmental summit. The great eighteenth- and nineteenth-century story (the "Scottish Enlightenment" story[12] whose general outlines are still so

[10] This proposition is probably also the single most disputed one within liberal legal scholarship: Many writers see the attribution of "needs" to societies as excessively reifying, and they therefore try to break societies down into their constituent individuals or interest groups. *See* text accompanying note 38 *infra.*

[11] For the purposes of this article, I'm reserving the term "functionalism" for the particular type of explanation outlined here, i.e., one that first posits a set of "primary," more-or-less objective needs or dynamic processes and then explains "secondary" historical phenomena as responses to those needs or processes.

Some legal writers seem to use "functionalism" in a sense different from mine, to mean any way of explaining legal forms or practices by reference to social "purposes" or "interests" – indeed by reference to anything other than the formal, internal materials of the legal system. This usage seems to me both too broad and too narrow. It's too broad because *any* practice is "functional," and none dysfunctional, if that means it serves somebody's interest or can be seen as part of a system or pattern or process. And it's too narrow because it arbitrarily excludes attempts to show how the "function" of a legal practice might be to meet the formal requirements of (i.e., serve someone's "ideal interest" in) the elegance or completeness of an abstract system. I'd prefer to call this general type of explanation "external" or "contextual" and to label as "instrumental" the particular subset of external explanations that account for legal practices as products of the desires or demands of social classes, groups, or individuals.

[12] *See* John Burrow, *A Liberal Descent: Victorian Historians and the English Past* 21–35 (1981); Albert Hirschman, *The Passions and the Interests: Political Arguments for Capitalism Before Its Triumph* 81–93 (1977).

firmly rooted in our culture) told of the gradual liberation of the individual from the shackles of feudalism and superstition – from restraints on trade, on free alienation of land, and on free movement of labor; from the oppressions of feudal dues and tithes and of perpetual subordination to customary hierarchies of ecclesiastical and noble orders; and from established religions. According to this story, the concurrent spread of liberty and commerce yielded a commonwealth of men who were actually or potentially (with some exceptions such as slaves) politically equal property-holders, securely owning and freely exchanging land, labor, and capital.[13]

By the start of our own century, the growth of propertyless classes caused the historians' emphasis to shift away from the concept of progress as the growth of yeoman freeholders and toward the concept of progress as improvement in technology, organization of production, and creation of opportunities for immigrants to rise in society. In our own age of dampened enthusiasms, the labels attached to basic historical changes tend to be more neutral: "industrialization," "modernization," or just "political and economic development." In usage, however, these labels retain a strong normative flavor and occasionally, as in some legal economists' interpretation of the history of societies as one long series of "efficiency" gains,[14] an unabashed Victorian optimism.

What all these histories have in common is their determinist teleologies, whose elemental parts – the "extension of the market," the "breakdown of

[13] The story was always ambiguous as to whether an ideal element (the love of liberty) or a material one (extension of the market) was the driving force behind this liberation.

[14] One can take as an example the following statement:

> The efficient society is wealthier than the inefficient – that is what efficiency means – and a wealthier society will support a larger population. This effect of greater wealth can be decisive in the competition among primitive societies, where the methods of warfare are simple and numbers of people count for much more than in modern warfare. Archaic societies sufficiently durable to have left substantial literary or archaeological remains and primitive societies sufficiently durable to have survived into the nineteenth century (when serious anthropological study began) are likely, therefore, to be societies whose customs are efficient.
>
> ...
>
> Clearly, however, the primitive social equilibrium is less efficient, at least in the long run, than that of advanced societies: consider the very small proportion of the world's population that lives in primitive societies today. This situation is due in some part to coercion, rather than peaceful competition, from advanced societies (dramatically so in the case of the North American Indians, for example), but in greater part to the adaptive responses of primitive society to its economic environment. These responses include practices, such as denying people privacy and preventing them from amassing wealth, which are inimical to economic progress and in turn to population growth. This is a point to give the romantic anarchist pause.

Richard Posner, "A Theory of Primitive Society, With Special Reference to Law," 23 *J. L. & Econ.* 1, 53 (1980).

I suppose that if Society A invents the Maxim gun, which it uses to massacre the natives of Society B, or develops an immunity to its own virulent venereal diseases, which then spread among and wipe out the population of Society B, we could say that Society A is more "efficient." Other adjectives also come to mind.

traditional communities and status hierarchies," the "shift from ascribed to achieved social status," the "triumph of the middle class," the "revolution of production in the factory system," the "rise of the administrative state," and the "development of the multi-divisional form of corporate organization" – are all linked together in a master process of social evolution.[15]

Lawyers once played a moderately important role in actually writing these histories. Recent legal writing is more likely just to assume that some objective, generally understood process of development has been working away in the background, and to leave the actual details of the process to vague implication.

4. *Legal systems should be described and explained in terms of their functional responsiveness to social needs.*

Functionalist sociological legal history has an exceedingly distinguished lineage, beginning with Montesquieu and Adam Smith, continuing through Karl Marx, Max Weber, and Rudolph von Jhering, and virtually all lesser nineteenth-century writers on law,[16] and including among twentieth-century lawyers such figures as Oliver Wendell Holmes, Roscoe Pound, Karl Llewellyn, Franz Neumann, and Willard Hurst. The general functionalist method is to construct (or, as is rather more common, to assume without much discussion) a typology of stages of social development and then to show how legal forms and institutions have satisfied, or failed to satisfy, the functional requirements of each stage. Obviously, an enormous gap in sophistication and conceptual power separates the best and worst examples of this method. At its best, as in Weber's work, complex bundles of rules are tied through explicit theorizing to elaborate accounts of social development. At its comically vulgar worst, the method produces wholly speculative functional rationales for legal rules in underlying social changes – vacuously described rationales such as "the evolution of the right of privacy was a response to the increasing complexity and interdependence of modern society."[17]

Of all the generalizations produced by this method, one so familiar that it has become a cliché of our common discourse is that capitalist development (or as our forebears preferred to put it, the expansion of commerce) requires legal improvements that increase the certainty and predictability of exchange relationships. I will come back to this assertion, but I should first list the final identifying characteristic of the dominant vision, namely:

[15] It was of course not a lawyer, but the sociologist Talcott Parsons. who produced the *Summa* of modern accounts of this integrated process. *See, e.g.*, Talcott Parsons & Neil Smelser, *Economy and Society: A Study in the Integration of Economic and Social Theory* 284–294 (1956). Yet something like the Parsonian account is remarkably pervasive in modern legal scholarship though its optimism is occasionally qualified with a trace of tragic modernism.

[16] *See, e.g.*, Peter Stein, *Legal Evolution: The Story of an Idea* 122–127 (1980).

[17] For a marvelous collection of examples, see Mark Kelman, "Trashing," 36 *Stan. L. Rev.* 293 (1984); *see also* notes 53–60 *infra* and accompanying text.

5. The legal system adapts to changing social needs.
This concept expresses the confidence that, in the advanced Western nations and especially in the United States, the legal system has in fact responded to evolving social needs. Save for egregiously Panglossian writers (Blackstone in some moods is one of these), the proponents of this notion do not feel a need to attribute a social function to every piece of law in the system; most writers will concede that even major legal forms and processes can be dysfunctional for short periods. But a committed functionalist will maintain that, despite undeniable instances of lag and reaction, adaptation is the normal course. The perspective thus tends to produce statements such as the following (presented here for the sake of illustration in their simplest and most unqualified form), which discuss specific changes in legal rules or forms:

- Tort law rules such as the negligence standard and the fellow-servant rule were adopted to meet the needs of early industrial development. (They allowed employers and transportation entrepreneurs to externalize a portion of their costs.) But as technological increased the risks of accidents stemming from employment and from the use of consumer goods, the law responded with rules of strict liability.
- Warranty rules such as "caveat emptor" reflected a society in which most commercial trading was face-to-face. But with the rise of mass consumer transactions between remote sellers and purchasers and with increasing ignorance about the risks of defects, the law implied warranties of merchantability.
- The corporate form developed in order to fulfill the need for capital accumulation during the period of industrial take-off.
- Various features of modern corporate organization, including the "business judgment" rule and the rules specifying areas of management "prerogative" exempt from collective bargaining, developed in order to give management broad discretionary decision-making power necessary for efficient maximization of profits in advanced industrial societies.
- Courts and legislatures were competent to handle the problems of regulating the early nineteenth-century economy of competitive individuals. By the late nineteenth century, however, the concentration of corporate enterprise was raising problems of such complexity that administrative agencies were required to handle them.
- Professionalization of the bar – the development of bar associations, law schools, formalized training and entry requirements, the large urban law office, etc. – was necessary to enable lawyers to take on the complex specialized tasks of law in a modern economy.

This perspective also produces some very large claims indeed. The first two examples listed below were commonplace in legal rhetoric through the end of the last century; the third is asserted by some lawyer-economists in our own time:

- The common law over time tends to work itself pure.
- Progressive improvements in legal science have tended to clarify legal doctrine, making it ever more certain and predictable, as well as more adaptable to social needs.
- Common law rules have tended to become more and more efficient.

B. Divisions Within Functionalism

By now it will be evident that my "dominant tradition" is a very broad umbrella, covering legal writers whose views on many issues differ radically, some of whom would be appalled to find themselves sharing even a limited-purpose category with the others. In particular, I mean to group under the common shelter of "evolutionary functionalism" both of the great antagonistic parties of modern American legal thought, labeled here for simplicity's sake "Formalism" and "Realism." Each of these parties has, I think, worked out contrasting visions of what social development consists of and how law has adapted to that development without disturbing the fundamental assumption of progressive adaptation that they hold in common. The parties have clashed instead over such issues as the definition of law and the autonomy of legal decision-making.[18]

The Formalist side has a very restrictive notion of law as judge-made law: "The legal system is the domain of the legal specialist; the legislature is in general not part of the legal system but a source of the goals that the legal system is to carry out."[19] Legislation and usually administration as well are thus relegated to the "social" sphere of the great law/society dichotomy. On the Realist side, however, law is "what officials do about disputes,"[20] or even more broadly, the work of anyone, including the private bar, whose task is the administration of public policy.

Formalists and Realists also divide over the issue of the "autonomy" of legal decision-making processes in relation to political, social, and economic decision-making. Formalists think that it is both usual and desirable for legal decisions to follow an internal professional agenda such as "a

[18] Incidentally, the fact that legal Formalism has been politically conservative and Legal Realism more liberal-reformist is only an accident of our recent history. It is easy to imagine a radical formalism, such as the French Revolution's program to remake society in accordance with abstract legal rights, or a conservative Realism, such as German historicism.

[19] Robert Means, *Underdevelopment and the Development of Law: Corporations and Corporation Law in Nineteenth-Century Columbia* xii (1980) (footnote omitted). This book is an exemplary performance in the functionalist/evolutionist mode of legal history (lacking, however, the normative notions of progress common to that mode).

[20] Karl Llewellyn, *The Bramble Bush: On our Law and its Study* 20 (1951). For a clear idea of what Llewellyn meant by this famous phrase, see William Twining, *Karl Llewellyn and the Realist Movement* 148–152 (1973).

taught legal tradition"[21] of the common law. The idea is that such decisions will best perform their social/functional task of adaptation if lawyers and judges are not thinking about society at all but only about perfecting their own craft, because a logic of liberty or efficiency is inherent in the practice of that craft. Realists think that this proposition is nonsense, that policy-making can't be socially functional unless it is self-consciously directed toward the satisfaction of social needs. Realists do, however, have their own notion of legal "autonomy": Policy-makers ought to be, and sometimes actually are, insulated from the immediate pressures of short-term political or economic interests so they can concentrate on their society's long-run needs.[22]

These differences lead to differing Formalist and Realist approaches to legal history. Formalist legal history focuses exclusively on the development of legal doctrine, while Realist legal history considers doctrine as one component of a general, if not always well-coordinated, policy-making enterprise.[23] Further, formalist legal history considers phenomena outside the legal craft as distorting judicial decision-making or as simply irrelevant to the important story to be told; the Formalist hero is the judge or treatise-writer who best clarifies doctrinal categories. Realist history, on the other hand, takes as its main subject the relations of function or dysfunction between law and major trends of social development; the Realist hero is the social engineer who masterfully wields law as an instrument of policy.[24]

Naturally, these differences lead to fundamental disagreements about the course of recent history. For many Formalists, the high point of legal development was reached around the end of the nineteenth century when the ideal of the rule of law as primarily enforced by judges through an autonomous legal order was at its peak of influence.[25] But the Formalists' high is the Realists' low: At that time, abstraction from concrete social forces had put the legal system badly out of synch with the evolving requirements of society, and we only climbed out of this trough of dysfunction through the implementation of the policies of Progressivism and the New Deal.[26]

[21] Roscoe Pound, *The Formative Era of American Law* 82 (1978).

[22] *See, e.g.*, James Landis, *The Administrative Process* 111–117 (1938) (discussing why agencies were organized so as to insulate them from the administration that appointed agency officials).

[23] *See, e.g.*, James Willard Hurst, *The Growth of American Law: The American Law Makers* 439–446 (1950) (adopting a broad view of law and of the tasks of legal history).

[24] *See, e.g.*, James Willard Hurst, "Alexander Hamilton, Law Maker," 78 *Colum. L. Rev.* 483 (1978).

[25] *See generally* 1 Friedrich Hayek, *Law, Legislation, and Liberty: Rules and Order* 94–123 (1973).

[26] *See, e.g.*, James Willard Hurst, *Law and the Conditions of Freedom in the Nineteenth Century United States* 84–108 (1956).

II. INTERLUDE FOR QUESTIONS ABOUT THE POINT OF THIS PROJECT

Before going on to say something about the attacks that have been eating away at the evolutionary-functionalist vision of legal history, it is worth pausing a moment to ask why anyone should bother to attack the vision at all. Social scientists who have heard previous versions of this piece wonder why I worry so much about evolutionism (our dominant vision's points 3 and 5) and functionalism (2 and 4), the mainstays of the liberal sociology of the 1950s; these views have been so thoroughly discredited in modern social theory, they argue, as to be left almost without serious defenders. On the other hand, some of my legal colleagues, who have spent their working lives trying to slay the Formalist hydra that is still powerfully present in legal-academic and professional thought generally, think it perverse and ungrateful to attack the Realist versions of functionalism, for these versions have proven to be the most reliable weapons against the dogma that legal forms can be understood apart from their social context: If the weapons are broken, won't the hydra stalk the law schools unafraid?

To the first question, the second is itself a partial answer: Evolutionary functionalism, in both the Formalist and Realist versions, has been kept going much longer in legal thought than in social thought generally. This isn't only because the law schools tend to pick up mainstream intellectual opinion ten to fifteen years late. The notion that law always is, or at least ought to be, functionally adapting to evolving social needs is so deeply embedded in standard legal speech that one isn't likely to make a legal argument of any length without at least mentioning it. This notion presumably persists because of its serviceability to the liberal idea of law as the neutral arbiter of social conflict: It tells the managers of the legal system that their basic instructions are specified by a social process outside of the legal system and that they have no responsibility for that process except to solve the technical problems of devising functional responses that will help rather than hinder it. Hence, the inevitable ambiguities of legislative command, prior case law, custom, or constitutional text need never force a legal system to the pain of political choice because its managers can always claim to be serving the logic of an historical process, or immanent social consensus that exists beyond and prior to politics.[27]

[27] For example, dominant visionaries argue that in "modern" or "developed" societies, innovations in technology and the organization of the work force are continually expanding the size of the total economic pie. *Political* conflict properly takes place only over issues of secondary importance, such as how the pie is to be divided; expansion is both the natural course of development for a modern society and something that is in everyone's interest. The job of the legal system, absent (evidently misguided) authoritative political directions to the contrary, is to facilitate the needs of the production process (e.g., "efficient management." "industrial peace"), which by definition are universal needs rather than those of a particular faction or class. See, for a fuller description of this example, Katherine Van Wezel Stone, "The Post-War Paradigm in American Labor Law," 90 *Yale L. J.* 1509, 1545 (1981).

What's more, not only is evolutionary functionalism still a living force in traditional legal argument, but it has in recent years received a terrific hormone boost from some of the fanciest and most interesting new work coming out of the law schools: the Chicago law and economics movement,[28] Williamson's "transaction cost" approach to legal institutions,[29] Bob Clark's explicitly evolutionary approach to the history of the modern corporation,[30] and Selznick and Nonet's theory of "responsive law."[31]

Perhaps by now the second question, "Why knock functionalism when it's been so good to you?," is on its way to being answered. Realist functionalism has unquestionably been a politically progressive and intellectually liberating force; it has moved us away from the occasionally useful but ultimately sterile studies of technical forms evolving in a cultural vacuum and from the idea that lawyers and judges will always and automatically do the most possible good through complacent inattention to the society in which they live. Its empirical investigations of the law "in action" have exploded forever the Formalist fantasy that a universal scheme of neutral, general rules controls equally and impersonally the discretion of every class and faction of civil society. We owe to the Realist tradition of scholarship most of our understanding of variations in the effectiveness of law according to the power and wealth of the people it touches or who seek to use it, of "legal pluralism" (the fact that real social life is prodigal of sovereigns – different governments, officials at different levels of government, "private" associations – each making its own brand of law in cooperation or competition with the others), and of the complexity and perversity of legal/social relations (how it so often happens that a legal form seemingly designed to strengthen A's at the expense of B's ends up wiping out A's and entrenching B's more immovably than ever). So much indeed have the Realist functionalists accomplished that it's hard not to sympathize with their resentment of Critics who seem to be trying to displace them just as Law-and-Society studies are beginning to make a dent on the mainstream lawyers who, until recently, showed little more than scorn for Realist empiricism. "Must we always," the empiricists ask despairingly, "be patronized by lawyers with fancy theories in their heads and no respect for facts? Might not our movement be

[28] *See, e.g.*, George Priest, "The Common Law Process and the Selection of Efficient Rules," 6 *J. Legal Stud.* 65 (1977); *see also* John Goodman, "An Economic Theory, of the Evolution of Common Law," 7 *J. Legal Stud.* 393 (1978); Paul Rubin, "Why Is the Common Law Efficient?," 6 *J. Legal Stud* 51 (1977); Peter Terrebone, "A Strictly Evolutionary Model of Common Law," 10 *J. Legal Stud.* 397 (1981).

[29] *See* Oliver Williamson, *Markets and Hierarchies: Analysis and antitrust Implications* (1975).

[30] *See* Robert Clark, "The Four Stages of Capitalism: Reflections on Investment Management Treatises," 94 *Harv. L. Rev.* 561 (1981); Robert Clark, "The Interdisciplinary Study of Legal Evolution," 90 *Yale L. J.* 1238 (1981).

[31] *See, e.g.*, Philippe Selznick & Philip Nonet, *Law and Society in Transition: Toward Responsive Law* (1978).

allowed its dialectical moment of supremacy before the tides of Critical negativity drag it away?"[32]

The Critics can give this *cri de coeur* a straightforward answer: Any intelligent Critical approach will make use of the insights and empirical findings of Realist functionalism,[33] but there are apologetic aspects even to the Realist versions of the dominant vision that the Critics feel compelled to resist. For example, by emphasizing law as policy, Realist functionalism almost unconsciously reserves even what it believes to be the very marginal opportunities for legal influence on the direction of social change to an elite of policy-makers: Mass movements and local struggles are not ordinarily thought of as makers of legal change.[34] Because it assumes a natural harmony of interests in the fulfillment of social needs, it has trouble seeing conflict as other than dysfunctional disturbance of equilibrium. And, with all regard for its heroic contributions, I believe its essential working assumptions misleadingly objectify history, making highly contingent developments appear to have been necessary.

The Critics' basic argument – elaborated more fully below – is that by taking the world as we know it as largely determined by impersonal social forces, evolutionary-functionalists obscure the ways in which these seemingly inevitable processes are actually manufactured by people who claim (and believe themselves) to be only passively adapting to such processes.[35] If there are evolutionary processes in social life, they are processes whose logic is one

[32] David Trubek, "Critical Legal Studies and Empiricism," 36 *Stan. L. Rev.* 575 (1984) is an especially useful statement of the differences, both real and supposed, between CLS and the Law-and-Society movement.

[33] I give examples of such uses at text accompanying notes 61–71, *infra*.

[34] How ironic it is that the country whose People, by their official ideology, have delegated only limited powers to their State; whose political origins lie in revolutionary protests organized by "the people out of doors," crowds explicitly claiming legal status and legitimacy; and whose history is so full of mass reform movements should have produced such a Tory legal literature, narrowly focused on official agencies, especially the courts, and almost completely indifferent to extra-institutional law-making. On the different conceptions of reform within and "outside" the "system" informing liberal and Critical thought, see William Simon, "Visions of Practice in Legal Thought," 36 *Stan. L. Rev.* 469 (1984).

[35] For example, the functionalist lawyers who helped to design the ground rules regulating labor-capital conflict after World War II assumed that the expansion of the total economic pie (which was in everyone's interest) required unconstrained management discretion over investment decisions and general working conditions, leaving to resolution through collective bargaining only the residual issue of how to divide the resulting surplus. Critical historians treat this more or less unexamined background *assumption* of a relationship of social necessity (efficient production requires legal forms preserving managerial prerogatives) as an ideological practice that helped to *produce* social necessity because it suppressed alternative methods of governing production as unthinkable or unrealistic. Thus, in company with many other social actors, lawyers were more or less unwittingly reproducing the world they were used to – actually helping to create what they imagined to be the given, pre-existing "hard social reality" of the situation – because they were trapped in a functionalist logic that told them the basic conditions of the production process had to remain much as they already were.

of multiplicity, not uniformity of forms. The social nature of human beings reveals itself not through constant responses to their environments but through an astonishing diversity of cultural responses and, most remarkable of all, a repeatedly demonstrated capacity to reimagine their situations so as to generate novel responses still.[36] We invent shorthand labels like "modernization" as a way of summarizing what has happened in and trying to generalize about the history of particular societies. Then, by a trick of the mind, we suddenly reify our label into a process that had to happen the way it did. The next thing you know, we start explaining the whole contingent miscellany of contemporary social practices (especially the nasty ones) as the natural outcome of the "modernization process." But if there is no such single process, there can't be any single set of functional responses to it either. Surely there are other ways of thinking about history that don't trap us into supposing we're permanently stuck with what we happen to be used to, with only the tiniest margins for maneuvering. The hope of getting out of that trap and of exploring the alternatives is what fuels the enterprise of criticizing the dominant vision.

III. PARTIAL CRITIQUES: VARIATIONS ON THE DOMINANT THEME

I call the sample of views that follow "partial" critiques because they remain faithful to many elements of the dominant vision while rejecting others. These critiques come from all colors of the political spectrum.

A. Variation #1: Collapse "Needs" into "Interests"

This move is so common that it could be called a subtheme rather than a variation of the dominant view. It consists simply of breaking down the universal category of societal needs into the particular conflicting desires or interests of society's members. The function of law then becomes that of responding to some balance of those interests.

This variation has an interesting history of appearances in modern legal scholarship. Toward the beginning of this century, a writer who identified the factional pressures behind the creation of a legal form was usually describing either an abnormal and regrettable situation or one that had happened a comfortably long time before. Explaining the political and economic origins of old law was all right so long as you made clear that recent law had developed independently of all pressures save the "taught tradition" of the profession. If you did attribute a class or special-interest origin to contemporary law, you did so

[36] *See* Stephen Gould, *The Mismeasure of Man* 324–334 (1981) (what is biologically determined is a brain capable of creative variation in its cultural environment), Clifford Geertz, "The Impact of the Concept of Culture on the Concept of Man," in Clifford Geertz, *The Interpretation of Cultures* (1973) (the human species realizes its "nature" not through uniformity but diversity of cultural forms).

in order to condemn it. Thus, legal conservatives condemned wages-and-hours laws as "class legislation," and Progressives condemned judicial invalidation of such laws as caving in to the Interests at the expense of the People.

But with time and growing disillusionment with the regulatory welfare state, one could hear more scholars, of whom perhaps the most influential were Lawrence Friedman and Gabriel Kolko, explaining not just bad law but all law as the product of interest-group pressures.[37] These writers were soon joined by the Chicago-school economists, the sires of the modern law and economics movement, in rapidly increasing numbers. And if today you hear a voice claiming that a legal rule was adopted because its adoption served the interest of some regulated industry, or that a complex procedure exists only because it makes money for the legal profession – explanations of a kind once despised by mainstream lawyers as the paranoid cynicism of Populist and Marxist vulgarisateurs – the voice as likely as not belongs to a right-wing economist.[38]

There are several different ways of characterizing the interests that law tries to satisfy. Right-wing economism says that interests are just the arbitrary desires of individual subjects, revealed through crude behavioral proxies such as "willingness to pay" or votes. This school has no theory at all of how such desires originate, except perhaps a vague notion that people in a given occupational or institutional role will want to maximize the interest the theorist casually attributes to that role.[39] Centrist-liberal pluralism discovers what interests are by looking at the programs of organized groups and largely explains legal enactments as compromises among those interests. While this view is certainly a big advance over the view of society as isolated individuals or roles, its mainstream forms have been famously vulnerable to the charge of lacking any plausible account of power or social structure that would help explain why some groups get their way more than others, or why some groups never get to be "interests" at all because they can't organize.[40] Finally, various economisms, not all on the left, do pay attention to power and social structure and explain law as the instrument of ruling groups. These last merit their own subheading and are treated under Variation #2.

[37] See, *e.g.*, Lawrence Friedman, *A History of American Law* (1973); Gabriel Kolko, *The Triumph of Conservatism: A Reinterpretation of American History, 1900–1916* (1963).

[38] *See, e.g.*, Peter Pashigian, "Regulation, Preventive Law, and the Duties of Attorneys," in *The Changing Role of the Corporate Attorney* 3 (W. Carney ed. 1982); George Stigler, "The Theory of Economic Regulation," 2 *Bell J. Econ. & Mgmt, Sci.* 3 (1971). The economist can afford this kind of candor about political pressures on law because he's got the suprapolitical norm of "efficiency" to fall back on. The left-wing writer, on the other hand, is much more likely to argue that the legal system is "relatively autonomous," not completely to be explained by this sort of influence. *See* notes 86–88 *infra* and accompanying text.

[39] For example, stockholders "want" profit on their investment and easy exit; workers "want" higher wages and benefits; neither "wants" a stake in management of the enterprise.

[40] *See* Richard Parker, "The Past of Constitutional Theory – and its Future," 42 *Ohio St. L. J.* 223 (1981).

But before going on to the rest of the Variations, it's worth pausing to ask if this first one, the reduction of needs to interests, represents an intellectual advance over the dominant vision. In some ways it clearly does: By assuming that conflict is a normal feature of social interaction, this view focuses attention on the distributional struggles underlying legal enactment and implementation and helps to identify who wins and who loses from different regimes of law. It also encourages descriptions of law-in-society that are populated with individuals and groups with aspirations and strategies and that are thus more concrete than the frequently vague allusions to the impersonal background forces of development that serve as the primary motors of change in the dominant tradition. After long immersion in writing that grounds legal change in the ghostly pressures of evolving doctrines or in such causes as "increasing social complexity and inter-dependence," one feels an amazed and delighted gratitude at coming across an account that tells you that some piece of law took the form it did because a shipper's lobby, or homesteaders, or a coal company, or a Senate committee chairman wanted it to.

Almost needless to say, such accounts are often fatal to the normative element in legal histories.[41] Yet the switch from needs to interests is by no means all gain. For all its problems, the functionalist perspective recognizes that societies have to be understood as systems and structures, not just as a series of collisions among the preferences and strategies of their constituent members: All these people participate in and are constrained by structures of discourse, ways of thinking about reality and right, cultural inheritance, and political and organizational forms that shape desire and channel its expression. The subtler exponents of "instrumental" theories of law (as this Variation's theories are commonly called) have always recognized this. The more reductionist exponents, principally the economists, seem to think that one is puncturing all the vagueness involved in reifying "society" into a thing with "needs" by getting down to the nitty-gritty reality of concrete individuals and groups. But the "interest groups" of pluralist theory and the "individuals" of economic theory are no less reified and no more real entities than is the "society" of functionalists; they are just as much products of socially created and maintained categories of thought and conventional practices.

[41] But not necessarily. It's quite possible, and indeed frequently happens, that a legal writer may combine an interest-group perspective with a functionalist one. The writer could argue, for instance, that needs appearing at some stage of historical development generate interests to assert those needs; the legal system then responds to those interests. Alternatively, the writer could take the view that the "market" for law-responsive-to-the-demands of-interests tends toward a long-run equilibrium; and this view could (though it need not) be a normative one such as that of interest-group pluralism, in which the primary if not exclusive virtue of a legal system consists in its responsiveness to such demands.

B. Variation #2 – Transpose "Needs" into "Domination"

In other words, every time a mainstream writer says a legal rule or process or institution serves the needs of society, show instead how it serves to maintain the power of a dominant class or group. Opponents of this variation are inclined to call it "Marxist," although the classical Marxist theory of law is just one highly specific subset of this variation.[42] In reality, this general proposition would be adopted as well by many non-Marxists: by elite theorists, including conservatives like Alexander Hamilton, who think the ruling classes ought to control the legal system, and by fatalists, who think that for good or ill elites will always be in control and indeed that having control of the legal system is one of the things that helps identify those elites.[43] On the other hand, modern *marxisant* theorists of law and the state, as well as most Critical Legal Studies people, have become so disenchanted with the project of trying to explain law as nothing more than the tool of the ruling class that their ideas can't be adequately treated under this subheading.

The great contribution of this variation has been to put social structure, class, and power – whose very existence much liberal legal writing seems so astonishingly to deny – back into our accounts of law. Histories of legal oppressions – of slavery, Indian Removal laws, Black Codes, labor injunctions – are indispensable reminders that there's often nothing subtle about the way the powerful deploy the legal system to keep themselves organized and their victims disorganized and scared.[44] But the crude versions of the law-as-an-elite-tool theory are as vulnerable as mainstream functionalism to the critique which points out how incredibly difficult it is to relate events in the realm of "law" in any straightforward causal way to those in the realm of "society."

C. Variation #3 – Weaken the Instrumental Links Between Law and Society

Instrumentalist theories of law – which here include mainstream functionalism as well as the right-wing economics of Variation # 1 and the orthodox Marxism of Variation #2 – generally aspire to a positivist style of explanation. The idea is that someday (that Jubilee when all the data have been gathered in) we will be able to generalize convincingly and fairly abstractly about what social conditions will produce what legal responses and what effects upon society those responses will have in their turn. Yet I think it's fair to say that on the whole

[42] The classical Marxist theory closely resembles the dominant liberal vision in that it holds legal institutions to be functionally responsive to the needs of the basic modes of production which define successive stages of a macrohistorical evolutionary process. For a useful summary account of the theory, see McLennan, *supra* note 4, at 3–23, 45–65.

[43] See, *e.g.*, Gaetano Mosca, *The Ruling Class* 130–134, 409–410 (1939).

[44] An especially fine and subtle work this genre is John Gaventa, *Power and Powerlessness* (1980) (describing use of terror, intimidation, control of the media, and manipulation of the legal and political processes in employers' campaign against striking Appalachian mineworkers).

such statements of regularity in legal-social relations don't stand up very well to historical criticism.[45] These statements keep running up against (a) comparative studies showing that social and economic conditions that are apparently similar in relevant respects[46] have actually produced radically different legal responses and (b) demonstrations that the social effects of adopting a legal form are never predictable from the form itself, because the interpretation of a form, its enforcement by lower-level officials, and the response it's likely to elicit (enthusiasm, indifference, resistance) may all vary with the minutest particulars of context.[47]

Take, for example, the once familiar proposition that the negligence principle was a functional response to the social needs of industrialization in its earlier phases (because it protected infant industry by externalizing its costs onto farmers, workers, city residents, etc.). The problems with this proposition are that (a) lots of societies industrialized without the negligence principle or after the principle had been around so long that it could hardly be a response" to industrialization,[48] and (b) the fact that there was a "negligence principle"

[45] This is a rather large assertion, for which thorough documentation would require combing mainstream legal scholarship for propositions suggesting functional linkages between legal forms and material conditions and then trying to show what was wrong with every such proposition. What I've done here instead is to pick out some commonplace examples of such propositions, all of them backed by respectable sponsors, in the supposition that they are representative samples of the whole bulk. Readers who think the examples are unfairly chosen are urged to produce better ones.

[46] Of course one could argue that situations are never similar enough in type to afford a basis for such comparisons, but so strong a form of historicism would doom forever the possibility of a historical sociology of law along functionalist lines.

[47] I should stress here that the most valuable criticism of this type has not come from radical critics, nor from CLS people, but from within mainstream liberal scholarship itself – from (a) functionalist social theorists such as Weber, who conscientiously raise difficulties with their own positions; (b) legal historians such as Scheiber and Hurst, who seem to have a general commitment to the notion that law responds to social needs, but whose particular narratives undercut any strong version of functionalism by revealing how various the responses have been; (c) legal historians who tend to explain law as the product of interest – group conflict, especially Friedman, who has always emphasized how many different techniques, legal or nonlegal, can serve an economic function and refused to give any legal form a position of causal necessity. *See, e.g.*, Friedman, *supra* note 37, at 234 ("It is doubtful that majestic capitalism would have smothered in its crib without the rule of *caveat emptor.* It is doubtful whether specific doctrines of commercial law were cause, effect, or condition of American capitalism; or all or none of these." (footnote omitted)); (d) institutional-economic historians, such as those cited *infra* note 62, who have done comparative work on the role of the state in promoting and regulating economic development; (e) the work of the law-and-society movement on the "gap between law on the books and the law in action," stressing the study of implementation of legal rules; and finally (f) the Legal Realists' critique of Formalist conceptualism, stressing the dependency of textual meaning on context and convention.

[48] *See, e.g.*, Robert Rabin, "The Historical Development of the Fault Principle: A Reinterpretation," *Ga. L. Rev.* 925 (1981); Gary Schwartz, "Tort Law and the Economy in Nineteenth Century America: A Reinterpretation," 90 *Yale L. J.* 1717 (1981).

doesn't by itself imply any determinate set of social consequences because the principle can be interpreted (or ignored) by judges, administrators, jurors, or employers so as to produce any imaginable combination of liability and damages (including none of either).[49] These signs of indeterminacy naturally do not daunt the committed functionalist; they only spur him on to more refined hypotheses that will account for most of the variations. But in practice the progressive refinement of general statements about causal relationships between legal and social forms tends rapidly to decompose such statements into the detailed histories of particular societies. One's brave and sweeping original hypothesis of the necessary relation between industrialization and a negligence standard of liability gets boiled down to something like this: "In those places where the negligence principle was recognized and routinely applied in a certain way, it may have helped somewhat to facilitate capital accumulation; in other places, where there seems to have been lots of capital accumulation under different legal conditions, (a) some other form served the same function as the negligence principle, or (b) for various special reasons it wasn't necessary to the accumulation process to have that function served, or (c) perhaps there would have been still more accumulation if there had been a negligence principle." There's nothing wrong with this modest sort of proposition; it's the common stuff of historical writing. But it is an awfully long distance from demonstrating that economic requirements produced the form and that it duly performed its functional services to those requirements.[50]

A Functionalist thus subdued can continue to argue for a scaled-down determinism: the legal forms that actually emerged in a particular society were necessary to that society's particular requirements. Even if a negligence rule was not necessary for industrialization, perhaps the fellow-servant rule, as administered to workers on the railroads or just the Pennsylvania Railroad in the 1870s, was critical to that industry's ability to finance its expansion.[51] One can't disprove such an assertion. Because everything that has happened in

[49] "There were and always are rules and counterrules, rules with exceptions of such scope as to threaten the rule itself, rules whose force can be eliminated by drawing creatively on analogies to apparently unrelated areas of law, and so on." Mark Tushnet, Book Review, 69 *Cornell L. Rev.* 281, 281 (1983).

[50] Of course, lawyers or entrepreneurs of the time often *believed* that a given legal form was an indispensable condition of material progress or social stability and pressed for its adoption or retention because of that belief. But the historian who casts her project as that of reconstructing such beliefs has abandoned functionalism entirely for the historiography of legal ideology or consciousness. *See* Variation # 7 *infra*.

[51] Robert Fogel, *Railroads and Economic Growth* (1964) is an extended cliometrician's *tour de force* purporting to demonstrate that *the railroad itself* was unnecessary to nineteenth-century economic growth. The thesis is violently controversial, but the arguments in its favor are not trivial. And if a leading economic historian doubts the functional contribution of the railroad, are lawyers, equipped with perhaps one percent of that historian's technical sophistication and empirical data, likely to succeed in making the case for the functional necessity of the fellow-servant rule?

history is causally connected to everything else, there's no way to be sure that the connections were not forged by a logic of necessity. Even actions that seem chosen or simply accidental may just look that way because we haven't yet discovered the secret logic underlying them.[52] Yet, without for a moment disputing that the forms that industrial capitalism and the negligence principle took in the nineteenth-century United States might be related, is the evolutionary-functionalist hypothesis (law meets the needs of the developing economy) the most plausible means of relating these two things? It is here that the comparative data revealing all the myriad paths to capital accumulation and the legal-realist data revealing all the myriad permutations that a legal form undergoes in practice should at least make the functionalist hesitate.

Let me illustrate what I mean through what I mentioned earlier as probably the most frequently asserted functionalist proposition about law: the claim that various regimes of legal rules were necessary or at least very useful to capitalist development because they provided the certainty that facilitated rational calculation. The strongest versions of this claim propose, for example, that the rules of nineteenth-century contract law functionally responded to the need for certainty: When commerce summoned loud, "Thou must!," contract whispered low, "I can!" One hears this claim all the time,[53] but it is very difficult to sustain. Such evidence as we have suggests that tracing the common law doctrines and institutions for enforcing contracts to businessmen, those whom one might expect to be society's preferred mouthpiece for voicing her needs, is very difficult. When businessmen say what they want from an enforcement mechanism, it's usually something along the lines of an arbitration process.[54] To be sure, the legal system may have been wiser than the businessmen about their true needs: Lawyers undeniably thought so, as they liked to promote their products – the common law of contracts, treatises, Restatements, and commercial codifications – for their presumed tendency to "increase the certainty and predictability" of commercial transactions. Yet, in retrospect, the lawyers' goal of certainty appears to have been largely a legal fantasy. Formal rules framed in juristic categories, such as "offer and acceptance" and "consideration," that have no regard for the specific usages of real businesses are not predictable. Nor are rules phrased in terms of general standards of customary fairness,

[52] Compare, for example, the hypothesis that both the negligence principle and the organizational structures of industry were products of a common political/legal ideology that liked to pretend that everything that happened in corporations was the product of voluntary individual choice.

[53] The claim most recently appeared in Patrick Atiyah, *The Rise and Fall of Freedom of Contract* 420–424 (1979). This aspect of Atiyah's work is shrewdly criticized in Betty Mensch, Book Review, 33 *Stan. L. Rev.* 752 (1981).

[54] *See, e.g.*, Jerold Auerbach, *Justice Without Law: Nonlegal Dispute Settlement in American History* 95–114 (1983); Jay Feinman, "Critical Approaches to Contract Law," 30 *U.C.L.A. Law Rev.* 829, 847–852 (1983); Robert Ferguson, "Legal Ideology and Commercial Interests: The Social Origins of the Commercial Law Codes," 4 *Brit. J.L. & Soc'y* 18 (1977); Sugarman *supra* note *.

such as "reasonableness" and "good faith," so as to incorporate those usages. And even if such rules were predictable, businessmen don't seem to pay much attention to them until the (rare) prospect of litigation looms.[55]

Further, when one looks at the early nineteenth-century legal system as a whole, rather than just at contract law, and to the system in operation, rather than just its formal doctrinal expressions, can one really say that this system made life more predictable for rational capitalist planning? Sometimes, perhaps. Other times, surely not. The law of that time, for example, rapidly divested a whole slew of previously vested legal rights – rights to monopolize resources, to enjoin nuisances created by new industry, to collect compensation for "indirect" property damage, and so forth.[56] Should one therefore say, "The legal system was a functional response to the capitalist need to destabilize everyone's expectations, to put all property rights at the risk of devastation from competition or from exposure to spillovers from capitalist enterprise?" Early nineteenth-century governments also created commons out of large bundles of previously vested individual entitlements, insisting on the community's power to subject property to takings or regulations for public uses.[57] Should one thus say, "The legal system responds to the need to sacrifice individual expectations to capitalist needs for social overhead capital?" And what if one takes a closer look at what lawyers actually did for their commercial clients? One would find, it appears, that one of their main jobs in their roles as debt-collectors was to mediate in bad times between their creditor clients and the debtors, not pushing collection to the limit but trying to reschedule and scale down debts in order to keep everyone afloat until the upswing of the business

[55] *See, e.g.*, James Gordley, "European Codes and American Restatements: Some Difficulties," 81 *Colum. L. Rev.* 140 (1981); Stewart Macaulay, "Non-Contractual Relations in Business: A Preliminary Study," 28 *Am. Soc. Rev.* 55 (1963); Robert W. Gordon, Book Review, 36 *Vand. L. Rev.* 431, 447–449 (1983).

Max Weber, who wrestled with these problems more than anyone else, never claimed that lawyers, in creating these rules, were *responding* to the functional needs of capitalists. He argued instead that lawyers were carrying out their project of legal rationalization for intellectual and status reasons of their own and that the culmination of their project happily coincided with the needs of capitalists for predictable rules. But the conscientious Weber had to back away from even this less deterministic, more cautious, and more convincing theory of legal/social relations when he confronted the problem of England, a society with lots of capitalist development within an apparently woefully underrationalized legal system. This discovery led him to reflect that perhaps the practical-minded, business-oriented lawyers of England had devised a body of rules that was operationally *more* predictable than the highly formal rule-schemes of the Continent. Yet if *that* were so, his main thesis about the calculability of highly formal rule-schemes was itself thrown into doubt, as he himself acknowledged. For exceptionally good treatments of these aspects of Weber's work, see Anthony Kronman, *Max Weber* 118–125 (1983); David Trubek, "Max Weber and the Rise of Capitalism," 1972 *Wis. L. Rev.* 720.

[56] *See* Morton Horwitz, *The Transformation of American Law 1780–1860*, at 31–62 (1977).

[57] *See* Harry Scheiber, "The Road to *Munn*: Eminent Domain and the Concept of Public Purpose in the State Courts," 5 *Perspectives in American History* 329 (1971).

cycle – in effect helping to redistribute losses among the whole trading community.[58] Should one then conclude, "The legal system responds functionally to the needs of capitalism not to have legal rules enforced too strictly?" And one still has to account for what look like a large number of anticapitalist rules, such as those restricting corporate powers, capitalization, and attempts to limit liability.[59] Perhaps here the explanation should be, "The legal system responds to the functional needs of capitalism to make concessions to its anticapitalist opponents." If one should be tempted to dismiss such rules (which I think would be a serious mistake) as aberrant spasms of dysfunctional Luddism, one can hardly do the same with the entire law of slavery or with the crop-lien system, which effectively tied farm labor to the land, that replaced it.[60]

It's worth repeating, since arguments like these are so often misunderstood, that this case for the indeterminacy of legal-economic relations is directed against certain typical propositions of relations of functional necessity, usually expressed in statements that some economic process "required" support from the legal system, which then responded to "meet the needs" of that process. The argument is not that "legal" and "economic" practices bear no or purely random relations to one another (though many Critics doubt that these categories are very helpful). Regular, patterned, and moderately predictable (at least in the short- to-medium-term) causal relations are always springing up between specific legal and economic practices – though the lessons of Realism are that one has to get down to very concrete situations before one can describe what they are. These causal relations seem to contemporaries and to historians who study them later to work loosely together into some sort of system. Lawyers make their livings from their experienced insights into the operations of these patterns or systems; policy-makers and investors make informed guesses, which are certainly not always wrong, that the patterns will continue to hold. This Variation's argument is that – though contemporaries and historians often believe the contrary – all the pieces of the system are very loosely articulated: Individual pieces, even quite large ones such as the fundamental premises of civil liability, the organization of enterprise in the corporate form, worker's compensation schemes, or even the progressive income tax, could

[58] *See* 1 *The Papers of Daniel Webster* 101–104 (Konefsky & King eds. 1982).

[59] *See, e.g.*, John Cadman, *The Corporation in New Jersey: Business and Politics, 1791-1875* 341–362 (1949); Edwin Dodd, *American Business Corporations Until 1860* 373–390 (1954); James Willard Hurst, *The Legitimacy of the Business Corporation in the Law of the United States, 1780–1970*, at 12–57 (1970).

[60] There is actually a fairly strong functional case for slavery's contribution to the capitalist economy, though it's not one that modern liberal lawyers often make. For one thing, slavery seems to have been quite an "efficient" system of production in itself, as well as the primary generator (through cotton exports) of the foreign exchange that financed Northern industrial development. For another, it was slavery that made it possible for whites to be the independent individual proprietors who are the heroes of the Scottish enlightenment story of the expansion of liberty and commerce. Edmund Morgan, *American Slavery – American Freedom* (1975).

have been even radically different without drastic consequences to the master social/economic processes that the functionalist has supposed to require them. The next Variation's argument is that the master social-economic processes themselves could have been different, even radically different.

D. Variation #4 – Turn Background Social Necessity into Contingency

The preceding discussion pointed out the perils of matching legal responses to social needs: You end up having either to concede that the law has responded differently to the same needs or to multiply the number of needs in order to account for the differences. The first move calls into question the "functional" nature of the legal responses, the second whether it's useful to attribute "needs" to societies at all, especially needs emerging from the "logic" of some stage of historical development.

Let me illustrate this second point by continuing the example I used in my earlier discussion – the claim that legal rules promoted capitalism by providing certainty. The earlier discussion showed that it was dubious that the legal rules provided certainty at all. That is, the rules as implemented often did not have their intended effect. Further, there were many legal rules that actually created *un*certainty. And the functional explanations for these rules involve a variety of hypothesized social "needs," which are sometimes conflicting.

The true functionalist, the functionalist *sans peur et sans reproche*, may at this point refine her theory so as to explain how all, or almost all, of these diverse legal phenomena meet social needs.[61] But she may now slide into the position that law just satisfies particular interests, rather than broadly defined needs, unless she can somehow objectify her notion of needs. This task, however – the specification of a general legal sociology of economic development – will not be an easy one. For she will immediately run across highly evolved dynamic capitalist societies that got that way through (despite?) radically different government policies toward capitalist enterprise: refusal of subsidies for transport ventures, intolerance toward the corporate form, state-sponsored insurance of workers against the risks of unemployment and industrial accidents, coordination of major investment decisions through central bureaucracies, and promotion of social and political stability through legal reinforcement

[61] She may now say, for example, that a legal system that is responsive to the needs of capitalism helps to construct both the technological (e.g., subsidies and immunities to transportation networks and institutional (commerce-clause-based demolitions of local trade barriers, negotiable paper, security devices, and corporations and partnerships to mobilize capital) infrastructures for the development of enterprise. Such a system also delegates major investment decisions to decentralized firms which are free to respond to market incentives: stabilizes *entrepreneurial* expectations but destroys *rentier* ones; builds in adjustment mechanisms to relax its rules when strict enforcement mechanisms to relax its rules when strict enforcement would pull everybody down; pacifies opponents through strategic concessions, welfare palliations, or symbolic gestures; and so forth.

of the "feudal" rights of great agricultural proprietors.[62] Of course, a nimble mind can invent a functional explanation for anything, reserving a residual category of "dysfunctional law" for the really tough cases, but such an explanation would hardly square with the original "predictability of transactions" hypothesis and would be in danger of falling into complete banality. Banality becomes pure tautology when the functionalist claim is reduced to one that the legal system responded to the needs of capitalism with rules securing to individuals large bundles of exclusion/exploitation/alienation rights that could be traded in markets because such a legal regime is one of the main characteristics most people use to define capitalism.[63] But within that large definitional frame there have been many historical capitalisms. And there might have been thousands more still.

I won't spend much time on this point because an immense critical literature has done the job. The governing idea of structural-functionalist sociology that all societies have needs to maintain equilibrium has been sufficiently battered out of countenance, and the grand evolutionary stage theories of eighteenth- and nineteenth-century social thought have been gradually picked to pieces. As I said before, legal writers have had too big an ideological stake in assuming that objective background forces supply the basic directives in social life to have contributed much to debunking such assumptions,[64] but the

[62] *See, e.g.*, Kenneth Barkin, *The controversy over German Industrialization 1890–1902, passim* (1970); Chalmers Johnson, *MITI and the Japanese Miracle: The Growth of Industrial Policy, 1925–1975, passim* (1982); Charles Kindleberger, *Economic Growth in France and Britain 1851–1950*, at 183–208; Alan Milward & S. B. Saul, *The Development of the Economies of Continental Europe* 1950-1914, at 318–322 (1977); David Landes, "The Structure of Enterprise in the Nineteenth Century: the Cases of Britain and Germany," in 5 *Rapports: Comité Internationale des Sciences Historiques, XL Congrès Internationale des Sciences Historiques* 107 (1960).

[63] The funny thing is that even the definition doesn't really fit the historical experiences from which it was extracted. David Sugarman, "Law, Economy, and the State in England, 1750–1911: Some Major Issues," in *Legality, Ideology, and the State* 223–230 (Sugarman ed. 1983) contains an especially useful discussion of the commonly held view that "absolute rights of property" are preconditions or defining traits of developed capitalist societies. These authors synthesize the results of many studies of English property, showing that property forms approached very close to absolute individual ownership in medieval times, and that a great diversity of restrictions and qualifications on property-holding forms persisted through late phases of capitalist development. *See* Duncan Kennedy & Frank Michelman, "Are Property and Contract Efficient?" 8 *Hofstra L. Rev.* 711, 764–769 (1980) (elegant demonstration that societies claiming to give full legal protection to private property and freedom of contract will also be found to legally promote (1) zones of unrestricted "states-of-nature," in which people are privileged to destroy one another's property at will (e.g., competition), and (2) commons, in which wealth is owned collectively and people are forced to share in gains and losses).

[64] There are distinguished exceptions. *See, e.g.*, 1 Frederick Pollock & Frederic William Maitland, *The History of English Law* 627–634, 653–657, 669–678 (1895) (confounding the conventional wisdom on the evolution of property from communal to individual forms by asserting the "individualism" of medieval property).

whole debunking literature is at hand any time we want to tap into it.[65] So let me leave this topic with a couple of quick examples of functionalist theories that assume objective social necessity and of the critiques that point out the contingent nature of that "necessity."

Some legal writers have recently been captivated by Alfred Chandler's thesis about the emergence of large, vertically integrated, multi-divisional forms of corporate enterprise in the United States.[66] This captivation is not surprising: Chandler's thesis in its most unqualified form perfectly suits the criteria of the dominant vision. It hypothesizes that these developments in the corporate form are functional responses to a set of objective-sounding, universalizable, historical conditions (the attainment of a given stage of development of technologies and markets). But Chandler has taken his evolutionary model abroad and found that, in various European countries at roughly comparable stages of market and technological development, many of the features of American managerial capitalism were missing, though some of them did show up much later, after World War II.[67]

A determined evolutionist wouldn't be upset by this discovery; she'd just attribute the late developments in the European experience to an evolutionary "lag"[68] and invent some ad hoc special reasons for the missing ones. To his credit, Chandler is not content with such a solution. He concludes instead that the differences are not entirely attributable to flaws or deviations in the development of European capitalism: They stem at least in part from differences in "cultural attitudes and values, ideologies, political systems, and social structures."[69] The reason that this full range of complex variables wasn't used in the first place to explain the American experience (and it wasn't; there is literally not a word about culture or social structure in *The Visible Hand*, and only a few sentences about ideologies and political systems) is that Chandler is committed to the determinism of "organizational imperatives." He thinks of the other factors as affecting only the design details of the functionally mandated

[65] For a representative sample, see the works cited in notes 1–4. *See also* Joyce Appleby, "Modernization Theory and the Formation of Modern Social Theories in England and America," 20 *Comp. Stud. in Soc'y & Hist.* 259 (1978) (discussing the different ideologies of "modernization" adopted in England and America and the consequences of those differences for politics, economic policies, and social change).

[66] *See* Alfred Chandler, *The Visible Hand* (1977).

[67] *See* Chandler, "The United States: Seedbed of Managerial Capitalism," in *Managerial Hierarchies: Comparative Perspectives on the Rise of The Modern Industrial Enterprise* 37–39 (Chandler & Daems eds. 1980).

[68] To me, however, a more promising sort of explanation might be found, for instance, in the political/ideological/cultural reasons why French entrepreneurs resisted copying Americans before, but not after, World War II. *See generally* Richard Kuisel, *Capitalism and the State in Modern France* (1981) (discussion of French economic management in the twentieth century).

[69] Chandler, *supra* note 67, at 39. To give due credit to Chandler and the history-of-entrepreneurship school from which he descends, they have always avoided the causal reductionism of economic history as the rational maximizing of everything.

proto- typical form in different societies: You can take it with or without options, soup it up or make it ride low; but these alterations are, as Marxists say, "superstructural": Underneath them all is the same old Chevy. One could have no quarrel with a method that combined the various elements of the American experience into an "ideal type," a model of organizational change self-consciously constructed for the sake of comparative study; but there's a huge difference between finding model explanatory patterns and reifying them into immutable laws of historical development. The illegitimate move, the move that turns history into apologetic ideology, is to start supposing that one's ideal/typical pattern, actually made up of thousands of tiny contingent practices, represents a universal historical force.

There are two basic kinds of determinist stories now circulating about the evolution of legal/social forms for the organization of the labor force in modern American society. The first of these, now much in vogue among lawyer-economists, stems from neoclassical theories of the firm and "transaction-cost" economics. It theorizes that rational profit maximizing fuels the search for cost-reducing innovations in organizational form as well as in technology. In this account, the various hierarchical arrangements that have been used to organize the work force appear as successions of progressively more efficient methods of lowering costs of production, such as the cost of monitoring workers to see they are doing as they are told.[70] The other main determinist story comes from the counter tradition, now almost as venerable as the first, of Marxist accounts of industrial capitalism. A school of modern historians following the lead of Harry Braverman's pathbreaking work;[71] has transposed the optimistic theme of cost reduction into the dark minor key of domination. For these historians, the evolution of work organization is the story of the breaking of skilled workers' control over the labor process in the late nineteenth century and of the inexorable homogenization of labor through the deskilling of jobs. As it is for the complacent functionalists, a historical logic is at work here: not the logic of cost reduction but the logic of the subjugation and degradation of labor under the conditions of monopoly capitalism.

[70] *See, e.g.*, Oliver Williamson, "The Organization of Work: A Comparative Institutional Assessment," 1 *J. Econ. Behav. & Org.* 5 (1980). This story is the latest in a series now more than two centuries old of complacent functionalist accounts of how it's best for everyone that workers are treated as they are in industrial societies. It even seems to be on the point of displacing its immediate predecessor, the Weber-Parsons-inspired industrial sociology explaining how the specialized work tasks and bureaucratic hierarchies of modern production are results of the progressive "rationalization" of social life in modern society. (The sting in this sociological tradition – Weber's own horror at the claustrophobic imprisonment of the freedom of creative movement in the "cage" of rationality – was carefully drawn before export.) *See also* Duncan Kennedy, "Cost Reduction Theory as Legitimation," 90 *Yale L. J.* 1275 (1981) (discussion of the politics of this evolutionary world).

[71] *See* Harry Braverman, *Labor and Monopoly Capital* (1974).

If forced at gunpoint to choose between these two stories, one should probably choose the second, if only because it's backed up by historical research into a lot of real industries, job reorganizations, and labor struggles: it has not been generated, as the first largely has, a priori out of a formal model with only a casual smattering of allusions to the abundant empirical literature. The "efficiency" story is also vulnerable on other grounds. For instance, many of the specific features of early twentieth-century work organization, such as artificial job ladders fragmenting similar jobs into hierarchies of different grades or the recruitment of many different ethnic groups followed by the minute subdivision of departments by race and ethnicity, seem far more plausibly explained as designed to divide and subjugate the work force than to reduce costs. Indeed, contemporaries often observed that preventing labor from organizing *was* management's purpose.[72] In any case, the general thesis that hierarchical forms of work organization are more efficient because they reduce transactions costs is oddly inattentive to the possibilities of the counter hypothesis that the best way to minimize costs of supervision might be to delegate tasks to people you trust with lots of discretion to work out the details of the job on their own, or for that matter, to have them design the tasks in the first place.[73]

Yet the story of the degradation of work under the logic of monopoly capitalism has problems of its own. That logic, if it was there at all, worked itself out in remarkably various forms. Many studies of specific labor-management struggles have appeared since Braverman wrote, studies that have stressed the importance of the relatively underdetermined variable of working-class solidarity, trying to explain why that consciousness (which itself wasn't one thing, but lots of different things, with different cultural/religious/political roots) emerged in some settings rather than in others and how its presence and the variant forms it took affected the counter strategies of employers and the resultant capital-labor bargain.[74] In addition, some of the most impressive studies we now possess, the historical contributions of the segmented-labor-market economists, tell a more complex story than Braverman's, one in which

[72] For discussions of these explanations, see Stephen Marglin, "What do Bosses Do?," *Rev. Radical Polit. Econ.*, Summer 1974 at 60; Katharine Stone, "The Origin of Job Structures in the Steel Industry" *Rev. Radical Polit. Econ.* Summer 1974, at 113, 127–151; *see also* David Gordon, Richard Edwards & Michael Reich, *Segmented Work, Divided Workers: The Historical Transformation of Labor in the United States* 112–164 (1982) (summarizing the evidence of this phenomenon).

[73] For some interesting empirical support for this counter hypothesis, *see e.g.*, Samuel Bowles, David Gordon & Thomas Weisskopf, *Beyond the Wasteland* 122–78 (1983) (on high costs of centralized supervision of the workforce); Alan Fox, *Beyond Contract: Work, Power and Trust Relations* 66–119 (1974) (on the importance of trust in workplace organization); Charles Sabel, *Work and Politics* 220–231 (1982) (on emerging alternatives to "Fordist" ways of organizing production in decentralized quasi-"cottage" industries).

[74] *See, e.g.*, Herbert Gutman, *Work, Culture and Society in Industrializing America* (1976); David Montgomery, *Workers' Control in America* (1979).

employers found the strategy of controlling labor by degrading and homogenizing jobs increasingly futile by the 1930s and then promoted the reskilling of certain jobs into an "independent primary segment" of privileged labor, thus both registering concessions to the gathering union movement and effectively limiting its spread.[75] Finally, a glance at the comparative evidence casts the usual doubts on whether any single set of forms is required to serve a given social function. If the goal was to pacify labor movements, other means might have served than the degradation of work. The companies could have co-opted the unions through co-determination, or got the state to fold the unions into a tightly controlled junior role in a corporatist partnership, or treated labor as a fixed rather than variable cost and given workers stable wages and secure jobs in return for their undeviating discipline and loyalty.[76] Or, for that matter, the unions might actually have won a measure of control over the labor process that satisfied at least some of their aspirations for honorable work at a decent wage. The unions didn't win what they hoped for, and one can suggest many reasons why they didn't (including lots of reasons having to do with law and the legal system), but the closer one looks at the process, the harder it is to find an inexorable logic to it.

E. Variation #5 – Fill the Vacuum Left by the Collapse of Functionalism with Disengagement, Legitimating Ideologies, or Symbolic Ritualism

Now that historical experience has turned out to be too prodigal of multiple developmental paths and of multiple legal adaptations to those paths for the comfort of traditional functionalist explanations, where can one turn in the hope of finding some coherent explanation of law-in-history? One possibility I've mentioned already: Explain anything that happens in the legal system by referring to someone's interest (Variation #1). This method, subtly employed, yields narratives that are both subtle and exciting, but sooner or later, as every legal change is attributed in turn to a different set of bargains among interests, as a form of explanation it's going to seem discouragingly ad hoc. Moreover, one must at some point deal with what's known as the "autonomy" problem – the fact that legal norms and practices aren't completely plastic and don't alter every time another set of interests gets its paws on them because they do have some resilience, some long- or medium-term continuity of inner structure.[77]

[75] *See* Gordon, Edwards & Reich, *supra* note 72.

[76] For a useful analysis of mixed strategies of repression and co-optation adopted by European states, see Charles Maier, *Recasting Bourgeois Europe* 19–225 (1975); for the Japanese variation, see S.B. Levine, "Labor Markets and Collective Bargaining in Japan" in *The State and Economic Enterprise in Japan* 633, 647–649 (Lockwood ed. 1965).

[77] If – just to focus on the most dramatic instance – one wants to explain the content of the Federal Constitution, the Beardian method of analyzing the class positions and financial stakes of the Framers is a perfectly valid first approach to the task (however snottily it may have been treated by people who wince to see sacred writings traced to material interests). But I think most people

Indeed, one of the properties that makes them legal norms and practices is that they at least appear to stand aloof from the everyday conflicts of civil society and to provide stable structures for the mediation of those conflicts. The classic preoccupation of legal sociology has been to try to pin down what's in this "autonomous" realm and theorize about its relation to the rest of society. I present three theories that are especially relevant to the background of the Critical approaches to legal history.

1. Disengagement

By "disengagement" I mean beating a retreat to the position that although law is something that happens within societies, it doesn't have any important relations with the rest of society. Law is a realm of its own with its own history and categories and professional habits, and the only other thing you can compare. it to is another legal system. You can't hope to explain anything that goes on in it except by reference to its own peculiar internal details or to its borrowings from the details of other legal systems.[78]

would now concede that this method yields results of strictly limited value and that one can understand the framers' projects much better after trying to reconstruct the general political language – the categories of thought and the basic assumptions about reality – in which the Constitution was written. *Compare* Charles Beard, *An Economic Interpretation of the Constitution* (1913) *with* Gordon Wood, *The Creation of the American Republic*, 1776–1787 (1969).

In some of the very best recent work in legal history, even writers thoroughly committed to placing legal form in social and economic context have stressed how important it is to understand the internal structures and logics of such forms on their own terms. *See, e.g.*, Charles McCurdy, "Justice Field and the Jurisprudence of Government-Business Relations: Some Parameters of Laissez-Faire Constitutionalism, 1863–1897," 61 *J. Am. Hist.* 970 (1975); Harry Scheiber, "The Road to *Munn*: Eminent Domain and Public Purpose in the State Courts," in 5 *Perspectives in American History* 329 (Fleming & Bailyn eds. 1971).

[78] The "disengaged" have this much in common with the old Formalist doctrinal historians; but they've lost the Formalists' confidence that it's the very aloofness of law that gives it central importance as the functional mainstay of the unfolding norms of property and liberty. Our modern disengaged are a chastened bunch. Alan Watson actually subscribes to the dominant vision's basic functionalism but believes that the legal system's imperviousness to any but professionally ingrown practices makes it perpetually dysfunctional. *See* Alan Watson, *Society and Legal Change* (1977); *see also* Richard Abel, Book Review, 80 *Mich. L. Rev.* 785 (dissecting not only Watson's thesis but legal functionalism generally). Charles Fried has lost some of his old conviction that legal rules were derivable from Kantian norms and now seems inclined to think that law doesn't resonate with anything but its own "artificial reason," and that law's social role is modestly confined to filling in the residual details of regulatory schemes in the course of settling marginal disputes. *See* Charles Fried, "The Artificial Reason of the Law: or What Lawyers Know," 60 *Tex. L. Rev.* 35 (1981). And Richard Epstein has recently written a very good (except for its failure to acknowledge any of the work of the law-and-society movement, which has been making similar points for years in the *Law and Society Review*) piece on how common law rules don't seem to have any important social consequences and are therefore best understood as belonging to the transhistorical discourse of a peculiar fellowship of specialists, those charged with resolving those minor problems that occasionally get tossed to the courts. *See* Richard Epstein, "The Social Consequences of Common Law Rules," 95 *Harv. L. Rev.* 1717 (1982).

There are grave problems with this approach. For one thing, as legal sociologists like Friedman and Macaulay point out, these writers, writing about the insular lawyer's law of cases, seem to be talking about awfully tiny corners of the law in any age (compared to legislation, administration, decrees, local law and custom, etc.) and especially in the current age of statutes and regulations.[79] If this is the only "law" that legal intellectuals are going to write about, they will weirdly and incomprehensibly restrict their field to topics that, at least by their own hypothesis, aren't very important to anyone, including lawyers themselves, who actually spend most of their time dealing with statutes and regulations.

More seriously, I believe that disengagement is an obscurantist approach to the autonomy problem. First, autonomy in my original sense of long-run structural characteristics that make legal practices outlast short-term swings in political pressure is hardly unique to lawyer's law. Entire subdisciplines are committed to studying the autonomous characteristics of state structures such as bureaucracies and armies to show how constraints of organizational forms, ingrown traditions, professional ideologies, etc. affect how political agendas are formed, options perceived, urged, or suppressed, and so forth.[80] Just as Realism

I can't help believing – though of course I can't even begin to prove it – that the strategy of disengagement is partly a reaction to left-wing work (especially Morton Horwitz's. *See* Horwitz, *supra* note 56, and to a lesser extent Douglas Hay's, *see* Douglas Hay, "Property, Authority, and the Criminal Law," in *Albion's Fatal Tree: Crime and Society in Eighteenth Century England* 17 (Hay, Rule, Linebaugh & Thompson eds. 1975) that depicts law as an instrument of ruling-class authority; it's the reaction of mainstream scholars saying indignantly, "Well if *that's* the social meaning you're going to give to law, we're going to show it doesn't have any at all." Years earlier, Roscoe Pound had the same reaction: confronted with theories that tort law served the capitalist class, the one-time functionalist retreated to the stance that tort law was a lawyer's creation irrelevant to *anyone's* needs. *See* Roscoe Pound, "The Economic Interpretation and the Law of Torts," 53 *Harv. L. Rev.* 365 (1940). Another way of attacking the thesis that law serves the interest of ruling classes is, instead of disengaging law from outside influence altogether, madly to proliferate outside influences, so that every interest gets a crack at shaping the legal system. The "ruling-class-influence" is then buried under an avalanche of other variables.

79 *See, e.g.*, Lawrence Friedman & Stewart Macaulay, "Contract Law and Contract Teaching: Past, Present, and Future," 1967 *Wis. L. Rev.* 805. Friedman and Macaulay do agree with the disengaged that some law is autonomous lawyer's law and, to that extent, it is socially trivial, being the "law of leftovers" that nobody cares enough about to regulate in some other way.

80 *See e.g.*, Theda Skocpol, *States and Social Revolutions* (1979). I mean to say much more here than that bureaucrats and legislators have their own "interests" that sometimes cut across, warp, or neutralize the pressures of "outside" interest groups. I mean that, like courts, bureaucracies and legislatures develop commitments to doctrine and "principles" – that is, to relatively abstract clusters of concepts that constrain their imaginations and actions. I really think it's pure lawyers' conceit to suppose that courts are *fundamentally* different in this respect from other legal institutions. True, our upper courts by tradition are supposed to be more self-conscious and to publish at least the formal reasons for their decisions. Yet if "autonomy" means, among other things, demonstrated capacity to stick to internal priorities and settled ways of thought in the face of intense short-term political pressure, isn't it likely that, say, the doctrines of the Pentagon's procurement and strategic planning establishments are at least as "autonomous" as those of most appellate courts? Maybe even more so, because these establishments have more effective ways of suppressing dissenting opinions. For many useful examples of "autonomous" bureaucratic practices, see *The Politics of Regulation* (Wilson ed. 1980).

taught us that judging, like legislation and administration, was political policy-making, it ought to have taught us that legislation and administration were, like judging, relatively autonomous.[81] Thus, focusing on the autonomy of law to deny its relevance seems somehow unsupportable.

Second, I find it very hard to believe that autonomous legal forms are best understood as the product of a culturally isolated tribe of beings. Would any society tolerate lawyers as mediators of disputes, practical problem-solvers, or instruments of legitimate rule if the lawyers' practices didn't resonate at all with anyone else's? It seems much more probable that the specific legal practices of a culture are simply dialects of a parent social speech and that studying the speech helps you understand the dialect and vice-versa. Even a legal system clotted with arcane technicalities is unlikely to depart drastically from the common stock of understanding in the surrounding culture in the methods it uses to categorize social realities, the arguments about facts and values that it recognizes as relevant and persuasive, and the justifications it gives for its exercises of power.

The position of the disengaged seems to me to rest on two confusions. One is the confusion of a possibly valid methodological precept with a wholly invalid social theory. The precept is that when you want to account for a legal form, you should start your search for explanations in legal materials. This precept makes sense because the form is bound to be embedded in a whole contextual structure. For example, if you want to know what Cicero meant by "the public good" it's a good idea to look for other uses he makes of the phrase, what he contrasts it with, and how other lawyers use it. The theory is that discourse that is autonomous in this sense must therefore be peripheral or irrelevant to everything else going on in the society. But this theory doesn't follow from the precept at all. It's like saying that because Cicero has a specialized usage of "the public good" his usage must not have anything to do with contemporary Roman political controversies.[82]

[81] In fact, the Realists never got that far because most of them turned out to be stuck as fast to the case-law tarbaby as their Formalist predecessors. It may not be an exaggeration to say that the relative inattention (despite honorable exceptions and what looks like a growing interest in such subjects) to the "deep structures" cutting across diverse substantive fields of legislation and administration is the major disgrace of modern legal scholarship. But I would want to see such studies carried out *not* on the ground sometimes urged by my law-and-society friends, that because appellate cases are freaky and exceptional legal scholars should write about more typical legal products, but on the ground that such other products are in essential respects no different from appellate cases.

[82] Sometimes one even hears legal historians argue for a method on the basis of the precept alone, claiming that since lots of law has a high technical content, the discipline of legal history should be confined to explicating the content that lawyers best understand. But "stuff outsiders can't understand" cannot be seriously proposed as a useful category for the study of social life, especially since laymen do come regularly into contact with these particular bundles of esoterica. At best, this very narrow view might be appropriate for people who saw their competence as purely auxiliary, similar to numismatics, epigraphy, or "quantitative and statistical methods." As legal specialists, they would stand ready to act as technical advisors to real historians. But the most insular of legal historians, far from being anxious to attach their specialties to general historiography, don't pay any attention to it at all!

The other confusion is between law as particular enactments or events and law as clusters of practices and packages of enactments, processes repeated not once but many times over. Law in the sense of isolated enactments, decisions in a single case, or one proposition on page 351 of a hornbook, is rarely of any immediate instrumental significance.[83] Epstein is surely right to claim that a few contract or tort rules more or less in the nineteenth century wouldn't have mattered much to anyone.[84] But the whole complex of contract, tort, and property rules? The whole apparatus of debt collection? Slave codes and fugitive slave laws? One might suppose, without falling back into the functionalist position that all this law had to exist in order to serve the needs of basic economic or evolutionary processes, that it was pretty important in constituting social life as actually experienced, and that removing any of these big pieces might well have drastically altered that experience.[85]

83 This statement itself is confused. There really isn't any such thing as an isolated enactment. Every case or statute is just one event in a complex series leading up to and away from that event as well as a piece of the giant puzzle-structures of social interpretation that categorize the event and give it a meaning in relation to other "like" and "unlike" events. Hence, it's not a little misleading to speak of the "effect of a legal rule" as if the rule were just a single blip on the legal grid; the rule-event wouldn't have happened at all if people in the social sphere hadn't been preparing for it in some way. Much legal enactment just "ratifies" conventions that have already crystallized in social relationships. By the time the rule appears, the social struggle to produce it is already over, so the enactment doesn't appear to have any "effect." For an example in the context of family law, see Lawrence Friedman, "Law Reform in Historical Perspective," 13 *St. Louis U.L.J.* 351, 362–364 (1969) (passage of the Married Women's Property Acts).

84 *See* Epstein, *supra* note 78. Individual statutes also may not have mattered, though Epstein, curiously, distinguishes these. *See id.* at 1718–1720.

85 Even more methodologically questionable than the fragmentation of legal causes and effects into isolated events – hardly of course a problem confined to the disengaged alone – is the positivist attitude that encourages such fragmentation: the assumption that the only kinds of statements about reality that are worth coming up with are empirically falsifiable statements about the probabilities under varying specified conditions that certain "legal behaviors" will elicit "social behaviors" (or vice-versa) in response. Sometimes this attitude deepens into the absurd claim that whatever you can't make such a statement about must not be there at all! This attitude is not confined to the disengaged; indeed, it has recently been voiced within CLS itself, in an exceptionally interesting piece by Alan Hyde that questions the utility of the concept of "legitimation" in legal sociology, essentially on the ground that the theory that people obey laws because they think them legitimate lacks convincing empirical support. *See* Alan Hyde, "The Concept of Legitimization in the Sociology of Law," 1983 *Wis. L. Rev.* 379.

This isn't the place to attempt a comprehensive critique of Hyde's careful and detailed argument. But I would like to relate the following story, adapted from John Womack's great history of the Mexican Revolution: The Revolution started because sugar planters began to expand their landholdings in order to rationalize the practice of commercial agriculture. They used force to expel peasants from their lands, but took care to back up every expulsion with land registration legislation, recording acts, and condemnation proceedings, all ratified by local courts. The villagers, for their part, saw themselves as defending legal title to their lands. The chief of the Morelos pueblo passed on to his successor, Emiliano Zapata, the pueblo's most precious possession, a packet of title documents. Zapata and his followers joined the revolution because they could not get "justice" (true law) through existing forms of law. They fought to establish national and

The disengaged have added persuasively to the critiques of functionalism, at least in the area of lawyer's law. But those of us whom they have failed to convince of law's total irrelevance to social life have to look elsewhere for our theory. One obvious place to look for a theory of the social relevance of law is at theories of the law as legitimating ideology.

2. *Law as (legitimating) Ideology*

Like the theory that law serves the interest of dominant groups, this one has come to be associated with the left, but again there's no necessary connection. Mainstream liberal functionalism has its own, Durkheimian version of the legitimating role of law: Legal norms are primary expressions of and means of reproducing the "shared values" that function as the integrating glue in liberal societies, orienting everyone's highly differentiated tasks toward a set of common social purposes.[86] But concededly it has been the left-wing theories, theories that have emerged to deal with the difficulties posed by the "autonomy" problem for any account of law as the direct instrument of class oppression, that have attracted the most attention. Let me, for convenience's sake, try to arrange some of these theories on a spectrum, starting with those closest to straight instrumental theories, and ending with those emphasizing the most diffuse and indirect ways in which law makes up the elements of a culture:

"All law is pig law dressed up in judges' robes." That is, law is a means for organizing the ruling class and for coercing, cheating, and disorganizing the working class. Thus, law allows capital freely to collectivize but sets limits on labor combinations; it allows "capital strikes" (disinvestment) but restricts labor strikes; it confirms capitalist control over the organization of work; it criminalizes "vagrancy" as a means of keeping docile the urban unemployed; and it provides that employment is "at will" so that the unorganized work force has no job security.

"The ruling class induces consent and demobilizes opposition by masking its rule in widely shared utopian norms and fair procedures, which it then distorts to its own purposes." For example, the classical bourgeois legal norms of "private property," "free contract," "free speech," and "due process" express universal longings for security, privacy, autonomy, free choice about what to

local governments that would do justice. Throughout the struggle the villagers would surrender positions held by force in return for legal guarantees (which if given were always betrayed). *See* John Womack, *Zapata and the Mexican Revolution* 44, 52–66, 371–382 (1968).

The planters and their political allies would not move except under the forms of law – to reassure foreign countries, the potentially hostile middle class, and (as much as anyone else) themselves that the rights of property were on their side. The pueblo rose in revolt because their rights of property had been violated. I really don't know whether the concept of "legitimation," admittedly vague, overused, stretched to fit far too many different purposes, is the best concept to use in explaining why legal forms mattered so much to these people, but I can't help thinking that some kindred notion must be.

[86] *See, e.g.*, Talcott Parsons, *The Structure of Social Action* (2nd edn. 1949).

buy and sell and whom to work for, the right to speak one's mind freely, and the universal desire for protection against arbitrary coercion. But in a class society these supposedly universal norms are deployed for the benefit of a particular class. Private property, free contract, (complex and expensive) due process, (well-heeled-and-organized-interest-group-responsive) democratic procedures, and even (expensive-and-technology-dependent) free speech operate de facto to reinforce the advantages of wealth and power. The victims of these outcomes feel powerless to complain because the outcomes seem to have been produced by legitimate rules and procedures.

"The ruling class confirms its rule by actually making good on enough of its utopian promises to convince potential opposition that the system is tolerably fair and capable of improvement, even with all its faults." This proposition is essentially Machiavellian. The ruling class periodically sets up demonstrations to convince people that it really does rule in the universal interest.[87]

"The ruling class itself is taken in by legal ideology; it believes that it's acting justly when it acts according to law, that everyone is getting approximately the best possible deal, and that change would make everyone worse off." This formulation is getting closer to the meaning of ideology in classical social theory: a partial vision of the world that appears to its proponents as well as to its victims as a universal vision. (In fact, in the case of the ideology of the "rule of law," middle-class people are rather more sold on it than working or lower-class people.)

"Law isn't just an instrument of class domination, it's an arena of class struggle." The content of legal rules and practices is ideologically tilted in favor of class rule (or, more generally, the reproduction of current modes of

[87] Some scholars who equate all left-wing legal thought and even "Marxism" with this ruling-class-conspiracy notion complain about how unfair it is: The ruling class is damned if it screws the underclass and damned again if it treats it justly; what evidence would show that the ruling class *wasn't* oppressive? *See, e.g.*, John Langbein, "*Albion's* Fatal Flaws," *Past & Present*, February 1983, at 96, 114–115. I would respond to this criticism in several ways: First, historical ruling classes have often behaved exactly as Machiavelli said they should. That is, they have self-consciously reformed legal practices, making them more impartial and equitable, for the precise purpose of staving off popular risings or of stealing the wind from political opponents. The strategy is surely part of the prudential repertoire of any ruler, although it may not always figure in the motivations behind the setting up of any particular regime of apparently impartial justice. Much more important, the complaint simply misses the point of the radical's analysis of legal practices, which is usually meant not to criticize the rulers for ruling nicely or to impugn their motives, but to help explain how a ruling class (especially a small one in a large population, or one without a large standing army or police force) maintains its rule? "By force and fraud," is always a part of the radical's answer, but especially in advanced Western societies where the direct threat of force is uncommon, the usual answer is "by consent (however grudgingly it may sometimes be given)." How does the ruling class induce consent? By persuading people that they are getting, if not a good deal, at least the best one they are likely to get, or perhaps the best one they are likely to get relatively easily (because anything better would require much struggle, disruption, and above all the risk of catastrophic failure).

hierarchical domination, class-based or otherwise), but ruling classes don't have everything their own way when it comes to specifying that content. The concessions that cause legal systems to respond to the interests and ideal aspirations of the dominated result from bargains struck after hard struggle. The norms embodied in legal rules therefore are always double-edged: The underdogs who have won them can also be co-opted by them; the overdogs who concede them in order to co-opt are always vulnerable to being undermined by their radical potential.[88]

"The discourse of law – its categories, arguments, reasoning modes, rhetorical tropes, and procedural rituals – fits into a complex of discursive practices that together structure how people perceive and that therefore act to reproduce or to try to change people's social reality." Because this assertion goes well beyond partial critique, and is one of the core views of many of the Critics, I'll postpone elaboration of it until the next section.

3. *Law as Symbols and Rituals*

This is a catch-all heading for those writers who see much of what goes on in the legal system as theatrical or religious public spectacles and story-telling sessions that infuse ordinary social life with dramatic meanings and messages: the triumph of Virtue over Corruption, the marking off of a "sacred" sphere of ideals from the "profane" world of fallen self-interest, the purification of society of polluting deviance, the proclamations that most economic transactions are fair and decent implicit in the stigmatizing of a few deals as exceptionally rotten, the instruction that life is a game to be played according to rules, and the trappings that tell you that authority is authority.

I'm not sure why cultural anthropology of this kind, which seems to me to be potentially one of the most exciting and fruitful sources of new insights about law, is so undeveloped in our scholarship, especially since of what little there is, so much is marvelous work.[89] Doubtless part of the reason is our scholarship's occasionally constricted positivist criteria for its rare excursions into social description, which sometimes suppose that whatever "effects" of law you can't measure precisely must not be there at all; the rest is perhaps simply that this sort of work is very hard to do.

[88] An important strand of critical historical writing descends from this set of insights. *See, e.g.*, Elizabeth Fox-Genovese & Eugene Genovese, *Fruits of Merchant Capital* 337–387 (1983); E. P. Thompson, *Whigs and Hunters* 258–269 (1975).

[89] *See, e.g.*, Thurman Arnold, *The Folklore of Capitalism* 185–188 (1935) (corporate reorganization rituals); Michel Foucault, *Discipline and Punish* (1977) (dramaturgy of executions); Lawrence Friedman, *The Roots of Justice: Crime and Punishment in Alameda County, California*, 1870–1910, at 150–195 (1981) (felony processes making hapless vagrants into cardboard villains); Ernst Kantorowicz, *The King's Two Bodies* (1957) (medieval kingship); Hay, *supra* note 78, at 17–18 (terror-theater of criminal assizes); Arthur Leff, "Law and," 87 *Yale L. J.* 989 (1978) (litigation rituals).

F. Variation #6 – Drawing upon Different Story-Lines

I have argued that the dominant vision of the meaning of modern history is an optimistic liberal vision.[90] Its principal story-line is one of the gradual recession of error before the advance of commerce, liberty, and science – an advance modestly but invaluably assisted by ever more efficiently adaptive technologies of law. There have been failures and setbacks, and work remains to be done; but we have triumphed over the major obstacles, and the remaining work is remedial reform of the details. To be sure, opposing schools within optimistic liberalism have developed somewhat conflicting stories: One sees the late nineteenth-century common law as the summit of legal enlightenment and the regulatory welfare state as a (presumably temporary) slide into Serfdom and Inefficiency; the other sees the late nineteenth century as a colossally misguided aberration and the regulatory welfare state not only as a useful corrective but as a continuation of the true American tradition of positive state interventions in the interest of the commonwealth.

Such sharply conflicting views even within mainstream functionalism had already shattered the tranquil complacency possible only to those in possession of uncontested mythic-historical ground, but this discord was nothing compared to the cries of distress that followed the appearance of Morton Horwitz's *The Transformation of American Law*.[91] As an event in the history of American legal/intellectual culture, this book is most interesting for its substitution of some of the major pessimistic story-lines available in our culture for the optimistic ones of the dominant vision:[92] first, the story of the dark side of capitalist development – the destruction of communal bonds and meaningful faiths, the wrenching apart of families, the abolition of honorable crafts, the routinization of work, the displacement of norms of equitable dealing by an ethic of self-seeking as the highest good;[93] second, the story of the declension from the Founders' vision of Republicanism as the participation of independent

[90] The vision, as it has approached our own time, has modulated its optimism into a kind of grimly resigned complacency, which finds its tragic consciousness of flawed and futile human capacities an inexhaustible stock of reasons why it would be futile to try to imagine any better forms of social life than those that we happen to be accustomed to.

[91] Horwitz, *supra* note 56. For reviews explicitly critical of the book for its pessimism (though coming to diverse overall judgments), see Charles McClain, "Legal Change and Class Interests: A Review Essay on Morton Horwitz's *The Transformation of American Law*," 68 *Calif. L. Rev.* 382 (1980); Grant Gilmore, Book Review, 86 *Yale L. J.* 788 (1977); John Reid, Book Review, 55 *Tex. L. Rev.* 1307 (1977); Peter R. Teachout, Book Review, 53 *N.Y.U. L. Rev.* 241 (1978).

[92] To my mind, however, the permanent importance of this book to scholarship lies in its subtlety and richness as a history of legal *ideology* – an aspect of Horwitz's argument that the many hostile reviewers who have pointed out its very real vulnerabilities as social and economic history have chosen to ignore almost completely.

[93] For an excellent survey and analysis of this deviant story-line, see Albert Hirschman, "Rival Interpretations of Market Society: Civilizing, Destructive, or Feeble?," 20 *J. Econ. Lit.* 1463 (1982).

citizens in civic association for the public good to a business society of profit-maximizing privatistic individuals;[94] third, the Populist story of the betrayal of the Revolutionary promise of democracy by plutocrats who have, since the first Constitutional Convention, managed to wrest the machinery of law and government away from the People and press it into the service of the wealthy and powerful.[95]

I attribute a good deal of the horror in the critical reaction to Horwitz, not to mention the absurd label of "Marxism," to his violating so many of the traditional canons of story-telling all at once. After all, these story-lines had been expressed previously by other writers.[96] It was all right for "social policy" to be instrumental to economic purposes so long as these purposes were benign (industrialization, economic growth, the needs of development) and so long as one was mostly talking about legislatures. Horwitz, however, made over the purposes into capital accumulation through expropriation and protection of profits from redistribution. He also implicated elite lawyers and judges, and with them the common law tradition of which they were the curators, as among the ringleaders of this dubious business. It was even all right (in the Realist tradition) to charge common law judges with class-biased rulemaking, so long as one safely limited the indictment to the ephemeral craziness of late-nineteenth-century Formalism. Horwitz carried the charge back to the early nineteenth century, the period that common lawyers had previously celebrated as their heroically "formative" era. I don't deny, and neither at this date would Horwitz himself, that there are problems with his thesis, and that some of the specific criticisms of his evidence and conclusions are sound. But it's hard to

[94] For a discussion of the persistence of the "republican" themes of the establishment of civic virtue and its corruption in American life, see, e.g., Dorothy Ross, "The Liberal Tradition Revisited and the Republican Tradition Addressed," in *New Directions in American Intellectual History* 116 (Higham & Conkin eds. 1979).

[95] The cornerstone work in this tradition is Beard, *supra* note 77.

[96] All of these are staple crops of mainstream Atlantic culture – so much so that I'm staggered by hearing their use in Horwitz's book so constantly called "Marxist." For God's sake, at any bar dinner you can listen to the most conservative lawyers talking about how the fellowship of the bar (community), sense of professionalism (craft ethic), and devotion to the public good (republicanism) have declined as the practice of law has become a business devoted to making money. Other legal historians had sounded these themes as well. Hurst told how the capitalist ethic had destroyed public-regarding values as well as the Wisconsin timberland in the mid-nineteenth century. *See* James Willard Hurst, *Law and Economic Growth* (1964). Nelson and Reid lamented the sinking of the idea of law as expressive of communal morality in the atomistic individualism of a commercializing nation. *See* William Nelson, *Americanization of the Common Law* (1975); John Reid, *In A Defiant Stance*; *see also* Hendrik Hartog, "Distancing Oneself from the Eighteenth Century: A Commentary on Changing Futures of American Legal History," in *Law in the American Revolution and the Revolution in Law* 229 (Hartog ed. 1981). Scheiber showed how early corporate enterprise had manipulated law to expropriate traditional rights as it marched onwards. *See* Harry Scheiber, "Proper Law, Expropriation, and Resource Allocation by Government," 33 *J. Econ. Hist.* 232 (1973). But somehow none of them ever provoked anything like the hostility that Horwitz did.

account for the volume and intensity of the adverse reactions without understanding why the thesis should have touched so many nerves.

The reason all this matters is that the new availability of major deviant story-lines about the main action in modern social/legal history has the effect of relativizing the old story-lines, of making them look not like uncontroversial assumptions but like what they are: some among many possible interpretive frameworks in which to stick historical evidence.

G. Variation #7 – Historicize Consciousness

The final twist on the dominant tradition that I'd like to mention here, one that ends up playing a central role in Critical thought, is simply the "Kuhnian"[97] or "Collingwoodian"[98] idea that the most basic ways in which people conceive of the natural and social universes in which they live, the most elementary categories that people use to organize everyday life, are culturally and historically contingent; that is, they are specific to given places and times. Pure functionalism, as we've seen, objectifies both social needs and adaptive responses, claiming that these are universal categories of real life: hypothetically, you can always tell, if you get enough data on a society, what its needs are and whether its social forms efficiently meet them. The historicist perspective, on the other hand, teaches that even the conceptual language in which the functionalist advances her claim of universal needs and adaptations is a time-and-culture-bound language with a history – not a gentle progressive history in which superstition gradually gives way to science, but a history with revolutions and disruptions in it.

There are two basic ways of pursuing the historicist approach. One is simply to write the history of our own modes of thought, to try to identify when our categories for organizing how we speak about law solidified into something like their present shape. When, for example, did we separate a private realm of "market" activity from a public realm of "state" activity and come to think of the latter as "intervening" in the former? When does the term "regulation" begin to be used in its modern sense? When did tort separate from contract, "corporation" come to mean mostly "private business enterprise," and "efficiency" achieve its present significance for antitrust lawyers? When did lawyers start speaking of the need to "balance" a multiplicity of "interests" in order to decide hard cases?[99]

[97] *See* Thomas Kuhn, *The Structure of Scientific Revolutions* (2nd edn. 1970).

[98] *See* R. G. Collingwood, *The Idea of History* (1946).

[99] Perhaps the closest analogues to the histories of legal consciousness now being written by many of the Critical legal historians are the histories of economic thought which study the historical emergence of its fundaments, such as the grounding of social action in individual subjects rationally pursuing self-interest through exchange. *See, e.g.*, Joyce Appleby, *Economic Thought and Ideology in Seventeenth Century England* (1978); Louis Dumont, *From Mandeville to Marx* (1977); Hirschman, *supra* note 12; Karl Polanyi, *The Great Transformation* (1944).

The other technique is the reconstruction of historical or cross-cultural modes of thought in such detail as to illustrate (a) that other societies have not shared the ways of thinking that we believe to be essential and obvious (they just don't have a counterpart conception to our idea of a "market" or of a "free individual," they don't think a "corporation" is legally any different from a family or a city, and either they don't distinguish between a "public" and a "private" realm or they mean something completely different by the distinction), and (b) that these views were completely plausible for the people who held them.[100] Such work can have a real political edge to it, as when the historian takes a set of ruling ideological conceptions that his own time condemns as cruel or mistaken – legal rationalizations of slavery, for instance, or the due process Formalism of the Lochner era – enters into their world with (provisional) sympathy, and then shows how much sense those conceptions make on their own terms.[101] The ways in which well-meaning gentlemen justified their social order – the social order that had so well situated them – as just and efficient may look uncomfortably familiar. But the leading edge of historicism cuts deeper still: it tells us that the difficulties we have in imagining forms of social life different from and better than those we are accustomed to may be due to the limits on our conceptions of reality rather than to limits inherent in reality itself. After all, perfectly smart and forward-looking Americans of about a century ago habitually believed such things as that social order and economic prosperity depended absolutely on the maintenance of permanent class divisions or slavery; that it was absurd utopianism to suppose that blacks and whites could ever associate on terms of social intimacy or equality (or if they did, the results would be biological degradation of the species); that the physical constitution of women unfitted them for attendance at colleges, that unemployment insurance would take all the discipline and will to work out of the labor force; and that judicial failure to enforce harsh bargains to their rigorously formal letter would bring on the imminent collapse of capitalism.

Such historicism is not, in its weaker versions, actually incompatible with functionalism. One could continue to suppose that universal processes generate needs for ideally adaptive responses while conceding that both needs and responses will be perceived at different times and places through different-colored, and more-or-less distorting, conceptual lenses and filters. The strong position, on the whole that adopted by Critical writers, is that both needs and

[100] Some of the very best legal/historical writing does exactly this: Maitland's or McIlwain's reconstruction of medieval world-views; Hurst's description of nineteenth-century American "bastard pragmatism"; Gordon Wood's recreation of the conceptual world of the Constitution-writers. Hurst, *supra* note 96 at 206; Charles McIlwain, *The High Court of Parliament and Its Supremacy* (1910); Pollock & Maitland, *supra* note 64; Wood, *supra* note 77.

[101] *See, e.g.*, Eugene Genovese, *The World the Slaveholders made* 114–244 (1969); Mark Tushnet, *The American Law of Slavery, 1810–1860* (1981); Duncan Kennedy, "Toward an Historical Understanding of Legal Consciousness: The Case of Classical Legal Thought in America, 1850–1910," in 3 *Research L. & Soc.* 3 (1980).

responses, and indeed the idea of needs-and-responses itself, must be seen as the cultural products of contingent modes of thought.

IV. GENERALIZING AND DEEPENING THE CRITIQUES: CRITICAL LEGAL HISTORIES

Having at last completed the catalogue of variations, let me restate in summary form those that have done the most to inform the varieties of Critical historiography:

1. The conditions of social life and the course of historical development are radically underdetermined, or at least not determined by any uniform evolutionary path.
2. The causal relations between changes in legal and social forms are likewise radically underdetermined: Comparable social conditions (both within the same and across different societies) have generated contrary legal responses, and comparable legal forms have produced contrary social effects.
3. If a society's law can't be understood as an objective response to objective historical processes, neither can it be understood as a neutral technology adapted to the needs of that particular society. Legal forms and practices are political products that arise from the struggles of conflicting social groups that possess very disparate resources of wealth, power, status, knowledge, access to armed force, and organizational capability.
4. Although they are the product of political conflict, legal forms and practices don't shift with every realignment of the balance of political forces. They tend to become embedded in "relatively autonomous" structures that transcend and, to some extent, help to shape the content of the immediate self-interest of social groups.
5. This relative autonomy means that they can't be explained completely by reference to external political/social/economic factors. To some extent they are independent variables in social experience and therefore they require study elaborating their peculiar internal structures with the aim of finding out how those structures feed back upon social life. Given what so often appears to be the indeterminacy of instrumental effects, a promising approach for such study may be to treat legal forms as ideologies and rituals whose "effects" – effects that include people's ways of sorting out social experience, giving it meaning, grading it as natural, just, and necessary or as contrived, unjust and subject to alteration – are in the realm of consciousness.
6. Our accustomed ways of thinking about law and history are as culturally and historically contingent as "society" and "law" themselves. Though we can never completely escape from the limitations of our environment, we can to some extent protect against the risk of simply projecting our

parochial categories onto the past with a self-conscious effort to relativize our own consciousness, by trying to write the story of its formative context and development and by trying to reconstruct as faithfully as possible the different mentalities of past societies before translating them into our own.

7. It will also help us to relativize our understanding of the past's relation to the present if we see that our conventional views of that relation are mediated by familiar narrative story-lines, that are so deeply entrenched in our consciousness that we are often unaware of their rule over our conception of reality. These story-lines, like other mentalities, have a history filled with ideological purposes, and there always exist – and so we always may draw upon – competing stories that impress the same historical experience with radically divergent meanings.

Taken en bloc rather than separately, this set of partial critiques adds up to a position that most people who see themselves as doing Critical legal historiography would probably accept.[102] Many, though by no means all,[103] would want to push the critique still further.

A. Blurring the "Law/Society" Distinction

You might think that after the ravages of partial critique there would not be much left of the dominant tradition. But there is. Its skeletal frame, its division of the world into social and legal spheres, tends to endure. Thus, even the more

[102] I want to be clear that I am not making the absurd claim that particular people affiliated with the Critical Legal Studies movement have *originated* these critiques. On the contrary, those critiques are virtually all of long historical standing, to be found in Hegel or Marx if not before; incorporated into the normal working assumptions of many social theorists (e.g., Weber, Durkheim, Gramsci, Foucault, Giddens, Offe); historians of political and economic thought (e.g., Maitland, McIlwain, Ernst Kantorowicz, Pocock, Quentin Skinner, Karl Polanyi, Hirschman); social historians (e.g., Bloch, Genovese, E. P. Thompson, M. I. Finley); virtually any modern intellectual historian; philosophers of science (e.g., Kuhn); and cultural anthropologists (e.g., Geertz, Turner, Sahlins); as well as many legal intellectuals, specifically among Legal Realists, sociologists, and historians. (This is my own, doubtless idiosyncratic list: others might well put together a different one.)

What some CLS people *have* done, I think, is (a) to *combine* these critiques in an interesting way; (b) to attempt to go somewhat beyond them, as specified in the next section; and (c) to apply the results to the historiography of American legal doctrine and institutions. (Even in these respects their work has been anticipated by others: I re-read recently a book published nearly forty years ago that seemed to me to fit most of the characteristics of what I'm here calling "Critical" legal historiography: Louis Hartz's *Economic Policy and Democratic Thought: Pennsylvania, 1776–1860* (1948).) Critical work may thus perhaps best be described as "distinctive" rather than "original," for surely it was only a matter of time before approaches already so well developed in other fields of learning would be applied to law. I mention this because scholars hostile to CLS work so often say, "Well, that's all old hat: there's nothing original about that," using (as I see it) the accusation of unoriginality as a reason for not engaging with the substance of the work. Let's all simply stipulate that it's not "original," that it's within a "school" or "tradition," and leave it at that.

[103] See for example the debates summarized at notes 127–140 *infra*.

severe of the partial critics continue to assume – although conceding that all over the landscape of social life we can see the imprints, some deep and others almost imperceptible, of feedback reactions from the "autonomous" outputs of the legal system – that at bottom the really basic terms of community life are set by conditions and relations we can, and should, describe independently of law: family ties, personal affections, power struggles, technology, consumption preferences, association in interest groups, and the organization of production. These conditions and relations – the realm of "material life" in some formulations; of "basic needs" of all societies or of particular evolutionary stages in evolutionary functionalism; of "the forces of production" in some Marxisms; of the "interests" of individuals or groups in liberal pluralist theory; and finally of the "preferences" of self-constituting individual subjects in the ultimate reduction of classical and neoclassical economics – comprise the "real world" which law may serve or disserve or even partially twist out of shape but to which law is ancillary. The fundamental operations of this world originate before law and go forward independently of it; they fashion in general outline (if not in tiny detail) the agendas and limits of legal systems and are beyond the power of law to alter.

Yet, in practice, it is just about impossible to describe any set of "basic" social practices without describing the legal relations among the people involved – legal relations that don't simply condition how the people relate to each other but to an important extent define the constitutive terms of the relationship, relations such as lord and peasant, master and slave, employer and employee, ratepayer and utility, and taxpayer and municipality. For instance, among the first words one might use to identify the various people in an office would likely be words connoting legal status: "That's the owner over there." "She's a partner; he's a senior associate; that means an associate with tenure." "That's a contractor who's come in to do repairs." "That's a temp they sent over from Manpower." This seems an obvious point, but if it's correct how can one square it with the standard view of law as peripheral to "real" social relations? Could one, for example, seriously assert that "the law of slavery has tended to play only a marginal role in the administration of slave societies"? Slavery is a legal relationship: It is precisely the slave's bundle of jural rights (or rather lack of them) and duties vis-à-vis others (he can't leave, he can't inherit, he has restricted rights of ownership, he can't insist on his family being together as a unit, etc.) that makes him a slave.[104] Change the bundle significantly and you have to call him something else. And how could one say something like

[104] *See* Moses Finley, "The Servile Statuses of Ancient Greece," in *Economy and Society in Ancient Greece*, 133, 134–135, 148–149 (Shaw & Saller eds. 1981) (using the "juristic" method, accompanied by proper cautions about its limits, to analyze the spectrum of servile statuses in the ancient world). I see no reason to change this conclusion after reading Orlando Patterson's important new study attacking strictly "legal" accounts of the master-slave relation. *See* Orlando Patterson, *Slavery and Social Death: A Comparative Study* 1–62 (1982). For one thing, neither I nor any of the Critics would ever describe a set of social relations in *exclusively*

"medieval law bolstered (or undermined) the structure of feudal society"? Again, a particular (though concededly in this case very hazily defined) set of legal relations composes what we tend to call feudal society. If those relations change (commutation of in-kind service to money rents, ousting of seignorial jurisdiction to punish offenses, etc.) we speak not simply of changes in "the legal rules regulating feudal institutions," but of the decline of feudalism itself.

I would guess that the notion of the fundamentally constitutive character of legal relations in social life is probably a lot easier to understand when made about slave or feudal societies than about liberal societies. After all, in liberal societies, differences of legal status are not supposed to define social relationships, but merely to channel and facilitate them. In theory, one can, in a liberal society, choose one's legal status to suit one's underlying, material, functional, real purposes; with "freedom of contract," one even gets to create that status within the limits set by public law. But a whole generation of Realists taught us to see that a regime of free contract delegates to those who contract legal powers, subject to a host of important legal exceptions, to coerce performance according to the contract;[105] and the establishment of private property gives the proprietor a set of legal powers, again subject to important legal limitations, to dictate to others the terms of access to his property:[106] and the chartering of a corporation entitles the managerial few to make binding decisions affecting the lives and fortunes of the laboring and shareholding Many.[107] These bundles of rights and powers, diminished by exceptions and limitations, with which members of liberal societies are endowed, are critical determinants of the terms of their relations with one another. For instance, it usually matters a lot in an employment relationship whether or not Employee is or is not employed at will, a major stockholder of the business, an illegal immigrant, married to Employer, protected against being fired for trying to organize other employees, and so forth. In each case, a different complex of background legal entitlements factors into the power relations between the parties. Of course, nobody is going to claim that law explains more than a fraction of the power differences between these people. The employee may be the only person who understands the filing system, or be irresistibly attractive or physically intimidating, or just have been there for ages, or have lots of alternatives in the market (though of

legal terms. For another, Patterson's attack is really only on a particularly misleading legal account of slavery as "property rights in human beings"; as he truly says, slavery is only a special case, a peculiar bundle of such rights. The real question for him is how such a set of legal relations is created, which he argues is by a process of "symbolic appropriation" resulting in the slave's "social death." For the consistency of this approach with that of the Critics, see text accompanying notes 115–124 *infra*.

[105] *See. e.g.*, Wesley Hohfeld, *Fundamental Legal Conceptions* (1923).

[106] *See, e.g.*, Morris Cohen, "Property and Sovereignty," 13 *Cornell L.Q.* 8 (1927); Robert Hale, "Coercion and Distribution in a Supposedly Non-Coercive State," 38 *Pol. Sci. Q.* 470 (1923).

[107] Arthur Jacobson, "The Private Use of Public Authority, Sovereignty and Associations in the Common Law," 29 *Buffalo L. Rev.* 599 (1981).

course that "market" itself is importantly structured by the legal regulations of what may be owned and traded in it, subject to limitations, and by the property entitlements of all the traders in it).[108] It is, of course, possible to imagine, as for example G. A. Cohen has done in his extremely ingenious attempt to demonstrate that one can describe a "material" core of social relations without any "law" in them at all,[109] a Hobbesian power balance of force that is destabilized every time somebody sharpens a stick or lifts a weight. But in actual historical societies, the law governing social relations – even when never invoked, alluded to, or even consciously much thought about – has been such a key element in the constitution of productive relations that it is difficult to see the value (aside from vindicating a wholly abstract commitment to "materialist" world views) of trying to describe those relations apart from law. Power is a function of one's ability to form and coordinate stable alliances with others that will survive setbacks and the temptations of defection to satisfy opportunistic interests. Such organization and coordination are bound to involve something legal. Indeed, one is likely to find the conditions of the Hobbesian state of war precisely in those instances where law has explicitly or by silence established a combat zone in which people are endowed with (in Hohfeldian terms) privileges to inflict harm upon one another and are denied any legal means of restricting that harm – (as when the legal regime says a wife can't be raped or that contracts between husband and wife are not enforceable). Clearly (as Cohen for example points out[110]) people can struggle to improve their position vis-à-vis others by changing the rules that define their entitlements, but that doesn't alter the fact that the bundle of legal endowments they start out with positions them for the struggle, and may make all the difference as to whether they win, lose, or get a good compromise deal. The new deal, when sufficiently stabilized in practice, will simply be the new legal constitution of their relationship.

More prosaically, the "interests" in the instrumental account that make demands upon the legal system are not self-constituting prelegal entities. They

[108] To give another example, assume two people are having an argument in a car. One says, "Get out of my car." The other says, "It's not your car, it's the company's car. I have as much right to be here as you do." The first: "I'm driving today, so as far as you're concerned it's my car; and I want you to get out." This is of course a fairly complex, if utterly commonplace legal argument – unusual if at all only in that the claims and counterclaims are very explicit instead of being just silent background assumptions. Of course, factors other than legal relations may be involved. One of these guys may be a lot bigger than the other or have a long-run stake in the other's amiability or good opinion. But the law of the situation is a potentially critical factor in its resolution.

[109] *See* Gerald Cohen, *Karl Marx's Theory of History: A Defence* 216–248 (1978). The book as a whole is a brilliant attempt to rehabilitate an orthodox-Marxist version of functionalism, in which, as in the dominant vision, law is one of the ideological superstructures called into being by the requirements of the material forces of production, which then reacts upon and mingles with those material forces. For a particularly useful (and to me, convincing) response to Cohen, see Hugh Collins, *Marxism and Law* 81–85 (1982).

[110] Cohen, *supra* note 109, at 216–248.

owe important aspects of their identities, traits, organizational forms, and sometimes their very existence to their legal constitution. For example, "taxpayers" are partially families, partnerships, or individuals, because of the legal definition of these units; "New England gas consumers" pressing the Congress for relief from high prices are partially a "regional interest" because of the legal form of territorial representation; "Communists" are not an interest represented as such in labor unions because of legal excommunication; whereas the true identity of the "corporate client" to whom a corporation's lawyer owes her undivided loyalty is an unsolved mystery, because of conflicts in legal theory. For the most part, the legal creation of "interests" and the selection of their representatives proceed too quietly for notice – save on those occasions where formal choice must be made, as in deciding whether the "Sierra Club" may represent people who care about the environment in class actions or administrative proceedings.[111]

Understanding the constitutive role of law in social relationships is often crucial not only in characterizing societies but in accounting for major social change. Robert Brenner's remarkable work on preindustrial Europe,[112] for instance, identifies two general patterns of social adjustment to the population declines of the late Middle Ages: a (typically) Western pattern in which the labor shortage resulted in more favorable labor terms for the peasantry, and a (typically) Eastern pattern in which the same shortage brought about an intensification of serfdom, a tightening of the lords' control over their serfs. Brenner's (richly detailed and here much simplified) explanation for this dichotomy is that the landlords' ability to tighten control instead of having to grant concessions depended critically upon the balance of class power that had come to prevail in their particular society. A central component of this power balance was the set of legal relationships that had been established between the classes. Where peasant communities were strongly organized, they had, over the centuries, managed to wring concessions from their lords, which had been institutionalized as law. Thus institutionalized as rights, these concessions could not be withdrawn without provoking massive resistance.[113] Brenner goes on to argue that where (as in France and parts of western Germany) these customary rights of peasant proprietorship persisted through the early modern period

[111] *See, e.g.*, Joseph Vining, *Legal Identity* (1978); Al Katz, "Studies in Boundary Theory: Three Essays in Adjudication and Politics," 28 *Buffalo L. Rev.* 383 (1979); Stephen Yeazell, "From Group Litigation to Class Action Part II: Class and Representation," 27 *U.C.L.A. L. Rev* 1067 (1980).

[112] Robert Brenner, "Agrarian Class Structure and Economic Development in Pre-Industrial Europe," *Past & Present*, February 1976 at 30.

[113] Whoever objects at this point that the "law" involved in this description is only epiphenomenal to the "social fact" of "organization" will have to try to find some way to describe that organization without mentioning the rules whose maintenance was its *raison d'etre* or the institutional forms in which its tasks were carried out – not to mention "Fight to Protect Your Rights!" as a means of organization itself.

they did so because centralizing states helped to secure these rights against the lords and thus retarded the process of capitalist consolidation of landholdings. In England, by contrast, where such rights had been eroded for a complex of reasons, small proprietors were unable to resist eviction.

Maybe the point that law and society are inextricably mixed seems hard for legal writers to grasp because they sometimes restrict their view of what law is to a bunch of discrete events that occur within certain specialized state agencies (in the most restrictive view, the courts alone) and therefore assume that the only question for a social history of law is the relation between the output of these agencies and social change. But if that output is all there is to law, how on earth are we going to characterize all the innumerable rights, duties, privileges, and immunities that people commonly recognize and enforce without officials anywhere nearby? Slavery, for instance, may well make its first appearance in the temporary emergency practices of a settlement, harden over the next few planting seasons into invariable custom, and, decades later, when the localities decide they want the help of centralized enforcement authority, become the subject of legislation in slave codes. When should a sociologically minded historian (as opposed, for example, to a legal-positivist jurisprudent) start to speak of the emergence in this society of the legal institutions of slavery? At any point, I should think, when she finds the ordinary practices and discourses of that society assuming or appealing to the collectively shared and maintained notions of right and obligation that support that institution, the moment when power becomes institutionalized as "right." Thus, the social/legal historian who began her account of slave law in these settlements with the codifications would rightly be accused of leaving out the most important part of the story.[114] Furthermore, even if the historian refused to recognize custom as law until it was ratified by some official agency, she won't get very far toward understanding the role of law in social change if she looks only for the immediate social effects of marginal changes in discrete enactments and ignores the whole invisible background network of rules (like the basic law of property) that are silently incorporated into people's lives.

Again, since it all seems so incredibly obvious once it's said, what explains the persistent view of law's marginality in social life? Partly, it comes from the view of generations of disillusioned reformers – liberal reformers mostly, I suspect – who have come to doubt whether more than marginal social change can be achieved through deliberate promotion by those in control of the mechanisms of the liberal state. But this proposition is not really about the limits

[114] Actual historical societies have conveniently simplified her task in some cases by adopting prefabricated bundles of officially legal relations. The way slavery came to the Virginia settlements, for instance, was by importation of blacks who were already enslaved somewhere else. Winthrop Jordan, *White Over Black* 71–82 (1968); Morgan, *supra* note 60, at 295–337. The story nicely illustrates the point that when people go about putting together their "material" economies, they use the "ideal" building blocks of legal relations.

of law; it is about the limits of selective types of attempts to reorient, usually from the top down, selective formal institutions. Most legal change takes place all through civil society, in thousands of small interactions, usually with no official visibly present at all. It's strange, in a way, that the Realist and Law-and-Society scholars, who taught us to see the law "in action" as well as the law "on the books," should so often be the very same people who revert to restrictive Formalist views of law when they stress, in Pound's words, "the limits of effective legal action." There is a real disjunction here between their sociological analysis of the law constituting the status quo as dynamic, informal, and political, and their programmatic analysis of the law needed to bring about change as static, formal, and bureaucratic.

The view that law is marginal in social life probably also registers an overreaction to the preceding generation of Formalists, who often behaved as if once you described the legal form of an institution or practice, you had described the whole thing. A "corporation" or a "city" appeared as nothing more than a shell of legal rights and powers. The Realist successors to these Formalists yearned to break through the formal shell to (as they often expressed it) the "living" reality beneath it: the "realities" of trade practices, power politics, emotional ties, "behavior," and, of course, social needs. But there is no way to detach essences from their forms: The law (in the catholic sense that I've been using) was all along a part of the reality. If the program of Realists was to lift the veil of legal Form to reveal living essences of power and need, the program of the Critics is to lift the veil of power and need to expose the legal elements in their composition.

B. Law as Constitutive of Consciousness

Many Critical writers would, I think, claim not only that law figures as a factor in the power relationships of individuals and social classes but also that it is omnipresent in the very marrow of society – that lawmaking and law-interpreting institutions have been among the primary sources of the pictures of order and disorder, virtue and vice, reasonableness and craziness, realism and visionary naiveté and of some of the most commonplace aspects of social reality that ordinary people carry around with them and use in ordering their lives. To put this another way, the power exerted by a legal regime consists less in the force that it can bring to bear against violators of its rules than in its capacity to persuade people that the world described in its images and categories is the only attainable world in which a sane person would want to live. "Either this world," legal actions are always implicitly asserting, "some slightly amended version of this world, or the Deluge."

A familiar example of the way in which legal categories affect social perceptions would be the carryover into common speech and perceptions of the legal distinction between Public and Private realms of action, the Public being the sphere of collective action for the welfare of all through the medium of government (and thus the only realm of legitimate coercion), and the Private being the sphere of individual self-regarding action.[115] Those who have internalized this distinction as part of the natural order of things, as all of us have to some extent, are perfectly capable of deriving from it conclusions such as this: It is an invasion of the privacy and autonomy of a (private) corporation for (public) OSHA inspectors to come upon its premises without a warrant, but the same company's management can post time-study monitors in the workers' washrooms because the workers have (impliedly) consented to this in advance by private contract.

I don't for a moment mean that this particular set of conclusions – in which readers are bound to recognize the classic late-nineteenth-century mind-set, recently dusted off for revival – flows inexorably from the Public/Private distinction. One could certainly also conclude, as many people have, that corporations, being organized collectives endowed by law with effective coercive power over people within their jurisdiction (on their property), are like states and may therefore exercise their power only through politically accountable forms.[116] The crucial point here is that both sets of conclusions are inferred from the same Public/Private classification (coercive-collective states versus freely choosing individuals) that sets fairly severe limits on the ways in which we can imagine the world and how to change it.[117]

Let me try another, perhaps slightly less abstract, example which I hope might illuminate some of the differences between functionalist and Critical styles of historical explanation. A nineteenth-century state that we'll call "Wisconsin" enacts a "lumber-lien" law – that is, a statute giving loggers of wood a priority lien for their wages in the proceeds from the sale of cut timber.[118] How might an historian approach the interpretation of this bit of law?[119] A good straightforward functionalist approach would look for the context of a social "problem" to which the law was an attempted response or solution. Let

[115] For representative Critical treatments of the Public/Private distinction as it has been applied to specific areas of law, see the articles by Paul Brest, Gerald Frug, Morton Horwitz, Duncan Kennedy, and Karl Klare in the recent Pennsylvania Law Review Symposium on the Public/Private Distinction. 130 *U. Pa. L. Rev.* 1246 (1982).

[116] *See, e.g.*, William O. Douglas, *Democracy and Finance* (1940), Adolf Berle, "For Whom Corporate Managers are Trustees: A Note," 45 *Harv. L. Rev.* (1932); Adolf Berle, "Constitutional Limitations on Corporate Activity – Protection of Personal Rights from Invasion Through Economic Power," 100 *U. Pa. L. Rev.* 933 (1952).

[117] Indeed the separation of law from society in what I have called the dominant vision of legal scholarship is *itself* a product of the Public/Private distinction. No matter how much Realist and post-Realist scholars blur the distinction in their empirical work on the "law in action," they usually end up reasserting it when they describe the "limits of effective legal action." See text accompanying note 26 *supra*.

[118] As the choice of this example probably reveals, it was developed in conversation with James Willard Hurst.

[119] The following paragraph is not my proposed history of the log-lien law but merely a sketch of how one might approach the task of interpreting its history.

us suppose that our functionalist historian finds such a problem in the circumstance that logging enterprises were short of liquid capital out of which to pay wages but needed to attract labor into the forests for a long winter's work. The solution to this problem was to give some additional security for wages in the lien, which was somewhat easier to enforce legally and less subject to trumping by other claims than was an ordinary action for breach of contract. There is nothing wrong, it seems, with this explanation as far as it goes. But then one starts to wonder: Why this solution rather than others one could think of – others that were actually adopted in nearby times and places? Here's a quick offhand list of potential solutions that doesn't even begin to exhaust the possibilities: (1) use slave labor in the forests; (2) use conscript labor – either as part of compulsory militia service or as a statutory duty of every able-bodied man in the state; (3) raise the capital fund for wage payments out of taxes; (4) refuse to "intervene in the private contracts" between logger and employer, and let the loggers contract, if they can, for their security interest in the wage bargain; (5) run logging as a state enterprise, paying loggers out of general revenues or out of an excise tax on log sales; (6) make the loggers general partners in the enterprise, entitled to manage company concerns and to share in company profits. In the perspective created by some of these alternatives, the lumber-lien law appears to have been the product of a political consciousness in which, for example, "enterprise" was "private," though the state might be expected to help it out and even "regulate" a bit, and in which labor was "free" but definitely subordinate. The main point I want to make here is that this statute was not only the product of such a consciousness but helped to reproduce that consciousness by confirming it. The statute's enactment made some political alternatives that the society had already discarded as bad or unworkable (slavery, conscription, state enterprise) just a tiny bit more unthinkable and made it a tiny bit more difficult to imagine something altogether outside the scope of familiar possibilities (such as the option of laborers as equal partners). In short, the legal forms we use set limits on what we can imagine as practical options: Our desires and plans tend to be shaped out of the limited stock of forms available to us: The forms thus condition not just our power to get what we want but what we want (or think we can get) itself.[120] This perspective

[120] I have no reason, incidentally, to think that Hurst himself would disagree with this analysis, since his work has always been devoted to showing how lawmakers' notions of the practical and functional have been shaped and constricted by the basic categories of their political consciousness. I think the important difference between him and the Critics is something like this: He takes the consciousness of nineteenth-century lawmakers – consisting of such elements as distrust for executive authority, faith in the market, a Promethean urge to dominate nature, etc. – as the product of a liberal, middle-class mindset forged in European historical conflicts of the seventeenth and eighteenth centuries, and pretty much fixed since then. To express this perhaps rather too grandly, for him, consciousness ceases to have a history after it reaches the American shore; it has only a series of instantiations. The view of many Critics, on the other hand, is that: (a) no political consciousness can persist simply because of inertia; enormous energy and effort (though rarely, to be sure, fully self-conscious effort) must be poured into

completely collapses the distinction that legal writers sometimes make – that indeed I made earlier in this article when discussing the Variations – between "instrumental" and "symbolic" uses of law. One never has more power than when one has so successfully appropriated the symbols of authority that one's actions are not seen as exercises of power at all, but simply as expressions of sound pragmatic common sense.[121]

Another way of looking at what seems to be the key difference of approach between functionalists and their Critical opponents is that the functionalist examines what has actually happened and explains how it all "works," how each development fits into the pattern created by all the others, while the Critic takes each event as situated not on a single developmental path but on multiple trajectories of possibility, the path actually chosen being chosen not because it had to be but because the people pushing for alternatives were weaker and lost out in their struggle or because both winners and losers shared a common consciousness that set the agenda for all of them, highlighting some possibilities and suppressing others completely. How can one identify the counterfactual trajectories, the roads not taken? From the experience of other societies, from the hopes of those who lost the struggle, from routine practices that the same society has tried in other spheres of life without ever dreaming they might be applied to the situation at hand, and from imagination disciplined, as one hopes, by the knowledge of past failures.

I take Karl Klare to be practicing something like this method in his history of the conservatizing Supreme Court interpretations of the Wagner Act.[122] Klare has been criticized for seeming to assume that the Wagner Act was radical legislation to start out with. It was, say his critics, as mildly reformist (or, if you prefer, designed to co-opt) in inspiration as in later interpretation.[123] To the extent that Klare's account is one of the corruption of a radical vision, the

reproducing it and protecting it from competition and disintegration; (b) in any case, the content of the basic American liberal ideology has not been constant over the last two centuries, but has undergone important transformation; and (c) even in what appear to have been its moments of greatest stability and most widespread consensual adoption, the liberal ideology was shot through with so many contradictions, so many implications leading the society in opposing directions, that the maintenance of consensus cannot be explained simply by the dominance of that ideology. These Critics see their task as explaining how the basic political ideology, the unexamined background common sense of the time, was reproduced and transformed and its centrifugal tendencies kept under control; and they see legal forms and practices as central to these processes. In a nutshell, Hurst sees law as a *product* of an ideological consciousness applied to practical problem-solving; the Critics see law as a primary *producer* of that consciousness. The difference is partly one of emphasis, of diverging views of what most urgently needs explaining.

[121] *See* Steven Lukes, *Power: A Radical View* (1974).

[122] Karl Klare, "Judicial Deradicalization of the Wagner Act and the Origins of Modern Legal Consciousness, 1937-1911," 62 *Minn. L. Rev.* 265 (1978)

[123] Comment, "The Radical Potential of the Wagner Act: The Duty to Bargain Collectively" 129 *U. Pa. L. Rev.* 1392 (1981).

criticism has some bite. Yet the main problem with the criticism is that it takes for granted a single-trajectory view of historical change; it assumes that things must evolve along the path they start out on. In the case of legislation, this path is sometimes identified by a curiously Formalist method as the "intent" of the enacting legislature, as if that legal construct had both some definite substance and some privileged claim to set the course of history! Klare, however, situates the Wagner Act at the junction of myriad potential tracks of departure – one could identify some of these by the programs of labor leaders of the time, others by the experiments of labor movements elsewhere, and still others by the "corporatist" models being practiced in the major European states and in some American industries – and then shows how the Supreme Court decisions, informed by a pervasively held general postwar consciousness on how to secure the conditions of "industrial peace," systematically helped lead the society down one track rather than any of the possible others.[124]

C. Indeterminacy Located in Contradiction

The partial critiques attack the twin determinisms of functionalism and evolutionism mostly by means of empirical counterexamples drawn from Legal Realism and the Law-and-Society movement in the case of functionalism (in practice, the effect of law varies enormously with differences of power politics, cultural predisposition to accept it, strength of local custom, etc.) and from comparative historiography in the case of evolutionism (there are many paths of development and of legal response; indeed variation in developmental path is partly a function of legal variation). Taken together, these partial critiques add up to the proposition that when you situate law in social context, it varies with variations in that context. Some of the most original and powerful recent Critical writing, however, carries the claim of law's indeterminate relation to social life a significant step further. The same body of law, in the same context, can always lead to contrary results because law is indeterminate at its core,

[124] Another, and separate, issue raised by the article is whether any important part of the history of labor relations is revealed by Supreme Court opinions at all: Are these mandarin dictates not absurdly remote from the "real" world of labor struggles? I will try to deal with this issue in general terms, *see* notes 127–140 *infra* and accompanying text; for now, let me just say that Klare wouldn't claim to have done anything more than to explore a fractional contribution to the formation of conventional ways of thinking among the elites about "the labor problem." The Justices borrowed from, and thus hardened by their authoritative example, some of the prevailing mentalities of their time. In conjunction with hundreds of other acts of consciousness-formation, these set the agenda for the ways in which many decision-makers in that generation framed issues having to do with labor. If one wanted to expand on Klare's work, one could look for other manifestations of the mentality he describes on the Court in other institutional settings, as well as for deviating and opposing mentalities. Mark Kelman, "Trashing," 36 *Stan. L. Rev.* 293 (1984) contains a valuable speculative sociology of high-level legal doctrine.

in its inception, not just in its applications. This indeterminacy exists because legal rules derive from structures of thought, the collective constructs of many minds, that are fundamentally contradictory. We are, the theory goes, constantly torn between our need for others and our fear of them, and law is one of the cultural devices we invent in order to establish terms upon which we can fuse with others without their crushing our identities, our freedom, even our lives. One way, therefore, of writing the histories of legal systems is to examine successive attempts to build structures that will facilitate good and prevent bad fusion. Such histories can reliably be expected to exhibit two properties: First, because the structures have usually been built by dominant elites (though with input from those struggling from below), their content will be ideological. That is, their methods of sorting out good from bad interactions will contain a bias in favor of existing orders. Second, and more important because the fundamental contradiction between the needs for fusion and for individuality has never been (perhaps can never be?) overcome, legal structures represent unsuccessful and thus inherently unstable mediations of that contradiction. Over time, therefore, these legal structures will tend to become unglued and to collapse.

According to this vision, modern American legal history is in part the story of how the latest of these great cultural constructs, "liberal legalism," arose and developed its own characteristic set of mediating devices (chief among these being the division of social life into a private sphere of contracting individuals, e.g., "the market," and a strictly limited sphere of constitutional/democratic collective coercion, "the state"); how the construct was purified of its pre-liberal elements and elaborated to its highest pitch in the late nineteenth century; and how, at the moment of its perfection, it started to decay under attacks from without and the pressure of its own internal contradictions – ultimately leaving us where we are now, living in its ruins, no longer believing in its mediating powers, and clinging to it still because we have found nothing to replace it, and being faithless moderns, doubting that we ever can. The general framework of this story has served as the background to a growing number of histories of particular bodies of legal doctrine and theory, each of which locates its special set of rules and principles within the fundamental contradiction and shows how one attempt after another to mediate that contradiction results in failure.[125]

[125] Duncan Kennedy, "The Structure of Blackstone's Commentaries," *Buffalo L. Rev.* 205 (1979), the pioneer venture in this mode, may be said to have founded an entire school. *See e.g.*, James Kainen, "From Vested to Substantive Rights," 31 *Buffalo L. Rev.* (1982); Frances Olsen, "The Family and the Market: A Study of Ideology and Legal Reform," 96 *Harv. L. Rev.* 1497 (1983); Joseph Singer, "The Legal Rights Debate in Analytical Jurisprudence from Bentham to Hohfeld," 1982 *Wis. L. Rev.* 975; Kenneth Vandevelde, "The New Property of the Nineteenth Century: The Development of the Modern Concept of Property," 29 *Buffalo L. Rev.* 325 (1980); Note, "Tortious Interference with Contractual Relations in the Nineteenth Century: The Transformation of Property, Contract, and Tort," 93 *Harv. L. Rev.* 1510 (1983).

For those unfamiliar with the method, an introduction to it notable for its lucidity and cleanness of line is Elizabeth Mensch's essay on contract law as a mediator between the contradictory desires to promote freedom of action and to guarantee the security of expectations. *See* Mensch, *supra* note 53.

The common thread of these histories is the observation that the contradiction makes available for the decision of every case matched pairs of arguments that are perfectly plausible within the logic of the system but that cut in exactly opposite directions. The managers of the legal system preserve their sense that law is actually relatively orderly and predictable by assembling a bunch of devices to keep these oppositions from becoming too starkly obvious (even to themselves). They classify some of the oppositions as "anomalies and exceptions." They stick others in separate categories (e.g., law/equity). They rule out still others (the capitalist wage-bargain is invalid, at least in times of high unemployment, because concluded under duress; the equal protection clause prohibits rationing scarce social goods by ability to pay) by a separation between law and politics or simply by arbitrary ideological fiat (interpretations of rules that would too much alter the status quo are wrong per se). Nonetheless, these fudging devices are subject to strains that eventually crack them apart. Enemies of the status quo expose obviously ideological contrivances for what they are and develop arguments based on utopian counterpossibilities of the system. ("Freedom of contract" as administered is just the rule of the stronger; contracts can't be really free unless entered into by parties with "equal bargaining power"; hence, "freedom of contract" norms require regulatory schemes equalizing bargaining power.) Ordinary lawyers and judges with no wish whatever to destroy the system lay bare its contradictions in adversary arguments or dissents. And jurists whose main ambition is to justify the system by showing how clear and orderly it is at its core end up expounding it so well that its faults appear in plain view.[126] Anyone who has come to adopt this approach has left functionalism far behind. For if it turns out to be true that law is founded upon contradictions, it cannot also be true that any particular legal form is required by, or a condition of, any particular set of social practices. And, in fact, one of the skills that the fans of this method have developed to an abnormal extent is that of supplying, whenever they hear a claim of functional relation between a legal rule and a social practice, the standard counterclaim, with counterexamples, for an exactly inverse relationship.

V. CRITICIZING THE CRITICS: SOME POINTS OF CONTROVERSY

One of the melancholy truths about Critical Legal Studies generally seems to be that its students, although many of them try hard to write free of jargon for wide audiences, have for the most part not succeeded in communicating their ideas clearly enough to attract much relevant criticism from outside opponents. Most of the interesting controversies that I've become aware of have taken

[126] It would be inconsistent with the Critics' inclination to relativize all historical stories for them to claim any privileged status for their own, and they don't. Their story is, presumably, as time-bound in its assumptions and as subject to displacement by other, more persuasive stories, as any other historical account.

place within CLS, among people who consider themselves part of the movement. I will devote the space remaining here to a brief account of some of these controversies and will scatter remarks here and there to indicate where I stand on them. These controversies tend to swirl around the validity of the approach described in the last section: legal historiography as the intellectual history of the rise and fall of paradigm structures of thought designed to mediate contradictions.[127] This special kind of doctrinal history is surely the most distinctive Critical contribution, as well as the one that has caused most of the arguments.

A. Argument #1: "The history of DOCTRINE? This is the big Liberating move? You've got to be kidding!"

This argument is more complex than first appears and usually turns out to consist of several different points:

(1) "You're just doing the history of legal ideas; what we need is the history of the law's effects on actual behavior in the real world." This point I think has been sufficiently addressed already: It's another version of the false law/society dichotomy. "The economy" is no more "real" than "legal ideas." It's an assemblage of conventions of which "legal ideas" such as property, contract, promissory and fiduciary obligation, not to mention money itself, are indispensable elements and propagators.

(2) "But assuming that you're right, that the Material is inextricably mixed up with the Ideal, isn't all this doctrinal history still excessively Idealist? For one thing, it seems so abstract and bloodless, so far removed from the world of concrete social experience. For another, the method makes it look as if the history of these legal/intellectual structures were somehow self-determining – as if the structures rose and fell because of some objective inner dynamic unrelated to the world of social struggle or, for that matter, to real people of any kind. Doesn't this just substitute another set of evolutionary determinisms for the social evolutionism that it rejects?" This point is troubling, though it is perhaps more about appearance than about substance. It's true, I think, that the kind of structuralist historiography that some of the Critics have written sometimes reads as if these impersonal structures had a life of their own and human beings were enslaved to the needs of that life-cycle, building or demolishing as the World-Spirit might dictate. This appearance is quite unfortunate

[127] Again, this is by no means the only way in which Critics write history. Every type of partial – or extended – Critical mode that I've mentioned in this piece has defenders and adherents; and the chief rival to the intellectual-history-of-doctrinal-contradictions approach is probably the history-from-the-bottom-up account of oppressed groups struggling against ruling-class versions of law and for their own versions, inspired mainly by the brilliant example of E. P. Thompson's work. *See* E. P. Thompson, *The Making of the English Working Class* (1963); Thompson, *supra* note 88.

> because I don't believe that these Critics want to divorce the life-cycle of their structures from human agency. On the contrary, their point is that people build these systems to satisfy their needs for cooperation with, while protecting against their terror of, one another. As people build, they reify, attributing to their own creations an impersonal determining force ("the logic of freedom of contract requires that legal lines be drawn strictly limiting the state's power to affect the substantive terms of the bargain"). But the Critics, far from believing that these structures determine everything, spend all their time showing how indeterminate they are – how they always lead to contradictory consequences. What the structures "determine" is not any particular set of social consequences but the categories of thought and discourse wherein political conflict will be carried out.

If you accept, or at least are willing to listen sympathetically for a moment to this defense of the structuralist method, you'll see why it would be hard for the Critics to do as their opponents ask – to tie in the story of the rise and fall of structures to narratives of particular social struggles between concrete interests. The Critics are trying to describe something that partly transcends concrete interest because it helps create the conceptual universe shared by all parties to the struggle. What the parties are struggling over is the power to interpret and to have applied in their favor the (contradictory) implications of a common set of premises. For example, because most of the actual work of elaborating the basic terms of political discourse is done by people at the top of the social pyramid, a historian would, to a limited extent, be able to tell the story of the rise of a structure as an elite's attempt to rationalize elite privileges and the story of its fall as the collapse of the elite's Empire of Reason under siege from the enemies below. Thus, the "classical" legal thought of the late nineteenth century was the creation of elite, mostly Republican or conservative Mugwump, lawyers and judges. The critiques that exposed it as ideology did often originate in reform movements considerably to the left of that elite (left-wing urban Progressivism, academic left-liberalism, Populism, the social-planning wing of the New Deal), which were expressing interests and programs of classes and groups somewhat further down in the social structure. Yet, as this particular example vividly demonstrates, such a simplistic narrative would be incomplete and fundamentally misleading if it cast elite conservatives as the sole architects of ideological mystification and their (relatively) left-wing critics or representatives of lower social classes as the bearers of Critical truth. Such an account would obscure the extent to which leftists and lower social classes shared the basic premises of the ideological structure. And it would obscure the role that elite conservatives themselves – think for example of Holmes, hardly a social reformer! – played in the demolition of that structure.

Nevertheless, the structuralist historians are partly to blame for the ways in which their work has been misunderstood. They do sometimes write the driest possible *Ideengeschichte* of doctrinal concepts evolving and dissolving over time, without paying nearly enough attention to the applications to which these doctrines were put in everyday practical reasoning or to the specific controversies or political events that suddenly opened up the doctrines to question. The structuralists would, I think, again respond that legal structures, because of their indeterminacy, can't be expected to connect in any predictable fashion with the interests of any particular class or group. Thus, a writer couldn't put the history of structures in the context of political events in any way that would make a coherent narrative. "Consideration" doctrine, for example, has played some part in building Anglo-American private law structures,[128] but it would be hard to attribute developments in the doctrine very convincingly to any one side's political interests.[129] (Nobody would write: "Agrarian radicals called for popular takeover of the banks and immediate abolition of the Pre-Existing Duty Rule.") One could concede this point to the structuralists and still ask them to embed their story in a narrative context that would at least supply subjects and occasions to the narrative to show that it is human beings with reasons and motives, not disembodied Spirits, who drive the manufacture of legal concepts: Who pushed which arguments on what occasions and why? What happened to set off the arguments? What happened to destabilize previously stable conventions?[130] We ought to have a rule of style: no sentence without a subject; no intellectual move without a reason – even if the particular subject and reason may sometimes be largely incidental to the grander thematic history of legal consciousness.[131]

(3) "All right then, I can see why you want to write legal history as the history of legal consciousness, and I can even understand why you think

[128] On the "latent functions" of consideration, see, e.g., David Brion Davis, *The Problem of Slavery in the Age of Revolution* 1770–1823 (1975).

[129] This does *not* mean, although the people I've called the disengaged think it does, that "consideration" doctrine has no social importance and should be treated solely as a piece of legal esoterica; the structuralist approach says that it matters all right, not all by itself, to be sure, but as a piece of a structure, a complex cultural code.

[130] Joseph Singer does this contextualizing very usefully. For example, in the middle of an extremely abstract history of modern analytical jurisprudence, he uses the context of the law of labor injunctions to show why it might matter to anyone whether "rights" entailed correlative "duties" or not. Singer, *supra* note 125, at 989. A model for this sort of approach to intellectual history is Quentin Skinner, *The Foundations of Modern Political Thought* (1978), which takes ancient arguments on authority, its legitimate exercise, proper limits, and redress for violating those limits, etc. through the successive political crises and controversies in which the arguments were deployed, warped, bent out of shape, and finally completely recast by the strategies of the disputants.

[131] When I say "subjects," it should be clear that I don't just mean *individual* subjects; legal concepts are made collectively, and the makers may be officials, judges, subcultures of professionals or intellectuals, the ideologues of political factions, workingmen's associations, religious groups, heavy-industry board chairmen, mass movements, or other collectives of whose existence our limited categories have left us unaware.

I am uneasy about this formulation even as I utter it. My colleague Tom Heller has vigorously argued that my attachment to narratives with subjects is a sentimental reaction to

> that, although that history is made by real people in social life, it can be told without reference to pressures of immediate interest. But what I can't understand is why you chose to write about these particular forms of legal consciousness – case law and treatise literature produced by the high mandarins of the legal system – in the first place. After all, isn't part of your theory that everyone in society – not just lawyers and certainly not just jurists and appellate judges – produces, applies, and interprets 'law.' And isn't it therefore perverse of you to stick with the mandarin materials beloved of the most reactionary of Formalists?"

This is not an easy criticism to answer, but as a start I might say that I've never heard any Critic argue (as some traditional legal historians have been known to do) that Critical histories ought to focus exclusively on mandarin materials. But for an historiographical practice just setting off on its travels, the choice of these materials does make a certain amount of sense for several reasons. First, case law and treatises are relatively accessible. Thus, you don't have to do a lot of digging to get materials to practice the method on, and newcomers, your students for example, can learn the method and produce finished pieces of research in a reasonable time. (In a field like law, which doesn't give people a long dissertation period to do research and develop their ideas, this is a real advantage.)

Second, the mandarin materials are among the richest artifacts of a society's legal consciousness. Because they are the most rationalized and elaborated legal products, you'll find in them an exceptionally refined and concentrated version of legal consciousness. Moreover, if you can crack the codes of these mandarin texts, you'll often have tapped into a structure that isn't at all peculiar to lawyers but that is the prototype speech behind many different dialect discourses in the society.[132] For one example, the elite legal thought of the late nineteenth century ("classical" legal thought, as it's sometimes called) is strikingly parallel in its basic structure to classical political economy.[133] For another, the transformations in the structure of legal thought which eventually led to Realism and the legal ideology of the administrative state have very close analogues in the rise of institutional economics.[134] But the crucial question is whether studying elite legal thought will equip you only to study other elite dialects or whether it will also help you understand the vernacular, the common forms of legal discourse. It would take a lot of nerve to answer this with much confidence because I know of very few attempts so far to apply the structuralist method

a prestructuralist past. For his reasons in detail, see Thomas C. Heller, "Structuralism and Critique," 36 *Stan. L. Rev.* 127 (1984).

132 Tushnet, *supra* note 101, exposes such a structure.

133 *See* Atiyah, *supra* note 53, at 660–669; Issac Balbus, "Commodity Form and Legal Form: An Essay on the "Relative Autonomy" of the Law," 11 *L. & Soc'y Rev.* 571 (1977).

134 *See* Thomas C. Heller & Jacques Pelkmans, "The Federal Economy: Law and Economic Integration and the Positive State," in *Integration Through Law: Europe and the American Federal Experience* 248 (Cappelletti ed., 1986).

to legal discourse at the field levels of lower-order officials, practitioners, or private lawmakers, but it seems plausible to suppose that the method would work at that level also.[135] My guess is that field-level studies would reveal a lot of trickle-down effects – a lot of mandarin ideology reproduced in somewhat vulgarized forms,[136] and doubtless also mixed up with a lot of foreign elements (as nineteenth-century American labor organizers, for example, assimilated the mainstream ideologies of their culture but mixed them up with elements less often found at the elite levels – evangelical religion, precapitalist ideas of work, time, and community, and some solidarist strains of European socialism[137]). Actually, these effects may not be trickle-down effects at all, but rather refracted trickle-up effects. That is, the mandarin ideology may represent simply an elaborated, purified, and formalized version of a consciousness whose primary producers are to be found all over the society. If either of these suppositions is even partially correct, regardless of the actual directions of influence, people interested in popular legal consciousness would be making a serious mistake to ignore studies of elites.

Third, in the particular context of the law schools, it has made good strategic sense for Critics to focus their energies on the deconstruction of mandarin materials because their method gives each other and their students alternative ways of thinking about the very materials that law teachers have traditionally cared about: the core doctrinal subjects of the first year curriculum. Although the Law-and-Society movement tried for years to convince traditional law teachers that these core subjects were "irrelevant" because they didn't "have anything to do with the real world," it had very little effect on the teaching and writing that went on in law schools. The Critics, by contrast, have engaged traditional doctrinalists on their own turf and have in the process stirred up a fabulous ruckus. My guess, however, is that this strategic usefulness will not last much longer; I predict that the forces of the orthodox will simply abandon their traditional doctrinal ground to the Critics, claiming that "it doesn't matter anyway, because it doesn't have anything to do with the real world."

[135] *See, e.g.*, William Simon, "Legality, Bureaucracy and Class in the Welfare System," 92 *Yale L. J.* 1198 (1983) (structural analysis originally developed in context of private law doctrine applied to study of lower-level welfare bureaucrats); *see also* John Reid, *Law for the Elephant: Property and Social Behavior on the Overland Trail* (1980) (basic elements of formal legal rules of property and contract internalized by laypeople and routinely applied in contexts remote from officials and courts); Al Katz & Lee Teitelbaum, "PINS Jurisdiction, the Vagueness Doctrine, and the Rule of Law," 53 *Ind. L. J.* 1 (1977–1978) (disposition of juvenile offenders); Robert Weisberg, "Deregulating Death," 1983 *Sup. Ct. Rev.* 303 (1983) (counsels' arguments to juries in death cases).

[136] The common speech of practically minded people, as Keynes famously remarked, is often composed largely of the theories of long defunct intellectuals. John Keynes, *General Theory of Employment, Interest and Money* (1936).

[137] *See, e.g.*, Gutman, *supra* note 74, at 3–117 (1976); David Montgomery, *Beyond Equality: Labor and the Radical Republicans* 237–241 (1967).

Empirical arguments, which used to be the stock in trade of left-liberal reformers trying to expose the gap between legal principles in high-sounding pretension and in seamy operation, will increasingly be heard from conservatives claiming "there's no evidence" that elite legal ideology affects anyone's "behavior." Simple anti-intellectualism, the claim that all these academic debates over doctrine are doubtless fascinating to the Rapunzels of the ivory tower but irrelevant to the practical tasks of lawyering, will also be adopted by these conservatives. When this happens, the Critics will have to find new ways of bringing home to mainstream lawyers the historicity and ideological nature of those lawyers' ordinary ways of thinking, and this need will force the Critics to try to decode the vernacular.

The Critics should try to do that anyway. I love the work that the Critical doctrinal historians have been doing. I think it's among the most exciting intellectual work being done anywhere and that it has revolutionized our vision of our legal past. But I also think that, just as the Critical narrative mode of intellectual history has misled readers into supposing that the Critics have bought into the idealism of the old Formalists who thought that legal ideas just "evolved" according to some mysterious inner dynamic, its focus on mandarin materials has led readers to suppose Critics to be trapped in the old Formalist belief that only specialized-law-stuff-separate-from-politics is law. My point is – and I hope this piece has been persuasive – that the Critics don't at all think that way about law. As E. P. Thompson has said about his own work,

> I found that law did not keep politely to a "level," but was at every bloody level; it was imbricated within the mode of production and productive relations themselves (as property-rights, definitions of agrarian practice) and it was simultaneously present in the philosophy of Locke; it intruded brusquely within alien categories, reappearing bewigged and gowned in the guise of ideology; it danced a cotillion with religion, moralizing over the theater of Tyburn; it was an arm of politics and politics was one of its arms; it was an academic discipline, subjected to the rigor of its own autonomous logic; it contributed to the definition of the self-identity both of rulers and of ruled; above all, it afforded an arena for class struggle, within which alternative notions of law were fought out.[138]

Specialized elites may exercise a disproportionate influence on the manufacture of the forms that go into the constitution of legal relations, but the forms are manufactured, reproduced, and modified for special purposes by everyone, at every level, all the time. Critics are not going to get this insight across if they don't switch their focus.[139]

[138] Edward P. Thompson, *The Poverty of Theory* 96 (1978).

[139] Some examples of what research into legal consciousness at the field level might yield are already available. Leon Litwack's study of Southern planters' relations with their newly emancipated slaves after the Civil War contains a wealth of evidence of how both planters and freedmen thought about (legal) "freedom" and "property" and "contract" and of how they tried to put their ideas into practice. For instance, Litwack describes in thorough detail the kinds of contracts that planters used to bind their freedmen to the land, how planters, freedmen,

There are already signs of such work being done within Critical Legal Studies,[140] and more is doubtless to come. The more, the better, not because workers' or freedmen's consciousnesses are somehow more "real" than Samuel Williston's consciousness (that belief is a sentimentalization that obscures how much the consciousness of all these people springs from the same cultural taproots) but because we'll never understand the power that legal forms hold over our minds unless we see them at work up close, in the most ordinary settings.

B. Argument #2 – The Critics who do intellectual-history-of-doctrinal-structures haven't got any theory of the causal relations between legal/doctrinal change and other social change, except their claim that the contradictions within legal structures make such relations completely indeterminate. But this claim of indeterminacy is surely exaggerated – there are lots of regularities in legal/social relations.

This argument has to be broken down a bit to be responded to. I think that, at this stage, the response can be very short because much of it has been answered

local courts, and the Freedmen's Bureau interpreted those contracts, and what all sides thought about them. He shows, in short, the social/legal relations of contract labor in the very act of their manufacture. Leon Litwack, *Been in the Storm So Long: The Aftermath of Slavery* 336–449 (1979). William Sewall's study of French labor movements in the early nineteenth century shows how French workers carried forward from the Ancien Regime various ideas of workers' "corporations" founded on a sense of craft communities and how, in the throes of successive political and economic crises, post-Revolutionary movements converted these traditional ideas into republican, and then revolutionary, ideologies of solidary corporate association. This is, in effect, a study of the social/ideological content of the legal form of the "corporation" from a new angle, the angle of those who borrowed some of their forms and practices from their rulers but refashioned and combined them with forms of their own to suit their own purposes and special view of their situation. William Sewell, *Work and Revolution in France: The Language of Labor from the Old Regime to 1848* (1980). And Michael Burawoy's extraordinary participant observation study of a modern industrial factory exposes the microscopic detail of the processes that engage the workers' consent and loyalty to the way the work place is managed. One of the many sets of such processes are those of what he calls the "internal state," the plant's internal equivalent (grievance procedures and collective bargaining) of the "rule of law" in the wider society – apparently impersonal institutions through which workers are granted a limited share in governing and to whose rules all the "citizens" of the plant, workers and management alike, are expected to adhere for the common good. Michael Burawoy, *Manufacturing Consent: Changes in the Labor process under Monopoly Capitalism* 109–120 (1979).

140 Duncan Kennedy, *Legal Education and the Reproduction of Hierarchy: A Polemic Against the System* (1983), for example, is a brilliantly described polemical anthropology of the micro-society of American law schools, which argues that the micro-society's patterns of hierarchy reproduce and thus reinforce similarly structured patterns of hierarchy in other social "cells." Elizabeth Mensch, "The Colonial Origins of Liberal Property Rights," 31 *Buffalo L. Rev.* 635 (1982) is a study of the practical applications of ideologies of legal property-relations at all levels of colonial New York society, from the highest and most abstract level of general political theory, through mandarin legal doctrine, down to the most commonplace contexts of legal/political disputes.

already. It's true that, for example, the Critics have not produced an analysis along the lines of the traditionalist functionalist histories or of instrumental Marxism that relates changes in the legal system to changes in the economy. The whole point, recall, of the Critics' critique is that the "economy" isn't something separate from the "law," which reacts on law and is in turn reacted upon by it; the idea of their separation is a hallucinatory effect of the liberal reification of "state" and "market" (or "public" and "private") into separate entities. Because the economy is partially composed of legal relations, legal and economic histories are not histories of distinct and interacting entities but simply different cross-cutting slices out of the same organic tissue. Again, if the Critics want to make this point convincingly, they will have to start slicing their narratives out of field-level uses of law.

The other argument rests, I think, on a misunderstanding of what the Critics mean by indeterminacy. They don't mean – although sometimes they sound as if they do – that there are never any predictable causal relations between legal forms and anything else. As argued earlier in this essay, there are plenty of short- and medium-run stable regularities in social life, including regularities in the interpretation and application, in given contexts, of legal rules. Lawyers, in fact, are constantly making predictions for their clients on the basis of these regularities. The Critical claim of indeterminacy is simply that none of these regularities are *necessary* consequences of the adoption of a given regime of rules. The rule-system could also have generated a different set of stabilizing conventions leading to exactly the opposite results and may, upon a shift in the direction of political winds, switch to those opposing conventions at any time.

V. CONCLUSION

As this guided tour comes to an end, what shall we say about the contribution of the Critical historians? Perhaps this: that they have added powerfully to the critique of the functionalist-evolutionary vision that has so long dominated legal studies and that they have produced their own distinctive and exciting brand of doctrinal historiography and successfully taught others how to apply their method. The Critics are still a long way from being able to deliver the brightest promises of their Critical program: thickly described accounts of how law has been imbricated in and has helped to structure the most routine practices of social life. But they are trying; they are getting there.

12

The Past as Authority and as Social Critic: Stabilizing and Destabilizing Functions of History in Legal Argument*

[*Unlike most of the other pieces in this collection, this one was written for an audience not of lawyers and legal scholars but of historians and social scientists. It resulted from an invitation to a conference organized in 1990 by the Program in Comparative Study in Social Transformations at the University of Michigan, a remarkable group of scholars from many different disciplines. Contributors to the conference were invited to speculate on the "turn" toward historical inquiry that seemed to be common to all these disciplines. This essay was written for that conference and the revised version of it published in Terrence J. McDonald (ed.),* The Historic Turn in the Human Sciences *(University of Michigan Press, 1996), 339–67.*]

In the last twenty years, there has been a remarkable revival of interest worldwide in history among lawyers and legal scholars and dramatically so in the United States, the country that Europeans like to accuse of lacking any consciousness of its past. Here, legal and constitutional history are unquestionably living subjects, the indispensable resources of the characteristically legalized forms of our political argumentation.

There is nothing at all new, of course, in the fact of lawyers resorting to history for their argumentative materials. Lawyers and historians have always cohabited in a relationship of intimate antagonism. Lawyers have always needed history, appealed to it for authority, and made significant contributions to writing it. They have also persistently been accused – especially since the emergence among professional historians of the historicist viewpoint that the past is a "foreign country" (Lowenthal 1985) different from the present and to be understood "on its own terms" – of abusing history, distorting the past, and making demands upon it to carry burdens of current relevance that it

* Grateful thanks to Stephen Diamond, Terrence McDonald, and Gunther Teubner for comments on earlier drafts, and to Laura Dickinson for help in preparing the manuscript.

cannot possibly sustain. The revival that is now taking place relies mostly on ways of making history relevant to legal argument that have been around for some time, some of them from early modern Europe, others of more recent eighteenth- and nineteenth-century invention (see generally Kelley 1970; Kelley 1990; Franklin 1963; Pocock 1957; Walker 1981; Wieacker 1967; Grossi 1981; Burrow 1981; Stein 1980; Dawson 1968; Whitman 1990; Lieberman 1990; Siegel 1990). Much of this essay will be given over to sketching some of these recurrent modes by which lawyers have resorted to history, along with some modern examples. But I will also want eventually to suggest, though very tentatively, that there may be something new in the current revival after all, some ways of using history that do not quite repeat familiar patterns.

LAWYERS' HISTORY – SOME STANDARD MODES

First to explain the apparent paradox, namely, why lawyers keep going back to history and keep – as the historians see it – abusing it. The need to resort to history is obvious: law derives its authority from things that happened in the past, sometimes the quite distant past, from ancient documents or enactments, precedents, customs, or traditions. Yet however ancient, these texts must usually be given present effect, forcibly ripped from their originating contexts and put to work for purposes, and under circumstances that their framers could quite literally not have imagined. Past practices are also looked to as sources of tradition as well as direct authority, especially in the Anglo-American legal culture with its preference for reasoning from precedent rather than from conceptual system. The common law method of adjudication – often extended to statutory and constitutional interpretation as well, so that in construing an old text the judges will look as often to their own past constructions as to the text itself – is inescapably to some extent backward-looking. But the invocation of tradition in law is usually for conservative rather than reactionary purposes. The legal enterprise is usually committed to stabilizing present advantages and expectations – or at most to encouraging incremental reforms – rather than to rolling back to the past in a way that would require radical un-doings of the present dispensation. Law is often called upon to legitimate entitlements that have vested only after considerable social dislocations.[1] The past is therefore chiefly serviceable to lawyers only insofar as it can be seen as being of a homogeneous – or at least continuous – piece with the present.

A closer look at some of the conventional modes of lawyers' history will quickly reveal why it is – indeed, usually must be – tortured history by the standards of historians.

[1] Legal elites of the industrializing societies of the nineteenth century, for example, used their roles as guardians of the "traditional rights of property" to help rationalize the process of wholesale destruction of existing property rights and their transfer and consolidation into the hands of entrepreneurial users (see, e.g., Horwitz [1977]).

1. The most basic and unavoidable lawyers' resort to historical materials is to texts that are themselves the operative law, that is, whose authoritative reading will actually resolve (or anyway bear on) a legal dispute – a constitution, statute, charter, grant, contract, or testamentary instrument, and the like. The lawyer-historian's contribution may be actually to discover the text, or simply to help interpret it, possibly with the aid of whatever contemporaneous records that may be helpful to the task. Sometimes the question posed to the text is authentically antiquarian ("What distinction was understood by the Constitution's drafters and their contemporaries to exist between the powers to 'make' and to 'declare' war?"). But much more often it is aggressively anachronistic ("Did the Framers of the Constitution confer upon the federal government the power to construct an interstate highway system?" "Would they have approved the legislative veto as a device to maintain congressional oversight over bureaucratic rule-making?" "Would the framers or ratifiers of the Fourteenth Amendment have wanted racial integration of the public schools?"), a question that a conscientious historian cannot really help to answer – or, to put this more cautiously, can help to answer only very indirectly – given that the present dispute is likely to be one that the text's authors could hardly have been able to approach with anything like a modern's experience, tacit knowledge, or pictures of the probable consequences of putting their views into practice.

The lawyer's easiest as well as most orthodox course, naturally, is to textualism – to reading the document as if it had been uttered in her own time, wrenching it out of history altogether and relocating it in a modern context The main alternative usually proposed, reconstruction in detail of the contemporaneous understandings of its original authors or audience, is attended by terrific practical difficulties (see Brest 1978; Powell 1987; Tushnet 1988): for example, their intentions may be undiscoverable, they may have disagreed fundamentally, they may have left intentions deliberately or unintentionally vague or ambiguous in order to accommodate conflicting opinions or the possibility of changing circumstances, or they may have drastically revised their views after a very short experience observing how they worked out in practice. If the lawyer bypasses these difficulties and partially succeeds in reconstructing intentions with some particularity, she is likely to find herself in an alien and unrecapturable social and conceptual world, one in which the most elementary terms such as *liberty* and *property* have connotations that have long since vanished and whose political concerns seem at least in some respects parochially preoccupied with transient problems and are in any case quite remote from those they have been resurrected to address. (No wonder that when such detailed reconstructions actually are accomplished by historians, they are often ignored in the profession and the courts.)

2. One middle way between anachronism and antiquarianism is to reconstruct the consciousness of the text's historical authors at a level of generality

that will comfortably straddle both past and present so as to be able to claim with apparent truth that legal principles do not change, though their applications must vary with changing circumstances. The level of generality may sometimes rise very high to make the straddle ("The founders were suspicious of concentrated power"), so high indeed as to soar above the specific intentions of historical legislators to the general mode of thinking of their age or even to the "spirit" or "genius" of "our Constitution and institutions" (e.g., "Teutonic democracy," "Anglo-Saxon norms of fair procedure").

Within this middle way there have been two major variations, one stressing the timelessness of the basic principles, the other their adaptation over time to changing circumstances. The choice of one path or the other can lead – as Pocock has shown in his contrast of seventeenth-century English conceptions of "immemorial" common law custom, one (Sir Edward Coke's) insisting on its foundation in the ancient Gothic constitution, the other (Sir Matthew Hale's) emphasizing its ceaseless adaptability – to radically divergent views of legal change (Pocock 1957).

(a) The first method usually privileges a particular historical moment or age – Rome in the period of classical legal science, pre-Conquest Anglo-Saxon England, the founding American generation of 1787 – as having exemplified the principles in an exceptionally pure form. Everything since must, if not decline from, at least struggle to recover that idyllic purity. Again, this sort of lapsarian history is not necessarily or even usually a reactionary method in the hands of a jurist willing to believe, let's say, that the ur-principles of common law or Roman law legal science or the American Constitution are devoted to the promotion of individual free will through protection of the owner's security and powers to dispose of private property. Thus interpreted, the principles have proved as recruitable to the same service as any ahistorical and a priori positivism or natural law theory or even for that matter any aggressively modernist project to shuck off the deadweight of the past. But it is obviously an anti-historical method for all its privileging of past authority (and despite the fact that much valuable historical research has been done, as it were, on the side by those who believed in it). As a method, it casually links together records from completely different periods and contexts as evidence of the same timeless principles. Its only notion of historical change is of lapses from and restorations of the true constitution.

(b) The second method of dynamic rather than static tradition, given somewhat variant forms in Matthew Hale, Edmund Burke, and Friedrich Karl von Savigny's Historical School, seems at first much friendlier to the historical sensibility. And of course Hale, Savigny, and Savigny's disciples did distinguished historical work. But the story of legal change as one in which law (mostly) unconsciously records the spontaneous underground modifications of thousands of particular customs to adapt to changing circumstances can be extremely resistant to historical analysis. Hale's view in fact seemed to be that the history of the common law was unknowable in that it has been fed by so many springs and sources over so long a time. One can never say therefore whether a given application is of fresh or ancient origin and what contextual influences or causes may have shaped it. Moreover, on this view the authority of law lies in its unbroken continuity, which repels any type of historical account of discontinuous change. The German school had no doubt that legal history was accessible to science. But ultimately for many members of that school the aim of studying multiple manifestations of legal forms over time was once again to distill their essential core of principle, to weed out the inessential (the arbitrary, anomalous, purely contingent debris of history) from the essential and, once this was done, to abandon historical inquiry altogether for the more urgent task of weaving the historically derived principles together into a system (see Reimann 1990).

(c) Much conventional legal argument of the last two centuries has relied on a lazy synthesis of these two competing views, seeing law as both unchanging in root principles but adaptive in particulars. It has combined the two views with a Whiggish notion of law as progress, so that, by means of gradual adaptation, the ancient and essential principles of legal order may be seen as ever more efficiently and purely realized (with some allowances for lapses and setbacks) in practice. In this synthesis, legal history is often written as the story of the genetic ancestors or "origins" of the legal forms of the present and of the gradual developing of these embryos into their mature modern condition.

3. There did, nonetheless, develop a mode of legal-historical writing that for some considerable time bridged the gulf between the dogmatic, authoritarian, stabilizing purposes of the lawyers and the integrity of a dominant historical method. This was the historiography of the "comparative method" of study, by means of comparative legal history as well as anthropology and linguistics, of societies from the relatively "primitive" to the most "advanced," with the purpose of discovering the laws governing the evolution of "progressive" societies (see Burrow 1966; Stein 1980). In fact, some of the great contributors to comparative evolutionary theory were lawyers like Adam Smith and Henry Sumner Maine. This symbiosis held enormous advantages for both historiography and law. Lawyers could write respectable historical scholarship of the most advanced kind without falling into anachronism yet also put it to use without threatening the conservatizing functions of their vocation.

By the mid-nineteenth century, it was no longer necessary to insist that private property had been the basis of ancient societies in order to legitimate it as the basis of modern societies. Communal property simply belonged to an earlier "stage" and was functional to society in that stage as absolute individual property is functional to civilization in its present and more advanced condition.[2]

Such studies, if their subtleties were pruned away, were also congenial to Whiggish views of legal evolution as being a central component of the simultaneous progress of commerce, liberty, and science. So useful in fact has been this mode of history – in which progressive societies evolve in stages and in each stage develop legal forms that are functional to their social needs – to lawyers that it has remained the dominant mode in legal argument and scholarship in this country ever since, even after many of the universalistic and deterministic premises on which it is based have been blasted into bits by scholars in other fields. But the lawyers often adopted the mode of thinking behind evolutionary functionalism without making any commitment to continuing the type of research on which that thinking was based. Thus, for the most part the promise of Adam Smith's and Henry Maine's efforts, that lawyers might develop a tradition of comparative historical sociology, was never fulfilled. The work of scholars like Theodor Mommsen, Max Weber, and Paul Vinogradoff, for example, was almost completely ignored by legal scholars in their own time, and no attempt was made to integrate it into conventional legal argument.[3] So instead of continuing to investigate the relations between changes in legal and in social forms, most legal writers were content simply to assume that such relations existed and that they were (save for some instances in which legal change "lagged" behind social and economic change) functional. A common reason for ignoring context – social history in the writing of legal history – was simply to posit that courts or jurists have been the authoritative recorders of customary practices, the best and truest representatives of the *Volk*, so there was no need to go behind their writings. One could even take this view if one believed – as Oliver Wendell Holmes, Jr. did, for example – that legal change was conflict-ridden and Darwinian rather than harmonious and consensual, that the courts and jurists simply registered the outcome of the struggle, the practices of the winners. The social change that supposedly drives legal change through its functional requirements thus tends to appear in legal writing only

[2] This is not to say that at the time these historical conclusions were not violently controversial. On the nineteenth-century debates among historians and lawyers on the history of property and its legal forms, see especially Grossi (1981) and Burrow (1974).

[3] Otto von Gierke's work on medieval associations as "group-persons" (Gierke [1913]) is a remarkable exception to this tale of neglect; it supplied the materials for reconceptualizing corporate personality in the era of giant concerns.

as vaguely specified background processes or "forces" – "the decline of feudalism," "modernization," "the rise of industrial capitalism," "the growth of the regulatory welfare state," and so forth – rather than as richly described environmental influences.

STABILIZING AND CRITICAL FUNCTIONS OF LAWYERS' HISTORY

As I said earlier, and as the preceding examples mostly demonstrate, lawyers' uses of history have generally been apologetic, designed to endow currently dominant claims to entitlements and distributions of legal advantage and modes of legitimating property and power with the authority of the past. Yet, that is only part of the story. In actual deployment, many legal-historical modes, including some of the modes just discussed, have (though not always intentionally) served critical and destabilizing functions, operating to challenge ruling authorities and assumptions about how the world works. In promoting a customary common law, Lord Coke and his fellows were opposing to centralized royal power what could be taken as, and later was often turned into, an ideology of popular pre-Norman liberties against central royal power. Adam Smith was of course challenging the entire system of mercantilist regulation and what he believed to be dysfunctional "feudal" survivals such as entails. Even Savigny, though an aristocratic conservative politically, was, as James Whitman has shown (Whitman 1990) concerned to develop a view of Roman property principles as gradually ripening possession into ownership in order to emancipate the German peasantry from serfdom without the need for either legislation or revolution. Modern "conservatives" like Robert Bork appeal to the authority of the "original understanding" in the hope of undoing a generation of settled constitutional precedent.

Some of the standard modes of historically based argument in law have always assumed an inherently critical rather than complacent stance toward the past. This is the commonplace argument that an old text should not be applied to present circumstances because its originating context is too alien from our own. At the end of the nineteenth century, lawyers such as F. W. Maitland and O. W. Holmes tried to generalize this critical-historicist mode of argument into the main purpose of legal history: that is, the modernist project of liberating the present from the past by revealing how much current law was merely "survivals" of ancient forms that had lost their functions or else by showing up authority as having been rooted in a context of ugly or barbaric or obsolete social practices. They also shook up the hardening complacency of evolutionary views of history by using their research into the history of legal forms to *invert* the conventional patterns of "progressive" social development. Maitland, for example, concluded that English law had evolved away from the "individualism" of medieval village societies toward more cooperative and communal forms in modern associational life, while Holmes concluded that the common law in the same period had abandoned its concern for individual moral culpability to treat persons as standardized units in the service of collective social welfare. The fact that lawyers may be recruited to serve different power centers and opposing economic and social interests has meant that these critical uses of history have also found their outlets in legal argument.

Even when lawyers adopted historical models for primarily apologetic purposes the resulting engagement with history could not help but bring with it destabilizing consequences. For example, when nineteenth-century historiography began to identify the Germanic collectivistic *Mark* rather than the Roman *dominium* as the "basic" or "original" form of European landholding, it removed one of the primary authoritative props to the order of absolute individual ownership – even though the same historians, like Maine, had the ready response that modern needs required new forms of ownership. As Paolo Grossi has pointed out in his great study of nineteenth-century debates over the history of property law (Grossi 1981), collectively held property through these researches acquired an entirely different status from any it had held before. It was no longer just a utopian fantasy or dangerous socialist projection but represented the actual lived experience of ancestors – and, as it turned out, of quite a lot of forgotten or marginalized though still existing European communes as well. The same could be said, to cite more recent examples, of the lawyers and historians who revived the extensive history of pre-Civil War state planning to demonstrate that the New Deal violated no sanctified American tradition of laissez-faire or for that matter, of legal scholars who have been raiding the historical revival of the "republican" tradition of civic virtue in the hope of finding counterweights to the politically regnant modes of unbridled "liberal," self-serving individualism. Just as conservative lawyers' appeals to tradition invite critical lawyers to discover counter traditions, so the conservatives' picture of the law of their own time as the result of a gradual evolutionary process encourages critics to argue that many existing areas of law are backward or lagging sectors that have failed to keep pace with the general tendencies of evolutionary change.

In other words, whenever the lawyers embraced historical methods and evidence, they could never get rid of them, even when their company became uncomfortable. The historicizing of the legal-dogmatic categories of property relations and the acceptance of non-legal evidence regarding them moved them into the domain of historical, sociological, and political-economic debate, where they became vulnerable to intellectual revisionists who sometimes shared none of the lawyers' stabilizing agenda.

EXAMPLES FROM RECENT AMERICAN HISTORIES OF LAW

My discussion so far has been somewhat abstract. In this section, I will try to give it more body and immediacy by matching up some of the recent work in American legal history to the main modes of lawyers' history just described. I will also try to indicate where this work falls on the divides between historically based argument that reinforces and stabilizes current dominant authorities and advantages and argument that seeks to challenge and destabilize. I should warn that the recent literature is vast; the examples that follow are illustrative rather than exhaustive and are confined to a few selected fields and omit mention of many works of high quality; and finally (and most earnestly) that sorting by crude labels such as those employed here does not begin to capture the complexity or variety of most of this work.

THE CORE NARRATIVE OF LIBERAL PROGRESS: A THEME WITH VARIATIONS

Americans, of course, venerate their federal Constitution and sacralize the moment of its making. Its text is their polity's supreme law. Nonetheless, the dominant mode of history among American lawyers has been dynamic rather than static – not surprising in a culture that prefers more to extol than to deplore progress, to see the present as, at least potentially, a fulfillment rather than a betrayal of the past. This needs some qualification: the founding period has the status of a golden age, and below the major themes of progress in American legal writing there has always been a strong minor subtheme of the jeremiad, lamenting declension from our origins. But the basic story told in American legal writing – until, as we shall see, quite recently – is the story of Western liberalism, the story told by the Scottish Enlightenment political thinkers of the hand-in-hand progress of commerce and liberty, the gradual emancipation of individual freedom and reason from the shackles of feudal and mercantilist restraints on land, labor, and capital and from the tyranny and superstition of the rule of despots, nobles, and established churches. This story in turn has effortlessly modulated in legal narratives into the generally accepted paradigm of Western history as a movement "from status to contract" or simply of "modernization" and of legal history as the gradual evolution of forms functional to that modernizing process. The middle classes rise, and after a long struggle with the ancien regime, finally triumph. (In America, of course, the ancien regime was pretty weak and vestigial to start with.) The remnants of the regime – primogeniture, established churches, seditious libel, imprisonment for debt and hostility to bankruptcy, customary monopolies, labor-conspiracy prosecutions, married women's disabilities, indentured servitude, eventually even slavery itself, and after slavery Jim Crow – gradually disappear under the modernizing pressures of commercial development. The basic theme is the emancipation of the freely choosing self: the release of individual energy, the opening of opportunity, the removal of restrictions on choice, gradual progress to the point where virtually all social relations in which people may find themselves may be seen as instituted by their voluntary consent. More and more groups shed special incidents of status and become eligible to participate as legal equals in the polity and economy. In these histories, the merit badges for lawyers go to those who help transform economic and political institutions in the direction of liberal development. Even lawyers who in their time may have been perceived as fairly conservative, such as Alexander Hamilton, John Marshall, Joseph Story, Lemuel Shaw, or James Kent, are cast as liberal pioneers, statesmanlike architects of the frameworks for a liberal-pluralist market society (see, for example, Hurst 1978; Newmyer 1985; and Levy 1957).

Needless to say, there are deep political splits even within the liberal tradition. The biggest divide is between parties one might call Classics and Progressives. Classical legal liberalism flourished around the end of the nineteenth century and is now experiencing a major revival. For its major nineteenth-century exponents, lawyers like Thomas M. Cooley, John Norton Pomeroy, and James Coolidge Carter, the gradual evolution of judicially recognized custom, assisted by a legal science devoted to eliciting its core of principle, had produced a system of common law and constitutional principles that came close to perfecting the framework for a libertarian polity (see Siegel 1990; Horwitz 1992 for good accounts of the Classical mindset). For its modern admirers, it remains the high point of liberal development: most legal change since then has been a slide into the "serfdom" and inefficiency of the regulatory welfare state.[4]

But it was the Progressives who began to criticize the Classical generation in the 1890s and whose ideas came gradually to be institutionalized in state social legislation and administrative commissions and ultimately in the New Deal, whose view of history achieved something close to total domination after World War Two. Progressivism dominated not only the work of professional legal historians but much of the ordinary rhetoric of legal argument and judicial opinions. Its hegemony has been subjected to serious challenge only in the last twenty-five years. For the Progressives, the Classics' late-nineteenth-century high point – symbolized by *Lochner* v *New York*[5] the case that in modern liberal-legal mythology is equivalent to the worst excesses of Stuart despotism – is our legal system's all-time historical low, a terrible deviation from the general pattern of advance. Some versions have it that there was a massive failure of policy and imagination during a "lag" period in which law failed to come to grips with the realities of large-scale capitalism and its effects of urban squalor, unassimilated immigrant populations, destruction of the natural resource base, industrial accidents, labor strife, monopoly power,

[4] The most influential Classical liberal in modern times is, of course, F. A. Hayek (see, e.g., Hayek [1960]). More recently the mission of bolstering a libertarian legal theory with historical models has fallen to Richard Epstein (see, e.g., Epstein [1983, 1984, 1985]). Yet with the significant exception of work by Chicago School economists on the history of regulation, surprisingly little legal history has as yet been written from a Classical-liberal perspective. As the ranks of right-libertarian academics increase, we may expect this to be one of the growth areas of legal historiography in the near future.

[5] 198 U.S. 45 (1905). In this famous case, the U.S. Supreme Court struck down a New York state law limiting work in bakeries to ten hours a day on the ground that the law violated the "liberty of contract" protected by the Fourteenth Amendment to the federal Constitution.

periodic depression and mass unemployment, and skewed wealth-and-income distribution. Other versions believed that well-organized corporate interests captured the legal system and made it do their bidding until underdog groups could counter-organize. The course of liberalization could only resume once the managers of the legal system accepted that state and federal governments would have to supply specialized regulatory mechanisms coordinating economic activity and controlling its worst side effects. After the New Deal, the Progressive legal historians returned to the antebellum period to find a rich variety of state interventions into economic life, so that the New Deal could be seen not as drastic innovation on a landscape of laissez-faire tradition but as one more stage in a long tradition of pragmatic state policies toward the economy (see, for example, Handlin and Handlin 1947; and Hartz 1948; and see Scheiber 1972 for an excellent critical synthesis of this body of work).

The masters of modern American legal history have been on the whole Progressives,[6] but rather somber and disenchanted ones. Their dour outlook befits a generation that has lived through the cold war, Vietnam, and many failures or shortfalls of Progressive-minded policies. These have included the failed war on poverty; the collapsed collective-bargaining regime (now shrunk to cover only 15 percent of the workforce); disappointed aspirations to racial integration, affordable housing, a universal social wage redistribution through progressive taxation, effective public education, and taming the political power of big business through antitrust policy; and waning confidence in regulatory bureaucracy as the instrument of such policies. It is not surprising that from the 1950s onward some Progressive historians would be stressing maturation as an important element of progress, meaning coming to terms with the tragic limits of human capacities and rational planning and the imperfections of legal and administrative institutions as instruments of policy (see, for example, Hurst 1979).

Soon after the Progressives began to sense the limitations of their political vision, the vision itself came under bruising assaults from both right- and left-wing critics, who offered remarkably convergent reasons to question the beneficence of Progressive state policies in "the public interest." The state, critics on both sides contended, had simply been captured by special interests for their own ends: economic regulation was thinly disguised cartel enforcement; spending programs were mostly subsidies for corporate or middle-class beneficiaries; and taxing policies riddled with special deals neither promoted economic growth nor genuinely redistributed income.[7] The critiques paved the way for both radical and conservative challenges to the long-standing Progressive story.

[6] I am thinking here primarily of Willard Hurst, Lawrence Friedman, Oscar and Mary Handlin, Louis Hartz, Harry Scheiber, Morton Keller, and even for some purposes (though his Progressive-liberal persona alternates with a radical one) Morton Horwitz.

[7] Disillusioned liberal historians themselves played a leading part in this revision: for a classic treatment of law as the product of interest group politics, see Friedman and Ladinsky (1967). But the pendulum of historical revision always swings back (and some of the critiques were

THE RADICAL CHALLENGE: PROGRESS THWARTED, PROMISES BETRAYED

Perhaps the earliest of the recent pressures to revise the Progressive narrative came from left-liberal and radical legal activists and scholars, inspired by the civil rights and antiwar movements and the general ferment of the 1960s.[8] In the last ten years it has been these radical reinterpretations that have been among the most consequential for legal-historical scholarship. They have had relatively little influence, compared to the older Progressive-liberal and the newly influential conservative paradigms, on the work of the practicing bar outside small enclaves of activists such as the National Lawyers Guild. But in the legal academy they have transformed the field. Many of the generation who came of intellectual age in the late 1960s or 1970s trained as historians under the stars of Christopher Hill, E. P. Thompson, Eric Hobsbawm, Eugene Genovese, Herbert Gutman, and David Montgomery. Seeing there were no jobs in history, they went to law school and ended up as legal scholars. These were scholars who explicitly sympathized with the subordinated groups of history and sought to recreate not only their distinctive patterns of life but their struggles with their overlords and their political, economic, and moral ideals.

Most conservative and some liberal historians tend somewhat to identify with the lawyers and judges and jurists they write about or at least with their situation.[9] For such historians, clearly, legal and constitutional history is in part professional training in statecraft:[10] we look to past masters to see what to emulate, what mistakes they made, and what to avoid and to learn maxims of prudential wisdom. Lawmaking has often been misguided, but well-made law, sound doctrine, and sensible policy is basically benign.

rather overbroad anyway). In recent years, historians have begun to rehabilitate the Progressive vision. Some have reemphasized the idealistic aims of Progressive reforms, as opposed to their self-interest-promoting and social control aims, and presented them as, though flawed, still basically admirable (see, e.g., Crunden [1982]; Kloppenberg [1986]). Others, notably including some legal writers, have reexamined specific policies and programs of the Progressive and New Deal eras, finding in them both evidence of motives to pursue the public interest (see, e.g., Hovenkamp [1988c] on Progressive railroad regulation) and continuing relevance for the remedy of current policy failures (see, e.g., Simon [1985] on the New Deal social workers).

8 The 1960s generation did not, of course, invent radical or populist critiques of the law and its history: these have been generated, especially by labor movements and their lawyers, since the beginning of the republic. And indeed the rediscovery of these critiques has been one of the accomplishments of the new critical legal histories. But with rare exceptions, such critical views did not reach the ordinary arguments of practicing lawyers or the profession's major journals until the late 1960s.

9 There is a clear generational difference here. Hurst clearly sees legal history as the handmaiden to current policy-makers. In his *History of American Law* (2nd edn. [1987]) Friedman is considerably less engaged, more ironic and detached.

10 For Hurst, to be sure, it is *democratic* statecraft, decision making at the humdrum administrative and state-legislative levels, not just the commanding heights.

Radical-populist history, by contrast, sees law from the bottom up, from the perspectives of oppressed or disempowered groups.[11] It thus sees it as ruling-class measures to repress or co-opt such groups, qualified only by whatever concessions such groups have managed to extract by struggle. Legal history in this mode is a dialectical story of progressively self-conscious but repeatedly thwarted, subordinated-group insurgency. The early workingmen's associations, for example, meet with indictments for criminal conspiracy. They overcome these only to enter a fearful new regime of regulation by injunction. They mobilize to win state legislative protections for labor picketing and organization and then see these statutes nullified by hostile courts. Finally, they achieve national defeat of injunctions and the legal rights to organization and recognition in the New Deal. But the New Deal protections are rolled back by the Taft-Hartley Act of 1947, by a series of adverse court rulings, and, since 1970, by renewed employer militance and a Labor Board ranging from ineffective to positively hostile (see, for example, Tomlins 1985; Holt 1984; Avery 1988; Forbath 1989; Klare 1978; Stone 1981; and Rogers 1990). Victims of industrial accidents run up against fellow-servant and assumption-of-risk defenses to tort suits in the mid-nineteenth century, only just begin to erode the defenses when the system is sidetracked onto low-payout workers' compensation and ultimately win a generic right to safe workplaces in the Occupational Safety and Health Act of 1970, only to find it unenforced (see, for example, Weinstein 1968; Abel 1985; and Noble 1986). Organizers for black rights see the ambitious hopes of Radical Reconstruction go down the drain with the Supreme Court's encouragement, the Southern legal system rebuilt around Jim Crow segregation maintained by corrupt officials and juries and the toleration of unofficial violence; and the Southern economy organized around the legal forms of sharecropping and tenant farming that trap blacks at the bottom of the occupational ladder. The *Brown* decision integrating the schools, painfully extracted from the courts after thirty years of patient NAACP litigation, runs into "massive resistance" from Southern political leadership, is left unenforced until a black civil rights movement organizes to challenge segregation, and remains unenforced to this day to the extent that integration and affirmative

[11] I say "populist" rather than "Marxist" because very little work by American legal historians is strongly or distinctively Marxist in approach, if one means by that history that seeks to explain most legal forms and outcomes as epiphenomena of the class struggle incident to the "relations of production," which are in turn determined by material-technological "forces of production." These days, ironically, it is likely to be right-wing Chicago economists who suggest that law is best explained as instrumentally fashioned by groups pursuing their material interests or as functional adaptations to master processes of economic change. The radical historians, by contrast, usually treat law as expressing ideologies and ideals that are partly "autonomous" from economic interests and "forces." I bring this up because the term *Marxist* is carelessly applied, often as a smear label, to almost any writer who shows sympathy with the underdogs of history or indignation at the ways in which political and economic elites used the legal system against them.

action may substantially threaten interests of middle-class whites (see, for example, R. Kennedy 1989a; Tushnet 1987; Bell 1980; Burns 1981; Crenshaw 1988; Freeman 1990). These are just a few examples. Obviously one could add similar stories for women, paupers and welfare recipients, immigrant groups, or radical dissenters.

In the radical legal histories law appears in (at least) two somewhat different and conflicting guises, an ambivalence nicely captured in a well-known passage from E. P. Thompson's *Whigs and Hunters* (Thompson 1975, 258–69) that characterizes the law as *both* a medium of ruling-class oppression *and* as a practically effective expression of the ideal of limits on such oppression. (*a*) In one of its aspects, law appears as broken promises. Law embodies universally good norms of equal rights and of fair procedures, protection against arbitrary and tyrannical rule, and protection of the conditions of self-realization – such as individual autonomy, solidarity in association with others, and participation in self-government. The problem is that these norms have been twisted and manipulated by dominant groups to their own advantage. Lawyers, who ought to have been the standard-bearers of the norms embodied in law, have instead repeatedly perverted them on behalf of powerful clients. (The theme of lawyers as betrayers of legal ideals is prominent in Horwitz 1977, chap. 5; Konefsky 1983; and especially Auerbach 1976.) Nonetheless, subordinated-groups can make use of the utopian and unfulfilled norms of justice as resources. They can refashion, out of the same norms they nominally share with their oppressors, constitutions and rights that effectively articulate their grievances and ideals – property rights in employment or in squatters' tenure or as traditional use – rights in grazing or fishing grounds; or freedom of contract defined as legal equalization of bargaining advantages. (*b*) Law also appears less advantageously as a bundle of snares and delusions, albeit with some exploitable loopholes. In this view, the utopian promises of the legal system are just ideological window dressing, masks for power. Yet the needs of the powerful to make them *seem* benign, to frame them in formal terms of general rights and obligations, delivers some resources to employ the norms and procedures of the system against itself. The danger of such tactics, however, is that they may only serve to reinforce the ideological legitimacy of the system as a whole.

This ambivalent attitude toward the legal system, like the history it generated of legal change as periodically resurgent and repeatedly thwarted subordinated-group mobilization, perfectly expressed the professional and political situation of legal activists for social movements. These activists had witnessed a remarkable blossoming of opportunities for law-driven (indeed court-driven) social change in the 1950s and 1960s, only to see them wither away or come to disaster in the 1970s and 1980s.

That same experience of disillusionment also delivered some real benefits to the radicals' legal-historical writing. It freed them from one of the besetting diseases of legal history, its filiopietism toward tradition and the heroic lawyers and judges of the past. It also markedly changed the portrayal of background "social forces." Appropriating the work of left social historians, the radicals emphasized the suffering and violence underlying what had often been told as a story of gradual and impersonal social changes – "evolution," "modernization," and "development."[12] "The re-organization of industry around mass-production techniques," to take one example of phrase describing a disembodied process, was in reality a prolonged and bloody business: ragged armies of strikers, often by the tens of thousands, confronting troops and armed guards for months at a time in violent standoffs (see, for example, Montgomery 1987; Edwards 1979; and Forbath 1989). Legal elites, who in the most complacent orthodox accounts figure as the statesmanlike vanguard of progressive policies ceaselessly adapting law to the evolving needs of society, in fact often actively participated in and apologized for the worst injustices, or tried not to see them. Progress toward equal and decent treatment of minorities and a more inclusive democracy usually came, when it came at all, from disruptive movements from below, aided in their early phases by few lawyers and those few as often as not considered outcasts and pariahs.[13] Moreover, there is never any assurance that ground thus gained will not be lost again and the gainers again dispossessed of power. There is no reliable trend toward ever increasing pluralism, incorporation of new groups into the economy and polity as equal players. Rather there are periods of struggle for incorporation, often followed by periods of intense reaction, sometimes xenophobic and hysterical, sometimes quite nicely calculated by established powers.[14]

[12] This exaggerates, as the critical generation of the 1960s was prone to do, the complacency of the previous accounts. In legal as in general historiography, the principal charge was that the historians of the 1950s had emphasized ideological "consensus" at the expense of "conflict" in the American past and had uncritically celebrated that consensus. The charge might have been valid enough against certain works of the period – let's say, for instance, Daniel Boorstin's *The Genius of American Politics* (Boorstin [1953]) – but vastly overdrawn with respect to its best work. James Willard Hurst, for example – like Richard Hofstadter and Louis Hartz – was acutely aware of the defects of the liberal consensus. Hurst characterized the dominant nineteenth-century consensus as "bastard pragmatism," fixated on market calculation, incapable of any but the most short-term assessment of the consequences of action, and basically irresponsible in ways that imposed heavy social costs (see Hurst [1964]). Later histories in tune with the liberal-progressive sensibility, like Lawrence Friedman's *A History of American Law* (2nd edn. [1985]), fully incorporate the "bottom-up" perspectives of the New Social History.

[13] The Boston legal establishment of the antebellum years, with a few notable exceptions, supported the segregation of the city's school system, setting a precedent that was to be fatally drawn upon in the construction of postbellum Jim Crow institutions (see Kousser [1988]). After the Civil War, most of the leaders of the Northeastern city bar cheered on the judicial evisceration of the Reconstruction amendments (see van Ee [1986]). In the post-*Brown* South, despite the stirring example of courage and firmness set by the Eisenhower-appointed judges of the Fifth Circuit in dismantling racial segregation, it was almost impossible to find white lawyers willing to take on a civil rights case (see Bass [1981]).

[14] One obvious example is the turn, after rapid progress had been made in the courts toward a libertarian view of the First Amendment in the 1930s and 1940s, to prosecutions of and legislative and administrative sanctions against dissidents and supposed "subversives" in the loyalty-security investigations and purges of the 1950s – many of which, though fortunately not all, survived judicial review (see Belknap [1977]; Kutler [1982]; and Caute [1978]).

The picture of law as a historical instrument of class, race, and gender subordination and even more of its history as a story of thwarted progress and broken promises, remains of course very important to the projects of lawyers, judges, and politicians trying to extend the reach of equal protection and due process norms to subordinated groups. There is no claim with more practical effect than one that generally accepted legal norms have been regularly perverted so as to systematically benefit privileged insiders at the expense of despised or helpless outsiders. Simple justice, say the claimants, requires ending the unequal treatment, restructuring the offending institutions, and redistributing wealth and social advantage to ensure equality. But on the whole the *scholarly* enterprise of left-of-center legal history has moved somewhat beyond this set of concerns – to historical accounts of law as a set of ideological representations of social reality and to accounts of the indigenous notions of legality fashioned by subordinated groups themselves. I will return to this later scholarship in a moment.

NEOTRADITIONALISM

In mainstream legal writing and argument, as distinct from academic legal history, the most pronounced tendency of the last two decades has been to move away from dynamic views of history-as-progress to look for authority and inspiration in a rediscovered past. This neotraditionalist revival has taken many different forms.

There are still some modern representatives of the adaptationist school of customary law. Some conservative legal historians stress the Burkean qualities of the legal system. They celebrate the common law as encoding the gradually evolving "spontaneous order" of society (in F. A. Hayek's phrase, frequently echoed in Bridwell and Whitten 1977). They echo the early Federalist (and Tocqueville's) *thèse nobiliaire*: that in America, lawyers and judges are an aristocracy with a social-stabilizing function; they restrain popular enthusiasms and leveling legislatures; they maintain, by means of transmitted professional habits and adherence to precedent, traditional principles and continuity with the past against radical revisions, sharp discontinuities, and excessively "abstract" principles; they are agents of social integration, promoting cultural and national unity and customary morality through the shared values of legalism and the constitutional norms of liberty, property, and due process. (For neo-Burkeanism, see, for example, Bickel 1975; McClellan 1971; Bridwell and Whitten 1977; and Presser and Hurley 1984; see Horwitz 1973 for a critique). The Burkean temper also briefly surfaced in a milieu where one would least expect to find it, namely, among Chicago lawyer-economists, who for a season formalized adaptationism as the "efficiency of the common law hypothesis." The hypothesis was that common law decision making had an inherent tendency to reach increasingly efficient – wealth-maximizing or transaction-cost-reducing – results over time. And considerable ingenuity went into describing the mechanisms that might explain how the common law could have relentlessly pursued economic efficiency even though its judges obviously hadn't a clue that that's what they were doing (see, for example, Priest 1977; Rubin 1977). The difficulty with all the "conservative" schools of adaptationism was that the last thing most of them wanted to do was to sanctify the most recent phase of evolution, the Progressive transformations of law and government over the last seventy-five years. Generally, they defend nineteenth-century corrective justice against twentieth-century redistributive justice, nineteenth-century common law rules against social-welfare legislation, and morals legislation against novel constitutional rights to sexual self-expression. The closest thing to a truly Burkean state of mind, in fact, belongs to the Progressive defenders of the legacy of the New Deal and Warren Court and the reformist, "evolving" Constitution.

The most prominent as well as most remarkable neotraditionalist movement – remarkable because one would have thought it had been so long and so thoroughly discredited among historically sophisticated lawyers – has been the revival of "originalism": the view that the *exclusive* guide to the current legal meanings of legal texts (especially the federal Constitution) should be the specific intentions of their historical framers or ratifiers. Obviously, there is nothing new or surprising in the appeal to original intentions, especially of the founders of 1787. In American (unlike British) legal practice, legislators' statements of their views are one among several acceptable supplemental sources – along with evidence of the broad historical context of enactment that reveals the "mischiefs" that the law was designed to remedy and of subsequent constructions of the law that show how judges and other officials have applied it in practice over time – in which judges may hunt for guidance for the meaning of ambiguous or vague textual provisions. In the case of federal constitutional interpretation, the prestige of the drafters and the sacralization of the drafting moment naturally lend the exegesis of intentions unusual rhetorical force. The oddity of the new originalism lies in its insistence that historical reconstruction of drafters' or ratifiers' intentions must be the sole guide to judicial interpretation – even if the effect would be to undo generations of precedent – and in its vigorous assertions that the historical method will in fact usually yield a single determinate meaning.

This robust version of originalism seems to have come into being in response to the race relations decisions of the Supreme Court under Chief Justice Earl Warren. The Warren Court undertook an expansive re-reading of the Reconstruction amendments and civil rights acts as not only mandating an end to official segregation but as authorizing civil and criminal remedies against even "private" discrimination in areas like restaurants and housing. Some of these decisions relied in part on detailed if somewhat tortured analyses of the historical intentions of the Reconstruction congresses (see, for example, *Bell* v. *Maryland* [1964], and *Jones* v. *Alfred H. Mayer* [1968]). To critics of these decisions it seemed not only that the court had got its history wrong but was dangerously out of control. The reaction grew sharper as federal judges in the 1960s and 1970s pioneered the "rights revolution" – the fashioning of novel legal rights and remedies on behalf of blacks, women, aliens, welfare recipients, inmates of prisons and mental asylums, schoolchildren, and other excluded or dependent groups; and the invention of new constitutional rights to contraception and abortion. History – meaning here, not history as historians understand it, but the narrow project of the search for intentions – was proposed as the corrective to judicial discretion run riot. If the meanings of the great open-ended "due process" and "equal protection" clauses could be tied down to the specific views of the enacting generation, the whole rights revolution could be branded an illegitimate outbreak of "government by judiciary" (Berger 1977) and could be repudiated by later, more conservative executive action and judicial rulings.

The "originalist" position achieved the rare distinction for a hermeneutic theory (at least, in a secular polity) of becoming official government policy in the Justice Department under Attorney General Edwin Meese (see Meese 1985). It was Judge Robert Bork's rallying cry in his unsuccessful campaign for confirmation to the Supreme Court (Bork 1990).[15] Originalism in the Reagan era attracted many supporters: the young Federalist Society lawyers in the Justice Department (some of whom went on to form a new cadre of conservative law teachers and think tank scholars), the older Straussian scholars favored for constitutional-bicentennial grants by the National Endowment for the Humanities, fundamentalist Christians with their own attachments to textual literalism, and – not least – the new chief justice of the United States William Rehnquist (elevated in 1986) and a new associate justice, Antonin Scalia (appointed in 1986).[16]

Inevitably, as soon as the conservatives had designated the past, particularly the eighteenth-century founding, as the terrain on which modern constitutional quarrels would be settled, their ground was immediately invaded by contending armies with entirely different political and intellectual aims.[17] Suddenly,

[15] Judge Bork was a fairly recent convert to originalism, a method that earlier in his career he had often derided as an unsatisfactory guide to interpretation. See Boyle (1991) for a comprehensive guide to Bork's intellectual migrations.

[16] It should be mentioned that the most intellectually sophisticated of the Reagan appointees, such as Judge Richard Posner (of the Court of Appeals for the Seventh Circuit and formerly of the University of Chicago Law School) and Professor Charles Fried (of Harvard Law School and Solicitor General of the United States under Reagan), never adopted the originalist position.

[17] The politicians not surprisingly failed to maintain much interest in originalism except as a vague rhetorical aspiration. Nobody really wants to revive the political culture of the eighteenth century in any detail, to turn Washington, DC, into some sort of Colonial Williamsburg. Some conservatives may want to repeal the New Deal, but few if any would seriously maintain what the framers clearly believed, that the issuance of paper money violates the Constitution. The Reagan Administration's legal scholars and ideologues were doubtless sincere in their faith in original intent. But for their political masters, presumably, originalism was only useful so long as it was expedient and was forgotten the moment it began to yield the wrong answers. Conservatives are very fond of original-intent analysis when it suggests that the framers approved of the death penalty, sodomy laws, and state efforts to promote religion or that they would have been baffled by the idea of procreative liberty or abortion as a fundamental right. The originalist approach

every school of constitutional theory, not just conservatives, felt the need to be regrounded in historical tradition. Valuable, fresh work was done by all parties on the venerable issues of framers' intentions – especially on the background of the religion clauses (see, for example, McConnell 1990; Laycock 1986, 1991), the Reconstruction amendments (see, for example, Kaczorowski 1986; Maltz 1985; and Nelson 1988), and the framers' views of property (Nedelsky 1990). Many of the most interesting disputes between parties searching for versions of the past to put to immediate use shift to a higher level of abstraction, over how best to characterize the general principles or "spirit" of the ancient constitution and founding age, either to shore up selected aspects of the present dispensation or to redeem the present from decadence through the founders' wisdom. Thus, the more sophisticated conservatives reconstruct eighteenth-century systems less so that we can slavishly imitate the details than that we may appreciate the principles and attitudes of mind informing them. Some examples of this include the conception of liberty as customary law restraining governmental power (Reid 1988a); the separation of law from politics in John Marshall's jurisprudence (Haskins and Johnson 1981); the Federalists' marvelous balance of temperament that could combine realism about self-interest with faith in civic virtue, respect for theory with distrust of overabstract systems, suspicion of political power with confidence that complex institutional mechanisms could both contain ambition and channel it productively, and disdain for the masses with optimistic projects for educating them to responsible citizenship (Lerner 1979); and even the High Federalist vision of an organic-hierarchical political community founded on deference to patrician men of virtue (Presser 1991). Perhaps the most ambitious (as well as the most resolutely anti-historical although purportedly based on history) conservative attempt to synthesize an unchanging ancient constitution for modern use has been Richard Epstein's assertion of a absolute libertarian right to property secure from all private and public encroachments, which he claims took the same basic form in Roman law, the liberal philosophies of Hobbes and Locke, the thought of the constitutional framers, and the (mostly late-nineteenth-century) "common law" (Epstein 1985)! Epstein's vision, though often cited as ideological authority by

is a lot less friendly to conservatives' claims of a broad presidential prerogative in foreign and national security affairs in that it is fairly clear that the original Constitution supposed that the Congress would share with the President primary authority over the design of foreign and war-making policy. More generally, the key originalist claim that original-intent research will fetter judges because it yields clear, single answers to legal questions cannot plausibly survive any serious scholarly enterprise in a field where there are no agreed-upon criteria even on what evidence should count as legally authoritative (e.g., should arguments in the Philadelphia Convention be given determinative weight? Weight only as evidence of contemporary views of meaning? No weight at all because the convention's proceedings were secret and uncommunicated to ratifiers?) and where every issue of historical fact is so hotly contested. It is thus hardly surprising that Judge Bork's recent book, even while affirming originalism as the only sure guide to constitutional interpretation, should fail to cite a single historian's work (Bork [1990]).

powerful people – libertarian policy-makers and lawyers – is of course in most respects in the modern world a radical one in that its literal realization would entail the demolition of all the taxing, spending, and regulatory activities of the modern state.

Meanwhile, responding in kind to the Reaganite intellectuals' excavation of eighteenth-century tradition to buttress cultural-conservative and libertarian-economic views, center-left liberals have come up with their own ancient constitution. The key components have been lifted from the revival of interest in "republican" or "civic-humanist" thought in the pioneering work of J. G. A. Pocock (Pocock 1975). Republicanism seems to solve a lot of problems (while raising some new ones) for modern heirs to Progressive liberalism. It infuses the Constitution-making moment with a communitarian, public-welfare-regarding ideology not handicapped by associations with European socialism. The legal scholar Cass Sunstein, for example, extrudes from the republican tradition as represented by Madison the norm of "deliberative democracy" in order to argue – against reductionist liberal conceptions such as those of public-choice theory – for a conception of politics as an arena in which preferences are shaped and transformed as well as simply given effect. Republicans, like liberals, favor legal rights such as rights to property but prefer that rights be allocated to facilitate the participation in self-government of independent and relatively equal citizens (Sunstein 1985, 1988; for other influential pieces in the "republican revival," see Michelman 1986; Sherry 1986).[18] Other scholars, most notably Bruce Ackerman, have found even more ingenious devices for adjusting their commitments to the regulatory-welfare state legacy of the New Deal to the exigencies of the new traditionalism. Ackerman advances a theory of "dualist democracy," distinguishing normal politics, the ordinary tug-and-haul of self-interested groups, from transformative political moments in which the people refashion the basic constitutional framework. He suggests that the Constitution has been "amended" by such transformations twice since the founding – once after the Civil War and again in the New Deal. He takes the task for constitutional theory to be one of creative synthesis of the core principles of each transformation (Ackerman 1991). By such devices, the authority of original foundations is preserved as the basis of our legal system without entailing the undoing of the modern state.

Even populist legal scholarship has been pulled into the search for the authority of original intentions and traditions. As I said earlier, the governing convention of radical work has been to tell legal history as a tale of thwarted progress and betrayed promises – that is, to construct a radical-egalitarian version of legal origins (for example, out of the Declaration of Independence's

[18] There has even been a revival – in one of those interesting legal historians' invocations of a lost cause as a competing source of tradition – of the thought of the opponents of the federal Constitution, the Anti-Federalists (Symposium [1989]).

assertion that "all men are created equal") against which present uses of law may be judged and seen to fall woefully short. First-rate work in this vein continues to appear. One thinks of Lea VanderVelde's recovery of the "free labor" ideology that informed the drafting of the Thirteenth Amendment, making that amendment capable of being read as a standing constitutional argument against all kinds of intensely subordinate or dependent labor relations as remnants or "badges" of slavery (Vandervelde 1989); or Karl Klare's story of how the original radical potential of the National Labor Relations (Wagner) Act was leeched away by later conservative Supreme Court interpretations (Klare 1978); or Akhil Amar's populist-libertarian theory of the original Bill of Rights (Amar 1991). Such work has lately been supplemented by legal history taking a rather different approach – reconstructing what Hendrik Hartog has called "the Constitution of aspiration" (Hartog 1988), an underground tradition of radical social-legal ideas that rarely had a chance of authoritative enactment when first uttered. These are accounts that show how subordinated groups appropriate the symbols and norms and procedures of legality from the dominant culture and use them to manufacture materials for their own emancipation out of the very systems meant to subdue them – as the slaves in Eugene Genovese's classic account (Genovese 1974) were said to have appropriated the Christianity of the slaveholders to fashion images of benevolent protective masters and their own release from bondage to the Promised Land (for legal histories with such themes, see, for example, Crenshaw 1988; Forbath 1989; Hartog 1985, 1988a,b; R. Kennedy 1989b; Luban 1989; Minow 1985; Siegel 1992; Simon 1991; Weisbrod 1986; and Wiecek 1977. For similar work by non-lawyer historians see, for example, Litwack 1979; Kerber 1980; Lebsock 1984; Sewell 1980; Hahn 1983; Pollack 1987; and Wilentz 1984.) Some of those counter-constitutions eventually achieve some recognition in the dominant legal culture; most are crushed or co-opted and lost to history. This is history that incorporates the legal realists' and legal sociologists' insights that the law of any period is not a fixed constellation of rules, articulated from the top, but is rather a plastic medium whose actual content is fought over and practically shaped by thousands of interpreters at all levels of society.

LAW AS PLURAL, CONTESTED, CONSTRUCTED

As the last set of examples shows, history in the legal academy is, broadly speaking, taking two different roads.

One road leads to direct engagement with the conservative revival of origins and traditions. Following long-standing custom in critical legal thought scholars on this path advance rival and, they claim, superior interpretations of the same traditional sources. Or they seek to establish different and additional sources as competing fonts of tradition. Or, finally, they use the time-honored techniques of historicist criticism to discredit particular fonts of traditional authority as obsolete and unworthy of present preservation.

But another set of critics is using both conventional methods of social, cultural, and intellectual history and the more modish methods of the "new historicism" to undermine the very idea of authoritative traditions. The project of the historicizers is to show legal ideas, rules, institutions, and procedures as contingent products of time and circumstances: contested in their content, multiple in their forms, variable across time, place, and social group in the ways they are put to practical use. Some of these scholars have no conspicuous agenda save the historicist one of rescuing the past from the distortions of the present-minded and of emphasizing the embeddedness of legal forms in the particularities of context. These have produced groundbreaking studies of the legal culture of the American Revolution and early republic (see especially Reid 1988a, 1988b, and 1989 on the Revolution; Conrad 1984, 1988, and 1989 on the legal thought of James Wilson; and White 1988 on the cultural matrix of John Marshall's Supreme Court).

For many legal historians critical of the revival of tradition, however, the demonstration of contingency has a political as well as intellectual purpose: to try to convince living lawyers and other civic actors that the jumble of forms of legal-social life and thought that we have become used to are not the ones that we are stuck with. The premise is that if we can show how past forms were made and unmade, and how present forms in their turn came to be put together, we can make the present seem more plastic, more amenable to present re-imagination and change. That premise clearly drives much of the work already described on the counter-constitutions of the oppressed. The aim of such work is to displace altogether ruling modes of legal thought, past and present, from their privileged position on center stage, to supplement or even displace the customary hieratic sources such as the appellate courts or elite treatise writers with popular sources of legal tradition ("Everyman's Constitution"), and to replace their master narratives with alternative stories whose heroes and heroines endure and resist dominant ideas of legality and struggle to forge their own normative orders.

The same premise may be seen at work in studies of dominant legal ideologies themselves. Until quite recently, most critical legal history approached dominant legal ideas and institutions in a debunking spirit. The aim was to show ruling systems as biased and hypocritical, dressed up in the costumes of neutral legality, but actually devoted to reinforcing the ability of the powerful to protect their privileges and subordinate the weak. Clearly, law and the state have frequently been recruited to exactly this service, and legal historians have continued to do valuable work uncovering the grimy details (see, for example, Harring 1983; Holt 1984, 1986; Tomlins 1988 on labor law; Siegel 1992 on laws restricting abortion and contraception; and Williams 1990 on European legal ideas about native American peoples). But some of the most exciting critical legal history of the last few years adopts a quite different approach: namely, taking dominant legal ideologies at their own estimation and trying to see how their components are assembled (see, for example, Olsen 1983; Steinfeld

1991). One of the large dividends of this approach has been a dramatic revision of the received (Progressive) view of the core ideas of the law of the Classical period of 1870–1920[19] (see Friedman 1985, 358–63; Paul 1960; D. Kennedy 1980; Benedict 1985; Keller 1977, 362–70; Jones 1967; McCurdy 1975; Siegel 1984; Urofsky 1985; Casebeer 1985; May 1989; Hovenkamp 1988a, 1988b; and Soifer 1987). The revisionists found that the Classical lawyers and judges had been unduly demonized by their Progressive critics as partisan ideologues of big capital. Classical common and constitutional law, they argued, was the stepchild of Jacksonian, Free Soil, and abolitionist "equal rights" ideology, not of the "trusts." It distrusted all forms of legal privilege and legal disability; it aimed at classless formal-general neutrality, such as perfectly symmetrical treatment of capital and labor combinations. Some of the Classical lawyers and judges were hostile toward or at least troubled by the rise of large business enterprises, believing that they threatened individual autonomy and political independence. Corporations as parties often lost in the courts while most Progressive social legislation survived judicial review under the quite expansive scope that Classical judges gave to the state police power to regulate health, safety, and morals. The effect of this rehabilitation, if one may call it that, of the Classical system, establishes it not as some sort of massive conspiracy or period of collective myopia but as a formidably plausible system for organizing perceptions of reality – sorting experience into categories that highlighted some types of economic pressure (such as labor boycotts) as intolerably coercive and others (such as employers' power to hire and fire) as simply natural facts about the world. It was only after a sustained assault by generations of Progressive critics that a new common sense could emerge – namely, that the Classical system's apparent neutrality was illusory, that it inevitably papered over a mass of unacknowledged biases and implicit policy judgments, that it privileged as somehow natural a particular and very controversial distribution of social power – and every key premise of the Classical world could be challenged and transformed (see Peller 1985; Horwitz 1992). The lesson, whether or not it was made explicit in the historian's work, is clear: what happened to the Classics can and will happen to us; our commonsense legal views of fault and necessity, accident and causation, consent and coercion, property and trespass, the public sphere and the private, the domains of the market and the family, are what they are under the sun of governing paradigms that structures perception and constrains imagination in certain systematic ways. The lesson is doubtless all the more sharply pointed because the reigning conservative lawyers and judges have been urging the reinstatement of so many features of the old Classical scheme – without however recognizing the wide scope even the

[19] Contrary to what one might expect, most of this work has not been done by free market conservatives trying to revive the pre-Progressive status quo ante as a model for present imitation but by scholars who seem mostly left-liberal in their general sympathies.

Classics allowed for regulation or the cogency of the most acute Progressive critiques of the scheme's basic premises.

Perhaps the most original as well as controversial of these efforts to reveal the backstage devices employed in the construction of dominant legal forms is the work of one school of the critical legal studies movement (for a fuller account see Gordon 1984), which argues that legal systems from Blackstone's time to the present day may be seen as a series of successive attempts to mediate between objectives that liberal thought holds to be in fundamental tension – for example, fusing with others in cooperative association versus preserving a sphere of autonomy against others' invasion; doing justice as rule-following versus justice as equitable particularism; promoting freedom of action in contracting versus protecting security; and so on; Each generation of lawyers holds out the hope that the objectives can be harmoniously reconciled or balanced through appropriate rule-systems. But each attempt at mediation proves to be unstable as it breaks down along the fault line of the contradiction. The school was founded by a brilliant (albeit so gnomic as to have remained almost unread) essay by Duncan Kennedy on Blackstone's *Commentaries* (D. Kennedy 1979). That essay helped spawn several monographs on very diverse topics (colonial property, preferences in bankruptcy, conditional gifts to heirs, tortious interference with contracts, among others), but which all shared an organization of the history of subfields of legal doctrine around attempts to mediate, minimize, or make disappear a basic structural contradiction, (see, for example, Frug 1980; Nockleby 1983; Olsen 1983; Mensch 1982; Alexander 1985; Bone 1986; Singer 1982; Kainen 1982; and Weisberg 1986).

The potentially constructive as well as critical bite to this work derives from the insight that if the legal rules and processes that in part constitute the workings of a liberal-capitalist society are contradictory at the core, there must always be alternative arrangements – already built in, as it were – to those that a society at any given time happens to privilege. To make this more concrete: the law defines what "private property" is and which "harms" to property may be compensated and enjoined and which must be suffered in silence. It sets the ground rules of economic conflict, marking the limits on how competitors and employers and workers may combine to do each other damage, and it supplies processes for resolving such issues (juries, administrative boards, adversary litigation, etc.) that also distribute advantages to those best able to manipulate them. The critical historians' main point about these legal arrangements is that the basic principles behind them are so indeterminate, and their historical interpretations so variable and multiform, that one cannot plausibly speak of a single "capitalist" order at all. A commitment to "private property rights" in the abstract can tell you nothing about whether homeowners can stop a coal company from polluting their groundwater; downstream riparian owners can sue upstreamers for diversion; or workers, creditors, suppliers, or customers have a right to participate in corporate decisions affecting their interests. The legal system has to decide how to define the property rights in question and to whom it will assign them. It has to decide whether the rights will be lumped together in one "owner" or spread among many, whether they will be protectable by injunction or only by damages, or not at all. In its actual history – as several excellent recent histories of property rights have confirmed (see, for example, Horwitz 1977; Scheiber 1984; Selvin 1980; and Rose 1986) – our legal system has resolved these questions and thousands more like them in strikingly different ways, reaching contradictory answers at different times and even in the same periods. It has moved property rights around to different categories of owners and continually abolished old rights and invented new ones. Thus, in the United States as elsewhere in the capitalist world, there have been many actual historical capitalisms – and one might add, many forms of patriarchy, many variations on the theme of white racial supremacy – and there might have been many more. Such legal histories usefully supplement work in comparative political economy that sharply challenges determinist accounts of the emergence of such institutional forms as eventually achieved predominance in the American economy[20] like "Fordist" methods of workplace organization or the giant multidivisional enterprise. Such work argues instead that there was nothing in the least inevitable about the appearance of these particular forms, that there have been plenty of variations on them within "capitalist" societies, and that the emergence of particular forms has been tied to quite contingent variations in politics, ideology, culture, and – not least – legal ideas and institutions (see, for example, Piore and Sabel 1984; Sabel and Zeitlin 1985; Berk 1994; Kuisel 1981; Reddy 1984; Wright 1986; Maier 1987; Goldthorpe 1984; and Rogers 1990). The point is that our current economic and legal institutions got to be the way they are not through some logic of linear development but through a process rather more nearly resembling that of biological evolution. Multiple forms are continually being produced. Some disappear, killed off by predators or random external shocks; some survive for contingent reasons, and some are selected for certain functional purposes then sidetracked and co-opted for other purposes entirely. The political lesson of such demonstrations, clearly, is to illustrate what might be called the radical potential of conservative arrangements: to show that there exist, already immanent in such familiar ideals and institutions as private property and free contract, possibilities for transforming the society and economy in more democratic and egalitarian – as well as to be sure more autocratic and unequal – directions.[21]

[20] Such accounts may take many forms, from liberal efficiency-based accounts (e.g., Chandler [1977]) to Marxist accounts of the logic of monopoly capitalism (e.g., Braverman [1974]).

[21] See, for example, D. Kennedy (1982) (revealing tradition of paternalist and redistributive motives in ordinary contract and tort doctrine); Lynd (1988); and Singer (1980) (showing how traditional contract and property doctrine justify giving workers and communities affected by plant closings a property interest in the plant). The legal scholar most insistent on the plasticity of economic institutions and the most conscientiously detailed in proposals for reconstruction is Roberto Mangabeira Unger (see especially Unger [1987]).

CONCLUSION

The reader will have noticed that most of the examples of recent American uses of history by lawyers and legal scholars follow the familiar patterns I sketched in the first section of this essay. For most of this century, the dominant resort to history was the Progressives' appeal to the notion of law as the product of a gradual and incremental evolutionary progress. This mode of history was readily adapted to critical purposes by legal activists claiming that progress had not moved far or fast enough or that the Progressive telos had been fundamentally sidetracked or sabotaged. The modest payoffs from this very activism in the "rights revolution" of the 1960s and 1970s prompted a backlash in the form of a rejection of modernism and the teleology of progress and the renewed interest in history as a source of traditional legal authority. But the conservatives' turn to history in search of authority, as has usually been the case, has been disappointing and ultimately somewhat subversive of its own ends. The project of recovering the past invites the participation of more critical lawyers with a historicist agenda that is often intensely anti-mythological. For example, the Magna Carta, once professionally reconstructed, is presented as a baffling technical quarrel over feudal privileges and the founding fathers as a diverse collection of politicians enmeshed in complex factional, regional, and ideological squabbles carried on in almost archaic political language. The search for tradition serves as an incitement to restore radical traditions as well as conservative ones, to appeal to the authority of the polity's past antiauthoritarianism and its eagerness to break radically with the encumbering past of the wicked Old World.

So far, as I say, these uses of history repeat familiar themes. Every time conservatives invoke the past for the purpose of shutting down further change, reform-minded lawyers dredge the same sources to brand the present as a corrupt deviation from its true principles, to recover buried counter-traditions or counter-constitutions to oppose to present orthodoxy, to suggest that evolutionary long-term trend lines point toward the triumph of reformist society, or finally just to suggest that the future is not determined by the past at all but is within the control of present generations. The main differences that I perceive about much modern work, particularly the radical or critical work, is a much sharper awareness, in the form of a kind of post-modern skepticism, about the contingency, fragility, and revisability of all models of the past, their own as well as the established ones they are trying to displace. This skepticism is by no means universal. There is still plenty of legal history that uses critical-historicist methods to destroy claims that some dominant conservative position is rooted in tradition or original intentions. But such history then goes on to assert that its own counter-traditions are more authoritative because more authentically rooted in lived experience or in normative longings that would be generally shared if no longer repressed by the powerful, or simply in the virtue and clarity of perception that results from injustice and suffering. On the whole, however, one less often has the sense now of dogma being swept aside so that a new dogmatics may take its place and counter-authority set on the throne of authority. The point seems to be rather simply (1) to soften up existing structures by becoming aware of the conflicts and ambiguities in the very foundations of the way they were constructed, (2) to recover suppressed alternatives less to establish them as a new orthodoxy than to suggest the perpetual malleability of structures and the possible experimental directions for their revision, (3) to stress the multiplicity of legal traditions and the perpetually contested and contradictory nature of basic legal ideals, (4) to reveal the backstage mechanics of how ideals are constructed in order to dissipate myths that they are natural or determined by the course of history, and (5) to spin out alternative narratives to break the spell of dominant master narratives. But with this loss of dogmatism, this newly playful awareness of contingency, has also come some sense of loss of direction. The erosion of faith in the Progressive paradigm of progress has weakened the moral force of the older critique's claim that the cause of progress had been unacceptably delayed or betrayed. The notion that every form of legality is a constructed artifact rather than a natural or determined fact is useful for understanding the genealogy of current conditions but at the same time tends, understandably, to deprive people of any strong basis for confidence in transcendent standpoints for critique of the present order. Thus, at this writing, the potential contributions of historical learning to rebuilding society – as contrasted simply to combating the fatalistic sense that no change is possible – are still not so clear.

REFERENCES

Abel, Richard. 1985. "Risk as an Arena of Struggle." *Michigan Law Review* 83: 772–794.

Ackerman, Bruce. 1991. *We the People. Vol. 1: Foundations*. Cambridge: Harvard University Press.

Alexander, Gregory. 1985. "The Dead Hand and the Law of Trusts in the Nineteenth Century." *Stanford Law Review* 37: 1189–1266.

Amar, Akhil. 1991. "The Bill of Rights as a Constitution." *Yale Law Journal* 100:1131–1210.

Auerbach, Jerold. 1976. *Unequal Justice: Lawyers and Social Change in Modern America*. New York: Oxford University Press.

Avery, Dianne. 1988. "Images of Violence in Labor Jurisprudence: The Regulation of Labor and Boycotts, 1894–1921." *Buffalo Law Review* 37:1–117.

Bass, Jack. 1981. *Unlikely Heroes: The Dramatic Story of the Southern Judges of the Fifth Circuit Who Translated the Supreme Court's Brown Decision into a Revolution for Equality*. New York: Simon and Schuster.

Belknap, Michael. 1977. *Cold War Political Justice: The Smith Act, the Communist Party, and American Civil Liberties*. Westport, CT: Greenwood Press.

Bell, Derrick. 1980. *Race, Racism, and American Law*. 2nd edn. Boston: Little, Brown.

Bell v Maryland 378 U.S. 226 (1964).

Benedict, Michael Les. 1985. "Laissez-Faire and Liberty: A Re-Evaluation of the Meaning and Origins of Laissez-Faire Constitutionalism." *Law and History Review* 3:293–331.

Berger, Raoul. 1977. *Government by Judiciary: The Transformation of the Fourteenth Amendment*. Cambridge: Harvard University Press.

Berk, Gerald. 1994. *Alternative Tracks: The Corporation and the Constitution of American Industrial Order, 1865–1917*. Baltimore: Johns Hopkins University Press.

Bickel, Alexander. 1975. *The Morality of Consent*. New Haven: Yale University Press.

Bone, Robert. 1986. "Normative Theory and Legal Doctrine in American Nuisance Law: 1850–1920." *Southern California Law Review* 59:1101–1226.

Boorstin, Daniel. 1953. *The Genius of American Politics*. Chicago: University of Chicago Press.

Bork, Robert. 1990. *The Tempting of America*. New York: Free Press.

Boyle, James. 1991. "A Process of Denial: Bork and Post-Modern Conservatism." *Yale Journal of Law and the Humanities* 3:263–314.

Braverman, Harry. 1974. *Labor and Monopoly Capital: The Degradation of Work in the Twentieth Century*. New York: Monthly Review Press.

Brest, Paul. 1978. "The Misconceived Quest for the Original Understanding." *Boston University Law Review* 25:75–110.

Bridwell, Randall, and Ralph U. Whitten. 1977. *The Constitution and the Common Law*. Lexington, MA: Lexington Books.

Burns, Haywood. 1981. "From Brown to Bakke and Back: Race, Law, and Social Change in America." *Daedalus* 110 (spring): 219–231.

Burrow, J. W. 1966. *Evolution and Society: A Study in Victorian Social Theory*. Cambridge: Cambridge University Press.

1974. "The 'Village Community' and the Uses of History in Late Nineteenth Century England." In Neil McKendrick, ed., *Historical Perspectives: Studies in English Thought and Society in Honor of J. H. Plumb*, 260–275. London: Europa.

1981. *A Liberal Descent: Victorian Historians and Their Past*. Cambridge: Cambridge University Press.

Casebeer, Kenneth. 1985. "Teaching an Old Dog New Tricks: *Coppage* v. *Kansas* and At-Will Employment Revisited." *Cardozo Law Review* 6:765–797.

Caute, David. 1978. *The Great Fear: The Anti-Communist Purge under Truman and Eisenhower*. New York: Simon and Schuster

Chandler, Alfred. 1977. *The Visible Hand: The Managerial Revolution in American Business*. Cambridge: Harvard University, Belknap Press.

Conrad, Stephen A. 1984. "Polite Foundation: Citizenship and Common Sense in James Wilson's Republican Theory." *Supreme Court Review* 1984:359–388.

1988. "Metaphor and Imagination in James Wilson's Theory of Federal Union." *Law and Social Inquiry* 13:1–70.

1989. "James Wilson's Assimilation of the Common-Law Mind." *Northwestern University Law Review* 89:186–219.

Crenshaw, Kimberle Williams. 1988. "Race, Reform, and Retrenchment: Transformation and Legitimation in Anti-Discrimination Law." *Harvard Law Review* 101:1331–1387.

Crunden, Robert. 1982. *Ministers of Reform: The Progressives' Achievement in American Civilization, 1889–1920*. New York: Basic Books.

Dawson, John P. 1968. *Oracles of the Law*. Ann Arbor: University of Michigan Law School.

Edwards, Richard. 1979. *Contested Terrain: The Transformation of the Workplace in the Twentieth Century*. New York: Basic Books.

Epstein, Richard. 1983. "A Common Law for Labor Relations: A Critique of the New Deal Labor Legislation." *Yale Law Journal* 92:1357–1408.

1984. "In Defense of the Contract at Will." *University of Chicago Law Review* 51:947–82.

1985. *Takings: Private Property and the Power of Eminent Domain*. Cambridge: Harvard University Press.

Foner, Eric. 1988. *Reconstruction: America: Unfinished Revolution, 1863–1877*. New York: Harper and Row.

Forbath, William. 1989. "The Shaping of the American Labor Movement." *Harvard Law Review* 102:1111–1256.

Franklin, Julian. 1963. *Jean Bodin and the Sixteenth Century Revolution in the Methodology of Law and History*. New York: Columbia University Press.

Freeman, Alan. 1990. "Antidiscrimination Law: The View from 1989." In David Kairys, ed., *The Politics of Law: A Progressive Critique*, 121–150. New York: Pantheon Books.

Friedman, Lawrence. 1985. *A History of American Law*. 2nd edn. New York: Simon and Schuster.

Friedman, Lawrence, and Jack Ladinsky. 1967. "Social Change and the Law of Industrial Accidents." *Columbia Law Review* 67:50–82.

Frug, Gerald. 1980. "The City as a Legal Concept." *Harvard Law Review* 93:1059–1154.

Garrow, David. 1986. *Bearing the Cross: Martin Luther King Jr. and the Southern Christian Leadership Conference*. New York: W. Morrow.

Genovese, Eugene. 1974. *Roll, Jordan, Roll*. New York: Pantheon.

Gierke, Otto Friedrich von. 1913. *Political Theories of the Middle Age*, F. W. Maitland, trans. and intro. Cambridge: Cambridge University Press.

Goldthorpe, John. 1984. *Order and Conflict in Contemporary Capitalism*. Oxford: Clarendon Press.

Gordon, Robert W. 1984. "Critical Legal Histories." *Stanford Law Review* 36:57–125.

Grossi, Paolo. 1981. *An Alternative to Private Property: Collective Property in the Juridical Consciousness of the Nineteenth Century*, Lydia C. Cochrane, trans. Chicago: University of Chicago Press.

Hahn, Stephen. 1983. *The Roots of Southern Populism: Yeoman Farmers and the Transformation of the Georgia Upcountry, 1850–1890*. New York: Oxford University Press.

Handlin, Oscar, and Mary Handlin. 1947. *Commonwealth: A Study of the Role of Government in the American Economy: Massachusetts, 1774–1861*. Cambridge: Harvard University Press.

Harring, Sidney. 1983. *Policing a Class Society*. New Brunswick, NJ: Rutgers University Press.

Hartog, Hendrik. 1985. "Pigs and Positivism." *Wisconsin Law Review* 1985:899–935.

1988a. "Mrs. Packard on Dependency." *Yale Journal of Law and the Humanities* 1:79–103.

1988b. "The Constitution of Aspiration and the 'Rights that Belong to Us All.'" In David Thelen, ed., *The Constitution and American Life* 353. Ithaca: Cornell University Press.

Hartz, Louis. 1948. *Economic Policy and Democratic Thought: Pennsylvania, 1776–1860*. Cambridge: Harvard University Press.

Haskins, George Lee, and Herbert A. Johnson. 1981. *Foundations of Power: John Marshall 1801–1815, Part One*. New York: Macmillan.

Hayek, Friederich A. von. 1960. *The Constitution of Liberty*. Chicago: University of Chicago Press.

Holt, Wythe. 1984. "Labour Conspiracy Cases in the United States: Bias and Legitimation in Common Law Adjudication, 1805–1842." *Osgoode Hall Law Journal* 22:591–663.

1986. "Recovery by the Worker Who Quits: A Comparison of the Mainstream, Legal Realist, and Critical Legal Studies Approaches to a Problem of Nineteenth Century Contract Law." *Wisconsin Law Review* 1986:677–732.

Horwitz, Morton. 1973. "The Conservative Tradition in the Writing of American Legal History." *American Journal of Legal History* 17:275–294.

1977. *The Transformation of American Law, 1780–1860*. Cambridge: Harvard University Press.

1992. *The Transformation of American Law, 1870–1960: The Crisis of Legal Orthodoxy*. New York: Oxford University Press.

Hovenkamp, Herbert. 1988a. "Labor Conspiracies in American Law, 1880–1930." *Texas Law Review* 66:919–965.

1988b. "The Political Economy of Substantive Due Process." *Stanford Law Review* 40:379–447.

1988c. "Regulatory Conflict in the Gilded Age: Federalism and the Railroad Problem." *Yale Law Journal* 97:1017–1072.

Howe, Daniel Walker. 1979. *The Political Culture of the American Whigs*. Chicago: University of Chicago Press.

Hurst, James Willard. 1964. *Law and Economic Growth: The Legal History of the Lumber Industry in Wisconsin, 1836–1915*. Cambridge: Harvard University Press.

1978. "Alexander Hamilton, Law Maker." *Columbia Law Review* 78:483–547.

1979. "Old and New Dimensions of Research in United States Legal History." *American Journal of Legal History* 23:1–20.

Hyman, Harold, and William M. Wiecek. 1982. *Equal Justice under Law: Constitutional Development, 1835–1875*. New York: Harper and Row.

Jones, Alan. 1967. "Thomas M. Cooley and Laissez-Faire Constitutionalism." *Journal of American History* 53:751–771.

Jones v Alfred H. Mayer, 392 U.S. 409 (1968).

Kaczorowski, Robert J. 1985. *The Politics of Judicial Interpretation*. Dobbs Ferry, NY: Oceana Publications.

1986. "Revolutionary Constitutionalism in the Era of the Civil War and Reconstruction." *New York University Law Review* 61:863–940.

Kainen, James. 1982. "Nineteenth Century Interpretation of the Federal Contract Clause: The Transformation from Vested to Substantive Rights against the State." *Buffalo Law Review* 31:381–480.

Kairys, David. 1982. *The Politics of Law: A Progressive Critique*. New York: Pantheon Books.

Keller, Morton. 1977. *Affairs of State: Public Life in Late Nineteenth Century America*. Cambridge: Harvard University, Belknap Press.

Kelley, Donald. 1970. *Foundations of Modern Historical Scholarship*. New York: Columbia University Press.

1990. *The Human Measure: Social Thought in the Western Legal Tradition*. Cambridge: Harvard University Press.

Kennedy, Duncan. 1979. "The Structure of Blackstone's Commentaries." *Buffalo Law Review* 28:209–382.

1980. "Toward an Historical Understanding of Legal Consciousness: The Case of Classical Legal Thought in America, 1850–1940." *Research on Law and Society* 3:3–24.

1982. "Distributive and Paternalist Motives in Contract and Tort Law, with Special Reference to Compulsory Terms and Unequal Bargaining Power." *Maryland Law Review* 41:563–658.

Kennedy, Randall. 1989a. "Reconstruction and the Politics of Scholarship." *Yale Law Journal* 98:521–539.

1989b. "Martin Luther King's Constitution: A Legal History of the Montgomery Bus Boycott." *Yale Law Journal* 98:999–1067.

Kerber, Linda. 1980. *Women of the Republic*. Chapel Hill: University of North Carolina Press.

Klare, Karl. 1978. "Judicial Deradicalization of the Wagner Act." *Minnesota Law Review* 62:265–339.

Kloppenberg, James. 1986. *Uncertain Victory: Social Democracy and Progressivism in European and American Thought, 1870–1920*. New York: Oxford University Press.

Kluger, Richard. 1976. *Simple Justice: The History of Brown v. Board of Education and Black America's Struggle for Equality*. New York: Alfred Knopf.

Konefsky, Alfred S. 1983. Preface to Alfred S. Konefsky and Andrew King, eds., *The Papers of Daniel Webster: Legal Papers, Vol. 1*. Hanover, NH: University Press of New England.

Kousser, J. Morgan. 1988. "The Supremacy of Equal Rights: The Struggle against Racial Discrimination in Ante-Bellum Massachusetts and the Foundations of the Fourteenth Amendment." *Northwestern Law Review* 82:941–1010.

Kuisel, Richard. 1981. *Capitalism and the State in France: Renovation and Economic Management in the Twentieth Century*. New York: Cambridge University Press.

Kutler, Stanley I. 1982. *The American Inquisition: Justice and Injustice in the Cold War*. New York: Hill and Wang.

Laycock, Douglas. 1986. '"Non-Preferential' Aid to Religion: A False Claim about Original Intent." *William and Mary Law Review* 27:875–923.

1991. '"Noncoercive' Support for Religion: Another False Claim about the Establishment Clause." *Valparaiso University Law Review* 26:37–67.

Lebsock, Suzanne. 1984. *The Free Women of Petersburg: Status and Culture in a Southern Town, 1784–1860*. New York: W.W. Norton.

Lerner, Ralph. 1979. "Recovering the Revolution." Prologue to Ralph Lerner, *The Thinking Revolutionary: Principle and Practice in the New Republic*, 1–38. Ithaca, NY: Cornell University Press.

Levy, Leonard Williams. 1957. *The Law of the Commonwealth and Chief Justice Shaw.* Cambridge: Harvard University Press.

Lieberman, David. 1990. *The Province of Legislation Determined.* Cambridge: Cambridge University Press.

Litwack, Leon. 1979. *Been in the Storm So Long: The Aftermath of Slavery.* New York: Alfred Knopf.

Lofgren, Charles. 1987. *The Plessy Case: A Legal-Historical Interpretation.* New York: Oxford University Press.

Lowenthal, David. 1985. *The Past Is a Foreign Country.* Cambridge: Cambridge University Press.

Luban, David. 1989. "Difference Made Legal: The Court and Dr. King." *Michigan Law Review* 87:2152–2224.

Lynd, Staughton. 1988. "The Genesis of the Idea of a Community Right to Industrial Property in Youngstown and Pittsburgh, 1977–1987." In David Thelen, ed., *The Constitution in American Life*, 266–298. Ithaca: Cornell University Press.

Maier, Charles. 1987. *In Search of Stability: Explorations in Historical Political Economy.* New York: Cambridge University Press.

Maltz, Earl M. 1985. "The Concept of Equal Protection of the Laws: A Historical Inquiry." *San Diego Law Review* 22:499–540.

May, James. 1989. "Antitrust in the Formative Era: Political and Economic Theory in Constitutional and Anti-Trust Analysis: 1880–1918." *Ohio State Law Journal* 50:257–395.

McClellan, James. 1971. *Joseph Story and the American Constitution.* Norman: University of Oklahoma Press.

McConnell, Michael. 1990. "The Origins and Historical Understanding of Free Exercise of Religion." *Harvard Law Review* 103:1409–1517.

McCurdy, Charles. 1975. "Justice Field and the Jurisprudence of Government-Business Relations." *Journal of American History* 61:970–1005.

Meese, Edwin. [1985] 1990. "Interpreting the Constitution." In Jack N. Rakove, ed., *Interpreting the Constitution: The Debate Over Original Intent*, 13–22. Boston: Northeastern University Press.

Mensch, Elizabeth. 1982. "The Colonial Origins of Liberal Property Rights." *Buffalo Law Review* 31:635–735.

Michelman, Frank I. 1986. "Foreword: Traces of Self-Government." *Harvard Law Review* 100:4–77.

Minow, Martha. 1985. "Farming Underneath Everything That Grows: Toward a History of Family Law." *Wisconsin Law Review* 1985:819–898.

Montgomery, David. 1987. *Fall of the House of Labor: The Workplace, the State, and American Labor Activism, 1865–1925.* New York: Cambridge University Press.

Moore, Barrington. 1966. *Social Origins of Dictatorship and Democracy: Lord and Peasant in the Making of the Modern World.* Boston: Beacon Press.

Nedelsky, Jennifer. 1990. *Private Property and the Limits of American Constitutionalism.* Chicago: University of Chicago Press.

Nelson, William. 1988. *The Fourteenth Amendment: From Political Principle to Judicial Doctrine.* Cambridge: Harvard University Press.

Newmyer, Kent. 1985. *Supreme Court Justice Joseph Story: Statesman of the Old Republic.* Chapel Hill: University of North Carolina Press.

Noble, Charles. 1986. *Liberalism at Work: The Rise and Fall of OSHA*. Philadelphia: Temple University Press.

Nockleby, John. 1983. "Tortious Interference with Contractual Relations in the Nineteenth Century." *Harvard Law Review* 93:1510–1539.

Olsen, Frances. 1983. "The Family and the Market: A Study of Ideology and Legal Reform." *Harvard Law Review* 96:1497–1578.

Paul, Arnold. 1960. *Conservative Crisis and the Rule of Law: Attitudes of Bar and Bench, 1887–1895*. Ithaca, NY: Cornell University Press.

Peller, Gary. 1985. "The Metaphysics of American Law." *California Law Review* 73:1152–1290.

Piore, Michael, and Charles Sabel. 1984. *The Second Industrial Divide: Possibilities for Prosperity*. New York: Basic Books.

Pocock, J. G. A. 1957. *The Ancient Constitution and the Feudal Law*. Cambridge: Cambridge University Press.

1975. *The Machiavellian Moment: Florentine Political Thought and the Atlantic Republican Tradition*. Princeton: Princeton University Press.

Pollack, Norman. 1987. *The Just Polity: Populism, Law, and Human Welfare*. Urbana: University of Illinois Press.

Powell, T. Jefferson. 1987. "Rules for Originalists." *Virginia Law Review* 73:659–699.

Presser, Stephen. 1991. *The Original Misunderstanding: The English, the Americans, and the Dialectic of Federalist Jurisprudence*. Durham, NC: Carolina Academic Press.

Presser, Stephen, and Becky Bair Hurley. 1984. "Saving God's Republic: The Jurisprudence of Samuel Chase." *University of Illinois Law Review* 1984:771–822.

Priest, George L. 1977. "The Common Law and the Efficient Selection of Legal Rules." *Journal of Legal Studies* 6:65–82.

Reddy, William. 1984. *The Rise of Market Culture: The Textile Trade and the Rise of French Society, 1750–1900*. New York: Cambridge University Press.

Reid, John Phillip. 1986–91. *Constitutional History of the American Revolution*. Vol. 1–3. Madison: University of Wisconsin Press.

1988a. "Liberty and the Original Understanding," In *Essays in the History of Liberty: Seaver Institute Lectures at the Huntington Library*. Vol. 1. Pasadena, CA: Huntington Library.

1988b. *The Concept of Liberty in the Age of the American Revolution*. Chicago: University of Chicago Press.

1989. *The Concept of Representation in the Age of the American Revolution*. Chicago: University of Chicago Press.

Reimann, Mathias. 1990. "Nineteenth Century German Legal Science." *Boston College Law Review* 31:837–897.

Rogers, Joel. 1990. "Divide and Conquer: Further Reflections on the Distinctive Character of American Labor Laws." *Wisconsin Law Review* 1990:1–147.

Rose, Carol. 1986. "The Comedy of the Commons: Custom, Commerce, and Inherently Public Property." *University of Chicago Law Review* 53:711–781.

Rubin, Paul H. 1977. "Why Is the Common Law Efficient?" *Journal of Legal Studies* 6:51–64.

Sabel, Charles F., and Jonathan Zeitlin. 1985. "Historical Alternatives to Mass Production." *Past and Present* 108 (August):133–176.

Scheiber, Harry. 1972. "Government and the Economy: Studies of the Commonwealth Policy in Nineteenth Century America." *Journal of Interdisciplinary History* 3:135–151.

1984. "Public Rights and the Rule of Law in American Legal History." *California Law Review* 75:415–444.

Selvin, Molly. 1980. "The Public Trust Doctrine in American Law and Economic Policy, 1789–1920." *Wisconsin Law Review* (1980):1403–1442.

Sewell, William H., Jr. 1980. *Work and Revolution in France: The Language of Labor from the Old Regime to 1848*. New York: Cambridge University Press.

Sherry, Suzanna. 1986. "Civic Virtue and the Feminine Voice in Constitutional Adjudication." *Virginia Law Review* 72:543–616.

Siegel, Reva. 1992. "Reasoning from the Body: A Historical Perspective on Abortion Regulation and Questions of Equal Protection." *Stanford Law Review* 44:261–381.

Siegel, Stephen. 1984. "Understanding the Lochner Era: Lessons from the Controversy over Railroad and Utility Rate Regulation." *Virginia Law Review* 70:187–263.

1990. "Historism in Late Nineteenth-Century Constitutional Thought." *Wisconsin Law Review* (1990):1431–1447.

Simon, William. 1985. "The Invention and Reinvention of Welfare Rights," *Maryland Law Review* 44:1–37.

1991. "Social-Republican Property." *UCLA Law Review* 38:1335–1413.

Singer, Joseph. 1980. "The Reliance Interest in Property." *Stanford Law Review* 40:611–751.

1982. "The Legal Rights Debate in Analytical Jurisprudence from Bentham to Hohfeld." *Wisconsin Law Review* 1982:975–1059.

Soifer, Aviam. 1987. "The Paradoxes of Paternalism and Laissez-Faire Constitutionalism: United States Supreme Court, 1888–1921." *Law and History Review* 5:249–279.

Stein, Peter. 1980. *Legal Evolution: The Story of an Idea*. Cambridge: Cambridge University Press.

Steinfeld, Robert. 1991. *The Invention of Free Labor: The Employment Relation in English and American Law and Culture, 1350–1870*. Chapel Hill: University of North Carolina Press.

Stone, Katherine van Wezel. 1981. "The Post-War Paradigm in American Labor Law." *Yale Law Journal* 90:1509–1580.

Story, Joseph. 1835. Inaugural discourse, "The Value and Importance of Legal Studies." In William W. Story, ed., *The Miscellaneous Writings*, 503–548. Boston: J. Munroe and Company.

Sunstein, Cass. 1985. "Interest Groups in American Public Law." *Stanford Law Review* 38:29–87.

1988. "Beyond the Republican Revival." *Yale Law Journal* 97:1539–1590.

Symposium. 1989. "Roads Not Taken: Undercurrents of Republican Thinking in Modern Constitutional Theory." *Northwestern University Law Review* 84:1–249.

Thompson, E. P. 1975. *Whigs and Hunters: The Origin of the Black Act*. New York: Pantheon Books.

Tomlins, Christopher. 1985. *The State and the Unions: Labor Relations, Law, and the Organized Labor Movement in America, 1880–1960*. Cambridge: Cambridge University Press.

1988. "A Mysterious Power: Industrial Accidents and the Legal Construction of Employment Relations in Massachusetts, 1800–1850." *Law and History Review* 6:375–438.

Tushnet, Mark. 1987. *The NAACP Campaign against Segregated Education, 1925–1950*. Chapel Hill: University of North Carolina Press.

1988. *Red, White, and Blue: A Critical Analysis of Constitutional Law*. Cambridge: Harvard University Press.

Unger, Roberto Mangabeira. 1987. *Politics: Part I, False Necessity – Anti-Necessitarian Social Theory in the Service of Radical Democracy*. Cambridge: Cambridge University Press.

Urofsky, Melvin. 1985. "State Courts and Protective Legislation during the Progressive Era." *Journal of American History* 72:63–91.

VanderVelde, Lea. 1989. "The Labor Vision of the Thirteenth Amendment." *University of Pennsylvania Law Review* 138:437–504.

van Ee, Daun. 1986. *David Dudley Field and the Reconstruction of the Law*. New York: Garland.

Walker, Mack. 1981. *Johann Jakob Moser and the Holy Roman Empire of the German Nation*. Chapel Hill: University of North Carolina Press.

Weinstein, James. 1968. *The Corporate Ideal in the Liberal State: 1900–1918*. Boston: Beacon Press.

Weisberg, Robert. 1986. "Commercial Morality, the Merchant Character, and the History of the Voidable Preference." *Stanford Law Review* 39:3–138.

Weisbrod, Carol. 1986. "Images of the Woman Juror." *Harvard Women's Law Journal* 9:59–82.

White, G. Edward. 1988. *The Marshall Court and Cultural Change: 1815–1835*. New York: Macmillan.

Whitman, James. 1990. *The Legacy of Roman Law in the German Romantic Era*. Princeton: Princeton University Press.

Wieacker, Franz. 1967. *Privatrechtsgeschichte der Neuzeit*. 2nd edn. Goettingen: Vandenhoek & Reprecht.

Wiecek, William. 1977. *The Sources of Antislavery Constitutionalism in America, 1760–1848*. Ithaca, NY: Cornell University Press.

Wilentz, Sean. 1984. *Chants Democratic: New York City and the Rise of the American Working Class*. New York: Oxford University Press.

Williams, Robert A. 1990. *The American Indian in Western Legal Thought: The Discourse of Conquest*. New York: Oxford University Press.

Wright, Gavin. 1986. *Old South, New South: Revolutions in the Southern Economy since the Civil War*. New York: Basic Books.

13

Taming the Past: Histories of Liberal Society in American Legal Thought*

[This essay is a somewhat revised and expanded version of the Thomas M. Cooley Lectures given at the University of Michigan Law School in February of 1993.]

LECTURE 1: THE FOUNDING NARRATIVE; CLASSICAL AND PROGRESSIVE VARIATIONS

Legal argument cannot do without history. Anyone who invokes the authority of law – and this applies especially to lawyers – needs to establish a relationship with the past. In argument, judicial decisions, legislative debate, and juristic writing, lawyers are constantly invoking visions of the past and its relation to the present. Sometimes past enactments or events – constitutions, statutes, charters, treaties, precedents – are direct authority for current law, and their history must be explored to illuminate their meaning. More often the uses of history in legal argument are less direct, as taken-for-granted background framing narratives of where we have been, and where we are heading. Lawyers sometimes construct the past as a Golden Age or exemplary time which we would do well to recover and revive, as a storehouse of timeless principles or immemorial traditions, or as a way-station along a path of progress leading toward the present and opening toward the future, or even as an attic full of corrupt or barbaric or simply outmoded practices best abandoned and forgotten, or preserved only to serve as solemn warnings of ancient follies. On some occasions, history is invoked to justify present practices as consistent with tradition or progressive development; on others to criticize the practices as lapses

* I am grateful to Dean Lee Bollinger of the University of Michigan Law School for the invitation to give these lectures and his hospitality during my visit, and to Richard Friedman, Tom Green, Debra Livingston, Rick Pildes, and Joseph Vining for helpful comments and criticisms.

from good old customs or as survivals of bad and obsolete ones. Even strict textualists, committed to read the words of legal enactments as if they had been uttered in their own time, must take a position on history: that is, to deny its relevance, to assert that the gulf in time that separates the present from the past doesn't matter – either because the text is actually immune from changes in linguistic usages or social context, or because our interpretive conventions require us to presume so.

The rhetoric of law is generally a rhetoric of fidelity to and continuity with past authority. We may admire "forward-looking" legislatures and "creative" judges, but even they are expected to maintain continuity with the essentials – the basic texts, the key precedents, the grounding principles.

Yet the past is a land of swamps, snares, and mines: relying too much on it for guidance is dangerous. As pervasive in our legal tradition as the rhetoric of continuity and fidelity is the rhetoric of warnings against being mired in the past, having its ghosts rise up to bite us in the rear. Blind obedience to older laws and traditions leads to stagnation, anachronism, the perpetuation or revival of obsolete and barbaric norms and practices. The most literally faithful applications of old texts to modern contexts in which social circumstances, legal and political institutions, cultural practices and values, have changed utterly, might have grotesque consequences. Even the most diehard "originalists" – that is, people who believe that Constitutions must be interpreted as their framers or ratifiers would have understood them – acknowledge that we could not now countenance interpretations of the Federal Constitution that would prohibit the federal government from issuing paper money or financing an interstate road system; or tolerate flogging, branding and ear-cropping as routine punishments; or that supposed the free speech clause was perfectly consistent with prosecutions for seditious libel and the non-establishment of religion clause with state taxation for the compulsory support of Protestant churches, and legislated disabilities for Catholics, Jews, and Muslims.

Because history is so important to legal argument, it is always greatly contested. Legal thinkers are always trying to establish some particular construction of an ancient text, or vision of past development, or general theory of interpretation or historical reconstruction, against rival notions. And often they succeed: for a season, an orthodox or canonical view of the past will triumph and become the general common sense of the legal profession, until it too is challenged and revised. Through all the revisions, however, certain basic themes keep recurring; so that modern lawyers' and jurists' arguments about the significance of the past strikingly resemble much older ones.

USES OF HISTORY IN LEGAL ARGUMENT – A BRIEF TAXONOMY

It will help to put the current debates in perspective if we can see them as variations on some of the standard modes in which lawyers make use of history. For simplicity, I'll classify the basic modes as static, dynamic, and critical.

In the **static** modes, lawyers argue that a legal norm or rule or practice has a fixed meaning that has been established by past usage. This may be an anti-historical argument for following a rule that is unchanging because it is timeless and universal, such as a natural-law norm. It also may be simply an argument for following precedent, for maintaining continuity, for doing things the way they have been done before: amplified, this becomes the argument from tradition or long-established custom, or time immemorial. Perhaps most often, however, the argument refers to a definite historical location: it calls for adherence to the original understanding of a text or the original intentions of a founding legislator. Sometimes it privileges a particular time and place as having special authority because especially worthy of respect or imitation. In the static modes, lawyers tend to treat the past as on a timeless horizontal plane with the present: past texts and practices are to be read exactly in their times as they are in ours, or exactly in our times as in theirs. Strict textualism – the view that interpreters should look only to the words of the text and ignore the context – often poses as a static mode ("The words of the Constitution mean today what they have always meant"), but in actual practice this a dynamic mode, since the reader of words who is allowed to ignore their context will necessarily read into them the conventional meanings of his own time and place. The words are left free to float and soak up later and changing meanings.

In the **dynamic** modes, lawyers argue that the interpretation and practical content of legal texts and rules and principles does and must change over time, to adapt to changing conditions. Lawyers working in this mode recognize historical change, but establish connections between past and present through narratives that integrate them into a reassuring story of continuity. In American legal practice, dynamic argument usually relies upon narratives of recovery, progress, or teleology. A narrative of recovery – often accompanied by a jeremiad lamenting recent lapses and corruptions – is in one which the legal system is seen as ready to be guided to recover the purity of its original principles. A narrative of progress or Whig History is one in which the law is seen as obeying a long-term process of historical transformation – e.g., from feudalism to liberal capitalism, status to contract, hierarchy to equal rights, irrational to rational modes of proof, formal rules to functional rules, full legal rights for the few to equal rights for all. A teleological narrative is one which shows legal forms working themselves pure over time to reveal their essence of immanent principle. Of course, there are also dynamic narratives of *decline* – the decline of republics, the fall of empires – but in our optimistic nation these have been until recently muted and minor themes.

Static and dynamic modes have in common that the lawyer appeals to history for *authority* – to the authority of an original text or tradition or founding moment, or to the authority of the course of history itself – changing circumstances or long-run evolutionary trends that dictate the need for a change in rules or a novel interpretation. History is read not simply as exemplary, a source of examples of right and noble laws to admire and of horrors to avoid, but as normative: if we interpret the past correctly, we will know what the law commands us to do now.

What I will call **critical** modes by contrast are used to destroy, or anyway to question, the authority of the past. They assert discontinuous breaks – epistemic and normative, changes in contexts and changes in values – between past and present. So if legal interpreters need narratives of continuity and fidelity (or of restoration) that bring the past into the present, they also need narratives of change, refurbishing, modernization, even transcendence, that shuck the skin of the dangerous past and leave its radioactive traces safely behind. To serve life, as Nietzsche says in his great essay "On the Utility and Liability of History for Life,"[1] the historian must both preserve and destroy. Nietzsche admires within limits the "antiquarian" historian, who "looks back with loyalty and love on the origins through which he became what he is... By attending with caring hands to what has subsisted since ancient times, he seeks to preserve for those who will emerge after him the conditions under which he came into being... The history of his city becomes his own history... 'It was possible to live here,' he says to himself, 'because it is possible to live here, and will in the future be possible to live here, for we are tough and cannot be broken overnight.'"[2] We cannot have an identity, personal, ethnic, professional, national, without memory establishing connections to origins and ancestors, an idea of where we have come from that suggests where we may be, or should be, going next. Yet human beings, Nietzsche says, need another mode, that of critical history: "In order to live he must... employ the strength to shatter and dissolve a past: he accomplishes this by bringing this past before a tribunal, painstakingly interrogating it, and finally condemning it."[3]

In conventional legal argument the most familiar of these critical modes is simply the argument from obsolescence: that the original reasons or purposes of a rule have ceased to exist, or that the rule sprang from motives or a context that are no longer acceptable to modern eyes, are rooted in ugly, barbaric, primitive conceptions or practices.

EXAMPLES FROM AMERICAN PRACTICE: REVOLUTIONARY AND ANTEBELLUM LEGAL ARGUMENT

What I'll present here is some compressed excerpts from, and brief reflections on, how history has been used in American legal argument. After a very brief account of the uses of history in the American Revolution, I'll skip to the middle of the story with the late nineteenth century or "Classical" jurists, and the generation of "Progressives" who spent their professional careers trying

[1] Friedrich Nietzsche, "The Utility and Liability of History for Life," *Unfashionable Observations* 85 (Richard T. Gray tr., 1995).

[2] *Id.* at 102–103.

[3] *Id.* at 106.

to undo and revise the classical picture of the world. Then, skimming rapidly over most of the period between the New Deal and the present, I want to pause to look at the histories of the conservative lawyers of the Reagan Revolution, how they have sought to revive something resembling the legal doctrines and policies of the classical era, and how they have been challenged in their turn. Finally I'd like to ask about why any of this matters, why anyone should care what lawyers think of history, any more than they do what accountants think of music, or musicians of accounting.

I won't have a lot to say here about the most familiar ways in which lawyers get tangled up with history: with the arguments over the right way to interpret legal texts – over whether courts should ignore originating context altogether and attend only to the "plain words"; or should try to reconstruct the "original meanings" of legal texts; and if so whether these should be meanings intended by authors or understood by readers, meanings narrowly confined to applications specifically expected by contemporaries or read as broad charters of general purposes or principles; meanings pinned down to practices around the period of enactment or enlarged or modified in the light of subsequent experience and later glosses; and over whether in any case such original meanings can really be accessible to us across the distances of time and perspective; whether we are not inevitably and damnably such strangers in the foreign country of the past that we can't ever really understand its customs or bring them into the present without gravely distorting their purposes. There are interesting things to say about all these issues; but the best grapes have been well trampled by others working this vineyard.

My interest rather is in the large assumptions about the course and direction of historical change – the embedded stories or narratives, sometimes made explicit, just as often implicit, having to be teased out from between the lines – in the discourse of lawyers and judges and legal scholars, the informal understandings about how the past connects to the present, of where current legal and social arrangements came from and where they may be going. And I'm sure it won't surprise anyone to learn that at any given time there's a limited stock of such narratives, or common stories, in legal rhetoric, usually several different ones coexisting in the same moment and often in the same people, and that these are controversial, fought over, and that the fighting produces innovations. The particular stories that lawyers tell when they resort to history obviously change in their details, but the general structure often remains the same. The stories connect the history of legal change to histories of political, social, economic, and intellectual change in certain systematic ways: so that the evolution of law, in our legal culture, is embedded in broader narratives of the origins, formation, and development of liberal society. In fact until the rise of history as a professional discipline in very recent times, lawyers were among the principal creators of these narratives.

In the American legal thought of the nineteenth century the master narrative was, of course, bound up with the common law tradition. There were however several different common law traditions, living side by side but each obeying a different logic or tempo of time. There was the static tradition of Coke's immemorial Gothic Constitution or ancient rights of Englishmen, given expression as general public-law maxims of the common law. But even that tradition was yoked to a dynamic story, the Whig histories of the recovery of original Anglo-Saxon liberty through centuries of struggle against feudalism and tyranny toward the mixed Constitution. And that dynamic story by mid-century had been grafted on to a genuinely progressive history, the Scottish Enlightenment's four-stage theory of the development of modern society, in which law evolved in ways that were thought to be functionally suitable to each stage, hunters, shepherds, agrarian, and commercial society as they succeeded one another. These dynamic themes – one specific to English history, the other a more general hypothesis of the progressive development of societies – were given a specifically national meaning, and destiny, by the American republican experiment, whose purpose was to preserve the static or timeless principles of English liberty, expressed in the common law, against any further corruptions; and also to carry the dynamic ones toward a more perfect realization than the world had ever seen. In this last theme we perceive, even in the inherent conservatism of legal discourse, traces of the American millennial dream, that in the New World the weight of history may be shed altogether, and men and women freed to natural liberty.

In American legal-historical thought all these different sources flowed together into the same narrative, the story of modern history, and especially American history, as an evolution toward the perfected legal framework of liberty.

This story is a dynamic story, the story of the rise of liberal society. The main *political* story is the evolution of the mixed Constitution; restoration of the Saxon Constitution; perfection of Teutonic representative institutions; the dethronement of arbitrary power of lords, bishops, prerogative courts; establishment of legal restraints on power in the form of rights enforced by ordinary judges; but also evolution of the capacity of magistrates to establish public order and promote the public welfare through the common-law, statutory and municipal regulatory powers grouped under the heading of "police." The main *economic* story, that of the legal constitution of the market, is of the movement from communal to separate property, agglomeration of partial and fragmented interests into the hands of a single disposing owner; removal of restrictions on mobility of labor and capital and the alienability of land; and the erosion of mercantilist restrictions on and regulations of trade, work, and manufactures. The *social* story, that of the legal constitution of civil society, is of the breakdown of hierarchical relations of status, the removal of special privileges and disabilities peculiar to special orders of persons; the tendency toward a growing formal equality of rights. The story of *legal procedures* is: in criminal procedure, the evolution from barbaric (irrational) modes of proof, trial and punishment to rational proof and proportionate punishments; in civil procedure, from the technical (over-formal) "forms of action" to "liberal" (simple and substantive) pleading and procedure.

The dynamic narrative was of course already well established in English legal argument well before Americans got their hands on it. The notion of the common law as accretions of recognized evolving customary practices, gradually adapting to circumstances so that its content is ceaselessly changing, was given classic expression in the seventeenth-century work of Matthew Hale; both Blackstone and the Scottish writers described a common law gradually shedding its feudal excrescences and evolving to suit the functional convenience of commercial society. The American revolutionary lawyers appropriated this general narrative structure, but then substituted their own terms. Take, for example, John Adams' *Dissertation on the Canon and the Feudal Law*. Adams relies on the consensus Whig storyline, as found for example in Blackstone's history of English law: Saxon liberty threatened by Norman "feudalism," Papal superstition, and baroque legal technicality; despotism set back in Magna Carta; the Pope happily expelled in the Reformation; but political tyranny and church establishments returning with as vengeance under the Tudor and Stuart despots acting through High Commission and Star Chamber; finally checked for good and all after some turmoil by the settlement of the Glorious Revolution – Toleration acts, bill of rights, abolition of prerogative courts, and the mixed constitution – and, as part of the package of blessings of modernity, a less cramped and more liberal and scientific common-law method. But Adams takes some, though not all the standard terms of the story, as Blackstone would tell it, for example, and gives them different values: the "Norman jurists" get no credit at all for liberalization of the feudal regime, or hereditary landowners for political progress; the main agents of modern liberties are the Puritan revolutionaries; and residual feudalism is still alive and well, in the Anglican, rather than the Roman, establishment, in the continuing technicality of common law, and above all of course in mercantilist restrictions on free trade. Feudalism, as something happily left behind, as something whose resurgence was always to be feared, as something that we were, or ought to be, continuously moving away from, and above all as something that liberty was *not* – it was the commonly agreed negative sign, though for Blackstone the specific great evil was wardships, and for Adams it was quit-rents and the Stamp Act.

The different stories all had somewhat differing accounts of what liberty entailed, but the master narrative of progress usefully obscured those differences in agreement on what it was not, what it had been evolving away from, which was "feudalism." (Later in the century "feudalism" was replaced with "socialism" as liberty's great opposite.) In the reactionary dynamic story of history as the recovery of ancient liberty, "feudalism" was the excrescence imposed on the free Saxons by the Norman jurists; in the Scottish story, it was the legal system belonging to the economic stage left behind in progress from agrarian to commercial society; it was obviously anti-republican because of its reduction of yeomen to dependency; finally, it was perfectly emblematic of the "artificial" privileges and disabilities inconsistent with natural liberty, the burdens of European historical experience that we are trying to throw off.

The "common law" had a wonderfully elastic and multiform character in this master narrative: it was the repository of basic and ancient principles of English liberty; it also stood for conservative (or Burkean-historicist) principles of slow growth of communal-customary law, with a deeper basis in popular consent than mere legislation, and a proved capacity for spontaneous self-reformation by adaptation to changing circumstances. But at the same time it had been badly perverted and corrupted by "feudal," ecclesiastical and monarchical influences. Americans believed that the English Crown and Parliament had been plotting to reverse the course of history and once again conspiring against traditional liberty in their treatment of the colonies.[4] John Adams argued:

> [S]till more calamitous to human liberty, was a wicked confederacy between the two systems of human tyranny [the canon and the feudal law]... [A]s long as this confederacy lasted, and the People were held in ignorance; Liberty, and with her, Knowledge and Virtue too, seem to have deserted the earth; and one age of darkness, succeeded another, until GOD in his benign providence, raised up the champions, who began and conducted the *reformation* ... The people grew more and more sensible of the wrong that was done them, by these systems; more and more impatient under it; and determined at all hazards to rid themselves of it; till, at last, under the execrable race of the *Steuarts*, the struggle between the people and the confederacy aforesaid of temporal and spiritual tyranny, became formidable, violent and bloody. It was this great struggle, that peopled America ... [But now, there] seems to be a direct and formal design on foot, to enslave all Americans. The first step that is intended seems to be an entire subversion of the whole system of our Fathers, by an introduction of the cannon and feudal law, into America. The cannon and feudal systems, tho' greatly mutilated in England, are not yet destroy'd. Like the temples and palaces, in which the great contrivers of them, once worship'd and inhabited, they exist in ruins; and much of the domineering spirit of them still remains.[5]

The colonists' basic argument, therefore, called for resuming progress toward the recovery of the past. After the Revolution, American canons of interpretation, as well as post-Revolutionary reception statutes, provided that Americans had only adopted the common law insofar as it was suitable to its circumstances and republican principles. Thus the task of American lawyers was to *preserve* the common law's timeless principles and gradually adapting slow-growing

[4] *See generally* Bernard Bailyn, *Ideological Origins of the American Revolution* (1992); John Phillip Reid, "The Jurisprudence of Liberty: The Ancient Constitution in the Legal Historiography of the Seventeenth and Eighteenth Centuries," in *The Roots of Liberty* 147 (Ellis Sandoz ed., 1993).

[5] John Adams, "A dissertation on the Canon and the Feudal Law," in *Papers of John Adams* I:127 (Robert J. Taylor, Mary-Jo Kline, and Greg L. Lint (eds.), 1977).

good customs; but also to *accelerate* its dynamic aspects to move it forward out of feudalism and the hierarchies of the corrupt old world.

As republican lawyers forged links of continuity with the good past, they sought to accomplish Nietzsche's work of creative destruction, to sever or obliterate ties to the bad past. The evolving story had not only to erase the American common law's traces of its feudal past, but the radical revolutionary nature of its own creation. Among our most powerful and inspiring traditions are those of anti-traditionalist radicalism, or anti-legalist legalism, the examples of the "people out of doors" mobilizing to alter and abolish their form of government, or resisting legal enactments in the name of the higher laws of nature and of conscience; or, as Bruce Ackerman's work likes to emphasize, a history of the extra-legal construction of new constitutional foundations, which drive the novel system through by force and fiat and leave it to time and popular support to ratify and provide legitimacy. Lawyers felt constrained to reinterpret these episodes to smooth over the discontinuities. Nineteenth-century lawyers like Daniel Webster, retelling the story of our Constitutional founding, told it as if the Revolution had hardly even happened, or had only happened to repair a momentary lapse on the part of the British imperial government from attention to the gradual unfolding of constitutional protections of liberty and property. Arguing against the legitimacy of the Dorr Rebellion in Rhode Island, Webster said:

> American Liberty has an Ancestry, a Pedigree, a History. The leaders of Plym[outh] and Jamestown were Englishmen; leaving oppression & misrule, but bringing all the buds, & blossoms, & fruits of civil and religious liberty, at that time to be had ... They had close & controlling Colonial feelings, but they had also English feelings; learning, tastes, literature & prejudices ... Where the form of Govt. was already well enough, they let it alone; where necessary, they reformed it. Every where & in all things, they acted in a true *conservative* spirit.

Yet even such conservative extra-legal acts of rebellion that might have been justified then as emergency repair measures could hardly be justified now.

> Men cannot get together, count themselves, say they are hundreds or thousands, judge of their own qualifications, call themselves the *People* & then proclaim alterations of the fundamental law, or any other law ... Who wishes a tempestuous, stormy, violent liberty, without power, except in its spasms, tumultuary, mobocratic, terrifying the timid, & alarming the prudent: a South American liberty; supported by arms, today, crushed by arms tomorrow.[6]

Throughout the nineteenth-century republic this dynamic story would change little in its general outline. It was continuously rewritten to include

[6] Daniel Webster, Notes for Oral Argument [in *Luther* v. *Borden*, adjudicating the legality of the Dorr Rebellion of 1842 in Rhode Island], *The Papers of Daniel Webster: Legal Papers* (Andrew J. King, ed. 1989) III:751, at 753, 754 (1848).

later installments of liberalizing law: abolition of primogeniture and entail; of established churches, tithes, ecclesiastical courts and taxes to support religious teachers; of game laws; of imprisonment for debt and distress for rent; of indentured servitude and specific performance of the employment contract; of some of the disabilities of married women, such as the inability to own property, and contract on their behalf; of most forms of wage and price regulation; of the slave trade; and eventually, of course, of slavery itself, along with peonage. At each rewriting, the most recently discarded practice was relegated to the "feudal" past. As it was continuously rewritten, it was also generalized – lifting Sir Henry Maine's phrase out of its context as an account of the ancient patriarchal family – as a movement from status-to-contract, the story of the breakup of tribes, patriarchal families, fiefs, guilds, monopolies, legally maintained status relations; and their replacement by a legal regime of formally free equals whose social relations were instituted and governed by their wills, or consent (subject to the like rights of others and the requirements of public order and welfare).

This system, or rather, field of overlapping systems, could be turned at any moment to apologetic or critical purposes. Where it relied on static original principles, either those of the immemorial Gothic constitution, the written constitutions of the 1780s, or the Revolution's spirit of republican liberty, the apologist or conservative would urge its maintenance against subversion. The reformer by contrast could argue that the principles had already been corrupted or subverted, and that radical reformation was required to restore them, as for example antislavery lawyers used *Somersett's Case*, the Declaration of Independence, and Constitutional principles in order to deny Congressional power to establish slavery in the territories and to require Northern states to collaborate in the capture and return of fugitive slaves. Or the reformer could argue that what was defended as a static principle was an instance of cultural lag, a maladaptive or obsolete vestige of feudalism. In the antebellum U.S. these divergent possibilities of the narrative were played out in a conflict between Whig and radical narratives of legal history: Whigs told the story of slow continuity, of the common law as adaptive and self-reforming; the Revolution flattened down to an episode in a continuous history of settlement from colonial times, the Constitution and its subsequent development as a further chapter in the evolution of the common law. Radicals tended to emphasize discontinuity and break with tradition, the feudal and barbaric aspects of the common law, the desire to break with it altogether and escape from its artificial restraints – to replace legally-regulated social bonds between private parties by free contract, and the necessary collective restraints and regulations of communal life by legislation by means of wholesale codification – to escape from the artificial past altogether into a society in which individual and social obligations were created only by individual or majority will.

CLASSICAL LEGAL HISTORY

This is all – rather breathlessly – by way of background to the legal thought of what we now call the Classical period, roughly, 1860 to 1920. In Classical legal thought, the historical narratives of Whigs and radicals were blurred together in a teleological synthesis: the gradual development of the common law had been toward realization of radical principles. Judges were no longer considered the enemy, but the force best entrusted with those principles.

Later Progressive critics, looking back at the Classical system at its height, tended to misrepresent it as basically anti-historical in its modes of thought – devoted to large generalities of "natural rights of property" and "freedom of contract," or, alternatively, as something like Weber's notion of a formally rational legal system, a body of systematic principles aiming at complete autonomy from the social system; or else as embodying, in Justice Holmes's memorable phrase, "Mr. Herbert Spencer's Social Statics," that is, not autonomous at all but colonized by principles of classical political economy or Social Darwinism. What's common to all these accounts is the notion of a body of legal thought grounded in a priori principles. This view is pretty plainly mistaken – the classical period was saturated in historical thinking. Stephen Siegel has recently argued and I think rightly, that this is even and maybe especially true of the Constitutional thought of the time: theirs was an evolving Constitution, located in historical time.[7] The confusion arises because the logic of historical development, in the classical scheme, was leading a core group of legal principles toward a sort of historical climax, a form so pure that they could be abstracted from their development and treated as a priori principles.

The work of Thomas M. Cooley, the patron saint of these lectures and probably the greatest influence on Classical jurists' constitutional thought, supplies some good examples. As an old time Barnburner Jacksonian Democrat, Cooley was no apologist for corporate concentration, but he was intensely concerned to extract from the course of the unruly mass of common law decisions some general liberal principles to serve as a foundation for constitutional limits on the powers of legislatures to regulate economic activity.

Cooley concedes the general right and duty of government to regulate property and – then a novel term in legal analysis – "business"; and that the rules of property are inevitably regulations of property; that there are many such regulations and many of these are necessary. But there must be limits. Where are these to be found? In express constitutional limits, of course, but where else? One can look to history, that is, to common law precedent; but the problem with this is that one can find precedents for every conceivable kind of regulation – wage and price controls, sumptuary laws, restrictions on landholdings.

[7] Stephen Siegel, "Historism in Late Nineteenth Century Constitutional Thought," 1990 *Wisc. L. Rev.* 1431 (1990).

Cooley's principal bane, it turns out, is price regulation; but of course he knows that in world history, including that of the common law, usury has been more often condemned, and the price of money regulated, than not. Cooley has to argue for lifting restraints on trade despite their ubiquity in our mercantilist past. His solution is to show that the law, meaning constitutional as well as common law has been evolving, and the direction of its evolution is known. His arguments (like those of Justice Stephen Field) that the new Thirteenth and Fourteenth Amendments were designed to emancipate business enterprisers from excessive regulation, relied on a historical narrative according to which the common law had for centuries been working itself free of the twin evils of slavery and state-imposed monopolies, both interferences with the right of free men to choose their vocations.[8] The undeniable fact that so many residues of feudal and mercantilist interferences with free commerce and labor remained in the law could be explained, paradoxically, as one of the virtues of a system that evolved gradually rather than by violent irruptions of abstract codification in the French style. Thus Cooley on usury:

> The present argument has no concern with the policy of usury laws; but this may be safely affirmed, that no conclusion in favor of the constitutional right to limit the profits from kinds of property that were never in thrall can be drawn from the fact that corresponding restrictions are not yet wholly removed from property that was never emancipated... [T]here must be kept in view the manner in which the constitutional principles have come to America. They have not, to use the language of Burke in his Letter to the Old Whigs, "been struck out at an heat by a set of presumptuous men," but they have been evolved slowly, and under great trials and difficulties; some of them attained full and rounded proportions before others came to be more faintly recognized; the growth of all has been historical, circumstances first giving to one a prominence and a vigor, and afterwards another. With such a growth, a barbarous anomaly, never yet wholly eradicated, and standing among free principles as a great and striking exception, ought to be neither surprising nor misleading ...The historical development of a constitution... never was and never can be entirely symmetrical; and it must be admitted that the grand old common law, of which the American constitutional principles formed a part, and for which the fathers perilled and some of them gave up their lives, had embodied in it more than one feature of barbarism, and indeed, as many believe, is not yet wholly relieved of serious anomalies ...

The important thing, Cooley thought, was not to admit any more such aberrations.

> Whatever in modern times has generally been looked upon as being outside the sphere of legislation, should be regarded as finally eliminated from state authority. To do this is only to take notice of the steady growth of the free principles which have come from

[8] See among innumerable examples the argument for the butchers against the regulated monopoly in the *Slaughterhouse Cases*, 83 U.S. [16 Wall] 36 (1873), as a type of "involuntary servitude" [J. A. Campbell, Brief and Argument for the Plaintiffs in Error], and the opinion of Field, J. in dissent.

common-law rules and usages, and of their gradual expansion with the general advance in intelligence and independent thought and action among the people. The gradual transition from despotism to freedom has been mainly accomplished by the dropping out one by one of obnoxious and despotic powers, and by recognition of the changes effected as permanent modifications of the constitutional system.[9]

Most of the remaining known instances of regulation of prices and terms of service – such as the newly created constitutional doctrine permitting state regulation of industries "affected with a public interest" – can all be put into the special and exceptional category of monopolies, "natural" monopolies like grain elevators, of franchises established for public purposes, like innkeepers, common carriers, or licensed occupations. History here is used – as it often was by the Classical writers – in two ways. One is through its revelation of immemorial principles – the common law's hostility to monopoly – which is the Jacksonian hostility to chartered corporations projected back onto Whig history. The other is through the common law's gradual course of evolution away from artificial restraints. (Some juristic writers, though not Cooley himself, located American legal developments in other teleologies, such as the "Aryan" roots of Anglo-American civilization, carrying legal institutions in the blood of the "race"; or more prosaically with the prototype of American political institutions in the Teutonic forests.)

Yet when we look back at the body of classical law as a whole, its common law and statutory law as well as constitutional principles, we can see that this progress out of history to unrestricted liberty describes only a limited – though ideologically central – core of legal relationships. Different sectors of social life occupy different strata, different timelines of historical development. Take for example the labor contract or wage bargain.

In the general status-to-contract story, "history" with respect to a contracting person was a gradually disappearing encrustation of special privileges and disabilities. With respect to ordinary men, these were governed by the dynamic liberalizing story, to be sheared off as artificial and archaic. The ordinary contracting *sui juris* man – women of course were still burdened by legal disabilities believed appropriate to their dependent condition – was the outcome of an historical process that had divested him of historical attributes. He had no past that mattered; for legal purposes he was the American Adam, self-reliant and self-inventing, what Thomas Haskell calls an "uncaused cause."[10] In the most radical versions, the evolutionary process offered an escape from history as the final outcome of historical development – defined as the Old World's confining

[9] Thomas M. Cooley, "Limits to State Control of Private Business," *Princeton Review* 54:233, at 246, 269 (1878).

[10] Thomas L. Haskell, "Persons as Uncaused Causes: John Stuart Mill, the Spirit of Capitalism, and the "Invention" of Formalism," in *The Culture of the Market: Historical Essays* 474 (T. Haskell & Richard F. Teichgraeber eds., 1993).

webs of the artificial – altogether. Freed of artificial restraints, he could make contracts on any terms another would agree to.

Yet – back in the real world of the actual employment law of the time, revealingly called "master-servant" law, once having accepted a job, the workingman was enmeshed in a dense web of statutory and common law regulation, governing the relations of master and servant, taken from the pre-liberal context of domestic household relations. The servant was plainly subordinate in the relation, under the master's direction and control and bound to follow any reasonable order. His mobility was legally as well as practically limited – by his inability to recover partial wages if he quit before his term was up, by the tort of enticement, founded on the master's property in his labor, which would make another employer liable for trying to hire him away; by vagrancy statutes, which made his being visibly unemployed in public a crime.[11] The political scientist Karen Orren has used the suggestive label of "belated feudalism" to describe this law of labor relations. But the point to make is that this web of restraints was explained in the cases and treatises as simply the ordinary common law, the dense legacy of centuries of slow time. The enticement tort in the treatises, for example, was accompanied by wholly unembarrassed references to its origins in the medieval Statutes of Laborers (1351) and Apprentices (1353).

Progressive critics of the Classical system thought it nothing more than a fancy ideological cloak for laissez-faire, designed to insulate business from desirable regulation. Later historical work has clarified that this was a caricature, at least insofar as it accused the Classics of toadying to big business: most of them were hostile to corporate power as potentially illegitimate monopoly, and thought the political domination of corporations was inconsistent with the common law spirit of individual liberty. Indeed, as James May has pointed out, antitrust policy, first at the state and then at the federal level, designed to target and eliminate anti-competitive distortions of the market, was an essential component of the Classical framework of liberty and equality.[12] Ultimately it was the Progressives who came to accept and to legitimate corporate concentration, so long as it was regulated. We, looking back at the Classical system, may be just as likely to see an intensely hierarchical, authoritarian legally maintained network of both public and private regulation – relational hierarchies and "public order." It is both individualist and collectivist in its legal policies: the contracting individual is *sui juris* in the contracting moment; but both within the categories and in the law maintaining public order and "moral order" the

[11] On American law's folding of the employment relationship back into the preliberal status of Master and Servant, the best account is Christopher Tomlins, *Law, Labor and Ideology in the Early American Republic* (1993).

[12] James May, "Antitrust in the Formative Era: Political and Economic Theory in Constitutional and Antitrust Analysis, 1880–1918," 50 *Ohio St. L. Rev.* 257 (1989).

constitutive orders of the market and civil society, he is regulated and disciplined and molded by bundles of very specific laws.

PROGRESSIVE USES OF HISTORY

Progressive (or New Liberal) lawyers and jurists (of approximately 1890–1937) tried to define themselves in opposition to the Classical scheme. Yet their uses of history were remarkably similar. The Progressives preserved the basic dynamism of the narrative. Some of the Progressive lawyers, to be sure, were aggressively modernist in outlook, treating the past as a disposable nuisance. The only use for history in this mode was critical – to help shed the law of its cobwebs by showing it up as antique, irrelevant, rooted in barbaric or obsolete social contexts and outgrown conceptions. Some of our greatest jurists, like Justices Holmes and Cardozo, were modernists, if rather conservative modernists.[13] Holmes spoke for a generation in saying:

> From a practical point of view [history's] use is mainly negative and skeptical... [I]ts chief good is to burst inflated explanations. Every one instinctively recognizes that in these days the justification for a law for us cannot be found in the fact that our fathers have always followed it. It must be found in some help which the law brings toward reaching a social end which the governing power of the community has made up its mind that it wants... [H]istory is the means by which we measure the power which the past has had to govern the present in spite of ourselves, so to speak, by imposing traditions which no longer meet their original end. History sets us free and enables us to make up our minds dispassionately whether the survival which we are enforcing answers any new purpose when it has ceased to answer the old.[14]

History helps "you get the dragon out of the cave on to the plain and in the daylight you can count his teeth and claws, and see just what is his strength. But to get him out is only a first step. The next is either to kill him, or to tame him and make him a useful animal."[15] In this critical and modernist mode of Progressive history, it would be *legislation*, based on the latest social science, that would break the cake of custom and refashion the legal framework according to the dictates of utilitarian reason. The end-point in the most optimistic versions was the escape from history: and the promise of beginning anew with scientific social-welfare legislation.

But most Progressive jurists did not seek to escape from history, but rather pragmatically to reshape the law to conform to what they saw as the pace and tendencies of historical change. Legislation in their view was not against or out of custom, but *followed* custom, was now to be the primary method for

[13] *See*, e.g., Oliver Wendell Holmes, Jr., "The Path of the Law," in *Collected Legal Papers* 167 (1920); Benjamin Cardozo, *The Nature of the Judicial Process* (1921).

[14] Oliver Wendell Holmes, Jr., "Law in Science – Science in Law," in *Collected Legal Papers* 210, 225 (1920).

[15] Oliver Wendell Holmes, Jr., "The Path of the Law," in *Collected Legal Papers* 167, 187 (1920).

adapting law to social evolution. The old common law system had become dysfunctional, overtaken by events, had evolved too slowly to cope with the rapidly changing conditions of industrial society. They argued that the "individualist" premises of Classical legal thought, which had originated in the natural-law thinking of the seventeenth and eighteenth centuries, had functioned well enough in an older America – an agrarian society on an open frontier with abundant land, a society of small independent producers – but was wholly unsuited to an industrial society of giant organizations.[16] The realization of individual freedom in such a society, as Chief Justice Hughes put in a famous New Deal case, required "increased use of the organization of our society in order to protect the very bases of individual opportunity..."[17] Thus they revised the story of stages of development to which legal change should functionally adapt by inventing a new stage – that of industrial or collective society. Its implications for many Progressives were that the giant corporation should be legally naturalized – transformed from a monopoly or conspiracy into a person – but so should the labor union, and a new role recognized for the state in regulating both.[18]

In a deliberate ironic play on the standard narrative of liberty, the Progressives sometimes called the new social order a "New Feudalism."[19] What they meant by that was that in modern social conditions persons increasingly assumed a large part of their social identities and functions by virtue of memberships in collectives that imposed upon them standardized prescribed duties in their relations with others. Some of these relational duties were imposed by the custom or rules of the collective, others by the state. Some Progressives, like Pound himself, viewed the new feudalism as a basically benign development: its legal implications were simply that such new relations had made obsolete the classical codes of general rights and duties, and required more specialized regulation precisely configured to the relation – what Max Weber called "substantively" as opposed to "formally rational" law. For others, like Louis Brandeis, Walton Hamilton or Friedrich Kessler, the New Feudalism, like the old, posed novel threats of overweening private power: Lockean property had become corporate property, requiring new forms of regulation. Corporate interests used law, as Justice Brandeis put it in a case where an employer sought a labor injunction against picketing strikers, "not ordinarily to prevent property from being injured nor to protect the owner in its use, but to endow property with active, militant power which would make it dominant over men; in other words...

[16] *See* e.g., Roscoe Pound, "Liberty of Contract," 18 *Yale. L. J.* 454, 464–466 (1909).

[17] *Home Insurance Co.* v. *Blaisdell*, 290 U.S. 398, at 442 (1934). Hughes borrowed this language from his colleague Cardozo.

[18] *See*, among innumerable examples, Jeremiah Smith, "Crucial Issues in Labor Litigation," 20 *Harvard L. Rev.* 253 (1907); Walton Hamilton, "Property – According to Locke," 41 *Yale L. J.* 864 (1932).

[19] Roscoe Pound, "The New Feudalism," 16 *A.B.A. J.* 553 (1930).

under the guise of protecting property rights, the employer was seeking sovereign power."[20]

This was a cruel irony: The Progressives accused their Classical predecessors, who had taken so much trouble to locate their system as the end product of a gradual historical development, of being unhistorical "natural law" thinkers! But probably the most effective Progressive critique of Classical history was that that it had misread both tradition and tendency. To the extent it relied on tradition, it had often got it wrong: the essential spirit of the common law was to regulate market dominance and correct for market failures; regulation of usury was not an anomalous exception but a leading example; all callings, not just an exceptional few, were potentially affected with a public interest; the corporation owes its existence to state-granted privileges; the "*sic utere*" principle (so use your own as not to injure another's) in operation leads to regulated commons like riparian rights, and limits to contracting freedom like duress and fraud and to common law actions for restraint of trade. The new Progressive historians took apart the classics' generalized "liberty" to do as one will with one's property, to contract on whatever terms or pursue whatever vocation one pleases; such a generalized liberty, they argued, was never part of traditional "due process" or "the law of the land" but a modern invention.

Progressive legislation was thus of a continuous piece with common law tradition. It was also consistent with the broader course of legal evolution: the classical jurists' stories of status to contract, strict liability to negligence, collective liability to individual moral fault, communal to separate property, were all – many Progressives argued – misdescriptions of the course of actual legal development.

LECTURE 2: THE RIGHTS REVOLUTION AND CONSERVATIVE CHALLENGES

By the 1950s, the Progressive historical narratives had triumphed almost unopposed in American legal culture. The realization of the Progressive program at the national level in the New Deal seemed the fulfillment of legal progress: either as a successful adaptation of law to the changed circumstances of a more interdependent modern economy; as a perfection of the ideals of liberalism as Alexander Hamilton and John Marshall's "energetic national government" in the public interest that had unhappily been interrupted in the classical era of default; or, as with liability-expanding private law, as the common law adapting to new social conditions. This story was reinforced by a body of pioneering historical work uncovering a tradition of pragmatic state government planning in the public interest before the Civil War – the mercantilist-Whig or "commonwealth" tradition of financing public works

[20] *Truax* v. *Corrigan*, 257 U.S. 312 (1921), at 368 (Brandeis, J. dissenting)

by granting out public franchises.[21] The entire classical era, newly rechristened the "Lochner Era" in Constitutional Law casebooks edited by ex-New Dealers, was seen as an aberration, the era of "formalist" or "mechanical" jurisprudence; its low points, the *Lochner*, *Adkins*, *Adair*, and *Hammer* decisions, took the place that the excesses of Stuart or Hanoverian despotism had occupied in the Whig story.

THE RIGHTS REVOLUTION

The third great wave of liberal-legal ideologies, the "Rights Revolution" of the 1960s and 70s, engineered by the civil rights and feminist movement and by the Supreme Court under Chief Justice Earl Warren and the federal government under Presidents Lyndon Johnson and (surprisingly!) Richard Nixon, was also faithful to the dynamic narrative of liberal progress. This phase added a still further stage in the evolution of liberal societies: one in which the state had to act affirmatively to bring groups who had been excluded or subordinated into full legal citizenship: women, blacks and other minorities, underrepresented voters, aliens, the illegitimate, those accused of crimes, prisoners, mental inmates, welfare recipients; and also to impose new legal controls on bureaucratic government to make it more transparent and responsive. Some lawyers and judges pressed – though ultimately unsuccessfully – more radical claims as well: to the effective fulfillment of economic and social rights such as the right to a minimum standard of living.[22] But much of this rights-rhetoric was entirely tradition-based: the rights were not new, but simply required to fulfill America's original liberal promise under changed conditions – such as the traditional right to the protection of "property" in an age where property increasingly took the form of grants of state privileges, licenses, benefits or employment.[23] Justice William Brennan put it this way:

> Until the end of the 19th century, freedom and dignity in our country found meaningful protection in the institution of real property... [A] piece of land provided men not just with sustenance but with the means of economic independence, a necessary precondition of political independence and expression... But the days when common law property relationships dominated litigation and legal practice are past... [E]conomic existence now depends on less certain relationships with government... Now hundreds of thousands of Americans live... without any real prospect of the dignity and autonomy that ownership of real property could confer. Protection of the human dignity of

[21] Oscar & Mary Handlin, *Commonwealth: A Study of the role of Government in the American Economy: Massachusetts, 1774–1861* (1969); Louis Hartz, *Economic policy and democratic thought: Pennsylvania, 1776–1860* (1968); James Willard Hurst, *Law and the Conditions of Freedom in the Nineteenth Century United States* (1956).

[22] *See* Samuel Krislov, "The OEO Lawyers Fail to Constitutionalize a Right to Welfare," 58 *Minn. L. Rev.* 21 (1973).

[23] *See* Charles Reich, "The New Property," 73 *Yale L. J.* 733 (1964).

such citizens requires a much modified view of the proper relationship of individual and state.[24]

The overall historical story was reframed as that of the growth or modernization of "free" or "Western" societies, dropping, for obvious reasons, the older terminology of "Anglo-Saxon," "Teutonic," and "Aryan" peoples. With the passage of the Civil Rights Acts of 1964, 1965 and 1968, African-Americans resumed their journey out of slavery that had been interrupted by Redemption and Jim Crow; with the passage in Congress of the Equal Rights Amendment (by a vote of 354 to 245 in the House and 84 to 8 in the Senate) women continued their journey, which had begun with the Seneca Falls Declaration and continued with Married Women's Property and Earnings Acts and the Nineteenth Amendment, out of coverture.

CHALLENGES TO LIBERAL PROGRESS

To summarize: American legal argument from the Founding onward consistently relied upon a core narrative of liberal progress: the story of liberal modernization, by which law both followed and facilitated the evolution of society away from feudalism, tyranny and superstition, and toward increasing freedom. To reconcile this dynamic narrative with the need to assert continuity with fundamental principles, the story was often told in a teleological mode, as the gradual fulfillment of perfection of principles already immanent at the time of the Founding. As Abraham Lincoln said of the Declaration of Independence, which had declared all men to be created equal even as it established a polity that legalized slavery, the Declaration's authors:

> did not mean to assert the obvious untruth, that all were then actually enjoying that equality, nor yet, that they were about to confer it immediately upon them. In fact they had no power to confer such a boon. They meant simply to declare the *right*, so that the *enforcement* of it might follow as fast as circumstances should permit. They meant to set up a standard maxim for free society, which should be familiar to all, and revered by all; constantly looked to, constantly labored for, and even though never perfectly attained, constantly approximated, and thereby constantly spreading and deepening its influence, and augmenting the happiness and value of life to all people of all colors everywhere.[25]

The core narrative underwent important mutations in its phases as Classical-liberal, Progressive, and Rights-Revolution ideology. Each phase always had its critics – reactionaries claiming that a new mutation was a betrayal of liberal principles, radicals that progress was not moving nearly fast or far enough to effective realize the core principles.

[24] Justice William J. Brennan, "The Constitution of the United States: Contemporary Ratification," in *The Debate over the Constitution* 23, at 29 (Jack Rakove, ed., 1990).

[25] Abraham Lincoln, Speech on Dred Scott Decision, Jun. 26, 1857, in Abraham Lincoln, *Speeches & Writings, 1832-1858* 390, at 398 (1989).

By the late 1960s and 1970s, the radical critiques intensified. At first the critiques came from the Left – from civil rights lawyers, organizers of poor communities and workers, feminists and anti-Vietnam-War activists, who, embittered by growing conservative resistance and backlash to the insurgent social movements of the 1960s, began to lose faith in liberal progress; and to diagnose economic, racial, and gender inequality as stemming from *permanent* structures of oppression (capitalism, racism, patriarchy) – structures that might vary over time in particular details, but constantly took on new and virulent mutant forms.[26] Some of these activists kept alive utopian-socialist hopes of Revolution; more often they were inclined to settle into a kind of grim historical pessimism or – as in the case of black radicals who adopted the rhetoric of Third World anticolonialist nationalism – to pursue a limited political strategy of separation from, rather than reform of, the wider society.[27]

THE CONSERVATIVE CHALLENGE

In the meantime another set of challenges was brewing on the Right – one that was to be much more consequential, since Reagan's victory in 1980 suddenly swept into the federal executive and judiciary a cadre of legal intellectuals: libertarians and law-and-economics scholars from the University of Chicago and various conservative think-tanks. The lawyers of the Reagan Revolution came to power determined to do to the entrenched Progressive histories what the Progressives had done to the Classics: to substitute a new story, with different heroic agents and a different ending, into the standard narrative structure of the history of liberal society. Theirs was an undertaking against obstacles. They captured less of the judicial and political machinery; and much less of the legal-academic intelligentsia; and have had to make their way in an intellectually hostile environment (indeed they behaved as a persecuted remnant even at height of their power). In Constitutional law they have had to compromise on some of their most visible agenda items – such as recriminalization of abortion and an end to affirmative action. But elsewhere in legal thought and practice their influence has been deep and pervasive – and has posed the most serious challenge yet to the long reign of Progressive orthodoxy.

At first glance, the most striking feature of conservative legal thought seems to be its historical pessimism – its apparent rejection of the dynamic narratives of legal change, especially as embodied in the notions of an "evolutionary" or "living" Constitution that the Classical and Progressive jurists had held in common. Modern conservative legal thought has a decidedly nostalgic impulse, to reproach modernist culture by reaching back into something before it: its discourses on social life follow the form of the jeremiad: a lament

[26] *See*, e.g., Derrick Bell, *Race, Racism and American Law* (1973).
[27] *See* Gary Peller, "Race-Consciousness," *Duke L. J.* 758 (1990).

over the declension of current generations from some exemplary golden age or founding principles, usually followed, in the optimistic American vein, by an account of how, despite backsliding, with repentance and discipline, the principles may be restored in an even better form. Progress and restoration are ingeniously combined, as in the teleological mode in which the evolution of common law and constitution are always working themselves pure toward the realization of the highest version of their own truest and most ancient virtues – as many of the Revolutionary generation for example believed that thanks to the Whiggish spirit of commerce and liberty American society was gradually realizing – or re-realizing – the principles of free alienability of land labor and capital embodied in ancient Anglo-Saxon allodial tenures. So the designers of the legal-political ideological imagery of the Reagan Revolution made it out that, with effort, we could be ceaselessly moved forward into our virtuous past of intact and solidary family life, shared and rigorously enforced moral and religious convictions, and the unregulated pursuit of acquisition.

Of course the historical view with which conservative lawyers are mostly identified is not a dynamic one at all – even a reactionary dynamism – but the static, reactionary one of frozen time: the various "originalist" theories of Constitutional interpretation – in their extreme forms, the views that the contemporary drafters' intentions or ratifiers' understandings or "public meanings" of the Constitutional texts of 1787, 1793 and 1868 should be the exclusive resources of Constitutional interpretation. Judging by gross volume of paper produced, originalist exegesis is where President Reagan's lawyers invested most of the resources they had to spend on history. The Attorney-General in a well-reported speech announced originalist hermeneutics as official government policy; and for a while the Justice Department's Office of Legal Policy resembled the anteroom of a seventeenth-century Stuart Parliament, humming with antiquarian researchers reporting excited discoveries in ancient parchments.[28]

The originalist virus never infected many of the most prominent jurists of the 1980s – Judge Richard Posner and Solicitor General Charles Fried, for example, remained immune; but it had brilliant and influential promoters in Chief Justice William Rehnquist, Justice Antonin Scalia and almost-Justice Robert Bork. As many observers of these judges have noticed, their originalism owes little to reverence toward the past or to the Founding Moments for their own sake. These are not Straussian conservatives who believe that the Founders were possessed of exemplary virtue or wisdom. Though Bork frequently invokes the name of Burke, and Scalia the binding force of "tradition," neither has much tincture of the common-law mentality, the respect for the irreducible particulars of customs accreting over slow time, the disposition to

[28] *See* Office of Legal Policy, Department of Justice, *Report to the Attorney General: The Constitution in the Year 2000 – Choices Ahead in Constitutional Interpretation*, October 11, 1998.

accept what is because it has been a long time building. With notable exceptions such as Professor Michael McConnell, they have much more in common with Bentham than with Hale or Burke or even Blackstone; they are positivists, who search the legal universe for authoritative commands, preferably those reducible to the form of code-like rules of general application. The past is valuable only insofar as it can furnish us with definite rules of decision: if it cannot, look elsewhere. Justice Scalia has a very complex package of hermeneutic formulae: to read specific enumerated Constitutional rights, use evidence of original context: to test claims of rights based on broad Constitutional texts or "penumbras," look for specific supporting or refuting "traditions," preferably state statutes on the subject enacted around the 1780s or 1860s; but to read statutes, go by their texts – that is, lift them altogether out of their originating context and follow their plain meanings.

Ironically, in their insistence that the "rule of law is a law of rules," the originalist jurists are swimming somewhat against what we have seen is the actual tradition of American historical jurisprudence, which is that of common-law dynamic adaptationism, given content and direction by a healthy hormone injection of liberal modernization theory. Many conservative nineteenth-century lawyers resisted codification because they supposed that its formulae would straitjacket legal development: the last thing they wanted was to anchor the Constitution and common law to America's mercantilist (and pro-slavery) past. Progressive jurists' most telling objections to the most analytic versions of classical legal science were similar: rule-formalism is "mechanical," inflexible, prevents adaptation to changing conditions.

Of course even codified texts in a legal regime that instructs judges to look each time only at the code and not at the subsequent glosses have a built-in flexibility – as social contexts and linguistic usages change, applications will change regardless of anyone's intentions. Strict originalism seems to want to freeze meanings against erosion by time; and this is rather hard to achieve. One can of course seek to state the original principle at a high enough level of abstraction so that it can be lifted above context altogether, which leaves it free to float and soak up later experience; or, more imaginatively, to work toward a faithful "translation" of the principle, so that it will have similar or analogous effects in the new context to those aimed for in the old;[29] but in choosing either of these strategies one will leave strict originalism far behind. If one takes one's originalism as a serious project of historical reconstruction, if one goes back in time to dredge up all the concrete practices of reading and applying the rule that once defined its practical meaning – one will usually discover a quite unmanageable degree of conflicting and ambiguous views. One will also find that the meanings of even the most basic terms – "property" and "liberty"

[29] See Mark Tushnet, "Following the Rules Laid Down," 96 *Harvard L. Rev.* 781 (1983); Lawrence Lessig, "Fidelity in Translation," 71 *Texas L. Rev.* 1165 (1993).

and "legislature" and "court" – have been greatly altered between that day and this.

And of course one will also find a lot of stuff that one really dislikes and cannot possibly convert to modern use. New Right jurists like to point out, for example, that in 1787 nobody could have dreamed that one day lawyers would be able to persuade some courts that the Constitution prohibits legislatures from enacting the death penalty, or criminal penalties for abortion or for homosexual acts: on such issues arguments from "original meanings" seem to have clear present value. But the original Framers also believed some much less convenient things: that their Constitution forbade the national government to issue paper money or to build a national road system; that its protections for "freedom of speech" did not prevent governments from criminal prosecutions of their political enemies for libels against officials; that the Constitutional protection of "free exercise of religion" was compatible with state legislation of civic disabilities for Catholics and Jews; that property in slaves and even the slave trade were to be protected against emancipators; that the President must conduct foreign policy, especially wars and other hostile engagements, under the close supervision of Congress. We could not restore that world of eighteenth-century political culture if we wanted to – and nobody, including the New Right, seriously wants to. Just quoting snippets of words sliced out of the past, eighteenth-century gentlemen barking at us half-intelligible commands that we are supposed to obey without question, with no account of what happened in between then and now that might speak to their application (or lack of it) to our current condition, seems to be a recipe for making us credulous idiots, cultists trying to interpret inscrutable commands from Dephi. The more dynamic readings of history have the advantage over originalism of giving us a method – however mythic and simple-minded that method may sometimes be – of connecting our present to our past in such a way as to argue that some story of progress or intervening experience has made pieces of the original understanding irrelevant, dead, anachronistic, obsolete.

As a practical matter the New Right jurists' commitments to originalist method could only be inconstant and fitful, and so indeed it has turned out. They use history when it suits their purposes, distort it or abandon it when it doesn't. In short, their uses of history are like those of any other lawyers – forensic and highly selective. It turns out that it is only quite recent history, not the nation's entire history, which the New Right wants to undo. Judge Bork – although convinced that the original scheme had been deformed almost at the very start by the Marshall Court – would have been largely content if we repealed only recent atrocities, such as *Roe* v. *Wade* – and refrained from deforming it any further. Bork's theory added riders that accepted most subsequent Constitutional changes as validated by prescription and long usage, which a prudent regard for structures built around reliance interests would hesitate to disturb; and accepted still other departures from original readings, such as the *Brown* case, as validated by changes in circumstances – though he continued to insist that changing *values* could not count as relevant changing circumstances.[30] In interpreting the anti-trust statutes he wholly ignored the historical context of their framing, and presumed them to enact a general "efficiency" norm whose content is to be supplied by modern Chicago-economic theory rather than the enacting Congress's.[31] Justice Scalia, as already mentioned, likewise rejects the use of history altogether to interpret statutes; and deploys it very selectively in Constitutional interpretation. In separation-of-powers cases he is given to rather grand freehanded improvisation of principles from the structure of the document, which leads him to such conclusions as that the Congress may not create a special prosecutor supervised by the courts instead of the President because prosecution is a "core executive" function, and that Congress may not give standing to citizens to sue for on Federal statutes unless they have been personally injured by the violation – conclusions quite contrary to well-established eighteenth- and nineteenth-century legal conventions.

The heart of the conservatives' legal program is not really, except perhaps in a few areas like religion and capital punishment, animated by a hankering after eighteenth-century values. Originalism began its career less a method of giving content to Constitutional rights than of limiting the invention of new rights to liberty and property. Here the Reagan-era judges mostly took as their models Progressive-generation jurists, Holmes, Brandeis and Frankfurter, the critics of *Lochner* and "judicial activism" and "substantive due process." This emphasis was perhaps at least partly tactical: most of the excesses of the regulatory-welfare state could be more effectually dealt with through gaining control of the executive than by reorienting the judiciary to a theory of Constitutionalized economic liberties. The overall formula of "restraint" could satisfy the twin conservative agendas of deregulation in economic matters and the restoration of "traditional" authority in social ones: the courts have been more inclined to "defer" to executive agency decisions that soften or nullify regulatory legislation by interpretation or inaction; to executive assertions of authority based on national security; and above all to the authority of public agencies at every level to direct (or neglect) the lives of subordinates and dependents like schoolchildren, asylum inmates, nursing home residents, public housing tenants, prisoners, schoolchildren, welfare recipients, public employees – all the old wards of the Warren Court. In the social polemics of conservatives, the federal courts' role in loosening traditional-hierarchical bonds maintained by these authorities is often pointed to as the root cause of the malaise of the 1960s and 70s – crime and defiance of law, permissiveness, idleness, the collapse of families, the decay of morals, litigiousness, and dependence on the state rather than individual efforts for the hope of improvement. By this means conservatives could tar their liberal opponents with the reactionary sin of Lochnerism.

[30] *See generally* Robert Bork, *The Tempting of America: The Political Seduction of the Law* (1989).
[31] *See generally* Robert Bork, *The Antitrust Paradox: A Policy at War with Itself* (1993).

Examined more closely, conservative legal histories fit nicely into the conventional narrative structures of American legal argument. Often they begin with the jeremiad, but end up promising redemption: the story of legal liberalism has only been sidetracked, and with proper adjustments can be rerouted back to the main line. The problems with the legal system can be largely analyzed as departures from some set of historically validated "traditional" baselines – past beliefs or practices, past trajectories.

Yet the call to restore "original intent" was obviously much more than a legal strategy: it was meant to underscore the theme of declension, to summon the past to reproach the present.

Chiefly, the attempt is to revive the condition not of late-*eighteenth*-century law but what they imagine to have been late-nineteenth-century law, or Classical liberal legalism. Most of the New Right intellectuals admire that regime for what they believe to have been its devotion to laissez-faire capitalism and the minimal state.[32] Some of the very same intellectuals admire the authoritarian social control of that period, by both state and civil society, of deviant behavior. Many legal intellectuals of the New Right have sought faithfully to revive almost all the main features of (what they imagine to have been[33]) the Classical-liberal legal regime, in private law as well as public law: tort law restored to the regime of minimal liability for harms caused by business enterprises; contract law restored to the principle of strict formal enforcement limited only by the most narrowly defined defenses of force and fraud; labor law restored to the unrestricted employment-at-will doctrine (that is, the doctrine that employees may be fired at any time for any reason or no reason); the corporation conceived as nothing more than an aggregation of individual contracts. In public law: a well-policed public–private boundary, strictly limiting the government's capacity to invade or regulate property without compensation, but removing all limits to the capacity of private owners to regulate those on their property; in the criminal law, an increased unwillingness of judges to supervise the police, or to regulate searches, arrests, detentions, interrogations, and conditions of confinement. In general: the restoration of the nineteenth-century belief in the superior efficiency of judge-declared common law to legislation as a mode of law-making. The resemblances in form are as striking as those of substance: the neoclassicals emulate the Classical taste for decontexualized principles at a high degree of generality, indeed for seeing the entire body of law as a system capable of being organized by a few basic conceptions that cut across doctrinal categories like contract, tort, and property, and across the divide between public and private law; for formally realizable, bright-line rules. They echo as

[32] *See* e.g., Bernard Siegan, *Economic Liberties and the Constitution* (1980).

[33] This qualifying phrase is needed because late-nineteenth-century private-law doctrine is often badly misdescribed by both its admirers and detractors. It was by no means so consistently favorable to the interests of business enterprises, or so strict and formal in contract enforcement, as it is often pictured.

well the classical distaste for the main tool of post-Progressive jurisprudence, the open-ended standard, the highly context-specific multi-factor balancing test. Above all perhaps the neoclassics share with the Classics – but one has to say they share it with the most self-assured Progressives too – a remarkable confidence in the power of correct scientific and legal methods to yield right answers uncorrupted by inappropriate judgments of value and politics; and in the determinacy of linguistic and social texts: the plain and objective meaning of statutory language or original intentions; rules and facts as hard data rather than constructed artifacts; and the disposition to respond to skepticism and claims of indeterminacy with bluff assertion.

With these and many similar doctrines much of the Classical edifice has been rebuilt brick by brick by legal intellectuals[34] – and in much of the legislation proposed by the current Congress and in decisions by the emerging New Right majority of the current Supreme Court, and especially in routine private-law decisions of state courts, many of these ideas are once again becoming law.

The most astonishing of the revivals – the more so because it seems to be a completely unconscious imitation of its nineteenth-century predecessors, the historical jurists – has been the revival among Chicago law-and-economics scholars of a customary-evolutionary theory of the common law: the Hayekian theory that judge-made law, unlike legislation, evolves by a process of natural selection or "spontaneous order" toward "efficient" legal rules.[35] Once naturalized in this way, common law property, tort, and contract rules could again function as the default legal constitution of the "private" market, any major changes in which by legislation would appear as excrescences, superimpositions, "artificial" acts of "intervention."

While conservative lawyers were renaturalizing something like the classical common law, they were also devastating the statutory and administrative legacies – the regulatory welfare state – left by its Progressive critics. In this they were aided by real history: a series of historical case-studies showing that regulation has usually been sought by regulated interests for their own ends: economic regulation was thinly disguised cartel enforcement; spending programs were mostly handouts to special business or middle-class beneficiaries. In its strong versions, the theory condemns almost all the legislative output of Parliamentary democracies as a kind of legalized theft.[36]

[34] The leading figure in the classical reconstruction is Professor Richard Epstein of the University of Chicago. *See*, e.g., Epstein, *Takings: Private Property and the Power of Eminent Domain* (1985); *Forbidden Grounds: The Case Against Employment Discrimination Law* (1995).

[35] *See* George L. Priest, "The Common Law and the Efficient Selection of Legal Rules," 6 *Journal of Legal Studies* 65 (1977); Paul H. Rubin, "Why is the Common Law Efficient?" 6 *Journal of Legal Studies* 51 (1977).

[36] *See* Daniel Farber and Philip Frickey, *Law and Public Choice* (1991) for an overview and informed critique of such theories.

To summarize, then: the New Right makes at least three kinds of historical claims. (1) There is a set of basic norms and principles that should be treated as the basic ground-rules of the American political, economic and social system: entitled to authority because they have been historically encoded in foundational legal forms (the original Constitutions, and common-law and legislative traditions). (2) At some point in historical time – exactly *which* point shifts around quite a bit, but the preferred location is the mid-to-late-nineteenth century – these basic ground-rules were actually in force, with beneficial results for individual freedom, national prosperity, and social cohesion and morals. (3) In more recent periods (in economic regulation, the 1930s to the present; in race relations, the period of "affirmative action" beginning in 1965; in social policy, the 1960s) the basic rules have been radically departed from, violated or distorted, with predictably horrible effects on freedom, prosperity, and morals. In these narratives – to cite the most striking example – the United States' tragic and bloody history of racial oppression, from slavery through legally enforced segregation, can be interpreted as a misguided departure from laissez-faire principles: that is, as having resulted from as excessive use of the state's police power to limit the free market competition that would in short order have eradicated racial discrimination.

CONSERVATIVE NARRATIVES OF CIVIL RIGHTS

The revival of something resembling the Classical-market-framework rules and the critique of legislation unduly altering those rules as unwarranted and self-destructive interferences, has carried over into public law – and especially to the civil rights debate. Again judging by volume of output, no legal issue has been more important to the conservative lawyers than government policies targeted at improving the life-chances of African-Americans and other marginalized ethnic groups; and none save perhaps economic regulation and church-state separation – has called forth a greater volume of historical narrative.[37]

For about the first two-thirds of the twentieth century, most conservative lawyers were unrelentingly hostile to liberal movements and legal doctrines promoting black equality.[38] Their history was Dunning-School history: the Civil War was fought to preserve states' rights; Reconstruction was a corrupt shambles of carpet-bagger-Negro misgovernment imposed by Northern radicals

[37] I have cobbled together the narrative that follows from several sources – briefs filed by President Reagan's Justice Department in the Supreme Court, speeches of William Bradford Reynolds and other Justice Department lawyers, a book by Terry Eastland and William Bennett, *Counting by Race: Equality from the Founding Fathers to Bakke and Weber* (1979) and the dicta of Supreme Court Justices in some of the major cases.

[38] I'm excepting a tiny handful of conservative lawyers like Moorfield Storey, the first President of the NAACP, who took the Reconstruction Amendments and the norm of formally-equal-treatment seriously enough to adopt the cause of black equality.

at the point of a gun; Redemption and its Jim Crow laws protecting white supremacy, disenfranchising blacks and excluding them from government and juries, and segregating schools and public spaces, promoted peace and good order valued by both races. The Southern states were special regions with their own customs, which states-rights doctrine allowed them to preserve; Southern blacks, under the benevolent tutelage and supervision of whites, were gradually progressing to higher stages of education and competence. The Supreme Court's command in *Brown* to end segregation was an unconstitutional federal interference by race radicals and Communists, which called for massive resistance. Yet massive resistance slowly yielded to grudging acceptance of the antisegregation principle announced in *Brown*, coupled with subtle evasive actions designed to prevent its effective implementation. By the 1960s, conservative leaders like Barry Goldwater and Ronald Reagan agreed that discrimination by race was morally wrong, but opposed the sections of the Civil Rights Acts forbidding private businesses to discriminate in employment and terms of service and homeowners to discriminate in sales or rentals, on the grounds that they violated states' rights and interfered with people's basic rights of property and liberty to deal with anyone they choose.

By the time of Reagan's election in 1980, however, conservatives had largely accepted not only *Brown*, but also the Civil Rights Acts of 1964 and the Voting Rights Act of 1965, and settled on a new historical narrative, one of gradual progress toward the realization of a basic norm of moral and legal equality – formal equality or "colorblindness." Their histories of the law of race relations now ran as follows: A basic norm of formal equality was memorably announced in the Declaration of Independence: the compromise on slavery in the Constitution was a regrettable deviation made necessary as the original price of Union. The norm nonetheless continued to be articulated by diverse prophets such as abolitionists and Quakers, and was adopted by Lincoln. Progress toward fulfilling the norm by prohibiting slavery in the territories was thwarted by an irresponsible outburst of judicial activism, Chief Justice Taney's opinion in the *Dred Scott* case. The norm however eventually triumphed in the Reconstruction Amendments; and was given its best formulation by the elder Justice Harlan's dissent in *Plessy* v. *Ferguson*: "Our Constitution is colorblind." Thereafter the norm unfortunately languished unrealized for decades in the South under Jim Crow, until triumphantly vindicated in the *Brown* case, the civil rights movement led by Dr. King, and the Civil Rights Act of 1964 – all of which were directed at removing race-based classifications from the law. In 1965 however civil rights policy took a disastrously wrong turn, deviating from the ideal of colorblindness and embracing instead "equality of result" in policies like busing of schoolchildren to ensure racial balance, hiring and admissions programs setting quotas to ensure proportional representation, and rules requiring "set-asides" for minority contractors. Such misguided policies have perpetuated the evils both of race-consciousness and of the paternalist welfarism that promotes dependence and subverts the dignity of reward by merit. In fact, even well-intentioned race-conscious policies favoring African-Americans result from the *same kinds of errors*, and are ultimately *just as evil*, as legal segregation and disenfranchisement. To be sure, some vestiges of racism persist, but in isolated pockets. Such differences in outcome as might remain under an ideally administered colorblind system would result chiefly from natural differences in talents and preferences; only to a slight extent from residual racial animus, which will disappear in the long run and in the short can be remedied through lawsuits brought under the Civil Rights statutes, limited to targeting intentional acts of discrimination, perpetrated by identifiable parties against identifiable victims.

This story has several aspects of great interest to the collector of historical narratives.

1. One is the way in which it isolates a single norm of legal equality – the norm of "moral equality" or perhaps of "meritocracy" expressed in the notion of "colorblindness" – and projects it into the past as the consensus or dominant norm. The colorblindness principle is validated by deep time: History is used here to certify the norm as one of long standing and general acceptance in our culture. Unfortunately for this view the official location for the norm can hardly be the original Constitution, with its carefully constructed political arrangements designed precisely to forestall emancipation. Therefore, like the abolitionists and Frederick Douglass and Lincoln before them, conservatives relocate it in the Declaration of Independence. Nor can the norm find much support, over most of our history, in the common consensus of white Americans, which as Rogers Smith has shown in exhaustive detail was overwhelmingly that the United States was a white man's republic in which, if blacks were to be allowed at all, they must occupy naturally subservient places.[39]

Indeed so far from being a mainstream or consensus norm, the norm of legal equality of the races has had to be carried for much of its history by radical dissidents, protestors, outsiders, like the Quaker abolitionist Anthony Benezet, democratic socialists like Bayard Rustin or Martin Luther King, Jr., or Communist activists like Angelo Herndon. Of course such genealogies aren't unusual in reform movements: many of the heroic agents of the Whig story of liberty are disreputable riffraff – Puritan dissenters like John Lilburne or rabble-rousers like John Wilkes or Sam Adams. But "colorblindness" has an exceptionally frail pedigree as a candidate for a mainstream American norm: race, like sex, almost always was subject to anomalous legal treatment. The Northern states gradually abolished slavery via the common law or statutory emancipation acts, but at the same time segregated and disenfranchised their black populations. And as Harlan wrote, his country was not only ratifying Jim Crow,

[39] Rogers Smith, *Civic Ideals: Conflicting Visions of Citizenship in U.S. History* (1997).

but adopting explicitly race-based immigration restrictions and allowing the Southern states to cancel the right of blacks to vote and the Northern states to segregate their neighborhoods.

Perhaps the most difficult hurdle the theory of colorblindness as a traditional American norm has to clear is not so much that of contrary practices – social practice after all often contradicts ideals, even consensus ones – is that although some white Americans did perceive slave or subordinate status for blacks as a betrayal of the American Creed, for many more whites, and not only in the South, black subordination was perceived not as a contradiction but a condition of their freedom. It was the condition, as Edmund Morgan put it, that enabled them to be the self-sufficient independent yeoman freeholders that they aspired to be.[40] During the Reconstruction era it's pretty clear that most whites, including Northerners, did not think formal equality of civil rights incompatible with continuing "de facto" segregation; though the blatant segregation of facilities by Jim Crow laws might make Northern whites wince, they could achieve the same results by various exclusionary practices: concerted refusals to deal and hire, union rules, restrictive real estate covenants, official government policy of refusing to underwrite mortgages on properties in black neighborhoods, and officially tolerated violence.

Advocates of the colorblindness norm argue, if only implicitly, that the historical norm has been one of "merit," that we are too judged by our individual capacities (natural and acquired), as Martin Luther King, Jr. memorably put it, the "color of our character," not of our "skin." Of course meritocracy is a notoriously slippery concept; and capacities can never in any case be wholly "individual;" but let's take the assertion in its narrowest sense, to mean that at least certain inherited characteristics (race, ethnicity, religion, national origin) are to be treated as irrelevant in decisions to grant access to avenues of opportunity – especially education and jobs. I have yet to find a conservative text in which anyone tries to specify when this norm was supposed to have prevailed. Of course one can find general expressions of the norm in the Revolutionary and Jacksonian attacks on traditional distinctions of rank and kinship and monopoly privileges as artificial barriers to the career open to talents; and then again in the "merit" norms for civil service examinations. But the abiding practice has always been to evaluate capacity and distribute opportunity in part by racial and ethnic (and gender) stereotypes. Under the legal threat and moral pressure of civil rights laws, the incidence has been waning, though there's plenty of evidence that it's still pervasive.

Some conservatives do of course have an answer to this, that in the absence of state-maintained discrimination, concerted private exclusion is always unstable – most of it will break down under competitive pressure. A chapter

[40] Edmund Morgan, *American Slavery – American Freedom – The Ordeal of Colonial Virginia* (1975).

of Professor Epstein's book on antidiscrimination law, called "History," argues that if *Lochner* had been applied consistently, Jim Crow would have been struck down as exceeding the state police power.[41] Some employers of the period in the South hired blacks and would have hired more if not for private violence (clearly prohibited under his scheme) and union threats.

Sometimes all that's meant by the norm is that the state is forbidden to use formal racial classifications (except, the usual qualification goes, to order specific perpetrators to correct specific acts of discrimination). Here the history that's left out is the long history of how much racial oppression can be accomplished by underground means without the benefit of legislative racial classifications. Southern sheriffs did not need Black Codes or Jim Crow laws to keep blacks off the voting rolls or jury pools; nor employers to confine them to the most menial jobs; nor farmers to cheat black contract laborers or sharecroppers out of their wages; nor coalitions of politicians, neighborhood groups, businesses and real-estate agents to confine northern blacks of whatever class within the boundaries of urban ghettoes; nor business or professional associations to exclude them from membership.

2. The norm of colorblindness is validated, in the conservative legal histories, not just by its (rather shaky) pedigree as a traditional consensus norm, but by its adoption by the civil rights movements themselves, before they strayed off the track in 1965. In itself the invocation of movement ideals is admirable: there is no reason why the equivocal and often resistant white majority should have the authority to give approved content of legal victories won through the struggles of others. But the civil rights movements' ideals have obviously been much broader than "colorblindness" for formal equality and reducing them to colorblindness means shearing off many of their distinctive elements.

(a) One is the antisubordination norm The Thirteenth Amendment itself, it is now generally accepted, reflects the "free labor" ideal, which was as much an anti-subordination ideology as one promoting mobility on the basis of "individual" talents and achievements: the aim was to promote in smallholders and workingmen republican independence, autonomy from the authority and control of others.[42] Conservatives regularly invoke the name of Martin Luther King, Jr. to sacralize the colorblindness norm – but never mention of the democratic-socialist second phase of his movement – which acknowledged that racial subordination would never be overcome through legal equality, but would require a redistribution of property and material advantage.

[41] Richard Epstein, *Forbidden Grounds: The Case Against Employment Discrimination Laws* 98–99 (1992).

[42] *See* Lea S. VanderVelde, "The Labor Vision of the Thirteenth Amendment," 138 *U. Pa. L. Rev.* 437 (1989).

(b) Another normative aspiration of the movements whose omission is really astonishing is that of integration! In nearly all the materials, I've examined, integration as a goal of the civil rights movement outside the context of public accommodations like buses, trains, parks, hotels, restaurants and stores is just not mentioned! – as if the uses of federal power to integrate schools and colleges had never happened.

(c) Less surprisingly, conservatives say nothing about race-relations aspirations that emerged in the later phases of the civil rights movement: that blacks within American society had become an "estate" (or "nation"), requiring either formal separation from the white-dominated polity, or proportionate or corporatist representation within it. This although hardly contrary to American historical practice – consider distribution of public contracts or employment or welfare benefits by political patronage, corporatist representation of various groups on public bodies and in unions, de facto representation in pluralist bargaining in the administrative process – never achieved the status of a respectable legal claim.

3. So much for the history of the norm. What of the history of its realization? One usually expects of conservative narratives a feeling for the sheer weight of history, the slowness to respond to efforts to cut across accumulated custom, the gradual nature of evolutionary change. And in fact the initial conservative objections to *Brown* and the Civil Rights Acts were that long-embedded social customs could not be altered overnight through legislation and court orders. In the current narratives however, the weight of history disappears almost entirely – now the 1964 Act is supposed to have achieved its purposes of equalizing opportunity almost from the moment of its enactment. The premises are those of Classical theory: without the distortions created by legally imposed disabilities, everybody is as free and prosperous as he can be, and is rewarded in proportion to his talents and efforts.

Yet if all the colorblindness norm means is that state agencies may not explicitly classify people by race as they distribute benefits, opportunities, privileges, and penalties, one might argue that it still permits – perhaps even sometimes encourages – everyone else to do so. Real, socially accepted colorblindness – colorblindness as a matter-of-fact taken-for-granted aspect of social life – colorblindness that would mean being black or brown was no more significant than being of Italian or Polish origin – colorblindness meaning that nobody in a position to grant access to economic or social opportunities would make assumptions about individual capacities on the basis of skin color alone – such a condition would have required a revolution in perceptions that could only happen after a massive sea-change eliminating, not simply "prejudice," but all sources of systemic inequality. Perhaps something like that social revolution, an elimination of the structural barriers to upward mobility and equal treatment and respect for all the poor, was the ultimate goal of

Lyndon Johnson's Great Society. That program however ran out of money and political support. It was both too expensive, and too disruptive to vested rights, to dismantle structural barriers, to equalize economic opportunity in some meaningful sense. The conservative critics of affirmative action, one might argue, got their critique exactly backwards – the problem with the program for the promotion of African-Americans into the middle class and elite professions through affirmative-action enforcement was not that it was a radical leap beyond the traditional norm of equalizing opportunity, but a disappointing retreat from it – an attempt to improve life-chances for a few beneficiaries rather than equalize them for all.

LECTURE 3: THE STAKES OF LEGAL HISTORY

In the big public theater of arguments over constitutional law, most conservative lawyers staked out relatively limited claims. Only a few libertarian academics and politicians tried to make a constitutional case for invalidation of all the regulatory, taxing, and welfare functions of the modern state. Sporadic attempts to revive the Commerce Clause and Contracts Clause as limits on federal and state regulatory powers were contained. The Supreme Court's new majority's Constitutional decisions had the more immediate pragmatic objective of using originalist arguments and Frankfurterian doctrines of judicial restraint in order to roll back, or at least curtail any further expansion, of the Rights Revolution. Their approach succeeded in crippling, though not entirely eliminating, race-conscious remedies like affirmative-action admissions policies, public contracting set-asides and school integration plans, and in limiting, but also not eliminating, rights to abortion. Conservatives managed to slow down, but not roll back, judicial expansion of the rights of women and gays. The conservative agenda of protecting business from regulation was pursued through a more modest ground game, restocking the federal courts with judges committed to restrictive readings of statutes and administrative rules regulating business, and placing procedural roadblocks in the way of plaintiffs' tort and antidiscrimination claims against business defendants.[43]

[43] [This assessment of relatively contained damage was made in 1993. More recent Supreme Court majorities have intensified the judicial campaign against the legacies of the New Deal, Great Society, and Rights Revolution. The Court came very close to invalidating the Obama Administration's signature achievement, the Affordable Care Act, as an abuse of the federal commerce power. *NFIB* v. *Sebelius*, 132 S.Ct 2566 (2012). The Court actually did invalidate the key enforcement provisions of the federal Voting Rights Act, enacted by an almost-unanimous Congress. *Shelby County* v. *Holder*, 133 S. Ct 2886 (2013). It struck down local school-integration plans as violations of the Fourteenth Amendment's principle that government action must be colorblind, on the ground that trying to achieve racial balance is not a valid object of state policy. *Parents Involved in Community Schools* v. *Seattle School Dist. No. 1*, 551 U.S. 701 (2007). It severely restricted access to the courts to redress injuries to consumers or employees

Limited though it was, the conservative initiative to reclaim Constitutional interpretation (occurring around the same time as the bicentennial celebrations) touched off a scholarly Kulturkampf for the soul of the American legal system. Having established original Constitutional meanings as the main cultural prize, the conservative originalists saw their ground invaded by hosts of alien interpreters with entirely different aims. The contest opened up our legal history to a fresh wave of revisionists, each trying to establish against competitors *the* authoritative reading of these Constitutional moments. These debates, it has become clear, are not just about law. Americans tend to sacralize their historical experience. Like Christian history, American history has to have a meaning, preferably a single meaning, a Platonic essence. The Constitution – at the time of its adoption only a set of momentary political compromises over a structure of government – has come over time to be a central symbol of our civilization. By appealing to history, American public intellectuals hope to find the answers to such questions as: Is the essence of our legal-Constitutional order the use of law to protect free markets and traditional values? Or is it to promote equality, civic inclusion, and free expression in personal life and an expansive role for government in promoting the general welfare?

The first impulse of Progressive Liberals in responding to the New Right, was to re-establish continuity with the Progressive story of liberal society – a story in which the modern state and its social policies could be vindicated and the Reagan Era put in its proper place as an unfortunate interruption. To retake Constitutional ground from the conservatives, many lawyers of the center-left – rather unfortunately in my view – abandoned the prevailing Progressive theory of the "living" and dynamically expanding Constitution and wandered back with the other time-travelers into the eighteenth century. Once there they made a happy discovery: the "republican" or civic humanist tradition of Atlantic political ideology elaborated by John Pocock and his school. In that tradition deriving from Polybius, Machiavelli, and James Harrington, which clearly greatly influenced the American Revolutionaries, individual personality is only fully realized through the experience of self-government, through participation in a *polis* or republic; for its maintenance the republic requires independent citizens capable of the civic virtue that causes men to identify their own interest with that of the common good.[44] Legal scholars like Cass Sunstein and Frank Michelman were inspired by the republican revival to a general conception of the constitutional design as something more than a framework for individual self-seeking through the market, a political system designed to promote,

by business entities, by limiting class actions and by upholding contract provisions mandating dispute-settlement by arbitrators chosen by the business. *Wal-Mart Stores, Inc.* v. *Dukes*, 131 S.Ct 2541 (2011); *ATT Mobility* v. *Concepcion*, 563 U.S. 321 (2011); *American Express Co.* v. *Italian Colors Restaurant*, 133 S. Ct. 2304 (2013).]

[44] J. G. A. Pocock, *The Machiavellian Moment: Florentine political thought and the Atlantic republican tradition* (1975).

through a filter of high-minded disinterested representation, "deliberative" democracy for the common good.[45] The appeal of civic-republicanism was that it offered a respectable, native-born, Founding-period-based communitarianism, a viewpoint from which to critique free-market libertarianism that was untainted by association with foreign socialisms or the Marxist tradition. Like all other historical revivals, this one had to leave out the inconvenient features of the civic republican tradition. It left out the tradition's very conservative aspects: military arms-bearing and the exercise of patriarchal authority within families as the basic qualifications for citizenship, exclusion of most persons as lacking in civic capacity, its strenuous critique of commerce and luxury, its culturally homogeneous conception of the public interest. And it elided its more radical implications – the need for social reforms leveling severe inequalities of property-distributions, imposing accumulation and alienation restraints on holdings, facilitating participatory economic democracy, in order to create a citizenry free enough of relations of dependence and subordination to be capable of sustaining a republic.[46]

Meanwhile more left-of-center historians began working up their own historically based counter-Constitutional histories, using as their working materials the new social "histories-from-the-bottom-up" to recover the political and legal *mentalités* of outgroups – outsiders, dissidents, rebels. This is an ancient technique of immanent critique – its user identifies insurgent outgroups as the bearers of the utopian norms that, it hopes, will eventually triumph as the dominant norms of the system. (In the last lecture we saw New Right lawyers using the same technique to identify early precursors of "colorblindness.") Of course if the outgroup does eventually triumph, its ideology becomes part of the official legal culture, and its despised radical precursors are retroactively sanctified as visionary prophets. The new social-legal histories take this method a logical step further, recovering the Constitutional ideas of groups that never won out, or who were briefly successful and then crushed and lost to history – nineteenth-century workingmen's associations, the movements of freed slaves for land redistribution after the Civil War and of the radical Northern political parties who supported them, the agrarian cooperative movements of the 1880s and 90s, the industrial unions of the 1930s, the feminist movements of the 1850s, 1930s and 1970s, the civil rights and farmworkers' movements of the 1960s and 70s, as the exponents – and conceivably prophets? – of an alternative, very differently constituted social order. For these historians the master narrative of American legal development is the struggle to realize the ideals of independent free labor (freedom from the control of powerful superiors, especially control over work and production) in the conditions of a modern

[45] Cass Sunstein, "Beyond the Republican Revival," 97 *Yale L. J.* 1539 (1988); Frank Michelman, "Foreword: Traces of Self-Government," 100 *Harv. L. Rev.* 4 (1986).

[46] The best account I know of the "republican revival" is in Laura Kalman, *The Strange Career of Legal Liberalism* (1996).

economy; and of equality of legal status, political participation, and economic opportunities for groups previously considered subordinates or outsiders.[47]

Every party to this debate, not just the conservatives, apparently hoped to find in eighteenth-century – or Reconstruction – Constitutionalism a new basis for forging consensus. What has happened instead, predictably, was that the historical controversies simply re-enact the modern ones. This Babel of contending originalisms has effectively precluded the hardening of a general consensus comparable to the Classical or Progressive narratives of progress in the Constitutional field – though each has achieved some local hegemony by ignoring the existence of the others.

But if I am right about the long-run New Right challenge to embedded historical memories, it is not – or anyway not entirely – in the field of Constitutional or public law at all. Of considerably more importance are their stealth campaigns in the areas of private law and statutory regulation. In these areas the New Right lawyers have re-invigorated something resembling nineteenth-century classical common law as the "natural" legal regime. The more successful is that effort at naturalization, the more departures from it are labeled (presumably illegitimate) "redistributions." So what I would guess to be the most important historical battles, though also the least visible ones, are being fought so low to the ground that almost nobody notices what is going on. The focus down there on the forest floor is on what common lawyers call custom, the routine doctrines and practices, common law, statutory and informal, which have made up the stuff of ordinary social relations, and have helped to constitute power, community, and meaning.

We recalled how nineteenth-century lawyers, under the spell of their long-term evolutionary paradigm, were mostly concerned to search for long-term trend-lines of legal development, originating in ancient and medieval times, but gradually perfecting in the present their immanent ideals of individual liberty. The current conservative stories, as I have mentioned, are considerably more vague in their historical assertions, but plainly rely on a – however idealized or stylized – version of nineteenth-century common law for their picture of the default legal framework. The assumption of an actual historical location, however vague, helps to give some solidity to that picture as the natural legal constitution of the market. The more successful that effort at naturalization is, the more departures from it may be called "interferences" and "redistributions," dubiously legitimate policies in need of justification. The conservative civil rights story takes race-conscious affirmative-action policies as departures from a natural state of affairs – an imagined neutral colorblind market – though one concededly disfigured by regrettable exceptions. Affirmative action is one

[47] See the essays contributed to a Symposium organized in 1989 by the Organization of American Historians, *The Constitution and American Life* (David Thelen ed. 1988).

deviation from that idealized state – just like the minimum wage, agricultural price supports, the legalized closed shop, and environmental regulation.[48]

Obviously this default picture has not gone unchallenged. Many of the challenges deploy the same techniques the Progressives used to denaturalize the Classical scheme, to make it appear to rest on illusory or unstable historical foundations. The most intellectually powerful techniques of critique are rather subtle ones that pick apart, bit by bit, the components of the picture. One technique is to simply keep chipping away at the surprisingly durable myth of laissez-faire – both by elaborating the myriad schemes of statutory and administrative regulation that are a constant throughout the nineteenth century, to demonstrate over and over again that as old forms of public regulation – wage and price controls, statutory governance of the labor contract, governance of corporate enterprise through conditions and limitations in charters – faded out, new and more extensive ones took their place. Another has been to reveal the regulatory doctrines at the heart of the common law rules themselves – customary default rules governing contract, labor, and tenancy relations, regulated commons in grazing or fishing grounds or riparian rights, doctrines of "public" rights limiting encroachments of private owners on public resources. The core doctrines of contract, tort, property, family law, labor relations, and unfair competition upon close inspection turn out to take not a single stable form, but shifting and multiple forms; to be elastic and highly contextualized in their applications, to vary from region to region, trade to trade. Contract law, which the classics and neoclassics tell us must take the form of a strict formal default regime, can be seen as a lush jungle of conflicting doctrines, many of them concerned with the substantive fairness of the bargain, others with restricting advantage-taking, others rapidly expanding excuses such as duress or misrepresentation or unconscionability under cover of a stern rhetoric of inflexible enforcement. Property law, which the classics and neoclassics tell us must consist of strict formal rules protecting absolutely delimited rights, turn out as often, in Carol Rose's terminology, to be "mud" – loose flexible standards – as "crystals"; to create zones of relative rights in commons rather than strict rights to exclude; or even zones of Hohfeldian privilege, where some may destroy the rights of others.[49] What the classics see as collective endeavors formed through individual-contracting parties – like the modern theory of the corporation as a "nexus of contracts" – revisionists are likely to reanalyze as communities or hierarchies, both more solidary and more authoritarian, more embedded and culture-laden: economic forms such as managed

[48] Environmental regulation seemingly would not belong on this list because it seeks to mitigate an "externality" of market dealings rather intervening directly in the market. But if one thinks of the market as "naturally" constituted by common law rules, environmental law is an "interference" with markets because it replaces or supplements common law nuisance with a statutory-administrative scheme.

[49] Carol Rose, "Crystals and Mud in Property Law," 40 *Stanford L. Rev.* 577 (1988).

commons, ethnically exclusive fishing grounds, the quasi-feudal structure of husband–household and master–servant relations, cooperative-producers associations, union-run factories. What is supposed to be the parsimonious hard spare classical piazza at the center of the customary common law laissez-faire constitution of the market, turns out to be a gypsy circus of strange and wonderful variety.

THE STAKES OF LEGAL HISTORY

All this has been meant to convey in a brief space some of the drama and intensity of lawyers' struggles over the history of their public and private law. Now we have to ask if any of this matters, whether it is not all wasted breath, the disputation of scholastics. I put aside here our real motivations for engaging in the enterprise, which F. W. Maitland called the "sheer thrilling interest" of the subject, to focus on the pragmatic payoffs from history for the daily legal business of justifying and remaking, pruning and replanting the little garden plots of social life.

Is it worth doing just because lawyers so often, we think, "get it wrong," and should "get it right" instead? The answer cannot be, though it is the answer often given, that it profanes the past to get it wrong, as lawyers so often do, by the criteria of professional historical practice. Every unkind word ever said about the defects of "law-office history" may be true. But getting history "wrong," distorting the past, relying on false analogies, wrenching verbal formulae from their originating contexts and putting them to different employments, has been one of the great forces of creative innovation in the law. As Toby Milsom puts it, "[t]he life of the common law has been in the abuse of its elementary ideas."[50] Holmes once argued that "ignorance is the best of law reformers"[51] – those who do not remember the past have the least work to do unlearning it. Sometimes bad history, with its selective oblivion, may be the best formula for promoting reconciliation and healing of social wounds after a period of great strife and trauma.

Is the virtue of historical inquiry that it destroys myth-making – for example, that it makes it hard to extract doctrine from the study of "original intentions"? or that by complicating the comforting bedtime stories of evolutionary progress it disabuses us of the notion that there is a simple linear progressive path of progress that we must adhere to? Certainly that's one of its virtues, so long as we don't expect too much from it. The hope of the Progressive modernists was that history would rid the present of the dead weight of survivals, leaving us free to purposefully refashion our futures. It is however difficult to believe any more in the possibility of this kind of total release from history: it is all too easy to historicize the modernists themselves, to see what a weight of

[50] S.F.C. Milsom, *Historical Foundations of the Common Law* 6 (2nd edn. 1981).
[51] Oliver Wendell Holmes, Jr., *The Common Law* 64 (Mark DeWolfe Howe ed., 1963).

unconscious inherited baggage they brought to the task of social-engineering, including their own set of mythic progressive narratives.

Anyway, does historical experience suggest that people, including lawyers, disabused of myths of progress do any better than those under their spell? The core legal story of liberal society as the gradual release of liberty from "feudal" restraints toward more personal liberty and political inclusion, has surely been an immensely powerful force for emancipation: ask Thurgood Marshall, who knew that the actual historical Constitution was a covenant with death and pact with hell, but that nonetheless American liberal-legality held immanent norms of freedom that could, with fighting human agents at their side, be gradually realized with unfolding time, so that in the words of the Langston Hughes' poem, "America, which never was, will be." The progressive's most effective ideological weapon has always been the metaphor of America's unfulfilled promise. Exploding this narrative as in some part mythical, one might well think, is not the most helpful advice the historian can bring to the Party of Humanity – especially because it's not *all* mythical, not by a long shot.

The core narratives of our legal history describe a process by which we repeatedly overcome the errors and abuses of the past. Every fresh version of the narrative requires some condemnation and censorship of its disreputable ancestors. Seventeenth-century legal radicals sought to lift from the law the Norman Yoke of infringements on Anglo-Saxon liberties and the fresher impositions of Tudor and Stuart tyranny. Blackstone viewed common law process as the gradual purging of excrescences imposed via the subtlety of Norman jurists. American revolutionaries saw the common law as still infected by feudal and hypertechnical elements, and novel tyrannical impositions, which it would be the mission of legal reformers in the new American republic to purge so as gradually to conform the law to republican principles. Mid- and late-nineteenth-century Classical liberals sought to work the law free of its persisting mercantilist-regulatory baggage; Progressive liberals to liberate it from what they saw as its anachronistic individualism in an age of giant organizations and its antagonism to beneficial social legislation; New Dealers to overcome local-parochial barriers to cope with the emergency of the Depression and to enact a national system of provision against economic insecurity. The Rights Revolution sought to make good on the promises of Emancipation and Reconstruction, to wash out the traces of slavery in Jim Crow and debt peonage; to eliminate the remnants of long-standing disabilities of women; and even, however feebly, to restore some of the lands stolen from Native Americans. The New Right sought to redescribe most of the Progressives' innovations as departures from the good path, to consign them, in their turn, to the bad past, and to restore a neoclassical regime of laissez-faire, federalism, and traditional moral codes. The Chicago law-and-economics movement pictured the common law as the evolution of ever-more-efficient rules.

Thus every fresh cycle brings an erasure of bad predecessors – but often as well an invocation of an older, nobler, purer spirit. We gradually erase the bad past so as to progress toward realization of the promise or spirit or principles of the good past. That doesn't sound so bad, does it?

And yet the core narratives, liberal as well as conservative, of legal history as the occasionally interrupted march of liberty, can do much harm to the extent they allow us to fog over and forget the bad past, to pretend that our abominations and errors never happened, or that if they did that they are safely left behind, locked up in the dead past. Selective oblivion is not always liberating, if it obscures continuing injustice. The deal struck by Northern with Southern whites after the Civil War, to pretend that the war had been fought on both sides for a noble cause, and that Reconstruction was an overreaching and corrupt intrusion into regional customs and states' rights, condemned African-Americans to a century of caste subordination. Nietzsche famously pointed to the danger that to feel too strongly the weight of the horrors of history may paralyze the will to carry on. In America the more likely dangerous temptations are to succumb to naïve nostalgic traditionalism, the view that all we have to do is to recover the sweeter, sturdier practices of our ancestors; or to Panglossian complacency about how we have overcome ancient transgressions to approximate the most just and beneficial set of arrangements possible on earth.

One argument then, for using history to bust up and complicate these simplifying and mythic core narratives is to show how multiple and conflicting the traditions are, all the different kinds of stories that can be told about the past, the kind of thing I've been trying to do in the last few days. We open up, one version of this argument goes, a space for freedom and innovation, not in the escape from history, but in choosing which traditions and trajectories to attach ourselves to.

Of course the availability of all these options may seem to deprive history of any independent value in political-legal argument: it's just another kind of rhetoric you resort to in order to argue for what you want. Having a different view of history in your arsenal is only good for convincing the incredibly rare judge or legislator whose mind is really going to be changed by another take on what happened in 1793 or 1868. The project to recover "original public meanings" to restore determinacy to Constitutional interpretation in the Supreme Court – to constrain "judicial activism" by binding judges to fixed meanings extracted by objective methods of historical reconstruction – has been fatally undermined by its own disciples. In case after case, majority and dissenting justices present dueling narratives – improvisations with footnotes, as often as not – of original meanings. History thus presented looks like a post-modern smorgasbord of past styles and practices, to be drawn from, mixed and matched, as expediency and political ideology dictate.

No: the point of deeper explorations of the past is not to triumphantly serve one's opponents with novel and trumping sources of *authority*. It is to invoke a more contextualized, complicated, multivalent, ironic, contradictory, historicized kind of history, to reveal a range of alternative choices and trajectories – roads actually taken but since forgotten or abandoned, possibilities once dreamed of but unrealized, social arrangements and understandings of startling variety. The aim is to shock people out of complacency about current arrangements (if they like them) or out of resignation to them (if they don't). We are not determined by our past – not because the past is so easily shaken off, but because our past is not one past but many. As Hobbes put it, "No man can have in his mind a conception of the future, for the future is not yet. But of our conceptions of the past, we make a future."[52]

We now occupy a historical situation in which, I think, a need for critical legal history, skeptically questioning and complicating taken-for-granted narratives, is especially urgent. That is because a particularly strong and dogmatic revival of the Classical version of the legal history of liberal societies is again coming into dominance in the Western world. This is the story of how "the West" grew prosperous and rich and free through the adoption of a strict framework of legal arrangements protecting "liberal capitalism" and "strict property rights;" and of how the world's societies, after failed experiments with socialism, central state planning, Keynesian redistribution, overregulation, and overgenerous social spending, are now, under the pressure of global competition, returning to their optimal political-economic foundations, and restoring "the market" to its central place.

In the actual domestic politics of Western societies, this neoclassical revival has met with only mixed success. Parties and governments that need the electoral support of labor and of beneficiaries of welfare policies like social insurance against unemployment, disability, and old age, have resisted the most aggressive schemes to privatize all public functions and dismantle the welfare state. But in zones of policy planning relatively insulated from domestic politics, such as conditions on grants and loans and trade agreements with developing countries, the neoclassical narrative is at high tide. In the versions promoted by the World Bank and the Agency for International Development, optimal governance demands a severely shrunken state, one whose functions are restricted to providing the "Rule of Law," meaning courts that protect property rights (remarkably under-specified, except for foreign direct investment), enforce contracts, and enforce constitutional restrictions on overregulation.

Evidently the historical model for this ideal legal regime is the late-nineteenth-century United States. That society is taken to be the one that most closely approximates the mixture of property-and-contract-protecting common law rules, and constitutional restraints preventing their revision by legislation and administration, that the neoclassical revival likes to celebrate. If all the world is to become America as it once was, then it would be well to know what that America really was.

[52] Thomas Hobbes, *The Elements of Law Natural and Politic*, Ch. 4, sec. 7 (1640) (in context this sentence makes a more modest claim than that implied by its quotation here: simply that past experience makes it possible to predict future consequences).

Now of course any legal framework – including the neoclassical model of the Rule of Law – needs for its installation and maintenance a lot more than the abstract commitment of political leadership. It needs to be accepted as just and legitimate, institutionalized in the everyday conventions of market relations and civil society, internalized as norm and habit. The framework will not work, for example, if all property, every contract deal, has to be policed by state force. The jurists of the actual Classical period were, as we have seen, historically and socially minded, not abstract natural lawyers. For them, markets were one piece of a whole array of institutions for socializing people into law-respecting, property-maintaining, work-disciplined and tolerably orderly and virtuous participants in civil society, institutions that were the product of a long-term evolution of Christian morals, the spirit of Anglo-Saxon (or "Aryan" or "Teutonic") liberty, and the common law gradually working itself pure. The Classics also drew on a venerable style of thinking from the Scottish Enlightenment: the *doux commerce* thesis that the growth of commerce will itself help to generate the character-traits of industry, thrift, obedience and work-discipline, competitiveness and ambition, required for its moral support; and the personal liberty and widely shared prosperity required for its political support. Traditional morality supports liberal capitalism; capitalism supports traditional morality. Or as modern conservatives say, the goal of legal-social policy in a well-regulated society is to reinforce the causal connections between personal virtue and economic reward.[53] Loosen those connections, as the Communist states spectacularly, and (they believe) the social-democratic welfare states more modestly, have done, and the results are clear: immorality and economic decline.

The operations of minimally regulated free markets, however, tend to produce great inequalities – as in fact they did during our Gilded Age. Why – especially in a democratic polity where the losers can vote – will the losers accept these? The answers, generally, given by the Classical tradition are: because they will see that market rewards in an unrigged system go to the most deserving – i.e., connect material with moral rewards – and that redistribution will hurt everyone by making geese less willing to lay golden eggs, and the pie of total social wealth smaller. Constitutional limitations on legislative revision of the free-market framework will also dampen temptations to redistributionist politics.

Yet is it ever credible that rewards under a market system actually go to the most economically deserving? Is it even remotely plausible that they go to the most morally deserving? At best they go to people in the adventitious situation of being the most marginally productive, while unemployment, poverty and misfortune often fall on the backs of the perfectly worthy but unlucky. Friedrich Hayek himself supposed that traditional moralities of desert and

[53] *See*, e.g., Charles Murray, *Losing Ground: American Social Policy, 1950–1980* (1984).

justice are pre-modern remnants that are quite dysfunctional in modern capitalist economies, where people ought to accept market outcomes, however immorally achieved, as the definition of justice. But why should they? Rather than swallow the insult that they are either undeserving and morally inferior, or even just the blameless casualties of an overall efficient system, one might suppose, they will see the game as rigged against them. They will take political action. If the constitutional arrangements prevent revision by peaceful means, they will seek to change those arrangements (think of the Sixteenth Amendment, or the Constitutional changes of the New Deal); and if they can't, they will rebel. And when they do, the coercive legal apparatus sustaining free markets becomes shockingly visible.

When admirers of the Classical age describe its legal framework, they tend to describe only its liberal elements. They systematically understate its authoritarian elements (and one might add its radical ones as well). Aside from the fact that laissez-faire capitalism was never all that laissez-faire – that it rested in fact on a proliferating and expanding archipelago of regulatory policies and bureaucratic agencies[54] – it was sustained by government more repressive and social conventions far more authoritarian, the threat and daily use of violence, the systematic subordination of groups within the polity – than would – one hopes – be tolerated in today's formally more inclusive democracy.[55] Labor unrest was met with court injunctions, enforced by state militias, federal troops, and deputized private armies. Subordinated racial groups were punished for exercising market freedoms to quit employment or accumulate property with jail and officially tolerated beatings and murder. The classical legal regime did not solve, but exacerbated the problem of distributional dissent. It was undone by the Progressives because its neutrality among classes was perceived to be a sham. It looks – as does much in the Progressive period that followed as well – appalling to us in its systematic preference for whites; and its continuing – though also eroding – presumptions of male superiority and privilege. Moreover the liberal principles of the self-making individual and formal equality that underwrote its market relations, as well as the actual operation of its markets, had a corrosive effect on the pre-liberal values and disciplines that had once made it work. To the extent that the older social order rested on the family, keeping middle-class women out of the wage economy to serve as curators of family values, and relying on the family collective to support its members through unemployment, disability and old age, new market pressures and opportunities began a long, slow process of its destruction.

Such would be the outlines of a historically based critique of the neoclassical revival. But the example is meant to illustrate a broader point. To return to

[54] For concise summaries of the regulatory innovations of the period, see, e.g., Morton Keller, *Regulating a New Society* (1998) and *Regulating a New Economy* (1996).

[55] For elaboration of this point, see a previous essay in this volume, "The Constitution of Liberal Order," *supra*, Ch. 9.

where we began, Holmes thought the use of history was to get the "dragon" of the past – inherited unexamined legal custom – out into the open; then either to kill him or tame him and make him a useful animal. But history does not make a good domestic pet. The past is too savage, too primitive, too tragic and too radical, too disorderly and too violent; both too utopian and too authoritarian, for the everyday uses to which lawyers habitually want to put it: as authoritative sources of safe principles, certain rules, sound doctrine and happy tales of progress. Evolving custom turns out not to be a process of gentle and efficient adaptation to changing needs, but a field of terror, pain, conflict, and scruffy, crazy utopians dreaming of escape to a better life.

But paradoxically, it is just these aspects of history that should make it most useful to lawyers. For lawyers the most valuable uses of history lie not in the ways in which it is safe, but in the ways in which it is dangerous – in which it refuses to confirm our prejudices, jolts us out of accepted assumptions, and allows us to imagine a wide array of possible futures.

14

Originalism and Nostalgic Traditionalism

[*This essay consolidates drafts of several public talks given in various venues, ranging from the scholarly (Wesleyan University, Yale Law School, University of Southern California) to the political (American Constitution Society meetings) between about 2005 and the present day. These talks were more frankly partisan and polemical than most of my writing and possibly less generous to opposing views than they should have been; but their main points still seem to me basically right.*]

Is there anything new or interesting to say about originalism – the doctrine that the Federal Constitution must be interpreted today exactly as people at the time of its ratification would have understood its terms? As a general and vague aspiration to be true to the visions, values, and political architecture of the Founders, of course, originalism is deeply embedded in American political consciousness, and especially prominent now. I don't recall in my lifetime so many calls summoning us to repent of our deviant ways and reclaim the political and social system of our origins. Originalist restorationism is a central plank in the platform and rhetoric of the Republican Party and especially its Tea Party wing. It receives at least lip service from Democrats and even liberals. Constitutional law professors say things like "We are all originalists now." Yet as a practical program, for lawyers and politicians and policy-makers, originalism is a zombie idea. It may once have seemed to have promise and plausibility, but it is exhausted as a program. Nobody faithfully and consistently tries to apply it as a working method, and this is especially true of those who most persistently and emphatically claim to be originalists. We are only "all originalists" if the concept elastically expands beyond all meaningful content.

Let me start with some reminders of the obvious. Originalism in its hard-edged form – that is that Founding-era understandings of the Constitutional text must be, after the text itself, the *exclusive* interpretative resource for recovering Constitutional meaning, did not begin as an abstract theory of judicial interpretation. In the form to which we are now accustomed, it was an ideology promoted by the Reagan Administration in the service of a political project, not just that of correcting the mistakes and excesses of liberal policies and court decisions of the 1960s and 70s era but – much more ambitiously – of actually recovering America as it was, or was imagined to have been, in some earlier era before everything fell apart.

The project had several different audiences, a popular and an elite-legal.

As a popular project the call to restore the Original Constitution had and still has a lot going for it – besides widespread general appeal it has the power to attract and unite different constituencies in the conservative coalition: It promotes fusionism by means of nostalgia – reconciling disparate elements of the conservative coalition by evoking an imagined past of libertarian economics in solidary Christian community – "traditional values" and "free markets" together at last. Originalism of course resonates deeply with Protestant fundamentalism: textual literalism with scriptural inerrancy; original meanings with the worship of the authority of founding ancestors – conceived of not as cosmopolitan Enlightenment gentleman but more as Old Testament patriarchs, symbols of a former state of society in which – it seemed – almost everyone was some kind of Christian, believed Christianity to be a necessary source of morality in Christian society, and engaged in Christian observances on public occasions and Christian teachings in the schools; in short where Christianity was so generally accepted that it needed no establishment; and in which socially compulsory heterosexual marriage was the only acceptable model for child-rearing and wealth-sharing. Yet originalism simultaneously appeals to business interests and economic libertarians, because it promises to delegitimize the regulatory and welfare state innovations of the New Deal and Great Society; and return us to some form of laissez-faire.

Originalism as a legal project – that is, a manifesto for judges and Justice Department and conservative movement lawyers, adopted by Attorney General Meese as the Reagan Administration's official hermeneutic – has been a bit more complicated; and its promoters flirted with several alternatives before settling on a formula that did most of what they wanted it to do.

Before the 1980s the dominant task to which originalist history was put was to try to roll back the constitutional innovations of the Warren (and Burger) Courts: expansive interpretations of the equality provisions of the Fourteenth Amendment (and its incorporated Bill of Rights) and the invention of new "unenumerated" rights protected against legislation. The general tone of the conservative critique was that of Burke reproving the wild abstract utopians of the French Revolution: the present-day Jacobins were liberal judges who put their personal/political preferences into the due process clause. The function of originalism was to show that the Warren and Burger Courts' innovations lacked historical foundations in the intent of those who drafted Constitutional provisions, especially the Fourteenth Amendment. (The same critique had been leveled in the 1950s and 60s at the Court that decided *Brown* v. *Board of Education*; but by the 1980s conservative lawyers had not only accepted *Brown*, but as judges cited it even more often than liberals.[1]) The leading illicit activist decisions were cases requiring busing to achieve racial integration; forbidding prayer (and the teaching of evolution) in public schools and state aid to religious schools; regulating police behavior in searches, arrests, interrogations by means of excluding relevant evidence and vacating state criminal convictions on habeas corpus; deregulating censorship and criminal controls on obscenity and pornography; subverting the authority of officials in charge of schools, prisons and welfare administration; and constitutionalizing a right to abortion. The charge was that arrogant activist liberal judges were subverting the will of democratic majorities. For this critique conservative lawyers continued to rely on older Progressive calls for judicial deference to elected legislatures, quoting judges like Holmes, Brandeis, and Frankfurter on the horrors of "Lochnerism," the oxymoron of "substantive" due process, the promiscuous invention of novel extra-textual "unenumerated" rights, and overreaching federal-judicial contravention of state statutes and state court decisions.

The critique evolved as the Democratic majorities who remained in charge of the federal Congress and of many state legislatures continued to enact liberal legislation; while Republican presidents restocked the federal judiciary with conservatives, for whom admonitions of restraint and deference to legislatures were losing much of their attraction. Originalism in the new, hard form became a formula that would not just prevent judges from inventing new rights good against legislation or official action; but would empower courts to strike down enactments or decisions that contravened the Constitution's text or original applications. The formula was that the courts should enforce *no more*, but also *no less*, than the original Constitution required. Views on what sources should be looked to for original meanings shifted from sources evidencing framers' intent to ratifiers' understandings, to applications near in time to ratification, to "original public meanings;" but there was agreement on two propositions: first that what was to be looked for was specific interpretations; and second that, after the text, usages near in time should be the *exclusive* guide to current meanings – thus ruling out faux-originalist pretenders who claim allegiance to the historical Constitution by attributing to it principles at a high level of generality, and those who use history as only one interpretive guide among many others.

The Reagan Justice Department's Office of Legal Policy put together a remarkable document called *The Constitution in the Year 2000*, which set out litigating strategies to address all the hot-button issues and causes of the conservative movement; and a *Sourcebook* of Founding-era documents to support the enterprise. They generally assumed that recovering the context for interpretation in the Founding Era would reliably lead to results conservatives would

[1] Brad Snyder, "How the Conservatives Canonized *Brown* v. *Board of Education*," 51 *Rutgers L. Rev.* 383 (2000).

like – less power for the national government (though ironically more for the President), fewer protections for minorities, women, poor people, and social outcasts, more support for religious and other social authorities.[2] This proved to be generally true but not invariably – criminals arguably got more procedural protections in the Founding era than they do now; Congress was a much stronger check on executive power; the legitimate scope and actual exercise of state regulatory power was in many respects more extensive – more morals regulation yes, but also a greater scope for the police power, including powers to closely regulate household labor and the prices of staple commodities.

Yet: Neither in its popular nor in its legal mode is originalism an effort to steep Americans in history, to recall them to their historical origins and remind them of their journey to the present. On the contrary: the calls to return to the world of the Founders are mostly attempts to escape from history altogether – from controversy, contingency, development, the painful and shameful elements of the past, and the troubling disturbances of modernity. The Tea Party movements whose fans carry copies of the Constitution in their pockets aim to restore a wholly imaginary pristine moment of concord, since hijacked by sinister forces for corrupt purposes. Like the "innocent life" of the unborn, the moment the new republic is born, it begins to undergo deformation and decay.

Originalism in this general popular key is nostalgic traditionalism – the fuzzy invocation of a mythic economic, social, and legal order – a lost Eden – somewhere back before our present discontents. The temporal location of this Eden shifts around quite a bit depending on the issue. In economic policy, it's somewhere before the New Deal, a time believed, though very inaccurately, to have been a period of consistently constitutionally guaranteed laissez-faire, the "*Lochner* era" of 1890–1937. In regulation of the family and sexual morality, I think it's pretty clearly the 1950s, though sometimes it seems more like the 1850s; in regulation of race relations, a *very* brief period between the adoption of the Civil Rights Act of 1964, and the onset of affirmative action in 1965; in criminal procedure, anytime before the Warren Court's Fourth, Fifth and Sixth Amendment cases; in welfare policy, the Victorian age's reliance on private charitable relief accompanied by aggressive religious sermonizing; in tort law, somewhere back before the 1940s, before strict products liability and the class action. So the location is variable, but it's always back then – back before some time when "liberal elites" took over and ruined everything. This imagined past then becomes the baseline from which deviation or decline is measured.

So conservative nostalgia recalls an older order of:

- An idealized laissez-faire market regime of constitutionalized "negative liberty," of judicially enforced limits on state action and authority; a state before the expansion of the powers of government, especially national government,

[2] *See* William N. Eskridge, Jr., Book Review, A Matter of Interpretation: Federal Courts and the Law by Antonin Scalia, 96 *Mich. L. Rev.* 1509 (1998)

to regulate business property and employer control of the workplace, to redistribute incomes through progressive taxation, and use the spending power to control state and local governments; and before the large-scale delegation of legislative power to administrative bureaucracies;
- An idealized patriarchal family, when the legal system supported unquestioned male authority over women and children, and sought to insure against family breakup by restricting divorce;
- An idealized ethic of "personal responsibility," that is, a society without social risk-pooling, in which people are supposed to provide on their own for the risks of disease, disability, workplace injury, unemployment and old age, and hope for charity if their resources run out;
- An idealized consensus on moral order, of shared values and absolute truths, reinforced by law criminalizing various forms of deviant non-procreative forms of sex, family formation, and methods of controlling reproduction, such as abortion, polygamy and homosexuality; and heavily regulating the lives of immigrants, women and the dependent poor;
- An idealized order of respect for established authority, Christian religious authority especially: a preferred position for religion and churches as socializing agencies; and a legal system underwriting the autocratic authority of teachers in the schoolroom and masters in the workplace;
- An idealized "common law" – both substantive and procedural (though not, interestingly, including jury trial), with traditional common law rules of contract defenses (narrow) and tort liability (fault-based or strict liability strongly laced with contributory negligence and assumption of risk defenses); and
- An idealized order (requiring I think in this case a fairly heroic feat of imagination) of color-blind equal opportunity, a regime of meritocracy, where people are rewarded for their talents and achievements, not by arbitrary criteria of ethnicity or class background or family connections. (For obvious reasons nobody has come up with a remotely plausible suggestion of when this regime might have been actually in effect).

Nostalgic traditionalism is of course very powerful. It appeals to anyone – and that means at one time or another probably almost everyone – who feels that the world is out of control and that forces in it are destroying ways of life that they have felt to be precious and valuable. The temptation is very strong to look to earlier times for sturdier and sweeter models of social life than the decadent ways into which we have fallen. And there's nothing wrong with that impulse, and it's certainly not always mistaken. But as Raymond Williams warns in *The Country and the City*, it is well to beware of nostalgic projections, mobilizing our collective longings for the security of childhood and home, in the service of someone's political project.[3]

[3] Raymond Williams, *The Country and the City* (1975).

The legal side of the originalist project, originalism as conservative jurists saw it, wasn't very historically minded either: as Stephen Griffin has put it, it was "history without historicism."[4] The most prominent judicial promoter of originalism, Justice Scalia, didn't adopt it out of regard for traditional authority, or the unconscious wisdom of immemorial tradition: he evinces no particular reverence for the Founders, or founding era as such. He simply likes rules as the basis for legal judgment; and originalism in his view reliably produces rules – formal positive rules. His aim is to treat the Constitution as a body of fixed commands that we must obey simply because they have been commanded. Rather than a "living Constitution" he prefers a "dead Constitution," the decrees of a remote and inaccessible sovereign. Attorney-General Edwin Meese by contrast was willing to ground the original Constitution's authority on its ratification by democratic assent.[5] That skips over a lot of problems – why should we be bound by the authority of long-dead people, particularly long-dead people consisting only of the propertied adult white males who were maybe 12 per cent of the new states' populations? – but at least Meese tries to provide some answer to the question of authority. Scalia provides none except an argument from efficiency: originalism, like textualism, is a relatively determinate method of ascertaining meaning: its chief virtue is to protect us from freewheeling judges. You can have either originalism, he proposes, or a Living Constitutionalism in which judges can read anything out of the Constitution that suits their personal or political preferences.[6] So this method is to identify some scraps of historical evidence that fix historical meaning in rule-like form sometime at a moment at or near the Founding, and then simply to import that meaning into the present. (His favorite example of his own method is his view that the Confrontation Clause of the Sixth Amendment requires that in the trial of an accused for sexual assault, a child accuser may not testify behind a screen but must sit face-to-face with the defendant. The Sixth Amendment says confront; so confront one literally must.[7])

This effort rapidly proved to create more difficulties than it solved, giving rise to a law review literature as tedious as it is massive. When different groups and legal authorities near in time to the Founding filled in gaps and ambiguities in the constitutional text with conflicting meanings, which was to prevail? How were we to integrate later with earlier Founding moments? Even hardcore originalists had to concede that the Constitutional structure did not freeze eighteenth-century legislative and executive practice, but rather sought to set in motion innovation and dynamic development; and in fact the responsibilities of the federal Congress, and especially of the Presidency, had expanded in scale

[4] Stephen Griffin, "Rebooting Originalism," 2008 *U. Ill. L. Rev.* 1185.

[5] Edwin Meese III, "Toward a Jurisprudence of Original Intent," 11 *Harv. J. L. & Pub.Pol'y* 5 (1988).

[6] Antonin Scalia, "Originalism – The Lesser Evil," 57 *U. Cin. L. Rev.* 849 (1989).

[7] *Maryland* v. *Craig*, 497 U.S. 836 (1990) (Scalia, J. dissenting).

and direction beyond anything the Framers would have anticipated or tolerated, especially the enormous national-security-military-intelligence apparatus and bureaucratic state. (Some conservative lawyers, like John Yoo, wrote histories purporting to show that unlimited executive power in war and national security matters was part of the original Constitutional design, but this was too transparently tendentious to be plausible.[8]) Many aspects of the original structural design, such as that Congress would check executive overreaching out of institutional self-interest (an incentive fatally undermined by the party system), that election to federal office would cause legislators to attend to enlarged national rather than local parochial interests, and that Congress would take the leading role in initiating war-making, became obsolete almost as soon as the republic started. What sense would it make for judges to give a static construction to a Constitution that the other branches, or changes in social context or institutions, have altered beyond recognition? (Especially since the judges' own authority to render judgments controlling the other branches was itself not part of the original design, but grafted on later!) Moreover the first was now no longer the only Founding period; it existed side by side with Reconstruction and arguably others, such as the New Deal and the Rights Revolution of 1954–1980. In interpreting the Bill of Rights, does the judge search the history around 1787–1791, around 1864–1868, or even later, when the right is question was recognized by the Supreme Court as having been incorporated against the states? (This last problem greatly perplexed the Court in the recent *McDonald* decision that the Second Amendment as incorporated by the Fourteenth protects an individual right to handguns against the states as well as the federal government.[9])

Indeed how does originalism consort with its sister formalist method, textualism? Textualism is necessarily a dynamic and not static method, since as linguistic usages and contexts change, so must the practical meanings of words. "Property" to take an important example, two hundred years included a man's right to his wife's exclusive domestic and sexual services, to the management of her property and the dictation of her domicile, and to the labor of his children, apprentices, and (except in states that had emancipated them by statute or common law) slaves, all protected by law against strangers who would appropriate or interfere with them; one hundred years ago it had come to include such rights as that of an investor in public utilities to a reasonable return on his investment, and an owner of business property to run it free of the interference of labor unions, all protected by Constitutional law against legislative or administrative regulation that would unduly infringe upon them; but no lawyer or lay interpreter of the word "property" would take it to include any of those rights today.

[8] *See*, e.g., John Yoo, *The Powers of War and Peace* (2005), and the trenchant review (one of several) of it by Stephen Holmes, "John Yoo's Tortured Logic," *The Nation*, May 1, 2006.

[9] *McDonald* v. *Chicago*, 561 U.S. 742 (2010).

The usual way people try to integrate bits of historical evidence from different periods is to work up a narrative that connects them – that accounts for how understandings altered over time in response to novel circumstances and novel responses to them: but this move is not permitted to hard originalists because they are committed to unchanging meanings. A real history of the relation of past to present requires a wobbly narrative, full of reversals, backlashes, unexpected twists and turns, ironic consequences, and most of all, the development of legal language to serve purposes its publics at the time of adoption could hardly have dreamed of. As Holmes – a Civil War veteran – memorably put it in *Missouri* v. *Holland*:

> [W]hen we are dealing with words that also are a constituent act, like the Constitution of the United States, we must realize that they have called into life a being the development of which could not have been foreseen completely by the most gifted of its begetters. It was enough for them to realize or to hope that they had created an organism; it has taken a century and has cost their successors much sweat and blood to prove that they created a nation.[10]

And Thurgood Marshall, in a bicentennial speech in 1987:

> I do not believe the meaning of the Constitution was forever "fixed" at the Philadelphia convention. Nor do I find the wisdom, foresight and sense of justice exhibited by the framers particularly profound. To the contrary, the government they devised was defective from the start, requiring several amendments, a civil war, and momentous social transformation to attain the system of constitutional government, and its respect for the individual freedoms and human rights, that we hold as fundamental today.[11]

In this process of development, some provisions (like the commerce and due process and equal protection clauses) undergo giant expansion; others (like privileges and immunities, or the guarantee of republican government, or Congress's war-declaring monopoly) become effective dead letters. Some of these changes follow the prescribed mode of change by constitutional amendment. But most of them change with shifts in customary practice and public opinion, many of these recognized and ratified by court opinions, others, like the executive's powers in rule-making and foreign affairs, acquired by usage and prescription. Yet if you permit evidence of how constitutional meanings change over time, you risk falling into the historicist swamp and the heresy of Living Constitutionalism. Hence the need for the Court to assert, as it has, that now disfavored cases like *Plessy* v. *Ferguson* and *Lochner* v. *New York* were "wrong the day they were decided": for if *Plessy* and *Lochner* were plausibly "correct" by the mores and lawyers' conventions of their times, how then could they be compatible with the fixed meaning of the fourteenth Amendment? If

[10] 252 U.S. 416, 433 (1920).

[11] Justice Thurgood Marshall, "Reflections on the Bicentennial of the United States Constitution," 101 *Harv. L. Rev.* 1 at 2 (1987).

Constitutional meanings always change with the dominant conventions of their times, would this not mean we had no fixed standpoint from which to critique them? The standpoint might of course be universal principles of natural law, but these are far too obviously malleable and indeterminate.

So we have this huge scholarly controversy over the merits of originalism, but it seems to me that the most convincing arguments against originalist method in fact is that those who most strongly favor it in theory rarely resort to it much in practice; and when they do engage in historical reconstruction, do it so haphazardly, and with such casual indifference to contradicting evidence and competing scholarly views, as to call into serious doubt their commitment to the project. A sound method, one would think, would offer better pragmatic proofs of its virtues. The New Right jurists go back to original meanings when it seems to suit their purposes, distort it or abandon them when they don't. Like those of any other lawyers, their uses of history are forensic and selective. Distortion is unavoidable, because lawyers and historians have different purposes: lawyers are looking for authoritative resolution – if they purport to find it in history, they have to choose among alternative sources of meaning, levels of abstraction, moments and contexts of application; law is a planting of staves in an onrushing stream. But much of what passes for originalist history is willful, flagrant, dishonesty that hardly even pretends to be anything else.

A very large literature has generated scores of examples. For a sample, let's look at the practice of originalism's most illustrious proponent, Justice Antonin Scalia. In the *Lucas* case of 1992,[12] the Supreme Court held that government restriction of developmental uses of beach-front property might be an unconstitutional taking. Historians provided a brief pointing out that in 1790–1800 nobody conceived of such regulatory restrictions as takings: the state was only considered to "take" property when it took it over and occupied and used it as its owner. Justice Scalia's opinion for the Court surprisingly pronounced all the historical practices illuminating eminent domain law around 1780 to be completely *irrelevant* – and said that what would determine what counted as property and what was a taking would be a "historical compact" around flexible, dynamic state-common law definitions of nuisance. And his preferred period for locating that doctrine seemed to be, as it often is, somewhere around the late nineteenth century.[13] The most extensive uses of history in recent Supreme Court practice are in the gun rights cases, *Heller* and *McDonald*, holding that the Second Amendment codifies a fundamental right to keep a handgun in the house for self-defense, and that this right has been incorporated via the fourteenth Amendment's due process (or, some argued, privileges and immunities)

[12] *Lucas* v. *South Carolina Coastal Comm'n.*, 505 U.S. 1003 (1992).

[13] Similarly, Scalia's view that Article III's case-and-controversy requirement and the separation of powers prohibit Congress from legislation that confers standing to sue the government on citizens at large defies long-standing eighteenth- and nineteenth-century practices of private and common-informer enforcement. *Lujan* v. *Defenders of Wildlife*, 504 U.S. 555 (1992).

clause to disallow state regulation limiting the right as well.[14] Most historians who have examined the majority's history think they made a hash of it – the majority simply blew off the actual text of the Second Amendment, "A well-regulated militia being necessary to the security of a free state," and the abundant evidence of its principal purposes, to reassure anti-Federalists that the new Federal government would not disarm the state militias and create a standing army.[15] The Court's actual opinion in *Heller* ignored all the evidence an originalist could be expected to find most useful, that of what the Founders' contemporaries thought the Amendment was designed to do, while drawing heavily upon evidence from much earlier English practice and much later nineteenth-century American practice – and, as Reva Siegel pointed out in a memorable article, actually ends up tracking pretty closely the scope of rights argued for by the more moderate elements of the modern gun rights movement.[16]

Neither Scalia's nor any other living judge's view of the First Amendment owes anything to eighteenth-century doctrines of free speech and press rights. Modern First Amendment law is all post-1930s – actually post-1970s – Constitutional law; just as the modern Constitutional law of Fourteenth Amendment-based racial discrimination is virtually all post-1950s, and of gender equality post-1970s. Justices opposed to affirmative action carefully avoid referring to the original history of the Reconstruction Amendments, for the obvious reason that that history is not one of color-blind enforcement, but replete with statutes and executive policies specifically targeted at advancing the welfare of black freedman. Indeed a Court claiming allegiance to original meanings has affirmed and revalidated a series of Redeemer decisions like the *Civil Rights Cases*[17] and *U.S.* v. *Cruikshank*[18], usually taken to ratify the *retreat* from the intentions of the Republicans who drafted and proposed the Reconstruction Amendments, and a repudiation of their promises to protect the freed slaves from subordination. One of the more breathtaking acts of blowing off eighteenth-century understandings was the recent *Citizens United*[19] case invalidating an Act of Congress that attempted to regulate corporate-financed political propaganda. On many matters the founding generation's views are

[14] *District of Columbia* v. *Heller*, 554 U.S. 570 (2008); *McDonald* v. *City of Chicago*, 561 U.S. 742 (2010).

[15] In McDonald, the arch-textualist Scalia actually mocked counsel in oral argument who proposed the Privileges and Immunities Clause as a vehicle for incorporating Second Amendment rights against the states: "Why are you asking us to overrule ... 140 years of prior law, when you can reach your result on substantive due [process]? I mean, unless you are bucking for a place on some law school faculty." Oral Argument in Macdonald v. City of Chicago, March 10, 2010, accessible at http://www.supremecourt.gov/oral_arguments/argument_transcripts/08-1521.pdf

[16] Reva Siegel, "Originalism as Popular Constitutionalism in *Heller*," 122 *Harv. L. Rev.* 191 (2008).

[17] 109 U.S. 3 (1883).

[18] 92 U.S. 542 (1875).

[19] *Citizens United* v. *FEC*, 558 U.S. 310 (2010).

obscure, but not that they had a healthy suspicion of corporations, insisted that they be chartered only to serve public purposes, and restricted their powers and capital to prevent them from oppressing their fellow citizens and corrupting governments. Justice Scalia, confronted by this history, breezily asserted that the Founders only distrusted corporations because they associated them with monopolies, and would have felt perfectly happy endowing modern ones with free-speech rights. This argument is questionable on its own terms – the founding generation didn't just fear monopoly, they feared the overbearing influence of concentrated private power and wealth, and the modern multinational colossi have far more of both than the founders ever could have imagined – but it's also pretty clear that once you allow speculation on how-the-founders-would-have-changed-their-minds-if-they-had-our-experience you have left anything resembling strict originalism far behind.

So although originalism remains deeply embedded in national conversations about the Constitution, its generative possibilities for legal argument seem pretty nearly exhausted. Many Constitutional cases still have a big historical component, requiring law clerks and Court advocates and warring groups of professional-historical amici to weigh in. But after thirty years' experience with originalism in constitutional adjudication and argument, nobody seriously thinks historical inquiry is a method for actually deciding important cases, as opposed to helping rationalize the outcomes. Certainly nobody argues anymore for its virtues as a *determinate* method for limiting the discretion of judges. Even the newest conservative recruits to the Court, Justices Roberts and Alito, refuse to swear allegiance to hard-core originalism as the exclusive interpretive method and sometimes actively make fun of it.

Yet if the legal wing of the originalist project seems to be drooping, the populist wing seems to be soaring. A new generation of commentators has arisen, hardly for the first time in our history, to denounce the entire liberal-Progressive modern regulatory-welfare state (and especially Barack Obama's rather modest extensions of it) and its encouragement of moral deviance a wholesale traducing of the original Constitution.

Constitutional fundamentalists like the Tea Partiers have learned to read the Constitution through the eyes of the Mormon-John-Bircher historian W. Cleon Skousen – whose work has been revived by the TV commentator Glenn Beck and serves as the curriculum for over 200 seminars a year offered to Tea Party groups. Skousen simply consolidates all these elements of conservative belief and transports them into 1787, when the Founders established an Anglo-Saxon Christian nation on Biblically based principles which (at the same time) sharply limited the federal government's authority to interfere with free markets or redistribute wealth – a theocratic libertarian state.[20] A similar account of the Founding is given by David Barton, a best-selling historian whose particular mission is to explode conventional accounts of the separation

[20] *See*, e.g., W. Cleon Skousen, *The 5000 Year Leap* (2009).

of church and state: the United States was founded not merely as a Christian society but as a Christian polity; and one dedicated to free-market principles.[21]

One might be entitled to wonder – and certainly many critics have wondered – why such a divinely inspired order should also not only have tolerated slavery, but even entrenched it in the Constitution itself; but in the Christian-libertarian vision of the Founding, slavery is a minor and transitory anomaly. When the House Republican majority opened the 113th Congress (in January 2013) by reading the Constitution aloud, they left out the bits about the 3/5th clause and recapturing persons bound to service or labor and not abolishing the slave trade before 1808. Congresswoman Michele Bachmann explained that although the Founders had reluctantly compromised on the slavery issue (with whom? Some cabal of non-Founders?) they then led the fight to abolish it; and Glenn Beck explained that the 3/5 clause actually was a step taken toward eventual abolition – rather than an attempt to protect it from future political interference.

In fact, of course, slavery was just getting going on its major phase when the Constitution was adopted. Slavery was essential to the development of the nineteenth-century American economy and the numbers of slaves grew from 600,000 in 1780 to 4 million in 1860. And slavery was only the most extreme of many subordinate and dependent statuses in Founding-era America. The United States may well have been in some respects the most free society in the world of its time, with a higher proportion of independent farmers, mechanics and tradesmen, and a more widespread ownership of land. Yet most of its population remained in one kind or another of servitude, subject to the effective rule of others, enmeshed in a great dense web of legal regulations and delegations of state authority that supported command over slaves, wives, indentured servants, household servants, servants in husbandry, apprentices, paupers, and children.[22] One can't see these unfreedoms as minor blemishes on a tableau of liberty: without them there would have been no liberty as understood in those times; the subordination of the many was what enabled the liberty of the few. The free republican citizen, the free enterprising individual, the "free market" of libertarian imagination all rested upon this bedrock of unfreedoms.[23] Originalism as popular nostalgia necessarily hazes over such details.

Now it might seem that the popular and legal forms of originalism inhabit such different social spheres as to have little connection with one another. And it's true that you're not likely to see prominent legal conservatives quoting Cleon Skousen or David Barton or wearing tricorn hats. But there is actually

[21] *See*, e.g., David Barton, *Separation of Church and State: What the Founders Meant* (2007).

[22] For a rich catalogue of such statuses and the law that backed them, *see* Christopher Tomlins, *Freedom Bound Freedom Bound: Law, Labor, and Civic Identity in Colonizing English America, 1580–1865* (2010).

[23] See Edmund Morgan, *American Slavery – American Freedom: The Ordeal of Colonial Virginia* (1995).

quite a lot of leakage from one sphere into another, as distinguished conservative jurists draw on the same fonts of nostalgia culture as some of the more populist spokesmen.

Take for example Judge Edith Jones of the Fifth Circuit Court of Appeals, frequently mentioned as a likely Supreme Court appointment, in a speech to the Federalist Society lamenting the falling away of traditional moral and religious values from modern legalism: "The first 100 years of American lawyers were trained on Blackstone, who wrote that 'The law of nature dictated by God is binding in all countries and at all times; no human laws are of any validity if contrary to this.' The Framers created a government of limited power with this understanding of the rule of law – that it was dependent on transcendent religious obligation."[24] She goes on to trace most of the current problems of the legal system – which she identifies as over-materialistic lawyers, meritless claims like employment discrimination suits, and lawyers' incivility – to the godless and relativistic post-modern mentality that rejects natural law as the basis of law.

There is Judge Janice Rogers Brown of the D.C. Circuit, who attributes all that has gone wrong with current law to the conceit of human perfectibility, which she says informs the French and Russian Revolutions and the New Deal. The false idea of "abstract human rights" leads to the "collectivist impulse," which is wholly foreign to the Framers' "conception of humanity" and the "classical conception of the Constitution."

> Writing 50 years ago, F.A. Hayek warned us that a centrally planned economy is "The Road to Serfdom."[3] He was right, of course; but the intervening years have shown us that there are many other roads to serfdom. In fact, it now appears that human nature is so constituted that, as in the days of empire all roads led to Rome; in the heyday of liberal democracy, all roads lead to slavery. And we no longer find slavery abhorrent. We embrace it. We demand more. Big government is not just the opiate of the masses. It is *the* opiate. The drug of choice for multinational corporations and single moms; for regulated industries and rugged Midwestern farmers and militant senior citizens. ...
>
> Where government moves in, community retreats, civil society disintegrates, and our ability to control our own destiny atrophies. The result is: families under siege; war in the streets; unapologetic expropriation of property; the precipitous decline of the rule of law; the rapid rise of corruption; the loss of civility and the triumph of deceit. The result is a debased, debauched culture which finds moral depravity entertaining and virtue contemptible. ...[25]

Most impressive of all, there is the late Robert Bork. Bork was one of the earliest prophets of a resurgent originalism, but of a rather mild variety. In *The*

[24] For the whole (remarkable) speech, see <http://www.massnews.com/2003_Editions/3_March/030703_mn_american_legal_system_corrupt.shtml>

[25] Janice Rogers Brown, "A Whiter Shade of Pale: Sense and Nonsense – The Pursuit of Perfection in Law and Politics," Speech to Federalist Society, University of Chicago Law School, April 20, 2000, at <http://ejournalofpoliticalscience.org/janicerogersbrown.html>

Tempting of America (1989), the book he wrote after failing to be confirmed to a seat on the Supreme Court, his originalism was so tempered by prudence as to almost disappear. The Constitution in his account had been deformed soon after the start by John Marshall's expansionist readings, and since that time repeatedly mangled by further departures from original understandings. But the deformations had been written into case law and could not now be undone without upsetting reliance interests. All we could now do was to overrule some of the more egregious recent deformations, such as *Roe* v. *Wade*, the abortion decisions, and not commit any more.

> But if a judge concludes a prior decision was wrong, he faces additional considerations. The previous decision on the subject may be clearly incorrect but nevertheless have become so embedded in the life of the nation, so accepted by the society, so fundamental to the private and public expectations of individuals and institutions, that the result should not be changed now... Thus it is too late to overrule not only the decisions legalizing paper money, but also those decisions validating certain New Deal and Great Society programs pursuant to the congressional power over commerce, taxation and spending. To overturn these would be to overturn most of modern government and plunge us into chaos. No judge would dream of doing it. It was never too late to overrule the line of cases represented by *Lochner*, because they were unjustifiable restrictions on governmental power, and allowing additional regulation of economic matters did not produce any great disruption of institutional arrangements. Similarly, it will probably never be too late to overrule the right of privacy cases, including *Roe* v. *Wade* [holding that the Fourteenth Amendment prohibits legislatures from restricting the right to abortion in the first trimester], because they remain unaccepted and unacceptable to large segments of the body politic, and judicial regulation could at once be replaced by restored legislative regulation of the subject.[26]

That was Bork in 1990. But in his later years Bork's Burkean prudence, his willingness (however grudging) to come to a pragmatic accommodation to modern society, vanished. *Slouching Towards Gomorrah* (1996) is a ferocious polemic against our contemporary condition, and its declension from virtue, order and reason into radical egalitarianism, pornography, multiculturalism, sexual degeneracy, crime, irreligion, and contempt for family values. Bork is drawn back, however, to a time even preceding the Founding, since he makes clear that the seeds of current decline were planted back at the new republic's beginning in the Declaration of Independence, the American Enlightenment's paean to liberty and equality. The worm was already in the apple; although it was then assumed that the urges to liberty and equality must be surrounded by customary and social restraints, and nobody foresaw what would happen when these restraints were loosened. It is precisely the teleological *realization* of these original principles – not their betrayal – which has gradually dissolved the chains that once bound them, that have produced the rough beast: the cultural revolution of the 1960s and the left extremists' capture of American

[26] Robert H. Bork, *The Tempting of America: The Political Seduction of the Law* 158 (1990).

values, a society that is corrupt, immoral, and decadent, full of "an increasing number of alienated, restless individuals, individuals without strong ties to others, except in the pursuit of ever more degraded distractions and sensations."[27] Only a revival of traditional restraints can save us, if anything can. So far Bork sounds like a genuine traditionalist conservative, a principled antagonist of modernity. But then he resorts to scapegoating, naming the chief cause of decline as a barbarian class of liberal-intellectuals who hate America and the Western tradition. (Given that Bork himself has just thoroughly trashed both modern America and its foundational liberal traditions, this is pretty rich.)

Yet Bork turned out to be at best an ambivalent traditionalist, for in other respects he was an unabashed celebrator of modernity, especially of modern capitalism, technology, and science, not giving even a hint of the recognition that the economic dynamism he celebrated might have had something to do with the dissolution of traditional social ties, hierarchies, shared religious convictions and authorities he deplored.

In Anglo-American culture evocations of tradition, of innocence lost, have often sounded in a pastoral key, like the Romantic critiques of modernity that blamed the decline of virtuous conduct and social customs supporting it to industrialization, the vices of the city, the commercial ethic that everything is for sale, and the competitive individualism that dissolves communal ties. But in American conservative jeremiads, the lost Eden is a purer and stricter form of capitalism itself. That helps to account for the peculiar hodge-podge of ideas in conservative polemics, quotations from F. A. Hayek, Milton Friedman and (the militant atheist) Ayn Rand, alongside echoes of Burke's rebuke to the abstract ideas informing the French Revolution and paeans to pre-modern morality and objectively discoverable natural law.

Indeed New Right jurists like to imagine American economic policy to have been generally laissez-faire from the Founding all the way to the New Deal, with the role of lawyers and the courts being to protect business property and entrepreneurial liberty from regulation and redistribution. Constitutional law existed largely to set strict limits on state power.

But this is part caricature, part fantasy. The myth of America's laissez-faire past is probably the most persistent and most damaging of all the imagined histories. Though repeatedly and consistently exploded by historians, the myth continues to dominate the fantasies of factions who promote the return of the "Constitution in Exile," the Classical regime of the "*Lochner* Era." The main purposes of the founding legal regimes, including federal constitutional law, were not to limit governmental power but to energize it – to empower the new states and federal government to promote economic development. The aim of state statute and case law in the early national period was not to protect traditional property rights but to qualify or destroy them in favor of dynamic

[27] *Slouching Towards Gomorrah: Modern Liberalism and American Decline* 63 (1996).

and competing users. Indeed the general norm pervading the law of most of our history has been that property is held subject to qualification or regulation for public ends and the public good.[28] America's history of government action has not been one of "hands off the market," but of aggressive promotion and regulation of economic activity.[29]

There were of course historical moments when courts aggressively struck down legislation regulating property. But these too have a history at odds with boosters of unrestrained business. Mid-nineteenth-century constitutional "due process" limits on state power actually originate with Jacksonians hostile to *corporate* power, who believed that the state and its resources and powers were being perverted to favor corporate domination and concentration. State power was to be restricted to rein in special interest legislation favoring corporations – to prevent states from conferring privileges, subsidies, and tax exemptions on business entities who were corrupting its legislatures. (This strain of American liberalism is continued in present-day libertarian critiques of regulation and corporate welfare as rent-seeking by special interests.) Even the slew of Constitutional decisions that did strike down legislative regulations of business was confined to a particular period in our history (the *Lochner* Era, for short) and at its height routinely approved a great and growing mass of regulatory legislation.

The complaint that we have declined from the Good Old Constitution is often accompanied by the complaint that we have declined from the Good Old Common Law. (The complaint is odd on its face, since by nature the common law is dynamic and evolving, constantly adapting to new social conditions, and not a static code; that the common law of the twenty-first century is not the same as the common law of the nineteenth, or of the fourteenth, would seem to be on the whole a good thing.) A typical complaint comes from one of the most widely quoted lawyers on tort and regulatory reform, Philip Howard. In a series of books and opinion columns, Howard criticizes giving to the jury the decision about whether doctors have been negligent, to set standards of care – suggesting that this is an innovation "since the earliest days of the common law." He also says that until recent times this didn't matter much, because "social mores kept people from suing except in egregious cases."[30] It's hard to know where to begin to address these claims. Until the early nineteenth century, juries in American courts decided all issues of law as well as fact. Even after

[28] For an excellent review essay summarizing the scholarship documenting the U.S.'s history of active government policy and uses of the eminent domain, police and taxing powers to pursue it, *see* Harry N. Scheiber, "Private Rights and Public Power: American Law, Capitalism, and the Republican Polity in Nineteenth-Century America" (1997) 107 *Yale L. J.* 823.

[29] For a recent survey of some of this activity, see Jacob Hacker and Paul Pierson, *American Amnesia: How the War on Government Led us to Forget What Made America Prosper* (2016).

[30] [I have not been able to recover the original source for these quotations, an Op-Ed in the N.Y. *Times*. Howard has made similar points in all his major publications, such as *The Death of Common Sense* (1994), *The Collapse of the Common Good* (2002).]

judges began to control juries with directed verdicts and instructions, the basic decision on negligence remained the jury's to make, as it is today. Furthermore, in the good old days of the last century, there were many *more* lawsuits per person, with much less at stake, than there are now. America was a very litigious society. To be sure, until the nineteenth century, there were few *personal injury* lawsuits of any kind, even for terrible injuries; because of impediments such as the lack of contingent fees, rules disqualifying parties from testifying, and the "fellow-servant" rule precluding liability of firms for industrial accidents; and even fewer *medical malpractice* suits until the late twentieth century, because doctors would not testify against one another. The actual Golden Age here is one in which there were no effective compensation mechanisms – no liability, no social insurance – for personal injury, and very badly damaged people accepted their injuries because they had no other options – not because people generally didn't resort to litigation: they did, when they had some hope of recovering something from it.[31]

Popular originalism works quite effectively as a vague nostalgic traditionalism, in which the "Founding Fathers" simply become placeholders for a general sense of loss and longing. Ronald Reagan's political genius lay in part in his ability to bathe an earlier America in a hazy golden light and to suggest that if post-New-Deal excrescences could be removed, that America could be recovered. But when, like the Tea Party, nostalgia-peddlers propose specific policies based upon specific wildly implausible history, they become – at least one hopes they become – a lot less persuasive. How many people are going to buy the hysterical claims that social democracy is the same as the French Terror or Soviet Communism, that accepting Social Security and Medicare reduces them to a dependent servitude worse than slavery, or that regulations seeking to protect their property and health from industries polluting their air and water are a form of tyranny? That the meaning of freedom is that if you get sick and old, unless you can get family or charity to support you, you must expect to die in the street? How many would really wish to return to the repressive sexual morality and the rigid sex roles of "traditional" society, with its strict barriers to divorce and its legal regime disabling women from managing their own property and earnings, entering the professions and most other occupations, and voting?

Returning now to the legal side of the project: People often ask critics of orginalism like me: So, if you don't like originalism, what's the alternative? Well, there's always the long-standing conventional view, that investigation of the history of a Constitutional provision is one tool among many in interpretation, along with text and structure and precedent. There's Bruce Ackerman's celebrated set of criteria for recognizing and ratifying Constitutional moments

[31] On this history see generally, Lawrence M. Friedman, *The Republic of Choice: Law Authority and Culture* (1990).

evidenced by critical elections.[32] There's Henry Monaghan and David Strauss's endorsement of common-law constitutionalism, the notion that the interpretation of the constitution should take the same ideally cautious, Burkean course of following precedents, generalizing them occasionally into principles, distinguishing and modifying applications to take account of changed circumstances.[33] I also find very attractive William Eskridge and John Ferejohn's recent variant, that constitutional interpretation should take its cues from evolving popular opinion as expressed in federal and state statutes: this view also has a Burkean component, cautioning courts against recognizing new rights until legislatures have done some preliminary work of recognition[34]; and Jack Balkin's "framework constitutionalism," using the founding generations as sources of broad principles.[35] All of these require as a practical matter taking account of the polity's whole history, not just little snippets of it plucked from "founding" periods.

Lawyers sometimes write as if the main alternative to originalism, Living Constitutionalism, keeping the Constitution up to date with changing conditions, were mainly a normative method, and a dubiously valid one at that. Actually it just seems to be a good description of the way constitutional interpretation actually happens and understandings change – as social movements are successful in pushing new litigation and legislative strategies, executives put them on the agenda of policy priorities, elected officials champion and administrative staffs implement them, and courts – swept up like everyone else in social and ideological change and refreshed by new appointees – recognize and ratify those changes. As Balkin says:

> There is no plausible account of living constitutionalism that does not involve the Court responding to popular culture, social movement mobilization, and electoral politics. Popular constitutionalism and partisan entrenchment drive doctrinal development. Doctrinal development, in turn, shapes the direction of social movement

[32] Bruce Ackerman, *We the People* (3 vols, 1993–2014)

[33] Monaghan, "Constitutional Common Law," 89 *Harv. L. Rev.* 1 (1976); Strauss, *The Living Constitution* (2010). Justice Scalia specifically disparages this approach: he wants to use "common law" as context for interpreting original meaning; but not "common law method or reasoning" as a method of interpretation. That's because he thinks that in late-eighteenth-century American colonies and new states, common law was something akin to a code, a system of definite rules uniform across the colonies, as reported in Blackstone. Bernadette Meyler has valuably demonstrated that it was not – common law was disuniform, open to divergent interpretation and debate, and above all dynamic, understood as adaptable to changing circumstances and new republican values. Thus understood, doing common law as eighteenth-century lawyers did common law provides a way of reconciling originalism with changing and living constitutionalism – one doesn't discard the eighteenth-century context as irrelevant, but as framing the questions that need answering. Meyler, "Towards a Common Law Originalism," 59 *Stan. L. Rev.* 551 (2006).

[34] *A Republic of Statutes: The New American Constitution* (2010).

[35] *Living Originalism* (2011).

and political activism. It does this sometimes by changing facts on the ground, sometimes by shaping popular consciousness, sometimes by opening up new channels and opportunities for constitutional claims, and sometimes by spawning backlash and counter-mobilizations that attempt to discipline the courts and change their direction. Constitutional politics influences constitutional courts; and in turn constitutional courts influence constitutional politics – both by what courts do and by what they refrain from doing.[36]

None of this is to say that the study of original meanings and original applications is utterly pointless: any legal document, especially on old one, may need historical investigation to discover what problems the text was meant to address. More broadly, law, like literary and political movements, can always benefit from refreshment at the source, reviving older traditions and expressions of ideals as inspirations for present reforms. In criminal procedure, for example, the institution that the Founding generation most counted upon to administer justice and defend liberty, the jury, has been allowed to wither away to almost nothing because of coercive plea bargaining; the grand jury, which was supposed to provide a check on prosecutors, has suffered a similar fate; sentencing guidelines have severely curtailed judges' sentencing discretion, so that discretion to prosecute and sentence is now entirely and unreviewably concentrated in the hands of assistant DAs, in violation of every principle of separated powers. Other atrophied original primary means of control over state abuse, suits against officers for misuse of office; and supervision of interrogations of suspects by magistrates; could be ripe for revival. It is also worth recalling – as David Golove and Daniel Hulsebosch have recently done – that the Enlightenment cosmopolitans who designed the Constitution viewed its "fundamental purpose ... to create a nation-state that the European powers would recognize, in a practical and legal sense, as a 'civilized state' worthy of equal respect in the international community"[37] – and sought to achieve this by embedding arrangements that would ensure the new republic would comply with its treaty obligations and the law of nations.

But of course it's also a useful enterprise for judges – like historians and politicians and everybody else – to check their impulses to ancestor-worship by recalling what is most alien, repellent, and unusable about them – not to mention what is unwieldy and dysfunctional in the parts of the original structure we can't shake off, much as some of us might want to (like two senators per state). The appeal to history needs to be critical as well as respectful, to liberate the mind from the dead weights both of inertia and of complacent modernism, the normative force of the actual. History can be used to reproach the present not only by reminders of exemplary founding principles but of how traces of

[36] Balkin, "Framework Originalism and the Living Constitution," 103 *Nw. L. Rev.* 549, at 597 (2009).

[37] Golove & Hulsebosch, "A Civilized Nation" 85 *N.Y.U. L. Rev.* 932 at 935 (2010).

the execrated past, the past that our progress has supposedly left behind for good, lives on in traces of the present.[38]

But it's not enough, it seems to me, simply to criticize the traditions invoked by conservative nostalgia – either by showing they never happened, or that if they did, once you describe them fully, they aren't anything you would want to preserve or return to. It's not enough to expose them as mythic. Progressives and Progressive lawyers need inspiring pasts and traditions of their own.

Now we are lucky enough to be heirs to a history that holds in it plenty of inspiring ideals embedded in legal practices. For progressives the great narrative of American legal development is the struggle to realize the ideals of independent free citizenship (that is, freedom from the domination of powerful superiors) in the conditions of a modern society and economy; and of equality of legal status, political participation, and economic opportunities for everyone, and especially for groups previously considered to be subordinates or outsiders. The ideals we look to in history are the immigrants' ideal of America as "the best poor man's country," the ideal of widespread ownership of property and fluid social mobility, the free labor ideal, the non-subordination ideal, the democratic critiques of aristocracy, oligarchy, concentrated wealth, and corrupt alliances between political and business elites; the long hard campaigns for civic inclusion and social recognition of marginals and pariahs; the struggle for a popular culture of civil liberties; and of law and law courts available to hear and redress claims of the weak against the strong. These are the traditions fought for by the great social movements: the nineteenth-century workingmen's associations, abolitionists, and women's rights campaigners; the movements of freed slaves for civil rights and land redistribution after the Civil War and of the radical Northern political parties who supported them, the agrarian cooperative movements of the 1880s and 90s, the industrial unions of the 1930s, Franklin Roosevelt's Second Bill of Rights, the radical dissenters in the Red Scares following both world wars and the anti-Vietnam war movement, the feminist movements of the 1850s, 1930s and 1970s, the civil rights and farmworkers' movements of the 1960s and 70s, among many others. Courts had little to do with any of these movements except to provide the status quo with weapons to hold them back – with the rare exception of the Warren Court period; but courts sometimes did, however belatedly, recognize their gains in legal doctrine. Hanging on to those gains – preventing them from being rolled back by nostalgia for a mostly imaginary or when real, frequently unattractive past, is a reasonable goal of progressive constitutionalism. But political action that builds on those gains is far more important.

[38] Both sides in the current race-policy debates make this reproach. Conservatives argue that affirmative action is *just like segregation*, official classification of persons by race; liberals argue that "colorblindness" has become the *functional substitute for "separate but equal,"* an assertion of formal equality that masks continuing practices of subordination.

Both sides in our present debates also resort to what Nietzsche called "monumental" history – the invocation of heroic examples to rouse us from stupor and stagnation and immersion in trivialities and timid comforts.[39] For some the monuments are the large-minded public-spirited lawyer-statesmen like the Founders; for others the leaders of great movements of civil rights and social reform. The appeal is to people who seemed to live without fear, who refused to shrug their shoulders and say, "That's just the way it is," who were able to risk their comforts for their beliefs and the possibility of a better world.

[39] "[E]ven if we were happy to accept our calling as descendants of antiquity, even if we were resolved to take this calling seriously and pursue it vigorously ... in spite of this we would still have to ask whether we are forever doomed to being the disciples of fading antiquity. At some time or other we may be allowed gradually to set our goal higher and farther; at some time or other we should be able to praise ourselves for having recreated in ourselves the spirit of Hellenistic and Roman culture ... [E]ven the often painful thought of being epigones can, when conceived grandly, guarantee both to an individual and to a people a hope-filled longing for the future: insofar, at least, as we understand ourselves as heirs and descendants of the remarkable powers of antiquity and see in this our honor, our incentive. That is to say, not as anemic and stunted late-born offspring of powerful generations, who eke out a cold existence as the antiquarians and grave diggers of these prior generations." Friedrich Nietzsche, "The Utility and Liability of History for Life," *Unfashionable Observations* 85, at 142 (Richard T. Gray tr., 1995).

15

Undoing Historical Injustice*

[*This piece appeared in a collection of essays edited by Austin Sarat & Thomas Kearns,* Justice and Injustice *(University of Michigan Press, 1996). It turned out to be a droplet in a flood of books and articles on "transitional justice," the ways in which countries that had recently emerged from communist or military or (as in South Africa) racial dictatorships into more democratic forms of rule chose to confront – or not to confront – their authoritarian pasts. My particular interest here was in the legal strategies that the new democracies employ to deal with their pasts and with the stories about the past that they tell to explain and justify those strategies. There is now a vast literature on these subjects. I can't claim to have read it all, but the books that I have read that seem to contribute most of value to these debates are Ruti Teitel,* Transitional Justice *(2000), Martha Minow,* Between Vengeance and Forgiveness: Facing History After Genocide and Mass Violence *(1998), and most especially Mark Osiel,* Mass Atrocity, Collective Memory and the Law *(1999). There have also been some notable new contributions to the particular historical examples in this article: on the framing of the false "reconciliation" narratives after the U.S. Civil War, David Blight,* Race and Reunion: The Civil War in American Memory *(2001); and on postwar Germany's management of its Nazi past, Norbert Frei,* Adenauer's Germany and the Nazi Past: The Politics of Amnesty and Integration *(2010).*]

* This essay is in memory of Alan Freeman, a piercing analyst of structural injustice. It is a revised and expanded version of a lecture given at Amherst College on March 8, 1994. Comments at the Amherst lecture, at a meeting of the University of Chicago's seminar on Comparative Legal History in April 1994 (especially those of Julius Kirshner, who began by asking, "What do you mean by 'justice', anyway?"), and of Owen Fiss, Ariela Gross, Thomas Heller, and Sophie Pirie in conversation, have helped me grope toward what I was trying to say. I want to acknowledge the admirable research assistance of Ariela Gross, without which I would never have gotten this far.

My subject in this essay is that of legal responses of liberal polities to epochal injustices. A regime comes to power – whether by conquest and occupation, by violent revolution, or by peaceful transition does not matter for the present – in a society whose previous rulers and people have practiced or permitted what the new regime judges to have been gross, systemic injustices. The legal responses chosen by the regime express a relation of the new society with its history, how legal systems try to make the future by redesigning the past and their connection with it. Most of my examples will come from four cases I have been trying to understand in detail: U.S. Federal Reconstruction policy after the Civil War; American anti-race-discrimination policies in the Second Reconstruction, focusing on affirmative action; Allied occupation policy in the American zone of Germany after World War II; and, briefly and in passing, the policies being debated and adopted by post-communist regimes in Germany and Eastern Europe to deal with their communist pasts.

Each type of response comes embedded in a history, a narrative that stitches together the society's past and future. In that narrative the period of injustice usually figures as a deviation from, or a distortion of, the history that should have happened instead – a departure from the society's traditional norms and practices or from some trajectory of evolutionary development that the society had previously followed or, alternatively, should have been following. When injustice is portrayed as a deviation from a counterfactual history – traditional, evolutionary, or even utopian – the regime's response to injustice is a way of defining the new society's identity by reweaving the severed threads of memory – or to vary the metaphor, by getting history back on track. To put this another way, every legal proposal to undo injustice comes with a story attached explaining what went wrong and how to reconnect to the normal and normatively acceptable path.

Indeed one way we commonly – though, as I'll argue, very misleadingly – classify modes of response to injustice is expressly in terms of relation to the past – as either backward looking or forward looking. I'm thinking of the familiar distinctions between justice and policy, adjudication and administration, righting of past wrongs and prevention of new ones, corrective compensation and social engineering. Such distinctions have been salient in debates in the context of arguments over the proper scope of judicial activism, whether courts are appropriate and capable agents to undertake social policy-making through the mechanisms and remedies of "public law litigation," the class action, and structural injunction.[1]

Let me suggest a somewhat different set of categories: I'll call these narrow agency, broad agency, and structural approaches to injustice. As the names

[1] See Abram Chayes, "The Role of the Judge in Public Law Litigation," 89 *Harvard Law Review* 1281 (1976); Owen Fiss, *The Civil Rights Injunction* (1978); Donald Horowitz, *The Courts and Social Policy* (1977).

suggest, they attribute injustice, respectively, to bad actors, bad groups, and bad structures.

1. The *narrow-agency* framing of injustice is as wrongs done by specific perpetrators to specific victims; the remedy is the limited and negative retributive sanction of the criminal process or the corrective remedy of the civil suit for compensatory damages. By these means the world is restored to normal by the exaction of an equivalence for the wrong done, the harm inflicted.

2. *Broad-agency* approaches aim at corrective or compensatory justice extended from individuals to collectivities – groups and entities: many wrongs have been done, by collective perpetrators to collective victims. Sometimes of course the agency paradigm can be stretched to accommodate broad-agency theories of liability and remedy in courts, such as the Nuremberg prosecutors' theories of Nazi war planning as a conspiracy and of groups such as the gestapo and SS as "criminal organizations."[2] Such theories have recently been revived in the Czech "lustration" laws declaring the Communist Party of Czechoslovakia from 1948 to 1989 a criminal organization, and presuming the incapacity for public service of persons whose names appeared on secret-police lists of collaborators.[3]

But just as often broad-agency arguments are urged not in pursuit of legal redress in court, but of official or unofficial actions effecting moral redress – compensation of a whole class of persons, or of people with some plausible claim to be their legal descendants, for wrongs done to them (or their ancestors) by another class. Such claims are evidently most manageable if they can be made both by and against identifiable persons or legal entities representing them or their successors in interest: for example, the reparations claims against the U.S. government by the Japanese Americans interned during World War II,[4] the claims of native American tribes for restitution of tribal lands,[5] the claims of present-day West Germans for return of property confiscated in the East zone after 1949,[6] the claims of freed slaves after the Civil War for a share of the

[2] Telford Taylor, *Anatomy of the Nuremberg Trials* 501–533, 583–587 (1992). For examples of collective or corporate liability in ordinary judicial contexts, both civil and criminal, see Larry May, *The Morality of Groups* (1987); Joseph Vining, *Legal Identity: The Coming of Age of Public Law* (1978); Stephen Yeazell, *From Medieval Group Litigation to the Modern Class Action* (1987).

[3] Tina Rosenberg, *The Haunted Land: Facing Europe's Ghosts after Communism* (1995).

[4] For a comprehensive account of the internees' claims and their legal basis by the lawyer who litigated the claims, see Peter Irons, *Justice at War* (1993).

[5] For a useful recent summary treatment of these claims, see Nell Jessup Newton, "Compensation, Reparations and Restitution: Indian Property Claims in the United States," 28 *Georgia L. Rev.* 453 (1994).

[6] The German Unification Treaty distinguishes between expropriations between 1945 and 1949 under Soviet occupation, which are considered irreversible (though, under a 1991 decision of the German Constitutional Court, requiring compensation) and by the German Democratic

very plantation, lands they had once worked,[7] or even the reparations paid in the 1950s by the West German government (as the legal successor to the Third Reich) to the state of Israel (as the moral representative of world Jewry).[8] But of course groups making such claims may conceive of victim and perpetrator classes much more generally and loosely – all freedmen and their descendants, for example, against all slaveholders and traders and their descendants, or all blacks (those who have suffered from the legacy of the wrong) against all whites (those who have profited).[9]

Actions taken to undo collective injustices don't always, to be sure, involve compensation or return of property. They may take the form of apologies, or acknowledgment of responsibility for harm, or official ceremonies of remembrance meant to prevent repetition of past errors. The "Truth Commission" that the Chilean government set up after the period of military rule to investigate the abuses of the Pinochet regime took as one of its tasks that of trying to record, as accurately as the files would allow, the fate of every dead or missing person who might have been the victim of the regime and the probable cause of death or disappearance.[10] Or just the opposite: the regime may try to cancel past sins by forgiving and forgetting, granting pardons or general amnesties, or by willing collective oblivion, by maintaining official silence, keeping references to the unjust period out of public discourse and education. The restorers of Chilean democracy – at the military's insistence – followed this path as well, granting a general amnesty for human rights abuses and naming only army or police units, not individual perpetrators, as their causes.

3. Last are what I'll call *structural* approaches: more concerned to attribute injustice to bad structures than bad agents and to attempt to undo the injustices by reforming the structures. The historical enterprise takes the form of a search for explanations rather than a search for villainous agents and attribution of blame; the remedial enterprise is directed to altering institutions, systems, and incentives rather than to exacting punishment or liability. The remedies may include the deliberate erasure of memory, such as when the public monuments and street names of the old regime are obliterated (as in East Berlin twice in modern times, once when the communists took over after the war and now again after they have fallen). That all sounds terribly mild, but naturally it needn't be: notoriously the leading examples of structural approaches to past injustices are Marxist-Leninist regimes, whose structural

Republic after 1949, which, subject to overriding legislation to encourage investments, must be restored.

7 See Eric Foner, *Reconstruction: America's Unfinished Revolution, 1863–1877* (1988).

8 Adenauer-Ben Gurion Agreement (1953).

9 Are Marxist-Leninist revolutionary expropriations of the bourgeoisie-as-whole in favor of workers and peasants examples? In their effects, yes, because they penalize one class of agents for another's benefit. In theory of course they are structural.

10 Phillip E. Berryman, trans., *Report of the Chilean National Commission on Truth and Reconciliation* (1993).

remedies have led them to expropriate and sometimes physically eliminate whole classes that have stood in the path of the march of history; the victims probably didn't feel any better about it because they were targeted as structures and not agents. Liberal regimes – the subject of the present chapter – also take structural approaches, but they are usually (though by no means always) constrained in their use of more drastic restructurings by liberal norms of legalism and democratic politics.

I started out by saying that each type of response to injustice is embedded in a history; it comes with a story attached of how history went off the track.

The view of history embedded in the corrective justice model is profoundly conservative, in the literal sense of the term. It reduces past or even continuing injustice to the isolated acts of a handful of bad agents: exceptional and abnormal disruptions of a normal law-abiding order. Nothing out of the way has happened except that a few villains or monsters spun out of control and in the process injured a few victims. Ingo Müller's recent work on German jurists after the war furnishes terrible examples of this mentality at its most extreme. The judges asserted their faith in the continuity of an autonomous legal community and doctrinal tradition even through the Third Reich, when the tradition was overlaid – but in the official view only superficially – with a thin layer of alien matter, distinctively Nazi statutes. For these judges, the only real interruption in tradition was that of the dark "tragic" period of occupation, 1945–1950. (The faith was sustained on a real continuity in personnel, for denazification efforts hardly touched the judiciary at all.) The courts purged very few statutes as "distinctively National Socialist" and confined the "criminal" agents of the regime to a tiny number of malefactors: Hitler and his immediate circle. Thus when postwar German courts tried even murders committed by lower-level Nazis, they took the view that only Hitler, Himmler, and a few others could be considered "perpetrators" of these crimes; anyone lower down, even if he pulled the trigger, was merely an "accomplice."[11]

Amnesties and pardons seem at first to be insisting on discontinuity rather than continuity with the past: it is time to put that unfortunate business behind us, to write a final line – or *Schlusstrich*, as the Germans say – under it, to make a fresh start. This is especially so when the new regime begins with an amnesty for leading perpetrators of the worst injustices – in some cases because the perpetrators, like the Chilean military, have insisted upon amnesty as a condition of the new regime's establishment; or, in other cases because the new regime, in a spirit of reconciliation, calls a halt to prosecution of perpetrators, as with the German and Allied wave of amnesties, pardons, and statutes of limitation for National Socialist crimes in the late 1940s and the 1950s.[12]

[11] Ingo Müller, *Hitler's Justice: The Courts of the Third Reich* 249–260 (1991).

[12] For example, Law on the Granting of Immunity (December 31, 1949; 1[1949] B.g.b. 37); Law of July 17, 1954 (1 [1954] B.g.b. 203).

But of course, as these examples suggest, willed oblivion is sometimes the most conservative story of all: it brackets the period of injustice as a historical accident, an outlying event in the general stream, so atypical as not to be worth mentioning, with no origins traceable to the prior period or implications for the present one. The injustice epoch drops out of memory altogether, and history resumes at the point where it left the track.

Treating the old injustices as ordinary crimes or torts, on the other hand, does at least send a signal to the world about historical discontinuity as well as continuity. The criminal trial with elaborate due process safeguards, modeled in Nuremberg, dramatizes the difference between the arbitrary cruelty of the unjust regime and the new regime's regard for truth and fair procedure. Adenauer's agreement to pay 3 billion Deutsche Marks in reparations to the state of Israel was less an attempt to compensate for the Final Solution, for which no compensation could ever have been enough, than to demonstrate to the Western nations with which Germany sought to integrate that the reconstructed Germany acknowledged its past and accepted responsibility for the predecessor regime's crimes, but was itself a reformed and chastened people, free of the Nazi taint. Still, there is no escaping the implicit conservatism of corrective justice, its implication that all debts are paid; and the period of reparations (*Wiedergutmachung*) is now generally regarded in Germany in a darker light, as a kind of exorcism by which the government tried to pay for "silence and a good conscience"[13] and to avoid confronting either the Nazi past or its many lingering traces.

In this chapter, I want to focus on a particular type of forward-looking response to epochal injustice: the restructuring response, the policies directed not at individuals but at institutions, cultures, and social structures, the social engineering strategies designed to rearrange the social system so that its organizations will lack the capacities and incentives to repeat the injustices. The most radical policies of restructuring would seem even more than the policy of deliberate forgetting to repudiate the past – or to treat it at best, as in Marxist eschatology, as merely a set of preparatory stages for a revolutionary present that, when actualized, will negate everything that has prepared the way. But just as backward-looking corrections of injustice also point forward to a society committed to justice in the future, so too do proposals for even radical restructuring rely on narratives of continuity – of traditions and trajectories of evolutionary change.

After the American Civil War the most radical proposals – the most radical, that is, aside from emancipation itself, which effected a massive uncompensated transfer of property from slaveholders to freedmen – were the various plans to confiscate large Southern plantations and break them up into forty-acre

[13] Saul Friedlander and Corinna Coulmas, "German Leftists Come to Grips with the Past," 6 *Holocaust & Genocide Studies* 33 (1991).

lots for distribution or sale-by-preemption to the freedmen. The nominal legal basis was corrective – punishment of rebellion and collection of delinquent Federal taxes. A few such lands actually were distributed through tax sales and Sherman's field orders. The most ambitious plan was Thaddeus Stevens's to confiscate 394 million acres from seventy thousand of the "chief rebels" (about 5 per cent of the South's white families) for distribution to freedmen. Stevens did put forward a compensatory rationale founded in Lockean labor theory: "[The freedmen] have earned this, they have worked upon the land for ages, and they are entitled to it."[14] Just compensation for long services rendered and never paid was apparently also the basis on which most of the freedmen claimed the right to their share of land.[15] But the radicals' main motive was to transform the political economy of the South and in consequence its political sociology. The analysis drew upon the central historical narratives of American political experience: the liberal, Scottish Enlightenment and civic-republican histories of the rise of liberty through the destruction of "feudal" estates, hierarchies, and "monopolies," and of the foundation of both personal freedom and democratic institutions on decentralized ownership, the economic independence of a self-sufficient "yeoman" middle class of freeholders and small traders. So long as the planter class controlled the land, the freed slaves could never attain enough "independence" to establish a political counterforce.

> Nothing is so likely to make a man a good citizen as to make him a freeholder. Nothing will so multiply the productions of the South as to divide it into small farms. Nothing will make men so industrious and moral as to let them feel that they are above want and are the owners of the soil which they till... No people will ever be republican in spirit and practice where a few own immense manors and the masses are landless. Small independent landholders are the support and guardians of republican liberty.[16]

With the economic basis of the planter class destroyed and the land occupied by yeoman farmers, the South could at last be launched on the evolutionary path to a free society (and not incidentally, ensure the Republican party an unbreakable lock on Congress for some time to come).

A very similar ideology and underlying set of historical assumptions informed an important school of policy-makers defining American structural reform objectives for the occupation and reconstruction of Germany and Japan. There were many conflicting American objectives.[17] Some officials – generally the most conservative, prizing above all the restoration of economic

[14] Thaddeus Stevens, quoted in Kenneth Stampp, *The Era of Reconstruction*, 1865-1877 122 (1965).

[15] See Leon Litwack, *Been in the Storm So Long: The Aftermath of Slavery* 399–408 (1979).

[16] Thaddeus Stevens, *quoted in* Eric Foner, *Politics and Ideology in the Age of the Civil War* 135 (1980).

[17] For useful summaries, *see* Walter Dorn, "The Debate over American Occupation Policy in Germany in 1944 to 1945," 72 *Political Science Quarterly* 481 (1957); Lutz Niethammer, *Entnazifizierung in Bayern* 32–68 (1972).

stability and civic order administered through existing elites – adopted a narrow-agency view of Nazism as a criminal "outlaw state" concentrated in a few top officials. Others favored a broader view that fascist and militarist ideologies had infected large numbers in mass and leadership institutions and required a wider purge. Structural approaches to history and reconstruction (setting aside the most drastic and soonest-abandoned structural approach, the Morgenthau Plan for the total destruction of German industrial capacity) seem to have been most common among intellectuals engaged in postwar planning,[18] and these approaches were briefly influential, if far from always dominant, in the first two years of occupation policy. The basic insight was the same as that of classical American liberal-republican history: that the paradigmatic movement of "progressive" societies was from status to contract, from the "feudalism" of fixed social statuses and of labor tied to land to the free movement of land, labor, and capital; from concentrated land ownership and state-sponsored monopolies to decentralized ownership and competitive enterprise; and that personal freedom and the stability of democratic political institutions in turn in the West, especially in the United States, had rested on the development of a broad property-owning middle class and sufficient social mobility to open access to that class through hard work and talent. By 1945 this history had been brought up to date with a Progressive addendum, in the recognition that the large-scale organizations of industrialized economies had fundamentally changed the political sociology of liberalism: evidently, the ideal of independent proprietorship of a farm of business for nearly everyone had become impossible, and wage-labor or tenant-farmer status the permanent condition of millions. In the conditions of industrial society, democracy had to be sustained on a different basis, and this basis, in Progressive-New Deal thinking, could be generated by public policies encouraging a wide distribution of wealth and access to educational opportunity and combining the breakup of "excessive" concentrations of economic power with the strategic creation of plural and countervailing sources of power, in opposition parties, trade unions, independent universities, and a free press. A new middle class would thus be created out of high-wage labor with job security, craft workers, industrial workers, and white-collar workers within the organizations. Thus, the twin dangers would be avoided of a state dominated by industrial plutocrats and of a marginalized and disaffected working class susceptible to communist agitators and fascist dictators. (It was not yet widely appreciated that Hitler had come to power on the votes of the middle-class, not the working-class, electorate.)

[18] The intellectuals were concentrated in the Office of Strategic Services: the core was a remarkable group of German émigré scholars: Franz Neumann, Hajo Holborn, Otto Kirchheimer, Felix Gilbert, and Carl-Joachim Friedrich. The bible of this group was Neumann's structural analysis of Nazism in *Behemoth: The Structure and Practice of National Socialism* (1942). See Barry Katz, *Foreign Intelligence: Research and Analysis in the Office of Strategic Services, 1942–45* (1989), for an account of this group and its work.

This then was what Progressive liberals and social democrats assumed to have been the exemplary history of Western democracies. By the terms of this model Germany and Japan had taken a deviant path to modernity – the thesis that historians now refer to as the "special path," or *Sonderweg*, thesis. In Germany especially industrialization had not been the project of a middle class committed to liberalism by its opposition to "feudal" landowners and an authoritarian and monopolistic state; it had rather been a "revolution from above," instigated by a thoroughly authoritarian state of officials recruited from hereditary great landowners and officer corps, devoted to traditional hierarchies and privileges, hostile to parliamentary democracy, and prone to expansionist foreign policies. In such a social structure, the state had created giant industrial cartels in its own image and cemented its power by alliance with them, the great landowning interests, and the army, against the threat of social democracy and independent trade unions.

This liberal Progressive view of history significantly influenced U.S. occupation policies in the American zone of Germany. The occupation set about what was probably the most comprehensive program of deliberate social engineering designed to produce the institutions, social structure, and culture of a liberal democratic republic in which Americans had ever engaged, even including the first decades of its own republic-building history and the radical plans for Southern reconstruction. Incidentally the more sophisticated of the reformers, who included a good many German exiles, denied that they were simply trying to remake Germany in the American image: they tried to establish continuities for all their reforms with prior experiments in German democracy, those of 1848 and especially the Weimar Republic. The acknowledged purpose was to break the hold of the old authoritarian elements – through land reform and the breakup of heavy industry, of the press syndicates, and of the elite-schooling monopolies that controlled access to the higher occupations – and to stimulate the formation of plural local from-the-bottom-up organizations: local political parties, regional newspapers, collective bargaining units at the plant level.

The most ambitious because by far the most administratively demanding component of the policy was denazification – which the liberal-progressive planners in the State Department, OSS, and SWNCC saw less as a punitive program than as the crucial prerequisite to positive reconstruction.[19] Key offices in the key institutions had to be staffed with people committed to the values of the new order.

As is well known, both these plans for radical reconstruction – in the post-Civil War South and U.S. zone of Germany – met with predictable fierce resistance and in any case came rapidly into collision with competing policies,

[19] See John H. Herz, "The Fiasco of Denazification in Germany," 63 *Political Science Quarterly* 569 (1948) and John H. Herz, "Denazification and Related Policies," in *From Dictatorship to Democracy*, 15–38 (Herz ed. 1982).

serving competing objectives, and attached to competing narratives of continuity, that in short order were to overwhelm them. The two experiences exhibit some remarkable likenesses. Promises under Reconstruction to redistribute plantation lands – to the vast disappointment of the freedmen who had trusted in them – never materialized; the few lands that had been distributed, as in the Sea Islands experiment, were returned to their former white owners. Instead of being yeoman freeholders, the freedmen found themselves once more subordinate farm laborers, initially as contract laborers coerced into Freedmen's Bureau-supervised contracts and tied to the land by vagrancy and enticement statutes, later as debt peons or sharecroppers.[20] Along the way, of course, they were also disenfranchised and resegregated by both law and custom.

For the Southern planters, the Civil War amendments had changed only the formal status of their black labor force; the task now was simply to work around the legal restrictions to reattach black laborers to their former masters and to preserve stratification by caste. Theirs was the narrative of "Redemption" – the reclaiming of "traditional" states' rights, customs, and labor practices after the interruptions of invasion and occupation policies: a recovery of continuity. For the Northern coalition that backed off the promise of Reconstruction to build a foundation for republican liberty by providing the freedmen with homesteads, the main strategy for linking the redeemed South to the liberal narratives of American history was through a much narrower construction of the end point of Western development as the possession of a formally equal chance at achieving, whatever the individual's starting point, self-sufficiency through free labor. Any additional attempts to distribute advantages to the freedmen would be a *reactionary* step backwards into a pre-liberal regime of dependence-inducing "paternalism" and race-based preferences and disabilities.[21] In the minds of Northern whites, the abolitionist view of the South as a pocket of feudal backwardness gave way to a "culture of conciliation" in which Northern whites combined deliberate forgetting – amnesty and amnesia for the rebellion and the "sins" of slavery – with adoption of Southern whites' own romantic myths of Redemption as recovery of a chivalric and aristocratic past, the continuing of a tradition in which blacks knew, and gratefully accepted, their servile place.[22]

The results of Allied occupation "democratization" policies in Germany were more mixed – and still very much disputed among historians: the occupation pushed through the adoption of the Basic Law; they did stimulate political party formation and competition, especially at the Land level; and they are generally credited with helping to create an independent press. The policies

[20] See Willie Lee Rose, *Rehearsal for Reconstruction* (1964); Foner, *supra* note 16.

[21] Gerald Jaynes, *Branches Without Roots* 16–23 (1986); Foner, *supra* note 7 at 237; Aviam Soifer, "The Paradox of Paternalism and Laissez-Faire Constitutionalism," 5 *Law & Hist. Rev.* 249 (1987).

[22] Nina Silber, *The Romance of Reunion: Northerners and the South, 1865-1900*, 108–109 (1993).

aimed at breaking the hold of traditional "authoritarian" elites and broadening the bases of social opportunity had very limited success. Radical decartelization and deconcentration policies were discarded by 1947 as obstacles to the more important goals of restoring German industrial capacity and integration with Western trade; though a milder form of decartelization directed at coal and iron was revived in 1950.[23] The U.S. preference for factory-level collective bargaining over bread-and-butter issues and its hostility to German efforts to construct institutions for corporatist bargaining (codetermination, workers' councils, centralized national unions) seem to have had the immediate effect of suppressing new grassroots initiatives for the governance of industry and thus of maintaining the hold of the old elites.[24] The educational reforms – directed at replacing the old system of class-based tracking and at modernizing the curriculum, especially in social sciences, languages, and history – aroused formidable conservative resistance and succeeded only in establishing the Free University in West Berlin and a handful of integrated comprehensive schools in a few Länder.[25] Only the officer corps was genuinely reconstructed, thanks in large part to the Soviet zone's destruction of its economic base in the Junker estates.

Denazification was a notoriously expensive fiasco. The most resented of all Allied occupation policies – opposition to denazification was the only issue that united all postwar German parties – it was also the most ineffectual. Administrative mass processing by inexperienced personnel inflicted fines and dismissals on thousands of small fry, while the larger fish were spared because they were urgently needed for rebuilding efforts, or were better equipped to take advantage of backlogs to delay their cases, or had emigrated from the East where no Westerner could know what they had done. Soon after the process was turned over to reluctant German tribunals to complete, it became largely a "follower-factory (Mitläuferfabrik)" process for reclassifying serious "offenders." By the time the U.S. Congress called a lurching halt to the process in 1948, sacrificing it to the more pressing need for reliable and unresentful allies against communism, the very meaning of the term *denazification* had changed from a

[23] Volker Berghahn, *The Americanization of West German Industry, 1945–73*, 84–110 (1986). See also Albert Diegmann, "American Deconcentration Policy in the Ruhr Coal Industry," in *American Policy and the Reconstruction of West Germany, 1945–55*, 197–215 (Diefendorf *et al.* ed. 1993).

[24] Diethelm Prowe, "German Democratization as Conservative Restabilization: The Impact of American Policy," in *American Policy and the Reconstruction of West Germany, 1945–55*, 307–329 (Diefendorf *et al.* ed. 1993).

[25] James Tent, *Mission on the Rhine: Reeducation and Denazification in American-Occupied Germany* (1983); Jutta-B. Lange-Quassowski, *Neuordnung oder Restauration? Das Demokratiekonzept der amerikanischen Besatzungsmacht und die politische Sozialisation der Westdeutschen* (1979); Lange-Quassowki, "Coming to Terms with the Nazi Past: Schools, Media, and the Formation of Opinion," in *From Dictatorship to Democracy*, 83–103 (Herz ed. 1982).

process for the purging of Nazis from positions of influence to a process for rehabilitating former Nazis to declare them eligible to return to their positions of influence.[26] The policies paid the penalty for overambition and confusion of aims. The liberal democratizers in the American zone had the largely structural aim, as in Japan, of replacing wholesale the top echelons of the German ruling class, and to this end drew up an appendix of high offices in bureaucracy, military, and industry [Control Council Directive #24]; but the Germans never accepted this appendix – and invariably characterized denazification in strictly agency-based terms as devoted to finding and punishing the worst Nazis. No matter how often the Allies characterized the tribunals as merely administrative, negative findings did after all carry penalties such as fines, confiscation, and deprivation of office with legal tenure. To the extent the proceedings were purportedly narrow-agency-based, targeting the worst offenders, they were visibly unjust, since the categories and presumptions on the questionnaires were necessarily crude, the administrative process necessarily summary, and the role of grudge informers in accusing and of good personal and clerical connections in exonerating so pervasive. To the extent they were based on broad-agency notions of collective liability, they were especially resented by a people already inclined, in the ruins of war, mass dislocation, and occupation, to see themselves collectively not as victimizers but as victims.

As structural remedies, at the same time, the denazification policies were vastly over- and underinclusive: by requiring all Germans older than eighteen to be screened instead of targeting high functionaries, they simply never got around to reviewing major institutions like the civil service; and by conflating the authoritarian elements they wished to purge with Nazi party membership, they passed over entirely traditional elites who had never joined the party but had done its bidding, had helped to undermine Weimar, and now sought to restore the institutions of the Kaiserreich. More decisively, the structural objectives of the purges conflicted fundamentally with other structural aims. As Volker Berghahn concisely put it:

> A de-Nazification policy which would have taken to task those individuals who made a major contribution to sustaining the Hitler regime would have touched the social and economic power structures of the Western zones much more radically than the Allies were prepared to permit. Neither the kind of economic system nor the society they were trying to reconstruct could exist without the expertise of the administrative, managerial and technical elites which had collaborated with Hitler.[27]

Resistance to the social reforms of the democratizers, and the shift of Allied policy focus from "reform" to stabilization with the division of Germany and the onset of the cold war, naturally drew upon alternative narratives of

[26] John Gimbel, *A German Community under American Occupation* (1961); John D. Montgomery, *Forced to be Free* (1957); Niethammer, *Entnazifizierung*.

[27] Volker Berghahn, *Modern Germany*, 187 (2nd edn. 1987).

Germany history and the placing of that history within the wider history of the West. The history of Germany as dangerous so long as it remained an authoritarian departure from the Western modernizing norm was temporarily shelved in favor of another much closer to the orthodox German view. In this view the mistakes not to be repeated were, first, those of Versailles, in which overly punitive peace terms had pushed the resentful German electorate into the grasp of a dictator who promised to restore national pride; second, the descent into economic chaos that had turned the stabilizing element of the middle class politically volatile; and finally, the weakness of the state, the inability of the fragile republic to defend itself against antidemocratic subversion – which in postwar conditions, under the prevailing analysis equating fascism and communism as variant forms of a single pathology of "totalitarianism," was subversion from the Left. American policy thus turned away from internal reform of German social structure to a strategy of integrating Germany with the Western Allies – with industry through the Schuman Plan, with trade through the Marshall Plan, with defense through rearmament under NATO command – and of subsidizing the economic miracle. This policy actually drew upon a much older narrative of Atlantic culture, the *doux commerce* thesis of Montesquieu and the Scottish Enlightenment, to the effect that turning to commercial pursuits is the best dissolver of a nation's warlike spirit. And in the meantime, the structural-reform ambitions of the democratizing liberals, especially decartelization and denazification, were discredited by being compared to the drastic and ruthless social restructurings that had been carried out on the other side of the Iron Curtain.

Some among the German elites, at the same time, were able to rescue from the failures and turnabouts of Allied policy an identity based on rather different, often very conservative, ideas of continuity. For some conservatives, membership in NATO reaffirmed Germany's historical geopolitical and cultural identity as the buffer Middle European state defending the humanistic values of the West from the barbarian hordes of the East. Traditional elites took care to affirm the positive value of Germany's deviant path (minus Hitler's regrettable excesses, which in this period were dealt with by silence): we like our Sonderweg, they said, we have no wish to be like America. The churches, which Americans in one of the most ludicrous cultural mistranslations had assumed to be "progressive" forces for democracy because of their dislike of Nazism, had most of all disliked Nazism for its ideology of progress and its populist policies: they undertook to retain the elite schooling tracks such as the Gymnasium and to ensure their devotion to Germany's ancient humanist past and "Christian values," most especially by requiring Latin and Greek. As of 1950, former Nazi party members were still in, or returned to, high positions in the civil service, judiciary, universities, and industry. Ingo Müller has described the official ideology as one of continuity of legal and civil-service traditions, the only interruption in continuity being denazification itself. Some "victims" of denazification received compensation in the civil courts; most important, a statute was passed (May 11, 1951) under the authority of Article 131 of the Basic Law, giving all those civil servants dismissed since 1945 a legal right to reinstatement and back pay. "For all practical purposes," as Müller comments acidly, "former membership in the Nazi party became a requirement for joining the civil service."[28] Yet though the most unregenerate of the elites, such as the judges and law professors, insisted on continuity, probably the most widespread strategy toward the Third Reich in the 1950s was deliberate oblivion. General amnesties were passed for Nazi crimes; the Allies pardoned or commuted sentences for most of the war criminals; the teaching of history in the schools and universities ended with Bismarck. Until the subject was sharply revived in the youth revolts of the 1960s, the Nazi period was treated as an inexplicable outbreak of exceptional criminality, and a general silence on the period descended.[29]

This has so far been an attempt to outline some general approaches that liberal societies have adopted to undoing historical injustice and the kinds of narratives of continuity and reformation that are attached to each approach, and also to begin to fill in the outline with some examples. Now I want to turn to the most enduring legacy of historical injustice in the United States, the subordination of its black people, and to ask how the conflicts over U.S. legal policy in the Second Reconstruction, especially affirmative action policies, fit into the general scheme I've outlined. These debates yield a rich if bewildering variety of positions.

Agency-based models, to recall the basics of the scheme, are those that frame the injustice as a harm committed by perpetrators upon victims, the undoing of which requires a make-whole remedy commensurate with the wrong. The result aims simply to remove blemishes that dot a landscape of historical normality.

Narrow agency is now the position commonly identified with legal conservatives, such as those who staffed the Office of Legal Policy and the Civil Rights Division of the Justice Department in the Reagan administration as well as the "right" wing of the U.S. Supreme Court, Justices Antonin Scalia and Clarence Thomas. The essence of the position is simple: slavery and Jim Crow were great historical injustices because they violated the historically established American basic norm of formally equal legal treatment of persons, or color blindness. These injustices were undone and the principle vindicated in the Reconstruction Amendments, *Brown* v. *Board of Education*, and the Civil Rights Act of 1964. Thus: (1) any state action (or private action subject to the antidiscrimination statutes) that directs preferential treatment of any racial group, including "affirmative action" intended to benefit historically

[28] Müller, *Nazi Justice*, 205.

[29] Richard Evans, *In Hitler's Shadow* 11–12 (1989); Ian Buruma, *The Wages of Guilt: Memories of War in Germany and Japan* 56 (1994).

disadvantaged groups, is unlawful as violating the color blindness principle prohibiting any use of racial categories as the basis of legal action; (2) the only persisting injustice that is legally cognizable is that of provable individual acts of racial animus directed against specific persons; and (3) whites who are disadvantaged by race-conscious policies are themselves victims of discrimination who must be legally made whole.[30] We are not to look back at older sins that may have contributed to present racial inequalities; and we are certainly not to contrive broad structural approaches to remedying them that benefit the victims of history: that is not justice, but "social engineering."[31]

The position seems at first glance completely anti-historical: After the Civil Rights Act of 1964, America is born anew and born into a presumptive condition of color blindness; the past has become simply irrelevant, except as its traces linger in the animus that occasionally flares into an isolated act of discrimination. Like much else in Reagan's ideology, the position owes something to the old myth of the American Adam, who upon arriving in America sheds the Old World's burdens of history and original sin and becomes free to reinvent himself. If the myth is an awkward fit to the situation of peoples descended from forcibly imported slaves, it can be made to fit by imagining 1964 as the date of their "arrival": once released from legal disabilities, blacks have since been free to compete on equal terms.

Yet inspected more closely, the position, like narrow-agency positions generally, is rooted in a conservative historical narrative of deep continuities subjected to temporary interruptions and deviations. The major civil rights tracts of President Reagan's lawyers and other conservative theorists of race relations consist in large part of elaborate historical justifications.[32] The main use of these histories is to establish that America's traditional, indeed Constitutional, Grundnorm of legal equality means color blindness and nothing else. Calling for authority on dead radicals, conservatives claim as precursors not only the authors of the Declaration of Independence, Lincoln, and the elder Justice Harlan, but also the abolitionists, Frederick Douglass, and the leaders of the early civil rights movement – Thurgood Marshall and the NAACP, Martin Luther King and the SCLC, and Hubert Humphrey and the other sponsors of the 1964 Civil Rights Act. If the deep continuity is in America's commitment to color blindness, any departure from it is a momentary deviation or anomaly. Indeed, in this view the original Constitution itself was an anomaly; a regrettable compromise with principle, unfortunately necessary at the time to bring

[30] The position has been advanced on innumerable occasions – perhaps in its purest and most powerful form in the Brief of the Solicitor General filed in *Wygant* v. *Jackson Board of Education*, 476 U.S. 267 (1986).

[31] Morris Abram, "Fair Shakers and Social Engineers," 99 *Harv. L. Rev.* 1312 (1986).

[32] For representative conservative histories of race relations, *see* Terry Eastland and William J. Bennett, *Counting by Race: Equality from the Founding Fathers to Bakke and Weber* (1979); Clink Bolick, *Changing Course* (1988).

the Southern states into the Federal Union. Slavery and state-mandated segregation were anomalies too.

On a par with those evils, and equally representing departure from historically established principle, is the general trend of federal civil rights policy after 1965 – judicial remedies in the form of "affirmative and comprehensive" school-integration plans intended to remedy not simply present discrete discriminatory acts but also the effects of historical discrimination: the adoption of statistical disparate-impact measures of employment discrimination and the imposition of novel requirements of federal contractors and grantees of numerical "quotas, goals, and timetables" measuring affirmative action favoring specific groups. The great discontinuity, as pictured in these conservative histories, is thus between American liberalism's "traditional" pursuit of color-blind equal treatment and the modern civil rights coalition's mania for quotas and proportional representation. "To pursue the concept of racial entitlement – even for the most admirable and benign of purposes – is to reinforce and preserve for future mischief the way of thinking that produced race slavery, race privilege, and race hatred."[33]

All histories select, but the omissions of this one are breathtaking. The most obvious problem with the narrative is its attempt to find firm ground in history for a basic norm to which, until quite recently, few whites ever subscribed. For most of our history it was generally assumed even in the free Northern states that blacks were, like women, a taken-for-granted exception to the norm of liberal equality; and indeed, especially in the South, that the confining of blacks to menial labor, either slave or free, was a necessary condition to the equal liberty and full citizenship of the white population. The norm of "color blindness" in the conservative narratives is at best a deeply buried immanent norm, a norm in long gestation, carried before its full realization only by a handful of mavericks, marginals, and outsiders: abolitionists, Radical Republicans, a lone dissenting Supreme Court justice (Harlan), and the moderate wing of the modern civil rights movements. In order to represent color blindness as the modern consensus norm, the conservative histories must leave out – and they do leave out – all the modern history that would help explain why liberal centrists after 1964 turned to affirmative action strategies. They represent the period from the 1954 *Brown* case as an irenic period of steady progress in race relations, in which one legal barrier after another fell to full legal citizenship and in which the irrationality of racism evaporated in the sunlight of modernity, rather than one of ferocious and continuing white resistance – including resistance by many people in the current conservative leadership, which that same leadership has exploited to its considerable political advantage.[34]

[33] *Adarand Constructors, Inc.* v. *Pena*, 63 U.S.L.W. 4523 (1995) (Scalia, J., concurring).

[34] *See generally* Thomas Byrne Edsall and Mary D. Edsall, *Chain Reaction: The Impact of Race, Rights and Taxes on American Politics* (1992). As Randall Kennedy has grimly pointed out, the record of opposition of conservative leaders like Ronald Reagan to virtually all past civil

The other major omission is any mention of the ways other than simple official color blindness in which civil rights movements and their supporters have defined justice for themselves. If names like King's are to be invoked as authority for the content of norms of justice, some notice should be taken of what the moderate civil rights activists actually believed: that the opposite of "segregation" was "integration," which has many possible meanings but clearly meant something more than the formally color-blind state of "desegregation," freedom from government race-based classifications. The injustice of segregation was not so much that the government made formal distinctions between races but that those distinctions served to enforce white supremacy, a caste system based on race, a system of pervasive economic, social, and cultural subordination. It was the evident failure of the purely formal and negative definition of justice as "color blindness" to make much headway against the institutions and customs of the caste system – practices that continued effectively to shut most blacks out of access to the jobs, schools, and neighborhoods that are the mobility channels of American society – which prompted the 1965 turn in civil rights policies.

Those post-1965 policies are very complex; but there's a mainstream or centrist set of justifications for them that is best described as *broad*-agency based. Their defenders agree with the narrow-agency view that the overall goal of civil rights policy is the remedy of past acts of discrimination but favor a much expanded method and scope of showing violations and obtaining relief, an approach that favors collective liability and group-based remedies. Broad-agency histories lay emphasis on the bitter experience with enforcement after *Brown*, which demonstrated that white resistance to integration was so fierce, tactics to evade court orders or fake compliance with hiring directives under cover of race-neutral devices so ingenious, as to make case-by-case proof of intent wholly ineffectual. The policy emphasis therefore shifted to wholesale enforcement, the substitution of statistical "effect" for individual "intent" as prima facie proof of discrimination, and measurable, monitorable, quantitative measures of relief in order to circumvent evasion and make enforcement burdens manageable. All these remedies could have been, and were, justified as an interim means to the ultimate end of color-blind equal treatment: "To get beyond race, we must first take account of race." (Eventually, of course, affirmative action policies developed their own vested interests and constituencies, some of whom began to rationalize the policies in very different terms: as programs designed to foster proportional representation of minorities in certain job categories and institutions – either as compensation for past injustice

rights legislation and enforcement tends to make people who believe in civil rights more than a little skeptical of present conservatives' claims to good faith on racial justice issues; Randall Kennedy, "Persuasion and Distrust: A Comment on the Affirmative Action Debate," 99 *Harv. L. Rev.* 1327 (1986). Nathan Glazer, in *Affirmative Discrimination* (1975) is one of the few neoconservative writers who deal at all candidly with the fact of white resistance.

or to meet the independent structural goal of "diversity.") As both judicial and executive branches were broadening both remedies and the classes entitled to them, the courts rapidly expanded the class of perpetrators well beyond present violators to those in the deep past – the officials who, even if long ago, had committed the fateful acts of intentional segregation that resulted in today's barriers to equal access.

Kathleen Sullivan has pointed out how the emphasis of the courts on "sins" of past discrimination, the framing of affirmative action claims as corrective responses to undo, repair, or compensate for past discrimination, helps maintain the perpetrator-victim (agency-based) focus of the public debate on affirmative action.[35] Whites say, We had nothing personally to do with the enslavement and oppression of blacks: indeed, our ancestors were being slaughtered by cossacks or starved out of Ireland at the time; it is now we who are victimized by departures from equal treatment and strict legality. Blacks respond in a similar discourse of agency, but broaden the frame: We are the descendants of those who were collectively victimized and we demand reparations; and we are still currently victimized by the continuing traces of historical wrongs and continued practice of the institutions and criteria of "merit" that were created in order to suppress us; and we demand access to the places we would have occupied but for this legacy. The earliest proposals for affirmative action, in fact, seem to have originated from civil rights leaders using this broad compensatory rationale. James Farmer of CORE, in testimony before the House Judiciary Committee in 1963, resolutely denied favoring either "quotas" or the displacement of white workers, but he did argue that in choosing between a white and black candidate of roughly equal qualifications, an employer should choose the black candidate. Rep. Rodino asked, "Isn't this preferential?"

FARMER: Well, you could call it preferential, you could call it compensatory, but sir, we have been seeking...

RODINO: Isn't that discriminating against a white who may have been innocent of any discrimination against anyone else in that time?

FARMER: You see, none of us are really innocent because we are caught in a society, the social system which has tolerated segregation, Negroes have received special treatment all their lives. They have received special treatment for 350 years. All we are asking for, all I am asking for now is some special treatment to overcome the effects of the long special treatment of a negative sort we have had in the past.[36]

If one conceives of the problem in such broad-agency terms, the make-whole remedy calls for a massive counterfactual thought experiment: imagine what positions in society and the economy living blacks would have attained had they not been subject to acts of racist injustice. The presumptive answer,

[35] Kathleen Sullivan, "Sins of Discrimination," 100 *Harv. L. Rev.* 78 (1986).

[36] Quoted in Hugh Davis Graham, *The Civil Rights Era: Origins and Development of National Policy, 1960–1972*, 109 (1990).

the late Ronald Fiscus argued, is that they would have been represented in all places in the class and occupational structure in proportion to their numbers in the population.[37] (The conservative objection to the counterfactual, that this assumption makes no allowances for generic differences in culture affecting economically valuable talents, abilities, and preferences is well taken; but so too is the response that, but for racism, those differences might not have developed.) The argument is a perfectly sensible one within the "bad actor" framework of legalism – one undoes the bad acts by undoing their effects, with the effects assessed by reference to where history would have brought the victimized group without the acts. But the assessment it calls for can only be performed very abstractly. The history of the United States, its entire economy, society, politics, and racial and ethnic composition, would have been so different without slavery that one couldn't even begin to guess what American society would look like now.

The argument from history then, has supported broad-agency claims to compensation or make-whole remedies for past injuries – in the form of grants of immediate access to positions of advantage. The response of some conservatives to this kind of argument is a sort of historical fatalism – history is a long unbroken recital of brutality and injustice, of ancient wrongs that cannot possibly be set right.[38] The legal system cannot possibly correct all these wrongs; all it can do is try to maintain the conditions for equal justice in the present and police current violations. But the usual conservative response relies on a much more optimistic set of assertions – that if the conditions of equal justice are satisfied, they actually operate so as to erase historical (and every other sort of unmerited) inequities in very short order. The equal treatment required by color blindness is coextensive with the conditions of "equal opportunity" to be evaluated according to merit, talent, ability, character. The problem, this very familiar argument goes, with post-1965 civil rights policy is that it replaced the goal of "equality of opportunity" with that of "equality of results," that is, proportional representation of minorities in all situations of advantage.

The argument is built on an important structural premise with its own supporting history: that American society has gradually but finally evolved to the stage where, now that formal race distinctions have been removed, and residual

[37] Ronald Jerry Fiscus, *The Constitutional Logic of Affirmative Action* (1992). For a recent extension of the argument, see Cheryl Harris, "Whiteness as Property," 106 *Harv. L. Rev.* 1709 (1993).

[38] In some recent decisions, courts have been giving as a reason for refusing to recognize Indian land claims the long, sorry, brutal history of white depredations of Indian lands; as if the repeated trampling of justice in the past could in itself be a justification for denying it now. Some judges are inclined to spread the blame: whites brutalized Indians, Indians brutalized whites, it all evens out. See Aviam Soifer, "Objects in Mirror are Closer Than They Appear," 28 *Georgia L. Rev.* 533 (1994); and Joseph Singer, "Well Settled? The Increasing Weight of History in American Indian Land Claims," 28 *Georgia L. Rev.* 481 (1994), for caustic and insightful reflections on this use of history in Indian lands cases.

acts of discrimination motivated by animus are legally forbidden, existing opportunity structures will in fact distribute rewards according to merit and talent. (Note: not according to "marginal product" – this is a moral argument, made in the moral language of classical liberalism, not a neoclassical economic argument.) The conditions of equal opportunity do not need to be created; they have arrived. Sometimes the assertion rests explicitly on a historical foundation, such as Thomas Sowell's thesis that the moment formal barriers were removed, blacks occupied the same relation to opportunity as any other immigrant groups. If then some blacks have not succeeded, we should not presume discrimination – many groups have faced that and succeeded, including West Indian blacks – but rather inherent deficiencies in African-American culture.

But of course the argument is much older than Sowell: it is the Jacksonian, or Free Soil, or simply classical liberal argument that welds liberal legalism to liberal political and moral economy: that in a society structured so that all have formally equal rights, and none have special disabilities or special privileges (in the form of "class legislation" of which the most important type is monopoly privileges), all will be free to compete on equal terms and to rise to the level befitting their efforts, virtues, and talents. In such a society history ceases to count; for we all are free to make our own destiny. It was exactly this argument that Northern conservatives used, after the Civil War, to defeat special legislation and protective measures on behalf of the black freedmen – that they were "paternalist" measures, obnoxious both as conferring special advantages on blacks and not on whites and as promoting in their beneficiaries habits of dependence rather than sturdy self-reliance.[39] Its genius lies in its equation of existing legal baseline entitlements with the condition of natural justice, any departures from which require extraordinary justification. What might be otherwise a controversial – and potentially very productive – structural argument about what the social preconditions of genuinely equal opportunity really might be is presented as a taken-for-granted premise, that the status quo baseline is required by the rule of law.[40]

[39] *See* Soifer, *supra* note 21; Eric Schnapper, "Affirmative Action and the Legislative History of the Fourteenth Amendment," 71 *Virginia L. Rev.* 753 (1985).

[40] For a typical, though valuable because unusually explicit, conflation of simple legality with equal opportunity (current race-neutral rules distribute opportunity equally; thus any redistribution would offend the rule of law) see Abram, "Fair Shakers and Social Engineers." The irony is that Abram is an old New Dealer, who would probably not object to structural alteration of the baselines to redistribute opportunity more equally, so long as the policy did not employ explicit racial criteria.

Of course, many conservatives do use structural and pragmatic arguments against affirmative action as well. In a bad mood, conservatives accuse rights activists of simply "rent seeking," securing places for themselves by law that they couldn't earn, creating jobs (or getting votes by creating jobs) for themselves in quota-monitoring bureaucracies. More generously, they allow that the policies are "well-intentioned" but have inefficient and perverse effects – the proliferation of offensive racial and ethnic categories in public life (Jim Crow redivivus) and unseemly intergroup competition for benefits accruing to victim status; damage to merit selection on the basis of individual worth; intrusive bureaucratic and judicial meddling in the decisions of

The use of history in this argument, then, is to show that by long-standing historical tradition – from which slavery and legalized segregation were unfortunate deviations[41] – the history of a group's situation is irrelevant to its legal status; those who would make it relevant again are repeating the errors of the racist past.[42] The legal history supporting the argument is that the formal-equality color-blind norm is the norm established by our traditions. The social history supporting the structural argument is that where the norm prevails, historical disadvantage can be overcome because opportunity structures have in fact operated to give everyone a fair shake.

Both the legalist and the structural positions have been challenged, from Right, Left, and Center. Each challenge uses history both to derive a different baseline norm and to assert that historical experience has either strayed from or never lived up to that norm.

The libertarian Right position is a purified version of the Center Right thesis that has dominated conservative policy. The Center-Right thesis, recall, holds that by 1964 the American polity had actually achieved the conditions of an equal treatment, equal opportunity society. It had finally fulfilled the norm from which post-1965 policy was to deviate. The more radical, or libertarian Right, position is that the norm came closest to fulfillment at the high point of classical-legal liberalism in the late nineteenth and early twentieth

employers and public authorities to run their shops as they see fit; adverse effects on quality, productivity, and competence of work; stigmatization of genuinely competent minorities. Yet the argument at the end usually returns to the perpetrator-victim perspective: affirmative action isn't simply bad policy, it's injustice to whites.

41 The modern conservative view of the history of racial subordination is one curiously detached from collective membership in the American polity: racial subordination never had much to do with people like us, and anyway it all happened a long time ago. In this aspect, American conservatism somewhat resembles the self-distancing of German conservatives from the Nazis as vulgar barbarians. In his reply to Justice Marshall's bicentennial speech charging that the Federal Constitution was "defective from the start" because of its entrenchment of slavery, William Bradford Reynolds argued that the Founding Fathers were regretfully forced to compromise with slavery in order to induce the southern states to join the Union; but that they really provided for its eventual extinction by enacting a structure of government designed to promote evolving liberties, and an amendment process in Article 5, whereby the fruits of that evolution could be, in time, constitutionally encoded. *See* Bradford Reynolds, "Another View: Our Magnificent Constitution," 40 *Vanderbilt L. Rev.* 1343 (1987). One might complain that this account rather too rapidly skates over the fact that the constitutional structure itself was intended to insure the southern states against the risk that the northern ones would someday confiscate their property by emancipation. Similarly, libertarian critics fault the "state," conceived as an alien excrescence, for the rules that have restricted black opportunity, almost as if the state and its rules were independent of society, as if Alabama government in the 1920s, for instance, were an entity wholly distinct from the white planter class.

42 The rich irony of this posture is that for many years the moderate conservative position on civil rights was a wholly Burkean one, that the accumulated weight of American traditions and customs of racial segregation lay so heavy on society that change must perforce be very slow; anyone who demanded equality now, even of the most formal kind, was an abstract radical with no historical sense!

century, the era of *Lochner* v. *New York*. Where it has been distorted is in the long history of government policies that exceed the proper constitutional limits of the police power: among these policies – in addition to regulation of wages, hours, and work conditions; occupational licensing and entry barriers to trades; legislation allowing union closed shops and other exercises of monopoly power – are laws enforcing segregation. The legal-historical argument is devoted to establishing not the current distribution of entitlements and institutions, but the laissez-faire regime as the baseline constitution of a liberal society.[43] Unfortunately, in this view, the ideal baseline conditions have been so disfigured by extensions of the police power that broad structural remedies will be needed to restore it – widespread repeal of regulatory laws, of the Wagner Act, of the public-school monopoly's claim to taxes, of the minimum wage, and of the antidiscrimination laws themselves.

This structural argument is a largely abstract one from political economy, albeit with some empirical-historical support. The basic argument is that cartels of whites to exclude blacks from opportunity are inherently unstable because competitive pressures make it rational to hire (recruit, educate) qualified blacks; that such discrimination as remains despite those pressures is likely to be only residual and in any case justified as an exercise of individual autonomy (an eccentric preference for racism over profits); and finally that any attempt to remedy residual discrimination through law will be, like virtually all forms of regulation, captured by special ("rent-seeking") interests and overextended as well as inefficiently intrusive into rational market calculations of employers. The history that backs this up is a general catalog of regulatory failures informed by Chicago public-choice and regulatory economics' very dim view of state capacity and proneness to capture; a much thinner – and highly contested – history supporting the point about the instability of racial cartels, and some economic studies purporting to show that industrialization and competition, not the civil rights laws, were the driving force behind black employment gains in the 1960s and 1970s.

The liberal-centrist argument dominated mainstream civil rights enforcement policy since 1965. It argues from a traditional legal baseline not of classical but of Progressive-New Deal liberalism that the government has to aggressively restructure some markets and institutions in order to equalize conditions of opportunity. The long history of discrimination has left a continuing legacy of disadvantage – racial stereotypes, educational deficits, isolation in environments spatially removed from jobs and prone to the self-destructiveness of despair. In the famous words of President Johnson's Howard University speech: "You do not take a person who for years has been hobbled by chains and liberate him, bring him up to the starting point of a race, and then say, 'You

[43] *See* Richard Epstein, *Forbidden Grounds: The Case against Employment Discrimination Laws* (1992); Clint Bolick, *Unfinished Business* (1990).

are free to compete with all the others,' and still justly believe you have been completely fair… We seek not just freedom, but opportunity – not just legal equity but human ability – not just equality as a right and a theory but equality as a fact and as a result."[44] In context, this is a perfectly centrist statement – not an argument for a legislated equality of everything (whatever that might mean) but for promoting the concrete conditions of an equality of opportunity, a race from an equalized starting point. The justification for affirmative action contained in it is partly agency-based – compensation in the form of preferences for handicaps or, as with veterans' preferences, for wounds incurred in consequence of one's country's policies – but is also structural: our job is to demolish these historically created barriers. In the structural view, affirmative action is simply one among many plans, as Kathleen Sullivan has put it, in "the architecture of a racially integrated future."[45] It was designed to help bypass traditional barriers to black advancement, like father-son sponsorship recruitment to craft unions, or political patronage or family network access to contracts and jobs, or tests or formal credentials bearing no provable relationship to job performance; it was designed to increase the size of the black middle class as rapidly as possible – by expanding the number of jobs in the public sector and encouraging recruitment to colleges and professional schools – partly to produce more professionals and businesses to serve black populations, but largely to help overcome racial stereotypes derived from the evident social fact that society whitens out toward the top, blackens out toward the bottom. Part of the historical argument backing this approach is that racism and social-economic exclusion and isolation have fed on each other; so conversely do integration and equal opportunity: "Green follows white" – resources go where the whites are; living in white communities and attending white schools have powerful neighborhood effects. The general notion is that the *ultimate end point* to be achieved is equal opportunity, meritocracy, and market rationality; but that progress toward this goal has had to be jump-started against cultural resistance (historically embedded racism, conscious, unconscious, and "statistical") and across structural barriers of isolation.

All the positions just described share the common structural goal of the equal opportunity society, although their divergences make abundantly clear how vague and elastic that goal is. Right-centrists, the current conservative majority in Congress and the Supreme Court, believe the conditions of equal opportunity have already been achieved, disfigured only by affirmative action preferences. Left-centrists, the dominant civil rights coalition until recently, believe in policies designed to construct those conditions against the lingering traces of racism. Libertarians believe that only radical restructuring of the legal framework can effectively restore the laissez-faire conditions of the equal opportunity society.

[44] I *Public Papers of the Presidents: Johnson*, 636 (1965).

[45] Sullivan, *supra* note 35 at 80.

Two other important traditions of thought and action regarding racial equality are in near-total eclipse at present but worth mentioning both for their prominence in the past of the struggle for racial equality and the critical insight they offer to the present.

One might be called a Left-social democratic view. This view uses a yet different baseline norm, an image of equality that also has deep roots in the American past: the antisubordination norm of American Revolutionary radicalism, artisanal republicanism, radical Reconstruction, the industrial labor movements, and, in the civil rights movement, the ideas of King and his chief theorist, Bayard Rustin. In this view the main obstacles to fulfillment of the norm of equality-as-antisubordination is the segmented economy – beginning with slavery itself, conceived of as a labor system structured by class as well as race distinctions, and continuing after emancipation as race is used by white capitalists to maintain the dual economy by dividing white laborers against black ones. At its peak of political influence in the Johnson administration, the civil rights coalition came close to persuading the federal government to undertake the massive full employment programs that would be needed to help overcome dualism; but it ran out of money and political support and had to settle for the War on Poverty program instead, in effect a very modest program combining a few jobs for black community activists with an expansion of traditional relief for the poor. Nixon's affirmative action programs, such as in public contract set-asides (the Philadelphia Plan), were a similar form of tokenism, an attempt to co-opt and buy out the most politically articulate blacks and gain some protection against urban protest, while not antagonizing the southern whites and northern white-ethnics who were his main political base.[46]

Another once-important vision of race-neutral equality has today – tragically – almost disappeared altogether: integration. A serious integrationist strategy would take the historically established baseline norm (of *Brown* and the 1960s civil rights movements) to be "color blindness" in the sense of a social state in which racial distinctions would simply cease to have much practical significance in the distribution of access to valuable social goods, opportunities, and respect. The achievement of such a state would actually require a social transformation of vast dimensions – one in which racial differences were not actually *perceived* as relevant. This would probably have to be an integrated, intermarried society in which pigmentation was distributed randomly across occupations, neighborhoods, and classes. For as long as one race persistently and disproportionately ends up at the bottom of the social ladder, with the highest crime and unemployment rates or, if employed, the crummiest, dead-end minimum wage jobs with no benefits and no advancement, society

[46] H. R. Haldeman's recently published *Diaries* (1994) suggest a considerably more cynical set of motives: that Nixon continued and intensified executive affirmative action policies because he well knew how divisive they were and hoped to reap the political benefits of backlash from their implementation.

can't possibly be "color blind;" everyone will notice this distribution and will draw strong conclusions from it – about either the capacities of members of the group or the injustice of race-based inequality. It is at least as plausible that policies on the model of the forced-integration model of the military, compelling different racial groups to associate, work together, and get to know each other, is likely to promote judgments on the content of one's character rather than the color of one's skin. Arguably something like this theory was historically tested in integration of the military, of the work forces of large public and private employers, in housing, and in education through school busing. Busing is now widely, but probably incorrectly[47] perceived as having been a complete failure, inducing massive "white flight" and disaffection with civil rights. Yet in the military, the perception is exactly the opposite, that forced integration has both worked and been accepted as legitimate.

Many in the civil rights movement have, however, become disillusioned with the ideal of race-neutral equality of opportunity altogether. They oppose to it a culturally pluralist norm of proportional representation, developed from a political model of social goods that also has a long history backing it up. The argument here is that the economy and society are and always have been riddled with special deals and preferences – that opportunity is distributed more by patronage and old-boys' networks, often based on ethnicity, than by "merit" (and indeed that what is called "merit" often has a large unspoken ethnic component); and thus what equal opportunity should mean as a practical matter is equal access to patronage. The demand for proportional representation is simply the demand to be included in the Great American Pork Barrel: We'll give up our claims to special treatment when you give up your ethnic political patronage, sponsorship of relatives for police and firefighter jobs, admission of legacies to colleges, tax preferences, veterans preferences, farm price supports, and the like. The supporting history argues that optimists like Sowell are mistaken in their basic proposition that outsider groups can advance only by adapting their cultures to produce skills in current demand by markets, for social advancement has in fact accrued to newcomer groups who were able to forge coalitions to obtain political power. When those groups have included blacks, blacks have advanced; when, as has happened much more frequently, blacks have been squeezed out of power, they have suffered. Affirmative action from this perspective is sometimes quite a conservative policy: it asks only for parity in patronage, slotting of minorities into established structures of jobs and access to jobs, rather than a restructuring of the labor market or a flattening of class divisions. There is, however, a more radical version that argues that what is valued as "meritorious" or skills is itself a product of cultural-racial

[47] *See* Jennifer Hochschild, *The New American Dilemma* (1984) for evidence suggesting the successes of compelled school integration where it was seriously tried and supported by local authorities.

categories; valued skills are just the skills that people on top happen to have, and what needs changing is what is valued – a redistribution of rewards based on a redistribution of recognition of value to plural cultural traits.

The civil rights experience has also given rise to some profoundly pessimistic views of history as an unbroken chronicle of hopes raised only to be dashed, promises made only to be broken, gains won only to be eroded, a grim testimony to the permanence of racism.[48] The dominant baseline norm in these narratives is white supremacy, a historical constant disturbed only by the occasional and ephemeral achievements of black struggle and resistance. The *Brown* case and the civil rights policies that followed it may look progressive but often serve only as covers for newer and subtler forms of racism: integrationism conveys the message that blacks living or educated apart from whites are necessarily inferior; equal opportunity norms privilege the forms of "merit" possessed by whites and thus serve to legitimate a racially skewed distribution of jobs and social goods; "color blindness" itself is simply a stratagem of subordination. The more optimistic believers in the permanence of racism hold out hope for separatist strategies of cultural preservation and economic development, sometimes coupled with broad-agency claims for financing by means of reparations or other concessions from white society. The more pessimistic often end up, ironically, in the same dark cul-de-sac as conservative historical fatalism – skepticism toward all claims of progress either achievable or already achieved; resignation to the inevitability of oppression in one or another of its endlessly mutable forms.

The examples have been intended to illustrate the kinds of policies and remedies to which those who would confront past injustices may be led by commitment to narrow-agency, broad-agency, or structural approaches. May one conclude anything from the examples about the relative value of the approaches? Nothing simple, anyway; certainly nothing like a clear recommendation for one approach over the others for general adoption.

I do, however, emerge from this exercise with strengthened, though not unqualified, respect for the structural modes of responding to great injustices and a sharper awareness of the deficiencies of the agency-based ones of either the broad or the narrow kind – with a qualified preference, that is, for both structural explanations and structural (or social-engineering) remedies over correction of wrongs or redemption of sin. Or, to express this in another way that less rigidly distinguishes law from morality and morality from politics: a society's most valuable response to historical injustice may often be to assume collective moral responsibility for structural understanding and, where this is possible, structural reform.

[48] *See, for example*, Harold Cruse, *Plural But Equal* (1987); Derrick Bell, *And We Are Not Saved* (1987).

The recent legal controversies over affirmative action are particularly good illustrations. There is a productive and substantive political debate about what structural barriers still impede the equal participation of blacks in American society and how those barriers may be removed. A small, but only small, fraction of that debate would worry about the wisdom or folly, the costs and benefits, of affirmative action – whether, as conservatives suggest, it helps mostly middle-class blacks and stigmatizes even them; whether, as liberals insist, it has not only helped create a substantial black middle and professional class but also significantly improved black working-class opportunities with no discernible adverse effects on productivity; whether, as some social democrats such as William Julius Wilson and Theda Skocpol suggest, race-targeted social programs have reached the limits of likely effectiveness and in view of their great political unpopularity should be replaced by class-based policies targeted to the poor. These are all issues well worth trying to resolve. But in general political rhetoric they have been swamped by a controversy, as unilluminating as it is politically explosive, about whether blacks are innocent victims or authors of their own misfortunes and whether whites are guilty perpetrators or themselves innocent victims of racist acts. For this is how the U.S. Supreme Court has chosen to frame the issue, setting limits supposedly derived from constitutional law on how policy-makers, private institutions, and employers may go about trying to remedy the problem of continuing de facto American apartheid. As Sullivan puts it, "If casting affirmative action as compensation invites protests about windfalls to nonvictims, casting it as punishment invites protests about unfairness to nonsinners. Viewed through the lens of retributive justice, a focus on sin begets claims of innocence."[49] The hunt for narrow agency then rapidly expands into broad, into general group blaming, and competing claims to the status of innocent victim. For blacks the morality of their claim is so obvious – all those generations of uncompensated slave labor; exploited sharecropper labor; exclusion from jobs, housing, and education; lynchings, false arrests, and unequal treatment by white courts and juries; and insult and humiliation have built up an enormous social debt. If, having been shoved to the back of the line for most of our history, they now ask for a place at the front, that is to ask for simple justice. But the agency model says, to displace anyone from the line, it is not sufficient that you be victims; they also have to be perpetrators. As Kyle Haselden put it more than twenty years ago: "It leaves with the descendants of the exploiters a guilt they cannot cancel and with the descendants of the exploited a debt they cannot collect."[50] Groups personalized as the eternal oppressor, who are asked to feel permanently guilty, turn instead angry and defensive, especially if they too belong to the struggling and victimized groups of history; while groups whose identity is constituted through the history of victimization and cannot claim material benefits except through their status

[49] Sullivan, *supra* note 35 at 94.

[50] Quoted in Graham, *supra* note 36 at 113.

of victim must fight to retain that status and to compete for it against other victimized groups. In such a system for allocating moral claims, to lose the status of innocent victim – which one begins to do the moment one achieves any place or power in society – is to risk losing not only preference but part of one's identity.[51]

Agency-based theories are really of very limited use as a framework either for understanding systemic or society-wide injustice or for ensuring it does not happen again. To take account of systemic injustice, the framework has sometimes to be expanded past the breaking point of plausibility – to make institutions and collective social movements into "defendants" by stretching notions of "conspiracy" and inventing new ones, such the Nuremberg prosecutors' theory of "organizational liability" for the SS and Gestapo; or, as in broad-agency theories, by the use of concepts such as "collective guilt" or "institutional racism," which confusingly deny agency at the instant of affirming it because they suggest that guilt inheres simply in being present in the historical situation, or in being descended from those who were, and is thus inescapable. The legalist notion of wrongs as departures from baseline norms, deviations from acceptable patterns of conduct, is an awkward conceptual fit to a regime that, with the support or complicity of most of civil society, is organized around the wholesale commission of wrongful acts. I don't mean, I hasten to say, that killing Jews or enslaving blacks by the millions is not wrong, that such acts can escape moral condemnation by virtue of having been approved by nation-states and engaged in by thousands of perpetrators. But if you see Nazism or slavery or segregation primarily as "violations" of some standard of natural or international law or "human rights," you are not making progress toward understanding them as social systems that made sense to and were accepted by many people at the time as authority relations, or labor systems, or caste systems, or bureaucratic routines, or simply regrettable necessities.[52] In the aftermath of the *Brown* decision, for instance, most lawyers entrapped in the legalist paradigm seemed to find it painfully difficult to explain what exactly *was* wrong with enforced apartheid, separate-but-[formally]-equal racial segregation. The

[51] For a particularly acute critique of group identity construction through history of victimization, see Guyora Binder, "Representing Nazism: Advocacy and Identity at the Trial of Klaus Barbie," 98 *Yale L. J.* 1321 (1989).

[52] In Germany, as Geoff Eley has pointed out, "concentrating opprobrium in the Nazi's crimes against the Jews" has served a right-wing agenda by obscuring Nazism's "relationship to a larger constellation of right-wing interests and belief. Once the problem of Nazism has been circumscribed in this way, questions of deeper origins and Germany's broader responsibility – that is, the more difficult and disturbing questions of Nazism's structural rootedness in German society at large – are easier to keep from the agenda." Geoff Eley, "Nazism, Politics and the Image of the Past," 121 *Past and Present* 174 (1988). Whether the Holocaust itself, as opposed to the other routine social-systemic practices of National Socialism, will always resist historical understanding, even of the structural kind, is a open question. *See* Dan Diner, ed., *Ist der NS Geschichte?* (1987).

Supreme Court itself came up with the rather odd theory that the wrong was infliction of psychological harm, but it gave no account of the context that would explain why the harm could not be avoided, as the old *Plessy* case had airily suggested, by simply having the black race put a different psychological construction on separation – a "multicultural" construction, for instance, to the effect that each racial "culture" was best preserved as a matter of policy by development in separate enclaves. The theory that compelled segregation violates the neutral "color blindness" norm by making racial status legally relevant does no better, for race distinctions are only obnoxious within a social structure that visits them with obnoxious consequences. In this strange legalist desert, it is a profound relief to come across Charles Black's celebrated article on "The Lawfulness of the Segregation Decisions,"[53] which pointed out what everyone already knew but could not say – partly because certain of its legal relevance, partly because unwilling to indict an entire region's habitual "way of life" – that segregation was one among many devices used to enforce a system of racial subordination, to keep blacks literally "in their place" in a hierarchy of orders.

Besides obscuring structural understanding, an emphasis on legal or moral redress can also inhibit structural solutions that may, in the end, accomplish much more. An obvious present-day example is the vogue for restitution of property to precommunist owners in Eastern Europe. Restitution is problematic enough on grounds of justice and fairness: why (as Jon Elster has asked) should it be those who have suffered this particular form of material loss, as compared to those denied the opportunity to contract or deprived of their privacy, dignity, liberty, and expressive freedom, who have first call on compensation?[54] More pragmatically, where restitution rights have been legislated, as in the former East Germany, they have sufficiently clouded titles so as to significantly inhibit investment (and as a result have been since largely overridden by subsequent statutes);[55] Some of the same difficulties, and even greater ones as well, surround the current revivals of interest (probably given fresh encouragement by the movements to reclaim Indian lands and compensate the Japanese-American internees) in reparations for American blacks, for their ancestors' forced transit, enslavement, and subsequent continuing legal subordination. Skepticism about reparations proposals commonly, and reasonably, tends to focus on issues of practical administrability, the problems of classification posed by trying to identify, at this remove, the current "victims of slavery," not to mention the beneficiaries of slavery who must be taxed to compensate them.[56] But the major objections seem to me structural. Group liability theories

53 Charles Black, "The Lawfulness of the Segregation Decisions," 69 *Yale L. J.* 421 (1960).

54 Jon Elster, "On Doing What One Can," 1 *E. Eur. Const. Rev.* 15 (1992).

55 Hans-Werner and Gerlinde Sinn, *Jumpstart* (1993); Ulrich Press, "Restitution vs. Investment," 1 *E. Eur. Const. Rev.* 22 (1992).

56 The administrability problem is addressed at length and with great ingenuity in Boris Bittker, *The Case for Black Reparations* (1973); and the classification problem in Mari Matsuda,

of such enormous breadth have to rely on such attenuated notions of blame and causation as to subvert their moral plausibility and thus undermine possibilities of political fraternity, creating resentment even between those who might be coalition partners in a politics that cast them as allies instead of historical villains. Groups who have suffered more immediate wrongs – including perhaps wrongs in which U.S. policies were complicit, such as torture or killing of their families by Salvadoran death squads – might wonder why *they* are being taxed to remedy such historically distant evils. Even more to the point: What would a one-time payment of compensation to the current generation accomplish? Wouldn't the money, if we could raise the political will for it, be better spent on institutional investment such as job training, drug treatment, scholarships, income credits for the working poor, public works, and other measures to address structural unemployment? Reparations payments, even when designed primarily as apology and symbolic atonement rather than literal compensation, are best given to the living victims of injustices that are firmly in the past; indeed, one of the messages intended by reparations is that the wrong is over and done with. When the wrong is continuing, the result of historically entrenched structural conditions, the last message the regime should be encouraged to send is that the current generation's obligations vis-à-vis the wrong can be satisfied with damages.

The familiar critique of structural explanations and of structural approaches to remedies is that they obscure the moral significance of social injustice: if the system is at fault, no one is at fault; if everything is structure, there is no agency; tout comprendre, c'est tout pardonner; the moral differences disappear between planning and following, between gross brutality and indifference, between fanatic enthusiasm and grudging complicity, between murder and guard duty, between profiteering and indirect benefit (getting the position that otherwise would have been occupied by the black or Jew or bourgeois), between those who enthusiastically supported and profited from the system, those who quietly but unhappily went along, those who performed small acts of kindness in the leeways of the system, and those who actively resisted. Most observers of President Reagan's peculiar speech at Bitburg Cemetery, which placed the Waffen-SS troops buried there on a moral equivalence with all the other "victims" of the Nazi regime, felt its terrible inappropriateness.[57] Without acknowledgment of wrongful, personal agency, there is no shame; without shame, no assumption of responsibility, no possibility of redemption.

"Looking to the Bottom: Critical Legal Studies and Reparations," 22 *Harvard Civil Rights-Civil Liberties Law Review* 323 (1987).

[57] For reflections on the moral meanings of the Bitburg ceremony, see Geoffrey Hartman, ed., *Bitburg in Moral and Political Perspective* (1986). Reagan's speech of course was anything but structural; it relied on the "outlaw" theory of Nazism as the work of a criminal gang, with neither roots in previous history nor continuities into the present, which had victimized all Germans.

(It is frequently said of the official German response to the Third Reich even to this day – that although there is increasing identification with the regime's victims, there is still little sense of implication in the death machinery of many "ordinary" Germans and almost no disposition to identify with active resistors as the true patriots trying to save Germany from itself.) If law describes injustice as abnormality and deviation, structural-historical explanation seems to do just the opposite. Although it may, as we've seen, describe the injustices as the product of a system that itself deviates from some macrohistorical norm or ideal, it nonetheless "normalizes" the unjust acts within the system as its banal and everyday practices.[58]

All true enough; yet in practice it has been the agency-based approaches, rather than the structural ones, that have tended to be exculpatory: the new regime turns on the bad agents as scapegoats for wrongs that really derived from the routine functioning of an entire social system. The trials of the worst offenders, the purges of the system's satraps and beneficiaries, even the reparations payments made to the most conspicuous victims, sometimes serve as ritual acts of exorcism of the monstrous, abnormal elements of a system with which, at the time, almost everybody in one way or another went along.[59] (Sometimes, alas, the purges serve no higher purpose than a personal settling of scores or pursuit of political advantage.) One thinks here of the ways in which the French people savagely punished "collaborators" after World War II or of the mass purges of Communist party functionaries that some of the new regimes are undertaking in Eastern Europe for the crimes committed by those regimes. Indeed, some observers have suggested that the quite efficient current West German purges of the former East German bureaucracy, legal system, and universities of political unreliables is intended in part to make up for the earlier failures of both the Weimar and denazification-era regimes to protect themselves against the enemies of democracy; others remark caustically that neither Weimar nor the Federal Republic ever found it difficult to protect themselves against threats from the Left. The proposal of reparations payments to black American for the injustices of slavery has drawn support from, among other sources, neoconservatives who see a one-time payment as a way of getting quit

[58] This was surely the most commonly made critique of Hannah Arendt's *Eichmann in Jerusalem*.

[59] Interestingly enough, in Eastern Europe it has often been the public figures (such as Adam Michnik and Vaclav Havel) with some of the best moral credentials as resistors to former communist regimes who now denounce "lustration" (purging of former communists and informers) – partly because that process would have to rely on the corrupt old regime's secret files to identify offenders, because the mass purge was an instrument of Communist party rule and "we are not like them," and because purging would be a "distraction" from the important business of rebuilding society, but also because in the old regime "everyone" was in some sense implicated: as Havel has put it, "we are all – though naturally to differing extent – responsible for the operation of the totalitarian machinery; none of us is just its victims; we are also its co-creators" (quoted in Maria Łos, "Lustration and Truth Claims: Unfinished Revolutions in Central Europe," 20 *L. & Soc. Inquiry* 117 (1995), an exceptionally penetrating analysis of the discourse of purges in East Europe).

of all future African-American claims on their republic's moral sense or purse strings.[60] The late Alan Freeman argued that American race relations policy in the Second Reconstruction adopted the perpetrator-victim model of racial wrongs as harmful deviations from the norms of equal treatment and meritocracy precisely so as to deflect attention from the contribution made by those very norms to maintaining a dual economy.[61] The condemnation of slavery as a departure from liberal norms obscures the extent to which, understood structurally and in context, slavery was indeed a departure from liberal norms and equality but also a precondition to their realization for most of the white population.[62]

Anyway, the moral distinctions are hardly irrelevant to structural responses: even if the new regime is primarily looking to structural reform rather than the punishment of individuals, if there is a choice in the matter it may not want to maintain in power those agents who in past times were the chief bearers of the old regime, carriers of its genes, as it were, agents who have developed attachments to its values and careers and vested interests around reproducing its habits and manipulative and duplicitous modes of operation, and who reflexively oppose anyone who would reform it. Even if most of them were just opportunists rather than true believers, do you want your own Rechtsstaat staffed with opportunists?[63]

> Is it fair, people ask, that those who had comfortable office jobs under the Communists should still have them today, when ordinary people are having to tighten their belts? Is it fair that members of the *nomenklatura* are exploiting the uncertain legal conditions of privatization to take over as capitalists the enterprises they had previously commanded as Communists?[64]

This example, however, does highlight one of the central problems with structural approaches: since they work upon institutions and groups (as broad-agency approaches do too), they involve wholesale treatment of the peoples in those groups without reference to particular deserts and thus treat them to some extent inevitably as objects. From the point of view of the people hurt, the impersonality of the reform process, its indifference to their

[60] Charles Krauthammer, "Reparations for Black Americans," 136 *Time* 18 (1990).

[61] Alan Freeman, "Legitimating Racial Discrimination Through Antidiscrimination Law," 62 *Minn. L. Rev.* 1049 (1978).

[62] Edmund S. Morgan, *American Slavery: American Freedom* (1975).

[63] Moral and structural concerns in this area may, however, irreconcilably conflict. From a moral point of view the ideological idealist who saw himself as selflessly building a classless utopia may be a considerably more attractive figure than the cynical apparatchik who joined the party for careerist privileges. (Admittedly by the time of the collapse of 1989 there were probably very few genuine idealists left.) The idealist, however, has no useful role in the new regime; like the many tenured professors of Marxism-Leninism in the universities, he will be out of a job, whereas the cynical apparatchik may make quite a competent capitalist manager.

[64] Timothy Garton Ash, "Eastern Europe: Après le Déluge, Nous," *New York Review of Books* 51 (August 16, 1990).

displacement and loss, is the most frightening thing about it. Whether or not the reformers legalize or moralize their aims, their victims will surely do so and accuse the new regime of behaving just like the old one, treating people as disposable because of their race, class, or institutional position. Members of liberal societies will, it seems, accept a considerable amount of such dislocation – loss of job, housing, neighborhood – if the structure that imposes it is an impersonal market; much less if it's seen as deliberate policy: they won't treat an affirmative action plan that costs them their job the way they would a plant closing. The Soviet occupiers of the East zone found it easy to denazify, since their structural policies were wholly unconstrained by legalist scruples; they did not feel it necessary to make fine distinctions between Nazis and the bourgeoisie generally or to be cautiously underinclusive in their internment, confiscation, and expulsion policies; and once the new structure was in place, they did not hesitate to declare an abrupt end to denazification and to reemploy in high party positions recanting Nazis who could be useful to them. The Allies, necessarily hampered by legalist concerns about due process, and at the same time far too ambitious in their structural goal of trying to replace wholesale the entire party apparatus while in fact having to make wholesale exceptions in order to staff the recovery, got the worst of both worlds: a mass administrative process that was too cautious and slow to be effective yet still created new martyrs and victims.

Neither is the relative impersonality of structural explanations of past injustice – historical explanations rather than legal or moral blame fixing – necessarily any less politically controversial than attribution to specific wrongdoers or groups. In the German Historikerstreit, the great "historians' controversy" of 1986–1987, the sides were divided by their attachments to diverging structural approaches to, explaining Nazism and the Holocaust: some conservatives (to simplify greatly a greatly complex debate) assimilating these events into a generalized twentieth-century crisis of modernity and pattern of mass horrors also exemplified by Stalin's and Pol Pot's massacres; liberals (and leftists) condemning that as a distraction from structural causes in Germany's own authoritarian (and capitalist) past.[65] Instead of focusing attention on needed reforms, history can become a massive subsidiary political battleground on which every monument, every date and proper name for hundreds of years past, is charged with polarized meanings.

There is also no guarantee that structural understandings will not undermine any reform impulse. It so happens that the structural views of history I have mostly been discussing are Whiggish views that see the "normal" past as pointing toward progress, so that the past correctly understood will indicate both the possibility and the directions of reform. One can rescue a similar optimism from critical views of history that assume structures are never

[65] On the Historikerstreit; see Charles Maier, *The Unmasterable Past* (1988); Evans, *supra* note 29.

determining, that there are always alternative paths to be chosen, that the contingent strategies of agents, especially collectively mobilized political agents, can make a difference at crucial junctures. But structural explanations could just as easily lead to fatalism, despair, and paralysis: we are in the grip of processes (the decline of the West, the globalization of the capitalist world system) in which domestic-political initiatives are pathetic scratchings on the surface of things. Coulmas and Friedländer have written movingly about the way many German youths, especially of the Left, feel not only overburdened but "mutilated": "the idea that German history is so overwhelming that it [has] crushed its offspring's personality, the free will and the freedom of the individual."[66]

Thus it may be that, quite paradoxically, the reformist possibilities of structural understanding may be restricted to societies whose own traditions make plausible a view of history in which good agents can triumph over bad structures. (The West German experience is now very appealing to some liberal reformers in Eastern Europe as an example of how a society with an authoritarian past can be discontinuously remade into a democratic one.) We are lucky enough to be beneficiaries of such traditions, yet in dealing with our racial heritage and dual economy we don't take advantage of our good fortune. Here is a puzzle: why is it that when conservatives excoriate social engineering schemes, the attempts at the "architecture of a racially integrated future," that they find a sympathetic ear? Why must structural claims to be politically acceptable adopt the vocabulary of legalism? After all, structural politics is hardly foreign to our history: America itself is a social engineering scheme, an experiment in liberal-republican society in which many legal policies untried almost anywhere else in world history – inheritance reform, wide distribution of public lands in homesteads, abolition of indentured servitude and imprisonment for debt, married women's property acts, the vast redistribution of property effected in uncompensated emancipation of slaves – have been carried out for the specific purpose of producing the social preconditions of a liberal polity – enhancing political stability, economic prosperity, and civil peace by creating a large middle class and reducing the distance between rich and poor. When we propose social changes for other societies, such as the former communist countries, we seem not to hesitate to recommend, or require as the condition of financial help and political support, very extensive restructurings of social and economic institutions – quite often, alas, in complete disregard of local traditions, continuities, and political consequences. But in our own society we seem to have reached a point of near paralysis in social experiments, less out of complacency than exhaustion.

[66] Friedlander and Coulmas, *supra* note 13 at 6.

Index